Key to En

☙ Children welcome (from age shown in brackets, if specified)

P Off-street car parking (number of places shown in brackets)

✗ No smoking

TV Television (either in every room or in a TV lounge)

🐾 Pets accepted (by prior arrangement)

✗ Evening meal available (by prior arrangement)

V Special diets catered for (by prior arrangement - please check with owner to see if your particular requirements are catered for)

▥
♿

✿ Christmas breaks a speciality

☕ Coffee/tea making facilities

▲ Youth Hostel

⌂ Camping Barn

🍱 Packed lunches available

// Drying facilities for wet clothes and boots

🚲 Safe cycle storage

The location heading - every hamlet, village, town and city mentioned in this directory is represented on the path map within each section.

Use the National Grid reference with Ordnance Survey maps and atlases. The letter(s) refer to a 100 kilometre grid square. The first two numbers refer to a North/South grid line and the last two numbers refer to an East/West grid line. The grid reference indicates their intersection point.

Penny Hassett   12

National Grid Ref: PH2096.

🍴 🍺 Cat & Fiddle, The Bull

These are the names of nearby pubs and restaurants that serve food in the evening, as suggested by local B&Bs.

The Old Rectory, *Main Street, Penny Hassett, Borchester, Borsetshire, BC2 3QT.*
C18th former rectory, lovely garden.
Grades: ETC 3 Diamond
Tel: **01048 598464** Mrs Smythe.
D: £18.00-£22.00 **S:** £20.00-£27.50
Open: All Year
Beds: 1F 1D 1T
Baths: 1 Pr 2 Sh
☙(4) **P**(2) ✗ **TV** 🐾 ✗ ▥ **V** ♿ ✿ ☕ 🚲

D = Price range per person sharing in a double room

S = Price range for a single person in a room

Bedrooms
F = Family
D = Double
T = Twin
S = Single

Bathrooms
En = Ensuite
Pr = Private
Sh = Shared

Grades - The English Tourism Council (**ETC**) grades B&Bs for quality in Diamonds (**1 Diamond** to **5 Diamond**, highest) and hotels in Stars (**1 Star** to **5 Star**). Bord Failte (**BF**, the Irish Tourist Board) grades guest houses in Stars (**1 Star** to **4 Star**); the Northern Ireland Tourist Board (**NITB**) rates them as Grade A (higher) or B. Both grade hotels in Stars (**1 Star** to **5 Star**). Both Tourist Boards for Ireland inspect B&B accommodation annually - such premises are entitled to show that they have been approved (**Approv**). Scottish and Welsh Tourist Board (**STB** and **WTB**) grades have two parts: the Star rating is for quality (**1 Star** to **5 Star**, highest), the other part designates the type of establishment, e.g. B&B, Guest House (**GH**), Country House (**CH**) etc. Ask at Tourist Information Centres for further information on these systems. The Automobile Association (**AA**) and Royal Automobile Club (**RAC**) both use, throughout the British-Irish Isles, the same system of Diamonds and Stars as the English Tourism Council.

CYCLEWAY COMPANION

PUBLISHER: TIM STILWELL

EDITOR: MARTIN DOWLING

STILWELL
Publishing

Distributed in Great Britain, Europe & the Commonwealth by Orca Book Services, Stanley House, 3 Fleets Lane, Poole, Dorset BH15 3AJ (Tel: 01202 665432) and available from all good bookshops. Distributed in North America by Seven Hills Book Distributors, 1531 Tremont Street, Cincinatti, OH 45214, USA (Tel: 513 471 4311).

ISBN 1-900861-26-7.

Published by Stilwell Publishing Ltd,
59 Charlotte Road, Shoreditch, London, EC2A 3QW.
Tel: 020-7739 7179. Fax: 020-7739 7191. E-mail: info@stilwell.co.uk

All maps in this book have been copied from pre-1948 mapping showing the National Grid.

Stilwell Publishing Ltd:
Publisher: Tim Stilwell
Editor: Martin Dowling

Design and Maps: Nigel Simpson

Printed in the Channel Islands by the Guernsey Press Company, Guernsey, Channel Islands.

Contents

Introduction

Several years ago, my wife and I set out to walk one of Britain's National Trails, the North Downs Way, over several weekends. Neither of us are born to camping, nor could we afford to stay in expensive hotels. We decided on B&Bs and found a problem straightaway. One could not find good value bed and breakfast accommodation along the route without going to a lot of trouble. Local libraries, directory enquiries, six different Tourist Information Centres and a large pile of brochures yielded nothing but a hotchpotch of B&B addresses, most of them miles out of our way. We abandoned the research and did the walk in one-day stretches, high-tailing it back to our London home each evening on the train.

The point is that we didn't really want to take the train back, especially when the time spent in waiting and travelling matched the time spent walking. A good weekend's walk would have been ideal, but we didn't know where to stay. The Law of Sod dictates that wherever you choose to finish your day's walking, there is either nothing in sight or a large country house hotel charging £100 for a one night stay. The train proved the logical option.

We therefore went on to create and publish a book called the *National Trail Companion* which publishes accommodation details for footpaths in the order that they appear along a path. Three years later, in 1998, the *Cycleway Companion* was launched, arranged along similar lines – for cyclists travelling along recognised cycle routes.

Long distance cycleways have become very popular over the last decade or so. County councils in particular have seen cycleways as a means of promoting tourism in the further-flung parts of their county. The Sustrans initiative has used the leisure-based cycle route as a flagship for their more wide-reaching campaign for sustainable transport. The travel pages of our weekend newspapers regularly feature cycle breaks at home and abroad. The popularity of mountain biking and off-road cycling is clear; they even have their own specialist magazines. All in all, there are three times as many people cycling for their holiday than there were 20 years ago.

So when a man from Cornwall telephoned us in 1997 to ask us whether we could bring out an accommodation book that catered for cyclists rather than for walkers, we finally jumped at the challenge. He had been the umpteenth person to ask us such a question that year. Here is the result, now in its third edition. 23 long distance cycle routes are featured in this book. They fall into two categories. The county cycleways are way-marked routes set up by the relevant county council. Only 9 counties and one National Park so far have had the imagination to set up their own cycleways. These routes are all waymarked except for those in Leicestershire (devised before the split with Rutland) and Essex.

The Sustrans routes are part of the widely-publicised National Cycle Network, supported by the Bristol-based Sustrans organisation. The National Cycle Network was one of the first projects to win financial backing from the Millennium Commission – a cool £42,500,000 up to the year 2000. Sustrans' objective is principally environmental: to create 7,000 miles of cycle routes with common standards in partnership with local government. The Sustrans routes shown here are conceived as leisure routes. In fact, Sustrans is at pains to point out that cycling is not just a leisure activity. It is a sustainable means of transport which does not rely on a finite resource – oil – and which produces no air pollution, no traffic jams, no billion-pound road schemes and no scrap disposal problems. In every sense, cycling costs less than motoring. Sustrans therefore has a loftier aim than happier holiday-making: it is to get us all out of automobiles and onto bicycles. This will not happen if there are no safe places to cycle – hence Sustrans' far-sighted and dedicated work in devising these routes. Sustrans also advise on and initiate civil engineering projects with local government to smooth the way further for the bicycle.

The *Cycleway Companion* does not attempt to tell the reader where to turn left or right, how far it is to the next stop or the steepness of the hills. This we leave to the admirable maps and guides already on the market (each chapter introduction tells you where to get hold of these). Instead, this book offers logistical help – where to stay and where to find pubs that serve evening meals along each route. It's my contention that once you've done one long distance cycle route, you want to do another, perhaps over a series of weekends rather than in one fell swoop. Planning and plotting the accommodation for such a journey is usually a long-winded affair. You have to ring Tourist Information Centres, wait for their literature, and then match unknown place-names to your mapped route. With this *Cycleway Companion* you can happily work out where to stay without the hassle, leaving you longer to devise a more extensive itinerary en route.

All information published in these pages has been collected over one year and provided by the owners themselves. The vast majority offer bed and breakfast at well under £27.50 per person per night, which we consider near the limit a cyclist would wish to pay. The pink highlight boxes are advertisements. Once again, we should make it clear that inclusion in these pages does not imply personal recommendation – we have not visited them all, merely written to them or phoned them. A simple glance over the salient details on any page, however, and the reader will be his or her own guide.

Owners were asked to provide their range of rates per person per night for the year in question. The rates are thus forecasts and are in any case always subject to fluctuation in demand. Of course, some information may already be out of date. Grades may go up or down, or be removed altogether. British Telecom may alter exchange numbers. Proprietors may decide on a whim to move out of the business altogether. That is why the *Cycleway Companion* has to be a yearbook; in general, though, the information published here will be accurate, pertinent and useful for a long time to come.

One of the most important considerations for any cyclist planning a night's rest at a hostel or B&B is 'how far off the route is it?' Our concern has been, of course, to research Youth Hostels and B&Bs that are at least close to a given route; the reader can gauge at a glance how far one village is from the route compared with another. The accommodation lists are published in the order in which they appear along the path. We have numbered the locations to make cross-referencing easier.

We have also included pubs and inns that serve food in the evenings. For many cyclists, the promise of an evening meal will be of prime importance in deciding where to stay. These pubs have been suggested as decent places to eat by the B&B owners themselves – we publish them here so that you know you'll have something to fall back on if that B&B doesn't serve dinner itself. The direction in which the locations are listed is determined by popular choice and not by personal preference. If you wish to cycle the C2C from East to West or the Lon Las Cymru from Holyhead to Cardiff, then you will simply have to flick backwards through the chapter's pages rather than forwards. As far as mapping is concerned, I have omitted giving Landranger map numbers, except in the introduction to each path. The Ordnance Survey's national grid references are more important; to this end we have indicated grid labels and lines at the edge of each map.

Throughout the book you will find boxes offering advice to cyclists staying at B&Bs. Some of you may think these a waste of time and in fact, they are partly a publishing trick. They fill space and tidy the page up. But we really have heard horror stories about all sorts of guests from B&B owners, mainly concerning disregard for other people's property. Much of this is done through thoughtlessness and not by intent. If a few words can remind someone of his or her obligations, then these boxes, however self-important, will have done the trick.

Tim Stilwell
Stoke Newington, April 2001

Cycleway Locations

Sustrans Carlisle to Inverness

At 402 miles, this massive crossing of Scotland from south to north is the longest route featured in this book. The **Scottish National Cycle Route** is a section of the planned Inverness to Dover route, the backbone of the new UK National Cycle Network. It runs on traffic-free paths and traffic-calmed roads from the English border city of Carlisle through the western Lowlands and Galloway Forest Park to Ayr on the west coast before reaching Glasgow, Scotland's metropolis. The northern section of the way will take you down the north bank of the Clyde Estuary to Dumbarton and the southern shore of Loch Lomond before you strike out into the varied and truly breathtaking scenery of the Scottish Highlands, from Loch Venachar to Loch Tay and across the Drumochter Pass, continuing through Strathspey below the Cairngorms to Inverness on the Moray Firth. The route is signposted by blue direction signs with a cycle silhouette and the number 7 in a red rectangle.

The indispensable **official route map and guide** for the Scottish National Cycle Route, which includes listings of cycle repair/hire shops along the route, comes in two parts, *Carlisle to Glasgow* and *Glasgow to Inverness*, and is available from Sustrans, 35 King Street, Bristol BS1 4DZ, tel 0117-926 8893, fax 0117-929 4173, @ £5.99 each (+ £1.50 p&p for both together or either one).

Maps: Ordnance Survey 1:50,000 Landranger series: 26, 27, 35, 36, 42, 43, 51, 52, 57, 63, 64, 70, 76, 77, 83, 84, 85

Transport: Carlisle, Glasgow and Inverness are all main termini on the Intercity network. There are connections to numerous other places on or near the route.

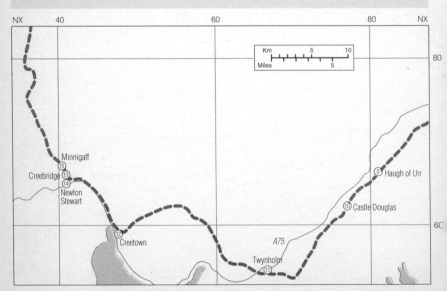

Carlisle 1

National Grid Ref: NY3955

🍴 🍺 Metal Bridge Inn, The Beehive, Mary's Pantry, Crown & Thistle, Coach & Horses, Golden Fleece, Black Lion

▲ **Carlisle Youth Hostel,**
University of Northumbria, The Old Brewery Residences, Bridge Lane, Caldewgate, Carlisle, Cumbria, CA2 5SR.
Actual grid ref: NY394560
Tel: **01228 597352**
Under 18: £8.75
Adults: £13.00
Self-catering facilities, Showers, Cycle store, Parking, Facilities for disabled people, No smoking, WC, Kitchen facilities
University accommodation in an award-winning conversion of the former Theakston's brewery. Single study bedrooms with shared kitchen and bathroom in flats for up to 7 people.

Howard Lodge, *90 Warwick Road, Carlisle, Cumbria, CA1 1JU.*
Actual grid ref: NY407558
Grades: ETC 4 Diamond, AA 3 Diamond
Tel: **01228 529842**
Mr Hendrie.
D: £15.00-£25.00
S: £20.00-£30.00.
Open: All Year
Beds: 2F 1D 2T 1S
Baths: 6 En 1 Sh
🛏 🅿 (6) 🛄 📺 ✕ 🌃 📖 💟 🚲
Friendly family-run guest house in comfortable Victorian town house in conservation area. Spacious rooms all fully ensuite with satellite TV, welcome tray, hairdryer and clock radio. Large breakfasts. 5 minutes' walk from station and city centre. Evening meals by prior arrangement. Private car park.

Craighead, 6 Hartington Place, Carlisle, Cumbria, CA1 1HL.
Actual grid ref: NY405559
Grades: ETC 3 Diamond
Tel: **01228 596767** Mrs Smith.
D: £17.00 **S:** £16.00.
Open: All Year (not Xmas)
Beds: 1F 2D 1T 1S
Baths: 1 En 2 Sh
🛏 🅿 🛄 🌃 📖 💟 🚲
You will receive a warm welcome at Craighead, a Grade II Listed spacious Victorian town house with comfortable rooms and original features. CTV, tea/coffee tray in all rooms. Minutes' walk to city centre bus and rail stations and all amenities. Friendly personal service.

Angus Hotel & Almonds Bistro, 14 Scotland Road, Stanwix, Carlisle, Cumbria, CA3 9DG.
Actual grid ref: NY400571
Grades: AA 4 Diamond
Tel: **01228 523546** Mr Webster.
Fax no: 01228 531895
D: £20.00-£27.00 **S:** £26.00-£42.00.
Open: All Year
Beds: 4F 3D 4T 3S
Baths: 11 En 3 Sh
🛏 🅿 (6) 🛄 ✕ 🌃 📖 💟 🅰 🚲
Victorian town house, foundations on Hadrian's Wall. Excellent food, Les Routiers Awards, local cheeses, home baked bread. Genuine warm welcome from owners. Licensed, draught beer, lounge, meeting room, internet cafe, direct dial telephones, secure garaging. Group rates for cyclists available.

All rates are subject to alteration at the owners' discretion.

Cherry Grove, 87 Petteril Street, Carlisle, Cumbria, CA1 2AW.
Lovely red brick building close to golf club and town.
Grades: AA 3 Diamond
Tel: **01228 541942**
Mr & Mrs Houghton.
D: £17.50-£20.00 **S:** £20.00-£30.00.
Open: All Year
Beds: 3F 2D
Baths: 5 En
🛏 🅿 (3) 🛄 🌃 📖 💟 🚲

Avondale, 3 St Aidans Road, Carlisle, Cumbria, CA1 1LT.
Attractive comfortable Edwardian house. Quiet central position convenient M6 J43.
Grades: ETC 4 Diamond
Tel: **01228 523012** (also fax no)
Mr & Mrs Hayes.
D: £20.00-£20.00 **S:** £20.00-£40.00.
Open: All Year (not Xmas)
Beds: 1D 1T **Baths:** 1 En 1 Pr
🛏 🅿 (3) 🛄 🌃 📖 💟 🚲

Dalroc, 411 Warwick Road, Carlisle, Cumbria, CA1 2RZ.
Small friendly house. Midway city centre and M6 motorway.
Tel: **01228 542805** Mrs Irving.
D: £16.00-£16.00 **S:** £16.00-£16.00.
Open: All Year (not Xmas/New Year)
Beds: 1T 1D 1S
🛏 (7) 🅿 🛄 ✕ 📖 💟 🅰 🚲

Chatsworth Guest House, 22 Chatsworth Square, Carlisle, Cumbria, CA1 1HF.
City centre Grade II Listed building, close to all amenities.
Grades: ETC 3 Diamond
Tel: **01228 524023** (also fax no)
Mrs Mackin.
D: £19.00-£22.00 **S:** £25.00-£25.00.
Open: All Year (not Xmas)
Beds: 1F 1D 2T 1S
Baths: 5 En
🛏 🅿 (2) 🛄 🌃 📖 💟

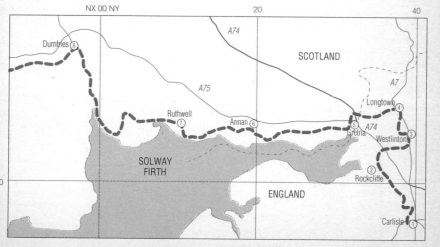

Kingstown Hotel, *246 Kingstown Road, Carlisle, CA3 0DE.*
Grades: AA 3 Diamond
Tel: **01228 515292** (also fax no)
Mrs Marshall.
D: £23.50 **S:** £35.00-£40.00.
Open: All Year
Beds: 1F 4D 2T
Baths: 7 En
⚡ 🅿 (14) ▢ ⌂ ⌘ ✕ 🔥 ▥ ⎙ & ▣ ⍓ 🚲
Just off the M6 (Jct. 44) we are a licensed hotel providing high-quality accommodation. You will find a friendly and relaxed atmosphere, freshly-prepared cuisine and fine wine at reasonable prices. A good base to explore Cumbria, Northumbria, Lake District, Scotland

Corner House Hotel & Bar,
4 Grey Street, Carlisle, CA1 2JP.
Grades: ETC 3 Diamond
Tel: **01228 533239** Mrs Anderson.
Fax no: 01228 546628
D: £17.50-£22.00 **S:** £20.00-£30.00.
Open: All Year
Beds: 3F 4D 4T 3S
Baths: All En
⚡ ▢ ⌂ ⌘ ✕ 🔥 ▥ ⎙ & ▣ ⍓ 🚲
Refurbished family run hotel. All rooms ensuite, colour TV, phones, tea/coffee, radio, toiletries etc. Cosy bar, Sky TV lounge, games room, easy access city centre, bus/train. Base for golf, walking, cycling, touring the Lakes, Roman Wall, Carlisle/ Settle line etc.

Ashleigh House, *46 Victoria Place, Carlisle, Cumbria, CA1 1EX.*
Beautifully decorated town house. Two minutes from city centre.
Grades: ETC 4 Diamond
Tel: **01228 521631** Mr Davies.
D: £19.00-£22.50 **S:** £25.00-£30.00.
Open: All Year (not Xmas/New Year)
Beds: 3F 1T 2D 1S
Baths: 7 En
⚡ (5) ▢ 🔥 ⎙ ▣

Cornerways Guest House,
107 Warwick Road, Carlisle, Cumbria, CA1 1EA.
Large Victorian town house.
Grades: ETC 4 Diamond
Tel: **01228 521733** Mrs Fisher.
D: £14.00-£18.00 **S:** £16.00-£18.00.
Open: All Year (not Xmas)
Beds: 2F 1D 4T 3S
Baths: 3 En 2 Sh
⚡ 🅿 (4) ▢ ⌂ ⌘ ✕ 🔥 ⎙ ▣ ▪ 🚲

Courtfield Guest House,
169 Warwick Road, Carlisle, Cumbria, CA1 1LP.
Short walk to historic city centre.
Close to M6, J43.
Grades: ETC 4 Diamond
Tel: **01228 522767** Mrs Dawes.
D: £18.00-£22.00 **S:** £25.00.
Open: All Year (not Xmas)
Beds: 1F 2D 2T
Baths: 5 En
⚡ 🅿 (4) ✂ ▢ 🔥 ▥ ▣ 🚲

East View Guest House,
110 Warwick Road, Carlisle, Cumbria, CA1 1JU.
Actual grid ref: NY407560
10 minutes' walking distance from city centre, railway station and restaurants.
Grades: ETC 3 Diamond, AA 3 Diamond, RAC 3 Diamond
Tel: **01228 522112** (also fax no)
Mrs Glease.
D: £18.00-£20.00
S: £20.00-£25.00.
Open: All Year (not Xmas)
Beds: 3F 2D 1T 1S
Baths: 7 En
⚡ 🅿 (4) ✂ ▢ 🔥 ⎙ ▥ ▣ 🚲

Cambro House, *173 Warwick Road, Carlisle, Cumbria, CA1 1LP.*
Grades: AA 3 Diamond
Tel: **01228 543094** (also fax no)
Mr & Mrs Mawson.
D: £17.00-£20.00
S: £20.00-£25.00.
Open: All Year
Beds: 2D 1T
Baths: 3 En
🅿 (2) ✂ ▢ 🔥 ⎙ ▣ ▪ 🚲
Guests can expect warm hospitality and friendly service at this attractively decorated and well-maintained guest house. Each ensuite bedroom includes TV, clock, radio, hairdryer and welcome tray. Private off-road parking available, non-smoking, close to golf course.

D = Price range per person sharing in a double room

Rockcliffe 2

National Grid Ref: NY3561

▥ ⌘ Metal Bridge Inn

Metal Bridge House, *Metal Bridge, Rockcliffe, Carlisle, Cumbria, CA6 4HG.*
Actual grid ref: NY356649
In country, close to M6/A74, quality accommodation, friendly welcome.
Tel: **01228 674695** Mr Rae.
D: £16.00-£18.00 **S:** £20.00-£22.00.
Open: All Year (not Xmas)
Beds: 1D 2T **Baths:** 1 Sh
⚡ 🅿 (6) ✂ ⌂ 🔥 ⎙ ▣ 🚲

Westlinton 3

National Grid Ref: NY3964

Lynebank, *Westlinton, Carlisle, Cumbria, CA6 6AA.*
Family-run, excellent food, ideal stop for England/Scotland journey.
Grades: ETC 4 Diamond
Tel: **01228 792820** (also fax no)
Mrs Butler.
D: £18.00-£22.00 **S:** £20.00-£24.00.
Open: All Year
Beds: 2F 3D 1T 3S **Baths:** 9 En
⚡ 🅿 (15) ▢ ✕ 🔥 ⎙ ▣ ⍓ 🚲

Carlisle to Dumfries

From the city centre of **Carlisle** (see the *Cumbria Cycleway*), the route proceeds to Rockcliffe on the Eden Estuary and Longtown on the Esk before crossing The Border to reach Gretna Green, the renowned border village whose Old Smithy was, during the eighteenth and nineteenth centuries, the site of numerous clandestine marriages of English people, in whose country marriage was the exclusive provenance of the Church. Heading west along the Solway Firth you reach **Annan** and then the village of Ruthwell, whose church houses a towering magnificently carved seventh-century cross. A little way further, Caerlaverock Castle is a beautiful thirteenth-century ruin built of pink stone, with a twin-towered gatehouse and surrounded by a moat. The nearby Wildfowl and Wetland Centre shelters bird species including the barnacle goose. Cycling up the beautiful Nith Estuary you reach the Queen of the South, **Dumfries**, much of which is built in the local red sandstone. Here behind the neoclassical columns of his mausoleum in St Michael's Churchyard lies Robert Burns, who lived in Dumfries for the last five years of his life. The Burns House has a collection of his paraphernalia and the Robert Burns Centre, located in a converted water mill, is a themed museum, with a cafe.

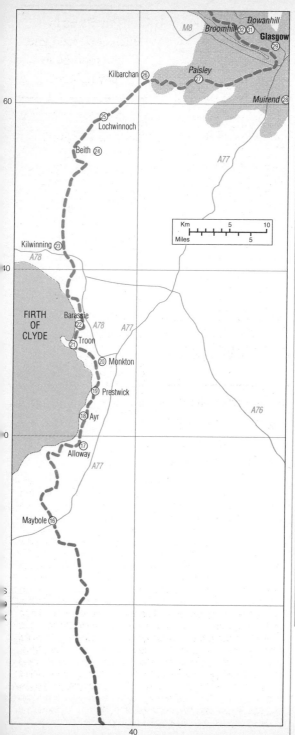

D = Price range per person sharing in a double room

Longtown 4

National Grid Ref: NY3868

🍴 🍺 Crossways Inn, Graham Arms

Briar Lea House, *Brampton Road, Longtown, Carlisle, Cumbria, CA6 5TN.*
A substantial country house in 1.75 acres of attractive grounds.
Grades: ETC 4 Diamond
Tel: **01228 791538** (also fax no)
Mr Gildert.
D: £19.50-£25.00 **S:** £25.00-£30.00.
Open: All Year (not Xmas)
Beds: 2D 1T
Baths: 3 En
🛇 🅿 (10) ⫼ 🖵 🛏 ✗ 🛀 🎹 ☕ ☑ ∥ ♻

Orchard House, *Blackbank, Longtown, Carlisle, Cumbria, CA6 5LQ.*
Spacious, tastefully furnished accommodation. Quiet wooded location near Gretna Green.
Grades: ETC 4 Diamond
Tel: **01461 338596** Mrs Payne.
D: £20.00-£22.50 .
Open: All Year (not Xmas)
Beds: 1D 1T
Baths: 2 En
🛇 🅿 (4) ⫼ 🖵 🛀 🎹 ☑ ∥ ♻

Gretna 5

National Grid Ref: NY3167

🍴 🍺 Solway Lodge

The Braids, *Annan Road, Gretna, Dumfriesshire, DG16 5DQ.*
Tel: **01461 337409** (also fax no)
Mrs Copeland.
D: £16.00-£18.00 **S:** £25.00-£28.00.
Open: All Year
Beds: 2T
Baths: 1 Sh
🛇 🅿 (2) 🖵 🛀 🎹 ☑ 🛢 ∥ ♻
Small friendly family B&B in bungalow inside the entrance to our (BGHP Grade 4) caravan park. Open all year. Gretna marriage centre, golf, Sunday market. Good area for birdwatching in winter months. Advice on fishing in the area.

Pay B&Bs by
cash or cheque and
be prepared to
pay up front.

All rates are subject to alteration at the owners' discretion.

Annan 6

National Grid Ref: NY1966

¶ ◀ Queensbury Arms

The Old Rectory Guest House,
12 St Johns Road, Annan,
Dumfriesshire, DG12 6AW.
Tel: **01461 202029** (also fax no)
Buchanan & J Alexander.
D: £22.00-£25.00
S: £22.00-£25.00.
Open: All Year
Beds: 2F 2D 1T 1S
Baths: 5 En 1 Pr
➤ (4) **P** (6) ⊬ ❑ ¶ ✕ ⌃ ⛁ ▥ ▣ 🅥 🛊 ⊀ ♻
Charming C19th manse in the centre of Annan, 7 miles from famous wedding town Gretna. Be assured of warm welcome, ensuite bedrooms, great Scottish breakfasts, home cooking, licensed, main Euro & Irish routes. Walkers, cyclist, small wedding parties welcome. Smoking lounge available.

Milnfield Farm, Low Road,
Annan, Dumfriesshire, DG12 5QP.
Working farm, riverside walks, large garden; ideal for touring base.
Grades: ETC 2 Star
Tel: **01461 201811** Robinson.
D: £16.00-£18.00
S: £16.00-£18.00.
Open: All Year (not Xmas)
Beds: 1F 1D
➤ **P** ⊬ ❑ ¶ ⌃ ⛁ ▥ 🅥 ♻ ⊀ ♻

Ruthwell 7

National Grid Ref: NY0967

Kirkland Country House Hotel,
Ruthwell, Dumfries, DG1 4NP.
Small country house hotel offering good food and friendly service.
Grades: ETC 3 Star
Tel: **01387 870284**
Mrs Coatsworth.
D: £25.00-£27.00
S: £35.00-£45.00.
Open: All Year
Beds: 1F 2T 3D
Baths: 6 En
➤ **P** (12) ❑ ✕ ⌃ ⛁ ▥ ⅊ 🅥 🛊 ⊀ ♻

Pay B&Bs by cash or cheque and be prepared to pay up front.

Dumfries 8

National Grid Ref: NX9776

¶ ◀ Hill Hotel, Auldgirth Inn, Station Hotel, Courtyard, Rat & Carrot, Queensbury, Waverley Bar, Aberdour Hotel

Hazledean Guest House, 4 Moffat
Road, Dumfries, DG1 1NJ.
4 star Victorian villa. Non-smoking. Parking. Near town centre.
Grades: ETC 4 Star
Tel: **01387 266178** (also fax no)
Mr & Mrs Harper.
D: £20.00-£20.00 **S:** £25.00-£28.00.
Open: All Year (not Xmas)
Beds: 2F 2D 2T 1S
Baths: 6 En
➤ **P** (8) ⊬ ❑ ✕ ⌃ ⛁ ▥ 🅥 🛊 ⊀ ♻

Fernwood, 4 Casslands, Dumfries,
DG2 7NS.
Victorian sandstone villa, close to golf course and town centre.
Grades: ETC 3 Star
Tel: **01387 253701** (also fax no)
Mrs Vaughan.
D: £17.50-£18.50 **S:** £17.50-£17.50.
Open: All Year (not Xmas)
Beds: 1F 1D 2S
Baths: 2 Sh
➤ **P** (6) ⊬ ❑ ⌃ ⛁ 🅥 ⊀ ♻

All cycleways are popular: you are well-advised to book ahead

30 Hardthorn Avenue, Dumfries,
DG2 9JA.
Grades: ETC 2 Star B&B
Tel: **01387 253502** (also fax no)
Ms Sloan.
D: £16.00-£18.00 **S:** £23.00-£25.00.
Open: Easter to Oct
Beds: 1D 1T
Baths: 1 Sh
P (2) ⊬ ❑ ⌃ ⛁ ▥ 🅥 ⊀ ♻
A warm Scottish welcome awaits you at No 30, a non-smoking private house with car parking in quiet residential area. Easy access from Dumfries bypass (A75) and less than a mile from town centre. Ideal base to explore SW Scotland.

Lindean, 50 Rae Street, Dumfries,
DG1 1JE.
Town centre house in quiet residential area, near railway station.
Grades: ETC 3 Star
Tel: **01387 251888** Mrs Stein.
D: £18.00-£20.00 **S:** £25.00-£25.00.
Open: All Year
Beds: 2T 1D
Baths: 2 En 1 Pr
➤ **P** ⊬ ❑ ⌃ ⛁ 🅥 🛊 ⊀ ♻

Brackenbridge, 67 New Abbey
Road, Dumfries, DG2 7JY.
Brackenridge bed and breakfast, walking distance into the town centre and all local attractions.
Grades: ETC 3 Star,
AA 3 Diamond
Tel: **01387 263962**
Mr & Mrs Thomson.
D: £18.50-£25.00
S: £20.00-£20.00.
Open: All Year
Beds: 3F 3T 1D 1S
Baths: 2 En 1 Pr
➤ **P** ❑ ¶ ✕ ⌃ ⛁ ▥ ⅊ 🅥 🛊 ⊀ ♻

Dumfries to Maybole

From Dumfries you head southwest through Haugh of Urr to reach **Castle Douglas** and nearby Threave Garden (National Trust for Scotland), with the sumptuous colours of its flowers and woodland, where there is also a restaurant. On to Tongland on the Dee and Gatehouse of Fleet, a pretty town in the lovely Fleet Valley. Nearby fifteenth-century Cardoness Castle is a typical Scottish tower house. From Gatehouse you head on to Creetown, where the River Cree flows into Wigtown Bay, before reaching Palnure on the edge of **Galloway Forest Park**, a beautiful 300-square-mile area of peaks in surroundings of forested hills and moorland with numerous lochs and a network of rivers. The Park's Kirroughtree Visitor Centre is nearby. Newton Stewart is a centre for salmon and trout fishing in the Cree; from here you follow the river upstream before heading into Glen Trool. Continuing through the Forest Park, the route wends its way over fairly gentle hills before a steeper climb and descent over Nick of the Balloch to the River Stinchar, and another climb to the summit below White Scaurins. You now descend steadily to reach Crosshill and **Maybole**. The climb out of Maybole yields splendid views out to sea – your first sight of the Firth of Clyde.

Waverley Guest House, 21 St
Mary's Street, Dumfries, *DG1 1HB.*
5 minutes from town centre, across
from Railway station. On main
road.
Tel: **01387 254080** Meikle-Latta.
Fax no: 01387 254848
D: £14.50-£20.00 **S:** £14.50-£24.00.
Open: All Year
Beds: 5F 3T 1D 5S **Baths:** 6 En
☜ ❑ ⊁ ⽕ Ⅲ. Ⓥ ⓘ ⚡

Cairndoon, 14 Newall Terrace,
Dumfries, *DG1 1LW.*
Elegant 1880 town house, gracious-
ly quiet. Warm and friendly wel-
come.
Tel: **01387 256991** Mrs Stevenson.
D: £20.00-£24.00 **S:** £21.00-£25.00.
Open: All Year
Beds: 3F 1S **Baths:** 2 En 1 Pr 1 Sh
☜ ₱ (1) ⊬ ❑ ⽕ ⓘ Ⅲ. Ⓥ ⓘ ⚡ ⚲

The Knock Guest House,
1 Lockerbie Rd, Dumfries, *DG1 3AP.*
Warm welcome. Convenient for
golfing, fishing, touring. Cyclists
welcome.
Grades: ETC 1 Star
Tel: **01387 253487** Mr Sutherland.
D: £16.00-£16.50 **S:** £16.00-£16.50.
Open: All Year
Beds: 3F 1D 1T 1S
☜ ₱ (1) ❑ ⽕ ✕ ⽕ Ⅲ. Ⓥ ⓘ ⚡ ⚲

Franklea Guest House, Castle
Douglas Road, Dumfries, *DG2 8PP.*
Actual grid ref: NX955757
Bungalow 1 mile from Dumfries;
ideal for golf next door, hill
walking, Galloway park.
Grades: ETC 3 Star
Tel: **01387 253004** Mrs Wild.
Fax no: 01387 259301
D: £18.00-£20.00 **S:** £20.00-£22.00.
Open: Easter to Nov
Beds: 1F 1D
Baths: 2 En
☜ (5) ₱ (5) ❑ ⽕ ✕ ⽕ Ⅲ. ⅙ Ⓥ ⓘ
⚲

Fulwood Hotel, Lovers Walk,
Dumfries, *DG1 1LX.*
Beautiful Victorian house opposite
railway station in the heart of Burns
country.
Tel: **01387 252262 / 0411 260246**
Fax no: 01387 252262
D: £17.00-£21.00 **S:** £20.00-£30.00.
Open: All Year (not Xmas)
Beds: 1F 2D 2T 1S
Baths: 3 En 1 Pr 1 Sh
☜ ❑ ⽕ Ⅲ. Ⓥ ⚡ ⚲

Haugh of Urr   9

National Grid Ref: NX8066

🍴 🍺 The Grapes, Laurie Arms

Corbieton Cottage, Haugh of Urr,
Castle Douglas,
Kirkcudbrightshire, *DG7 3JJ.*
Actual grid ref: NX795695
Charming country cottage, lovely
views, good food and a warm
welcome.
Tel: **01556 660413**
Mr Jones.
D: £16.00-£18.00
S: £17.00-£18.00.
Open: Feb to Dec
Beds: 1D 1T
Baths: 1 Sh
₱ (2) ⊬ ❑ ✕ ⽕ Ⅲ. Ⓥ

Castle Douglas   10

National Grid Ref: NX7662

🍴 🍺 Old Smugglers, King's Arms, Laurie Arms,
Douglas Arms, Grapes, Imperial Hotel, Thistle
Inn

Smithy House, The Buchan, Castle
Douglas, Kirkcudbrightshire,
DG7 1TH.
Actual grid ref: NX760614
Comfortable Galloway cottage
overlooking Carlingwark Loch.
Central for exploring Galloway.
Grades: ETC 4 Star
Tel: **01556 503841**
Mrs Carcas.
D: £20.00-£27.50
S: £30.00-£35.00.
Open: All Year (not Xmas/New
Year)
Beds: 1T 2D
Baths: 2 En 1 Pr
₱ (4) ⊬ ❑ ⽕ Ⅲ. Ⓥ ⚡ ⚲

Milton Park Farm, Castle
Douglas, *DG7 3JJ.*
A warm welcome and good food
await you in this comfortable farm-
house.
Tel: **01556 660212**
Mrs Muir.
D: £18.00-£20.00
S: £18.00-£20.00.
Open: Easter to Oct
Beds: 2D 1T
Baths: 2 Sh
☜ (9) ₱ (4) ❑ ⽕ Ⅲ. Ⓥ

Craigadam, Castle Douglas,
Kirkcudbrightshire, *DG7 3HV.*
Actual grid ref: NX801728
Elegant country house within work-
ing farm. Antique furnishings, log
fires and friendly atmosphere.
Tel: **01556 650233** (also fax no)
Mrs Pickup.
D: £23.00-£23.00
S: £28.00-£28.00.
Open: All Year (not Xmas)
Beds: 1F 2D 4T
Baths: 3 Pr
☜ ₱ (10) ❑ ⽕ ✕ ⽕ Ⅲ. Ⓥ ⚡ ⚲

Imperial Hotel, King Street, Castle
Douglas, Kirkcudbrightshire,
DG7 1AA.
Former coaching inn and Listed
building. All rooms ensuite. Warm
friendly welcome.
Tel: **01556 502086**
Fax no: 01556 503009
D: £27.00-£29.00
S: £35.00-£45.00.
Open: All Year (not Xmas)
Beds: 5D 5T 2S
Baths: 12 En
☜ ₱ (20) ❑ ⽕ ✕ ⽕ Ⅲ. Ⓥ ⚡ ⚲

Dalcroy, 24 Abercromby Road,
Castle Douglas,
Kirkcudbrightshire, *DG7 1BA.*
A warm Scottish welcome assured
in this long-established, spacious
detached house.
Tel: **01556 502674**
Mrs Coates.
D: £16.50-£17.50
S: £13.00-£13.00.
Open: May to Oct
Beds: 1D 1T
Baths: 1 Sh
₱ (3) ⊬ ❑ ⽕ ⽕ Ⅲ. Ⓥ ⚡ ⚲

Twynholm   11

National Grid Ref: NX6654

🍴 🍺 Murray Arms

Barbey Farm, Twynholm,
Kirkcudbright, Kirkcudbrightshire,
DG6 4PN.
Farmhouse accommodation with
beautiful gardens in quiet rural
area.
Tel: **01557 860229**
Miss Service.
D: £14.00-£14.00
S: £14.00-£14.00.
Open: Easter to Sep
Beds: 1F 1T
☜ ₱ (2) ❑ ⽕ ⽕ Ⓥ

Creetown 12

National Grid Ref: NX4758

🍴 🍺 Barholm Arms

Wal-d-mar, *Mill Street, Creetown, Newton Stewart, Wigtownshire, DG8 7JN.*
Tel: **01671 820369** Lockett.
Fax no: 01671 820266
D: £16.00-£16.00 **S:** £16.00-£16.00.
Open: All Year (not Xmas)
Beds: 1D 1S
Baths: 1 Sh
🛏 🅿 (3) 🖵 🏗 🍽 🛖 🕭 🖼 📷 ⅤⓋ 💷 ✏ ⚡ 🚲
Modern bungalow in quiet village location, ideal base for touring, walking, golf, etc. Comfortable beds, good breakfasts, private off-road parking, warm Scottish welcome assured. Situated between Dumfries and Stranraer on the Cree estuary.

Creebridge 13

National Grid Ref: NX4165

Villa Cree, *Creebridge, Newton Stewart, Wigtownshire, DG8 6NR.*
Quiet riverside family house, excellent for walking, wildlife, touring or business.
Tel: **01671 403914**
Mr Rankin.
D: £18.00-£20.00
S: £18.00-£20.00.
Open: All Year (not Xmas)
Beds: 2D 1T 1S
Baths: 1 En 1 Pr
🛏 🅿 (3) ✂ 🖵 🏗 🛖 🖼 ⓋV 💷 ✏ ⚡ 🚲

Newton Stewart 14

National Grid Ref: NX4065

Rowallan House, *Corsbie Road, Newton Stewart, DG8 6JB.*
Visit our website -
www.rowallan.co.uk - see what our guests say about Rowallan.
Grades: ETC 4 Star
Tel: **01671 402520**
Mrs Henderson.
D: £27.00-£30.00
S: £27.00-£40.00.
Open: All Year
Beds: 2D 2T
Baths: 4 En
🛏 (10) 🅿 (6) ✂ 🖵 🏗 🛖 🖼 ⓋV 💷 ✏ ⚡ 🚲

Kilwarlin, *Corvisel Road, Newton Stewart, Wigtownshire, DG8 6LN.*
Actual grid ref: NX408650
Victorian house, beautiful garden, central location, home-baking, golf, fishing.
Tel: **01671 403047**
Mrs Dickson.
D: £16.50-£16.50
S: £16.50-£16.50.
Open: Easter to Oct
Beds: 1F 1D 1S
Baths: 1 Sh
🛏 (3) 🅿 (3) 🖵 🏗 🛖 🖼 ⓋV 💷 ✏ ⚡ 🚲

Maybole to Glasgow

Descending to reach the coast at Doonfoot, you cycle along the seafront of its sandy beach into **Ayr**, birthplace of Robert Burns. The old town nestles around the fifteenth-century auld brig over the River Ayr, which features in Burns' poem 'Twa Brigs'. St John's Tower is the remnant of a church where Cromwell had an armoury. Scotland's most important racecourse is on the north bank of the river. The next stretch along the coast is peppered with golf courses – the game originated in Scotland. After Prestwick you reach Troon, one of the locations of the British Open golf championship. The Scottish Maritime Museum is at Irvine; from here you head inland to Kilwinning and up the Garnock Valley to Kilbirnie, before turning east through Lochwinnoch, Kilbarchan and Johnstone to **Paisley**. The interior of the town's abbey, which was originally founded in the twelfth century but overhauled in the Victorian era, is richly decorated. The stained glass dates from various periods. The Museum and Art Gallery has a large exhibition of shawls documenting the history of the famous Paisley Pattern, which was developed from Indian designs. At the Sma' Shot Cottages, a large themed exhibition recreates different aspects of life in the eighteenth and nineteenth centuries. From Paisley you weave your way mostly through urban sprawl, but pass close to Pollok Country Park, where the fantastic Burrel Collection, which includes Chinese porcelain, Egyptian antiquities, medieval tapestries and furniture, stained glass and a large collection of paintings among much else, is flooded with sunlight in its superb purpose-built gallery. Proceeding to the south bank of the Clyde, cross Bell's Bridge to reach the centre of Scotland's powerhouse and largest city, Glasgow.

---

skdale, Princess Avenue, Newton ewart, DG8 6ES.
ttractive detached house, very uiet residential area, 5 mins' walk wn centre.
el: **01671 404195**
rs Smith.
: £16.00-£18.00
: £16.00-£20.00.
pen: All Year
eds: 1D 1T 1S
aths: 1 Pr 1 Sh
(4) ✂ ⌷ 🛋 ▦ Ⅴ ▮ ⚡ ᗕ

---

linnigaff 15

ational Grid Ref: NX4166

Minnigaff Youth Hostel,
innigaff, Newton Stewart, igtownshire, DG8 6PL.
Actual grid ref: NX411663
el: **01671 402211**
nder 18: £7.01
dults: £8.26
lf-catering facilities, Shop arby, Facilities for disabled ople
alloway Forest Park and RSPB serve are nearby. Good area for lwalking, cycling and pony kking. Fishing in the River Cree; y trips to wild goat park and ture trails.

All cycleways are popular: you are well-advised to book ahead

---

Maybole 16

National Grid Ref: NS2909

🍴 ⬥ Welltrees Inn

Homelea, *62 Culzean Road, Maybole, Ayrshire, KA19 8AH.*
Actual grid ref: NS295100
Homelea is a spacious red sandstone Victorian family home, retaining many original features.
Grades: ETC 3 Star
Tel: **01655 882736** Mrs McKellar.
Fax no: 01655 883557
D: £17.50-£18.50 **S:** £20.00-£22.00.
Open: Easter to Oct
Beds: 1F 1T 1S
Baths: 2 Sh
⛵ ⧖ 🄿 (3) ✂ ⌷ 🛋 ▦ Ⅴ ▮ ⚡ ᗕ

Garpin Farm, *Crosshill, Maybole, Ayrshire, KA19 7PX.*
Comfortable family farmhouse in beautiful Ayrshire countryside. Home baking.
Tel: **01655 740214**
Mrs Young.
D: £18.00-£20.00 **S:** £21.00.
Open: All Year
Beds: 1F 1T 1D
Baths: 1 Sh
⛵ 🄿 ⌷ ✗ 🛋 ▦ Ⅴ ▮ ⚡ ᗕ

Nether Culzean Farm, *Maybole, KA19 7JQ.*
Beautiful Listed C18th farmhouse, spacious and comfortable. Near Culzean Castle, beaches, golf courses.
Tel: **01655 882269**
Mrs Blythe.
D: £15.00-£17.00 **S:** £15.00-£17.00.
Open: Easter to Oct
Beds: 2F
Baths: 1 Pr
⛵ 🄿 (2) ✂ ⌷ 🐾 🛋 ▦ ♿ Ⅴ ⚡ ᗕ

Alloway 17

National Grid Ref: NS3318

Garth Madryn, *71 Maybole Road, Alloway, Ayr, KA7 4TB.*
Alloway is a quiet residential area of Ayr within easy reach of the town.
Tel: **01292 443346** Mrs MacKie.
D: £16.00-£17.00 **S:** £16.00-£17.00.
Open: All Year
Beds: 2T
Baths: 2 En

Ayr 18

National Grid Ref: NS3422

🍴 ⬥ Tam O'Shanter, Kylestrome Hotel, Finlay's Bar, Burrofield's Bar, Carrick Lodge, Durward Hotel, Hollybush Inn, Balgarth, Littlejohns

▲ Ayr Youth Hostel, *5 Craigwell Road, Ayr, KA7 2XJ.*
Actual grid ref: NS331211
Tel: **01292 262322**
Under 18: £8.00 **Adults:** £9.25
Self-catering facilities, Shop nearby, Laundry facilities
An excellent family base, with a barbecue, a 3-mile sandy beach and plenty to see nearby, including Burns Cottage, Culzean Castle and a Gold Cup racecourse.

Please respect a B&B's wishes regarding children, animals & smoking.

Inverlea Guest House, *42 Carrick Road, Ayr, KA7 2RB.*
Tel: **01292 266756** (also fax no)
Mr & Mrs Bryson.
D: £15.00-£20.00 **S:** £18.00-£25.00.
Open: All Year
Beds: 3F 2D 2T 1S
Baths: 3 En 2 Pr 3 Sh
🛏 🅿 (5) 🖵 🏃 🕹 🛆 📖 🔽 ✔ ᚛
Family-run Victorian guest house
which has ensured personal
attention for 15 years. Few minutes
walk from beach and town centre.
Burns Cottage and 7 golf courses
nearby. Large enclosed car park at
rear of house.

Belmont Guest House, *15 Park Circus, Ayr, KA7 2DJ.*
Grades: ETC 2 Star,
AA 3 Diamond
Tel: **01292 265588** Mr Hillhouse.
Fax no: 01292 290303
D: £20.00-£22.00 **S:** £24.00-£24.00.
Open: All Year (not Xmas)
Beds: 2F 2D 1T **Baths:** 5 En
🛏 🅿 (5) 🖵 🏃 🕹 📖 🛆 🔽 ✔
Try a breath of fresh 'Ayr'. Warm,
comfortable hospitality assured in
this Victorian town house, situated
in a quiet residential area within
easy walking distance of the town
centre and beach. Ground floor
bedrooms available. Glasgow
(Prestwick) Airport 6 miles. Green
Tourism Silver Award.

Kilkerran, *15 Prestwick Road, Ayr, KA8 8LD.*
Friendly family-run guest house on
main A74 Ayr-Prestwick route.
Grades: ETC 2 Star
Tel: **01292 266477** Ms Ferguson.
D: £16.00-£20.00 **S:** £16.00-£20.00.
Open: All Year
Beds: 3F 2D 2T 2S
Baths: 2 En 1 Pr 3 Sh
🛏 🅿 (10) 🖵 🏃 🗙 🕹 📖 🛆 🔽 ᚛ ✔ ᚛

Finlayson Arms Hotel, *Coylton, Ayr, KA6 6JT.*
Tel: **01292 570298** (also fax no)
D: £22.50-£27.50
S: £25.00-£35.00.
Open: All Year (not Xmas/
New Year)
Beds: 1F 7T
Baths: 8 En
🛏 🅿 (12) ✔ 🖵 🗙 🕹 📖 🛆 🔽 ▮
Superbly located for golfing
holidays, with over 30 courses
nearby including Turnberry and
Royal Troon. Beautiful fresh
cuisine. Nearby to Ayr for
excellent shopping & relaxing
Ayrshire scenery. Ideally situated
for exploring Burns country. Fine
selection of malts.

Deanbank, *44 Ashgrove Street, Ayr, KA7 3BG.*
Convenient for town centre,
station, golf and Burns Country.
Grades: ETC 4 Star
Tel: **01292 263745**
Ms Wilson.
D: £18.00-£20.00
S: £20.00-£25.00.
Open: All Year (not Xmas)
Beds: 1F 1T
Baths: 1 Sh
🛏 (1) ✔ 🖵 🏃 🕹 📖 🔽 ✔ ᚛

Sunnyside, *26 Dunure Road, Doonfoot, Ayr, KA7 4HR.*
Actual grid ref: NS322185
Close to Burns Cottage, Brig
O'Doon; spacious rooms; family
welcome.
Grades: ETC 3 Star
Tel: **01292 441234** (also fax no)
Mrs Malcolm.
D: £20.00-£22.00
S: £26.00-£28.00.
Open: All Year (not Xmas)
Beds: 2F
Baths: 2 En
🛏 🅿 (4) ✔ 🖵 🕹 📖 🔽 ✔ ᚛

Ferguslea, *98 New Road, Ayr, KA8 8JG.*
Family run, good food, traditional
Scottish hospitality.
Grades: ETC 2 Star
Tel: **01292 268551** Mrs Campbell.
D: £14.00-£16.00 **S:** £14.00-£16.00.
Open: All Year (not Xmas/New
Year)
Beds: 2T 1S
Baths: 2 Sh
🛏 🅿 (3) 🖵 🏃 🕹 📖 🔽 ᚛

Tramore Guest House, *17 Eglinton Terrace, Ayr, KA7 1JJ.*
In C12th old fort area, 2 mins from
town centre.
Grades: ETC 3 Star
Tel: **01292 266019** (also fax no)
Tumilty.
D: £17.00-£18.00 **S:** £17.00-£19.00
Open: All Year
Beds: 1D 2T
Baths: 2 Sh
🛏 🖵 🏃 🗙 🕹 📖 🔽 ▮

Langley Bank Guest House, *39 Carrick Road, Ayr, KA7 2RD.*
A well appointed Victorian house.
Centrally situated.
Grades: ETC 3 Star
Tel: **01292 264246**
Mr & Mrs Mitchell.
Fax no: 01292 282628
D: £15.00-£25.00 **S:** £20.00-£45.00
Open: All Year
Beds: 1F 3D 2T **Baths:** 4 Pr 1 En
🛏 🅿 (4) 🖵 🕹 📖 🔽 ✔

Glasgow

The great city of **Glasgow** has long been
Scotland's industrial hub, historically the centre
of the European tobacco trade until
shipbuilding and heavy industry took over. The
city's Victorian civic architecture was built on
wealth that flowed from industries whose
employees were crammed into its notorious
squalid and insanitary tenements. The grand
public architecture of the eighteenth and
nineteenth centuries includes the City
Chambers, elegantly colonnaded Stirling's
Library, Hutcheson's Hall with its white spire,
designed by David Hamilton (now National
Trust for Scotland) and Trades House,
Glasgow's only surviving Robert Adam
building, with a green dome and trade-inspired
internal decoration. The earlier history of the
city is reflected by Provand's Lordship, a
fifteenth-century house (now a museum) and

thirteenth-century **St Mungo's Cathedral**.
Close by, St Mungo's Museum of Religious Life
and Art is an excellent display of the art of the
world's religions. In addition to the Burrell
Collection, Glasgow's many superb museums
include the **Hunterian** (archaeology and
Scottish art), **Kelvingrove Art Gallery** and
Museum (Scottish and European art and
Scottish natural history), the **Museum of
Transport** (including bicycles, trains and
trams) and the **People's Palace** (the city's
social history). The considerable legacy of art
nouveau architect and designer Charles
Rennie Mackintosh includes the **Glasgow
School of Art**, which demonstrates inside and
out his concept of a building as total work of
art, Queen's Cross Church and Scotland Street
School. Mackintosh House, an impressive
recreation of the interior of his home, is at the
Hunterian.

Dunedin, 10 Montgomerie *Terrace, Ayr, KA7 1JL.*
Comfortable family home from home.
Grades: ETC 2 Star
Tel: 01292 261224 Mrs Grant.
D: £18.00-£19.00 **S:** £36.00-£46.00.
Open: Easter to Sept
Beds: 1F 1D
Baths: 2 En
🛏🅿(2)⊬⬜🛉🎤🖩Ⅴ

Windsor Hotel, 6 Alloway Place, *Ayr, KA7 2AA.*
Town house hotel within 15 min drive of 14 golf courses.
Grades: ETC 2 Star,
AA 3 Diamond
Tel: 01292 264689 Mrs Hamilton:
D: £22.00-£25.00 **S:** £22.00-£35.00.
Open: All Year (not Xmas)
Beds: 4F 3D 1T 2S
Baths: 7 En 1 Pr 1 Sh
🛏⊬⬜🖈✕🛉🎤🖩♿Ⅴ🛗

Town Hotel, 9-11 Barns Street, *Ayr, KA7 1XB.*
Family run hotel, close to town centre and 10 local golf courses.
Tel: 01292 267595
D: £20.00-£25.00 **S:** £20.00-£25.00.
Open: All Year
Beds: 3F 1D 14T
Baths: 18 En
🛏(1)🅿(1)⬜🖈✕🛉🎤🖩♿Ⅴ🛗♦
🐾

Iona, 27 St Leonards Road, Ayr, *KA7 2PS.*
Actual grid ref: NS341203
Welcome to Iona for comfortable rooms and full Scottish breakfast.
Tel: 01292 269541 (also fax no)
Mr & Mrs Gibson.
D: £17.00-£20.00 **S:** £17.00-£20.00.
Open: Feb to Nov
Beds: 1D 1T 2S
Baths: 2 En 1 Sh
🛏🅿(3)⬜🖈🛉🎤🖩Ⅴ🐾

Failte, 9 Prestwick Road, Ayr, *KA8 8LD.*
Situated on the main road for Glasgow, 10 mins from Prestwick International Airport.
Tel: 01292 265282 (also fax no)
Mrs Jennifer Thomson.
D: £19.00-£22.00 **S:** £19.00-£22.00.
Open: All Year (not Xmas)
Beds: 1D 1T
Baths: 1 En 1 Pr
🛏🅿⬜🛉🎤🖩Ⅴ♦🐾

All rooms full and
nowhere else to stay?
Ask the owner if
there's anywhere
nearby

The Dunn Thing Guest House, 13 Park Circus, Ayr, *KA7 2DJ.*
Victorian house in quiet street near town centre.
Tel: 01292 284531 Mrs Dunn.
D: £17.00-£20.00 **S:** £18.00-£22.00.
Open: All Year
Beds: 2D 1T **Baths:** 3 En
🛏⬜🖈🛉🎤🖩Ⅴ♦🐾

Monaco Guest House, 41 Seafield *Drive, Ayr, KA7 4BJ.*
Comfortable family-run B&B in quiet seafront location with superb panoramic views.
Tel: 01292 264295 Lennon.
D: £19.00-£22.00 **S:** £20.00-£24.00.
Open: Easter to Oct
Beds: 1D 1T 1S
Baths: 1 En 1 Sh
🅿(6)⊬⬜🛉🎤🖩Ⅴ🐾

Prestwick   19

National Grid Ref: NS3425

🍴 🍺 North Beach Hotel, Golf Inn, Carlton Hotel

Knox Bed & Breakfast, 105 Ayr *Road, Prestwick, Ayrshire, KA9 1TN.*
Superb accommodation, homely welcome, excellent value, close to all amenities, airport and Centrum Arena.
Tel: 01292 478808 Mrs Wardrope.
D: £15.00-£18.00 **S:** £16.00-£20.00.
Open: All Year (not Xmas)
Beds: 1D 1T 1S **Baths:** 1 Sh
🛏(2)🅿(4)⊬⬜🛉🎤🖩Ⅴ♦🐾

Monkton   20

National Grid Ref: NS3627

🍴 🍺 Wheatsheaf, North Beach Hotel

Crookside Farm, Kerrix Road, *Monkton, Prestwick, Ayrshire, KA9 2QU.*
Comfortable farmhouse, central heating throughout, ideal for golfing, close to airport.
Tel: 01563 830266 Mrs Gault.
D: £12.00-£12.00 **S:** £12.00-£12.00.
Open: All Year (not Xmas)
Beds: 1F 1D **Baths:** 1 Sh
🛏🅿⬜🖈🛉🎤♿Ⅴ

Troon   21

National Grid Ref: NS3230

🍴 🍺 Old Loans Inn, Lookout, Wheatsheaf, South Beach Hotel, Anchorage, Towers

The Cherries, 50 Ottoline Drive, *Troon, Ayrshire, KA10 7AW.*
Beautiful quiet home on golf course near beaches and restaurants.
Grades: ETC 3 Star
Tel: 01292 313312 Mrs Tweedie.
Fax no: 01292 319007
D: £20.00-£24.00 **S:** £20.00-£25.00.
Open: All Year
Beds: 1F 1T 1S
Baths: 1 En 1 Pr 1 Sh
🛏🅿(5)⊬⬜🖈🛉🎤🖩Ⅴ♦🐾

Rosedale, 9 Firth Road, Barassie, *Troon, KA10 6TF.*
Quiet seafront location - ideal for Sea Cat ferry to Ireland.
Grades: ETC 2 Star
Tel: 01292 314371 Mrs Risk.
D: £20.00-£20.00 **S:** £20.00-£20.00.
Open: All Year (not Xmas)
Beds: 1D 1T 1S
🛏(5)⊬⬜🛉🎤🖩Ⅴ🐾

Mossgiel, 56 Bentinck Drive, *Troon, KA10 6HY.*
5 minutes from beach, 10 minutes' walk from golf courses.
Grades: ETC 2 Star
Tel: 01292 314937 (also fax no)
Mrs Rankin.
D: £19.00-£22.00
S: £22.00-£25.00.
Open: All Year
Beds: 1F 1D 1T
Baths: 3 En
🛏🅿(3)⬜🛉🎤♿Ⅴ🛗♦🐾

The Beeches, 63 Ottoline Drive, *Troon, KA10 7AN.*
Bright spacious house, wooded gardens. Every amenity, beaches, golf, marina.
Grades: ETC 2 Star
Tel: 01292 314180
Mrs Sinclair.
D: £16.00-£18.00 **S:** £18.00-£20.00.
Open: All Year
Beds: 1D 1T 1S
Baths: 2 Pr
🛏🅿(4)⊬⬜🛉🎤🖩Ⅴ🐾

Barassie   22

National Grid Ref: NS3232

🍴 🍺 Tower Hotel

Fordell, 43 Beach Road, Barassie, *Troon, KA10 6SU.*
Grades: ETC 3 Star
Tel: 01292 313224
Mrs Mathieson.
Fax no: 01292 312141
D: £18.00-£20.00
S: £20.00-£25.00.
Open: All Year (not Xmas/New Year)
Beds: 2T
Baths: 2 Sh
⊬⬜🖈🛉🎤🖩Ⅴ♦🐾
Relax in this Victorian house overlooking the sea or use it as a base to visit Ayrshire's famed golf courses or many other attractions. Comfortable rooms, good breakfasts, secure parking for cycles or motor bikes. A warm welcome awaits.

D = Price range per
person sharing in a
double room

Km ┣┼┼┼┼┼┼┼┤ 5   10
Miles ┣┼┼┼┼┤ 5

Aviemore ⑥②

A9

Kincraig ⑤⓪

⑤① Feshiebridge

Kingussie ④⑨

NH
00
NN

Newtonmore ④⑧

80

A9

Blair Atholl ④⑦

Killiecrankie ④⑥

60

④⑤

Pitlochry   A9

A827

Edradynate ④④

A827

④③

Aberfeldy

④②

Acharn

40

A827

80

Kilwinning   23

National Grid Ref: NS3043

🍴 🍺 Blair Inn, Claremont Hotel

Claremont Guest House,
27 Howgate, Kilwinning, Ayrshire,
KA13 6EW.
Friendly family B&B close to town
centre and public transport.
Tel: **01294 553905** Mrs Filby.
D: £17.00-£20.00 **S:** £17.00-£20.00.
Open: All Year (not Xmas)
Beds: 1F 1S **Baths:** 2 Sh
🛇 🅿 (10) ⅟ 🗙 🖥 ⚭ 🚲

Tarcoola, *Montgreenan,*
Kilwinning, Ayrshire, KA13 7QZ.
Actual grid ref: NS344440
Attractive country setting conve-
nient for Arran ferry and Ayrshire
golf.
Tel: **01294 850379** Mrs Melville.
Fax no: 01294 850249
D: £16.00-£18.00 **S:** £16.00-£16.00.
Open: All Year
Beds: 1T **Baths:** 1 Pr
🛇 (8) 🅿 (2) ⅟ 🗙 🕇 ⚏ 🖥 Ⓥ ⚭ 🚲

Beith   24

National Grid Ref: NS3553

🍴 🍺 Parrafin Lamp

Townend of Shuterflat Farm,
Beith, Ayrshire, KA15 2LW.
Comfortable farmhouse, warm
welcome, 15 minutes Glasgow
Airport and city centre.
Tel: **01505 502342** Mrs Lamont.
D: £17.50-£17.50 **S:** £17.50-£17.50.
Open: All Year
Beds: 1T 2D
Baths: 1 Sh
🛇 🅿 (4) 🗙 🕇 ⚏ 🖥 Ⓥ 🖪 ⚭ 🚲

Lochwinnoch   25

National Grid Ref: NS3559

🍴 🍺 Mossend Hotel, Gateside Inn, Brown Bull

East Lochhead, *Largs Road,*
Lochwinnoch, Renfrewshire,
PA12 4DX.
Beautifully restored farmhouse.
Loch views, gardens. Taste of
Scotland.
Grades: ETC 4 Star,
AA 5 Diamond, Premier Select
Tel: **01505 842610** (also fax no)
Mrs Anderson.
D: £30.00-£32.50 **S:** £30.00-£35.00.
Open: All Year
Beds: 1T 2D **Baths:** 3 En
🛇 🅿 (6) ⅟ 🗙 🕇 ✗ ⚏ 🖥 ♿ Ⓥ 🖪 ⚭ 🚲

Bringing children with

you? Always ask for

any special rates.

All cycleways are popular: you are well-advised to book ahead

---

Garnock Lodge, *Lochwinnoch,*
Renfrewshire, PA12 4JT.
Grades: ETC 4 Star,
AA 4 Diamond
Tel: **01505 503680** (also fax no)
Mr & Mrs McMeechan.
D: £18.00-£21.00
S: £25.00-£30.00.
Open: All Year
Beds: 1D 2T 1S
Baths: 2 En 1 Sh
🛏 🅿 (4) ⊬🗆 🖢 🎟 ⱱ ♦ ⬥ ⊰
A warm welcome awaits you at detached house in rural situation easy access to Glasgow Airport via main route also Loch Lomond and Ayrshire coast, walking, fishing, golf, cycling and bird watching, home baking, log fires, ensuite, off road parking.

Kilbarchan   26
National Grid Ref: NS4063

📍 🍴 Trust Inn

Gladstone Farmhouse,
Burntshields Road, Kilbarchan,
Johnstone, Renfrewshire, PA10 2PB.
Quiet countryside, 10 minutes
Glasgow airport on direct route.
Tel: **01505 702579** (also fax no)
Mrs Douglas.
D: £18.00-£18.00
S: £20.00-£20.00.
Open: All Year
Beds: 1F 1D 1T
Baths: 1 Sh
🛏 🅿 (6) 🗆 🖢 ✗ 🖢 🎟 ⬥ ⱱ ♦ ⬥ ⊰

Paisley   27
National Grid Ref: NS4863

📍 🍴 Lord Lounsdale, Paraffin Lamp

Accara Guest House,
75 Maxwellton Road, Paisley,
Renfrewshire, PA1 2RB.
Grade II Listed building close to
airport, museum, university, hospital.
Grades: ETC 2 Star
Tel: **0141 887 7604** Mrs Stevens.
Fax no: 0141 887 1589
D: £20.00-£20.00 **S:** £25.00-£25.00.
Open: All Year
Beds: 1F 1T 1S
Baths: 2 Sh
🛏 (4) ⊬🗆 🖢 🎟 ⱱ

S = Price range for a single person in a room

Myfarrclan Guest House,
146 Corsebar Road, Paisley,
Renfrewshire, PA2 9NA.
Nestling in leafy suburb of Paisley, lovingly restored bungalow offering many thoughtful extras.
Tel: **0141 884 8285**
Mr & Mrs Farr.
Fax no: 0141 581 1566
D: £32.50-£35.00
S: £40.00-£60.00.
Open: All Year
Beds: 2D 1T
Baths: 2 En 1 Pr
🛏 🅿 (2) ⊬🗆 ✗ 🖢 🎟 ⱱ

Glasgow Muirend   28
National Grid Ref: NS5760

16 Bogton Avenue, *Muirend,*
Glasgow, G44 3JJ.
Quiet red sandstone terraced private house adjacent station, 12 mins city centre.
Tel: **0141 637 4402** (also fax no)
Mrs Paterson.
D: £20.00-£20.00
S: £22.00-£22.00.
Open: All Year (not Xmas)
Beds: 1D 2S
Baths: 2 Sh
🅿 (2) ⊬🗆 ✗ 🖢 🎟 ⱱ

Planning a longer stay? Always ask for any special rates.

Glasgow Central   29
National Grid Ref: NS5865

📍 🍴 Dorsey's, Park Bar, Mitchell's, Stravaigan's, Orchard Park, Bellahoustan Hotel, Garfield House, Highlanders Park, Snaffil Bit

🔺 **Glasgow Youth Hostel,** *7/8*
Park Terrace, Glasgow, G3 6BY.
Actual grid ref: NS575662
Tel: **0141 332 3004**
Under 18: £8.50
Adults: £10.00
Self-catering facilities, Shop nearby, Laundry facilities, Evening meal for groups only
Glasgow has something for everyone, from city parks to free museums and galleries, and great nightlife. Good base for touring the Trossachs, the Clyde Coast and Loch Lomond.

🔺 **Euro Hostel Glasgow,** *318*
Clyde Street, Glasgow G1 4NR.
Actual grid ref: NS593645
Tel: **0141 222 2828**
Adults: £13.75
Laundry facilities, Games room, Security lockers, Cycle store, Facilities for disabled people, No smoking
Centrally located, overlooking River Clyde. All rooms ensuite: 3 single, 70 twin, 3 triple, 32 x 4 person/family, 3 x 8 person, 4 x 14 person - most combinations of requirements can be catered for. Close Central/Queen Street rail stations/Buchanan Street Bus Station; overnight parking available at nearby St Enoch Square.

Glasgow to Loch Tay

Proceeding through the decaying shipyards of the north bank of the Clyde, you reach **Dumbarton** before heading north to Balloch Castle Country Park by Loch Lomond. Having left metropolitan Clydeside spectacularly behind, you continue to Drymen before cycling through Queen Elizabeth Forest Park, where there are red deer, to reach Aberfoyle. Climbing northward you are in the heart of the Trossachs, a wild and wonderful region of craggy hills, forest and secluded waterfalls. Hugging the southern shore of Loch Venachar you arrive at **Callander**, a small town with excellent facilities, where the Rob Roy and Trossachs visitor centre introduces the region and offers an audiovisual presentation on its famous son, the most renowned of the MacGregors and hero of Sir Walter Scott's novel. From here you cycle along the west bank of Loch Lubnaig to reach Balquhidder at the eastern end of Loch Voil and Lochearnhead at the western end of Loch Earn. Climbing to the summit of Glen Ogle and descending to Lix Toll, you reach **Killin**, where the River Dochart cascades over the town's pretty waterfall into Loch Tay. The mountain **Ben Lawers** glowers across from the other side as you undertake the long ride down the southern shore of the loch.

Kirkland House, *42 St Vincent Crescent, Glasgow, G3 8NG.*
Grades: ETC 3 Star
Tel: **0141 248 3458** Mrs Divers.
Fax no: 0141 221 5174
D: £27.00-£30.00
S: £27.00-£30.00.
Open: All Year
Beds: 3D 2T 2S **Baths:** 6 En 2 Sh
☎ (1) ⊁ ♥ 🍽 V
City centre guest house with excellent rooms on beautiful Victorian Crescent in Finnieston (Glasgow's 'little Chelsea'). Short walk to Scottish Exhibition Centre, Museum/Art Gallery, Kelvingrove Park and all West End facilities. Glasgow airport 10 minutes. Member of the Harry James society.

Kelvingrove Hotel,
944 Sauchiehall Street, Glasgow, G3 7TH.
Grades: ETC 3 Star,
AA 3 Diamond, RAC 3 Star
Tel: **0141 339 5011** Mr Wills.
Fax no: 0141 339 6566
D: £24.00-£29.00
S: £33.00-£38.00.
Open: All Year (not Xmas)
Beds: 8D 4T 4F
Baths: 10 En
☎ ₱ (20) ⊁ ♥ ♥ ♣ ♣ 🍽 V ▮ ♿
Centrally located family-run hotel, set in Glasgow's fashionable West End. Close to pubs, clubs, art galleries, museums, University, shops, rail and bus links - all within walking distance.

Adelaide's, *209 Bath Street, Glasgow, G2 4HZ.*
Central location, close to all major attractions of revitalised city.
Grades: ETC 2 Star
Tel: **0141 248 4970** Meiklejohn.
Fax no: 0141 226 4247
D: £25.00-£28.00
S: £35.00-£45.00.
Open: All Year (not Xmas/New Year)
Beds: 2F 2T 2D 2S
Baths: 6 En 2 Sh
☎ ⊁ ♥ ♣ V ▮ ♿

Number Thirty Six, *36 St Vincent Crescent, Glasgow, G3 8NG.*
Situated in a Georgian terrace on the edge of Glasgow city centre.
Tel: **0141 248 2086** Mrs MacKay.
Fax no: 0141 221 1477
D: £25.00-£30.00
S: £30.00-£35.00.
Open: All Year (not Xmas)
Beds: 4D 2T
Baths: 4 En 2 Pr
⊁ ♥ ♣ 🍽 V

Please don't camp
on *anyone's* land
without first obtaining
their permission.

Glasgow Dennistoun   30

National Grid Ref: NS6065

¶ ♨ Fire Station Resturant, Dorsey's, Park Bar, Mitchell's, Stravaigan's, Orchard Park, Bellahoustow Hotel, Garfield House, Highlanders Park, Snaffil Bit

Seton Guest House, *6 Seton Terrace, Glasgow, G31 2HU.*
Warm and friendly welcome assured. Five minutes from city centre.
Grades: ETC 2 Star
Tel: **0141 556 7654** Mr Passway.
Fax no: 0141 402 3655
D: £16.00-£17.00 **S:** £17.00-£18.00.
Open: All Year (not Xmas)
Beds: 4F 2D 2T 1S
Baths: 3 Sh
☎ ♥ ♣ 🍽 V

Rosewood Guest House, *4 Seton Terrace, Glasgow, G31 2HU.*
Victorian House near City Centre, close to many city attractions.
Grades: ETC 2 Star
Tel: **0141 550 1500**
Ms Turner.
Fax no: 01555 393876
D: £17.00-£20.00
S: £19.00-£22.00.
Open: All Year
Beds: 3F 2T 1D 2S
Baths: 3 Sh
☎ ₱ ♥ ♥ ♣ 🍽 V ♿

Glasgow Dowanhill   31

National Grid Ref: NS5667

¶ ♨ Orchard Park Hotel, Bellahoustow Hotel

The Terrace House Hotel, *14 Belhaven Terrace, Glasgow, G12 0TG.*
Grades: ETC 2 Star
Tel: **0141 337 3377** (also fax no)
Mrs Black.
D: £29.00-£39.00
S: £49.00-£65.00.
Open: All Year
Beds: 4F 3D 5T 1S
Baths: 12 En 1 Pr
☎ ⊁ ♥ ♥ ✗ ♣ 🍽 V
'B' Listed terraced townhouse, built circa 1860, boasting fine period features, such as ornate cornices, wall friezes and columned entrance. Well connected to transport links to city centre, Glasgow Airport and Loch Lomond. A friendly welcome awaits you.

Glasgow Broomhill   32

National Grid Ref: NS5467

¶ ♨ Air Organic, Bellahoustow Hotel, Dino's, Dorsey's, Garfield House, Highlanders Park, Mitchell's, Orchard Park, Pablo's, Park Bar, Stravaigan's, Snaffil Bit

Lochgilvie House, *117 Randolph Road, Broomhill, Glasgow, G11 7DS.*
Grades: ETC 3 Star
Tel: **0141 357 1593**
Mrs Ogilvie.
Fax no: 0141 334 5828
D: £25.00-£30.00 **S:** £25.00-£35.00.
Open: All Year
Beds: 1F 2D 3T
Baths: 4 En
☎ (10) ₱ ⊁ ♥ ♣ 🍽 V
Luxurious Victorian town house situated in Glasgow's prestigious West End, adjacent to rail station, beside the art galleries, university, SECC, convenient for International Airport.

Park House, *13 Victoria Park Gardens South, Glasgow, G11 7BX.*
Magnificent Victorian residence overlooking private parkland in quiet residential area.
Grades: ETC 4 Star
Tel: **0141 339 1559**
Mrs Hallam.
Fax no: 0141 576 0915
D: £25.00-£27.50
S: £32.00-£37.50.
Open: All Year
Beds: 2D 1T
Baths: 2 En 1 Pr
☎ ₱ (3) ♥ ✗ ♣ 🍽 V

Balloch   33

National Grid Ref: NS3982

¶ ♨ Roundabout Inn, Balloch Hotel, Corries, Stables, Clachan Inn

Glyndale, *6 McKenzie Drive, Lomond Road Estate, Balloch, Alexandria, Dunbartonshire, G83 8HL.*
Easy access to Loch Lomond, Glasgow Airport, public transport.
Grades: ETC 3 Star B&B
Tel: **01389 758238** Mrs Ross.
D: £16.50-£17.50 **S:** £20.00-£20.00
Open: All Year (not Xmas)
Beds: 1D 1T
Baths: 1 Sh
☎ ₱ (2) ⊁ ♥ ♥ ♣ 🍽 V ♿

Anchorage Guest House, *Balloch Road, Balloch, Alexandria, Dunbartonshire, G83 8SS.*
Situated on the banks of Loch Lomond. Ideal base for touring, fishing, sailing & walking.
Grades: ETC 1 Star
Tel: **01389 753336** Mr Bowman.
D: £18.00-£25.00 .
Open: All Year
Beds: 1F 2D 4T
Baths: 5 En 2 Sh
☎ (1) ₱ (6) ♥ ♥ ✗ ♣ 🍽 & V ▮ ♿

Pay B&Bs by cash or
cheque and be prepared
to pay up front.

Dumbain Farm, *Balloch, Alexandria, Dunbartonshire, G83 8DS.*
Newly converted byre on working farm. Aga cooked breakfast. Homemade raspberry jam.
Grades: ETC 3 Star
Tel: 01389 752263
Mrs Watson.
D: £20.00-£22.00 **S:** £18.00-£25.00.
Open: All Year
Beds: 1F 1T 1D
Baths: 3 En
🛇 🅿 (5) ⅍ ◻ ☕ 🎂 🏧 Ⅴ ✦ 🚲

Gowanlea Guest House, *Drymen Road, Balloch, Alexandria, Dunbartonshire, G83 8HS.*
Grades: ETC 4 Star
Tel: 01389 752456
Mrs Campbell.
Fax no: 01389 710543
D: £19.00-£23.00
S: £22.00-£30.00.
Open: All Year (not Xmas/New Year)
Beds: 1T 3D
Baths: 4 En
🛇 🅿 (4) ⅍ ◻ 🎂 🏧 Ⅴ ✦
Warm welcome awaits you at Campbell's award winning family run guest house B&B. Superior accommodation, excellent hospitality. Ideal touring base.

Heathpete, *24 Balloch Road, Balloch, Alexandria, Dunbartonshire, G83 8LE.*
Superb hospitality offered in luxurious accommodation central to all amenities.
Grades: ETC 3 Star
Tel: 01389 752195
Mrs Hamill.
D: £12.00-£25.00 **S:** £18.00-£25.00.
Open: All Year
Beds: 2F 2D
Baths: 4 En
🛇 🅿 (5) ◻ ☂ 🎂 🏧 🔥 Ⅴ ✦ 🚲

Auchry, *24 Boturich Drive, Balloch, Alexandria, Dunbartonshire, G83 8JP.*
Actual grid ref: NS395822
Set in quiet cul de sac; walking distance to Loch Lomond.
Grades: ETC 3 Star
Tel: 01389 753208 Mrs McIntosh.
D: £17.00-£19.00 **S:** £18.00-£20.00.
Open: All Year (not Xmas/New Year)
Beds: 1D 1S
Baths: 1 En 1 Sh
🅿 (4) ⅍ ◻ 🎂 🏧 Ⅴ ✦ 🚲

7 Carrochan Crescent, *Balloch, Alexandria, Dunbartonshire, G83 8PX.*
A warm welcome awaits you; ideally situated for touring etc.
Grades: ETC 3 Star
Tel: 01389 750078 Mrs Campbell.
D: £16.00-£16.00 **S:** £18.00-£18.00.
Open: Easter to Oct
Beds: 2D
Baths: 1 Sh
🛇 🅿 (2) ◻ 🎂 🏧 Ⅴ 🔥 ✦ 🚲

S = Price range for a single person in a room

Gartocharn 34

National Grid Ref: NS4286

🍴 🍺 Hungry Monk, Clachan Inn

Mardella Farm, *Old School Road, Gartocharn, Loch Lomond, Alexandria, Dunbartonshire, G83 8SD.*
Actual grid ref: NS438864
Friendly, welcoming, homely atmosphere. Come and meet the quackers (ducks)!
Grades: AA 4 Diamond
Tel: 01389 830428
Mrs MacDonell.
D: £18.50-£22.00 **S:** £31.00-£37.00.
Open: All Year
Beds: 1F 1D 1T
Baths: 1 En 1 Sh
🛇 🅿 (4) ⅍ ◻ ☂ 🎂 🏧 Ⅴ ✦

Croftamie 35

National Grid Ref: NS4786

🍴 🍺 Clachan Inn, Wayfarers

Croftburn, *Croftamie, Drymen, Glasgow, G63 0HA.*
Actual grid ref: NS402860
Former gamekeeper's cottage in one acre of beautiful gardens overlooking Strathendrick Valley & Campsie Fells.
Grades: ETC 3 Star, AA 4 Diamond
Tel: 01360 660796 Mrs Reid.
Fax no: 01360 661005
D: £18.00-£22.00 **S:** £20.00-£25.00.
Open: All Year
Beds: 2D 1T
Baths: 2 En 1 Pr
🛇 (12) 🅿 (20) ⅍ ◻ ☂ ✕ 🎂 🏧 Ⅴ 🔥 🚲

Drymen 36

National Grid Ref: NS4788

🍴 🍺 Buchanan Arms, Clachan Inn, Pottery, Wayfarers, Winnock Hotel

---

Green Shadows, *Buchanan Castle Estate, Drymen, Glasgow, G63 0HX.*
Tel: 01360 660289 Mrs Goodwin.
D: £21.00-£21.00 **S:** £24.00-£24.00.
Open: All year (not Xmas)
Beds: 1F 1D 1S
Baths: 2 Sh
🛇 🅿 (8) ⅍ ◻ 🎂 🏧 Ⅴ 🔥 ✦ 🚲
Warm, friendly welcome in a beautiful country house with spectacular views over golf course and the Lomond Hills. Buchanan Castle to the rear. 1 mile from Drymen Centre, 2 miles from Loch Lomond. Glasgow Airport 40 mins away.

Easter Drumquhassle Farm, *Gartness Road, Drymen, Glasgow, G63 0DN.*
Actual grid ref: NS486872
Traditional farmhouse, beautiful views, home cooking, excellent base on the West Highland Way.
Grades: ETC 3 Star, AA 3 Diamond
Tel: 01360 660893 Mrs Cross.
Fax no: 01360 660282
D: £18.00-£25.00 **S:** £25.00-£30.00.
Open: All Year
Beds: 1F 1D 1T
Baths: 2 En
🛇 🅿 (10) ⅍ ◻ ☂ ✕ 🎂 🏧 Ⅴ ✦ 🚲

Ceardach, *Gartness Road, Drymen, Glasgow, G63 0BH.*
Tel: 01360 660596 (also fax no)
Mrs Robb.
D: £18.00-£20.00 **S:** £18.00-£20.00.
Open: All Year (not Xmas)
Beds: 1D 1T
Baths: 1 Sh
🛇 (1) 🅿 (3) ◻ ☂ 🎂 🏧 👟 Ⅴ 🔥 ✦ 🚲
250 year old Coach house. Situated near the shores of Loch Lomond large garden. Good home cooking, a warm and friendly welcome awaits you.

Glenava, *Stirling Road, Drymen, Glasgow, G63 0AA.*
A warm welcome, stunning scenery, comfortable rooms, lovely local walks.
Grades: ETC 3 Star
Tel: 01360 660491 Ms Fraser.
D: £18.00-£20.00 **S:** £30.00-£30.00.
Open: Easter to Oct
Beds: 1D 1T
Baths: 1 Sh
🛇 🅿 (4) ⅍ 🎂 🏧 Ⅴ 🔥 ✦ 🚲

17 Stirling Road, *Drymen, Glasgow, G63 0BW.*
Actual grid ref: NS476883
Family home in village near West Highland Way; lovely garden.
Tel: 01360 660273 (also fax no)
Mrs Lander.
D: £15.00-£18.00 **S:** £18.00-£23.00.
Open: All Year
Beds: 1F 1T **Baths:** 1 Sh
🛇 🅿 (1) ◻ ☂ 🎂 Ⅴ 🔥 ✦ 🚲

Aberfoyle 37

National Grid Ref: NN5200

🍴 🍺 Black Bull, Byre, Old Coach House, Inverard Hotel, Forth Inn

Creag Ard House B&B, *Aberfoyle, Stirling, FK8 3TQ.*
Actual grid ref: NN502015
A beautiful Victorian house with extensive and colourful gardens, set in magnificent scenery.
Grades: ETC 4 Star
Tel: 01877 382297 Mrs Wilson.
D: £27.00-£40.00 **S:** £35.00-£70.00.
Open: All Year
Beds: 4D 2T
Baths: 6 En
🛇 🅿 (7) ⅍ ◻ ✕ 🎂 🏧 Ⅴ 🔥 ✦ 🚲

Mayfield, *Main Street, Aberfoyle, Stirling, FK8 3UQ.*
Large Victorian private house in centre of Aberfoyle.
Grades: ETC Listed, Comm
Tel: **01877 382845** Mrs Oldham.
D: £18.50-£22.00 **S:** £20.00-£25.00.
Open: All Year (not Xmas/New Year)
Beds: 2D 1T 1S
Baths: 3 En 1 Pr
⏲🅿(4)⬜🏠🛏🎢💻🖳📺⬚🚲

Oak Royal Guest House,
Aberfoyle, Stirling, FK8 3UX.
Beautiful Trossachs countryside.
Ideal base for touring & outdoor enthusiasts.
Tel: **01877 382633** (also fax no)
D: £20.00-£22.50 **S:** £25.00-£30.00.
Open: All Year
Beds: 2D 1T **Baths:** 2 En 1 Sh
⏲🅿(6)✍⬜🏠🛏🎢💻📺⬚🚲

Loch Achray   38

National Grid Ref: NN5106

Glenbruach Country House, *Loch Achray, Trossachs, Callander, Perthshire, FK17 8HX.*
Tel: **01877 376216** (also fax no)
Mrs Lindsay.
D: £22.00-£25.00 **S:** £22.00-£25.00.
Open: All Year
Beds: 2D 1T
Baths: 2 En 1 Pr
⏲(12)🅿(3)✍🏠🛏🎢💻📺⬚⬚🚲
Unique country mansion in the heart of Rob Roy country. All rooms with Loch views. Interesting interior design and collections in this Scots-owned home.

Callander   39

National Grid Ref: NN6307

🍴⬚ Abbotsford Lodge Hotel, Myrtle Inn, Crags Hotel, Bracklin Fall, Bridge End, Byre

▲ **Trossachs Backpackers,**
Invertrossachs Road, Callander, Perthshire, FK17 8HW.
Actual grid ref: NN606072
Tel: **01877 331200**
Under 18: £10.00 **Adults:** £12.50
Self-catering facilities, Television, Showers, Central heating, Shop, Laundry facilities, Wet weather shelter, Lounge, Dining room, Games room, Grounds available for games, Drying room, Cycle store, Parking, Facilities for disabled people, No smoking
Luxurious hostel in idyllic national park setting. Many local attractions.

Arden House, *Bracklinn Road, Callander, Perthshire, FK17 8EQ.*
Tel: **01877 330235** (also fax no)
Mr Mitchell & Mr W Jackson.
D: £27.50-£30.00 **S:** £30.00-£30.00.
Open: Easter to Nov
Beds: 3D 2T 1S
Baths: 6 En
⏲(14)🅿(6)✍⬜🛏🎢💻📺⬚
Tranquillity in the Trossachs. Peaceful Victorian country house with stunning views. Home of BBC TVs 'Dr Finlay's Casebook'. Comfortable, elegant ensuite rooms with TV, tea/coffee and many thoughtful touches. Few minutes walk to village. Generous breakfasts and genuine hospitality.

Planning a longer stay? Always ask for any special rates.

Campfield Cottage, *138 Main Street, Callander, Perthshire, FK17 8BG.*
Tel: **01877 330597** Mrs Hunter.
D: £18.00-£18.00 **S:** £18.00-£18.00.
Open: All Year (not Xmas/New Year)
Beds: 2D 1T 1S **Baths:** 1 Sh
⏲🅿✍⬜🏠🛏🎢💻📺⬚🚲
Charming C18th cottage in the heart of Callander, down a quiet lane, for a good night's sleep. Highly recommended by people from all over the world, colour TVs in double rooms, washing facilities, tea/coffee, visitors' lounge, conservatory, parking.

Burnt Inn House, *Brig o' Turk, Callander, Perthshire, FK17 8HT.*
Actual grid ref: NN537066
Situated in the heart of the Trossachs. Quiet rural location.
Grades: ETC 3 Star
Tel: **01877 376212**
Mrs Trzebiatowski
Fax no: 01877 376233
D: £20.00-£25.00 **S:** £20.00-£25.00.
Open: All Year (not Xmas/New Year)
Beds: 2T 1D **Baths:** 3 En
⏲(12)🅿(3)⬚💻📺⬚🚲

Glengarry Hotel, *Stirling Road, Callander, Perthshire, FK17 8DA.*
Tel: **01877 330216**
D: £22.00-£25.00 .
Open: All Year
Beds: 3F 1D **Baths:** 4 En
⏲🅿(15)⬜🏠🛡🛏💻📺⬚🚲
Family-run hotel in its own grounds in the picturesque town of Callander where the Lowlands meet the Highlands. Large comfortable bedrooms. A warm welcome, a hearty breakfast, traditional home-cooked evening meals. Easy access.

Loch Tay to the Pass of Drumochter

From Kenmore at the northeastern end of Loch Tay you follow the River Tay to the sixteenth-century fortified tower house Castle Menzies, historic seat of the Menzies clan, and Aberfeldy, where the restored water mill dates from the early nineteenth century. From here you continue to **Pitlochry**. Here the Edradour Distillery is Scotland's smallest whisky distillery and the Pitlochry Festival Theatre stages a different play every night from May to October. By the hydroelectric power station is a fish ladder, by which the salmon can bypass the dam on the Tummel to reach their breeding grounds. A short way through the Tummel Forest Park, the spectacular Pass of Killiecrankie was the setting in 1689 for the Battle of Killiecrankie, a great Jacobite victory in the period when such things happened. A little further on is Blair Atholl, where there is a working water mill, and nearby Blair Castle, seat of the Dukes of Atholl. Over the long period since its foundation in the thirteenth century, this striking white fortress has undergone much alteration. It is the scene every May for the parade of the Atholl Highlanders, Britain's only legal private army. The route through Glen Garry culminates in a steady ascent to the **Pass of Drumochter**. This will test your stamina. There is no alternative to the A9 and there is only one hotel listed in this book - at Dalwhinnie.

The Grid Reference beneath the location heading is for the village or town - *not* for individual houses, which are shown (where supplied) in each entry itself.

Riverview House, *Leny Road, Callander, Perthshire, FK17 8AL.*
Grades: ETC 3 Star
Tel: **01877 330635** Mr Little.
D: £21.00-£22.00 **S:** £22.00-£24.00.
Open: All Year (not Xmas)
Beds: 3D 2T 1S **Baths:** 5 En
🅿 (6) ⊬ ⏶ 🛏 🎘 🏛 Ⅴ ♻
Attractive, stone-built villa in own grounds within easy walking of town centre and cycle/pathway. Good home cooking. We also offer self catering cottages in beautiful Trossachs area.

Linley Guest House, *139 Main Street, Callander, Perthshire, FK17 8BH.*
Grades: ETC 3 Star
Tel: **01877 330087** McQuilton.
D: £16.00-£18.50 **S:** £20.00-£25.00.
Open: All Year
Beds: 1F 1T 3D
Baths: 2 En 2 Sh
🛏 🅿 ⊡ 🛏 🎘 🏛 Ⅴ 🍴 ♻ ♿
Comfortable Victorian terraced house close to Callander busy centre. Good for overnight stop/touring base for the magnificent scenery of the Trossachs renowned for hill walking, fishing, cycling and water sports. Stirling 25 minutes drive, Glasgow and Edinburgh only 1 hour.

East Mains House, *Bridgend, Callander, Perthshire, FK17 8AG.*
C18th mansion house, mature garden.
Grades: ETC 3 Star
Tel: **01877 330535** (also fax no)
Ms Alexander.
D: £22.00-£24.00 **S:** £29.00-£29.00.
Open: All Year
Beds: 2F 4D
Baths: 4 En
🛏 🅿 (6) ⊬ ⊡ 🛏 🎘 🏛 Ⅴ 🍴 ♻ ♿

Brook Linn Country House, *Callander, Perthshire, FK17 8AU.*
Lovely comfortable Victorian house with magnificent views and personal attention.
Grades: ETC 4 Star,
AA 4 Diamond
Tel: **01877 330103** (also fax no)
Mrs House.
D: £23.00-£27.00 **S:** £23.00-£27.00.
Open: Easter to Oct
Beds: 1F 2D 2T 2S
Baths: 6 En 1 Pr
🛏 🅿 (8) ⊬ ⊡ 🛏 🎘 🏛 Ⅴ ♻ ♿

White Cottage, *Bracklinn Road, Callander, FK17 8EQ.*
Situated in one acre garden. Magnificent views of Ben Ledi.
Grades: ETC 3 Star
Tel: **01877 330896**
Mrs Hughes.
D: £17.50-£19.00
S: £22.00-£25.00.
Open: Apr to Nov
Beds: 2D
Baths: 1 Sh
🅿 (3) ⊬ ⊡ 🛏 🏛 Ⅴ ♻

Roslin Cottage, *Lagrannoch, Callander, Perthshire, FK17 8LE.*
Beautiful C18th stone cottage & garden on outskirts of town.
Tel: **01877 330638** Mrs Ferguson.
Fax no: 01877 331448
D: £15.50-£16.00 **S:** £18.50-£18.50.
Open: All Year
Beds: 1D 1T 2S
Baths: 1 Sh
🛏 🅿 ⊡ 🛏 🎘 🏛 Ⅴ ♻

Lamorna, *Ancaster Road, Callander, Perthshire, FK17 8JJ.*
Detached bungalow, panoramic views of Callander and surrounding countryside, quiet location, close all amenities.
Tel: **01877 330868**
D: £18.00-£20.00.
Open: Easter to Oct
Beds: 1D 1T
Baths: 1 Sh
🅿 (2) ⊬ ⊡ 🛏 🏛 Ⅴ

Strathyre   40

National Grid Ref: NN5617

🍴 ⏚ Strathyre Inn, Ben Shian Hotel

Coire Buidhe, *Strathyre, Callander, Perthshire, FK18 8NA.*
Family Bed and Breakfast, centrally located for Stirling, Trossachs.
Tel: **01877 384288**
Mr & Mrs Reid.
D: £17.00-£20.00 **S:** £17.00-£20.00.
Open: All Year (not Xmas)
Beds: 3F 1D 1T 1S
Baths: 1 Pr 3 Sh
🛏 🅿 (6) ⊬ ⊡ 🛏 🎘 🏛 Ⅴ 🍴 ♻ ♿

Dochfour, *Strathyre, Callander, FK18 8NA.*
Award-winning B&B in scenic glen, specialising in being the best!
Grades: ETC 3 Star
Tel: **01877 384256** (also fax no)
Mr & Mrs Ffinch.
D: £17.00-£20.00 **S:** £23.00-£26.00.
Open: All Year
Beds: 2D 1T
Baths: 2 En 1 Pr
🛏 🅿 (6) ⊡ 🎘 🏛 Ⅴ 🍴 ♻ ♿

Rosebank House, *Strathyre, Callander, Perthshire, FK18 8NA.*
Actual grid ref: NN563174
Rosebank house is a fine example of Victorian architecture.
Tel: **01877 384208**
Mr & Mrs Moor.
Fax no: 01877 384201
D: £18.00-£20.00
S: £18.00-£25.00.
Open: Mar to Dec
Beds: 1F 2D 1T 1S
Baths: 2 En 1 Pr
🛏 🅿 (3) ⊬ ⊡ 🎘 🛏 🏛 Ⅴ 🍴 ♻ ♿

D = Price range per person sharing in a double room

S = Price range for a single person in a room

Killin   41

National Grid Ref: NN5732

🍴 ⏚ Bridge Of Lochay, Coach House, Killin Hotel, Shutters

▲ **Killin Youth Hostel,** *Killin, Perthshire, FK21 8TN.*
Actual grid ref: NN569338
Tel: **01567 820546**
Under 18: £6.00 **Adults:** £8.75
Self-catering facilities, Shop nearby, Facilities for disabled people
Picturesque Killin has the impressive Falls of Dochart and standing stones from the Bronze Age. Good walks with views of Ben Lawers and Loch Tay and a wide range of wildlife.

Falls of Dochart Cottage, *Killin, Perthshire, FK21 8SW.*
Grades: ETC 2 Star
Tel: **01567 820363**
Mr & Mrs Mudd.
D: £16.00-£17.00 **S:** £17.00-£17.00.
Open: All Year (not Xmas)
Beds: 1D 1T 1S
Baths: 2 Sh
🛏 🅿 (1) 🅿 (4) ⊬ ⊡ 🛏 🎘 🏛 ♻
C17th cottage, overlooking the falls and river - home cooking - comfortable and friendly atmosphere. Open all year: central to magnificent mountain area - renowned for hill walking.

Allt Fulieach, *Maragowan, Killin, Perthshire, FK21 8TN.*
Comfortable, modern house at the head of Loch Tay.
Tel: **01567 820962**
Mr Judd.
D: £19.00-£19.00 **S:** £19.00-£19.00.
Open: All Year
Beds: 2T 1D
Baths: 3 En
🛏 🅿 (4) ⊬ ⊡ 🛏 🏛 Ⅴ 🍴 ♻ ♿

Main Street, *Killin, Perthshire, FK21 8TP.*
Grades: ETC 2 Star
Tel: **01567 820296**
Mr & Mrs Garnier.
Fax no: 01567 820647
D: £19.00-£35.00
S: £19.00-£35.00.
Open: All Year
Beds: 3F 6T 17D 6S
Baths: 32 En
🛏 🅿 (20) ⊬ ⊡ 🛏 🎘 🏛 ⅷ Ⅴ 🍴 ♻ ♿
The setting is magnificent, overlooking the river Lochay, we have a bistro restaurant specialising in home cooked dishes, all rooms are ensuite, lounge bar with stock of malt Whiskies. A friendly welcome from the owners guaranteed.

The Coach House Hotel, *Lochay Road, Killin, Perthshire, FK21 8TN.*
Family-run hotel surrounded by mountains overlooking the river.
Tel: **01567 820349** (also fax no)
D: £20.00-£26.00 **S:** £20.00-£26.00.
Open: All Year
Beds: 1F 1D 2T **Baths:** 2 En 2 Sh
🛏 🅿 (40) ⊬ ☐ 🛒 🏢 Ⅵ ♣ ⚡ ⚲ ♻

Drumfinn House, *Manse Road, Killin, Perthshire, FK21 8UY.*
Warm, friendly country house in the centre of the highland village of Killin.
Tel: **01567 820900** (also fax no)
Mrs Semple.
D: £16.00-£20.00 .
Open: All Year (not Xmas)
Beds: 1F 1D 2T **Baths:** 3 En 1 Sh
🛏 (12) 🅿 (6) ⊬ ☐ 🛒 🏢 Ⅵ 👜 ⚡ ♻

Acharn 42

National Grid Ref: NN7543

🍴 ⚑ Croft-na-caber Hotel

12 Ballinlaggan, *Acharn, Aberfeldy, Perthshire, PH15 2HT.*
Warm welcome awaits in quiet lochside village of Acharn, surrounded by beautiful scenery.
Tel: **01887 830409** Mrs Spiers.
D: £16.00-£16.00 **S:** £16.00-£16.00.
Open: All Year
Beds: 1T 1S **Baths:** 1 Sh
🛏 🅿 (2) ⊬ ☐ ✕ 🛒 🏢 Ⅵ 👜 ⚲

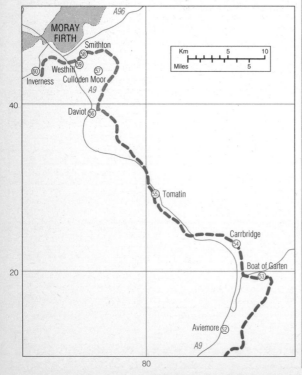

Planning a longer stay? Always ask for any special rates.

Aberfeldy 43

National Grid Ref: NN8549

🍴 ⚑ Black Watch, Aileen Chraggan Hotel, Coshieville Hotel

Ardtornish, *Kenmore Street, Aberfeldy, PH15 2BL.*
In beautiful friendly Highland Perthshire with walking, golf, cycling, water sports and more.
Grades: ETC 3 Star
Tel: **01887 820629** Mrs Ross.
D: £16.00-£19.00 **S:** £16.00-£19.00.
Open: All Year (not Xmas/New Year)
Beds: 1D 1T 1D/F
Baths: 1 En 1 Sh
🅿 (3) ⊬ ☐ 🛒 🏢 Ⅵ ⚲ ♻

D = Price range per person sharing in a double room

Tomvale, *Tom of Cluny Farm, Aberfeldy, Perthshire, PH15 2JT.*
Modern farmhouse with outstanding views of the Upper Tay Valley.
Tel: **01887 820171** (also fax no)
Mrs Kennedy.
D: £17.00-£17.00 **S:** £18.00-£18.00.
Open: All Year (not Xmas)
Beds: 1F 1D
Baths: 1 Sh
🛏 🅿 ☐ 🛒 ✕ 🏢 Ⅵ 👜 ⚡ ♻

Carn Dris, *Aberfeldy, Perthshire, PH15 2LB.*
Large Edwardian private house, ex manse, overlooking Aberfeldy golf course.
Tel: **01887 820250**
Mrs Bell Campbell.
D: £20.00-£25.00 **S:** £20.00-£25.00.
Open: Easter to Oct
Beds: 2D 1T
Baths: 1 En 1 Sh
🛏 (10) 🅿 (4) ☐ 🛒 🏢 👜 ⚡ ♻

Novar, *2 Home Street, Aberfeldy, Perthshire, PH15 2AJ.*
Novar is a comfortable stone house near golf course; good walks.
Tel: **01887 820779** Mrs Malcolm.
D: £17.00-£19.00 **S:** £25.00-£25.00.
Open: All Year (not Xmas)
Beds: 1F 1D 1T
Baths: 2 En 5 Pr 1 Sh
🛏 🅿 (3) ⊬ ☐ 🛒 🏢 ⚑ Ⅵ 👜 ⚡ ⚲

Edradynate 44

National Grid Ref: NN8852

Lurgan Farm, *Edradynate, Aberfeldy, Perthshire, PH15 2JX.*
Actual grid ref: NN880529
Traditional working farm, with stunning views over the Tay Valley.
Tel: **01887 840451** Mrs Kennedy.
D: £17.00-£22.00 **S:** £17.00-£22.00.
Open: All Year (not Xmas)
Beds: 1F **Baths:** 1 En
🛏 🅿 ⊬ ☐ 🛒 🏢 Ⅵ ♻

Pitlochry 45

National Grid Ref: NN9458

🍴 ⚑ Acarsaid Hotel, Pine Trees Hotel, Atholl Arms Hotel, Old Smithy, Old Armoury, Port-na-Craig Inn, Moulin Hotel, Westlands, Mill, McKay's, Ballinling Inn

▲ *Pitlochry Youth Hostel,* *Knockard Road, Pitlochry, PH16 5HJ.*
Actual grid ref: NN943584
Tel: **01796 472308**
Under 18: £6.00 **Adults:** £8.00
Self-catering facilities, Shop nearby, Laundry facilities, Evening meal for groups only
Pitlochry is a bustling small town at the very centre of Scotland. Scenic countryside ideal for climbing. The Festival Theatre is open May-October - outdoor shows all summer. The Highland Games are in September.

The Pass of Drumochter to Inverness

The way through Glen Truim leads to **Newtonmore** and **Kingussie**, where Ruthven Barracks was built in the early eighteenth century by the ascendant royal family to suppress the Jacobites. From here you head on through Strathspey, haven of ospreys and salmon, past Loch Insh to **Inverdruie** near Aviemore, and on to **Boat of Garten**; before turning west and then north to Carrbridge, and on to Slochd Summit. After descending to Tomatin across the River Findhorn you proceed to **Culloden**. Here in 1746 the last battle fought anywhere in Britain finally crushed the Jacobite rebellion, leading to the flight of Prince Charles Edward Stuart and the mass murder and pillage of the Highland Clearances. Before you reach the town the Culloden Visitor Centre, at the site of the battle, offers an audiovisual presentation. It is but a short way to **Inverness**, capital of the Highlands, where the route ends on the west bank of the River Ness. In front of the Victorian castle, built on the site of the earlier edifice razed by the Jacobites, stands a statue of Flora MacDonald, the local heroine who helped 'Bonnie' Prince Charles Edward Stuart escape from Benbecula to Skye after Culloden. The Museum and Art Gallery has displays of local interest; and Balnain House, a museum of Highland music, is well worth a visit. To the south of town, the northern section of Thomas Telford's Caledonian Canal leads into Loch Ness. To the north, you can take a cruise around the Moray Firth to spot seals and perhaps dolphins traversing the bay.

Auchlatt Steading, Kinnaird, Pitlochry, Perthshire, *PH16 5JL.*
Tel: **01796 472661** (also fax no)
Miss Elkins.
D: £17.00-£17.00.
S: £17.00-£17.00.
Open: Easter to Nov
Beds: 1T 1D
Baths: All En
🅿 (2) ⅍☐🛏📺.
Newly converted Scottish barn comfortable beds and a good honest breakfast overlooking Pitlochry and surrounding beautiful countryside. Close to Edradour and Scotland's smallest distillery, good hill walking and fishing, also the theatre and much historic interest.

Atholl Villa, 29 Atholl Road, Pitlochry, Perthshire, *PH16 5BX.*
Grades: ETC 3 Star
Tel: **01796 473820**
Mrs Bruce.
D: £17.50-£25.00
S: £17.50-£25.00.
Open: All Year
Beds: 3F 2T 2D
Baths: 7 En
🛏🅿(10)⅍☐🛏✖♨📺.♿🎥
🐾
This 10 bedroom Victorian detached stone house of typical highland construction, built 150 years ago, is situated right at the edge of town, close to rail and bus stations, an abundance of restaurants, shops and the most famous Festival Theatre.

Wellwood House, West Moulin Rd, Pitlochry, Perthshire, *PH16 5EA.*
Grades: ETC 2 Star,
AA 3 Diamond
Tel: **01796 474288** Ms Herd.
Fax no: 01796 474299
D: £19.50-£25.00 **S:** £25.00-£35.00.
Open: March to Nov
Beds: 1F 5D 4T **Baths:** 8 En 2 Sh
🛏🅿(25)☐🛏♨📺.🎥
The Wellwood is a Victorian mansion house set in 2 acres of splendid gardens, yet only a 5 minute walk from town centre, comfortable rooms, glorious views, secure open car park.

Balrobin Hotel, Higher Oakfield, Pitlochry, Perthshire, *PH16 5HT.*
Quality accommodation with panoramic views at affordable prices.
Grades: ETC 3 Star, AA 2 Star, RAC 2 Star
Tel: **01796 472901** Mr Hohman.
Fax no: 01796 474200
D: £25.00-£33.00 **S:** £25.00-£39.00.
Open: Apr to Oct
Beds: 1F 10D 3T 1S **Baths:** 15 En
🛏(5) 🅿(15)⅍☐🛏✖♨📺.🎥🐾

Easter Dunfallandy Country House B&B, Pitlochry, Perthshire, *PH16 5NA.*
Beautifully presented country house with fine views and gourmet breakfast.
Grades: ETC 4 Star
Tel: **01796 474128** Mr Mathieson.
Fax no: 01796 473994
D: £28.00-£28.00 **S:** £38.00-£38.00.
Open: All Year (not Xmas/New Year)
Beds: 1D 2T **Baths:** 3 En
🛏(12) 🅿(6)⅍☐📺.

S = Price range for a single person in a room

Planning a longer stay? Always ask for any special rates.

Pooltiel, Lettoch Road, Pitlochry, *PH16 5AZ.*
Quiet scenic location in Perthshire Highlands with panoramic views.
Grades: ETC 3 Star
Tel: **01796 472184** Mrs Sandison.
D: £17.00-£18.00 **S:** £17.00-£18.00.
Open: Easter to Oct
Beds: 1F 1T 1D
Baths: 1 Sh
🛏🅿⅍☐🛏♨📺.🎥✦🐾

Lynedoch, 9 Lettoch Terrace, Pitlochry, Perthshire, *PH16 5BA.*
Tel: **01796 472119** Mrs Williamson.
D: £16.00-£18.00 **S:** £16.00-£18.00.
Open: Easter to Oct
Beds: 2D 1T
Baths: 2 Sh
🅿 (3)⅍☐🛏♨📺.🎥
Stone-built semi-detached villa in beautiful Highland Perthshire, ideally situated for walking, golf, fishing etc. Close by are hydroelectric dam, fish ladder, world famous festival theatre and whisky distilleries. Views of Ben Vrackie and the Fonab Hills.

8 Darach Road, Pitlochry, Perthshire, *PH16 5HR.*
Semi detached house. Hill walking, theatre, various walks, central to cities.
Tel: **01796 472074**
Mrs Weyda-Wernick.
D: £15.00-£15.00 **S:** £18.00-£18.00.
Open: All Year (not Xmas/New Year)
Beds: 1D **Baths:** 2 Sh
🛏🅿(2)☐🛏📺.✦🐾

Carra Beag Guest House,
16 Toberargan Road, Pitlochry,
Perthshire, PH16 5HG.
Magnificent views; central
location; breakfast cooked to order;
period features.
Grades: ETC 3 Star
Tel: 01796 472835 (also fax no)
Mr Stone.
D: £13.00-£23.00 **S:** £13.00-
£23.00.
Open: All Year
Beds: 2F 3D 3T 2S
Baths: 9 Pr 1 Sh
🛇 🅿 (9) ⚡ 🗆 ⛌ ✕ 🍴 🖺 Ⅲ Ⅵ 🛆 🔌 ♻

Ferrymans Cottage, *Port-na-*
Craig, Pitlochry, Perthshire,
PH16 5ND.
Cosy riverside cottage below
Festival Theatre or stroll into town.
Grades: ETC 3 Star
Tel: 01796 473681 (also fax no)
Mrs Sanderson.
D: £19.00-£24.00 .
Open: Easter to Nov
Beds: 2F **Baths:** 1 Pr 1 En
🛇 🅿 (6) ⚡ 🗆 🍴 Ⅲ Ⅵ ♻

Killiecrankie 46

National Grid Ref: NN9162
🍴 🍺 Killiecrankie Hotel

Tighdornie, *Killiecrankie,*
Pitlochry, Perthshire, PH16 5LR.
Modern house in historic
Killiecrankie. 2.5 miles from Blair
Castle.
Grades: ETC 3 Star
Tel: 01796 473276 (also fax no)
Mrs Sanderson.
D: £22.00-£24.00 **S:** £27.00-£27.00
Open: All Year
Beds: 1T 2D **Baths:** 3 En
🛇 (12) 🅿 (4) ⚡ 🗆 🍴 Ⅲ Ⅵ 🛆 🔌

Blair Atholl 47

National Grid Ref: NN8764
🍴 🍺 Tilt Hotel, The Roundhouse

Dalgreine, *off St Andrews*
Crescent, Blair Atholl, Pitlochry,
Perthshire, PH18 5SX.
Attractive comfortable guest house,
set in beautiful surroundings near
Blair Castle.
Grades: ETC 3 Star,
AA 4 Diamond
Tel: 01796 481276
Mr & Mrs Pywell & Mrs F Hardie.
D: £16.00-£20.00 **S:** £17.00-£20.00
Open: All Year
Beds: 1F 2D 2T 1S
Baths: 2 En 1 Pr 1 Sh
🛇 🅿 (6) ⚡ 🗆 ✕ 🍴 Ⅲ Ⅵ 🛆 🔌 ♻

Pay B&Bs by cash or
cheque and be prepared
to pay up front.

S = Price range for a single
person in a room

Newtonmore 48

National Grid Ref: NN7199

🍴 🍺 Braeriach Hotel, Glen Hotel, Ballavalie Sport
Hotel

▲ **Newtonmore Independent**
Hostel, *Craigellachie House, Main*
Street, Newtonmore, Inverness-
shire, PH20 1DA.
Actual grid ref: NN713990
Tel: 01540 673360 Adults: £8.50.
No smoking

▲ **Strathspey Mountain Hostel,**
Main Street, Newtonmore,
Inverness-shire, PH20 1DR.
Actual grid ref: NN716993
Tel: 01540 673694
Adults: £7.50
Self-catering facilities, Television,
Showers, Central heating, Laundry
facilities, Wet weather shelter,
Lounge, Dining room, Drying
room, Security lockers, Cycle
store, Parking, Facilities for disabled people
Brilliant, central location for walk-
ers, cyclists, golfers, skiers, bird-
watchers, fishermen, families,
groups and individuals. Fully mod-
ernised highland villa. C/W, full
CH, excellent showers and compre-
hensive self-catering facilities. STB
2 Star Hostel Award and Eco
Tourism Award. Coal fire, cosy TV
lounge. Excellent local information
from outdoor activist owners. 6-
bed cottage also available.

▲ **Croft Holidays Hostel,** *Croft*
Holidays, Newtonmore, Inverness-
shire, PH20 1BA.
Actual grid ref: NH721001
Tel: 01540 673504
Under 18: £9.00 **Adults:** £9.00
Self-catering facilities, Television,
Showers, Central heating, Laundry
facilities, Lounge, Dining room,
Grounds available for games,
Drying room, Cycle store, Parking,
Facilities for disabled people, No
smoking
Flexible accommodation, half mile
from Newtonmore in foothills of
Monadhliaths.

Alder Lodge Guest House, *Glen*
Road, Newtonmore, Inverness-
shire, PH20 1EA.
Beautiful house, quiet situation,
0.25 mile from the shops and
hotels.
Tel: 01540 673376 Mr Stewart.
D: £15.00-£15.00 **S:** £15.00-£15.00.
Open: All Year
Beds: 2 T 2D **Baths:** 1 Sh
🛇 🅿 (6) ⛌ ✕ 🍴 Ⅲ Ⅵ 🔌 ♻

The Pines, *Station Road,*
Newtonmore, Inverness-shire,
PH20 1AR.
Tel: 01540 673271 Mr Walker.
Fax no: 01540 673882
D: £20.00-£25.00 **S:** £20.00-£25.00.
Open: Jan to Oct
Beds: 2D 2T 2S
Baths: 6 En
🛇 (12) 🅿 (5) ⚡ 🗆 ⛌ ✕ 🍴 🖺 Ⅲ Ⅵ 🛆 ♻
Comfortable Edwardian house with
river valley and mountain views.
Peaceful wooded gardens rich in
bird and wildlife. Conveniently
located for public transport,
touring, walking, cycling, golf,
Cairngorm Mountains and RSPB
reserves. Please phone for colour
brochure.

Kingussie 49

National Grid Ref: NH7500

🍴 🍺 Scot House Hotel, Tipsy Laird, Osprey
Hotel

▲ **Lairds Bothy Hostel,** *68 High*
Street, Kingussie, Inverness-shire,
PH21 1HZ.
Actual grid ref: NH758008
Tel: 01540 661334 Adults: £8.00
Evening meal available

The Osprey Hotel, *Kingussie,*
Inverness-shire, PH21 1EN.
Grades: ETC 3 Star Hotel,
AA 2 Star
Tel: 01540 661510 (also fax no)
Mr & Mrs Burrow.
D: £24.00-£30.00 **S:** £24.00-£30.00.
Open: All Year
Beds: 3D 3T 2S
Baths: 8 En
🛇 🅿 🗆 ⛌ ✕ 🍴 🖺 Ⅲ 🛆 Ⅵ 🔌 ♻
Small hotel in area of outstanding
beauty, offering a warm welcome,
ensuite accommodation and
award-winning food. Aileen &
Robert hold AA food rosettes and
are members of the 'taste of
Scotland'. Ideal base for touring,
walking, golf, fishing, etc.

Arden House, *Newtonmore Road,*
Kingussie, Inverness-shire,
PH21 1HE.
Excellent food and accommoda-
tion, delightful centrally situated
Victorian villa.
Grades: ETC 3 Star GH
Tel: 01540 661369 (also fax no)
Mrs Spry.
D: £18.00-£22.00 **S:** £18.00-£22.00.
Open: All Year
Beds: 2F 2D 1T 1S
Baths: 3 En 3 Sh
🛇 (1) 🅿 (7) ⚡ 🗆 ⛌ ✕ 🍴 🖺 Ⅲ 🛆 Ⅵ
🔌 ♻

D = Price range per person
sharing in a double room

The Hermitage, *Spey Street, Kingussie, Inverness-shire, PH21 1HN.*
Warm Highland welcome in heart of Badenoch & Strathspey. Excellent touring base.
Grades: ETC 4 Star
Tel: **01540 662137** Mr Taylor.
Fax no: 01540 662177
D: £21.00-£23.00 **S:** £26.00-£28.00.
Open: All Year (not Xmas)
Beds: 1F 1T 3D
Baths: 5 En
🛇📷🅿️⊬➶🏃✕♨🕮 V̶🛉⚡🚲

St Helens, *Ardbroilach Road, Kingussie, Inverness-shire, PH21 1JX.*
Built 100 years ago, St Helens is an elegant Victorian villa.
Grades: ETC 4 Star
Tel: **01540 661430** Mrs Jarratt.
D: £20.00-£20.00 **S:** £38.00-£38.00.
Open: All Year
Beds: 1D 1T
Baths: 1 En 1 Pr
🛇(12)🅿️(3)⊬➶♨🕮 V̶🛉🚲

Ruthven Farmhouse, *Kingussie, Inverness-shire, PH21 1NR.*
Spacious farmhouse set amidst an acre of landscaped grounds.
Grades: ETC 3 Star
Tel: **01540 661226**
Mr Morris.
D: £18.00-£20.00 **S:** £18.00-£20.00.
Open: All Year
Beds: 2D 1T
Baths: 1 En 2 Pr
🛇(10)🅿️(3)⊬➶♨🕮 V̶🛉⚡

Dunmhor House, *67 High Street, Kingussie, Inverness-shire, PH21 1HX.*
Centrally situated for numerous attractions in beautiful scenic Highland village.
Tel: **01540 661809** (also fax no)
D: £16.00-£18.00
S: £16.00-£20.00.
Open: All Year
Beds: 2F 2D 1S
Baths: 2 Sh
🛇🅿️(5)➶🏃✕♨🕮 V̶🚲

Bhuna Monadh, *85 High Street, Kingussie, Inverness-shire, PH21 1HX.*
Listed building in scenic area with many outdoor activities.
Tel: **01540 661186**
Ms Gibson.
Fax no: 01540 661186
D: £15.00-£20.00 **S:** £20.00-£25.00.
Open: All Year
Beds: 1D 1T
Baths: 2 En
🛇🅿️(3)⊬➶🏃♨🕮 V̶🛉⚡🚲

Greystones, *Acres Road, Kingussie, Inverness-shire, PH21 1LA.*
Actual grid ref: NH758012
Victorian family home, pleasantly secluded, a five-minute walk from Kingussie.
Tel: **01540 661052** Mrs Johnstone.
Fax no: 01540 662162
D: £18.50-£18.50 **S:** £18.50-£18.50.
Open: All Year (not Xmas)
Beds: 1F 1D 1T 1S
Baths: 1 Pr 2 Sh
🛇🅿️(6)⊬➶🏃♨🕮 V̶🛉⚡🚲

Rowan House, *Homewood, Newtonmore Road, Kingussie, Inverness-shire, PH21 1HD.*
Quiet hillside position; outstanding views of Spey Valley and mountains.
Tel: **01540 662153** Ms Smiter.
D: £17.00-£22.00 **S:** £17.00-£20.00.
Open: All Year (not Xmas)
Beds: 1D 2T **Baths:** 1 En 2 Pr
🛇(2)🅿️(3)⊬➶🏃♨🕮 V̶🛉🚲

Homewood Lodge, *Kingussie, Inverness-shire, PH21 1HD.*
Homewood Lodge, a beautifully decorated Victorian house set in mature gardens.
Tel: **01540 661507** Anderson.
D: £15.00-£15.00 **S:** £15.00-£15.00.
Open: All Year
Beds: 1F 1T 2D **Baths:** 4 En
🅿️(6)⊬➶🏃♨🕮 V̶🛉⚡🚲

Kincraig   50
National Grid Ref: NH8305

🍴🍺 Kith & Kin Inn, Ossian Hotel

🔺 **Badenoch Christian Centre,** *Kincraig, Kingussie, Inverness-shire, PH21 1QD.*
Tel: **01540 651373**
Under 18: £8.00 **Adults:** £9.50
Self-catering facilities, Television, Showers, Central heating, Lounge, Dining room, Games room, Grounds available for games, Drying room, Cycle store, Parking, Facilities for disabled people
Comfortable purpose built-centre with well-fitted bunk rooms for 2 or 4 people. Great area for water sports and mountain activities including skiing. Many visitor attractions close by. Suitable for groups or individuals, also family rooms and self-contained family suite. Occasional programmed activities and quiet retreat days.

🔺 **Kirkbeag Hostel,** *Kirkbeag, Milehead, Kincraig, Kingussie, Inverness-shire, PH21 1ND.*
Actual grid ref: NH840068
Tel: **01540 651298**
Under 18: £8.50 **Adults:** £9.00
Self-catering facilities, Television, Showers, Lounge, Dining room, Grounds available for games, Drying room, Parking
Sleeps max. 6. Quiet country location, ideal for walking/climbing.

Ossian Hotel, *Kincraig, Kingussie, Inverness-shire, PH21 1QD.*
Built in 1880s lochside village. Magnificent mountain views.
Grades: ETC 2 Star
Tel: **01540 651242** Mrs Rainbow.
Fax no: 01540 651633
D: £20.00-£31.00 **S:** £20.00-£31.00.
Open: Feb to Dec
Beds: 2F 3D 2T 2S
Baths: 8 En 1 Pr
🛇🅿️(20)⊬➶🏃✕♨🕮 V̶🛉⚡🚲

Braeriach Guest House, *Kincraig, Kingussie, Inverness-shire, PH21 1QA.*
Actual grid ref: NH824056
Beautiful riverside country house. Spacious comfortable rooms with incredible views.
Tel: **01540 651369** Mrs Johnson.
D: £20.00-£25.00 **S:** £20.00-£25.00.
Open: All Year
Beds: 2D 2T
Baths: 3 En 1 Pr
🛇🅿️(4)➶🏃✕♨🕮 V̶🛉⚡🚲

Kirkbeag, *Milehead, Kincraig, Kingussie, Inverness-shire, PH21 1ND.*
Friendly family B&B in converted C19th church. Quiet country location.
Tel: **01540 651298** (also fax no)
Mrs Paisley.
D: £16.50-£17.50
S: £20.00-£23.00.
Open: All Year
Beds: 1D 1T
Baths: 2 Sh
🛇🅿️(6)➶🏃✕♨🕮 V̶🛉⚡

Insh House, *Kincraig, Kingussie, Inverness-shire, PH21 1NU.*
Friendly family guest house in splendid rural location near loch & mountains.
Tel: **01540 651377**
Thompson.
D: £17.00-£20.00
S: £17.00-£20.00.
Open: All Year (not Xmas)
Beds: 1F 1D 1T 2S
Baths: 2 En 1 Sh
🛇🅿️⊬➶🏃✕♨🕮 V̶🛉⚡

Bringing children with you? Always ask for any special rates.

The Grid Reference beneath the location heading is for the village or town - *not* for individual houses, which are shown (where supplied) in each entry itself.

Feshiebridge 51

National Grid Ref: NH8504

Balcraggan House, *Feshiebridge, Kincraig, Kingussie, Inverness-shire, PH21 1NG.*
Wonderful setting where wildlife, walks and cycle routes abound.
Tel: **01540 651488**
Mrs Gillies.
D: £25.00-£25.00
S: £30.00-£35.00.
Open: All Year
Beds: 1D 1T
Baths: 2 En
⛺ (10) 🅿 (3) ⅋ 🖵 ✕ 🍽 ⅏ 🛏 Ⅲ. Ⅴ ⅋

Aviemore 52

National Grid Ref: NH8912

🍴 🍺 Glenmore Lodge, Cairngorm Hotel, Old Bridge Inn, Mackenzie's, Winking Owl

▲ **Aviemore Youth Hostel,** *25 Grampian Road, Aviemore, Inverness-shire, PH22 1PR.*
Actual grid ref: NH893119
Tel: **01479 810345**
Under 18: £6.00
Adults: £9.00
Self-catering facilities, Shop, Laundry facilities, Facilities for disabled people
Set in birch woodlands next to a nature reserve, ideal base to explore Strathspey. Gliding, skiing, snowboarding, canoeing, golf available locally.

Cairngorm Guest House, *Grampian Road, Aviemore, Inverness-shire, PH22 1RP.*
Tel: **01479 810630** (also fax no)
Mrs Conn.
D: £18.00-£25.00
S: £20.00-£28.00.
Open: Easter to Easter
Beds: 1F 5D 3T
Baths: 9 En
⛺ (2) 🅿 (10) ⅋ 🖵 🛏 Ⅲ. Ⅴ ⅋ ⚲
Experience a real Scottish welcome. Have coffee with us on arrival. Relax in our guest lounge in front of a real fire with views of the Cairngorm mountains. Handy for train/bus. Two minutes walk to the centre. 24 hour access to rooms.

Ravenscraig Guest House, *Aviemore, Inverness-shire, PH22 1RP.*
Central village location. Ideal for exploring highlands or just relaxing.
Grades: ETC 2 Star GH,
AA 3 Diamond, RAC 3 Diamond
Tel: **01479 810278**
Mr & Mrs Gatenby.
Fax no: 01479 812742
D: £18.00-£24.00
S: £18.00-£24.00.
Open: All Year
Beds: 2F 5D 4T 1S
Baths: 12 En
⛺ 🅿 (16) 🖵 🍽 🛏 Ⅲ. Ⅴ ⅋ ⚲

Rowan Tree Country Hotel, *Loch Alvie, Aviemore, Inverness-shire, PH22 1QB.*
C17th Coaching Inn. Characterful bedrooms. Comfortable lounges. A warm welcome.
Grades: ETC 3 Star
Tel: **01479 810207** (also fax no)
D: £26.50-£31.50 **S:** £36.50-£41.50.
Open: All Year
Beds: 2F 3T 4D 1S
Baths: 10 En 1 Sh
⛺ (12) 🅿 🖵 🍽 ✕ ⅏ 🛏 Ⅲ. Ⅴ ⅊ ⅋ ⚲

Eriskay, *Craig-na-gower, Aviemore, Inverness-shire, PH22 1RW.*
Quietly situated warm and comfortable house, good base for touring.
Grades: ETC 4 Star
Tel: **01479 810717**
Fax no: 01479 812312
D: £17.00-£20.00 **S:** £22.00-£26.00.
Open: All Year
Beds: 2D 1T **Baths:** 3 En
🅿 (4) 🖵 🛏 Ⅲ. Ⅴ ⅋ ⚲

Dunroamin, *Craig Gower Avenue, Aviemore, Inverness-shire, PH22 1RN.*
Comfortable, friendly, family-run home. Rooms tasteful and spacious.
Grades: ETC 2 Star
Tel: **01479 810698** (also fax no)
Mrs Sheffield.
D: £16.00-£25.00 **S:** £20.00-£40.00.
Open: All Year
Beds: 2F 2D
Baths: 3 En 1 Pr
⛺ 🅿 (4) ⅋ 🖵 🛏 Ⅲ. Ⅴ ⅋ ⚲

Waverley, *35 Strathspey Avenue, Aviemore, Inverness-shire, PH22 1SN.*
Modern comfortable bungalow in quiet area.
Tel: **01479 811226** Mrs Fraser.
D: £17.00-£20.00 **S:** £20.00-£25.00.
Open: All Year (not Xmas)
Beds: 1D 1T
Baths: 1 En 1 Pr
⛺ (8) ⅋ 🖵 🛏 Ⅲ. & Ⅴ ⅋ ⚲

Ardlogie Guest House, *Dalfaber Road, Aviemore, Inverness-shire, PH22 1PU.*
Centre of Aviemore views over River Spey to Cairngorm Mountains.
Grades: ETC 2 Star
Tel: **01479 810747**
D: £17.00-£17.00 **S:** £17.00-£17.00.
Open: All Year
Beds: 4D 1T
Baths: 5 En
⛺ 🅿 (3) 🖵 🐾 🛏 Ⅲ. Ⅴ ⅋ ⚲

Ryvoan, *Grampian Road, Aviemore, Inverness-shire, PH22 1RY.*
Beautiful modern bungalow with patio overlooking the Cairngorms situated at north end of village.
Tel: **01479 810805** Mrs Cristall.
D: £16.00-£16.00 **S:** £18.00-£18.00.
Open: Dec to Oct
Beds: 1T 1D
Baths: 2 En
🅿 (3) 🖵 🐾 🛏 Ⅲ. Ⅴ ⅊ ⅋ ⚲

Boat of Garten 53

National Grid Ref: NH9418

🍴 🍺 Boat, Craigard Hotel, Heatherbank, Lisi's

▲ **Fraoch Lodge,** *Deshar Road, Boat of Garten, Inverness-shire, PH24 3BN.*
Actual grid ref: NH938190
Tel: **01479 831331**
Under 18: £7.50 **Adults:** £7.50
Self-catering facilities, Showers, Central heating, Laundry facilities, Lounge, Dining room, Grounds available for games, Cycle store, Parking, Evening meal available, No smoking
Cairngorms route/weather info, local pub, breakfast available, friendly atmosphere.

The Old Ferrymans House, *Boat of Garten, Inverness-shire, PH24 3BY.*
Tel: **01479 831370** (also fax no)
Ms Matthews.
D: £19.50-£19.50 **S:** £19.50-£19.50.
Open: All Year
Beds: 1T 1D 2S **Baths:** 2 Sh
⛺ 🅿 (4) ⅋ 🖵 ✕ 🛏 Ⅲ. Ⅴ ⅊ ⅋
Which? recommended former ferryman's house, just across River Spey from village, welcoming, homely, comfortable. Sitting room with wood stove, many books, no TV. No set breakfast times, home-cooked meals with Highland specialities. Numerous walks, beautiful Strathspey countryside and Cairngorm mountains, castles, distilleries.

Avingormack Guest House, *Boat of Garten, Inverness-shire, PH24 3BT.*
Breathtaking views of the mountains, award-winning food - just perfect.
Grades: ETC 3 Star
Tel: **01479 831614** Mrs Ferguson.
D: £19.00-£22.00 **S:** £19.50-£19.50.
Open: All Year
Beds: 1F 2D 1T **Baths:** 2 En 1 Sh
⛺ 🅿 (6) ⅋ 🖵 🛏 Ⅲ. Ⅴ ⅊ ⅋

Chapelton Steading, *Boat Of Garten, Inverness-shire, PH24 3BU.*
Spacious rural retreat. Charming garden with views of Cairngorm Mountains.
Grades: ETC 4 Star
Tel: **01479 831327** Mrs Smyth.
D: £21.00-£22.00 **S:** £23.00-£25.00.
Open: March to Nov
Beds: 2T 1D **Baths:** 3 En
⛺ (10) 🅿 (4) ⅋ 🖵 🛏 Ⅴ ⅊ ⅋ ⚲

All rooms full and nowhere else to stay? Ask the owner if there's anywhere nearby

Heathbank - The Victorian House, Drumuillie Road, Boat of Garten, Inverness-shire, *PH24 3BD.*
Beautiful of character, house full of curiosities; each bedroom different in style and atmosphere.
Tel: **01479 831234** Mr Burge.
D: £25.00-£35.00 **S:** £30.00-£50.00.
Open: All Year
Beds: 5D 2T **Baths:** 7 En
⌖ (8) ▣ (8) ⌿⌖✕⚓⚲⛭ﬗ ⓥ ╟ ✦ ♂⛰

Glen Sanda, Street Of Kincardine, Boat of Garten, Inverness-shire, *PH24 3BY.*
Modern bungalow, rural setting, near RSPB and all sporting amenities.
Tel: **01479 831494** Mrs Lyons.
D: £20.00-£22.00 **S:** £20.00-£24.00.
Open: All Year
Beds: 2D 1T **Baths:** 3 En
▣ (3) ⌿⛬⚲⛭ﬗ ⓥ ╟ ♂⛰

Mountain Innovations, Fraoch Lodge, Deshar Road, Boat of Garten, Invernesshire, *PH24 3BN.*
Fully equipped drying room, mountain weather forecasts. No restrictive meal times.
Tel: **01479 831331** (also fax no)
Mr Bateman.
D: £9.00-£15.50 **S:** £9.00-£15.50.
Open: All Year
Beds: 3F 3T **Baths:** 3 Sh
⌖ ▣ (12) ⌿⛬✕⚓⚲⛭ﬗ ⓥ ╟ ♂⛰

Carrbridge 54

National Grid Ref: NH9022

⚏ ⚑ Cairn Hotel, Rowanlea, Struan Hotel

Cairn Hotel, Main Road, Carrbridge, Inverness-shire, *PH23 3AS.*
Actual grid ref: NH907228
Grades: ETC 3 Star
Tel: **01479 841212** Mr Kirk.
Fax no: 01479 841362
D: £19.00-£22.00 **S:** £19.00-£26.00.
Open: All Year (not Xmas)
Beds: 2F 2D 1T 2S
Baths: 4 En 1 Sh
⌖ ▣ (15) ⛬⚲⛭ ⓥ ♂⛰
Enjoy the country pub atmosphere; log fire, malt whiskies, real ales and affordable food in this family-owned village centre hotel close to the historic bridge. A perfect base for touring Cairngorms, Loch Ness, Whisky Trail and beyond.

Carrmoor Guest House, Carr Road, Carrbridge, Inverness-shire, *PH23 3AD.*
Actual grid ref: NH908227
Licensed, family-run, warm welcome. Popular restaurant, chef proprietor.
Grades: ETC 3 Star,
AA 4 Diamond
Tel: **01479 841244** (also fax no)
Mrs Stitt.
D: £19.50-£21.50 **S:** £22.00-£22.00.
Open:
Beds: 1F 3D 2T **Baths:** 6 En
⌖ ▣ (6) ⛬✕⚓⚲⛭ﬗ ⓥ ╟ ♂⛰

Craigellachie House, Main Street, Carrbridge, Inverness-shire, *PH23 3AS.*
Traditional house in centre of small Highland village on main tourist routes.
Grades: ETC 3 Star GH
Tel: **01479 841641** Mrs Pedersen.
D: £16.00-£19.00 **S:** £16.00-£25.00.
Open: All Year
Beds: 2F 2D 2T 1S
Baths: 3 En 2 Sh
⌖ ▣ (8) ⌿⛬✕⚲⛭ﬗ ⓥ ╟ ♂⛰

Pine Ridge, Carrbridge, Inverness-shire, *PH23 3AA.*
Pine Ridge is a beautiful 100 year old home.
Tel: **01479 841646** Mrs Weston.
D: £16.00-£20.00 **S:** £20.00-£25.00.
Open: All Year
Beds: 1F 1D 1T **Baths:** 1 En 1 Sh
⌖ ▣ (6) ⌿⛬⚓⚲⛭ﬗ ⓥ ╟ ♂⛰

Tomatin 55

National Grid Ref: NH8029

⚏ ⚑ Tomatin Inn

Millcroft, Old Mill Road, Tomatin, Inverness, *IV13 7YN.*
1850 modernised crofthouse in quiet village. Ideal base for touring.
Grades: AA 4 Diamond
Tel: **01808 511405** Mrs Leitch.
D: £18.00-£18.00 **S:** £20.00-£25.00.
Open: All Year
Beds: 1D 1F
Baths: 1 En 1 Pr
⌖ ▣ (3) ⛬⚓⛭ ╟ ♂⛰

Daviot 56

National Grid Ref: NH7239

⚏ ⚑ Deerstalker, Tomatin Inn

Torguish House, Daviot, Inverness, *IV2 5XQ.*
Former manse set in quiet rural area, childhood home of late author Alistair McLean.
Tel: **01463 772208**
Mr & Mrs Allan.
Fax no: 01463 772308
D: £16.00-£22.00 **S:** £20.00-£25.00.
Open: All Year
Beds: 3F 3D 1T **Baths:** 5 En 2 Pr
⌖ ▣ (20) ⛬⚓⚲⛭ ⓥ

Culloden Moor 57

National Grid Ref: NH7345

⚏ ⚑ Snow Goose, Cawdor Tavern, Culloden Moor Inn

Culdoich Farm, Culloden Muir, Inverness, *IV2 5EL.*
Old farmhouse in peaceful surroundings. Good farmhouse cooking.
Grades: ETC 3 Star
Tel: **01463 790268** Mrs Alexander.
D: £17.00-£17.00 **S:** £34.00-£34.00.
Open: May to Oct
Beds: 1F 1T/D **Baths:** 1 Sh
⌖ ▣ ⛬✕⚲ ⓥ

Westhill House, Westhill, Inverness, *IV1 5BP.*
Grades: ETC 2 Star
Tel: **01463 793225** Mrs Honnor.
Fax no: 01463 792503
D: £18.00-£20.00 **S:** £16.00-£18.00.
Open: Easter to Oct
Beds: 1F 1T 1S **Baths:** 2 En 1 Sh
⌖ ▣ (4) ⌿⛬⚓✕⚲⛭ﬗ ⓥ ♂⛰
Spacious, comfortable family home in lovely garden amidst trees, wildlife and glorious views. One mile Culloden Battlefield, three miles Inverness. Perfect for touring Highlands.

Bayview, Westhill, Culloden Moor, Inverness, *IV2 5BP.*
Grades: ETC 3 Star
Tel: **01463 790386** (also fax no)
Mrs Campbell.
D: £18.00-£22.00 **S:** £20.00-£25.00.
Open: Easter to Oct
Beds: 1T 2D **Baths:** 2 En 1 Pr
▣ (3) ⌿⛬⚓✕⚲⛭ﬗ ⓥ ⛰
Modern two storey house situated in 1/2 acre landscaped garden. Beautiful views to Ross-shire hills, Moray Firth and Inverness. 20 mins from Dalcross Airport. 1/2 mile from the famous Culloden Battlefield, 3 miles from Clava Cairns. Choice of breakfast, fresh produce used.

King of Clubs, Tigh-Na-Ceard, Culloden Moor, Inverness, *IV2 5EE.*
A warm, friendly welcome awaits you at King of Clubs. Central to all amenities.
Tel: **01463 790476** (also fax no)
Fraser.
D: £17.00-£19.00 **S:** £17.00-£19.00.
Open: All Year
Beds: 1F 1D 1T 1S **Baths:** 2 En 1 Sh
⌖ ▣ (6) ⛬⚓⚲⛭ﬗ ⓥ ♂⛰

Smithton 58

National Grid Ref: NH7145

3a Resaurie, Smithton, Inverness, *IV2 7NH.*
Actual grid ref: NH708452
Tel: **01463 791714** Mrs Mansfield.
D: £17.00-£21.00 **S:** £17.00-£21.00.
Open: All Year
Beds: 2D 1T **Baths:** 1 En 1 Sh
⌖ ▣ (3) ⌿⛬⚓✕⚲⛭ﬗ ⓥ ╟ ♂⛰
Quiet residential area 3 miles east of Inverness. Public transport nearby. GB National Cycle Route 7 passes door. Adjacent to farmland. Views to Moray Firth, Ben Wyvis and Ross-shire Hills. Home baking, high tea, Evening meals. A CHRISTIAN HOME.

High season,
bank holidays and
special events mean
low availability
everywhere.

Westhill 59

National Grid Ref: NH7144

🍴 🍺 Snow Goose, Cawdor Tavern

Easter Muckovie Farm House,
Westhill, Inverness, IV2 5BN.
Grades: ETC 3 Star
Tel: **01463 791556** MacLellan.
D: £18.00-£20.00 **S:** £25.00-£25.00.
Open: All Year
Beds: 2F
Baths: 1 En 1 Pr
🛇 🅿 (5) ⅍ 🖵 🕇 ✕ 🛓 🎹 ☑ ⓘ ⅊ ⌁
Original farmhouse, modernised,
set in a rural location overlooking
Inverness town, Moray & Beauly
Firth with Sutherland & Ross-shire
Hills in background. Culloden
Battlefield, Cawdor Castle & Clava
Cairns nearby. Excellent Scottish
breakfast provided in comfortable
dining room.

Inverness 60

National Grid Ref: NH6645

🍴 🍺 Beaufort Hotel, Castle, Cawdor Tavern,
Craigmonie Hotel, Finlay's, Girvans, Harlequin,
Heathmount Hotel, Johnny Fox's, Kilcoy Arms,
Loch Ness House, Mairten Lodge, No 27 Pub,
Redcliffe, Waterfront

🔺 **Inverness Milburn Youth
Hostel,** Victoria Drive, Inverness,
IV2 3BQ.
Actual grid ref: NH667449
Tel: **01463 231771**
Under 18: £6.00
Adults: £9.00
Self-catering facilities, Shop near-
by, Laundry facilities, Evening
meal for groups only, Facilities for
disabled people
*Modern hostel close to town centre
and all its amenities, the shops,
cafes and the lively Eden Court
Theatre. The gateway to the
Highlands.*

Please respect
a B&B's wishes
regarding children,
animals & smoking.

🔺 **Eastgate Hostel,** *38 Eastgate,
Inverness, Inverness-shire,
IV2 3NA.*
Tel: **01463 718756**
Under 18: £9.00
Adults: £9.00
Self-catering facilities, Television,
Showers, Licensed bar, Central
heating, Wet weather shelter,
Lounge, Dining room, Drying
room, Cycle store, Parking
*Eastgate Hostel is located in the
city centre - 5 mins from train/bus
station. Relaxed atmosphere,
friendly staff, newly opened
pub/restaurant with live music.
Free tea/coffee, no curfew, 5 mins
from pubs and clubs, supermarket.
Visit Loch Ness, Inverness Castle,
Culloden Battlefield and our lovely
dolphins.*

Eskdale Guest House, *41 Greig
Street, Inverness, IV3 5PX.*
Grades: ETC 3 Star
Tel: **01463 240933** (also fax no)
Mrs Mazurek.
D: £16.00-£25.00 **S:** £22.00-£25.00.
Open: All Year (not Xmas)
Beds: 2F 2D 1T 1S
Baths: 3 En 1 Sh
🛇 🅿 (5) ⅍ 🖵 🛓 🎹 ☑
Situated in the heart of Inverness
only 5 minutes from bus/rail
stations, this impeccably run guest
house offers all the comforts of
home and a warm Highland
welcome. Private parking, dis-
counts for stays over 3 days. Please
phone Vera & Alex.

Loanfern Guest House,
*4 Glenurquhart Road, Inverness,
IV3 5NU.*
Victorian house with character. 10
minutes walk from town centre.
Grades: ETC 3 Star
Tel: **01463 221660** (also fax no)
Mrs Campbell.
D: £16.00-£22.00
S: £18.00-£23.00.
Open: All Year (not Xmas/New
Year)
Beds: 1F 2T 2D
Baths: 1 En 2 Sh
🛇 🅿 (4) ⅍ 🖵 ☑

Pitfaranne, *57 Crown Street,
Inverness, IV2 3AY.*
Grades: ETC 3 Star
Tel: **01463 239338**
Morrison.
D: £16.00-£20.00
S: £18.00-£26.00.
Open: All Year
Beds: 1F 2D 4T
Baths: 1 En 1 Pr 2 Sh
🛇 🅿 (5) 🖵 🕇 🛓 🎹 ☑ ⅊ ⌁
5 minutes from town centre/rail/bus
stations. Find true Highland
hospitality in friendly relaxed
atmosphere of 100-year-old town
house in quiet location. Private
showers in all cosy guest rooms.
Daily room service. Extensive
varied menu. Full Highland
breakfast our speciality.

S = Price range for a single
person in a room

Strathmhor Guest House, *99
Kenneth Street, Inverness, IV3 5QQ.*
Grades: ETC 3 Star
Tel: **01463 235397**
Mr & Mrs Reid.
D: £20.00-£25.00 **S:** £18.00-£25.00.
Open: All Year
Beds: 2D 2T 1S
Baths: 2 En 1 Pr 1 Sh
🛇 🅿 (5) 🖵 🛓 🎹 ☑ ⓘ ⌁
Warm welcome awaits at refur-
bished Victorian home.
Comfortable bedrooms and good
food. 10 minutes walk into town
centre, theatres, restaurants, leisure
centre; golf course and fishing
nearby. Easy access for all traffic
off A9.

The Tilt, *26 Old Perth Road,
Inverness, IV2 3UT.*
Family home convenient for A9.
Ideal touring base.
Grades: ETC 3 Star B&B
Tel: **01463 225352** (also fax no)
Mrs Fiddes.
D: £15.00-£15.00 **S:** £17.00-£17.00
Open: All Year (not Xmas)
Beds: 1F 1D 1T 1S
Baths: 1 Sh
🛇 🅿 (4) ⅍ 🖵 🎹

Torridon Guest House, *59
Kenneth Street, Inverness, IV3 5PZ.*
Grades: ETC 3 Star B&B
Tel: **01463 236449** (also fax no)
Mrs Stenhouse.
D: £17.00-£17.00 .
Open: All Year
Beds: 3F
Baths: 2 En 1 Pr
🛇 (5) 🅿 (4) 🖵 🛓 🎹 ☑ ⓘ
Comfortable, family-run house,
5 minutes from town centre, good
food, good beds and a warm
welcome assured.

---

30 Culduthel Road, *Inverness,
IV2 4AP.*
Tel: **01463 717181** Mrs Dunnett.
Fax no: 01463 717188
D: £12.50-£15.00 **S:** £18.00-£22.0⃠
Open: All Year
Beds: 1D 1T
Baths: 1 En 1 Pr
🛇 (5) 🅿 (4) 🖵 🕇 ✕ 🛓 🎹 ♿ ☑ ⌁
1930s bungalow set in large garden, pleasant to relax in on summe⃠
evenings. Central heating. Lounge
with open fire which you may hav⃠
to share with a cat. Your hosts are
both qualified local guides.

D = Price range per perso⃠
sharing in a double room

Roseneath Guest House, *39 Greig Street, Inverness, IV3 5PX.*
Grades: ETC 3 Star
Tel: **01463 220201** (also fax no)
Mr Morrison.
D: £15.00-£25.00 .
Open: All Year
Beds: 3F 1T 2D
Baths: 5 En 1 Pr
♿ (7) 🅿 (3) 🛏 👤 🛁 ▥ 📶 📞 ♿
Over 100 year old building in centre location 200 yards from River Ness and Grieg Street Bridge. Only 5 minutes to town centre and all tourist excursions. Recently refurbished to very high standards.

Melness Guest House, 8 Old Edinburgh Road, Inverness, IV2 3HF.
Charming, award-winning guest house close to town centre.
Grades: ETC 3 Star
Tel: **01463 220963**
Fax no: 01463 717037
D: £20.00-£26.00 **S:** £25.00-£40.00.
Open: All Year
Beds: 1F 1T 1D
Baths: 1 En 1 Sh
🅿 (3) ⌁ 🛏 👤 🛁 ▥ 📞 ♿

Edenview, 26 Ness Bank, Inverness, IV2 4SF.
Comfortable friendly Victorian home on River Ness within 5 minutes town, 7 miles airport.
Grades: ETC 3 Star
Tel: **01463 234397** Mrs Fraser.
Fax no: 01463 222742
D: £20.00-£24.00 **S:** £22.00-£28.00.
Open: Mar to Oct
Beds: 1F 1D 1T
Baths: 2 En 1 Pr
♿ 🅿 (4) 🛏 👤 ▥

Abb Cottage, 11 Douglas Row, Inverness, IV1 1RE.
Central, quiet, riverside Listed terraced cottage. Easy access public transport.
Tel: **01463 233486** Miss Storrar.
D: £16.00-£18.00 **S:** £18.00-£25.00.
Open: Feb to Dec
Beds: 3T
Baths: 1 Sh
♿ (12) 🅿 (2) ⌁ 🛏 ✕ 👤 🛁 ♿ ▥

Winmar House Hotel, Kenneth Street, Inverness, IV3 5QG.
Full Scottish breakfast and friendly welcome. Ample parking.
Tel: **01463 239328** (also fax no)
Mrs Maclellan.
D: £16.00-£22.00 **S:** £16.00-£22.00.
Open: All Year (not Xmas)
Beds: 1D 6T 3S
Baths: 1 En 4 Pr 2 Sh
♿ 🅿 (10) ⌁ 🛏 🐾 👤 🛁 ▥ ♿ ♿

All cycleways are
popular: you are well-
advised to book ahead

S = Price range for a single
person in a room

MacGregor's, *36 Ardconnel Street, Inverness, IV2 3EX.*
We are situated minutes from River Ness, shops and castle.
Tel: **01463 238357**
Mrs MacGregor.
D: £14.00-£18.00
S: £15.00-£20.00.
Open: All Year (not Xmas/New Year)
Beds: 1F 3D 1T 3S
Baths: 2 En 3 Sh
🛏 🐾 👤 ▥ ▥

Hazeldean House, *125 Lochalsh Road, Inverness, IV3 5QS.*
Friendly Highland welcome. Only 10 mins' walk to town centre.
Grades: ETC 3 Star
Tel: **01463 241338**
Mr Stuart.
Fax no: 01463 236387
D: £14.00-£20.00
S: £16.00-£22.00.
Open: All Year
Beds: 2F 4D 3T 2S
Baths: 3 En 2 Sh
♿ 🅿 (6) ⌁ 🛏 🐾 👤 ▥ ▥ ♿

101 Kenneth Street, Inverness, IV3 5QQ.
Ideal base for day trips to North Highland and Islands.
Grades: ETC 2 Star
Tel: **01463 237224** Mrs Reid.
Fax no: 01463 712249
D: £16.00-£25.00 **S:** £20.00-£25.00.
Open: All Year
Beds: 2F 2D 1T 1S
Baths: 1 En 1 Pr 2 Sh
♿ 🅿 (6) ⌁ 🛏 👤 ▥ ♿ ▥

Strathisla, 42 Charles Street, Inverness, IV2 3AH.
2 minutes' walk to high street. 5 mins to rail and bus stations.
Grades: ETC 3 Star
Tel: **01463 235657** (also fax no)
Mr & Mrs Lewthwaite.
D: £15.00-£18.00
S: £16.00-£20.00.
Open: All Year (not Xmas)
Beds: 1D 1T 2S
Baths: 1 Sh
♿ (8) 🅿 (2) ⌁ 🛏 ✕ 👤 🛁 ▥ ♿

Ivybank Guest House, 28 Old Edinburgh Road, Inverness, IV2 3HJ.
Georgian home, near town centre and with parking.
Grades: ETC 4 Star
Tel: **01463 232796** (also fax no)
Mrs Cameron.
D: £20.00-£27.50
S: £20.00-£55.00.
Open: All Year
Beds: 1F 4D 2T 5S
Baths: 3 En 1 Pr 2 Sh
♿ 🅿 ⌁ 🐾 🛏 👤 🛁 ▥ 📞 ♿ ♿

---

5 Muirfield Gardens, Inverness, IV2 4HF.
Quiet residential area 15 mins walk to town centre. All rooms on ground floor.
Grades: ETC 3 Star
Tel: **01463 238114**
Mrs MacDonald.
D: £17.00-£20.00 **S:** £18.00-£20.00.
Open: Easter to Dec
Beds: 2D 1T
Baths: 2 Sh
🅿 (3) 🛏 👤 ▥ ▥

6 Broadstone Park, Inverness, IV2 3LA.
Family-run B&B. Victorian house 10 mins town centre, bus and railway station.
Grades: ETC 2 Star
Tel: **01463 221506**
Mrs Mackinnon.
D: £20.00-£25.00 **S:** £21.00-£25.00.
Open: All Year (not Xmas)
Beds: 1F 1D 1T 1S
Baths: 2 En 1 Pr
♿ (5) 🅿 (3) ⌁ 🛏 👤 ▥ ▥ ♿ ♿

Lyndon, 50 Telford Street, Inverness, IV3 5LE.
A warm and friendly welcome awaits you at the Lyndon.
Grades: ETC 3 Star
Tel: **01463 232551** Smith.
D: £15.00-£22.00 **S:** £30.00-£40.00.
Open: All Year (not Xmas)
Beds: 4F 1D 1T
Baths: 6 En
♿ 🅿 (6) 🛏 🐾 👤 🛁 ▥ ♿ ▥ ♿

Taigh Na Teile, 6 Island Bank Road, Inverness, IV2 4SY.
Overlooking the River Ness, this is a beautifully appointed Victorian-style house.
Grades: ETC 4 Star
Tel: **01463 222842**
Mr & Mrs Menzies.
Fax no: 01463 226844
D: £20.00-£20.00 **S:** £25.00-£30.00.
Open: All Year (not Xmas)
Beds: 1D 2T
Baths: All En
🅿 (4) ⌁ 🛏 👤 🛁 ▥ ▥ 📞 ♿

St Anns House, 37 Harrowden Road, Inverness, IV3 5QN.
Actual grid ref: NH658453
Friendly, small, clean, family-run hotel, 10 minutes' walk from town centre, bus & rail stations.
Tel: **01463 236157** (also fax no)
Mr Wilson.
D: £22.00-£24.00 **S:** £20.00-£30.00.
Open: Mar to Oct
Beds: 1F 2D 2T 1S
Baths: 5 En 1 Pr
♿ 🅿 (4) ⌁ 🛏 👤 🛁 ▥ 📞 ♿ ♿ ♿

Pay B&Bs by cash or
cheque and be prepared
to pay up front.

Tanera, *8 Fairfield Road, Inverness, IV3 5QA.*
Warm, comfortable house, close to River Ness, theatre and all amenities.
Tel: **01463 230037** (also fax no)
Mrs Geddes.
D: £18.00-£25.00 **S:** £20.00-£30.00.
Open: All Year
Beds: 2D 1T
Baths: 2 En 1 Pr 1 Sh
🛏 (10) 🅿 (3) ⌇ 🖵 🗡 ≛ 🛋 ▥ ⚡ ⚲

Crown Hotel, *19 Ardconnel Street, Inverness, IV2 3EU.*
Clean, warm, friendly. Excellent breakfast, four minutes from the station.
Tel: **01463 231135** (also fax no)
D: £17.00-£20.00 **S:** £17.00-£25.00.
Open: All Year (not Xmas)
Beds: 2F 2D 1T 2S
Baths: 3 En 2 Sh
🛏 🖵 ≛ 🛋 ▥ ⚲

Clach Mhuilinn, *7 Harris Road, Inverness, IV2 3LS.*
Comfortable no smoking B&B with luxury, charming ensuite bedrooms.
Tel: **01463 237059** Mrs Elmslie.
Fax no: 01463 242092
D: £24.00-£27.50 **S:** £35.00-£40.00.
Open: Easter to Oct
Beds: 1D 1T
Baths: 2 En
🛏 (10) 🅿 (3) ⌇ 🖵 ≛ 🛋 ▥

Ivanhoe Guest House, *68 Lochalsh Road, Inverness, IV3 6HW.*
Family-run, 10 mins' walk town centre. 'Highland Hospitality'.
Tel: **01463 223020** (also fax no)
Crerer.
D: £16.00-£18.00 **S:** £16.00-£18.00.
Open: All Year (not Xmas)
Beds: 2F 1T 2S
Baths: 2 En 3 Sh
🛏 (5) ⌇ 🖵 ≛ 🛋 ▥

Kendon, *9 Old Mill Lane, Inverness, IV2 3XP.*
Family bungalow in peaceful location with large garden and private parking.
Tel: **01463 238215** Mrs Kennedy.
D: £21.00-£25.00 .
Open: Apr to Oct
Beds: 2D 1T
Baths: 3 En
🅿 (4) ⌇ 🖵 ≛ 🛋 ▥ ▮

Hebrides, *120a Glenurquhart Road, Inverness, IV3 5TD.*
Quality graded B&B offering high standards, no smoking, private parking.
Tel: **01463 220062**
Mrs MacDonald.
D: £18.00-£25.00 .
Open: All Year
Beds: 2D 1T
Baths: 2 En
🅿 (3) ⌇ 🖵 ≛ ▥ ⚲

East Dene, *6 Ballifeary Road, Inverness, IV3 5PJ.*
Near Eden Court Theatre.
Tel: **01463 232976** (also fax no)
Mrs Greig.
D: £22.00-£27.00
S: £29.00-£35.00.
Open: All Year
Beds: 3D 1T
Baths: 3 En
🅿 (4) 🖵 🗡 ✕ ≛ 🛋 ▥

Cambeth Lodge, *49 Fairfield Road, Inverness, IV3 5QP.*
Comfortable detached Victorian house. Warm Scottish welcome assured.
Tel: **01463 231764**
Mrs Carson-Duff.
D: £17.00-£20.00 .
Open: All Year (not Xmas)
Beds: 2D 1T
Baths: 1 En 1 Pr 1 Sh
🛏 🅿 (5) ⌇ 🖵 ≛ 🛋 ▥ ⚲

Abbotsford, *7 Fairfield Road, Inverness, IV3 5QA.*
Comfortable friendly home, centrally situated, 2 mins town centre.
Tel: **01463 715377**
Mr Griffin.
D: £16.00-£20.00 **S:** £18.00-£25.00.
Open: All Year (not Xmas)
Beds: 1F 1D
Baths: 2 En
🛏 (12) 🅿 (1) 🖵 ≛ 🛋 ▥

Hawthorn Lodge House, *15 Fairfield Road, Inverness, IV3 5QA.*
The real taste of Scotland at Hawthorn Lodge.
Tel: **01463 715516** Mrs Davidson.
Fax no: 01463 221578
D: £20.00-£26.00 **S:** £20.00-£26.00.
Open: All Year
Beds: 2F 1D 1T
Baths: 3 En 1 Sh
🛏 🅿 (6) ⌇ 🖵 ≛ 🛋 ▥ ▮ ⚲ 🚲

D = Price range per person sharing in a double room

Carbisdale, *43 Charles Street, Inverness, IV2 3AH.*
Victorian family home, central location, ideal base for touring highlands.
Tel: **01463 225689** (also fax no)
Mrs Chisholm.
D: £16.00-£18.00
S: £20.00-£25.00.
Open: All Year
Beds: 2D 1T
Baths: 2 Sh
🖵 ≛ 🛋 ▥

Kinkell House, *11 Old Edinburgh Road, Inverness, IV2 3HF.*
Traditional Georgian family home full of charm and character. Spacious rooms, tastefully decorated.
Tel: **01463 235243**
Fax no: 01463 225255
D: £18.00-£46.00
S: £20.00-£24.00.
Open: All Year
Beds: 4F 1D 1S
Baths: 3 En 2 Sh
🅿 (8) 🖵 🗡 ≛ 🛋 ▥ ▮ ⚲

Charden Villa, *11 Fairfield Road, Inverness, IV3 5QA.*
Warm comfortable family-run house situated 10 mins' walk town centre.
Tel: **01463 222403**
Mrs Munro.
D: £18.00-£20.00
S: £22.00-£25.00.
Open: All Year
Beds: 4F, 3T or 1D
Baths: 2 En, 1 Sh
🛏 🖵 ≛ 🛋 ⅙ ▥ ▮ ⚲

Always telephone to get directions to the B&B - you will save time!

IRELAND: BED & BREAKFAST 2001

The essential guide to B&Bs in the Republic of Ireland and Northen Ireland

Think of Ireland and you think of that famous Irish hospitality. The warmth of the welcome is as much a part of this great island as the wild and beautiful landscapes, the traditional folk music and the Guiness. Wherever you go, town or country, North or South, you can't escape it.

There are few better ways of experiencing this renowned hospitality, when traveling through Ireland, than by staying at one of the country's many Bed & Breakfasts. They offer a great value alternative to expensive hotels, each has its own individual charm and you get a home cooked breakfast to help you start your day.

Stilwell's Ireland: Bed & Breakfast 2001 is the most comprehensive guide of its kind, with over 1,400 entries listed by county and location, in both Northern Ireland and the Republic of Ireland. Each entry includes room rates, facilities, Tourist Board grades, local maps and a brief description of the B&B, its location and surroundings.

Treat yourself to some Irish hospitality with **Stilwell Ireland: Bed & Breakfast 2001.**

Private Houses, Country Halls, Farms, Cottages, Inns, Small Hotels and Guest Houses

Over 1,400 entries
Average price £18 per person per night ($32 per person per night)
All official grades shown
Local maps
Pubs serving hot evening meals shown
Tourist Information Offices listed
Handy size for easy packing!

£6.95 from all good bookstores (ISBN 1-900861-24-0) or £7.95 (inc p&p) from Stilwell Publishing, 59 Charlotte Road, London EC2A 3QW (020 7739 7179)

Sustrans Clyde to Forth

The **Clyde to Forth Cycle Route** is a new section of the developing National Cycle Network, running for 90 miles on traffic-free paths and traffic-calmed roads through Scotland's central belt, linking the west and east coasts and the country's two most major cities, Glasgow, the metropolis, and Edinburgh, the capital. The route intersects with the Scottish National Cycle Route (Carlisle to Inverness) in Glasgow and Paisley. It is clearly signposted by blue direction signs with a cycle silhouette and the number 75 in a red rectangle.

Having started at the port of **Gourock**, with excellent views across the Firth of Clyde both north and west to the highlands of Argyll, the route from **Greenock** follows an almost entirely traffic-free railway path through Port Glasgow, Kilmalcolm and Bridge of Weir as far as **Paisley;** then alternates between shorter traffic-free paths and minor roads through **Glasgow**'s South Side to reach the Clyde at Bell's Bridge,which you cross to reach the city centre. The route now meanders with the river eastwards out of town through Rutherglen to reach Uddingston, from where you head north through Coatbridge to Airdrie. The central link in the route is the **Airdrie to Bathgate Railway Path**, a superb traffic-free path built out of the industrial decay of the former Junction Railway. Interspersed with the disused mines and quarries there is now a sculpture trail, featuring works which aim to use their industrial and natural setting to aesthetic advantage. The path takes you to Caldercruix and around the Hillend Reservoir across the country's central plateau via Blackridge and Armadale. After Bathgate the route crosses **Livingston** on landscaped paths

into Almondell and Calderwood Country Park, with its attractive wooded valleys. From East Calder there is a section on roads via Kirknewton to Currie, where you join the Water of Leith Walkway which you follow into outer **Edinburgh**. The Union Canal towpath takes you to the city centre, from where it's a short ride to the end of the route at **Leith**.

The indispensable **official route map and guide** for the route is available from Sustrans, 35 King Street, Bristol BS1 4DZ, tel 0117-926 8893, fax 0117-929 4173, @ £5.99 (+ £2.00 p&p).

Maps: Ordnance Survey 1:50,000 Landranger series: 63, 64, 65, 66

Trains: Glasgow and Edinburgh are both major termini on the Intercity network. Numerous other places on or near to the route are served by trains, including Gourock, from where there are also frequent ferry departures to Dunoon in Argyll.

Kilmacolm   **1**

National Grid Ref: NS3669

｜●｜ ◀▆ Pullman

Margaret's Mill Farm, *High Greenock Road, Kilmacolm, Renfrewshire, PA13 4TG.*
200-year-old farmhouse set in beautiful valley. Comfortable spacious bedrooms with colour TV.
Tel: **01505 873716** Mrs Henderson.
D: £15.00-£18.00 **S:** £15.00-£18.00.
Open: All Year **Beds:** 1F 1D 1T
🛏 🅿 (8) ✂ ❐ ♨ 🛉 🖤 ⅰ ∦ ♋

Greenock has a couple of interesting museums – the Custom House Museum, on the history of Customs and Excise, and the Mclean Museum of shipping and steam power, commemorating James Watt, the local boy who revolutionised the technology by inventing the first steam engine with separate condenser in 1765.

For information on **Paisley** and **Glasgow** see under *Sustrans Carlisle to Inverness*.

Kilbarchan 2

National Grid Ref: NS4063

⊮ ⛾ Trust Inn

Gladstone Farmhouse,
Burntshields Road, Kilbarchan,
Johnstone, Renfrewshire, PA10 2PB.
Quiet countryside, 10 minutes
Glasgow airport on direct route.
Tel: **01505 702579** (also fax no)
Mrs Douglas.
D: £18.00-£18.00 **S:** £20.00-£20.00
Open: All Year
Beds: 1F 1D 1T **Baths:** 1 Sh
🚸 🅿 (6) 🗔 🌴 ✗ 🛒 🎟 🛁 ⚓ Ⓥ ⚡ ⊶

D = Price range per person
sharing in a double room

All cycleways are popular: you are well-advised to book ahead

---

Paisley 3

National Grid Ref: NS4863

⊮ ⛾ Lord Lounsdale, Paraffin Lamp

Accara Guest House, *75*
Maxwellton Road, Paisley,
Renfrewshire, PA1 2RB.
Grade II Listed building close to
airport, museum, university,
hospital.
Grades: ETC 2 Star
Tel: **0141 887 7604**
Mrs Stevens.
Fax no: 0141 887 1589
D: £20.00-£20.00
S: £25.00-£25.00.
Open: All Year
Beds: 1F 1T 1S
Baths: 2 Sh
🚸 (4) 🗔 🛒 🎟 Ⓥ

Myfarrclan Guest House, *146*
Corsebar Road, Paisley,
Renfrewshire, PA2 9NA.
Nestling in leafy suburb of Paisley,
lovingly restored bungalow offer-
ing many thoughtful extras.
Tel: **0141 884 8285**
Mr & Mrs Farr.
Fax no: 0141 581 1566
D: £32.50-£35.00 **S:** £40.00-£60.00.
Open: All Year
Beds: 2D 1T
Baths: 2 En 1 Pr
🚸 🅿 (2) 🛒 🗔 ✗ 🛒 🎟 Ⓥ

Glasgow Muirend 4

National Grid Ref: NS5760

16 Bogton Avenue, *Muirend,*
Glasgow, G44 3JJ.
Quiet red sandstone terraced
private house adjacent station,
12 mins city centre.
Tel: **0141 637 4402** (also fax no)
Mrs Paterson.
D: £20.00-£20.00 **S:** £22.00-£22.00.
Open: All Year (not Xmas)
Beds: 1D 2S
Baths: 2 Sh
🅿 (2) 🛒 🗔 ✗ 🛒 🎟 Ⓥ

Glasgow Central 5

National Grid Ref: NS5865

⊮ ⛾ Dorsey's, Park Bar, Mitchell's, Stravaigan's, Orchard Park, Bellahouston Hotel, Garfield House, Highlanders Park, Snaffil Bit

▲ ***Glasgow Youth Hostel,*** *7/8*
Park Terrace, Glasgow, G3 6BY.
Actual grid ref: NS575662
Tel: **0141 332 3004**
Under 18: £8.50
Adults: £10.00
Self-catering facilities, Shop
nearby, Laundry facilities, Evening
meal for groups only
*Glasgow has something for
everyone, from city parks to free
museums and galleries, and great
nightlife. Good base for touring the
Trossachs, the Clyde Coast and
Loch Lomond.*

S = Price range for a single
person in a room

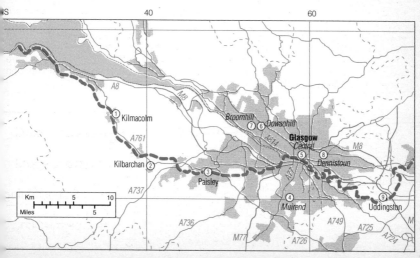

▲ *Euro Hostel Glasgow, 318 Clyde Street, Glasgow G1 4NR.*
Actual grid ref: NS593645
Tel: **0141 222 2828 Adults:** £13.75
Laundry facilities, Games room, Security lockers, Cycle store, Facilities for disabled people, No smoking
Centrally located, overlooking River Clyde. All rooms ensuite: 3 single, 70 twin, 3 triple, 32 x 4 person/family, 3 x 8 person, 4 x 14 person - most combinations of requirements can be catered for. Close Central/Queen Street rail stations/Buchanan Street Bus Station; overnight parking available at nearby St Enoch Square.

Kirkland House, 42 St Vincent Crescent, Glasgow, G3 8NG.
Grades: ETC 3 Star
Tel: **0141 248 3458**
Mrs Divers.
Fax no: 0141 221 5174
D: £27.00-£30.00 **S:** £27.00-£30.00.
Open: All Year
Beds: 3D 2T 2S
Baths: 6 En 2 Sh
🛇 (1) ⑭🖂❑♨💷.Ⅶ
City centre guest house with excellent rooms on beautiful Victorian Crescent in Finnieston (Glasgow's 'little Chelsea'). Short walk to Scottish Exhibition Centre, Museum/Art Gallery, Kelvingrove Park and all West End facilities. Glasgow airport 10 minutes, member of the Harry James society.

Kelvingrove Hotel, 944 Sauchiehall Street, Glasgow, G3 7TH.
Grades: ETC 3 Star,
AA 3 Diamond, RAC 3 Star
Tel: **0141 339 5011**
Mr Wills.
Fax no: 0141 339 6566
D: £24.00-£29.00 **S:** £33.00-£38.00.
Open: All Year (not Xmas)
Beds: 8D 4T 4F
Baths: 10 En
🛇 🅿 (20)⑭🖂❑♛✗♨💷.Ⅶ🌢⌇☙
Centrally located family-run hotel, set in Glasgow's fashionable West End. Close to pubs, clubs, art galleries, museums, University, shops, rail and bus links - all within walking distance.

Adelaide's, 209 Bath Street, Glasgow, G2 4HZ.
Central location, close to all major attractions of revitalised city.
Grades: ETC 2 Star
Tel: **0141 248 4970**
Meiklejohn.
Fax no: 0141 226 4247
D: £25.00-£28.00
S: £35.00-£45.00.
Open: All Year (not Xmas/ New Year)
Beds: 2F 2T 2D 2S
Baths: 6 En 2 Sh
🛇⑭🖂❑♨Ⅶ🌢☙

Number Thirty Six, 36 St Vincent Crescent, Glasgow, G3 8NG.
Situated in a Georgian terrace on the edge of Glasgow city centre.
Tel: **0141 248 2086** Mrs MacKay.
Fax no: 0141 221 1477
D: £25.00-£30.00 **S:** £30.00-£35.00.
Open: All Year (not Xmas)
Beds: 4D 2T
Baths: 4 En 2 Pr
⑭❑♨💷.Ⅶ

Glasgow Dowanhill 6
National Grid Ref: NS5667

⑭🍴Orchard Park Hotel, Bellahouston Hotel

The Terrace House Hotel, 14 Belhaven Terrace, Glasgow, G12 0TG.
Grades: ETC 2 Star
Tel: **0141 337 3377** (also fax no)
Mrs Black.
D: £29.00-£39.00 **S:** £49.00-£65.00.
Open: All Year
Beds: 4F 3D 5T 1S
Baths: 12 En 1 Pr
🛇⑭🖂❑♛✗♨💷.Ⅶ
'B' Listed terraced townhouse, built circa 1860, boasting fine period features, such as ornate cornices, wall friezes and columned entrance. Well connected to transport links to city centre, Glasgow Airport and Loch Lomond. A friendly welcome awaits you.

Glasgow Broomhill 7
National Grid Ref: NS5467

⑭🍴Air Organic, Bellahouston Hotel, Dino's, Dorsey's, Garfield House, Highlanders Park, Mitchell's, Orchard Park, Pablo's, Park Bar, Stravaigan's, Snaffil Bit

Lochgilvie House, 117 Randolph Road, Broomhill, Glasgow, G11 7DS.
Grades: ETC 3 Star
Tel: **0141 357 1593** Mrs Ogilvie.
Fax no: 0141 334 5828
D: £25.00-£30.00 **S:** £25.00-£35.00.
Open: All Year
Beds: 1F 2D 3T
Baths: 4 En
🛇 (10) 🅿⑭🖂❑♨💷.Ⅶ
Luxurious Victorian town house situated in Glasgow's prestigious West End, adjacent to rail station, beside the art galleries, university, SECC, convenient for International Airport.

Park House, 13 Victoria Park Gardens South, Glasgow, G11 7BX.
Magnificent Victorian residence overlooking private parkland in quiet residential area.
Grades: ETC 4 Star
Tel: **0141 339 1559** Mrs Hallam.
Fax no: 0141 576 0915
D: £25.00-£27.50 **S:** £32.00-£37.50.
Open: All Year
Beds: 2S 1T
Baths: 2 En 1 Pr
🛇🅿 (3)❑✗♨💷.Ⅶ

Glasgow Dennistoun 8
National Grid Ref: NS6065

⑭🍴Fire Station Resturant, Dorsey's, Park Bar, Mitchell's, Stravaigan's, Orchard Park, Bellahoustow Hotel, Garfield House, Highlanders Park, Snaffil Bit

Seton Guest House, 6 Seton Terrace, Glasgow, G31 2HU.
Warm and friendly welcome assured. Five minutes from city centre.
Grades: ETC 2 Star
Tel: **0141 556 7654**
Mr Passway
Fax no: 0141 402 3655
D: £16.00-£17.00 **S:** £17.00-£18.00
Open: All Year (not Xmas)
Beds: 4F 2D 2T 1S
Baths: 3 Sh
🛇⊐♛♨💷.Ⅶ☙

Rosewood Guest House, 4 Seton Terrace, Glasgow, G31 2HU.
Victorian house near city centre, close to many city attractions.
Grades: ETC 2 Star
Tel: **0141 550 1500**
Ms Turner.
Fax no: 01555 393876
D: £17.00-£20.00
S: £19.00-£22.00.
Open: All Year
Beds: 3F 2T 1D 2S
Baths: 3 Sh
🛇🅿❑♛♨💷.Ⅶ☙

Uddingston
National Grid Ref: NS6960

⑭🍴Windmill, Redstones

Phoenix Lodge Guest House, 4 Girdons Way, Uddingston, Glasgow, G71 7ED.
Grades: ETC 2 Star
Tel: **01698 815296** Mr Boyce.
Fax no: 01698 267567
D: £19.00-£22.00 **S:** £23.00-£25.00
Open: All Year
Beds: 6F 1T 1D
Baths: 3 En 2 Sh
🛇🅿 (8) ❑♛✗♨💷.&Ⅶ🌢🗲
Modern building, close to motorways north & south, rail station, lots of tourist attractions locally, walks, close to swimming pool, tenpin bowling, cinemas, parks, gymnasium, lots of pubs, clubs, various eating places, e.g. Indian, Italian, Chinese. Close to Glasgow Zoo.

Northcote Guest House, 2 Holmbrae Avenue, Uddingston, Glasgow, G71 6AL.
Large Victorian private house, quiet locality. Easily accessible.
Tel: **01698 813319** (also fax no)
Mrs Meggs.
D: £16.00-£17.00 **S:** £16.00-£17.
Open: All Year (not Xmas)
Beds: 1F 1D 1S
Baths: 1 Sh
🛇🅿 (3)❑💷.

Armadale 10

National Grid Ref: NS9368

Tarrareoch Farm, Armadale, Bathgate, W Lothian, EH48 3BJ.
C17th farmhouse all on one level. Midway Edinburgh/Glasgow. Beautiful countryside.
Grades: ETC 3 Star
Tel: **01501 730404** (also fax no) Mrs Gibb.
D: £16.00-£20.00 **S:** £20.00-£26.00.
Open: All Year
Beds: 1F 2T
Baths: 1 En 1 Sh
🛇 **P** (10) 🛏 🕇 🌣 ⬛ V ⅄ ॐ

Bathgate 11

National Grid Ref: NS9769

🍴 🍷 Kaim Park

Hillview, 35 The Green, Bathgate, W Lothian, EH48 4DA.
Quality and friendly accommodation with spectacular views of West Lothian.
Grades: ETC 2 Star
Tel: **01506 654830** (also fax no) Mrs Connell.
D: £15.00-£16.00 **S:** £20.00-£22.00.
Open: All Year (not Xmas)
Beds: 1F 1T
Baths: 1 Sh
🛇 ⅍ 🛏 🕇 🌣 ⬛ V ⅄ ᥣᥩ

Blackburn 12

National Grid Ref: NS9865

Cruachan Guest House, 78 East Main Street, Blackburn, Bathgate, West Lothian, EH47 7QS.
Relaxed, friendly, high-quality. Airport nearby, rail service to Edinburgh.
Grades: ETC 3 Star
Tel: **01506 655221** Mr Harkins.
Fax no: 01506 652395
D: £20.00-£23.00 **S:** £25.00-£30.00.
Open: All Year (not Xmas)
Beds: 1F 3D
Baths: 3 En 1 Pr
🛇 **P** (5) ⅍ 🌣 ⬛ V ⅄ ॐ

Balerno 13

National Grid Ref: NT1666

🍴 🍷 Tanners, Kestrel

Newmills Cottage, 472 Lanark Road West, Balerno, EH14 5AE.
Delightful house set in own grounds with ample private off-road parking.
Grades: ETC 4 Star, AA 4 Diamond
Tel: **0131 449 4300** (also fax no) Mrs Linn.
D: £20.00-£27.50 **S:** £25.00-£35.00.
Open: All Year
Beds: 2T
Baths: 1 En 1 Pr
P ⅍ 🌣 ⬛ V ⅄ ॐ

Edinburgh Morningside 14

National Grid Ref: NT2471

🍴 🍷 Montpeliers

Sandeman House, 33 Colinton Road, Edinburgh, EH10 5DR.
Non-smoking Victorian family home, conveniently situated, unrestricted street parking.
Tel: **0131 447 8080** (also fax no) Ms Sandeman.
D: £28.00-£36.00 **S:** £25.00-£45.00.
Open: All Year (not Xmas)
Beds: 1D 1T 1S **Baths:** 3 Pr
🛇 **P** 🌣 ⬛ V ⅄

Dunedin, 21-23 Colinton Road, Edinburgh, EH10 5DR.
Victorian terraced villa, furnished in period style. Princes Street, 15 mins.
Tel: **0131 447 0679** Mr Fortune.
Fax no: 0131 446 9358
D: £20.00-£30.00 **S:** £20.00-£30.00.
Open: All Year (not Xmas)
Beds: 4F 2D 1T 2S
Baths: 6 En 1 Pr 2 Sh
🛇 ⅍ 🌣 ⬛ ♿ V ॐ

Edinburgh Corstorphine 15

National Grid Ref: NT1972

Zetland Guest House, 186 St Johns Road, Edinburgh, EH12 8SG.
A splendid Victorian house situated on the west side of Edinburgh.
Grades: ETC 3 Star GH, AA 4 Diamond
Tel: **0131 334 3898** (also fax no) Mr Stein.
D: £20.00-£27.50 **S:** £20.00-£50.00.
Open: All Year
Beds: 1F 2D 4T 1S
Baths: 4 En 2 Sh
🛇 **P** (7) 🌣 ⬛ V

Edinburgh Slateford 16

National Grid Ref: NT2271

🍴 🍷 Dell Inn, Tickled Trout

13 Moat Street, Edinburgh, EH14 1PE.
Comfortable accommodation, colour TV, each room.
Grades: ETC 2 Star
Tel: **0131 443 8266** Mrs Hume.
D: £15.00-£20.00 **S:** £18.00-£20.00.
Open: Easter to Mar
Beds: 1D 1T
🛇 **P** 🌣 ⬛ V

Doocote House, 15 Moat Street, Edinburgh, EH14 1PE.
Victorian terraced house 2 miles from city centre, unrestricted parking.
Grades: ETC 2 Star
Tel: **0131 443 5455** Mr Manson.
D: £18.00-£20.00 **S:** £20.00-£30.00.
Open: All Year
Beds: 1F 1D 1T
Baths: 2 Sh
🛇 **P** 🛏 🕇 🌣 ⬛ V

On the way in **Livingston**, the Almond Valley Heritage Centre at Mill Farm has reconstructions tracing different aspects of past life in the West Lothian region, including an exhibition on the shale oil industry, a working water mill and a narrow-gauge railway. This one is particularly suitable for young children, with farm animals in child-friendly closures.

Just before **Currie**, Malleny Garden contains Scotland's national collection of bonsai trees, a large array of roses and four 400-year-old yew trees.

Edinburgh Merchiston 17

National Grid Ref: NT2472

🍴 🍷 Allison Hotel, Backstage Bistro, Belfry, Bennets Bar, Cafe Royal, Grannies Attic, Kings Wark, March Hall Hotel, Minto Hotel, Navaar House, Railto Restaurant, Seahaven Hotel, Suffolk Hall Hotel, Tatlers Golf Tavern

Villa Nina Guest House, 39 Leamington Terrace, Edinburgh, EH10 4JS.
Grades: ETC 1 Star
Tel: **0131 229 2644** (also fax no) Mr Cecco.
D: £18.00-£24.00 .
Open: All Year (not Xmas/New Year)
Beds: 1F 2D 2T **Baths:** 2 Sh
P 🌣 ⬛ V
Very comfortable Victorian terrace house situated in quiet residential part of city yet 15 minutes' walk Princes Street, Castle, theatres. TV in all rooms. Private showers. Full cooked breakfast.

Granville Guest House, 13 Granville Terrace, Edinburgh, EH10 4PQ.
Grades: ETC 1 Star
Tel: **0131 229 1676** Oussellam.
Fax no: 0131 227 4633
D: £19.00-£30.00 **S:** £20.00-£30.00.
Open: All Year (not Xmas)
Beds: 2F 1T 3D 1S
Baths: 2 En 2 Sh
🛇 **P** ⅍ 🌣 ⬛ V
A family run guest house situated centrally in Edinburgh, all local amenities are nearby - not to mention the Kings Theatre and a newly built leisure complex. We are around a ten minute walk from the city centre and the historic Edinburgh Castle.

Sustrans Clyde to Forth

Nova Hotel, *5 Bruntsfield Crescent, Edinburgh, EH10 4EZ.*
Victorian, city centre, quiet area, free parking, fully licensed, all rooms ensuite. Lovely views.
Grades: ETC 3 Star
Tel: **0131 447 6437** Mr McBride.
Fax no: 0131 452 8126 (preferred for bookings)
D: £25.00-£55.00 **S:** £35.00-£70.00.
Open: All Year
Beds: 6F 2D 2T 2S
Baths: 13 En
🛏️🅿️✕🍴🛉🗶🛆🎍⛆🔌📺🛆✿🚲

Leamington Guest House, *57 Leamington Terrace, Edinburgh, EH10 4JS.*
Elegant Victorian town house close to city centre. Warm welcome assured.
Grades: ETC 3 Star,
AA 3 Diamond
Tel: **0131 228 3879** Ms Stewart.
Fax no: 0131 221 1022
D: £25.00-£40.00 **S:** £25.00-£40.00.
Open: All Year
Beds: 3F 2D 1T 2S
Baths: 4 En 2 Sh
🛏️✕🍴🛉🎍⛆📺🔌

Kariba Guest House, *10 Granville Terrace, Edinburgh, EH10 4BQ.*
Victorian townhouse 15 minutes walk to city centre. Private parking.
Grades: AA 2 Diamond,
RAC 2 Diamond
Tel: **0131 229 3773** Mrs Holligan.
Fax no: 0131 229 4968
D: £18.00-£28.00 **S:** £25.00-£50.00.
Open: All Year
Beds: 2F 4D 3T **Baths:** 2 En
🛏️(1)🍴🛉🎍⛆🛆📺

D = Price range per person sharing in a double room

All details shown as supplied by B&B owners in Autumn 2000.

Edinburgh Newington 18

National Grid Ref: NT2671

🍴 Old Bell Inn, Suffolk Hall Hotel, Cragg, Braidburn Inn

Rowan Guest House, *13 Glenorchy Terrace, Edinburgh, EH9 2DQ.*
Grades: ETC 3 Star,
AA 3 Diamond
Tel: **0131 667 2463** (also fax no)
Mr & Mrs Vidler.
D: £23.00-£32.00 **S:** £24.00-£29.00.
Open: All Year (not Xmas)
Beds: 1F 3D 2T 3S
Baths: 3 En 3 Sh
🛏️(2)🅿️(2)🍴🛉🎍⛆📺
Comfortable Victorian home in quiet, leafy, conservation area, a mile and a half from city centre, castle and Royal Mile. Delicious breakfast, including porridge and freshly baked scones. A warm welcome and personal service from Alan and Angela. Free parking.

Ascot Guest House, *98 Dalkeith Road, Edinburgh, EH16 5AF.*
Comfortable family-run guest house close to all attractions.
Tel: **0131 667 1500** Williams.
D: £18.00-£30.00 **S:** £20.00-£40.00.
Open: All Year
Beds: 2F 2T 2D 1S
Baths: 2 En 2 Pr 2 Sh
🛏️(10)🅿️(3)🍴🛉🎍⛆📺🚲

Gifford House, *103 Dalkeith Road, Edinburgh, EH16 5AJ.*
Elegant Victorian house. Superior rooms with Edinburgh's attractions within easy reach.
Grades: ETC 4 Star
Tel: **0131 667 4688** (also fax no)
Mrs Dow.
D: £20.00-£38.00 **S:** £23.00-£50.00.
Open: All Year
Beds: 2F 2D 2T 1S
Baths: 7 En
🛏️✕🍴🛉🎍⛆📺🛆✿🚲

17 Crawfurd Road, *Edinburgh, EH16 5PQ.*
Victorian family home, friendly welcome - easy access to city centre.
Grades: ETC 2 Star
Tel: **0131 667 1191** Ms Simpson.
D: £17.50-£25.00 **S:** £17.50-£25.00.
Open: May to Sep
Beds: 1D 1T 1S
Baths: 2 Sh
🛏️🅿️(1)✕🍴🎍⛆📺

Kingsley Guest House, *30 Craigmillar Park, Edinburgh, EH16 5PS.*
Friendly-family run house on excellent bus route for sightseeing.
Grades: ETC 3 Star,
AA 3 Diamond
Tel: **0131 667 8439** (also fax no)
D: £20.00-£35.00 **S:** £25.00-£40.00.
Open: All Year
Beds: 1F 2T 3D **Baths:** 3 En 2 Pr
🛏️(3)🅿️(5)✕🍴🎍⛆📺

7 Crawfurd Road, *Newington, Edinburgh, EH16 5PQ.*
Beautiful centrally located house. Guest rooms overlook well-maintained gardens.
Tel: **0131 667 2283** Mrs McLean.
D: £19.00-£25.00 **S:** £22.00-£25.00.
Open: Easter to Oct
Beds: 1F 1T 1S **Baths:** 1 Sh
✕🍴🎍

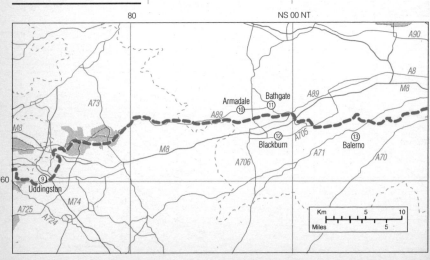

Edinburgh, for unbroken centuries the centre of Scotland's judicial system and church, has just been restored to pre-eminence in the country's administration and legislature. The new Scottish Parliament will eventually sit in a brand new building, currently under construction, designed by the Catalan architects Enric Miralles Benedetta Tagliabue. It will stand close by the Palace of Holyroodhouse, at the eastern end of the Old Town's historic main thoroughfare, the Royal Mile, and will be an open, fragmented arrangement which is designed to complement both the Palace itself, and Salisbury Crags to the south. Holyrood Palace itself, official residence of the monarch in Scotland, is a mainly sixteenth- and seventeenth-century building with a turreted façade and Palladian courtyard. Access is restricted to guided tours, which include the rooms once inhabited by Mary, Queen of Scots. In the grounds stand the ruins of Holyrood Abbey, which arose in the twelfth century from origins shrouded in mystery. Of the earliest, Norman part of the building there survives one doorway. The Royal Mile leads westwards up to the rock, with sheer drops on three sides and yielding the best views over the city, on which stands Edinburgh Castle. It was here that the city began, and for centuries the castle had enormous strategic importance; its military significance remains, as the headquarters of the Scottish Division. The castle's oldest building is St Margaret's Chapel, an atmospheric small Norman church.

There is much to explore long the Royal Mile itself, including the churches of St Giles, a hotch-potch of styles thanks to multiple restorations, and Canongate, built in the seventeenth century to an anachronistic Renaissance design, which has a number of notables buried in its graveyard, including Adam Smith. Elsewhere in the Old Town, Greyfriars Kirkyard is one of the most atmospheric graveyards you're likely to find, and is famous for Greyfriars Bobby, the archetypal loyal dog who refused to leave his master's grave. The Old Town's museums include the wide-ranging Royal Museum of Scotland, the Museum of Childhood and the Scotch Whisky Heritage Centre – yes, they have got a shop. Stretching north from Princes Street, in Edinburgh's smart Georgian New Town you can find the excellent National Gallery of Scotland and the Scottish National Portrait Gallery and Museum of Antiquities. Further afield, the Scottish National Gallery of Modern Art was the first purely twentieth-century galley in Britain when it opened forty years ago.

Edinburgh's port of **Leith** has a high concentration of pubs and eateries on or near the waterfront, and is, as such, the ideal journey's end.

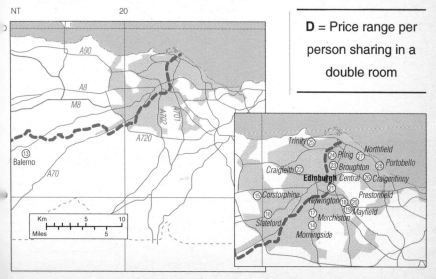

D = Price range per person sharing in a double room

Edinburgh Mayfield 19

National Grid Ref: NT2672

Braidburn Inn, Leasley, La Campana, Old Bell Inn

The International, *37 Mayfield Gardens, Edinburgh,* EH9 2BX.
Grades: ETC 4 Star, AA 4 Diamond
Tel: **0131 667 2511** Mrs Niven.
Fax no: 0131 667 1112
D: £20.00-£40.00 **S:** £25.00-£45.00.
Open: All Year
Beds: 2F 2D 2T 3S
Baths: 9 Pr
An attractive stone built Victorian house situated 1.5 miles south of Princes Street. Lying on main bus route, access to city centre is easy. The decor is outstanding, some rooms enjoy magnificent views across to the extinct Arthur's Seat volcano. Direct dial telephones.

Lorne Villa Guest House, *9 East Mayfield, Edinburgh,* EH9 1SD.
Festival city residence, serving fine Scottish cuisine with Scottish hospitality.
Grades: ETC 3 Star
Tel: **0131 667 7159** (also fax no) Mr McCulloch.
D: £18.00-£32.00 **S:** £18.00-£32.00.
Open: All Year
Beds: 1F 2D 3T 1S
Baths: 3 En 1 Pr 3 Sh
(6)

Hopetoun Guest House, *15 Mayfield Road, Edinburgh,* EH9 2NG.
Actual grid ref: NT265717
Grades: ETC 3 Star
Tel: **0131 667 7691** Mrs Mitchell.
Fax no: 0131 466 1691
D: £20.00-£27.00 **S:** £25.00-£40.00.
Open: All Year (not Xmas)
Beds: 1F 1D 1T
Baths: 1 En 1 Pr 1 Sh
(6) (2)
Completely non-smoking. Small, friendly, family-run guest house, close to Edinburgh University. Excellent bus service. Royal Mile/Castle 25 mins on foot. Personal attention in a relaxed, informal atmosphere. Good choice of breakfast. Owner a fund of local information! Which? Books B&B Guide.

All rooms full and nowhere else to stay? Ask the owner if there's anywhere nearby

Lauderville Guest House, *52 Mayfield Road, Edinburgh,* EH9 2NH.
Grades: ETC 4 Star
Tel: **0131 667 7788** Mrs Marriott.
Fax no: 0131 667 2636
D: £25.00-£40.00
S: £28.00-£48.00.
Open: All Year
Beds: 1F 6D 2T 1S
Baths: 10 En
(6)
Restored Victorian town house minutes from the city sights, Royal Mile, Castle, Princes St. Elegant non-smoking bedrooms and excellent breakfast awaits, with varied menu including vegetarian. Secluded garden and secure car park. Traditional pubs and quality restaurants nearby.

Tania Guest House, *19 Minto Street, Edinburgh,* EH9 1RQ.
Comfortable Georgian guest house, very good bus route, Italian spoken.
Grades: ETC 1 Star
Tel: **0131 667 4144** Mrs Roscilli.
D: £18.00-£25.00
S: £20.00-£27.50.
Open: All Year (not Xmas)
Beds: 3F 1D 1T 1S
Baths: 2 En

Ivy Guest House, *7 Mayfield Gardens, Edinburgh,* EH9 2AX.
Grades: ETC 3 Star, AA 3 Diamond, RAC 4 Diamond
Tel: **0131 667 3411** Mr Green.
Fax no: 0131 620 1422
D: £17.00-£35.00
S: £17.00-£65.00.
Open: All Year
Beds: 2F 3D 2T 1S
Baths: 6 En 2 Pr
(7)
Quiet, family-run Victorian villa guest house, many local restaurants, close to all Edinburgh's major cultural attractions, golf courses, Commonwealth swimming pool and university. A hearty Scottish breakfast and a warm welcome is assured.

Glenalmond Guest House, *25 Mayfield Gardens, Edinburgh,* EH9 2BX.
Grades: ETC 4 Star
Tel: **0131 668 2392** (also fax no) Mr & Mrs Fraser.
D: £20.00-£35.00
S: £25.00-£40.00.
Open: All Year (not Xmas)
Beds: 3F 4D 2T 1S
Baths: 10 En
(5)
Deb & Dave warmly welcome you to their superb accommodation. Ground, four poster, en-suite rooms available. Close to Waverley Station. Varied breakfast served daily with home-made scones.

Ben Doran Guest House, *11 Mayfield Gardens, Edinburgh,* EH9 2AX.
Beautiful refurbished Georgian house. Elegant, cosy, comfortable, central. Family run hotel.
Grades: ETC 4 Star, AA 4 Diamond, RAC 4 Diamond, Sparkling
Tel: **0131 667 8488** Dr Labaki.
Fax no: 0131 667 0076
D: £25.00-£60.00 **S:** £25.00-£60.00.
Open: All Year
Beds: 4F 3D 2T 1S
Baths: 6 En 4 Sh
(17)

Crion Guest House, *33 Minto Street, Edinburgh,* EH9 2BT.
Family run guest house near city centre. Most tourist attractions.
Grades: ETC Approv
Tel: **0131 667 2708**
Fax no: 0131 662 1946
D: £20.00-£27.00 **S:** £20.00-£27.00.
Open: All Year
Beds: 1D 2T 1S
Baths: 1 Sh
(2)

Parklands Guest House, *20 Mayfield Gardens, Edinburgh,* EH9 2BZ.
Comfortable well maintained Victorian guest house near city centre.
Grades: ETC 3 Star, AA 3 Diamond
Tel: **0131 667 7184** Mr Drummond.
Fax no: 0131 667 2011
D: £22.00-£30.00
S: £25.00-£40.00.
Open: All Year
Beds: 1F 2D 2T 1S
Baths: 5 En 1 Pr
(1)

Sylvern Guest House, *22 West Mayfield, Edinburgh,* EH9 1TQ.
Situated near the city centre. Good bus routes, car park.
Grades: ETC 2 Star
Tel: **0131 667 1241** (also fax no) Mr & Mrs Livornese.
D: £17.00-£24.00 .
Open: All Year
Beds: 2F 2T 2D
Baths: 4 En 2 Sh
(8)

Fairholme Guest House, *13 Moston Terrace, Edinburgh,* EH9 2DE.
Nestled away from noisy traffic, yet only 1.5 miles from Castle.
Grades: ETC 3 Star
Tel: **0131 667 8645** Mrs Blows.
Fax no: 0131 668 2435
D: £23.00-£35.00
S: £25.00-£40.00.
Open: All Year
Beds: 1F 1D 1T 1S
Baths: 3 En 1 Pr
(1)

St Conan's Guest House, *30 Minto Street, Edinburgh, EH9 1SB.*
A handsome, stone-built, Listed, end-terrace Georgian town house on three floors.
Tel: **0131 667 8393** (also fax no)
Mr Bryce.
D: £20.00-£27.00
S: £20.00-£30.00.
Open: All Year
Beds: 3F 1D 3T
Baths: 1 En 4 Pr 1 Sh
🛇 �Ⓟ (7) ⌷ ⅋ 🏊 ⅏ Ⓥ

Classic Guest House, *50 Mayfield Road, Edinburgh, EH9 2NH.*
Friendly, family-run Victorian house, totally non-smoking.
Personal service, Scottish hospitality.
Tel: **0131 667 5847**
Mrs Mail.
Fax no: 0131 662 1016
D: £20.00-£30.00 **S:** £20.00-£40.00.
Open: All Year
Beds: 7F 1D 1T 3S
Baths: 7 En
🛇 (3) Ⓟ ⅋ ⌷ 🏊 ⅏ ⅙ Ⓥ ⊶

Abcorn Guest House, *4 Mayfield Gardens, Edinburgh, EH9 2BU.*
Detached Victorian villa, one mile from Edinburgh city centre.
Tel: **0131 667 6548**
D: £25.00-£35.00 **S:** £25.00-£35.00.
Open: All Year
Beds: 2F 2D 2T 1S
Baths: 7 En
🛇 Ⓟ (6) ⌷ 🏊 ⅏ Ⓥ

Kingsway Guest House, *5 East Mayfield, Edinburgh, EH9 1SD.*
Warm, friendly, terraced Victorian villa quietly situated near Castle & Princes Street.
Tel: **0131 667 5029**
Mrs Macdonald.
Fax no: 0131 662 4635
D: £18.00-£35.00 **S:** £25.00-£35.00.
Open: All Year
Beds: 2F 2D 2T 1S
Baths: 4 En 1 Pr 1 Sh
Ⓟ ⌷ ⊱ 🏊 ⅏ Ⓥ ⅋ ⊶

Edinburgh Prestonfield 20

National Grid Ref: NT2771

🍴 🍺 Golf Tavern, Bennets Bar, Tapas Ole, Minto Hotel, Navaar Hotel, Allison Hotel, Grannies Attic, Seahaven Hotel, Hotel Ceilidhonia

Airdenair, *29 Kilmaurs Road, Edinburgh, EH16 5DB.*
Fabulous views of Edinburgh.
Recently refurbished, family-run.
Quiet location
Grades: ETC 3 Star
Tel: **0131 668 2336**
Mrs Mclennan.
D: £22.00-£30.00
S: £30.00-£40.00.
Open: All Year
Beds: 2T 2D 2S
Baths: 5 En
Ⓟ ⅋ ⌷ 🏊 ⅏ Ⓥ

Always telephone to get directions to the B&B - you will save time!

Cameron Toll Guest House, *299 Dalkeith Road, Edinburgh, EH16 5JX.*
Eco-friendly family guest house on A7, 10 minutes from city centre.
Grades: ETC 4 Star
Tel: **0131 667 2950** Deans.
Fax no: 0131 662 1987
D: £20.00-£35.00 **S:** £25.00-£37.00.
Open: All Year
Beds: 3F 2T 3D 3S
Baths: 10 En 1 Pr
🛇 Ⓟ (4) ⅋ ⌷ ✗ 🏊 ⅏ ⅙ Ⓥ ⅋ ⅌ ⊶

Edinburgh Central 21

National Grid Ref: NT2573

🍴 🍺 Golf Tavern, Bennets Bar, Minto Hotel, Navaar Hotel, Allison Hotel, Seahaven Hotel

🔺 **Edinburgh Eglinton Youth Hostel,** *18 Eglinton Crescent, Edinburgh, EH12 5DD.*
Actual grid ref: NT238735
Tel: **0131 337 1120**
Under 18: £10.50 **Adults:** £12.00
Self-catering facilities, Shop, Laundry facilities, Evening meal for groups only
Edinburgh's cobbled streets provide a wealth of history, superb restaurants and spectacular views. The Arts festival runs every summer.

🔺 **Edinburgh Central Youth Hostel,** *Robertson Close/College Wynd, Cowgate, Edinburgh, EH1 1LY.*
Tel: **08701 553255**
Under 18: £14.00 **Adults:** £14.00
Self-catering facilities, Shop nearby, Laundry facilities

🔺 **Edinburgh Pleasance Youth Hostel,** *New Arthur Place, Edinburgh, EH8 9TH.*
Tel: **08701 553255**
Under 18: £14.00 **Adults:** £14.00
Self-catering facilities, Shop nearby, Laundry facilities

🔺 **Brodies Backpackers Hostel,** *12 High Street, Edinburgh, EH1 1TB.*
Actual grid ref: NT262737
Tel: **0131 556 6770**
Adults: £10.20
Showers, Central heating, Laundry facilities, Lounge, Security lockers, No smoking
Edinburgh's friendliest wee hostel. Superb location, quality facilities, great atmosphere.

🔺 **Cowgate Tourist Hostel,** *112 Cowgate , Edinburgh, EH1 1JN.*
Tel: **0131 226 2153**
Under 18: £11.00
Adults: £11.00
Self-catering facilities, Television, Showers, Central heating, Laundry facilities, Wet weather shelter, Lounge, Dining room, Drying room, Security lockers, Cycle store, Parking
Located in the heart of the historic old town, close to attractions. This hostel is made up of large apartments with own bathrooms and kitchen, with TV. 10 mins from train/bus station. 5 mins from pubs/clubs. This hostel has a relaxed atmosphere with friendly staff.

Rothesay Hotel, *8 Rothesay Place, Edinburgh, EH3 7SL.*
Heart of Edinburgh's Georgian new town in the city centre, short walk Princes Street.
Grades: ETC 2 Star,
AA 3 Diamond
Tel: **0131 225 4125** Mr Borland.
D: £25.00-£45.00 **S:** £38.00-£65.00.
Open: All Year
Beds: 2F 4D 18T 12S
Baths: 36 Pr
🛇 ⌷ ⊱ ✗ ⅙

Averon Guest House, *44 Gilmore Place, Edinburgh, EH3 9NQ.*
Grades: ETC 1 Star, AA 2 Diamond, RAC 3 Diamond
Tel: **0131 229 9932** Mr Cran.
D: £18.00-£38.00 **S:** £25.00-£38.00.
Open: All Year
Beds: 3F 2D 3T 1S
Baths: 6 Pr
🛇 Ⓟ (10) ⌷ 🏊 ⅏ ⅙ Ⓥ ⊶
Fully restored Georgian town house, built in 1770. Central Edinburgh with car park. Standard and ensuite rooms available. STB, AA, RAC, Les Routiers recommended. 10 minute walk to Castle and Princes Street.

6 Dean Park Crescent, *Edinburgh, EH4 1PN.*
Warm friendly home. Large rooms. 10 mins walk to centre.
Grades: ETC 3 Star B&B
Tel: **0131 332 5017**
Mrs Kirkland.
D: £22.00-£29.00
S: £40.00-£55.00.
Open: Easter to Oct
Beds: 1F 1D 1T
Baths: 1 En 1 Pr 1 Sh
🛇 ⅋ ⌷ 🏊 ⅏ ⅙ Ⓥ

All cycleways are popular: you are well-advised to book ahead

---

Amaryllis Guest House, *21 Upper Gilmore Place, Edinburgh, EH3 9NL.*
Warm, comfortable, friendly, central all attractions. Walkable but quietly situated.
Grades: ETC 2 Star
Tel: **0131 229 3293** (also fax no)
Melrose.
D: £18.00-£30.00 **S:** £25.00-£40.00.
Open: All Year (not Xmas)
Beds: 3F 1D 1T
Baths: 4 En 1 Pr
▷ (10) **P** (2) **□** ≛ ▥ ⓥ

17 Hope Park Terrace, *Edinburgh, EH8 9LZ.*
Fifteen minutes' walk city centre. H&C in bedrooms.
Grades: ETC 1 Star
Tel: **0131 667 7963**
Mrs Frackelton.
D: £25.00-£25.00 **S:** £25.00-£25.00.
Open: All Year
Beds: 2D **Baths:** 1 Sh
▷ (10) ✕ ≛ ▥ ⓥ ▮

28 London Street, *Edinburgh, EH3 6NA.*
Central Georgian 1st floor flat 5 minutes walk from station.
Grades: ETC 2 Star
Tel: **0131 556 4641**
Mr & Mrs Campbell.
D: £18.00-£25.00 **S:** £20.00-£27.00.
Open: Easter to Oct
Beds: 1F 1T 1D 1S **Baths:** 3 Sh
▷ (5) **P** (1) **□** ▥

Ailsa Craig Hotel, *24 Royal Terrace, Edinburgh, EH7 5AH.*
Elegant city centre Georgian town house hotel. Walking distance major attractions.
Grades: ETC 3 Star
Tel: **0131 556 1022**
Fax no: 0131 556 6055
D: £25.00-£45.00 **S:** £25.00-£60.00.
Open: All Year
Beds: 5F 5D 3T 4S
Baths: 14 En 1 Pr 2 Sh
▷ **□** ✕ ≛ ▥ ⓥ ▮

Castle Park Guest House, *75 Gilmore Place, Edinburgh, EH3 9NU.*
Charming Victorian guest house ideally situated close to King Theatre & city centre.
Grades: ETC 2 Star
Tel: **0131 229 1215**
Fax no: 0131 229 1223
D: £17.50-£25.00 **S:** £17.50-£22.50.
Open: All Year
Beds: 1F 4D 1T 2S
Baths: 4 En 2 Sh
▷ **P** (4) **□** ≛ ▥ ⓥ

37 Howe Street, *Edinburgh, EH3 6TF.*
Listed building the the heart of Edinburgh in historic New Town.
Grades: ETC 2 Star
Tel: **0131 557 3487** (also fax no)
Mrs Collie.
D: £20.00-£20.00 .
Open: Easter to Oct
Beds: 1D **Baths:** 1 Sh
□ ≛ ▥ ⓥ

Aries Guest House, *5 Upper Gilmore Place, Edinburgh, EH3 9NW.*
Small central friendly, all attractions walkable. TV, tea in rooms.
Tel: **0131 229 4669** Mrs Robertson.
D: £17.00-£28.00 **S:** £25.00-£35.00.
Open: All Year (not Xmas)
Beds: 1F 2D 2T
Baths: 2 Sh
▷ **□** ≛ ▥ ⓖ ⓥ

Edinburgh Craigleith   22

National Grid Ref: NT2374

St Bernards Guest House, *22 St Bernards Crescent, Edinburgh, EH4 1NS.*
Victorian town house. 15 minute walk from city centre. Quiet location.
Tel: **0131 332 2339**
Mr & Mrs Alsop.
D: £22.50-£30.00 **S:** £25.00-£30.00.
Open: All Year
Beds: 3D 4T 1S
Baths: 4 En 2 Sh
✕ **□** ≛ ▥ ⓥ ▮ ∕ ✰

Edinburgh Broughton   23

National Grid Ref: NT2575

🍽 🍺 Clarmont Bar

Ben Cruachan, *17 Mcdonald Road, Edinburgh, EH7 4LX.*
Grades: ETC 3 Star
Tel: **0131 556 3709** Stark.
D: £25.00-£35.00 .
Open: April to Oct
Beds: 1F 1T 1D
Baths: 3 En
▷ (10) **P** ✕ **□** ≛ ▥ ⓥ
Be assured of a very warm welcome at our family-run centrally situated guesthouse within walking distance of all main attractions. Bedrooms are fully equipped with your every comfort in mind. Excellent breakfast served. Free street parking.

Elas Guest House, *10 Claremont Crescent, Edinburgh, EH7 4HX.*
Georgian house, central Edinburgh. Free street parking. Traditional Scottish breakfasts. Groups and families welcome.
Grades: ETC 2 Star
Tel: **0131 556 1929** Mrs Elas.
D: £20.00-£30.00 **S:** £20.00-£30.00.
Open: All Year
Beds: 3F 2D 2T 1S **Baths:** 8 En
▷ **□** ≛ ✕ ≛ ▥ ⓥ ▮ ∕ ✰

Brodies Guest House, *22 East Claremont Street, Edinburgh, EH7 4JP.*
A warm Scottish welcome awaits you at our Victorian town house.
Tel: **0131 556 4032** Mrs Olbert.
Fax no: 0131 556 9739
D: £22.00-£35.00 **S:** £22.00-£30.00.
Open: All Year (not Xmas)
Beds: 1F 1D 1T 1S **Baths:** 2 Pr 1 Sh
▷ **□** ≛ ▥ ⓥ

Edinburgh Pilrig   24

National Grid Ref: NT2675

🍽 🍺 Oyster Bar

Claymore Guest House, *68 Pilrig Street, Edinburgh, EH6 5AS.*
Warm, welcoming, personally run, centrally situated, close to all attractions.
Grades: ETC 2 Star GH
Tel: **0131 554 2500** (also fax no)
Mrs Dorrian.
D: £18.00-£30.00 **S:** £22.00-£22.00.
Open: All Year (not Xmas)
Beds: 2F 2D 2T
Baths: 3 En 1 Pr 2 Sh
▷ ✕ **□** ≛ ▥ ⓥ

Sunnyside Guest House, *13 Pilrig Street, Edinburgh, EH6 5AN.*
Beautiful Georgian family-run guest house. An easy atmosphere and ample breakfast.
Grades: ETC 2 Star
Tel: **0131 553 2084**
Mr Wheelaghan.
D: £17.00-£30.00 **S:** £17.00-£30.00.
Open: All Year (not Xmas)
Beds: 2F 4D 2T 1S
Baths: 4 En 1 Pr 1 Sh
▷ **P** ✕ **□** ≛ ▥ ⓥ ✰

Glenburn Guest House, *22 Pilrig Street, Edinburgh, EH6 5AJ.*
Clean, welcoming, budget accommodation. 15 minutes from the city centre.
Tel: **0131 554 9818** (also fax no)
Mrs McVeigh.
D: £19.00-£26.00 **S:** £20.00-£36.00.
Open: All Year (not Xmas)
Beds: 3F 3D 4T 3S
Baths: 1 En 6 Sh
□ ≛ ▥ ⓥ

Balmoral Guest House, *32 Pilrig Street, Edinburgh, EH6 5AL.*
Excellent location for city centre, Leith Port and Royal Yacht 'Britannia'.
Tel: **0131 554 1857**
Fax no: 0131 553 5712
D: £17.00-£30.00 **S:** £25.00-£25.00.
Open: All Year (not Xmas)
Beds: 1F 2D 2T
Baths: 1 En 2 Sh
▷ **P** ✕ **□** ≛ ▥ ⓥ ✰

Edinburgh Trinity   25

National Grid Ref: NT2476

🍽 🍺 Peacock Inn

Falcon Crest, *70 South Trinity Road, Edinburgh, EH5 3NX.*
Victorian family home, 2 miles north of Edinburgh Castle.
Grades: ETC 1 Star
Tel: **0131 552 5294** Mrs Clark.
D: £15.00-£26.00 **S:** £16.00-£26.00.
Open: All Year (not Xmas)
Beds: 1F 2D 2T 1S
Baths: 3 En 2 Sh
▷ **P** (2) ✕ **□** ✕ ≛ ▥ ⓥ ▮

Edinburgh Craigentinny 26

National Grid Ref: NT2974

Glenfarrer House, 36 Farrer Terrace, Edinburgh, EH7 6SG.
Chalet bungalow close to excellent bus services. City centre 2 miles.
Tel: **0131 669 1265**
Mrs Smith.
D: £21.00-£21.00
S: £17.00-£17.00.
Open: Easter to Oct
Beds: 1D 1T 2S
Baths: 2 En 1 Sh
🅿 (2) ⊬ ⛌ 🌢 🏛 Ⓥ ⊬

Order your
packed lunches the
evening before you
need them.
Not at breakfast!

S = Price range for a single
person in a single room

Edinburgh Northfield 27

National Grid Ref: NT2973

🍴 🍺 Golf Tavern, Bennets Bar, Tapas Ole, Minto Hotel, Navaar Hotel, Allison Hotel, Grannies Attic, Seahaven Hotel

*Brae Guest House,
119 Willowbrae Road, Edinburgh, EH8 7HN.*
Friendly guest house. Meadowbank - Holyrood Palace, on main bus route.
Grades: ETC 3 Star,
AA 3 Diamond
Tel: **0131 661 0170**
Mrs Walker.
D: £18.00-£40.00
S: £18.00-£40.00.
Open: All Year
Beds: 1F 1T 1D 1S
Baths: 3 En 1 Pr
🕿 ⛌ 🏃 🌢 🏛 Ⓥ ⓘ ⊬ 🚲

Edinburgh Portobello 28

National Grid Ref: NT3074

🍴 🍺 Peacock Inn

Hopebank, 33 Hope Lane North, Portobello, Edinburgh, EH15 2PZ.
Tel: **0131 657 1149** Ms Williamson
D: £20.00-£20.00 **S:** £20.00-£20.00.
Open: Easter to Oct
Beds: 2D 1T **Baths:** 3 Pr 1 Sh
🕿 🅿 ⊬ ⛌ 🌢 🏛 Ⓥ ⊬
Victorian terraced villa, two minutes sea - beautiful promenade, 20 minutes city centre. Good food, Scottish hospitality, inexpensive bus service to centre. Non smoking, showers ensuite, TV in all rooms. Many golf courses nearby, good touring centre.

Cruachan, 6 Pittville Street, Edinburgh, EH15 2BY.
Elegant Georgian villa adjacent to beach, promenade, city centre 2.5 miles. Good parking.
Grades: ETC 2 Star B&B
Tel: **0131 669 2195** Mrs Thom.
D: £20.00-£22.00 **S:** £19.00-£21.00.
Open: Easter to Oct
Beds: 2D 1T 1S **Baths:** 2 Sh
🕿 (12) 🅿 (3) ⊬ ⛌ 🏃 🌢 Ⓥ

Sustrans Devon Coast to Coast

The new **Devon Coast to Coast Cycle Route** is a recently opened section of the developing National Cycle Network, running on traffic-free paths and traffic-calmed roads for 90 miles from Ilfracombe on Devon's rugged north coast to the historic city and port of Plymouth, in the south western corner of the county. The southern part of the route skirts the west side of Dartmoor National Park. A high proportion is on railway paths, exemplary of the work Sustrans has been engaged in over recent years in creating safe, enjoyable routes for cyclists. The route coincides with the West Country Way from Barnstaple through Bideford and up the Torridge Valley as far as Sheepwash. It is clearly signposted by blue direction signs with a cycle silhouette, numbered 31 from Ilfracombe to Barnstaple, 3 for the length of the intersection with the West Country Way and 27 from Sheepwash to Plymouth. There is a fair amount of up-and-down involved throughout.

The route starts with a climb inland before descending back to the coast to reach the attractive stone-built village of **Mortehoe** and then **Woolacombe**, from where you cycle beside the beach as far as Putsborough before the ride to **Braunton**,which involves a few climbs and descents. From Braunton the route shares a traffic-free path with the Tarka Trail walk into **Barnstaple**. This continues west along the coast through Instow and up the Torridge Estuary to the eastern part of **Bideford**, East-the-Water, where the Tarka Trail Centre is located; and on a railway path up the Torridge Valley to East Yarde and as far as Moormill, close by **Petrockstowe**, from where you follow roads to Sheepwash and Hatherleigh. On to Jacobstowe in the Okement Valley and through Abbeyford Woods to **Okehampton**, on the northern edge of **Dartmoor**. A bridleway leads to the Meldon Viaduct, which you cross to reach **Bridestowe**. From here you head on to **Lydford**, and pass above the gorge to reach **North Brentor**, where the route divides to give two alternatives through the south western edge of Dartmoor. The western route takes you below the bleak outcrop of Brent Tor, crowned by St Michael's church, and is reasonably straightforward as far as **Tavistock** but gets tougher and rather muddy between there and Yelverton. The eastern route, through Mary Tavy,

Peter Tavy, Walkhampton, Dousland and Meavy, is a little way up onto the moor so a bit more up-and-down throughout. The routes meet at Clearbrook, from where most of the rest of the way runs on another traffic-free railway path, the Plym Valley Path, as far as the mouth of the Plym. Cross the bridge into **Plymouth** and ride along the seafront to the Hoe and on to the end of the route at Millbay Docks.

The indispensable **official route map and guide** for the route is available from Sustrans, 35 King Street, Bristol BS1 4DZ, tel 0117-926 8893, fax 0117-929 4173, @ £5.99 (+ £2.00 p&p).

Maps: Ordnance Survey 1:50,000 Landranger series: 180, 181, 190, 191, 192, 201, 202

Transport: Plymouth is a main line rail terminus; Okehampton and Barnstaple are also served by trains. The **Devon Bike Bus** scheme, operated by Devon County Council between Barnstaple and Okehampton, and connecting from Okehampton to Exeter, runs throughout the months of June, July, August and September. This innovative new scheme makes use of specially converted buses to carry cyclists with their bicycles. Contact Devon County Council on 01392 383223 for details. Unfortunately the stretch from Ilfracombe to Barnstaple is not served, and drivers on regular bus services will not accept bicycles. Cycling the whole route from the designated start may therefore prove impractical.

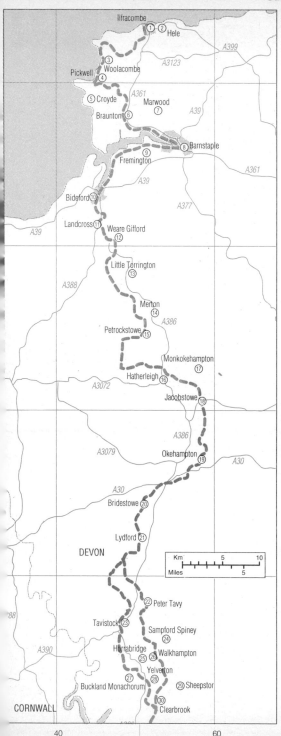

Ilfracombe 1

National Grid Ref: SS5147

🛏 🍴 Williams Arms, Agricultural Inn, Cider Apple, Crown, Sherbourne Lodge, Hele Bay, Ye Old Globe

▲ **Ilfracombe Youth Hostel,** *Ashmour House, 1 Hillsborough Terrace, Ilfracombe, Devon, EX34 9NR.*
Actual grid ref: SS524476
Tel: **01271 865337**
Under 18: £6.90 **Adults:** £10.00
Self-catering facilities, Showers, Licensed bar, Drying room, Cycle store, Evening meal at 7.00pm, No smoking, Kitchen facilities, Breakfast available, Credit cards accepted
End house on a fine Georgian terrace, overlooking the picturesque harbour and the Bristol Channel.

Cairn House Hotel, *43 St Brannocks Road, Ilfracombe, Devon, EX34 8EH.*
Grades: ETC 1 StarRAC 1 Star
Tel: **01271 863911** (also fax no)
Mrs Tupper.
D: £18.00-£21.50 **S:** £18.00-£21.50.
Open: All Year (not Xmas/New Year)
Beds: 3F 6D 1S
Baths: 10 En
🛏 🖪 🖵 🕿 🖢 ✗ 🗶 🔟 Ⓥ 🔒
The Cairn House Hotel is a beautiful Victorian hotel delightfully situated in its own grounds with extensive views over town, sea and surrounding countryside. There is a comfortable lounge/bar to relax in before or after your evening meal.

Beechwood Hotel, *Torrs Park, Ilfracombe, Devon, EX34 8AZ.*
Grades: ETC 2 Star
Tel: **01271 863800** (also fax no)
Burridge.
D: £22.00-£25.00 **S:** £22.00-£25.00.
Open: Mar to Oct
Beds: 2T 5D
Baths: 7 En
🖪 (8) ⅙ 🖵 ✗ 🖢 🔟 Ⓥ
Peacefully situated non-smoking Victorian mansion, own woods bordering spectacular National Trust lands and coast path. Superb views over town and countryside to sea. Just 10 minutes walk to harbour and town. Spacious well appointed guest rooms, good food. Licensed. Parking.

Pay B&Bs by
cash or cheque and
be prepared to
pay up front.

Lyncott Guest House, *56 St Brannock's Road, Ilfracombe, Devon, EX34 8EQ.*
Actual grid ref: SS517463
Grades: ETC 4 Diamond
Tel: **01271 862425** (also fax no)
Mr & Mrs Holdsworth.
D: £18.00-£21.00 **S:** £18.00.
Open: All Year
Beds: 2F 3D 1S
Baths: 6 En
🛏 (5) ⚲ 🗖 ✕ 🛉 🖳 Ⓥ ✦ 🐾
Join David and Marianna in their charming, lovingly refurbished Victorian house pleasantly situated near lovely Bicclescombe Park. Relax in elegant, smoke-free surroundings. Enjoy delightful, spacious, individually designed ensuite bedrooms and sample their scrumptious home-made fare.

Combe Lodge Hotel, *Chambercombe Park, Ilfracombe, Devon, EX34 9QW.*
Actual grid ref: SS530473
Quiet position, overlooking harbour, ideal for walking, cycling, golf holidays.
Tel: **01271 864518**
Mr & Mrs Wileman.
D: £16.50-£18.50 **S:** £20.50-£22.50.
Open: All Year (not Xmas)
Beds: 2F 4D 2S
Baths: 4 En 1 Pr 1 Sh
🛏 (1) 🅿 (8) ⚲ 🗖 🛉 ✕ 🛉 🖳 Ⓥ ✦ 🐾

Strathmore Hotel, *57 St Brannock's Road, Ilfracombe, Devon, EX34 8EQ.*
Grades: ETC 4 Diamond, AA 4 Diamond, RAC 4 Diamond
Tel: **01271 862248** Mr Smith.
Fax no: 01271 862243
D: £20.00-£28.00 **S:** £25.00-£33.00.
Open: All Year
Beds: 1F 5D 1T 1S **Baths:** 8 Pr
🛏 🅿 (7) ⚲ 🗖 🛉 ✕ 🛉 🖳 Ⓥ ✦ 🐾
Delightful Victorian Hotel near to Ilfracombe town centre, Bicclescombe Park, Cairn Nature Reserve and glorious beaches. All rooms are ensuite with colour TV and hospitality trays. We offer varied and delicious menus. All meals are freshly prepared on the premises.

The Grid Reference beneath the location heading is for the village or town - *not* **for individual houses, which are shown (where supplied) in each entry itself.**

Varley House, *Chambercombe Park, Ilfracombe, Devon, EX34 9QW.*
Period house with attractive ensuite accommodation, close to coastal walks.
Tel: **01271 863927**
Mrs S O'Sullivan & Mr D Small.
Fax no: 01271 879299
D: £24.00-£25.00
S: £23.00-£24.00.
Open: Easter to Oct
Beds: 2F 4D 1T 1S
Baths: 7 En 1 Pr
🛏 (5) 🅿 (7) 🗖 🛉 ✕ 🛉 🖳 Ⓥ

Westwell Hall, *Torrs Park, Ilfracombe, Devon, EX34 8AZ.*
Elegant Victorian gentleman's residence in own grounds - superb views.
Tel: **01271 862792** (also fax no)
Mr & Mrs Lomas.
D: £22.00-£24.00
S: £22.00-£24.00.
Open: All Year
Beds: 7D 2T 1S
Baths: 10 En
🛏 🅿 🗖 🛉 ✕ 🛉 🖳 Ⓥ

Harcourt Hotel, *Fore Street, Ilfracombe, Devon, EX34 9DS.*
Friendly licensed hotel, ensuite rooms, TV, tea coffee, sea views.
Tel: **01271 862931**
Mr Doorbar.
D: £17.00-£24.00
S: £17.00-£24.00.
Open: All Year
Beds: 3F 4D 1T 2S
Baths: 8 En 2 Sh
🛏 🅿 (4) 🗖 🛉 ✕ 🛉 Ⓥ ✦ 🐾

Sherborne Lodge Hotel, *Torrs Park, Ilfracombe, Devon, EX34 8AY.*
Friendly, fully-licensed family hotel providing good food, wine, comfortable accommodation.
Tel: **01271 862297**
Mr & Mrs Millington.
Fax no: 01271 865520
D: £15.50-£21.50
S: £15.50-£21.50.
Open: All Year
Beds: 1F 8D 2T 1S
🛏 🅿 (10) 🗖 🛉 ✕ 🛉 🖳 Ⓥ ✦ 🐾

Hele (Ilfracombe) 2

National Grid Ref: SS5347

🍴 🍺 Hele Bay Hotel, Ye Olde Globe

Moles Farmhouse, *Old Berrynarbor Road, Hele, Ilfracombe, Devon, EX34 9RB.*
Actual grid ref: SSS34474
Beautifully restored former farmhouse, situated in picturesque Hele Valley, near Ilfracombe.
Tel: **01271 862099** (also fax no)
Ms Grindlay.
D: £17.00-£20.00 .
Open: All Year
Beds: 1F 1T 1D
Baths: 2 En 1 Sh
🛏 🅿 (4) ⚲ 🗖 🛉 🖳 Ⓥ ✦ 🐾

Woolacombe 3

National Grid Ref: SS4543

🍴 🍺 Jubilee Inn, Chichester Arms, Red Barn, Stables, Golden Hind, The Mill

Ossaborough House, *Woolacombe, Devon, EX34 7HJ.*
Grades: ETC 3 Diamond
Tel: **01271 870297** Mr & Mrs Day.
D: £21.00-£25.00 **S:** £21.00-£25.00.
Open: All Year
Beds: 2F 2T 2D
Baths: 5 En 1 Pr
🛏 (8) ⚲ 🗖 🛉 ✕ 🛉 🖳 Ⓥ ✦ 🐾
Escape to our lovely C17th country house originating in the days of Saxon England - rustic beams, thick stone walls, inglenook fireplaces, candlelit dinners. All rooms sympathetically restored. Explore rolling hills, rugged cliffs, picturesque villages, stunning golden beaches and secluded coves.

Camberley, *Beach Road, Woolacombe, Devon, EX34 7AA.*
Actual grid ref: SS465437
Large Victorian house with views to sea and NT land. Use of indoor pool.
Grades: ETC 3 Diamond
Tel: **01271 870231**
Mr & Mrs Riley.
D: £20.00-£25.00 **S:** £19.00-£24.00.
Open: All Year (not Xmas)
Beds: 3F 3D 1T
Baths: 6 En 1 Pr
🛏 🅿 (6) 🗖 🛉 🖳 Ⓥ ✦ 🐾

Barton Lea, *Beach Road, Woolacombe, Devon, EX34 7BT.*
Warm welcome, sea views, big breakfast menu, close to Coastal Foot Path.
Tel: **01271 870928** Mrs Vickery.
D: £15.50-£20.00 **S:** £20.00-£25.00
Open: Easter to Oct
Beds: 1F 1D 1T
Baths: 3 En
🛏 🅿 (7) ⚲ 🗖 🛉 🖳 Ⓥ ✦ 🐾

Sunny Nook, *Beach Road, Woolacombe, Devon, EX34 7AA.*
Actual grid ref: SS466438
Delightful home in lovely situation wonderful views and excellent breakfasts. No smoking throughout.
Tel: **01271 870964** Mr Fenn.
D: £18.00-£23.00 **S:** £25.00-£30.00
Open: All Year (not Xmas)
Beds: 1F 1D 1T
Baths: 2 En 1 Pr
🛏 (8) 🅿 (5) ⚲ 🗖 ✕ 🛉 🖳 Ⓥ ✦ 🐾

All rates are subject to alteration at the owners' discretion.

Clyst House, *Rockfield Road,
Woolacombe, Devon, EX34 7DH.*
Friendly, comfortable guest house
close blue flag beach. Delicious
English breakfast. Beautiful
walking area.
Tel: **01271 870220**
Mrs Braund.
D: £20.00-£22.00 **S:** £20.00-£22.00.
Open: Mar to Nov
Beds: 1F 1D 1T
Baths: 1 Sh
⌂ (7) ▣ ⅌⛌✕♐Ⓜ Ⓥ ⚡

Pickwell 4

National Grid Ref: SS4641

⋈ ⛿ Rock Inn, Thatched Barn

Meadow Cottage, *Pickwell,
Georgeham, Braunton, Devon,
EX33 1LA.*
Tel: **01271 890938** (also fax no)
Mrs Holmes.
D: £20.00 **S:** £20.00.
Open: All Year
Beds: 1D 1S
Baths: 1 Private
⌂ ▣ (3) ⅌⛌Ⓜ ⚡ ❀
Meadow Cottage is in the tranquil
setting of Pickwell. Off the beaten
track with panoramic views of
patchwork fields to the sea, close to
the coastal path and beaches of
Woolacombe, Putsborough and
Croyde and the championship golf
course, Saunton.

Croyde 5

National Grid Ref: SS4439

⋈ ⛿ Manor, Thatched Barn Inn

Moorsands, *Moor Lane, Croyde
Bay, Braunton, Devon, EX33 1NP.*
Grades: ETC 3 Diamond
Tel: **01271 890781**
Mr & Mrs Davis.
D: £20.00-£26.00 **S:** £20.00-£26.00.
Open: All Year
Beds: 1F 1T 2D 1S
Baths: 5 En
⌂ ▣ (6) ⅌⛌♐Ⓜ Ⓥ ⚡
Originally a large Victorian coast
guard station with stunning views,
Moorsands offers short walks to
beach, village and local facilities.
Come and surf, ride, cycle etc. or
simply relax with our comfortable
ensuite rooms, guest lounge,
beautiful surroundings and superb
breakfasts.

Tamaru, *Down End, Croyde,
Braunton, Devon, EX33 1QE.*
500m from top surfing beach and
village. Relaxed friendly
atmosphere.
Tel: **01271 890765**
Mr & Mrs Jenkins.
D: £17.50-£25.00.
S: £17.50-£25.00.
Open: All Year
Beds: 1F 1D
Baths: 1 En 1 Pr
⌂ ▣ (6) ⅌⛌♐Ⓜ Ⓥ ❀

West Winds Guest House, *Moor
Lane, Croyde Bay,
Braunton, Devon, EX33 1PA.*
Actual grid ref: SS433396
Stunning water's edge location
with views over Croyde Beach.
Grades: ETC 4 Diamond,
AA 4 Diamond
Tel: **01271 890489** (also fax no)
Mr & Mrs Gedling.
D: £26.00-£31.00
S: £26.00-£31.00.
Open: Mar to Nov
Beds: 3D 2T
Baths: 3 Pr 2 Sh
⌂ ▣ (6) ⅌⛌♐✕♐Ⓜ Ⓥ ♠

Chapel Farm, *Hobbs Hill, Croyde,
Braunton, Devon, EX33 1NE.*
Actual grid ref: SS444390
C16th thatched farmhouse, 10
minutes to beach.
Tel: **01271 890429** Mrs Windsor.
D: £18.00-£26.00 **S:** £18.00-£30.00.
Open: Easter to Nov
Beds: 1F 2D
Baths: 3 En
⌂ ▣ (6) ⅌⛌♐Ⓜ Ⓥ ♠ ❀

Braunton 6

National Grid Ref: SS4936

⋈ ⛿ Agricultural Inn

St Merryn, *Higher Park Road,
Braunton, Devon, EX33 2LG.*
Tel: **01271 813805** Mrs Bradford.
Fax no: 01271 812097
D: £20.00-£22.00 **S:** £20.00-£22.00.
Open: Jan to Dec
Beds: 1F 1T 1D
Baths: 1 En 2 Pr
⌂ ▣ (5) ⅌⛌♐✕♐Ⓜ Ⓥ ⚡ ❀
Beautiful 1930s home set in
delightful large garden. Tranquil
setting with excellent parking and
within easy walking distance of
village. Excellent beaches and golf
courses within a short drive.

Pixie Dell, *1 Willand Rd,
Braunton, N. Devon, EX33 1AX.*
Large chalet bungalow and garden.
Warm welcome assured.
Tel: **01271 812233**
Mrs Dale.
D: £18.00-£18.00 **S:** £18.00-£20.00.
Open: All Year (not Xmas)
Beds: 1D 2T 1S
Baths: 2 Sh
⌂ ▣ (4) ⅌⛌♐Ⓜ Ⓥ ♠ ⚡ ❀

Marwood 7

National Grid Ref: SS5437

⋈ ⛿ New Ring O' Bells

Lee House, *Marwood, Barnstaple,
Devon, EX31 4DZ.*
Family-run Elizabethan manor
house. Wonderful views, secluded
grounds.
Tel: **01271 374345**
Mrs Darling.
D: £20.00-£22.00 **S:** £20.00-£22.00.
Open: Apr to Oct
Beds: 1T 2D
Baths: 3 En
⌂ (14) ▣ (8) ⅌⛌♐Ⓜ Ⓥ

Barnstaple 8

National Grid Ref: SS5633

⋈ ⛿ Windsor Arms, Williams Arms, Rolle Quay
Inn, North Country Inn, Pyne Arms, Ring
O'Bells, Chichester Arms

Crossways, *Braunton Road,
Barnstaple, Devon, EX31 1JY.*
Actual grid ref: SS555333
Detached house - town & Tarka
Trail 150 yards, bicycle hire.
Tel: **01271 379120**
Mr & Mrs Tyson.
D: £15.00 **S:** £17.00.
Open: All Year
Beds: 1F 1D 1T
Baths: 2 Pr 1 Sh
⌂ ▣ (6) ⅌⛌✕♐Ⓜ Ⓥ ♠ ❀

The pretty old market town of **Barnstaple** has some
interesting buildings, such as the medieval timber-framed
Pannier Market, where the market is still held, the
eighteenth-century colonnades of Queen Anne's Walk and
fourteenth-century St Anne's Chapel, a school where John
Gay, who wrote *The Beggar's Opera*, was once a pupil – it
now houses a museum of education. The town also hosts the
Museum of North Devon, and the Queen's Theatre.

At **Bideford**, on the Torridge Estuary, you will find a
fourteenth-century bridge and a statue commemorating
Charles Kingsley, who wrote the historical romance
Westward Ho!, set in the town (the eponymous nearby
coastal resort was named after the book). The Tarka Trail
Centre in East-the-Water provides information on the popular
walk which shares this part of the cycle route: named after
Henry Williamson's classic 1927 novel, *Tarka the Otter*
(which has been a bestseller ever since), it explores the
varied North Devon countryside through which Tarka was
pursued.

Mount Sandford, *Landkey Road,*
Barnstaple, Devon, EX32 0HL.
Georgian house in 1.5 acres gardens. 2 double, 1 twin, all ensuite.
Tel: **01271 342354** Mrs White.
D: £18.00-£22.00 **S:** £20.00.
Open: All Year (not Xmas)
Beds: 1F 1D 1T
Baths: 3 En
🛏 (3) �P (3) ⌇⌂ 🖥 👤 🎍 🖤 V ⌀ 🐾

Fremington 9

National Grid Ref: SS5132

🍴 🍺 New Inn, Boat House

Lower Yelland Farm, *Yelland*
Road, Fremington, Barnstaple,
Devon, EX31 3EN.
Tel: **01271 860101** (also fax no)
Mr Day.
D: £20.00-£20.00 **S:** £20.00-£20.00.
Open: All Year (not Xmas/New
Year)
Beds: 1T 2D
Baths: 3 En
🛏 ⊘ (6) ⌂ 👔 🎍 🖤 V ⌀ ⌀
North Devon Coast: beautifully
situated period house on Taw
Estuary. Ideal touring centre,
Instow beach/marina
approximately 1 mile, Bideford,
Barnstaple 4.5 miles. Several golf
courses in the vicinity. Adjacent to
bird sanctuary. Private off road
parking.

Bideford 10

National Grid Ref: SS4526

🍴 🍺 Tanton's Hotel, Farmers Arms, Crab & Ale,
Royal Hotel, Swan Inn, Joiners' Arms, Hunters'
Inn, Sunset Hotel

The Mount Hotel, *Northdown*
Road, Bideford, Devon, EX39 3LP.
Actual grid ref: SS449269
Grades: AA 4 Diamond
Tel: **01237 473748**
Mr & Mrs Laugharne.
D: £23.00-£25.00
S: £25.00-£33.00.
Open: Jan to Dec
Beds: 1F 3D 1T 2S
Baths: 7 En
🛏 ⊘ (4) ⌇⌂ 🎍 👤 🎍 ⅃ V ⌀ ⌀ 🐾
Charming Georgian licensed guest
house only 5 minutes' walk to town
centre, private lounge for guests'
use, all rooms ensuite, attractive
garden, car parking for guests.
Convenient for touring N Devon
coastline, Clovelly, Lundy, Exmoor
and Dartmoor. No smoking.

All cycleways are
popular: you are
well-advised to
book ahead

Landcross 11

National Grid Ref: SS4623

Sunset Hotel, *Landcross, Bideford,*
Devon, EX39 5JA.
Actual grid ref: SS461239
Small country hotel. Peaceful location overlooking spectacular
scenery and Tarka Trail.
Grades: ETC 3 Diamond, AA 3
Diamond
Tel: **01237 472962** Mrs Lamb.
D: £27.00-£30.00 **S:** £36.00-£40.00.
Open: Easter to Nov
Beds: 2F 2D 2T **Baths:** 4 En
⊘ (8) ⌇⌂ ✕ 🎍 👤 🖤 V ⌀ 🐾

Weare Giffard 12

National Grid Ref: SS4721

🔺 **Sea Lock Camping Barn &**
Tent Site, *Vale Cottage, 7 Annery*
Kiln, Weare Giffard, Bideford,
Devon, EX39 5JE.
Tel: **01237 477705 / 07866 026194**
Under 18: £5.00 **Adults:** £5.00
Self-catering facilities, Showers,
Parking, Facilities for disabled
people
Newly converted barn, offering
basic accommodation, in beautiful,
tranquil wooded valley overlooking
River Torridge, between Bideford
and Torrington. Private access to
Tarka Trail (NCN 3) and conserva-
tion area. Superb walking, cycling,
canoeing, fishing, birdwatching.
Pubs/shops within 2.5 miles. Book
individual beds/family rooms
(sharing facilities) or sole use.

Taking your dog?

Book *in advance*

ONLY with owners

who accept dogs (👔)

Just off the route (there is a link route) at **Great
Torrington**, *Torrington 1646* reconstructs the battle, in which
Cromwell's New Model Army was instrumental, that saw this
Royalist stronghold fall finally to the forces of Parliament. You
can also visit the Dartington Crystal factory (tours are available) and shop.

At **Hatherleigh** there is a gallery of local arts and crafts
and a pottery.

Okehampton has a ruined castle with a Norman keep
and the Museum of Dartmoor Life, with interactive exhibits.

Lydford Gorge, owned by the National Trust, boasts
some impressive natural features, from the raging Devil's
Cauldron whirlpool to the White Lady, a slender water drop
of 90 feet. The gorge shelters a wealth of wildlife, including
woodpeckers, herons and butterflies galore.

Little Torrington 13

National Grid Ref: SS4916

Smytham Holiday Park, *Little*
Torrington, Torrington, Devon,
EX38 8PU.
C17th manor house. beautiful tranquil grounds. Outdoor heated pool.
Tel: **01805 622110** Mr Bland.
D: £20.00-£30.00 **S:** £24.00-£36.00.
Open: All Year (not Xmas/New
Year)
Beds: 4D 3T
Baths: 5 En 1 Sh
🛏 ⊘ ⌇⌂ 🖥 👔 ✕ 🎍 👤 🖤 V ⌀ 🐾

Merton 14

National Grid Ref: SS5212

🍴 🍺 Bull & Dragon

Richmond House, *New Road*
(A386), Merton, Okehampton,
Devon, EX20 3EG.
Tel: **01805 603258** Mrs Wickett.
D: £15.00-£15.00 **S:** £15.00-£15.00.
Open: All Year
Beds: 3F 1T 2D
Baths: 1 Sh
🛏 (5) ⊘ (4) ⌂ 👔 ✕ 🎍 V ⌀ ⌀ 🐾
Country house within easy reach of
beach, moors, gardens, Tarka Trail.
Evening meal optional. H.C. in all
bedrooms.

Petrockstowe 15

National Grid Ref: SS5109

🍴 🍺 The Laurels Inn

Aish Villa, *Petrockstowe,*
Okehampton, Devon, EX20 3HL.
Actual grid ref: SS514089
Peaceful location, superb views,
ideal for visiting Dartmoor,
Exmoor, coast.
Tel: **01837 810581** Ms Gordon.
D: £17.00-£17.00 **S:** £17.00-£17.00
Open: All Year
Beds: 1F 1T 1D
Baths: 1 Sh
🛏 ⊘ (4) ⌇⌂ 🎍 👤 🖥 👤 🖤 V ⌀ 🐾

Hatherleigh 16

National Grid Ref: SS5404

Pressland Country House Hotel,
Hatherleigh, Okehampton, Devon,
EX20 3LW.
Grades: AA 5 Diamond
Tel: **01837 810871**
Fax no: 01837 810303
D: £20.00-£32.00 **S:** £28.00-£36.00.
Open: Mar to Nov
Beds: 2T 3D
Baths: 4 En 1 Pr
☎ (12) 🅿 (6) ⅋🗀✕ 🛊 Ⅲ Ⅵ 🛆 ⅋
Delightful and spacious Victorian
house set in 1.5 acres of landscaped
garden, with glorious views of
Dartmoor and surrounding
countryside. The family-run hotel
is licensed and there is a large,
comfortable lounge, separate bar
and a restaurant of growing repute.

Monkokehampton 17

National Grid Ref: SS5805

🍴 🍺 Duke Of York

Seldon Farm, Monkokehampton,
Winkleigh, Devon, EX19 8RY.
Charming C17th farmhouse in
beautiful, tranquil, rural setting.
Grades: ETC 2 Diamond
Tel: **01837 810312**
Mrs Case.
D: £20.00**S:** £23.00.
Open: Easter to Oct
Beds: 1F 2D
Baths: 1 Pr 1 En
☎ 🅿 🗀 ⅄ 🛊 Ⅵ 🛆 ⅋ ⅛

Jacobstowe 18

National Grid Ref: SS5801

Higher Cadham Farm,
Jacobstowe, Okehampton, Devon,
EX20 3RB.
Superb farmhouse accommodation
with country walks. Hearty
farmhouse food.
Grades: ETC 4 Diamond,
AA 4 Diamond
Tel: **01837 851647** Mrs King.
Fax no: 01837 851410
D: £18.50-£25.00
S: £18.50-£25.00.
Open: All Year (not Xmas)
Beds: 3F 2D 3T 1S
Baths: 5 En 1 Sh
☎ (1) 🅿 (10) 🗀 ⅄✕ 🛊 Ⅲ 🛆 Ⅵ 🛆
⅋ ⅛

The Grid Reference
beneath the location
heading is for the
village or town - *not*
for individual houses,
which are shown
(where supplied) in
each entry itself.

Okehampton 19

National Grid Ref: SX5895

🍴 🍺 Oxenham Arms, River Inn, Tors Hotel,
New Inn, Taw River, Sticklepath, Cellars,
Plume Of Feathers

▲ *Okehampton Youth Hostel,*
The Goods Yard, Okehampton
Station, Okehampton, Devon,
EX20 1EJ.
Actual grid ref: SX591942
Tel: **01837 53916**
Under 18: £7.75
Adults: £11.00
Self-catering facilities, Showers,
Licensed bar, Laundry facilities,
Lounge, Parking, Evening meal at
7.00pm, No smoking, WC, Kitchen
facilities, Credit cards accepted
Converted Victorian railway goods
shed on northern edge of Dartmoor
National Park.

North Lake, Exeter Road,
Okehampton, Devon, EX20 1QH.
Grades: ETC 3 Diamond
Tel: **01837 53100**
Mrs Jones.
D: £20.00**S:** £23.00.
Open: All Year (not Xmas)
Beds: 2D 1T
Baths: 2 En 1 Pr
☎ (6) 🅿 (10) ⅋🗀 ⅄ 🛊 Ⅲ Ⅵ 🛆 ⅋ ⅛
Set in large grounds with panoram-
ic views across Dartmoor.
Tastefully furnished, good food,
with a personal touch; come and go as you please. Superb
walking and riding base, stunning
scenery and cascading rivers.

Heathfield House, Klondyke Road,
Okehampton, Devon, EX20 1EW.
Grades: AA 4 Diamond
Tel: **01837 54211** (also fax no)
Mr & Mrs Gibbins.
D: £17.00-£30.00
S: £30.00-£35.00.
Open: Feb to Dec
Beds: 1F 2D 1T
Baths: 4 En
☎ 🅿 (8) ⅋🗀 ⅄✕ 🛊 Ⅲ Ⅵ 🛆 ⅋ ⅛
Situated high on north face of
Dartmoor, tucked away & private,
although only 10 mins from market
town of Okehampton. Chef owner,
direct access Dartmoor, spectacular
views. Fine food and wine. Heated
outdoor pool. Residential pottery
courses. Christmas breaks.

Order your
packed lunches the
evening before you
need them.
Not at breakfast!

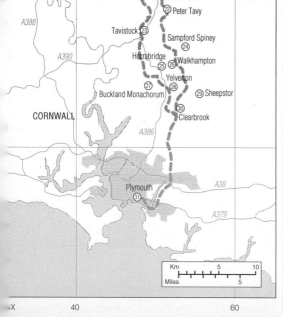

Arnley House, 7 Oaklands Park, Okehampton, Devon, *EX20 ILN.*
Modern luxury house, warm welcome, discount for 3 days plus.
Tel: **01837 53311**
Ms Masereeuw.
D: £23.50-£23.50 **S:** £23.50-£23.50.
Open: Jan to Nov
Beds: 1D **Baths:** 1 En
🅿 (1) 🍴☐ 🛋 🎗 Ⅲ ☑ ♦ ⚲ ♻

Bridestowe 20

National Grid Ref: SX5189

🍴 🍺 White Hart

The White Hart Inn, Fore Street, Bridestowe, Okehampton, Devon, *EX20 4EL.*
Actual grid ref: SX513893
C17th country inn, close to Dartmoor. Same owners for 39 years.
Grades: ETC 3 Diamond
Tel: **01837 861318** (also fax no)
Mr Owen.
D: £23.75-£23.75
S: £29.95-£29.95.
Open: All Year
Beds: 2D **Baths:** 2 En
🅿 (20) ☐ ✕ 🛋 ☑ 🖊 ⚲ ♻

Pay B&Bs by cash or cheque and be prepared to pay up front.

D = Price range per person sharing in a double room

Week Farm, Bridestowe, Okehampton, Devon, *EX20 4HZ.*
Actual grid ref: SX519913
C17th farmhouse home-from-home, guests returning annually.
Tel: **01837 861221** (also fax no)
Ms Hockridge.
D: £23.00-£24.00 **S:** £23.00-£24.00.
Open: All Year (not Xmas)
Beds: 2F 3D
Baths: 5 En
🐂 🅿 🍴 ☐ 🎗 ✕ 🛋 Ⅲ 🚿 ☑ 🖊 ♦ ⚲ ♻

Lydford 21

National Grid Ref: SX5184

🍴 🍺 Dartmoor Inn

Moor View House, Vale Down, Lydford, Okehampton, Devon, *EX20 4BB.*
Licensed Victorian country house, edge Dartmoor. Outskirts of Lydford, ideal touring Devon & Cornwall.
Grades: AA 5 Diamond, RAC 5 Diamond
Tel: **01822 820220** (also fax no)
Mr Sharples.
D: £25.00-£36.00 **S:** £30.00-£45.00.
Open: All Year
Beds: 3D 1T
Baths: 4 Pr
🐂 (12) 🅿 🍴 ☐ 🎗 ✕ 🛋 Ⅲ ☑ 🖊 ♦ ⚲

Peter Tavy 22

National Grid Ref: SX5177

🍴 🍺 Peter Tavy Inn

Churchtown, Peter Tavy, Tavistock, Devon, *PL19 9NP.*
Detached Victorian house standing in own large quiet garden.
Tel: **01822 810477** Mrs Lane.
D: £17.00-£18.00 **S:** £17.00-£18.00.
Open: All Year (not Xmas)
Beds: 2D 1S
Baths: 1 En 1 Sh
🐂 (10) 🅿 (6) ☐ 🎗 🛋 Ⅲ ☑ ♦ ⚲ ♻

Tavistock 23

National Grid Ref: SX4874

🍴 🍺 Blacksmiths' Arms, Cornish Arms, Peter Tavy Inn, Montery Jacks, Chip Shop Inn, Carpenters Arms, Ordulph Arms, Dartmoor Inn

Acorn Cottage, Heathfield, Tavistock, Devon, *PL19 0LQ.*
Actual grid ref: SX463787
Grades: ETC 4 Diamond
Tel: **01822 810038**
Mrs Powell-Thomas.
D: £15.00-£20.00
Open: All Year
Beds: 1D 2T **Baths:** 3 En 1 Pr
🐂 (6) 🅿 (20) 🍴 ☐ 🎗 🛋 Ⅲ ☑ ♦ ⚲ ♻
C17th Grade II Listed, many original features retained. Peaceful, rural location, beautiful views, just 3 miles from Tavistock on the Chillaton road. Quality accommodation near Lydford Gorge and Brentor medieval church. Central to many activities. Also self catering accommodation available.

At **Tavistock**, visit the church of St Eustace, where, close by the remains of eleventh-century Tavistock Abbey, the fifteenth-century church building is adorned by a William Morris window.

A couple of miles off the route, **Buckland Abbey**, a former Cistercian abbey, was converted to become the home of Francis Drake. There is an array of Drake memorabilia on show in the house, which stands amid beautiful grounds.

Between **Plympton** and Plymouth, Saltram House, the largest country house in Devon, features Robert Adam architecture, Chippendale furniture and portraits by Joshua Reynolds.

Plymouth is one of Britain's most important maritime cities. Plymouth Hoe, the historic promenade from which the city spreads out, gives magnificent views across Plymouth Sound, also at times catching strong winds. Here in 1588, having caught wind of the approaching Spanish Armada whilst in the middle of a game of bowls, Sir Francis Drake declared, "There is plenty of time to win this game and to thrash the Spaniards too". Allegedly. Close by are the Barbican, whose Tudor and Jacobean buildings form the heart of old Plymouth, with the Mayflower Steps from which the Pilgrim Fathers set sail; and the Royal Citadel, a fortification built during the Restoration to keep this Parliamentarian town in check.

The Country Code

Enjoy the countryside and respect its life and work

Guard against all risk of fire

Fasten all gates

Keep your dogs under close control

Keep to public paths across farmland

Use gates and stiles to cross fences, hedges and walls

Leave livestock, crops and machinery alone

Take your litter home

Help to keep all water clean

Protect wild-life, plants and trees

Take special care on country roads

Make no unnecessary noise

Bracken B & B, 36 Plymouth
Road, Tavistock, Devon, *PL19 8BU.*
Comfortable Victorian town house.
Adjacent Dartmoor National Park.
Warm welcome.
Tel: **01822 613914** Ms Spartley.
D: £16.00-£20.00 **S:** £20.00-£30.00.
Open: All Year
Beds: 1T 3D
Baths: 1 En 1 Pr 1 Sh
ᵰ (5) **P** (4) ⅙⏚✉🌐👥🖥️🖳🖵

Mount Tavy Cottage, Tavistock,
Devon, *PL19 9JL.*
Stone cottage in ten acres, own
walled garden, close to Dartmoor.
Tel: **01822 614253** Mr Moule.
D: £20.00-£22.50 **S:** £18.00-£22.50.
Open: All Year
Beds: 2D 1S
Baths: 2 Pr
ᵰ **P** (6) ⅙⏚🌐👥🖥️🖳🖵

Westward, 15 Plymouth Road,
Tavistock, Devon, *PL19 8AU.*
Listed Victorian house. Charming
wall garden bounded by Tavistock
Canal.
Tel: **01822 612094** Ms Parkin.
D: £16.00-£20.00 **S:** £16.00-£18.00.
Open: All Year
Beds: 1F 1S
Baths: 1 En 1 Sh
ᵰ **P** (3) ⏚🌐👥🖥️🖳🖵

Kingfisher Cottage, Mount Tavy
Road, Vigo Bridge, Tavistock,
Devon, *PL19 9JB.*
Riverside accommodation in char-
acterful cottage near town and
beautiful Dartmoor.
Tel: **01822 613801**
Mrs Toland.
D: £16.00-£21.00
S: £16.00-£35.00.
Open: All Year
Beds: 2D 1T
Baths: 1 En
ᵰ **P** (5) ⅙⏚🌐👥🖥️🖳🖵

Hele Farm, Tavistock, Devon,
PL19 8PA.
Comfortable accommodation at
fully organic dairy farm dated
1780.
Tel: **01822 833084**
Mrs Steer.
D: £18.00-£20.00
S: £20.00-£25.00.
Open: Apr to Oct
Beds: 1D 1T
Baths: 2 Pr
ᵰ **P** (3) ⅙⏚🌐👥🖥️🖳🖵

**All rooms full and
nowhere else to stay?
Ask the owner if
there's anywhere
nearby**

**All details shown
are as supplied
by B&B owners in
Autumn 2000.**

Sampford Spiney 24

National Grid Ref: SX5372

🍴 🍺 London Inn

Withill Farm, Sampford Spiney,
Yelverton, Devon, *PL20 6LN.*
Actual grid ref: SX548727
Tel: **01822 853992** (also fax no)
Mrs Kitchen.
D: £18.00-£21.00
S: £19.00-£23.00.
Open: All Year
Beds: 1D 2T
Baths: 1 En 1 Sh
ᵰ **P** (6) ⅙⏚🌾✖️🌐👥🖥️🖵
West Dartmoor. Relax at our
friendly, small working farm in an
secluded setting, surrounded by
woods, a tumbling brook, moorland
and granite tors. Ideal for walking,
riding, cycling, central for visiting
Devon & Cornwall.

Horrabridge 25

National Grid Ref: SX5169

🍴 🍺 Leaping Salmon, London Inn

Overcombe Hotel, Old Station
Road, Horrabridge, Yelverton,
Devon, *PL20 7RA.*
Enjoy beautiful views across the
Walkham Valley towards High
Tor.
Tel: **01822 853501**
Wright.
D: £22.00-£22.50
S: £22.00-£28.00.
Open: All Year
Beds: 2F 5D 3T 1S
Baths: 10 Pr 1 Sh
ᵰ **P** (10) ⏚🌾✖️🖳👥

The Old Mine House, Sortridge,
Horrabridge, Yelverton, Devon,
PL20 7UA.
Actual grid ref: SX510707
Peaceful grounds. Dartmoor views.
Woods, pond, chickens. Distinctive
house.
Tel: **01822 855586** (also fax no)
Ian Robinson.
D: £15.00-£20.00
S: £15.00-£20.00.
Open: All Year (not Xmas/
New Year)
Beds: 3F 3T 1D
Baths: 3 Pr
ᵰ **P** (20) ⅙⏚🌾✖️🌐👥🖳🖵
🖵

Walkhampton 26

National Grid Ref: SX5369

Town Farm, Walkhampton,
Yelverton, Devon, *PL20 6JX.*
Actual grid ref: SX533698
Tel: **01822 855145**
Mr & Mrs Morley.
Fax no: 01822 852180
D: £20.00
S: £25.00.
Open: All Year
Beds: 1T 1D
Baths: 2 En
ᵰ **P** (2) ⅙⏚✖️🌐👥🖥️🖵
Self contained accommodation in
recently refurbished Listed barn.
Attractive courtyard location.
Breakfast in main house.
Centre of moorland village.
Excellent base for exploring
Dartmoor on foot & by car. Close
to historic Plymouth & the market
town of Tavistock both connected
to Sir Francis Drake. Personally
guided tours.

Buckland Monachorum 27

National Grid Ref: SX4968

Uppaton Country Guest House,
Coppicetown Road, Buckland
Monachorum, Yelverton, Devon,
PL20 7LL.
Beautiful Victorian mansion
between Tavistock & Plymouth on
the edge of Dartmoor National
Park.
Tel: **01822 855511**
Mr & Dr McQueen.
D: £20.00-£25.00
S: £20.00-£25.00.
Open: All Year
Beds: 1F 2D 2T 1S
Baths: 3 En 2 Sh
ᵰ **P** ⅙⏚🌾✖️🌐👥🖥️🖵

Yelverton 28

National Grid Ref: SX5267

🍴 🍺 Drakes Manor, Rock Inn

The Rosemont Guest House,
Greenbank Terrace, Yelverton,
Devon, *PL20 6DR.*
Grades: ETC 3 Diamond
Tel: **01822 852175**
Mr & Mrs Eastaugh.
D: £21.00-£22.00
S: £21.00-£32.00.
Open: All Year (not Xmas)
Beds: 1F 3D 2T 1S
Baths: 7 En
ᵰ **P** (5) ⅙⏚👥🖥️🖥️🖳🖵
Overlooking moorland village
green within the glorious Dartmoor
National Park. Historic Plymouth,
Tavistock, Buckland Abbey,
Garden House and Lydford Gorge
all nearby. Excellent free range
breakfast using local produce.
Pubs, restaurants and other
amenities within village.

Stokehill Farmhouse, *Yelverton, Devon, PL20 6EW.*
Tel: **01822 853791** Mrs Gozzard.
D: £22.50-£25.00 **S:** £27.00-£30.00.
Open: All Year (not Xmas/New Year)
Beds: 1T 2D
Baths: 1Ensuite 1 Pr
🛏 (10) ▣ ⊬ 🖵 🗻 🎚 Ⅲ. Ⅵ ⊁ ♿
Beautiful country house set in lovely grounds in a quiet, rural setting. Large bedrooms and bathrooms richly furnished with stunning views across rolling countryside. On the edge of the Dartmoor National Park but close to Plymouth and the coast.

Knightstone Tea Rooms,
Crapstone Road, Yelverton, Devon, PL20 6BT.
Quiet, secluded, of historic interest, overlooking moors. Ideal for sightseeing.
Grades: ETC 2 Diamond
Tel: **01822 853679** Mrs Hayes.
D: £17.50-£17.50 **S:** £17.50-£17.50.
Open: All Year
Beds: 1F 1T 1S
Baths: 1 Sh
🛏 ▣ (20) ⊬ 🖵 ✕ 🗻 Ⅲ. Ⅵ ■ ⊁ ♿

Rettery Bank, *Harrowbeer Lane, Yelverton, Devon, PL20 6EA.*
Actual grid ref: SX519684
Quiet house with wonderful views, comfortable beds, jacuzzi, English breakfast.
Tel: **01822 855088** (also fax no)
Ms Leavey.
D: £20.00-£25.00 **S:** £16.00-£20.00.
Open: All Year (not Xmas)
Beds: 1D 1T
Baths: 1 En 1 Sh
🛏 (5) ▣ (2) 🖵 ✕ 🗻 Ⅲ. Ⅵ ■ ⊁ ♿

Sheepstor   29

National Grid Ref: SX5567

🍴 🍺 The Royal Oak

Burrator House, *Sheepstor, Yelverton, Devon, PL20 2PF.*
Secluded historic country house. Guest rooms overlook lake and gardens. Dartmoor Tourist Association Member.
Tel: **01822 855669** (also fax no)
Mr Flint.
D: £25.00-£27.50
S: £35.00-£37.50.
Open: All Year (not Xmas)
Beds: 3D 1T 1S
Baths: 3 En 1 Pr
🛏 (8) ▣ (12) ⊬ 🖵 🏇 ✕ 🗻 Ⅲ. Ⅵ ■
⊁ ♿

Bringing children with you? Always ask for any special rates.

Clearbrook   30

National Grid Ref: SX5265

🍴 🍺 Skylark Inn

Sunbeam House, *Clearbrook, Yelverton, Devon, PL20 6JD.*
Actual grid ref: SX521656
Tel: **01822 853871** Ms Newberry.
Fax no: 01822 855672
D: £17.50-£17.50 **S:** £20.00-£20.00.
Open: All Year (not Xmas)
Beds: 1D 1T **Baths:** 2 Sh
🛏 ▣ (6) ⊬ 🖵 🗻 Ⅲ. Ⅵ ■ ⊁ ♿
Direct access to Dartmoor. Large double fronted family house offering peace and tranquillity. Good-sized bay-windowed double bedrooms overlooking Dartmoor. Friendly welcome, hearty country breakfast. Close to local pub for evening meals. Ideal for walking, cycling, fishing, golf.

Plymouth   31

National Grid Ref: SX4756

🍴 🍺 West Hoe, Brown Bear, Odd Wheel, Eddystone Inn, The Walrus, Sippers, The Yardarm, Frog & Frigate, Waterfront, Notte Inn

▲ **Plymouth Youth Hostel,**
Belmont House, Devonport Road, Stoke, Plymouth, Devon, PL3 4DW.
Actual grid ref: SX461555
Tel: **01752 562189**
Under 18: £7.75 **Adults:** £11.00
Self-catering facilities, Television, Showers, Wet weather shelter, Lounge, Games room, Drying room, Cycle store, Parking, Evening meal at 7.00pm, Kitchen facilities, Breakfast available, Luggage store, Credit cards accepted
Classical Greek-style house built in 1820 for a wealthy banker, set in own grounds, within easy walking distance of the city centre.

▲ **Plymouth Backpackers' Hostel,** *172 Citadel Road, The Hoe, Plymouth, Devon, PL1 3DB.*
Actual grid ref: SX483537
Tel: **01752 225158** **Adults:** £7.50

Mountbatten Hotel, *52 Exmouth Road, Stoke, Plymouth, Devon, PL1 4QH.*
Grades: ETC 3 Diamond
Tel: **01752 563843** Mr Hendy.
Fax no: 01752 606014
D: £23.00-£25.00 **S:** £20.00-£27.00.
Open: All Year
Beds: 3F 6D 2T 4S
Baths: 7 En 2 Sh
🛏 ▣ (4) 🖵 🏇 ✕ 🗻 Ⅲ. Ⅵ ■ ♿
Small licensed Victorian hotel overlooking parkland with river views. Quiet cul de sac. Close city centre/ferryport. Good access Cornwall. Walking distance Naval base, Royal Fleet Club, FE College. Secure parking. Well appointed rooms. Tea/coffee, CTVs, telephones. Credit cards accepted.

The Old Pier Guest House, *20 Radford Road, West Hoe, Plymouth, Devon, PL1 3BY.*
Actual grid ref: SX472537
Convenient for ferry, Barbican, city centre, sea front. Offers exceptional value.
Grades: ETC 3 Diamond
Tel: **01752 268468** Mrs Jones.
D: £15.00-£19.00 **S:** £16.00-£25.00.
Open: All Year (not Xmas/New Year)
Beds: 1F 2T 3D 1S
🛏 (10) ⊬ 🖵 ✕ 🗻 Ⅲ. Ⅵ ⊁ ♿

Teviot Guest House, *20 North Road East, Plymouth, Devon, PL4 6AS.*
Excellent Bed & Breakfast in central location for non-smokers.
Grades: ETC 4 Diamond, Silver
Tel: **01752 262656** Mrs Fisher.
Fax no: 01752 251660
D: £18.00-£30.00 **S:** £18.00-£30.00.
Open: All Year (not Xmas)
Beds: 2F 2D 1T 1S
Baths: 2 En 3 Pr 1 Sh
🛏 (7) ▣ (2) ⊬ 🖵 🗻 Ⅲ. Ⅵ ■ ⊁

The Elizabethan Guest House, *223 Citadel Road, The Hoe, Plymouth, Devon, PL1 2JY.*
Central location. Close to Hoe, harbour, Barbican and city centre.
Tel: **01752 661672** (also fax no)
D: £14.00-£20.00 **S:** £18.00-£22.00
Open: All Year
Beds: 1F 4D 2T
Baths: 1 En 2 Sh
🛏 ▣ (3) 🖵 🗻 Ⅲ. & Ⅵ ⊁ ♿

Caraneal, *12-14 Pier Street, The Hoe, Plymouth, Devon, PL1 3BS.*
Friendly, family run. Close to city centre, seafront, continental ferry port.
Grades: AA 3 Diamond
Tel: **01752 663589**
Mrs Crosland.
Fax no: 01752 212871
D: £19.00-£22.50 **S:** £25.00-£30.00
Open: All Year
Beds: 1F 6D 1T 1S
Baths: 9 En
🛏 ▣ (2) 🖵 ✕ 🗻 Ⅲ. Ⅵ ⊁ ♿

Sunray Hotel, *3/5 Alfred Street, The Hoe, Plymouth, Devon, PL1 2RP.*
Centrally located, convenient for theatre, shops, Barbican and National Aquarium.
Tel: **01752 669113** Mr Sutton.
Fax no: 01752 268969
D: £23.00-£26.00 **S:** £28.00-£35.00
Open: All Year (not Xmas/New Year)
Beds: 6F 4D 5T 3S
Baths: 16 En 2 Pr
▣ (6) 🖵 🗻 Ⅲ. Ⅵ ■ ⊁

S = Price range for a single person in a room

Olivers Hotel & Restaurant,
*33 Sutherland Road, Plymouth,
Devon, PL4 6BN.*
Actual grid ref: SX481555
Welcoming, restful Victorian hotel
convenient for City, Sea and
Moors.
Grades: RAC 4 diamond
Tel: **01752 663923** Mrs Purser.
Fax no: 01752 262295
D: £22.50-£25.00
S: £20.00-£30.00.
Open: All Year
Beds: 1F 2D 1T 2S
Baths: 4 En 1 Sh
🛏 (11) 🅿 (2) 🖵 ✕ 🧴 🎟 Ⅵ

Georgian House Hotel, *51 Citadel
Road, The Hoe, Plymouth, PL1 3AU.*
Family-run hotel in central location
near all Plymouth's amenities.
Grades: AA 3 Diamond
Tel: **01752 663237**
D: £19.00-£22.00
S: £22.00-£29.00.
Open: Feb to Dec
Beds: 6D 2T 2S
Baths: 10 En
🛏 ⅙ 🖵 🧴 🎟 Ⅵ 🍴

D = Price range per person
sharing in a double room

S = Price range for a single
person in a room

Osmond Guest House, *42 Pier
Street, West Hoe, Plymouth,
Devon, PL1 3BT.*
Seafront Edwardian house.
Walking distance to all attractions.
Courtesy pick-up from stations.
Tel: **01752 229705**
Mrs Richards.
Fax no: 01752 269655
D: £16.00-£20.00 **S:** £17.00-£25.00.
Open: All Year
Beds: 3D 2T 1S
Baths: 4 En
🅿 (2) ⅙ 🖵 🧴 🎟 ♿ Ⅵ 🍴 🐾

Hotspur Guest House, *108 North
Road East, Plymouth, Devon,
PL4 6AW.*
Victorian property, adjacent city
centre; bus/rail stations, historic
Barbican, Hoe, seafronts.
Tel: **01752 663928**
Taylor.
Fax no: 01752 261493
D: £16.00-£17.00 **S:** £16.50-£17.50.
Open: All Year (not Xmas)
Beds: 2F 1D 2T 3S
🛏 🖵 🐾 ✕ 🧴 🎟 Ⅵ 🍴

Sydney Guest House, *181 North
Road West, Plymouth, Devon,
PL1 5DE.*
Situated in the heart of the city near
the railway, ferry, port, university.
Tel: **01752 266541** Mrs Puckey.
Fax no: 01333 310573
D: £25.00-£45.00 **S:** £14.00-£25.00.
Open: All Year
Beds: 1F 2D 2T 3S **Baths:** 3 En
🛏 🖵 ✕ 🎟

Rusty Anchor, *30 Grand Parade,
West Hoe, Plymouth, Devon, PL1 3DJ*
Situated on the sea front, walking
distance city centre, Hoe.
Tel: **01752 663924** (also fax no)
Ms Turner.
D: £15.00-£25.00 **S:** £15.00-£30.00.
Open: All Year (not Xmas)
Beds: 4F 1D 2T 2S
Baths: 3 En 3 Pr 2 Sh
🛏 🖵 🐾 ✕ 🧴 🎟 Ⅵ 🍴 🐾

Cassandra Guest House,
*13 Crescent Avenue, The Hoe,
Plymouth, Devon, PL1 3AN.*
Ideally situated for city centre,
seafront, Barbican, Ferry, port,
theatres, stations.
Tel: **01752 220715** (also fax no)
D: £17.00-£20.00 **S:** £17.00-£26.00.
Open: All Year **Beds:** 3F 1D 1T 1S
Baths: 2 En 1 Pr 1 Sh
🛏 ⅙ 🖵 🐾 🧴 🎟 Ⅵ ♦ 🐾

Sustrans Hull to Harwich

The **Hull to Harwich Cycle Route** is a section of the new National Cycle Network, running on traffic-free paths and traffic-calmed roads between the Continental ferry ports of Hull in the East Riding of Yorkshire and Harwich in the northeastern corner of Essex. 370 miles long, it links the towns of Lincoln and Boston in Lincolnshire, Wisbech in Cambridgeshire and King's Lynn, Fakenham and Norwich in Norfolk with Beccles, Woodbridge and Ipswich in Suffolk and Colchester in Essex. The flat landscape of the Eastern counties yields long views and makes excellent cycling country: the only up-and-down of any degree (and this undemanding) comes in the route through the northern reaches of the Lincolnshire Wolds. The route is clearly signposted by blue direction signs with a cycle silhouette and the number 1 in a red rectangle.

The indispensable **official route map and guide** for the route comes in two parts, *Hull to Fakenham* and *Fakenham to Harwich*, and is available from Sustrans, 35 King Street, Bristol BS1 4DZ, tel 0117-926 8893, fax 0117-929 4173, @ £5.99 each (+ £1.50 p&p for both together or either one).

Maps: Ordnance Survey 1:50,000 Landranger series: 107, 112, 113, 121, 122, 131, 132, 133, 134, 155, 156, 168, 169

Trains: Hull, King's Lynn, Norwich, Ipswich, Colchester and Harwich are all main line termini; there are connecting services to many other places on or near the route.

Hull to Market Rasen

Kingston-upon-Hull is the major port of the Humber, the great deepwater estuary of England's East Coast. The poet Philip Larkin said the only good thing about the place is that it is 'very nice and flat for cycling'. For your purposes, that's a recommendation. The Streetlife Transport Museum may be of interest, as it has a recreation of a bicycle repair workshop from the early days of the beautiful machine. Of more general interest are the Town Docks Museum, the Ferens Art Gallery and the birthplace of William Wilberforce, who achieved the abolition of slavery in Britain. From the docks you head west, staying close to the river, to Hessle, where you join the Humber Bridge cyclepath to cross the resplendent Humber Bridge. The longest suspension bridge in the world, it was completed in 1981. The best view of the bridge is from the waterside at Barton-upon-Humber, on the other side. From Barton you head south, and into the Lincolnshire Wolds. From here it's a brief climb and then descent to Walesby, before you head down to the small market town of **Market Rasen**.

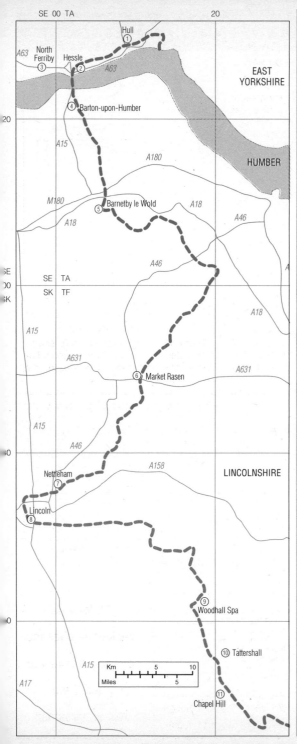

Allandra Hotel, 5 Park Avenue, Hull, *HU5 3EN.*
Grades: ETC 2 Diamond
Tel: **01482 493349**
Fax no: 01482 492680
D: £19.50-£19.50
S: £26.00-£26.00.
Open: All Year
Beds: 2F 1T 7D
Baths: 10 En
📷 🅿 (5) 🛏 ⊁ ✗ 🚲 🖳 Ⅴ ♿
Charming Victorian town house hotel, family run, close to all amenities. Delightfully situated, convenient universities and town centre opposite pleasant parking. All rooms ensuite.

Beck House , 628 Beverley High Road, Hull, *HU6 7LL.*
Traditional town house, B&B, fine accommodation, close to university etc.
Tel: **01482 445468**
Mrs Aylwin.
D: £19.00-£22.00.
S: £19.00-£22.00.
Open: All Year
Beds: 3D 3S
Baths: 1 En 1 Sh
📷 🅿 (4) 🛏 🚲 🖳 Ⅴ ♿

Hessle 2

National Grid Ref: TA0326

🍴 🍺 Country Park Inn, The Hase

Redcliffe House, Redcliffe Road, Hessle, E Yorks, *HU13 0HA.*
Beautifully appointed, riverside location close to Humber Bridge, Hull, Beverley.
Grades: ETC 4 Diamond
Tel: **01482 648655**
Skiba.
D: £20.00-£20.00
S: £20.00-£35.00.
Open: All Year
Beds: 2D 2T 1S
Baths: 4 En 1 Sh
📷 🅿 (6) 🛏 🚲 🖳 Ⅴ ♿

The Grid Reference beneath the location heading is for the village or town - *not* for individual houses, which are shown (where supplied) in each entry itself.

North Ferriby   3

National Grid Ref: SE9826

*B&B at 103, 103 Ferriby High
Road, North Ferriby, East Yorks,
HU14 3LA.*
Comfortable house, large garden,
overlooking river near Humber
Bridge and Hull.
Grades: ETC 3 Diamond
Tel: **01482 633637** Mrs Simpson.
D: £15.00-£15.00 **S:** £15.00-£15.00.
Open: All Year
Beds: 1D 1T 1S
Baths: 1 Sh
🛏 (7) ⓟ (2) �⏰ ⽊ ✗ ▥ Ⅲ. Ⅴ ℩ ⅋
⚲

Barton-upon-Humber   4

National Grid Ref: TA0321

🍽 ◁ White Swan

*White Swan Hotel, Fleetgate,
Barton-upon-Humber, N Lincs,
DN18 5QD.*
Local friendly pub, pool, darts,
doms etc.
Tel: **01652 632459**
D: £23.50-£23.50
S: £30.00-£30.00.
Open: All Year (not Xmas)
Beds: 1D 3T
Baths: 2 En 1 Sh
ⓟ (10) ▥ ✗ ▦ Ⅲ. Ⅴ ⚲

**All rooms full and
nowhere else to stay?
Ask the owner if
there's anywhere
nearby**

Barnetby le Wold   5

National Grid Ref: TA0509

🍽 ◁ Station Hotel

*Holcombe Guest House, 34
Victoria Road, Barnetby le Wold,
Lincs, DN38 6JR.*
Actual grid ref: TA059097
First class accommodation and a
warm welcome awaits you.
Tel: **01652 680655** Mrs Vora.
Fax no: 01652 680841
D: £16.25-£20.00 **S:** £20.00-£20.00.
Open: All Year
Beds: 2F 1T 5S
Baths: 4 Pr 2 Sh
🛏 ⓟ (7) ▥ ⽊ ✗ ▦ Ⅲ. ♿ Ⅴ ℩ ⅋ ⚲

*Reginald House, 27 Queen Road,
Barnetby le Wold, Lincolnshire,
DN38 6JH.*
Beautiful modern bungalow with
newly-built first floor ensuite guest
accommodation.
Tel: **01652 688566**
Fax no: 01652 688510
D: £17.50-£20.00 **S:** £22.50-£25.00.
Open: All Year
Beds: 1D 1T
Baths: 2 En
ⓟ (4) �▥ ✗ ▦ Ⅲ. Ⅴ ℩ ⅋ ⚲

Market Rasen   6

National Grid Ref: TF1089

🍽 ◁ The Chase, Gordon Arms, White Swan

*Waveney Cottage Guest House,
Willingham Road, Market Rasen,
Lincs, LN8 3DN.*
Small Tudor-style cottage. Ideal
base for walking and cycling.
Grades: ETC 3 Diamond
Tel: **01673 843236** Mrs Bridger.
D: £19.50**S:** £21.50.
Open: All Year
Beds: 1D 2T
Baths: 3 En
🛏 ⓟ (6) �▥ ✗ ▦ Ⅲ. Ⅴ ℩ ⅋

S = Price range for a single
person in a room

---

*White Swan Hotel, 29 Queen
Street, Market Rasen, Lincs,
LN8 3EN.*
Close to Racecourse, offering
warm, friendly atmosphere.
Tel: **01673 843356** Scuffam.
D: £17.50 **S:** £17.50.
Open: All Year
Beds: 1F 1D 2T 1S
Baths: 1 Sh
🛏 ⓟ (10) ▥ ✗ ▦ Ⅲ. Ⅴ ℩ ⅋ ⚲

Nettleham   7

National Grid Ref: TF0075

🍽 ◁ Black Horse

*Haymans Ghyll, 9 Church Street,
Nettleham, Lincoln, LN2 2PD.*
C18th cottage situated centre
village, private lounge. Lincoln ten
minutes.
Tel: **01522 751812** (also fax no)
Mr Dawkins.
D: £20.00-£22.00
S: £25.00-£30.00.
Open: All Year (not Xmas/New
Year)
Beds: 2D
Baths: 1 En 1 Pr
⅋▥ ▦ Ⅲ. Ⅴ ⅋ ⚲

**Please don't camp
on *anyone's* land
without first obtaining
their permission.**

Market Rasen to Boston

From Market Rasen it's a leisurely jaunt
through a series of Lincolnshire villages to
Lincoln. Here you can find the largest
collection of bicycles in Britain at the National
Cycle Museum. The massive cathedral, whose
three towers dominate the flat landscape for
miles around, originated in the Norman period,
but was ruined by an earthquake in the twelfth
century. The reconstruction dates from the Early
English period of the Gothic age. Most notewor-
thy is the intricate narrative carving of the frieze
on the west front. Lincoln Castle also dates from
the Norman period, and houses one of only four
existing original copies of the Magna Carta; but
from 1787 until 1878 it was used as the city jail.

The pews in the prison chapel resemble coffins
– a reminder of the era's not-so-progressive
attitudes towards criminal justice. The route
through southern Lincolnshire brings you to
Tattershall Bridge, close to Tattershall Castle,
an early brick building put up in the fifteenth
century, with late Gothic fireplaces and
tapestries. With the Boston Stump, the 288-foot
tower of the church of St Botolph (nicknamed
from its lack of a spire), rising ahead, you cycle
on to *St Botolph's Town*. **Boston**, standing
close to where the Witham flows into The Wash,
was the starting point for the first abortive
voyage of the Pilgrim Fathers, who were
imprisoned in the Guildhall, now a museum. The
link remains strong with the town's greater
namesake in Massachussetts.

Lincoln 8

National Grid Ref: SK9771

🏵 🍺 Lord Tennyson, Sun Inn, The Barge, Royal William, Horse & Groom, Burton Arms, Wig & Mitre

▲ *Lincoln Youth Hostel,* 77 *South Park, Lincoln, LN5 8ES.*
Actual grid ref: SK980700
Tel: **01522 522076**
Under 18: £6.90 **Adults:** £10.00
Self-catering facilities, Television, Laundry facilities, Lounge, Cycle store, Parking, Evening meal at 7.00pm, No smoking, Kitchen facilities, Breakfast available, Luggage store, Credit cards accepted
Victorian villa in a quiet road opposite South Common open parkland within easy reach of the centre, castle and cathedral.

Admiral Guest House, 16/18 *Nelson Street, Lincoln, LN1 1PJ.*
Actual grid ref: SK968715
Grades: RAC 3 Diamond
Tel: **01522 544467** (also fax no)
Mr Major.
D: £18.00-£20.00 -£22.00.
Open: All Year (not Xmas)
Beds: 1F 3D 2T 3S
Baths: 7 En 2 Pr
🛏 🅿 (12) 🖵 🏋 ✗ 🛢 🎵 🔥 🖦 & 🖸 🛗 ✦ 🚲

Admiral Guest House, also known as Nelsons Cottages, situated just off main A57 close to city centre and Lincoln University, offering large floodlit car park, also close to Brayford pool, cathedral and castle and all amenities. All rooms ensuite and private bath.

Edward King House, The Old Palace, Minster Yard, Lincoln, *LN2 1PU.*
Actual grid ref: SK978718
Grades: ETC 2 Diamond
Tel: **01522 528778** Rev Adkins.
Fax no: 01522 527308
D: £18.50-£20.50 **S:** £19.00-£21.00.
Open: All Year (not Xmas)
Beds: 1F 11T 5S
Baths: 8 Sh
🛏 🅿 (12) ⅏ 🖵 🏋 🛢 🖦 🖸 🚲
A former residence of the Bishops of Lincoln at the historic heart of the city and next to the cathedral and medieval old palace. We offer a peaceful haven with a secluded garden and superb views.

High season,
bank holidays and
special events mean
low availability
everywhere.

South Park Guest House, 11 *South Park, Lincoln, LN5 8EN.*
Tel: **01522 528243** Mr Bull.
Fax no: 01522 524603
D: £18.00-£26.00 **S:** £22.00-£25.00.
Open: All Year (not Xmas/
New Year)
Beds: 1F 2T 2D 1S
Baths: 6 En
🛏 (1) 🅿 (6) 🖵 ✗ 🛢 🖦 🖸 🛗
Fine Victorian detached house, recently refurbished to provide excellent quality accommodation, while maintaining many original features & character. Situated overlooking the South Common, only a short walk to shops, pubs, restaurants, city centre and tourist attractions. Ensuite rooms. Private parking.

Hamiltons Hotel, 2 Hamilton Road, St Catherines, Lincoln, *LN5 8ED.*
Friendly family-run hotel in a detached former Victorian home.
Tel: **01522 528243** Bull.
Fax no: 01522 524603
D: £18.00-£20.00 **S:** £18.00-£25.00.
Open: All Year
Beds: 1F 3T 2D 3S
Baths: 4 En 5 Sh
🛏 🅿 (9) 🖵 🏋 ✗ 🛢 🖦 🖸 🛗 🚲

A B C Charisma Guest House, 126 *Yarborough Road, Lincoln, LN1 1HP.*
Beautiful views overlooking Trent valley 10 minutes walk to tourist area.
Tel: **01522 543560** (also fax no)
D: £20.00-£22.50 **S:** £20.00-£25.00.
Open: All Year
Beds: 1F 2T 6D 2S
Baths: 3 En 4 Sh
🛏 (10) 🅿 (10) ⅏ 🖵 🛢 🖦 🖸 ✦ 🚲

Newport Guest House, 26-28 *Newport, Lincoln, LN1 3DF.*
A high standard establishment 500 metres from historic city centre.
Grades: ETC 3 Diamond,
AA 3 Diamond
Tel: **01522 528590** Mr Clarke.
Fax no: 01522 544502
D: £16.00-£20.00 **S:** £16.00-£28.00.
Open: All Year (not Xmas)
Beds: 2D 5T 1S
Baths: 5 En 2 Sh
🛏 (6) 🅿 (5) ⅏ 🖵 🏋 🛢 🖦 & 🖸 🚲 🛗

D = Price range per person
sharing in a double room

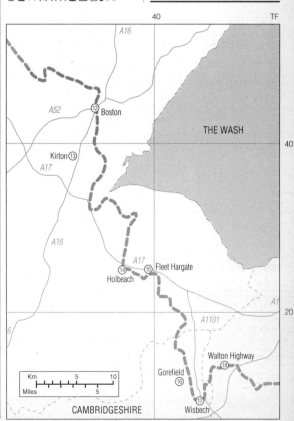

The Old Rectory, *19 Newport, Lincoln, LN1 3DQ.*
Large Edwardian home near cathedral, castle, pubs and restaurants.
Tel: **01522 514774**
Mr Downes.
D: £20.00-£20.00
S: £20.00-£25.00.
Open: All Year (not Xmas)
Beds: 2F 4D 1T 1S
Baths: 5 En 1 Sh
⛟ 🅿 (8) ⌁ 🖵 🛒 🏧 Ⓥ ⚲

Westlyn House, *67 Carholme Road, Lincoln, LN1 1RT.*
Late Georgian house close to university, marina, cathedral, castle, city centre.
Grades: RAC 3 Diamond
Tel: **01522 537468** (also fax no)
Mrs Shelton.
D: £17.50-£20.00
S: £20.00-£25.00.
Open: All Year (not Xmas)
Beds: 1F 1T 2D 1S
Baths: 5 En
⛟ (3) 🅿 (4) ⌁ 🖵 🐾 🛒 🏧 Ⓥ ⚐ ⚲

The Bakery Guest House, *26-28 Burton Road, Lincoln, LN1 3LB.*
Converted bakery only two minutes from Lincoln castle and cathedral.
Tel: **01522 576057** (also fax no)
D: £20.00-£30.00 **S:** £25.00-£40.00.
Open: All Year
Beds: 1F 2D 1T
Baths: 3 En 1 Pr
⛟ 🖵 🐾 🛒 🏧 Ⓥ ⚲

Elma Guest House, *14 Albion Crescent, off Long Leys Road, Lincoln, LN1 1EB.*
Quiet location, friendly family home with garden pond and willow tree.
Grades: AA 2 Diamond
Tel: **01522 529792** (also fax no)
Mrs Guymer.
D: £17.00-£20.00 **S:** £17.00-£20.00.
Open: All Year
Beds: 1D 1T 1S
Baths: 2 Sh
⛟ 🅿 (5) 🖵 ✕ 🛒 🏧 Ⓥ ⚲

Jaymar, *31 Newland Street West, Lincoln, LN1 1QQ.*
Close proximity to: city attractions, A46, A57. Early breakfasts available.
Tel: **01522 532934** Mrs Ward.
D: £15.00-£15.00 **S:** £15.00-£15.00.
Open: All Year (not Xmas)
Beds: 1D 1S
Baths: 1 Sh
⛟ ⌁ 🖵 🐾 🛒 Ⓥ ⚲

Ridgeways Guest House, *243 Burton Road, Lincoln, LN1 3UB.*
Actual grid ref: SK972727
Situated uphill within easy walking distance to the historic heart of Lincoln.
Tel: **01522 546878** (also fax no)
Mr Barnes.
D: £17.50-£25.00 **S:** £20.00-£25.00.
Open: All Year
Beds: 2F 1D 1T
Baths: 3 En 1 Pr
🅿 (6) ⌁ 🖵 🐾 🛒 ♿ Ⓥ ⚲

The Barbican Hotel, *11 St Marys Street, Lincoln, LN5 7EQ.*
Victorian hotel. Refurbished. Opposite railway station. An ideal central location.
Tel: **01522 543811**
D: £26.00
S: £39.00-£39.00.
Open: All Year (not Xmas)
Beds: 5D 2T 5S
Baths: 12 En
⛟ 🖵 🐾 🛒 🏧 Ⓥ ⚐ ⚲

Eardleys Hotel, *21 Cross O'Cliff Hill, Lincoln, LN5 8PN.*
Homely hotel, overlooking parkland & golf course. Guest bar & parking.
Tel: **01522 523050** (also fax no)
Mr Hill.
D: £17.50-£20.00 **S:** £20.00-£25.00.
Open: All Year
Beds: 2F 2D 1T 1S
Baths: 2 En 2 Sh
⛟ 🅿 (10) 🖵 🐾 ✕ 🛒 🏧 Ⓥ ⚐ ⚐ ⚲

Order your
packed lunches the
evening before you
need them.
Not at breakfast!

Boston to Beccles

Now you strike out southwards across the Fens, the low-lying country of southern Lincolnshire and northern Cambridgeshire which, before it was drained in the seventeenth century by Dutchmen, was inhospitable marshland. After crossing the River Welland at Fosdyke Bridge, it's over three marshes to Holbeach, before crossing into Cambridgeshire at Tydd St Giles and proceeding to **Wisbech** on the River Nene, the 'capital of the fens'. Here the Fenland Museum sports, among other things, a reconstructed Victorian post office. Leaving Wisbech to the north you come into Norfolk and head eastwards. After crossing the River Great Ouse at Wiggenhall St Germans, you cycle into **King's Lynn**, which lies a short way upstream from where the Ouse flows into the Wash. There is much to see here: St George's Guildhall, one of England's largest, dates from the fifteenth century and now houses an arts centre and a restaurant; the Customs House at Purfleet Quay is a small seventeenth-century Palladian building; and St Margaret's church boasts two impressive Flemish brasses. The Old Gaol House holds a display of treasures from the town's past; the True's Yard museum offers a glimpse of life in the old fishing community through two tiny preserved cottages. Attractions on the route northeast out of King's Lynn include **Castle Rising**, where the impressively well-preserved twelfth-century keep is surrounded by a large earthwork, and the village has a group of seventeenth-century almshouses. A little way further on stands **Sandringham House**, a private country retreat of the Royal family (but open to the public) built in the late nineteenth century in the neo-Jacobean style, set in sixty acres of pretty grounds. From here it's on to Ringstead, not far from the spectacular cliffs of Hunstanton, then Burnham Market, birthplace of Admiral Nelson (with three pubs carrying his worthy name), before you reach the market town of **Fakenham**. The route now takes you along the line of the River Wensum to the attractive village of Reepham, with its Georgian and half-timbered houses and the redbrick Old Brewery House, and on to **Norwich**. The capital of East Anglia was economically important for centuries before the Industrial Revolution; the city bears traces of every period of English history. Tombland is the old Saxon market place, close to the picturesque half-timbered houses of Elm Hill. The Norman keep of Norwich Castle, dating from the twelfth century, ranks with the Tower of London as England's best surviving Norman fortification. The city's cathedral is also a Norman foundation, with later additions - the vaulted roof, with illustratively carved bosses, and the spire (the tallest in England after Salisbury) date from the fifteenth century. The most important modern building is the Sainsbury Centre for the Visual Arts, designed in the 1970s by Norman Foster, which houses a brilliant display in which central figures of western modern art (Picasso, Modigliani, Giacometti) share space with African, Pacific and Native American exhibits. Having cycled through the city centre, you cross the River Yare and skirt the Norfolk Broads as far as Loddon, before heading south to the banks of the Waveney, which you follow downstream until the route enters Suffolk at **Beccles**.

Woodhall Spa 9

National Grid Ref: TF1963

🏠 The Mall, Abbey Lodge, Eagle Lodge

Claremont Guest House,
9-11 Witham Road, Woodhall Spa, Lincs, LN10 6RW.
Friendly personal service in a traditional unspoilt Victorian guest house.
Grades: ETC 2 Diamond
Tel: 01526 352000 Mrs Brennan.
D: £15.00-£20.00 **S:** £15.00-£20.00.
Open: All Year
Beds: 4F 2D 1T 3S
Baths: 3 En 2 Sh
🛏️🅿️(4)⛺🔥🍴🏥▥Ⅴ🌿🚲

Newlands Guest House, 56
Woodland Drive, Woodhall Spa, Lincs, LN10 6YG.
Grades: ETC 4 Diamond
Tel: 01526 352881
D: £18.00-£20.00 **S:** £20.00-£20.00.
Open: All Year (not Xmas)
Beds: 1D 2T **Baths:** 2 En 1 Pr
🛏️🅿️(8)🍴🔥🏥▥Ⅴ🚲
Luxury accommodation in quiet tree-lined lane. Very convenient for village and international golf courses. Special aviation room and guest lounge. Very attractive gardens, excellent centre for visiting Lincolnshire.

Tattershall 10

National Grid Ref: TF2158

🏠 Prattington Arms

Lodge House, Market Place, Tattershall, Lincoln, Lincs, LN4 4LQ.
Clean comfortable accommodation. Close RAF Coningsby. Walking, Cycling, Angling, Golf.
Tel: 01526 342575 (also fax no)
Mr Palethorpe.
D: £14.00-£16.00 **S:** £13.00-£17.00.
Open: All Year
Beds: 1D 1T 2S
Baths: 2 En 1 Sh
🛏️(1)🅿️(3)🍴🔥🏥▥Ⅴ🌿🚲

Chapel Hill 11

National Grid Ref: TF2054

The Crown Inn, Chapel Hill, Tattershall, Lincoln, LN4 4PX.
Ensuite rooms,varied menu, walks, fishing, boating, real ale, entertainment.
Tel: 01526 342262 (also fax no)
Mr Harrington.
D: £18.00-£18.00 **S:** £20.00-£20.00.
Open: All Year
Beds: 1F 2T 1S
🛏️🅿️(15)🍴🔥🏥▥Ⅴ🌿

Boston 12

National Grid Ref: TF3344

🏠 The Mill, White Hart, Four Crossroads, Red Cow, Good Barns, Cowbridge Inn

The New England Hotel, Wide Bargate, Boston, Lincolnshire, PE21 6SH.
Grades: ETC 3 Star, AA 3 Star
Tel: 01205 365255
Mr Maund.
D: £30.25-£36.25
S: £50.00-£62.50.
Open: All Year
Beds: 2F 5T 10D 8S
Baths: 25 En
🛏️🅿️⛺🔥🍴🏥▥Ⅴ🌿🚲
The New England is a top quality hotel with restaurant, bar, residents' lounge, good secure parking. Located in the town centre, we are close to Boston Stump, the Maud Foster Windmill and only 1/2 hour drive from Skegness and Lincoln.

S = Price range for a single person in a room

Lochiel Guest House,
69 Horncastle Road, Boston, Lincs,
PE21 9HY.
Comfortable, friendly, picturesque
waterside setting. Large garden.
Working windmill view.
Tel: **01205 363628**
Mr & Mrs Lynch.
D: £18.00-£18.00 **S:** £20.00-£20.00.
Open: All Year
Beds: 1D 1T 1S
Baths: 1 Sh
🛏 🅿 (3) ⊬ 🗔 🍴 🖾 V 🛈 ⊹ ♿

90 Pilleys Lane, *Boston, Lincs,*
PE21 9RB.
Actual grid ref: TF330464
Comfortable, detached bungalow.
Quiet. Close to Pilgrim Hospital.
Lovely residential area.
Tel: **01205 360723**
Mrs Claridge.
D: £22.00-£36.00
S: £22.00-£36.00.
Open: All Year
Beds: 1T
Baths: 1 Pr
🛏 (1) 🅿 ⊬ 🗔 🍴 🗶 🖾 & V ⊹ ♿

Kirton 13

National Grid Ref: TF3038

⊯ 🍺 Merry Monk

Westfield House, *31 Willington*
Road, Kirton, Boston, Lincs,
PE20 1EP.
Victorian house in large village, 4
miles from historic Boston
Tel: **01205 722221** Mrs Duff.
D: £15.00-£15.00 **S:** £15.00-£15.00.
Open: All Year
Beds: 1F 1D 1S
Baths: 1 Shared
🛏 🅿 (5) 🗔 🍴 🔔 🖾 V

The Nook, *45 Boston Road, Kirton,*
Boston, Lincolnshire, PE20 1ES.
Farm cottage c1900, village loca-
tion, 3 miles from historic Boston.
Tel: **01205 723419**
D: £16.00 **S:** £16.00.
Open: All Year (not Xmas)
Beds: 1F 1S
Baths: 1 Sh
⊬ 🗔 🗶 🔔 🖾 V 🛈

Holbeach 14

National Grid Ref: TF3625

⊯ 🍺 Chequers Hotel

Elloe Lodge, *37 Barrington Gate,*
Holbeach, Spalding, Lincs, PE12 7LB.
Spacious house, old market town,
close pubs & restaurants. Snooker
room, drawing room, delightful
gardens.
Tel: **01406 423207** (also fax no)
Mrs Vasey.
D: £19.00-£19.00
S: £25.00-£25.00.
Open: All Year (not Xmas)
Beds: 3D
Baths: 2 Pr
🛏 🅿 (10) ⊬ 🗔 🗶 🔔 🖾 V ⊹ ♿

Cackle Hill House, *Cackle Hill*
Lane, Holbeach, Spalding, Lincs,
PE12 8BS.
Actual grid ref: TF352262
Spacious, comfortable, tastefully-
furnished farmhouse set in a rural
position.
Tel: **01406 426721**
Mrs Biggadike.
Fax no: 01406 424659
D: £20.00-£22.00
S: £22.00-£24.00.
Open: All Year (not Xmas)
Beds: 1D 2T
Baths: 2 En 1 Pr
🛏 (10) 🅿 (5) ⊬ 🗔 🍴 🔔 🖾 V ⊹

Barrington House, *Barrington*
Gate, Holbeach, Spalding, Lincs,
PE12 7LB.
Spacious Georgian house 3 minutes
walk from pubs and restaurants.
Tel: **01406 425178** (also fax no)
Mrs Symonds.
D: £25.00-£22.50
S: £23.00-£25.00.
Open: All Year
Beds: 2D 1T 1S
Baths: 3 En 2 Pr
🛏 🅿 (4) 🗔 🍴 🔔 🖾 V ⊹ ♿

Fleet Hargate 15

National Grid Ref: TF3925

⊯ 🍺 The Bull, Rose & Crown

Willow Tea Rooms And B&B, *Old*
Main Road, Fleet Hargate,
Spalding, Lincs, PE12 8LL.
Tel: **01406 423112**
D: £16.00-£18.00 **S:** £20.00-£22.00.
Open: All Year
Beds: 2F 3D 1T
Baths: 5 En 1 Pr
🛏 🅿 (6) 🗔 🍴 🔔 🖾 V 🛈 ♿
Pretty English tea rooms renowned
for good food. Comfortable
accommodation.

Gorefield 16

National Grid Ref: TF4211

Maison De La Chien, *35 Churchill*
Road, Gorefield, Wisbech, Cambs,
PE13 4NA.
Actual grid ref: TF422122
Quiet village location overlooking
farmland on the beautiful
Cambridgeshire fens.
Tel: **01945 870789** (also fax no)
Mrs Barnard.
D: £15.00-£15.00
S: £15.00-£15.00.
Open: All Year
Beds: 1D 1T
Baths: 1 Sh
🅿 (2) ⊬ 🗔 🍴 🗶 🖾 V 🛈 ⊹ ♿

D = Price range per person
sharing in a double room

Wisbech 17

National Grid Ref: TF4609

⊯ 🍺 Blackfriars, Red Lion

Marmion House Hotel, *11 Lynn*
Road, Wisbech, Cambs, PE13 3DD.
Georgian town house hotel located
in the capital of the Fens.
Grades: ETC 3 Diamond
Tel: **01945 582822** Mrs Lilley.
Fax no: 01945 475889
D: £18.00-£22.00 **S:** £20.00-£26.00.
Open: All Year (not Xmas)
Beds: 20F 10D 2T 6S
Baths: 18 En 1 Pr 2 Sh
🛏 🅿 🗔 🔔 🖾 V ♿

Ravenscourt, *138 Lynn Road,*
Wisbech, Cambs, PE13 3DP.
Actual grid ref: TF466102
Quality accommodation, friendly
atmosphere, well situated for
business or holiday.
Tel: **01945 585052** (also fax no)
Mr Parish.
D: £16.00 **S:** £17.50-£20.00.
Open: All Year (not Xmas/New
Year)
Beds: 1F 2D 1T
Baths: 4 Pr
🛏 🅿 (3) ⊬ 🗔 🔔 🖾 V 🛈 ⊹ ♿

Algethi Guest House, *136 Lynn*
Road, Wisbech, Cambs, PE13 3DP.
Friendly family-run guest house
near town centre and river.
Tel: **01945 582278** Mrs McManus.
Fax no: 01945 466456
D: £15.00-£17.50 **S:** £15.00-£17.50.
Open: All Year
Beds: 2F 1D 2S
Baths: 2 Pr
🛏 🅿 (3) 🗔 🍴 🗶 🔔 🖾 & V 🛈 ⊹ ♿

Walton Highway 18

National Grid Ref: TF4912

⊯ 🍺 King Of Hearts

Homeleigh Guest House, *Lynn*
Road, Walton Highway, Wisbech,
Cambs, PE14 7DE.
Homeleigh Guest House built
1880s. All rooms ensuite.
Tel: **01945 582356**
Mrs Wiseman.
Fax no: 01945 587006
D: £20.00**S:** £20.00.
Open: All Year
Beds: 2D 2T 2S
Baths: 6 En
🛏 🅿 (6) 🗔 🍴 🗶 🔔 🖾 & V 🛈 ⊹ ♿

Maple Lodge, *Lynn Road, Walton*
Highway, Wisbech, Cambs,
PE14 7QE.
Modern family home on outskirts
of village, overlooking open fields.
Tel: **01945 461430**
D: £18.00-£21.00 **S:** £18.00-£21.00.
Open: All Year
Beds: 2D 1T 1S
Baths: 1 En 1 Sh
🛏 🅿 (5) ⊬ 🗔 🗶 🔔 🖾 V ♿

King's Lynn 19

National Grid Ref: TF6120

The Wildfowler

▲ ***King's Lynn Youth Hostel,*** *Thoresby College, College Lane, King's Lynn, Norfolk, PE30 1JB.*
Actual grid ref: TF616199
Tel: **01553 772461**
Under 18: £6.50 **Adults:** £9.25
Self-catering facilities, Showers, Lounge, Dining room, Drying room, Cycle store, Evening meal if pre-booked, No smoking, Kitchen facilities, Breakfast available, Credit cards accepted
This is the wing of a 500-year-old Chantry college building. It is a ideal base for walking and cycling as well as exploring the many historical and cultural attractions of King's Lynn itself.

The Old Rectory, *33 Goodwins Road, King's Lynn, Norfolk, PE30 5QX.*
Grades: ETC 4 Diamond
Tel: **01553 768544** Faulkner.
D: £21.00-£21.00 **S:** £32.00-£32.00.
Open: All Year
Beds: 2F 2T
Baths: 4 En
(5)
Elegant former rectory. Well-appointed, high quality ensuite accommodation. Guests have freedom of access at all times. Off street parking, storage for cycles, non-smoking, quietly situated, close to centre of historic attractive market town. Well-behaved pets welcome.

Maranatha Havana Guest House, *115 Gaywood Road, King's Lynn, Norfolk, PE30 2PU.*
Friendly family run. Special rates for children, groups catered for.
Grades: ETC 2 Diamond
Tel: **01553 774596**
Mr Bastone.
D: £15.00-£20.00 **S:** £20.00.
Open: All Year
Beds: 2F 2D 3T 2S
Baths: 4 En 2 Sh
(9)

Flints Hotel, *73 Norfolk Street, King's Lynn, Norfolk, PE30 1AD.*
Modern hotel.
Tel: **01553 769400** Mr Flint.
D: £18.00 **S:** £18.00.
Open: All Year
Beds: 1F 1D 1T 1S
(1) (7)

Pay B&Bs by cash or cheque and be prepared to pay up front.

Guanock Hotel, *Southgates, London Road, King's Lynn, Norfolk, PE30 5JG.*
Warm friendly hotel noted for cleanliness and good food. Close to town centre.
Tel: **01553 772959** (also fax no)
Mr Parchment.
D: £18.00-£19.00
S: £21.00-£24.00.
Open: All Year
Beds: 5F 4D 3T 5S
Baths: 5 Sh
(8)

Old Hunstanton 20

National Grid Ref: TF6842

Mariners Inn

Cobbler's Cottage, *3 Wodehouse Road, Old Hunstanton, Hunstanton, Norfolk, PE36 6JD.*
Quietly situated 500 yards from sandy natural beach. Birdwatching at Titchwell, Snettisham Holme.
Tel: **01485 534036**
Ms Poore.
D: £20.00-£27.00
S: £27.00-£32.00.
Open: Feb to Nov
Beds: 1D 2T
Baths: 3 En
(8)

Hunstanton 21

National Grid Ref: TF6740

Golden Lion, Marine Bar, Le Strange Arms, Ancient Mariner, Platters

▲ ***Hunstanton Youth Hostel,*** *15 Avenue Road, Hunstanton, Norfolk, PE36 5BW.*
Actual grid ref: TF674406
Tel: **01485 532061**
Under 18: £6.90
Adults: £10.00
Self-catering facilities, Television, Showers, Wet weather shelter, Lounge, Dining room, Drying room, Cycle store, Evening meal at 7.00pm, Kitchen facilities, Luggage store, Credit cards accepted
Large Victorian house in seaside resort with Blue Flag beach, famous for bird and seal watching and ecology studies.

Peacock House, *28 Park Road, Hunstanton, Norfolk, PE36 5BY.*
A large warm and comfortable Victorian house serving memorable breakfasts.
Grades: ETC 3 Diamond
Tel: **01485 534551**
Mrs Sandercock.
D: £17.50-£24.50
S: £24.00-£30.00.
Open: All Year
Beds: 1F 1T 1D
Baths: 3 En
(5)

Kiama Cottage, *23 Austin Street, Hunstanton, Norfolk, PE36 6AN.*
Grades: ETC 3 Diamond
Tel: **01485 533615**
Mr & Mrs Gardiner.
D: £18.00-£25.00 **S:** £20.00-£25.00.
Open: All year (not Xmas)
Beds: 2F 2D
Baths: 3 En 1 Pr
A warm welcome awaits you at our Victorian-style cottage located in a quiet residential area and ideally situated for visiting Hunstanton attractions and West Norfolk generally. Hosts Neville & Beverley are well travelled and are sensitive to your needs.

The Gables, *28 Austin Street, Hunstanton, PE36 6AW.*
Recently refurbished attractive Edwardian home retaining many original features.
Grades: ETC 4 Diamond, AA 4 Diamond
Tel: **01485 532514** Mrs Bamfield.
D: £17.00-£23.00 .
Open: All Year
Beds: 5F 1D 1T
Baths: 5 En

Rosamaly Guest House, *14 Glebe Avenue, Hunstanton, Norfolk, PE36 6BS.*
Warm, friendly atmosphere. Hearty breakfasts, tasty evening meals. Comfy ensuite bedrooms, quiet, convenient location.
Grades: ETC 3 Diamond
Tel: **01485 534187** Mrs Duff Dick.
D: £18.00-£23.00 **S:** £20.00-£25.00.
Open: All Year (not Xmas)
Beds: 1F 3D 1T 1S
Baths: 5 En

Burleigh Hotel, *7 Cliff Terrace, Hunstanton, Norfolk, PE36 6DY.*
Victorian family-run hotel, close to sea front and gardens.
Grades: ETC 4 Diamond
Tel: **01485 533080** Mr & Mrs Abos
D: £21.00-£25.00 **S:** £23.00-£25.00.
Open: All Year
Beds: 4F 4D 2T 1S
Baths: 9 En 2 Pr
(5) (7)

Sutton House Hotel, *24 Northgate, Hunstanton, Norfolk, PE36 6AP.*
Edwardian house near town/sea.
Tel: **01485 532552** (also fax no)
Mr Emsden.
D: £20.00-£27.00 **S:** £25.00-£25.00.
Open: All Year
Beds: 2F 2D 3T 1S
Baths: 8 En
(1) (5)

D = Price range per person sharing in a double room

Ellinbrook Guest House,
37 Avenue Road, Hunstanton,
Norfolk, PE36 5HW.
Friendly family establishment situated 5 minutes from seafront and shops.
Tel: **01485 532022** Mr & Mrs Vass
D: £15.00-£21.00 **S:** £15.00-£21.00
Open: All Year (not Xmas)
Beds: 2F 2D 1T 1S **Baths:** 1 Sh
🛏 🅿 (5) ⊬ 🗖 🗙 🖢 🛍 🔽 🛇 ♂

Thornham 22

National Grid Ref: TF7343

🍴 🍺 King's Head, The Lifeboat, Titchwell Manor

Orchard House, *Thornham,*
Hunstanton, Norfolk, PE36 6LY.
Tucked away in large garden, centre of conservation village.
Grades: ETC 4 Diamond
Tel: **01485 512259** Mrs Rutland.
D: £22.50-£30.00
S: £35.00-£45.00.
Open: All Year (not Xmas Day)
Beds: 2T 2D **Baths:** 3 En 1 Pr
🛏 (8) 🅿 (6) ⊬ 🗖 🖢 🛍 🔽 ♂

Burnham Market 23

National Grid Ref: TF8342

🍴 🍺 Host Arms

Wood Lodge, *Millwood, Herrings*
Lane, Burnham Market, King's
Lynn, Norfolk, PE31 8DP.
Peaceful, luxurious coastal lodge.
Grades: ETC 4 Daimond
Tel: **01328 730152** Mrs Leftley.
Fax no: 01328 730158
D: £27.50-£30.00 **S:** £35.00-£45.00
Open: All Year (not Xmas)
Beds: 1D 1T
🛏 (8) 🅿 ⊬ 🗖 🛪 🖢 🛍 🔽 ♂

Burnham Overy Staithe 24

National Grid Ref: TF8444

🍴 🍺 The Hero

Domville Guest House, *Glebe*
Lane, Burnham Overy Staithe,
Kings Lynn, Norfolk, PE31 8JQ.
Quietly situated family-run guest house. Home cooking a speciality.
Grades: ETC 3 Diamond
Tel: **01328 738298** (also fax no)
Mrs Smith.
D: £18.00-£23.00
S: £20.00-£25.00.
Open: All Year (not Xmas)
Beds: 2T 3S 2D **Baths:** 4 En
🛏 (6) 🅿 (10) ⊬ 🗖 🗙 🖢 🔽 🛇 ♂

Pay B&Bs by cash or
cheque and be prepared
to pay up front.

Wells-next-the-Sea 25

National Grid Ref: TF9143

🍴 🍺 Crown Hotel, The Edinburgh, Ark Royal, Lifeboat Inn, Three Horseshoes

Greengates, *Stiffkey Road, Wells-next-the-Sea, Norfolk, NR23 1QB.*
Actual grid ref: TF9243
C18th cottage with views over salt marsh to sea.
Tel: **01328 711040** Mrs Jarvis.
D: £19.00-£23.00
S: £20.00-£25.00.
Open: All Year (not Xmas)
Beds: 1D 1T
Baths: 1 En 1 Pr 1 Sh
🅿 (2) ⊬ 🗖 🖢 🛍 🔽 🛇

East House, *East Quay, Wells-next-the-Sea, Norfolk, NR23 1LE.*
Actual grid ref: TF921437
Old house overlooking marsh, creeks and boats to distant sea.
Tel: **01328 710408**
Mrs Scott.
D: £22.50-£22.50
S: £26.00-£26.00.
Open: All Year (not Xmas)
Beds: 2T
Baths: 2 En
🛏 (7) 🅿 (2) 🗖 🖢 🛍 🔽 ♂ 🛇

St Heliers Guest House, *Station Road, Wells-next-the-Sea, Norfolk, NR23 1EA.*
Actual grid ref: TF917436
Central Georgian family house in secluded gardens with excellent breakfasts.
Tel: **01328 710361** (also fax no)
Mrs Kerr.
D: £16.00-£25.00 **S:** £18.00-£30.00.
Open: 10 months
Beds: 1D 1T 1S
Baths: 2 Sh 1 En
🅿 (4) ⊬ 🗖 🖢 🛍 🔽 🛇 ♂

Mill House, *Northfield Lane, Wells-next-the-Sea, Norfolk, NR23 1JZ.*
Mill House: a former mill-owner's house in secluded gardens.
Tel: **01328 710739**
Mr Downey.
D: £17.00
S: £17.50.
Open: All Year
Beds: 1F 3D 3T 2S
Baths: 7 En 2 Pr
🛏 (8) 🅿 (10) 🗖 🖢 🛍 ♿ 🔽 ♂

The Warren, *Warham Road, Wells-next-the-Sea, Norfolk, NR23 1NE.*
Actual grid ref: TF922430
Ideally situated for ornithologists, walkers, cyclists, beach lovers and historians.
Tel: **01328 710273**
Mrs Wickens.
D: £20.00-£20.00
S: £22.00-£25.00.
Open: All Year (not Xmas)
Beds: 1D 1T
Baths: 1 En 1 Pr
🅿 (2) ⊬ 🗖 🖢 🛍 🔽

Please respect
a B&B's wishes
regarding children,
animals & smoking.

Brooklands, *31 Burnt Street, Wells-next-the-Sea, Norfolk, NR23 1HP.*
Charming beamed 250-year-old house. Delightful cottage garden.
Tel: **01328 710768** Mrs Wykes.
D: £16.00-£16.00 **S:** £20.00.
Open: Apr to Oct
Beds: 1F 1D
Baths: 1 Sh
🛏 (7) 🅿 (2) ⊬ 🗖 🛪 🖢 🛍 🔽

Warham 26

National Grid Ref: TF9441

🍴 🍺 Three Horseshoes

The Three Horseshoes / The Old Post Office, *69 Bridge Street, Warham, Wells-next-the-Sea, Norfolk, NR23 1NL.*
Dream country cottage adjoining award-winning village pub.
Tel: **01328 710547** Mr Salmon.
D: £24.00-£26.00 **S:** £24.00-£24.00
Open: All Year (not Xmas)
Beds: 3D 1S
Baths: 1 En 1 Sh
🛏 (14) 🅿 (10) ⊬ 🗖 🛪 🗙 🖢 🛍 🔽 🛇 ♂

Little Walsingham 27

National Grid Ref: TF9337

🍴 🍺 White Horse

St Davids House, *Friday Market, Little Walsingham, Walsingham, Norfolk, NR22 6BY.*
Actual grid ref: TF9437
Tudor house in medieval village; five miles from coast.
Grades: ETC 2 Diamond
Tel: **01328 820633**
Mrs Renshaw.
D: £21.00-£24.00 **S:** £26.00-£30.00
Open: All Year
Beds: 2F 1D 2T
Baths: 2 En 2 Sh
🛏 🅿 🗖 🛪 🗙 🖢 🛍 🔽 🛇 ♂

The Old Bakehouse, *33 High Street, Little Walsingham, Norfolk, NR22 6BZ.*
Restaurant with good food and attractive rooms in historic village.
Tel: **01328 820454**
Mrs Padley.
D: £22.50-£22.50 **S:** £27.50-£27.50
Open: All Year (not Xmas)
Beds: 2D 1T
Baths: 3 En
🛏 🗖 🛪 🗙 🖢 🛍 🔽

Fakenham 28

National Grid Ref: TF9230

Yew Tree House, 2 East View, Hempton, Fakenham, Norfolk, NR21 7LW.
Open spaces, birdwatching area. Close to Sandringham, North Norfolk Coast.
Tel: **01328 851450** Mr Beales.
D: £15.00-£18.00 **S:** £15.00-£18.00.
Open: All Year
Beds: 1F 1D 1T 1S
Baths: 1 Sh
🛏 (1) 🅿 (5) ⌿⌷🏄✗🛒🗑Ⓥ🛆⌿♨

D = Price range per person sharing in a double room

Great Ryburgh 29

National Grid Ref: TF9527

Highfield Farm, Great Ryburgh, Fakenham, Norfolk, NR21 7AL.
Actual grid ref: TF947279
Beautiful large farmhouse, peaceful location, welcoming hosts.
Tel: **01328 829249**
Mrs Savory.
Fax no: 01328 829422
D: £20.00
S: £25.00.
Open: All Year (not Xmas)
Beds: 1D 2T
Baths: 1 En 1 Sh
🛏 (12) 🅿 (8) ⌿⌷✗🛒🗑Ⓥ

S = Price range for a single person in a room

Gateley 30

National Grid Ref: TF9624

Centre Farm, Gateley, Fakenham, Norfolk, NR20 5EF.
Beautiful Georgian farm house set in quiet country village.
Tel: **01328 829618** (also fax no)
Mrs Savory.
D: £20.00-£25.00 .
Open: All Year
Beds: 3T
Baths: 2 Pr
🛏 (8) 🅷🛒Ⓥ

Bringing children with you? Always ask for any special rates.

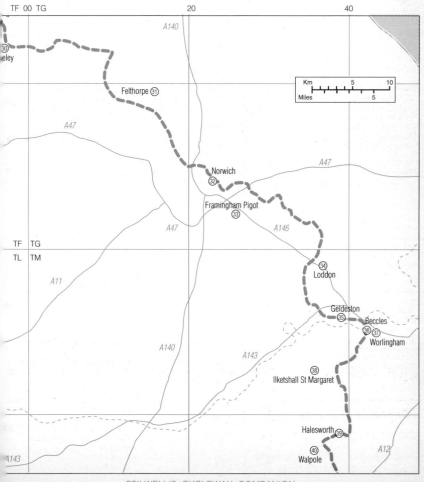

STILWELL'S CYCLEWAY COMPANION

57

Felthorpe 31

National Grid Ref: TG1618

|◎| 🍴 Red Lion, Parson Woodforde, Blacksmiths, Yeast & Feast, Ratcatchers, Marsham Arms, Dog

Spinney Ridge, Hall Lane, Felthorpe, Norwich, NR10 4BX.
Actual grid ref: TG168183
Tel: 01603 754833
Mr & Mrs Thompson.
D: £18.00-£20.00
S: £18.00-£20.00.
Open: All Year (not Xmas)
Beds: 2D 2T 1S
Baths: 2 En 1 Sh
🛇 (1) 🅿 (6) ⅍ 🖵 🛒 🎟 🖾 🗸 ♻
Characterful quiet house in a wooded rural setting with a warm and friendly welcome and service 6 miles north of Norwich off the A1149. Centre for North Norfolk and the Broads, convenient to recommended restaurants. No smoking, no dogs, please.

Lodge Farmhouse, 89 The Street, Felthorpe, Norwich, NR10 4BY.
Actual grid ref: TG170182
Comfortable friendly family house, edge of village location, good breakfast.
Tel: 01603 754896
Mrs Howe.
D: £15.00-£15.00 **S:** £15.00-£15.00.
Open: All Year (not Xmas)
Beds: 1D 1T
Baths: 1 Sh
🛇 🅿 (4) ⅍ 🖵 🛒 🎟 🖾 ⓘ 🗸 ♻

Norwich 32

National Grid Ref: TG2308

|◎| 🍴 Coach & Horses, Pickwick, Black Horse, Tuns, Falcon, Town House

▲ *Norwich Youth Hostel, 112 Turner Road, Norwich, NR2 4HB.*
Actual grid ref: TG213095
Tel: 01603 627647
Under 18: £6.90
Adults: £10.00
Self-catering facilities, Television, Showers, Lounge, Drying room, Cycle store, Parking, Evening meal at 7.00pm, Kitchen facilities, Breakfast available, Credit cards accepted
Just a short distance from the city centre, with its medieval cathedral and churches. From Norwich it is easy to reach the seaside and the Broads.

Please don't camp on *anyone's* land without first obtaining their permission.

Earlham Guest House, 147 Earlham Road, Norwich, NR2 3RG.
Grades: ETC 4 Diamond, AA 4 Diamond
Tel: 01603 454169 (also fax no)
Mr & Mrs Wright.
D: £20.00-£23.00 **S:** £22.00-£25.00.
Open: All Year (not Xmas)
Beds: 1F 3D 1T 3S
Baths: 2 En 2 Sh
🛇 (10) ⅍ 🖵 🛒 🎟 🖾 🗸 ♻
Susan & Derek Wright offer welcoming and friendly hospitality with comfortable modern facilities, close historic Norwich, University and Norfolk Broads. Vegetarian choices, personal keys. Short break rates available 1 Oct - 31 Mar. No smoking throughout. All cards welcome.

Arbor Linden Lodge, Linden House, 557 Earlham Road, Norwich, NR4 7HW.
Grades: ETC 4 Diamond
Tel: 01603 451303 Mr Betts.
Fax no: 01603 250641
D: £20.00-£25.00 **S:** £26.00-£35.00.
Open: All Year
Beds: 1F 1T 3D 1S
Baths: 6 En
🛇 🅿 (10) ⅍ 🖵 🛒 🎟 🖾 ⓘ 🗸 ♻
Family-run for quality and warmth of welcome. Secure parking. free parking near city centre. garden breakfast conservatory. Garden/play area. Convenient rivers, broads, UEA, Norwich and BUPA hospitals, Sports Park Olympic Centre, bus and fast food takeaway. refrigerator/microwave in guest lounge.

Beaufort Lodge, 62 Earlham Road, Norwich, NR2 3DF.
Grades: AA 4 Diamond
Tel: 01603 627928 (also fax no)
Mr Dobbins.
D: £25.00-£25.00 **S:** £35.00-£40.00.
Open: All Year (not Xmas/New Year)
Beds: 3D 1S
Baths: 3 En 1 Pr
🅿 ⅍ 🖵 🛒 🎟 🖾 ♻
Spacious Victorian house with ample parking. Within easy walking distance of city centre. A short drive away are the Broads and the Coastal towns of Cromer and Sheringham. Inland there are many historic and interesting houses to visit including Sandringham.

Trebeigh House, 16 Brabazon Road, Hellesdon, Norwich, NR6 6SY.
Warm welcome to quiet friendly house convenient for city, country, airport.
Tel: 01603 429056
Mrs Jope.
Fax no: 01603 414247
D: £18.00-£19.00 **S:** £18.00-£20.00.
Open: All Year (not Xmas)
Beds: 1D 1T
Baths: 1 Sh
🛇 🅿 (3) ⅍ 🖵 🛒 🎟 🖾 ⓘ

Rosedale, 145 Earlham Road, Norwich, NR2 3RG.
Comfortable, family-run guest house. Easy access to city, coast & university.
Tel: 01603 453743
Mrs Curtis.
Fax no: 01603 259887
D: £19.00-£40.00 **S:** £18.00-£25.00.
Open: All Year (not Xmas)
Beds: 2F 2T 2S **Baths:** 2 Sh
🛇 (4) ⅍ 🖵 🛒 🎟 🖾

Pine Lodge, 518 Earlham Road, Norwich, NR4 7HR.
Distinctive, cheerful and comfortable accommodation between university and the city centre.
Tel: 01603 504834
Mr & Mrs Tovell.
D: £18.00-£20.00 **S:** £25.00-£25.00.
Open: All Year
🅿 🖵 🛒 🎟 🖾 ⓘ 🗸 ♻

Harvey House Guest House, 50 Harvey Lane, Norwich, NR7 0AQ.
Comfy, no smoking with easy access to city and Broads.
Grades: ETC 3 Diamond
Tel: 01603 436575 (also fax no)
Pritchard.
D: £18.00-£21.00 **S:** £18.00-£25.00.
Open: All Year
Beds: 1F 1D 2T 1S
Baths: 3 En 1 Pr 1 Sh
🛇 (3) 🅿 (6) ⅍ 🖵 🛒 🎟 🖾

Butterfield Hotel, 4 Stracey Road, Norwich, NR1 1EZ.
We offer warm, friendly welcome to ensure your stay is a happy one.
Tel: 01603 661008 Ackhe Kamal.
D: £20.00-£35.00 **S:** £20.00-£35.00
Open: All Year
Beds: 4F 4T 6S 2D
Baths: 2 En
🛇 🅿 (5) 🖵 🛏 ✗ 🛒 🎟 ⅋ ♻

Framingham Pigot 33

National Grid Ref: TG2703

|◎| 🍴 The Gull

The Old Rectory, Rectory Lane, Framingham Pigot, Norwich, NR14 7QQ.
Friendly comfortable Victorian Rectory. Large garden. 10 mins Norwich centre.
Tel: 01508 493082 Mrs Thurman.
D: £21.00-£21.00 **S:** £21.00-£21.00
Open: All Year (not Xmas)
Beds: 1F 1D 1T
Baths: 2 En 1 Sh
🛇 🅿 (6) ⅍ 🖵 🛒 🎟 🖾 🗸 ♻

Planning a longer stay? Always ask for any special rates.

Loddon 34

National Grid Ref: TM3698

¶ Kings Head

Poplar Farm, *Sisland, Loddon, Norwich, NR14 6EF.*
Working farm pigs, cows. Quiet, rural setting near Broads.
Tel: **01508 520706** Mrs Hemmant.
D: £17.00-£25.00 **S:** £18.00-£25.00.
Open: All Year (not Xmas)
Beds: 1F 1D 1T **Baths:** 1 En 1 Pr
🛏 🅿 (4) ⅍ 🗗 ✕ 🕭 🎟 🖾

Geldeston 35

National Grid Ref: TM3992

¶ The Wherry Inn

Archway Cottage, *Geldeston, Beccles, Suffolk, NR34 0LB.*
Clean comfortable cottage with a warm welcome to all our guests.
Tel: **01508 518056** Mrs Dean.
D: £19.00-£19.00 **S:** £25.00-£28.00.
Open: All Year
Beds: 2D
Baths: 1 Sh
🛏 (2) 🅿 (2) ⅍ 🗗 🕭 🎟 🖾 🛡 🕇 ⚴

Beccles 36

National Grid Ref: TM4289

¶ Bear & Bells

Catherine House, *2 Ringsfield Road, Beccles, Suffolk, NR34 9PQ.*
Well furnished family home, excellent facilities, view over Waveney Valley.
Grades: ETC 4 Diamond
Tel: **01502 716428** (also fax no)
Mrs Renilson.
D: £20.00 **S:** £20.00.
Open: All Year
Beds: 3D
Baths: 2 En 1 Pr
🅿 (4) 🗗 🕭 🎟 🖾 🕇 ⚴

Worlingham 37

National Grid Ref: TM4490

Colville Arms Motel, *Lowestoft Road, Worligham, Beccles, Suffolk, NR34 7EF.*
Village location close to Lowestoft, Norwich, Yarmouth, Broads, golf and fishing.
Tel: **01502 712571** (also fax no)
Brooks.
D: £22.50-£27.50 **S:** £32.50-£40.00.
Open: All Year
Beds: 4T 5D 2S
Baths: 11 En
🗗 ✕ 🕭 🎟 🖾 🛡

= Price range per person
sharing in a double room

Ilketshall St Margaret 38

National Grid Ref: TM3585

¶ Rumburgh Buck

Shoo-Devil Farmhouse, *Ilketshall St Margaret, Bungay, Suffolk, NR35 1QU.*
Actual grid ref: TM351858
Enchanting thatched C16th farm house in secluded garden near St. Peters Brewery.
Tel: **01986 781303** (also fax no)
Mrs Lewis.
D: £18.50-£20.00
S: £20.00-£25.00.
Open: All Year (not Xmas)
Beds: 1D 1T
Baths: 2 En
🅿 (4) ⅍ 🗗 ✕ 🕭 🎟 🖾 🕇 ⚴

Halesworth 39

National Grid Ref: TM3877

¶ White Hart, Rumburgh Buck, Huntsman & Hound

Fen Way, *School Lane, Halesworth, Suffolk, IP19 8BW.*
Fen Way is set in its own 7 acres of meadowland.
Tel: **01986 873574** Mrs George.
D: £18.00-£21.00 **S:** £20.00-£25.00.
Open: All Year
Beds: 2D 1T
Baths: 1 En 1 Sh
🛏 (7) 🅿 (6) ⅍ 🗗 ✕ 🕭 🎟 🖾 🕇 ⚴

All rates are subject to alteration at the owners' discretion.

Rumburgh Farm, *Halesworth, Suffolk, IP19 0RU.*
Attractive C17th timber framed farmhouse on a mixed enterprise farm.
Grades: ETC 3 Diamond
Tel: **01986 781351** (also fax no)
D: £16.50-£19.00 **S:** £21.00-£25.00.
Open: All Year (not Xmas)
Beds: 1F 1D
Baths: 2 En
🛏 🅿 (3) ⅍ 🗗 🕭 🎟 🖾 🕇 ⚴

Walpole 40

National Grid Ref: TM3674

¶ Queen's Head

The Old Vicarage, *Walpole, Halesworth, Suffolk, IP19 9AR.*
Spacious bedrooms, lovely views from every room.
Tel: **01986 784295** Mr Calver.
D: £20.00-£25.00 **S:** £25.00-£30.00.
Open: All Year
Beds: 1T 1D **Baths:** 2 Pr
🛏 🅿 (6) 🗗 🕇 🕭 🎟 🖾 ⚴

Darsham 41

National Grid Ref: TM4169

¶ The Fox

White House Farm, *Main Road, Darsham, Saxmundham, Suffolk, IP17 3PP.*
Period farmhouse. Extensive gardens. Close Minsmere/ Dunwich/Southwold. All facilities.
Grades: ETC 3 Diamond
Tel: **01728 668632** Mrs Newman.
D: £20.00-£27.50 **S:** £25.00-£35.00.
Open: All Year
Beds: 1T 2D
Baths: 1 En 1 Sh
🛏 (5) 🅿 (20) ⅍ 🗗 🕭 🎟 🖾 🕇 ⚴

Halesworth to Dedham Vale

The way through the gently sloping rich farmland of Suffolk brings you to the market town of **Halesworth** and then the village of Peasenhall before you reach **Framlingham,** whose twelfth-century castle has a continuous curtain wall, from which there are fine views of the small town. From here it's on to the attractive town of **Woodbridge**, before you pass through the northwestern outskirts of **Ipswich**, Suffolk's county town. Ipswich Museum contains replicas of the Roman Mildenhall Treasure and the Sutton Hoo ship burial, both important local archaeological finds (the originals are in the British Museum in London), local studies exhibitions and anthropological galleries on Africa, Asia and the Americas. Christchurch Mansion is a Tudor house with substantial collections of Gainsborough and Constable, both local painters. The town's other celebrated Tudor building is the 'ancient house', faced with an outstanding seventeenth-century example of pargeting (sculpted plasterwork). Leaving town to the west, you go on to Whatfield and turn south through **Hadleigh**, before reaching **Stratford St Mary** in Constable's **Dedham Vale.**

Priory Farm, Priory Lane, Darsham, Saxmundham, Suffolk, IP17 3QD.
Grades: ETC 3 Diamond
Tel: **01728 668459** (also fax no)
Mrs Bloomfield.
D: £22.50-£30.00 **S:** £25.00-£35.00.
Open: Easter to Oct
Beds: 1D 1T **Baths:** 2 Pr
🛏 (12) 🅿 (2) ⊬ ⊡ 🔥 🛄 ⓥ
Bed and breakfast in comfortable C17th farmhouse situated in peaceful countryside. Ideal base for exploring the Suffolk coast. All rooms with private facilities. Breakfast made with quality local specialities. Excellent pubs and restaurants nearby. Sorry no pets. Cycle hire available.

All cycleways are popular: you are well-advised to book ahead

Pay B&Bs by cash or cheque and be prepared to pay up front.

Sibton 42

National Grid Ref: TM3669

🍴 🍺 The Griffin, Queen's Head

Park Farm, Sibton, Saxmundham, Suffolk, IP17 2LZ.
Enjoy a friendly farmhouse welcome with your every comfort assured.
Grades: ETC 4 Diamond
Tel: **01728 668324**
Gray.
Fax no: 01728 668564
D: £19.00-£22.00
S: £19.00-£22.00.
Open: All Year (not Xmas)
Beds: 1D 2T
Baths: 2 En 1 Pr
🅿 (6) ⊬ ⊡ ✗ 🔥 🛄 ⓥ ∞

Sibton White Horse, Halesworth Road, Sibton, Saxmundham, Suffolk, IP17 2JJ.
C16th inn. 3 acres secluded grounds. 8 rooms with private facilities.
Tel: **01728 660337**
Mr Dyke.
D: £22.50-£22.50
S: £27.00-£27.00.
Open: All Year
Beds: 3D 2T 3S
Baths: 7 En 1 Sh
🛏 🅿 🔥 ✗ 🔥 🛄 ♿ ⓥ ∎

Order your packed lunches the *evening before* you need them.
Not at breakfast!

ransford 43

ational Grid Ref: TM3164

White Horse, The Crown

*igh House Farm, Cransford,
ear Framlingham, Woodbridge,
uffolk, IP13 9PD.*
rades: ETC 3 Diamond
el: 01728 663461 Mrs Kindred.
ax no: 01728 663409
: £20.00 **S:** £25.00-£30.00.
pen: All Year
eds: 1F 1D
aths: 1 En 1 Pr
: P (4) ⌨ ⊀ ⚿ Ⅲ V ⚡ ⌗
eautiful oak-beamed C15th farm-
ouse on family farm. Spacious and
omfortable accommodation. Large
mily room with private bathroom.
ouble room ensuite. Inglenook
replaces. Attractive gardens.
uietly set. Ideal location to
plore the heart of rural Suffolk
d the Heritage coast. Children
elcome.

ramlingham 44

ational Grid Ref: TM2863

The Crown, Queen's Head

*immens Pightle, Dennington
ad, Framlingham, Woodbridge,
ffolk, IP13 9JT.*
rades: ETC 3 Diamond
l: 01728 724036 Mrs Collett.
£21.00-£22.00 **S:** £23.00-£25.00.
pen: Easter to Nov
ds: 2D 1T
ths: 1 Sh
(8) P (5) ⚿ ⌨ ⚁ Ⅲ V
omfortable family home set in an
re of landscaped garden, over-
oking fields. Within a mile of the
toric castle town of
amlingham with its famous castle
d church. Ground floor rooms
th wash basins. Local cured
con & home preserves. Guests'
inge with TV.

*undary Farm, off Saxmundham
ad, Framlingham, Woodbridge,
folk, IP13 9NU.*
7th farmhouse, open country-
e, ideal touring base. Brochure
request.
: 01728 723401
s Cook.
x no: 01728 723877
£18.00-£25.00 **S:** £20.00-£25.00.
en: All Year (not Xmas)
ds: 2D 1T
ths: 1 En 1 Sh
P (4) ⌨ ✕ ⚁ Ⅲ V ⚡ ⌗

Dallinghoo 45

National Grid Ref: TM2655

Three Horseshoes

*Old Rectory, Dallinghoo,
Woodbridge, Suffolk, IP13 0LA.*
Actual grid ref: TM263551
Rare, restful, rural retreat, relaxing,
remedial, regularly revisited, room
service.
Grades: ETC 3 Diamond
Tel: **01473 737700** Mrs Quinlan.
D: £16.00-£18.00 .
Open: All Year (not Xmas)
Beds: 1D 1T
Baths: 1 Pr 1 Sh
⚆ P (6) ⚿ Ⅲ ⚡ ⌗

Bredfield 46

National Grid Ref: TM2652

Wilford Bridge Inn

*Moat Farmhouse, Dallinghoo
Road, Bredfield, Woodbridge,
Suffolk, IP13 6BD.*
Grades: ETC 3 Diamond
Tel: **01473 737475** Mrs Downing.
D: £17.00-£17.00 **S:** £17.00-£17.00.
Open: Mar to Oct
Beds: 1D 1T
Baths: 1 Sh
⚆ (1) P (4) ⚿ ⌨ ⚁ Ⅲ V ⚡ ⌗
Ideal family home accommodation.
Reductions for children. Self con-
tained on ground floor, own sit-
ting/TV room. Extensive gardens
1 mile from A12 close to heritage
coast Ipswich 11 miles Woodbridge
3 miles and Aldeburgh Festival.

*Moat Barn, Bredfield, Woodbridge,
Suffolk, IP13 6BD.*
Converted barn with original
beams. Family atmosphere and
tranquil surroundings.
Grades: ETC 3 Diamond
Tel: **01473 737520** (also fax no)
Mr Allen.
D: £19.50-£24.50
S: £29.00-£34.00.
Open: All Year
Beds: 1F 1D 1T
Baths: 1 En 1 Sh
⚆ P (10) ⚿ ⌨ ⚁ Ⅲ V ⚡ ⌗

Woodbridge 47

National Grid Ref: TM2649

Coach & Horses

*Dehen Lodge, Melton Road,
Woodbridge, Suffolk, IP12 1NH.*
Victorian house, large garden,
stream, tennis court, riverside walk.
Tidemill and town.
Grades: ETC 3 Diamond
Tel: **01394 382740**
Mrs Schlee.
D: £18.00-£20.00
S: £18.00-£20.00.
Open: All Year
Beds: 1D 1T 2S
Baths: 2 Sh
⚆ P (4) ⚿ ⌨ ⊀ ⚁ Ⅲ V ⚡ ⌗

*Grove House Hotel, 39 Grove
Road, Woodbridge, Suffolk,
IP12 4LG.*
A warm welcome awaits everyone
at our newly extended and
renovated hotel.
Tel: **01394 382202**
D: £25.00-£27.50
S: £25.00-£37.50.
Open: All Year
Beds: 1F 5D 3T 3S
Baths: 11 En 1 Sh
⚆ P (15) ⌨ ⊀ ✕ ⚁ Ⅲ ♿ V ⚡ ⌗

Colchester to Harwich

Crossing the River Stour
into Essex, continue into
Colchester, the oldest town
in Britain. *Camulodunum* was
the first capital of Roman
Britain, and there are remains
of the Roman walls. The town
was sacked by Queen
Boudicca ('Boadicea') of the
Iceni tribe after the Romans
killed her husband and raped
her daughters. The honey-
coloured Norman castle
keep, the biggest in Europe,
was built on the foundations
of a Roman temple, and now
houses a museum with
Roman mosaics and statues.
There is a museum of social
history in the Saxon Holy
Trinity Church. Also worth
visiting is the Dutch Quarter,
established by Flemish
refugee weavers in the
sixteenth century, which has
tall Dutch-style houses. The
route out of town goes to
Wivenhoe, from where the
final stretch leads to
Harwich. The Harwich
Redoubt, a circular fort currently undergoing restoration,
was built against a feared
invasion by Napoleon.

Playford 48

National Grid Ref: TM2147

🍴 🍺 Admiral's Head, Falcon Inn

Glenham, *Hill Farm Road, Playford, Ipswich, Suffolk, IP6 9DU.*
Actual grid ref: TM215478
Situated in the Fynn valley. Warm welcome.
Grades: ETC 3 Diamond
Tel: **01473 624939**
Mr & Mrs Booker.
D: £16.00-£25.00
S: £16.00-£20.00.
Open: All Year (not Xmas)
Beds: 1F 1T 1S
Baths: 1 Pr 1 Sh
🛇 🅿 (3) 🗲 🗖 🛏 🖿 🕮 🖖 🚲

Ipswich 49

National Grid Ref: TM1644

🍴 🍺 Royal George, The Westerfield, The Swan, The Greyhound, The Ram, The Railway, Beagle Inn, Talk of the Town

Redholme, *52 Ivry Street, Ipswich, IP1 3QP.*
Grades: ETC 4 Diamond
Tel: **01473 250018** (also fax no)
Mr & Mrs McNeil.
D: £20.25-£24.00 **S:** £25.20-£31.00.
Open: All Year
Beds: 1F 2D 2T 1S
Baths: 5 En 1 Pr
🛇 🅿 (5) 🗲 🗖 🗙 🕮 🖿 🕮 🖖 🖾 🖖 🚲
Elegant Victorian house in large well maintained garden in quiet conservation area. 10 minutes' walk from town centre near Christchurch Park. Spacious bedrooms with complete bathrooms, we offer comfort in a friendly and helpful atmosphere. Good centre for visiting Suffolk.

Craigerne, *Cauldwell Avenue, Ipswich, Suffolk, IP4 4DZ.*
Large Victorian house, 3/4 acre pretty gardens. Friendly welcome.
Tel: **01473 714061** Mrs Krotunas.
D: £18.00**S:** £18.00-£26.00.
Open: All Year (not Xmas)
Beds: 1D 1T 2S
Baths: 2 En 2 Sh
🅿 (6) 🗖 🕮 🕮 🖾

Maple House, *114 Westerfield Road, Ipswich, Suffolk, IP4 2XW.*
Attractive house one mile to town centre; close to park.
Tel: **01473 253797**
Mrs Seal.
D: £25.00-£25.00 **S:** £15.00-£15.00.
Open: All Year (not Xmas)
Beds: 2D 2S
Baths: 2 En 1 Sh
🛇 🅿 (3) 🗲 🗖 🛏 🕮 🖿 🕮 🖾 🚲

Cliffden Guest House, *21 London Road, Ipswich, Suffolk, IP1 2EZ.*
Close to town centre. Full Sky TV. Family-run.
Tel: **01473 252689** Mr Billington.
Fax no: 01473 252685
D: £20.00-£30.00 **S:** £20.00-£30.00.
Open: All Year
Beds: 3F 1D 3T 8S
Baths: 7 Pr 3 Sh
🛇 🅿 (5) 🗖 🛏 🗙 🕮 🖿 🕮 🖾 🖖 🚲

Stelvio Guest House, *Crane Hill, London Road, Ipswich, Suffolk, IP2 0SS.*
Red brick Edwardian house close to A12, A14 junction.
Tel: **01473 602982**
Mr & Mrs Patrick.
D: £20.00-£25.00 **S:** £21.00-£25.00.
Open: All Year
Beds: 1F 1T 1S
Baths: 2 En 1 Pr
🛇 🅿 (10) 🗲 🗖 🖿 🕮 🖾 🖖

Sidegate Guest House, *121 Sidegate Lane, Ipswich, IP4 4JB.*
High quality ensuite rooms in beautiful house and gardens, family run.
Tel: **01473 728714**
Mr & Mrs Marriott.
Fax no: 01473 728714 (phone first)
D: £20.00-£25.00 **S:** £27.00-£30.00.
Open: All Year
Beds: 1F 2D 1T
Baths: 4 En
🛇 🅿 (5) 🗲 🗖 🛏 🕮 🖿 🕮 🖖 🖾 🖖 🚲

Kersey 50

National Grid Ref: TM0044

🍴 🍺 The Bell

Red House Farm, *Kersey, Ipswich, Suffolk, IP7 6EY.*
Comfortable farmhouse (c.1840).
Tel: **01787 210245**
Mrs Alleston.
D: £18.00
S: £20.00.
Open: All Year
Beds: 1D 1T
Baths: 1 Pr 1 Sh
🅿 (4) 🗖 🛏 🗙 🕮 🖿 🕮 🖾

Holton St Mary 51

National Grid Ref: TM0636

🍴 🍺 King's Head, The Angel

Stratford House, *Holton St Mary, Colchester, Essex, CO7 6NT.*
Luxury accommodation in Constable country; easy access for touring Suffolk & Essex.
Grades: ETC 4 Diamond
Tel: **01206 298246** (also fax no)
Mrs Selleck.
D: £20.00-£20.00
S: £20.00-£20.00.
Open: All Year (not Xmas)
Beds: 1D 1T 1S
Baths: 1 Sh
🛇 (10) 🅿 (10) 🗲 🗖 🖿 🕮 🖾 🖖 🚲

Dedham 52

National Grid Ref: TM0533

🍴 🍺 Marlborough Head

Mays Barn Farm, *Mays Lane, Dedham, Colchester, Essex, CO7 6EW.*
Actual grid ref: TM0531
A comfortable well-furnished old house with wonderful views of Dedham Vale.
Grades: ETC 4 Diamond
Tel: **01206 323191**
Mrs Freeman.
D: £20.00-£22.00
S: £25.00-£30.00.
Open: All Year
Beds: 1D 1T
Baths: 1 En 1 Pr
🛇 (12) 🅿 (3) 🗲 🗖 🖿 🕮 🖾 🚲

Langham 5

National Grid Ref: TM0233

🍴 🍺 Shepherd & Dog

Oak Apple Farm, *Greyhound Hill, Langham, Colchester, Essex, CO4 5QF.*
Actual grid ref: TM023320
Comfortable farmhouse tastefully decorated with large attractive garden.
Grades: ETC 4 Diamond
Tel: **01206 272234**
Mrs Helliwell.
D: £22.00 **S:** £22.00.
Open: All Year (not Xmas)
Beds: 2T 1S
Baths: 1 Sh
🛇 🅿 (6) 🗖 🖿 🕮 🖾 🖖 🚲

Colchester 5

National Grid Ref: TL9925

🍴 🍺 Forresters, George, Siege House, Red Li, Roverstye, Peveril Hotel

Salisbury Hotel, *112 Butt Road, Colchester, Essex, CO3 3DL.*
Grades: AA 2 Diamond
Tel: **01206 508508**
Fax no: 01206 797265
D: £25.00-£35.00.
S: £30.00-£40.00.
Open: All Year
Beds: 2F 4T 3D 3S
Baths: All En
🛇 🅿 🗖 🗙 🖿 🕮 🖾 🖖
Situated in the historical garrison town of Colchester and within ea reach of 3 cathedral cities. Despi being in the centre of town this p has a relaxed and informal atmosphere. The in-house bar an restaurant serve delicious and innovative meals

D = Price range per person sharing in a double room

S = Price range for a sing person in a room

St John's Guest House,
330 Ipswich Road, Colchester,
Essex, CO4 4ET.
Well situated close to town, conve-
nient for A12 and A120 Harwich.
Tel: **01206 852288** Mrs Knight.
D: £20.00-£25.00 **S:** £26.00-£45.00.
Open: All Year
Beds: 2F 2D 2T 2S
Baths: 5 En 3 Sh
🛏 🅿 (10) ⏰ 🖵 ⚲ 🔥 🛏 ▦ 🆅 ♿

11a Lincoln Way, *Colchester,*
Essex, CO1 2RL.
Friendly, comfortable modern
house in quiet residential area, five
minutes' walk from town centre.
Tel: **01206 867192**
Mrs Edwards.
Fax no: 01206 799993
D: £18.00-£20.00
S: £18.00-£22.00.
Open: All Year
Beds: 1T 1S **Baths:** 1 Sh
🛏 (4) 🅿 (1) ⏰ 🖵 ⚲ 🗡 🔥 🛏 ▦ 🆅 ♿

Peveril Hotel, *51 North Hill,*
Colchester, Essex, CO1 1PY.
Town centre holiday accommoda-
tion. Superb food, near castle.
Tel: **01206 574001** (also fax no)
D: £27.00-£45.00
S: £27.00-£45.00.
Open: All Year (not Xmas)
Beds: 4F 6D 2T 5S
Baths: 6 En 4 Sh
🛏 🅿 (10) 🖵 ⚲ 🗡 🔥 🛏 ▦ 🆅 ♿

8 Broadmead Road, *Parsons*
Heath, Colchester, Essex, CO4 3HB.
Friendly family home, quiet resi-
dential area. 10 mins bus/car from
town centre.
Tel: **01206 861818** (also fax no)
Mr & Mrs Smith.
D: £18.50-£18.50 **S:** £25.00-£25.00.
Open: All Year
Beds: 1D **Baths:** 1 Sh
🅿 ⏰ 🖵 🗡 🔥 ▦ 🆅

Wivenhoe 55

National Grid Ref: TM0421

🍴 🍺 William Boosey, Black Buoy Pub

2 Alma Street, *Wivenhoe,*
Colchester, Essex, CO7 9DL.
Grade II Listed early Victorian
house, close to River Colne.
Tel: **01245 380705** Mrs Tritton.
D: £21.00-£22.50 **S:** £21.50-£23.00.
Open: All Year (not Xmas)
Beds: 1T 1S **Baths:** 1 Sh
🛏 (9) 🅿 (4) 🖵 🗡 🔥 ▦ 🆅 🛡 ♿

Little Bentley 56

National Grid Ref: TM1125

🍴 🍺 Bricklayers Arms

Bentley Manor, *Little Bentley,*
Colchester, Essex, CO7 8SE.
C15th manor house, close to
Colchester, 15 mins port of
Harwich.
Tel: **01206 250622** Mrs Dyson.
Fax no: 01206 251820
D: £20.00-£22.00 **S:** £24.00-£26.00.
Open: All Year
Beds: 1F 1S 1T **Baths:** 2 En
🛏 🅿 ⏰ 🖵 🔥 ▦ 🆅 ♿

Wix 57

National Grid Ref: TM1628

🍴 🍺 Village Maid

Dairy House Farm, *Bradfield*
Road, Wix, Manningtree, Essex,
CO11 2SR.
Spacious quality, rural accommoda-
tion. A really relaxing place to stay.
Grades: ETC 4 Diamond, Gold
Tel: **01255 870322** Mrs Whitworth.
Fax no: 01255 870186
D: £18.50-£20.00 **S:** £26.00-£26.00.
Open: All Year (not Xmas)
Beds: 1D 2T **Baths:** 2 En 1 Pr
🛏 (12) 🅿 (4) 🖵 🔥 ▦ 🆅 🛡 ♿

Dovercourt 58

National Grid Ref: TM2531

🍴 🍺 Royal Oak Inn

Dudley Guest House, *34 Cliff*
Road, Dovercourt, Harwich, Essex,
CO12 3PP.
Family-run Victorian house.
Railway/buses short walk. Pubs,
restaurants, shops, banks close by.
Grades: ETC 2 Diamond
Tel: **01255 504927** Mr Rackham.
D: £14.00-£18.00 **S:** £18.00-£22.00.
Open: All Year
Beds: 1F 1D 1T 1S
Baths: 1 En 2 Sh
🛏 🅿 (4) ⏰ 🖵 🔥 ▦ 🆅 ♿

Harwich 59

National Grid Ref: TM2431

🍴 🍺 The Royal Oak

Tudor Rose, *124 Fronks Road,*
Dovercourt, Harwich, CO12 4EQ.
Harwich international port.
Seafront, Railway 5 minutes.
London 1 hour.
Tel: **01255 552398**
D: £17.50-£17.50 **S:** £20.00-£30.00.
Open: May to Aug
🛏 🅿 (2) ⏰ 🖵 🔥 ▦ 🆅 ♿

Order your
packed lunches the
evening before you
need them.
Not at breakfast!

Kingfisher Cycle Trail

The **Kingfisher Cycle Trail** is a new long-distance cycleway through Ireland's beautiful border lakelands, where the kingfisher is king. It straddles the Irish Border, running mainly through Fermanagh and Leitrim but with briefer forays into Cavan, Monaghan, Donegal and Tyrone. It has been developed primarily by Leitrim County Council in the Republic of Ireland and Fermanagh District Council in Northern Ireland, with assistance from Sustrans in Britain. The northern section forms part of the UK's National Cycle Network; the route as a whole is the first long distance cyleway in Ireland and the first link in a proposed All Ireland Cycle Network. The total length is 280 miles, and the route is signposted by a brown direction sign bearing a cycle silhouette and the image of a kingfisher, fish in bill.

The route is set out in a figure of eight. The northern circle takes you from **Enniskillen** through Fermanagh's south western corner to the shores of **Loch Melvin**, then north to **Belleek** and around the north bank of **Lower Lough Erne** through **Pettigo**, **Kesh** and the **Castle Archdale Forest** to **Irvinestown** and back to Enniskillen. The southern circle starts in **Carrick-on-Shannon** and takes you through Leitrim village and **Drumshanbo** past the shores of **Loch Allen**, and below the Cuilcagh Mountains to Derrylin before crossing **Upper Lough Erne** by ferry and continuing through Newtownbutler to **Clones**, County Monaghan, at the eastern extremity of the route. From here you head west through Cavan to **Belturbet** and **Ballyconnel** before you reach **Ballinamore** in County Leitrim and return to Carrick-on-Shannon. The two circles overlap in the Fermanagh countryside, through Florencecourt Forest and Marlbank National Nature Reserve.

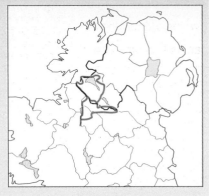

The indispensable **official route map and guide** for the route is available from Sustrans, 35 King Street, Bristol BS1 4DZ, tel 0117-926 8893, fax 0117-929 4173, @ £5.99 (+ £2.00 p&p). The Kingfisher Cycle Trail Holiday Guide, with information on organised cycle tours of varying lengths around the trail, is available free of charge from the Kingfisher Cycle Trail Office, Tourist Information Centre, Wellington Road, Enniskillen, Co Fermanagh BT74 7EF, tel 028 6632 0121, fax 028 6632 5511, email pat@cycleireland.com or visit them on the internet at www.cycleireland.com

Maps: 1:50,000 Irish OS Discovery/ OSNI Discoverer series: 12, 17, 26, 27, 33 (both ranges use the same system of serial numbers – some border country maps are available in both)

Transport links: Carrick-on-Shannon can be reached by rail from Dublin. Enniskillen can be reached by bus from Belfast (Ulsterbus) or from Dublin (Bus Eireann), both of which can carry bicycles in the luggage boot.

Enniskillen   1

National Grid Ref: H2344

|≡| ⊲ Horseshoe, Manor House, Inishclare, Mulligan's, Crow's Nest, Mulligan's, Franco's, Saddler's

Belmore Court Motel, *Tempo Road, Enniskillen, Co Fermanagh,* BT74 6HX.
Situated in the heart of the beautiful Fermanagh Lakelands.
Tel: **028 6632 6633** Mr McCartney.
Fax no: 028 6632 6362
D: £22.50-£27.50 .
Open: All Year (not Xmas)
Beds: 11F 13D 6T **Baths:** 30 En
⛟ 🅿 (30) 🖵 🏠 ✕ 🛒 Ⅲ. & Ⅴ ♣⊚

Drumcoo House,
32 Cherryville, Cornagrade Road, Enniskillen, Co Fermanagh, BT74 4FY.
Actual grid ref: H237458
Family-run B&B in Enniskillen, central to beautiful Lakeland county.
Tel: **028 6632 6672** Mrs Farrell.
D: £17.00-£19.00 **S:** £19.00-£24.00.
Open: All Year (not Xmas)
Beds: 1F 1D 1T 1S
Baths: 3 En 1 Sh
⛟ 🅿 (10) 🖵 🛒 Ⅲ. Ⅴ 🛅 ♣ ⊀ ⊚

D = Price range per person
sharing in a double room

S = Price range for a single
person in a room

Mountview Guest House,
61 Irvinestown Road, Enniskillen, Co Fermanagh, BT74 6DN.
Victorian house, large ensuite. Half mile to town. Sky TV, snooker room. Tel: **028 6632 3147**
Fax no: 028 6632 9611
D: £20.00-£21.00 **S:** £25.00-£30.00.
Open: All Year (not Xmas)
Beds: 3T
Baths: 3 En
⛟ 🅿 (6) 🖵 ✕ 🛒 Ⅲ. Ⅴ

Please respect a B&B's wishes regarding children, animals & smoking.

Abbeyville, *1 Willoughby Court, Portora, Enniskillen, Co Fermanagh, BT74 7EX.*
Modern B&B, convenient to National Trust properties, leisure facilities and Marble Arch Caves.
Tel: **028 6632 7033** Mrs McMahon
D: £17.00-£20.00 .
Open: All Year (not Xmas)
Beds: 2T 1D **Baths:** 3 En
🛏 🅿 (6) ⅍⬛ 🖳 ⬛ 🖳 Ⓥ 🛉

Tamlaght   2

National Grid Ref: H2741

🍴 🍺 Mulligan's

Dromard House, *Tamlaght, Enniskillen, Co Fermanagh, BT74 4HR.*
Award-winning B&B beautifully situated with woodland walk to lake shore.
Tel: **028 6638 7250** Mrs Weir.
D: £17.50-£17.50 **S:** £20.00-£20.00.
Open: All Year (not Xmas)
Beds: 1F 2D 1T 0S
Baths: 4 En 0 Pr 0 Sh
🛏 (8) 🅿 (4) ⅍⬛ 🐾 🖳 ⬛ Ⓥ

Enniskillen, *Inis Ceithleann*, means 'the island of Kathleen', the wife of Balor, the Celtic king who once took refuge from his enemies on the island upon which stands the town. Here you can find the Watergate, a seventeenth-century construction with Scottish characteristics, built by William Cole on the site of the old Maguire Castle. The building hosts a Heritage Centre, which contains exhibitions on the history and natural history of the area; and for military enthusiasts, the Regimental Museum of the Royal Inniskilling Fusiliers, boasting a wealth of paraphernalia including the bugle that sounded the charge at the Somme in 1916. Castle Coole is a late eighteenth-century Palladian house built in Portland stone by James Wyatt, with original plasterwork decoration intact; set in landscaped parkland with oak trees. The town's old buttermarket has been renovated to house a craft centre, where you can see craftspeople at work on vases, ceramics and Celtic jewellery, which are on sale in the shop.

Florencecourt   3

National Grid Ref: H1734

Tullyhona House, *59 Marble Arch Road, Florencecourt, Enniskillen, Co Fermanagh, BT92 1DE.*
Actual grid ref: H166347
Winner of 14 awards, Taste of Ulster Restaurant. Central for touring Ireland. **Grades:** AA 3 Diamond
Tel: **028 6634 8452** Mrs Armstrong
D: £19.00-£21.00 **S:** £20.00-£25.00.
Open: All Year
Beds: 2F 2D 2T **Baths:** 2 En 2 Pr 2 Sh
🛏 🅿 ⅍⬛ 🐾 ✗ 🖳 ⬛ Ⓥ 🛉 🚲

Belcoo   4

National Grid Ref: H0838
🍴 🍺 Leo's Bar

Corralea Forest Lodge, *Corralea, Belcoo, Enniskillen, Co Fermanagh, BT93 5DZ.*
Lakeside purpose built guest house on lake shore in 34 acres.
Grades: ETC 2 Star
Tel: **028 6638 6325** Mrs Catterall.
D: £21.00-£21.00 **S:** £21.00-£21.00.
Open: Easter to October
Beds: 1D 3T **Baths:** 4 En
🛏 🅿 ⬛ ✗ 🖳 ⬛ Ⓥ 🛉 🚲

Kingfisher Cycle Trail

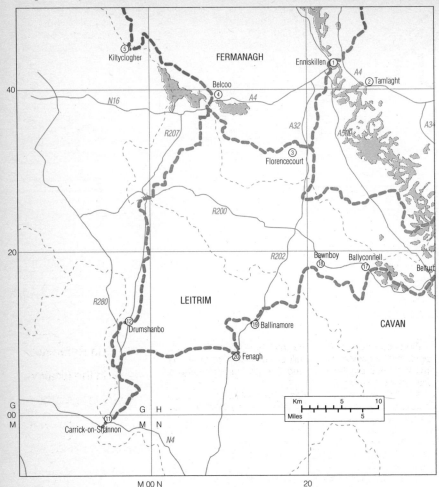

Kiltyclogher 5

National Grid Ref: G9744

▲ *Leitrim Lakes Hostel,*
Kiltyclogher, Sligo.
Tel: **072 54044 Adults:** £7.00

Pettigoe 6

National Grid Ref: H1066

Hill Top View,
Pettigoe, Donegal.
Spectacular view of Lough Erne.
Anglers', walkers' paradise. Lough
Derg pilgrimage.
Grades: ETC Approv
Tel: **072 61535** Mrs O'Shea.
D: £16.00 **S:** £19.00.
Open: All Year (not Xmas)
Beds: 1F 1T
Baths: 4 Ensuite
⛄ (1) 🅿 (6) ⊬ ☐ 🛏 ✗ 🖿 🛢 ∦

D = Price range per person
sharing in a double room

Kesh 7

National Grid Ref: H1863

🏠 🚲 Lough Erne Hotel, Drumshane Hotel,
Drumrush Lodge, Waterfront

Muckross Lodge, Muckross Quay,
Kesh, Enniskillen, Co Fermanagh,
BT93 1TZ.
Situated overlooking lake, beaches,
public jetty at end of driveway.
Tel: **028 6863 1887** Mrs Anderson.
D: £16.00-£19.00 **S:** £16.00-£19.00.
Open: All Year
Beds: 1F 1T 1D
Baths: 3 En
⛄ 🅿 ⊬ ☐ 🛏 🖿 🖿 🆅 🛢 ∦ ☌

Ardess Craft Centre, Ardess
House, Kesh, Enniskillen,
Co Fermanagh, BT93 1NX.
Craft centre for viewing or
participation. Rural views from
rooms.
Grades: ETC 2 Star
Tel: **028 6863 1267** (also fax no)
Mrs Pendry.
D: £22.50-£22.50
S: £27.50-£27.50.
Open: Jan to Dec
Beds: 4F 1T 3D
Baths: 4 En
⛄ 🅿 ⊬ ☐ 🛏 ✗ 🖿 🖿 🆅 🛢 ∦ ☌

Planning a longer
stay? Always ask for
any special rates.

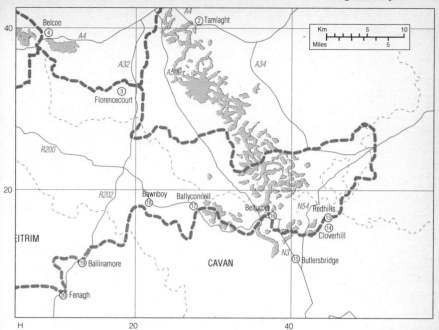

Florence Court, on the route south from Enniskillen, is an eighteenth-century mansion built by John Cole, noted for its lavish rococo plasterwork, and the grounds including a water-powered sawmill.

A little further on, in the Marlbank National Nature Reserve, tours are available through the stalactite-clad **Marble Arch Caves**, the most impressive of the many famous caves of County Fermanagh.

At **Garrison**, on the shores of Loch Melvin, the Loch Melvin Activity Centre offers a range of outdoor pursuits including caving and watersports.

A little way off the route beyond **Belleek** (take care on the busy road if you make this detour), the nature reserve at Castle Caldwell is the breeding ground of a number of rare birds, including the common scoter and the peregrine falcon.

From Castle Archdale Forest you can take a ferry to **White Island**, renowned for its ruined twelfth-century abbey with an eery collection of early Christian sculptures, believed to be caryatids (carved columns) from an earlier church on the site.

The Grid Reference beneath the location heading is for the village or town - *not* for individual houses, which are shown (where supplied) in each entry itself.

Ederney   8

National Grid Ref: H2264

⊯ ⏄ Lough Erne Hotel

Roscolban House, Enniskillen Road, Kesh, Enniskillen, Co Fermanagh, BT93 1TF.
Modern comfortable guest house. Quiet and conveniently situated for touring with a friendly welcome
Tel: **028 6863 1096** Mrs Stronge.
D: £16.00 **S:** £18.50.
Open: All Year (not Xmas)
Beds: 2F 1T
Baths: 2 En 1 Sh
⛄ 🅿 (6) ⫟⬜📕✗⬇📖.🆅🛈

All details shown are as supplied by B&B owners in Autumn 2000.

Greenwood Lodge, Erne Drive, Ederney, Kesh, Enniskillen, Co Fermanagh, BT93 0EF.
Well-appointed guest house, good food, personal service. Ideal for touring.
Tel: **028 6863 1366** (also fax no)
Mrs McCord.
D: £16.00-£18.00 **S:** £18.00-£20.00.
Open: All Year (not Xmas)
Beds: 3D 2T 1S
Baths: 5 En 1 Sh
⛄ 🅿 (10) ⬜✗⬇📖.🆅🛈🚲

Carrick-on-Shannon, County Letrim's main town, sits picturesquely on both sides of a wide stretch of the Shannon, and is a good location for watersports enthusiasts. Worth seeing here: the Costello Mortuary Chapel is the smallest chapel in Ireland and the second smallest in the world. Built in 1879 by a local businessman to commemorate his wife, the interior is beautifully tiled with Bath stone, with the couple's coffins on either side of the miniature aisle. The Irish Potato Famine is commemorated by a memorial garden behind the old St Patrick's Workhouse (now a hospital), whose inmates suffered particularly badly.

At **Drumshanbo**, on the south of Loch Allen, the Sliabh an Iarann Visitor Centre includes exhibits on the area's mining history.

On the site of the sixth-century monastery founded by St Tiernach at **Clones**, the vestiges of the twelfth-century Augustinian abbey can be found in Abbey Street. The town's religious heritage is further reflected in the richly carved (although weathered by age) High Cross, at 'the Diamond' in the centre of town, depicting biblical scenes.

Fenagh has a ruined monastery and two seventh-century churches founded by St Caillain.

Close to **Keshcarrigan**, where the route passes Loch Scur, the cairn and stone circle at Sheebeg is believed by some to be the grave of the Irish hero Finn MacCool.

Killadeas 9

National Grid Ref: H2054

|†○| ⬛ Manor House, The Inishclare

The Olde Schoolhouse, Tully Road, Killadeas, Enniskillen, Co Fermanagh, BT94 1RE.
Central for touring Fermanagh, Tyrone and Donegal. Good food, homely atmosphere.
Tel: **028 6862 1688** (also fax no)
Mrs Moore.
D: £19.00-£21.00
S: £20.00-£29.00.
Open: All Year
Beds: 2F 3D 1T
Baths: 6 En
🛇 🅿 (10) 🖵 ✗ 🖳 🕭 🔟 🛉 ✦

Rossfad House, Killadeas, Enniskillen, Co Fermanagh, BT94 2LS.
A Georgian country house on Lower Lough Erne. Lake views.
Tel: **028 6638 8505** Mrs Williams.
D: £17.50-£20.00
S: £20.00-£25.00.
Open: Mar to Nov
Beds: 1F 1D **Baths:** 1 En 1 Pr
🛇 (4) 🅿 ✦ 🖵 🔟 🖳 🛉 ✦ ✦

All rates are subject to alteration at the owners' discretion.

Irvinestown 10

National Grid Ref: H2358

|†○| ⬛ Castle Archdale Youth Hostel

▲ **Castle Archdale Youth Hostel,** *Castle Archdale Country Park, Irvinestown, Co Fermanagh BT94 1PP.*
Tel: **028 6862 8118 Adults:** £10.50
Self-catering facilities, Television, Central heating, Shop, Laundry facilities, Dining room, Cycle store, Evening meal available.
On the shores of Lower Lough Erne. The hostel is located in an C18th house within the Castle Archdale country park. It is suitable for visitors of all description, wanting to explore Co Fermanagh.

Carrick-on-Shannon 11

National Grid Ref: M9499

|†○| ⬛ Riverside Bar, Cryan's, Tig Brid

▲ **Town Clock Hostel,** *Town Centre, Carrick-on-Shannon, County Leitrim.*
Tel: **078 20068 Adults:** £6.00

The Shannon Valley, Carrick-on-Shannon, Co Leitrim.
Superb old house. Fine dining, own wooded grounds. Night club.
Tel: **078 20103** Fax no: 078 50876
D: £56.00-£72.00
S: £56.00-£72.00.
Open: All Year
Beds: 4F 6D **Baths:** 10 En
🛇 🅿 (200) 🖵 ✗ 🖳 🛉 ✦ ✦

Moyrane House, Dublin Road, Carrick-on-Shannon, Co Leitrim.
A truly Irish family home. Peaceful setting. Highly recommended.
Grades: ETC Approv
Tel: **078 20325** Mrs Shortt.
D: £19.00.
Open: Apr to Oct
Beds: 4F 2D/T 1S
Baths: 3 En
🛇 🅿 (5) 🖵 ✗ 🖳.

Gortmor House, Lismakeegan, Carrick-on-Shannon, Co Leitrim.
Excellent home cooking, good wines, quiet scenic location, laundry facilities on request.
Tel: **078 20489** Mrs McMahon.
Fax no: 078 21439
D: £18.50-£18.50 **S:** £25.00-£25.00.
Open: Jan to Nov
Beds: 2F 1D 1T
Baths: 1 En 3 Pr
🛇 🅿 (8) ✦ 🖵 ✗ 🖳 🛉 ✦ ✦

Corbally Lodge, Dublin Road N4, Carrick-on-Shannon, Co Leitrim.
Country peacefulness, antique furnishings, laundry, breakfast service. Fishing and walking.
Tel: **078 20228** (also fax no)
Mr & Mrs Rowley.
D: £16.00-£18.00 **S:** £20.00-£23.00.
Open: All Year (not Xmas)
Beds: 1D 3T
Baths: 3 En
🛇 🅿 🖵 ✦ ✗ 🖳 🛉 ✦

Drumshanbo 12

National Grid Ref: G9710

|†○| ⬛ Sorohan's, Allandale

Mooney's B&B, 2 Carick Road, Drumshanbo, Carrick-on-Shannon, Co Leitrim.
Stone two-storey house, home from home, scenic area in lovely Leitrim.
Grades: ETC Approv
Tel: **078 41013** Mrs Mooney.
Fax no: 078 41237
D: £15.00 **S:** £17.00.
Open: All Year (not Xmas)
Beds: 2D 1T 1S
Baths: 1 Sh
🛇 (12) ✦ 🖵 🖳 ✦

Redhills 13

National Grid Ref: H4416

|†○| ⬛ Old Post Inn, Derry Garra Inn

Hillside, Shannon Wood, Redhills, Cavan.
Beautiful modern home half mile Redhills village, 2 music pubs, horse riding, golf, fishing locally.
Grades: ETC Approv
Tel: **047 55125** Mrs Smith.
D: £17.00-£17.00 **S:** £20.00-£20.00.
Open: Apr to Oct
Beds: 2F 1T
Baths: 3 En
🛇 🅿 🖵 ✗ 🖳 🛉 ✦

Cloverhill 14

National Grid Ref: H4114

⊌◀ Derragarra Inn, Old Post

Fortview House, *Drumbran, Cloverhill, Belturbet, Co Cavan.*
Beautiful country house. Excellent home cooking. Farm walks. First class fishing.
Tel: **049 4338185** Mrs Smith.
Fax no: 049 4338834
D: £17.00-£17.00 **S:** £20.00-£20.00.
Open: Easter to Oct
Beds: 3F 1D 2T
Baths: 3 Pr 2 Sh 3 En
⊜ ₽ ⊬ ⊐ ✕ ♨ ▥. Ⅴ

Butlersbridge 15

National Grid Ref: H4110

⊌◀ Deragara Inn

Inishmore House, *Butlersbridge, Cavan.*
Top fishing area, own boat jetty & boats for hire.
Grades: ETC Approv
Tel: **049 4334151** Mrs Lynch.
D: £17.00-£22.00 .
Open: Easter to Nov
Beds: 3F 1T
Baths: 2 En
⊜ ₽ ⊬ ⊐ ✕ ▥. ♟ ✦ ⟳

Ford House, *Deredis, Butlersbridge, Cavan.*
Modern farm guest house, over-looking rivers and lakes in what is truly scenic countryside.
Tel: **049 4331427** Mrs Mundy.
D: £15.00-£18.00 .
Open: All Year
Beds: 6F
Baths: 3 En 1 Pr 1 Sh
⊜ ₽ ⊐ ♜ ✕ ▥. Ⅴ

Belturbet 16

National Grid Ref: H3617

Erne View House, *9 Bridge Street, Belturbet, Co Cavan.*
Town house by River Erne convenient to pubs, shops and bistros
Grades: ETC Approv
Tel: **049 9522289** Mrs McGreevey.
D: £15.00 **S:** £18.00.
Open: All Year (not Xmas)
Beds: 4 F
Baths: 2 Ensuite 2 Shared
⊜ ₽ (5) ⊐ ✕ ▥. Ⅴ

Ballyconnell 17

National Grid Ref: H2718

▲ **Sandville House Hostel,**
Ballyconnell, Co Cavan.
Actual grid ref: H291152
Tel: **049 9526297**
Under 18: £2.00 **Adults:** £7.50
Self-catering facilities, Television, Showers, Central heating, Laundry facilities, Wet weather shelter, Lounge, Dining room, Games room, Grounds available for games, Parking, Facilities for disabled people
Restored barn hostel in quiet setting. Beautiful, well equipped, totally informal. Large family rooms. gardens, play space. 4 km Ballyconnell, signed from Belturbet Road. Express bus Dublin 2.5 hrs. Explore rich landscape of Cavan and Leitrim. Lakes, hill walks, archaeology. Unmissable Marble Arch Caves 25 km. Good touring base. Occasionally private for retreats.

Bawnboy 18

National Grid Ref: H2119

The Keepers' Arms, *Bawnboy, Ballyconnell, Belturbet, Co Cavan.*
Tel: **049 9523318**
Mrs McKiernan.
Fax no: 049 9523008
D: £11.00-£15.00 **S:** £25.00-£30.00.
Open: All Year (not Xmas/ New Year)
Beds: 3D 2T 6D
Baths: 11 En
⊜ ₽ (15) ⊬ ⊐ ♜ ✕ ♨ ▥. Ⅴ ♟ ✦ ⟳
Come taste our wares . . . . in West Cavan. Enjoy the Shannon Erne waterway on land or by water. Day or evening cruising, angling on our lakes and rivers, pet farms, Irish music/dancing schools, or try 18 hole (championship) golf.

All cycleways are popular: you are well-advised to book ahead

---

Ballinamore 19

National Grid Ref: H1211

⊌◀ Smyth's

▲ **Ballinamore Holiday Hostel,**
Main Street, Ballinamore, County Leitrim.
Tel: **078 44955 Adults:** £7.50
Evening meal available.

Riversdale Farm Guest House,
Ballinamore, Co Leitrim.
Grades: ETC 3 Star
RAC 3 Diamond
Tel: **078 44122**
Ms Thomas.
Fax no: 078 44813
D: £28.00-£28.00
S: £33.00-£33.00.
Open: All Year (not Xmas)
Beds: 4F 3D 2T 1S
Baths: 10 En
⊜ (5) ₽ (12) ⊐ ♜ ✕ ▥. ♟ ✦ ⟳
Comfortable spacious residence in parkland setting alongside Shannon-Erne Waterway. Indoor heated swimming pool, squash, sauna, games room, fitness suite on premises. Local golf, horse-riding, boat trips. Good touring centre. Brochure available. Weekly terms. Canal barge holidays.

Fenagh 20

National Grid Ref: H1007

The Old Rectory, *Fenagh, Ballinamore, Co Leitrim.*
Grades: ETC Approv
Tel: **078 44089**
Mr & Mrs Curran.
D: £20.00
S: £25.00.
Open: Jan 10 to Dec 15
Beds: 2D 1T 1F
Baths: 3 En 1 Sh
⊜ ₽ (6) ⊐ ♜ ✕ ▥. ♟ ✦ ⟳
The Old Rectory built in 1827 is situated on 50 acres of wooded parkland overlooking Fenagh Lake a beautifully restored Georgian house, this secluded and elegant retreat is ideal for those who wish to relax and enjoy country living.

Sustrans Lon Las Cymru

The **Welsh National Cycle Route** is a section of the new UK National Cycle Network, running on traffic-free paths and traffic-calmed roads across the full length of Wales from the southeastern coast to the ferry port of Holyhead at the northwest of the Isle of Anglesey. It will take you through the full range of the Principality's breathtaking landscape, including two National Parks, the Brecon Beacons in the south and Snowdonia in the north. Much of the route is through sparsely populated regions. You should be prepared for a fair amount of climbing, particularly in the northern reaches, but don't let this put you off – Sustrans have designed the route with novice cyclists in mind. You can start at Cardiff, or at Chepstow on the English border; there are western and eastern alternative routes for most of the way, meeting and parting twice before meeting again for the final stretch from Porthmadog to Holyhead. The maximum distance is 288 miles; most of the route is signposted by blue direction signs with a cycle silhouette and the number 8 in a red rectangle.

The indispensable **official route map and guide** in English and Welsh for the Welsh National Cycle Route, which includes listings of cycle repair/hire shops along the route, comes in two parts, *Lon Las Cymru: Chepstow & Cardiff to Builth Wells* and *Lon Las Cymru: Builth Wells to Holyhead*, and is available from

Sustrans, 35 King Street, Bristol BS1 4DZ, tel 0117-926 8893, fax 0117-929 4173, @ £5.99 each (+ £1.50 p&p for both together or either one).

Maps: Ordnance Survey 1:50,000 Landranger series: 114, 123, 124, 135, 136, 147, 160, 161, 171, 172

Transport: Cardiff, Bangor and Holyhead are all main line rail termini; Chepstow is a stop on the line between Cardiff and Gloucester; there are connections to many other places on or near the route. Holyhead is a major ferry port to Ireland, serving Dublin and Dun Laoghaire.

Cardiff   1

National Grid Ref: ST1677

✋ ⚭ Beverley, Clifton Hotel, Halfway Hotel, Hayes Court, Poachers' Lodge, Robin Hood

▲ **Cardiff Youth Hostel,** Ty Croeso, 2 Wedal Road, Roath Park, Cardiff, CF2 5PG.
Actual grid ref: ST185788
Tel: **029 2046 2303**
Under 18: £10.20 **Adults:** £13.50
Self-catering facilities, Television, Showers, Shop, Laundry facilities, Lounge 2, Cycle store, Parking, Kitchen facilities, Breakfast available, Luggage store, Credit cards accepted
Conveniently located hostel near the city centre and Roath Park Lake, with cycling & sailing facilities.

D = Price range per person sharing in a double room

S = Price range for a single person in a room

▲ **Cardiff Backpacker Caerdydd,** 98 Neville Street, Riverside, Cardiff, CF11 6LS.
Actual grid ref: ST176763
Tel: **029 2034 5577 Adults:** £13.50
Self-catering facilities, Television, Showers, Licensed bar, Central heating, Shop, Laundry facilities, Lounge, Dining room, Games room, Security lockers, Cycle store, Parking, No smoking
Cardiff's only central tourist hostel, located within five minutes walk from train/bus stations and all civic amenities. Relax and socialise in a lively Welsh atmosphere with travellers from all over the world or explore the nearby Brecon Beacons National Park and breathtaking castles, museums and coastline. WTB 4 Star Hostel.

Rambler Court Hotel, 188 *Cathedral Road, Pontcanna, Cardiff, S Glam,* CF11 9JE.
Grades: ETC 2 Star
Tel: **029 2022 1187** (also fax no)
Mrs Cronin.
D: £17.00-£20.00 **S:** £17.00-£25.00.
Open: All Year
Beds: 3F 3D 1T 3S
Baths: 4 En 5 Sh
⛽ Ⓝ (4) 🛒 ⏳ 🗼 🍽 V ⋆ 🎫
Friendly family-run hotel, ideally situated in a tree-lined conservation area, close to all of the city's main attractions, 10 minutes' walk from the city centre and Millennium Stadium. Good local restaurants & pubs.

Bringing children with you? Always ask for any special rates.

*Preste Gaarden Hotel, 181
Cathedral Road, Pontcanna,
Cardiff, S Glam, CF11 9PN.*
Highly recommended, modernised
ex-Norwegian consulate offering
olde-worlde charm.
Grades: ETC 2 Star Hotel
Tel: **029 2022 8607** Mrs Nicholls.
Fax no: 029 2037 4805
D: £18.00-£22.00 **S:** £22.00-£27.00.
Open: All Year (not Xmas)
Beds: 1F 2D 3T 4S **Baths:** 7 En 3 Pr
⛵ P (3) 🖵 🍽 🛏 📺 Ⓥ

*Austins, 11 Coldstream Terrace,
City Centre, Cardiff, CF11 6LJ.*
In the centre of the city 300 yards
from Cardiff Castle.
Grades: ETC 2 Star
Tel: **029 2037 7148**
Mr Hopkins.
Fax no: 029 2037 7158
D: £17.50-£19.50
S: £20.00-£27.50.
Open: All Year
Beds: 1F 5T 5S **Baths:** 4 En 2 Sh
⛵ 🖵 🍽 🛏 📺 Ⓥ 🚲

*Annedd Lon Guest House,
157-159 Cathedral Road, Cardiff,
S Glam, CF1 9PL.*
Centrally located guest house in
elegant conservation area. Non
smoking throughout.
Grades: AA 4 Daimond
Tel: **029 2022 3349** Mrs Tucker.
Fax no: 029 2064 0885
D: £20.00-£22.50 **S:** £18.00-£30.00.
Open: All Year (not Xmas/New Year)
Beds: 2F 1D 2T 1S **Baths:** 2 En 2 Sh
⛵ P (7) 🚭 🖵 🛏 📺 Ⓥ 🚲

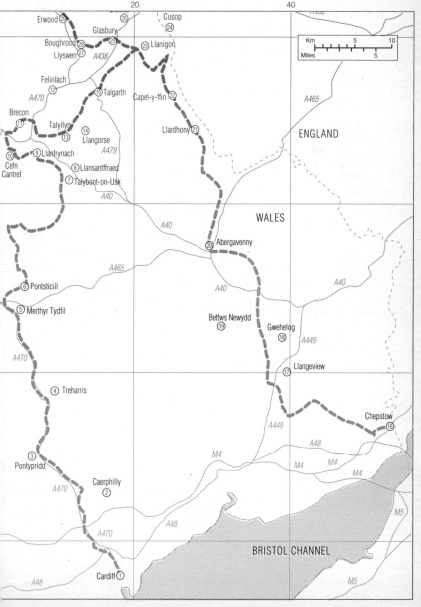

The Routes

The **western route** runs from **Cardiff** up the River Taff through the industrial heartland of South Wales to Pontypridd, Abercynon and Merthyr Tydfil, before wending through the beautiful wooded valleys below the Brecon Beacons range itself, within the **Brecon Beacons National Park**, to Brecon, where it turns east to join the other route close to the River Wye. From **Chepstow**, at the mouth of the Wye, the **eastern route** turns west to the River Usk, which it follows upstream to Usk before heading on to **Abergavenny**, where it enters the Brecon Beacons National Park to follow the River Honddu up the idyllic Vale of Ewyas to its source in the Black Mountains range, passing below Offa's Dyke and the border for much of the way until the two routes converge. After the stretch through the beautiful Wye Valley as far as **Builth Wells**, the route parts again as it heads into Mid Wales: the eastern way pursues the Wye Valley to Newbridge-on-Wye, Rhayader and Llangurig before turning eastwards to Llanidloes. The western section of this part of the route is unsignposted and tough going – only for experienced cyclists, preferably on a mountain bike: after **Llanwrtyd Wells** you take the Abergwysyn Pass up the 'Devil's Staircase' through dense forest, to reach the valley of the Towi with its breathtaking scenery. After following the Towi to its source you proceed to Devil's Bridge.

The two routes pass either side of the peak of **Plynlimon Fawr** in the Cambrian Mountains before they converge again at **Machynlleth**, where you cross the River Dovey into **Snowdonia National Park**. The western alternative turns west to Tywyn on the coast before heading north and crossing the Barmouth viaduct bridge into **Barmouth**. From here you continue to Dyffryn Ardudwy and Llanbedr, and proceed to the toll bridge over the River Dwyryd into Penrhyndeudraeth, and on to Garreg, where the routes finally join. The eastern route from Machynlleth goes to Corris, and continues, with the majestic mass of Cader Idris towering away to the left, to **Dolgellau**. From here you cycle through the lovely Coed-y-Brenin Forest Park, in the heart of southern Snowdonia, and on to Trawsfynydd, Gellilydan and Maentwrog on the Dwyryd before reaching Garreg. The final stretch of the way proceeds through **Porthmadog** and around the western side of the Snowdon massif to Caernarfon and Bangor; having crossed the great Menai Suspension Bridge, you traverse the southern side of Anglesey, an island scattered with the remains of ancient Celtic settlements, to reach **Holyhead**.

Georgian Hotel, 179 Cathedral Road, Pontcanna, Cardiff, S Glam, CF1 9PL.
All rooms tastefully restored to today's standards, each having a colour television.
Tel: **029 2023 2594** Mr Menin.
D: £20.00-£27.50 **S:** £27.50-£35.00.
Open: All Year (not Xmas)
Beds: 1F 2D 3T 2S
Baths: 8 En
🛇 🖵 🗶 ⬛ Ⅷ ⒱ ᴔ

Caerphilly   2

National Grid Ref: ST1586

🍴 🍺 Cedar Tree, Traveller's Rest, The Moat, Black Cock, Kings Arms, Rudry Hotel, Maenllloyd Inn

The Cottage Guest House,
Pwlly Pant, Caerphilly, Mid Glam, CF83 3HW.
300 year old Cottage. Castles, coastline, mountains nearby. Warm welcome.
Grades: ETC 3 Star,
AA 3 Diamond
Tel: **029 2086 9160** Mr Giles.
D: £17.00-£20.00 **S:** £26.00-£29.00.
Open: All Year
Beds: 3T
Baths: 2 En 1 Pr
🛇 🅿 (5) 🗶 🖵 ⬛ Ⅷ ⒱ ᴔ

Lugano Guest House, Hillside Mountain Road, Caerphilly, Mid Glamorgan, CF83 1HN.
Grades: ETC 3 Star, Highly Commended
Tel: **029 2085 2672**
D: £16.50-£17.50
S: £22.50-£25.00.
Open: All Year (not Xmas)
Beds: 1D 2T
Baths: 3 En
🛇 (1) 🅿 (2) 🗶 🖵 ⬛ Ⅷ ⒱
Charming character house, residents' own private garden and entrance. Upstairs bedrooms overlooking Caerphilly Castle, all rooms ensuite. Minutes' walk to town centre, castle, train and bus stations for regular services to the capital, Cardiff. Warm friendly welcome assured. No smoking.

All details shown
are as supplied
by B&B owners in
Autumn 2000.

Planning a longer
stay? Always ask for
any special rates.

Pontypridd   3

National Grid Ref: ST0789

🍴 🍺 Market Tavern

Market Tavern Hotel, Market St, Pontypridd, Mid Glam, CF37 2ST.
Tel: **01443 485331**
Mr John.
Fax no: 01443 491403
D: £19.00-£20.00
S: £28.00-£30.00.
Open: All Year (not Xmas)
Beds: 4D 3T 4S
Baths: 11 En
🛇 🖵 🗶 ⬛ Ⅷ ⚿ ⒱
All bedrooms ensuite and delightfully furnished. Tavern bar offers good range of ales, wines and food. Chilli Pepper Cocktail Bar & Strads Nightclub are open late Friday & Saturday evenings. Centrally located. Ideal base for Cardiff & the Valleys.

Treharris 4

National Grid Ref: ST0997

◔ ◖ Railway Inn, Cross Inn

Fairmead, 24 Gelligaer Rd, Treharris, Nelson, Mid Glam, CF46 6DN
A small family run quiet haven, offering a warm welcome.
Grades: ETC 4 Star
Tel: **01443 411174** Mrs Kedward.
Fax no: 01443 411430
D: £21.50-£35.00 **S:** £27.50-£35.00.
Open: All Year
Beds: 2D 1T **Baths:** 2 En 1 Pr
⌂ ▣ (5) ⊬ ⬜ ⼞ ✕ ♨ ▥ Ⅵ ▮ ⧸ ⚲

Merthyr Tydfil 5

National Grid Ref: SO0506

◔ ◖ Mountain Ash, Brunswick, White Horse

Maes Y Coed, Park Terrace, Pontmorlais West, Merthyr Tydfil, Mid Glam, CF47 8UT.
Tel: **01685 722246** (also fax no)
Mr Davies.
D: £16.00-£18.00 **S:** £18.00-£22.00.
Open: All Year
Beds: 4F 5T 1S **Baths:** 4 En
⌂ ▣ (4) ⬜ ♨ ✕ ♨ ▥ Ⅵ ▮ ⧸ ⚲
Large comfortable house on edge of Brecon Beacons in 1/4 acre of gardens. Edging the Taff Trail. Friendly welcome, good home cooked breakfast, evening meals. Ideal for golfing, fishing, walking and all outdoors pursuits.

Brynawel Guest House, Queens Road, Merthyr Tydfil, Mid Glam, CF47 0HD.
Actual grid ref: SO053065
Grades: ETC 3 Star
Tel: **01685 722573** Mrs Johnson.
D: £23.00-£23.00 **S:** £28.00-£28.00.
Open: All Year
Beds: 1D 2T
Baths: 3 En
⌂ ▣ (5) ⊬ ⬜ ♨ ▥ Ⅵ ▮ ⧸ ⚲
Large Victorian house, tastefully furnished, adjoining parks, family home, friendly atmosphere. Ensuite rooms, TV, tea/coffee. Non-smoking, 10 mins Brecon Beacons National Park. Excellent Welsh breakfast. Ideal location for walkers, cyclists, business or quiet break.

Pontsticill 6

National Grid Ref: SO0511

◔ ◖ Butchers Arms

Butchers Arms, Pontsticill, Merthyr Tydfil, CF48 2UE.
Actual grid ref: SO056113
Set in the beautiful surroundings of the Brecon Beacons National Park.
Tel: **01685 723544**
Fax no: 01685 388820
D: £18.50-£22.50 .
Open: All Year
Beds: 2D 1T **Baths:** 3 En
⌂ (1) ▣ (20) ⊬ ⬜ ✕ ♨ ▥ Ⅵ ▮ ⚲

Talybont-on-Usk 7

National Grid Ref: SO1122

◔ ◖ Traveller's Rest

Llanddety Hall Farm, Talybont-on-Usk, Brecon, Powys, LD3 7YR.
C17th Listed farmhouse in Brecon Beacons National Park, beautiful views.
Grades: ETC 3 Star Farm, AA 4 Diamond
Tel: **01874 676415** Mrs Atkins.
D: £22.00-£26.00 **S:** £25.00-£26.00.
Open: All Year (not Xmas)
Beds: 2D 1T
Baths: 2 En 1 Pr
⌂ (12) ▣ (5) ⊬ ⬜ ✕ ♨ ▥ Ⅵ

Llansantffraed 8

National Grid Ref: SO1223

The Allt, Llansantffraed, Talybont-on-Usk, Brecon, Powys, LD3 7YF.
Actual grid ref: SO123234
C18th farmhouse overlooking River Usk with magnificent mountain views.
Tel: **01874 676310**
Mrs Hamill-Keays.
D: £15.00-£16.50 **S:** £12.00-£15.00.
Open: All Year (not Xmas)
Beds: 1F 1D 1S
Baths: 1 Sh
⌂ ▣ (6) ⬜ ♨ ✕ ♨ ▥ Ⅵ ▮ ⧸ ⚲

Cardiff to Brecon

Cardiff, the national capital, was in the past important for its docks, which shipped out coal from the South Wales mines. With the decline of the docks, Cardiff Bay is now undergoing extensive redevelopment, including the construction of a barrage to create a giant freshwater marina. There is a visitors' centre, built into a hollow tube that overlooks the bay, which has displays on the various projects underway. Also at Cardiff Bay is the Welsh Industrial and Maritime Museum, with prominence given to mining and to the railways. Other museums in and around Cardiff are the National Museum of Wales, including the natural history of Wales and a sizeable art collection, which includes Italian and Flemish Renaissance paintings, Impressionism and sculpture; and the fantastic Welsh Folk Museum at St Fagan's, just west of town. This is a large site with reconstructed buildings, of all sorts and various periods, from all over the country. Other attractions are Cardiff Castle, an amalgam of Norman motte and bailey with an extensive Victorian

Neo-Gothic fantasy by William Burges; and Llandaff Cathedral, originally twelfth century but with substantial nineteenth-century restoration, including work by prominent Pre-Raphaelites.

On the route just north of Cardiff, **Castell Coch** is a Victorian medieval fantasy also by William Burges, constructed out of a thirteenth-century ruined fortress.

At **Pontypridd** you can find the Pontypridd Historical and Cultural Centre, dedicated to life in the Valleys.

Merthyr Tydfil has another Neo-Gothic castle, Cyfartha, a gallery of Welsh modern art and a museum which records the harsh conditions of nineteenth-century industrial life, the Ynysfach Engine House.

Every self-respecting Celtic nation produces whisky. If you've only heard of the Scotch and Irish varieties, you will be surprised to find the Welsh Whisky Visitor Centre at **Brecon**. The town also offers the Brecknock Museum, a document of past life in the region, and an intriguing cathedral, originally Norman but restored in the Victorian era.

S = Price range for a single

person in a room

Llanfrynach 9

National Grid Ref: SO0725

|⚑| ⬗ White Swan

*Llanbrynean Farm, Llanfrynach,
Brecon, Powys, LD3 7BQ.*
Actual grid ref: SO076254
Beautiful countryside, traditional
family farmhouse, ideal location
for Brecon Beacons.
Grades: ETC 2 Star
Tel: **01874 665222** Mrs Harpur.
D: £19.00-£21.00 **S:** £20.00-£25.00.
Open: Easter to Nov
Beds: 1F 1D 1T
Baths: 2 En 1 Pr
⛺ 🅿 (8) ⚡🛏️🕭🚲🌐🖩ⓥ🛉⚡🐾

Cefn Cantref 10

National Grid Ref: SO0426

▲ *Held Bunkhouse Barn, Cefn
Cantref, Brecon, Powys, LD3 8LT.*
Actual grid ref: SO036266
Tel: **01874 624646 Adults:** £7.50

Brecon 11

National Grid Ref: SO0428

|⚑| ⬗ Bentley's, Clarence, Camden Arms, Castle,
George, Lion, Three Horseshoes, Red Lion,
Traveller's Rest, Tai 'R' Bull

▲ *Canal Barn Bunk House, Ty
Camlas, Canal Bank, Brecon,
Powys, LD3 7HH.*
Tel: **01874 625361 Adults:** £8.35
Self-catering facilities, Showers,
Central heating, Shop, Laundry
facilities, Wet weather shelter,
Dining room, Grounds available
for games, Drying room, Cycle
store, Parking, Facilities for
disabled people, No smoking
*A great base for outdoor activities
in the Brecon Beacons.*

*Lansdowne Hotel, 39 The Watton,
Brecon, Powys, LD3 7EG.*
Grades: ETC 2 Star, AA 2 Star
Tel: **01874 623321** Mrs Mulley.
Fax no: 01874 610438
D: £23.50-£25.00 **S:** £27.50-£30.00.
Open: All Year
Beds: 2F 5D 2T
Baths: 9 Pr
🛏️🕭🌐🖩ⓥ🛉⚡
Our warm and friendly family-run
hotel and restaurant is located in
the centre of Brecon. You can
enjoy comfortable accommodation
and delicious freshly prepared food
in our fully licensed restaurant. The
perfect location for touring the
beautiful National Park.

*Beacons Accommodation and
Restaurant, 16 Bridge Street,
Brecon, Powys, LD3 8AH.*
Actual grid ref: SO142285
Grades: ETC 3 Star GH, AA 3
Diamond, RAC 3 Diamond
Tel: **01874 623339** (also fax no)
Mr & Mrs Jackson.
D: £18.00-£29.50 **S:** £20.00.
Open: All Year (not Xmas)
Beds: 6F 4D 3T 1S
Baths: 11 En 1 Sh
⛺🅿 (14) ⚡🛏️🐾🕭🚲🌐🖩🟊ⓥ🛉🐾
Recently restored Georgian town
house offering a variety of well
appointed standard ensuite and
luxury period rooms. A candlelit
restaurant serves fine food and
wines (5 nights). There is a cosy
cellar bar and a restful lounge, pri-
vate car park and a secure bike store.

*Pen-y-Bryn House, Llangorse,
Brecon, LD3 7UG.*
Actual grid ref: SO137275
Grades: ETC 4 Star
Tel: **01874 658606** Mrs Thomas.
Fax no: 01874 658215
D: £20.00-£20.00 **S:** £25.00-£25.00.
Open: All Year (not Xmas)
Beds: 1F 1T 1D
Baths: 2 En 1 Pr
⛺🅿⚡🛏️🐾🕭🌐🖩ⓥ🛉⚡🐾
Situated in the Brecon Beacons
National Park, overlooking
Llangorse Lake, with large gardens
and mountains beyond. Also, we
have nearby our own activity cen-
tre which offers riding, climbing
indoor and out (best indoor climb-
ing in Britain) and so much more.

*Flag & Castle Guest House, 11
Orchard Street, Llanfaes, Brecon,
Powys, LD3 8AN.*
Family run guest house near to
town centre and National Park.
Grades: ETC 3 Star
Tel: **01874 625860**
Mr & Mrs Richards.
D: £20.00-£25.00 **S:** £25.00-£25.00.
Open: All Year
Beds: 2T 1D **Baths:** 3 En
⛺🅿⚡🛏️🐾🕭🌐ⓥ🛉🐾

*Tir Bach Guest House, 13
Alexandra Road, Brecon, Powys,
LD3 7PD.*
Panoramic view of Brecon
Beacons. Quiet road near town
centre.
Grades: ETC 2 Star
Tel: **01874 624551** Mrs Thomas.
D: £18.00-£19.00 **S:** £25.00-£30.00.
Open: All Year (not Xmas)
Beds: 1F 1D 1T **Baths:** 1 Sh
⛺🛏️🐾🕭🌐🖩ⓥ🐾

Bringing children with
you? Always ask for
any special rates.

*Brecon Canal Guest House, Canal
Bank, The Watton, Brecon, Powys,
LD3 7HG.*
Grades: ETC 2 Star
Tel: **01874 623464**
Fax no: 01874 610930
D: £17.00-£20.00
S: £17.00-£17.00.
Open: Feb to Nov
Beds: 1D 2T 1S
Baths: 2 En
🅿 (6) 🛏️🐾🕭🌐🖩ⓥ🛉⚡🐾
Small, friendly, cottage-style guest
house, situated adjacent to the
Brecon canal close to new theatre.
Quiet, semi-rural position, yet only
5 minutes walk from town centre.
All rooms have TV, tea/coffee,
some ensuite. Private parking.

*Canal Bridge B&B, 1 Gasworks
Lane, Brecon, LD3 7HA.*
Actual grid ref: SO048282
Spacious and comfortable B&B
close to historic town centre,
museums, theatre, River Usk.
Grades: ETC 3 Star
Tel: **01874 611088** Ms Lake.
D: £18.00-£20.00 **S:** £20.00-£25.00
Open: Mar to Nov
Beds: 1F 3D 1T 1S
Baths: 4 En 2 Pr
⛺ (5) 🅿 (6) ⚡🛏️🕭🌐🖩ⓥ🛉⚡🐾

*Tir Bach, Libanus, Brecon, Powys,
LD3 8NE.*
Beautiful C17th Welsh Longhouse
in Brecon Beacons National Park.
Grades: ETC 3 Star
Tel: **01874 625675**
Mrs Norris.
Fax no: 01874 611198
D: £20.00-£20.00
S: £23.00-£25.00.
Open: All Year (not Xmas)
Beds: 1T 2D
Baths: 2 En 1 Pr
⛺ (12) 🅿 (6) ⚡🛏️🕭🌐🖩ⓥ🛉⚡🐾

*County House, 100 The Struet,
Brecon, LD3 7LS.*
C18th Georgian Grade II Listed
town house - served as judge's
lodgings for 150 years.
Grades: ETC 4 Star
Tel: **01874 625844** (also fax no)
Mr Cope.
D: £27.50 **S:** £37.50.
Open: All Year
Beds: 2D 1T
Baths: 3 En
⛺🅿 (6) 🛏️🐾🕭🚲🌐🖩ⓥ🛉⚡🐾

*Brynawel Guest House, 13 Crado
Road, Brecon, LD3 9LH.*
Impressive Victorian residence.
Beautiful views, ensuites, TVs,
drinks facilities.
Grades: ETC 3 Star
Tel: **01874 624363** (also fax no)
Rogers.
D: £20.00-£25.00
S: £20.00-£25.00.
Open: All Year (not Xmas)
Beds: 2D 1T
Baths: 3 En
⛺ (6) 🅿 (5) 🛏️🐾🕭🚲🌐🖩ⓥ🛉⚡🐾

Glanyrafon, *1 The Promenade, Kensington, Brecon, Powys, LD3 9AY.*
Riverside Edwardian house, view of Beacons, near town centre.
Tel: **01874 623302** (also fax no) Mrs Roberts.
D: £17.50-£19.00 **S:** £20.00-£22.00.
Open: Easter to Oct
Beds: 2D 1T **Baths:** 2 Sh
🛇 (11) 🅿 (3) ⊬🗆 🚽 🎟 🖳 🍴 ⚡ 🚲

Blaencar Farm, *Sennybridge, Brecon, Powys, LD3 8HA.*
Actual grid ref: SN933287
Tastefully restored farmhouse on working family farm. Quality ensuite accommodation in peaceful, accessible location.
Tel: **01874 636610**
D: £20.00-£22.00 **S:** £24.00-£24.00.
Open: Easter to Nov
Beds: 2D 1T **Baths:** 3 En
🅿 ⊬🗆 🚽 🎟 🖳 🍴 ⚡ 🚲

Felinfach 12

National Grid Ref: SO0933

🍴 🍺 Griffin Inn, Old Ford Inn, Plough & Harrow

Plough & Harrow Inn, *Felinfach, Brecon, Powys, LD3 0UB.*
Village inn offering comfortable ensuite accommodation, located 4 miles north of Brecon.
Tel: **01874 622709** Ms Warren.
D: £18.00-£20.00 **S:** £25.00-£25.00.
Open: All Year
Beds: 1F 1D 1T **Baths:** 2 En 1 Pr
🛇 🅿 (20) 🗆 🍴 ✗ 🚽 🎟 🖳 🍴 🖤 ⚡ 🚲

Talyllyn 13

National Grid Ref: SO1027

🍴 🍺 Red Lion, White Swan, Castle

Glascwm, *Talyllyn, Brecon, LD3 7SY.*
Tranquil rural setting, close to the Brecon Beacons and Llangorse Lake.
Grades: ETC 3 Star
Tel: **01874 658659** King.
Fax no: 01874 658649
D: £22.00-£22.00 .
Open: All Year (not Xmas)
Beds: 1F 1D 1T **Baths:** 3 En
🛇 🅿 (4) ⊬🗆 🚽 🎟 🖳 🍴

Llangorse 14

National Grid Ref: SO1327

🍴 🍺 Red Lion

Shiwa, *Llangorse, Brecon, Powys, LD3 7UG.*
Tel: **01874 658631** Mrs Gray.
D: £20.00-£25.00 **S:** £20.00-£30.00.
Open: All Year (not Xmas)
Beds: 2F 1D **Baths:** 3 En
🛇 🅿 (5) ⊬🗆 🚽 🎟 🖳 & 🖤 ⚡ 🚲
Overlooking Llangorse Lake but in a village location, 'Shiwa' offers comfortable accommodation in the activities centre of the Brecon Beacons. The African decor and memorabilia make it a special place for those on whom Africa has cast its spell!

Talgarth 15

National Grid Ref: SO1533

🍴 🍺 Mason's Arms, Castle Inn

The Olde Masons Arms Hotel, *Hay Road, Talgarth, Brecon, Powys, LD3 0BB.*
C16th hotel with country cottage ambience. Ideal for walking amidst Black Mountains & Brecon Beacons.
Grades: ETC 3 Star
Tel: **01874 711688** Evans.
D: £26.50-£29.50
S: £29.50-£32.50.
Open: All Year
Beds: 2F 2D 1T 2S
Baths: 7 En
🛇 🅿 (10) 🗆 🍴 ✗ 🚽 🎟 🖳 🖤 🍴 ⚡

Castle Inn, *Pengenfford, Talgarth, Brecon, Powys, LD3 0EP.*
Actual grid ref: SO174296
Traditional country inn with the Brecon Beacons national park.
Tel: **01874 711353** Mr Mountjoy.
D: £20.00-£23.00
S: £20.00-£31.00.
Open: All Year (not Xmas)
Beds: 1F 2D 1T 1S
Baths: 2 En 1 Sh
🛇 🅿 (50) 🗆 ✗ 🚽 🎟 🖳 🖤 🍴 ⚡ 🚲

**Please respect
a B&B's wishes
regarding children,
animals & smoking.**

Chepstow 16

National Grid Ref: ST5393

🍴 🍺 White Lion, Coach & Horses, Cross Keys

Lower Hardwick House, *Mount Pleasant, Chepstow, Monmouthshire, NP16 5PT.*
Actual grid ref: ST531935
Beautiful Georgian house, walled garden. Free car parking for duration walk.
Tel: **01291 622162** Mrs Grassby.
D: £15.50-£18.00 **S:** £18.00-£25.00.
Open: All Year
Beds: 1F 1D 1T 1S
Baths: 2 Pr 1 Sh
🛇 🅿 (12) 🗆 🍴 🚽 🎟 🖳 🖤 ⚡ 🚲

The Old Course Hotel, *Newport Road, Chepstow, Gwent, NP16 5PR.*
Modern hotel, convenient for the Wye Valley, Chepstow races and more.
Grades: AA 3 Star
Tel: **01291 626261**
Fax no: 01291 626263
D: £28.75-£32.25 **S:** £47.00-£53.00.
Open: All Year
Beds: 4F 10D 7T 10S
Baths: 31 En
🛇 🅿 (180) 🗆 🍴 ✗ 🚽 🎟 🖳 🖤 🍴 ⚡

The First Hurdle, *9-10 Upper Church St, Chepstow, Gwent, NP16 5EX.*
Enjoy comfortable, ensuite accommodation. Centrally situated, family owned B&B.
Tel: **01291 622189** Mrs Westwood.
Fax no: 01291 628421
D: £23.00-£25.00 **S:** £25.00-£27.50.
Open: Easter to Nov
Beds: 2D 2T 1S
Baths: 5 En
⊬🗆 🚽 🎟 🖳 🖤 ⚡ 🚲

Chepstow to Llanidloes

Chepstow Castle, built in the twelfth century, was the first stone castle in Britain. Its strategic location on a cliff overlooking the Wye, with a panorama of the area around the border, lends it considerable drama.

After flying to Scotland in 1941, Rudolf Hess was imprisoned in **Abergavenny** – Spandau was definitely a considerable comedown. The main attraction today is the Museum of Childhood and the Home, which has a haunted doll's house. The restored eleventh-century castle keep hosts a museum of local history.

Llanthony Priory in the Vale of Ewyas is a romantic ruin in an unworldly setting. An Augustine foundation dating from the twelfth century, the ruined arches frame the mountains to create a picture of tranquillity.

Rhayader is an attractive town with eighteenth-century coaching inns.

At picturesque **Llanidloes** there is a rare free-standing Tudor market hall and an interesting museum, as well as a church with a hammerbeam roof dating from the fifteenth century.

Langcroft, 71 St Kingsmark Avenue, Chepstow, Monmouthshire, *NP6 5LY.*
Actual grid ref: ST529938
Modern family friendly home. Town centre, four minutes' walk.
Tel: **01291 625569** (also fax no)
Mrs Langdale.
D: £18.00-£20.00
S: £20.00-£20.00.
Open: All Year
Beds: 1D 1T 1S
Baths: 1 Sh
🛇 🅿 (2) 🗖 🛏 🛉 🎹 Ⅴ ♦ ⚲

Llangeview   17

National Grid Ref: SO3900

The Rat Trap, Chepstow Rd, Llangeview, Usk, Monmouthshire, *NP5 1EY.*
In the beautiful setting of the Vale of Usk (adjacent to the Wye Valley).
Tel: **01291 673288** Mrs Rabaiotti.
Fax no: 01291 673305
D: £29.50-£34.50 **S:** £20.00-£24.00.
Open: All Year
Beds: 1F 5D 5T 1S **Baths:** 12 En
🛇 (2) 🅿 (50) 🗖 🛏 🛉 🎹 & Ⅴ 🖬 ⚲

Gwehelog   18

National Grid Ref: SO3804

Ty-Gwyn Farm, Gwehelog, Usk, Monmouthshire, NP5 1RG.
Quiet countryside location with magnificent views, surrounded by secluded lawns.
Tel: **01291 672878** (also fax no)
Mr & Mrs Arnett.
D: £19.00-£20.00 **S:** £25.00-£30.00.
Open: All Year (not Xmas)
Beds: 2D 1T **Baths:** 2 En 1 Pr
🛇 (5) 🅿 ⚲ 🗖 🛉 🎹 Ⅴ 🖬 ♦ ⚲

60   80   SH 00 SJ

Bettws Newydd 19

National Grid Ref: SO3605

⌕ ◀ Black Bear

*Thornbury Farm, Bettws Newydd,
Usk, Monmouthshire, NP5 1JY.*
Family farm. Warm welcome,
beautiful views, attractions -
castles, golf, walks.
Tel: **01873 880598**
Mrs Jones.
D: £20.00-£20.00 **S:** £22.00-£22.00.
Open: All Year (not Xmas/
New Year)
Beds: 1T 2D
Baths: 1Shared
⛫ ▣ ⍓ ⌷ ⚲ ⋯ ⎕ ⊻ ⌁

Abergavenny 20

National Grid Ref: SO2914

⌕ ◀ King's Arms, Crown Inn, Old Mitre, Lamb
Flag, Walnut Tree, Bear Hotel, Nant-y-fyn,
Red Hart

*Pentre Court, Brecon Road,
Abergavenny, NP7 9ND.*
Grades: ETC 2 Stars
Tel: **01873 853545**
Mrs Candler.
D: £18.00-£24.00
S: £18.00-£30.00.
Open: All Year
Beds: 3D
Baths: 3 En
⛫ ▣ ⌷ ⍓ ⚲ ⋯ ⎕ ⊻ ⌁
Spacious, welcoming Georgian
house with open fires, set in 3 acres
of pretty stream side interestingly
stocked gardens/paddock, spring
bulbs, shrubs and roses, with won-
derful views over the Usk valley.
Just inside the National Park beside
footpath to River Usk and
Sugarloaf Mountain.

*Tyn-y-bryn, Deriside,
Abergavenny, Monmouthshire,
NP7 7HT.*
Actual grid ref: SO301165
Magnificent views, a homely
atmosphere. Comfortable
accommodation & warm welcome.
Grades: ETC 3 Star Farm
Tel: **01873 856682** (also fax no)
Mrs Belcham.
D: £20.00 **S:** £25.00.
Open: All Year
Beds: 1F 1T 1D
Baths: 2 En
⛫ (6) ⌷ ⍓ ⚲ ⋯ ⎕ ⊻

All rooms full and
nowhere else to stay?
Ask the owner if
there's anywhere
nearby

All rates are subject
to alteration at the
owners' discretion.

*Pentre House, Brecon Road,
Abergavenny, Monmouthshire,
NP7 7EW.*
Actual grid ref: SO283151
Charming small Georgian
award-winning country house in
wonderful gardens.
Grades: ETC 3 Star
Tel: **01873 853435**
Mrs Reardon-Smith.
Fax no: 01873 852321
D: £17.00-£18.00
S: £20.00-£25.00.
Open: All Year (not Xmas)
Beds: 1F 1D 1T
Baths: 2 Sh
⛫ ▣ (6) ⌷ ⍓ ⚲ ⋯ ⎕ ⊻ ⌁

*Ty`r Morwydd House, Pen-y-
Pound, Abergavenny,
Monmouthshire, NP7 5UD.*
Actual grid ref: SO297147
Quality group accommodation,
conferences, training etc. Advance
bookings only.
Grades: ETC 3 Star
Tel: **01873 855959**
Mrs Senior.
Fax no: 01873 855443
D: £16.50-£16.50
S: £16.50-£16.50.
Open: All Year (not Xmas/
New Year)
Beds: 2F 18T 29S
⛫ ▣ (25) ⊻ ⌷ ⍓ ⚲ ⋯ ⎕ ⊻ ⌁
⌁

*The Guest House & Mansel
Restaurant, 2 Oxford Street,
Abergavenny, Monmouthshire,
NP7 5RP.*
Actual grid ref: SO303147
Near bus, railway station, town;
excellent accommodation, choice
of breakfast.
Tel: **01873 854823** Mrs Cook.
D: £16.00-£19.00
S: £19.50-£27.00.
Open: Mar to Dec
Beds: 3F 6D 6T 2S
Baths: 3 Sh
⛫ (6) ▣ (10) ⌷ ⚲ ⋯ ⎕ ⊻ ⌁ ⌁

*Maes Glas, Monmouth Road,
Abergavenny, NP9 9SP.*
Maes Glas is a detached bungalow,
within easy walking distance of
town centre.
Tel: **01873 854494** (also fax no)
Mrs Haynes.
D: £17.50-£20.00
S: £17.50-£20.00.
Open: All Year
Beds: 1F 1D
⛫ ▣ ⊻ ⌷ ⚲ ⋯ ⎕ ⊻ ⌁

Llanthony 21

National Grid Ref: SO2827

*The Half Moon, Llanthony,
Abergavenny, Monmouthshire,
NP7 7NN.*
Actual grid ref: SO286278
C17th, beautiful countryside.
Serves good food and real ales.
Tel: **01873 890611**
Mrs Smith.
D: £20.00-£22.00
S: £22.00-£25.00.
Open: All Year (not Xmas)
Beds: 2F 4D 2T 1S
Baths: 2 Sh
⛫ ▣ (8) ⌷ ⍓ ⚲ ⋯ ⎕ ⊻ ⌁

Capel-y-Ffin 22

National Grid Ref: SO2531

▲ *Capel-y-Ffin Youth Hostel,
Capel-y-Ffin, Abergavenny,
Monmouthshire, NP7 7NP.*
Actual grid ref: SO250328
Tel: **01873 890650**
Under 18: £5.75 **Adults:** £8.50
Self-catering facilities, Showers,
Shop, Lounge, Drying room, Cycle
store, Parking, Evening meal at
7.00pm, No smoking, Kitchen
facilities, Breakfast available,
Credit cards accepted.
*Old hill farm set in 40-acre
grounds on mountainside in Brecon
Beacons National Park.*

*The Grange, Capel-y-Ffin,
Abergavenny, NP7 7NP.*
Actual grid ref: SO251315
Small Victorian guest house
situated in the beautiful Black
Mountains.
Grades: ETC 1 Star
Tel: **01873 890215**
Mrs Griffiths.
Fax no: 01873 890157
D: £22.50-£23.00
S: £22.50-£23.00.
Open: Easter to Nov
Beds: 1F 1D 1T 1S
Baths: 3 En
⛫ (6) ▣ (10) ⌷ ⍓ ⚲ ⋯ ⎕ ⊻ ⌁
⌁ ⌁

Llanigon 23

National Grid Ref: SO2139

⍾ ◀ Black Lion

*The Old Post Office,
Llanigon, Hay-on-Wye,
Hereford, HR3 5QA.*
A very special find in Black
Mountains, superb vegetarian
breakfast.
Grades: ETC 3 Star GH
Tel: **01497 820008**
Mrs Webb.
D: £17.00-£25.00
S: £20.00-£45.00.
Open: All Year
Beds: 1F 1D 1T
Baths: 2 En 1 Sh
⛫ ▣ (3) ⊻ ⌷ ⍓ ⚲ ⋯ ⎕ ⊻ ⌁ ⌁

Llwynbrain, *Llanigon, Hay-on-Wye, Hereford, HR3 5QF.*
Warm, friendly family farmhouse with views of Black Mountains.
Tel: **01497 847266**
D: £18.00-£25.00 **S:** £18.00-£25.00.
Open: All Year (not Xmas)
Beds: 2F 1S **Baths:** 1 Sh
ॐ **P** (6) ⌷ ★ ☆ ▥ **V** ⓘ ⚡ ⊕ ⫶

Cusop 24

National Grid Ref: SO2341

Fernleigh, *Hardwick Road, Cusop, Hay-on-Wye, Hereford, HR3 5QX.*
Quiet location walking distance of the famous book town of Hay-on-Wye.
Tel: **01497 820459** Mr Hughes.
D: £15.00-£19.00 **S:** £19.00-£19.00.
Open: Easter to Oct
Beds: 2D 1S **Baths:** 1 En 1 Sh
ॐ **P** (4) ⅟ ⌷ ✕ ☆ ▥ **V** ⓘ ⚡ ⊕ ⫶

Glasbury 25

National Grid Ref: SO1739

Maes-Mawr, *Glasbury, Hereford, HR3 5ND.*
10 mins off A438 on a farm in countryside. Panoramic views of Black Mountains.
Tel: **01497 847308**
D: £15.00-£17.00 **S:** £16.00-£18.00.
Open: Easter to Nov
Beds: 1F 2D 1T
Baths: 1 Sh
ॐ **P** (5) ⌷ ★ ☆ ▥ **V** ⓘ ⊕ ⫶

Llowes 26

National Grid Ref: SO1942

† ◁ Maesllwch Arms

Ty-Bach, *Llowes, Glasbury, HR3 5JE.*
Ornamental ponds, woodland garden, breathtaking views, abundant wildlife, birds. Friendly.
Grades: ETC 3 Star
Tel: **01497 847759** Bradfield.
Fax no: 01497 847940
D: £22.50-£25.00 **S:** £30.00-£40.00.
Open: All Year (not Xmas/New Year)
Beds: 1T 1D
Baths: 2 Pr
ॐ (5) **P** (5) ⌷ ✕ ☆ ▥ ⊕ ⫶

Llyswen 27

National Grid Ref: SO1337

† ◁ Griffin Inn

Lower Rhydness Bungalow, *Llyswen, Brecon, Powys, LD3 0AZ.*
Very comfortable centrally-heated bungalow, working farm, views into valley.
Tel: **01874 754264** Mrs Williams.
D: £16.00 **S:** £16.00.
Open: Easter to Dec
Beds: 1D 1T 1S **Baths:** 1 Sh
ॐ **P** (3) ⌷ ★ ✕ ☆ ▥ ⅋ **V** ⓘ ⊕

Boughrood 28

National Grid Ref: SO1339

† ◁ Bridgend Inn, Griffin Inn

Balangia, *Station Rd, Boughrood, Brecon, Powys, LD3 0YF.*
On the Wye Valley walk. Homely welcome given to all.
Tel: **01874 754453** Mrs Brown.
D: £16.00-£17.00 **S:** £16.00-£34.00.
Open: Easter to Oct
Beds: 1D 1T 1S **Baths:** 1 Sh
ॐ **P** ⅟ ⌷ ★ ✕ ☆ ▥ ⅋ **V** ⓘ ⊕ ⫶

Upper Middle Road, *Boughrood, Brecon, Powys, LD3 0BX.*
Actual grid ref: SO140392
Quietly situated, 180-year-old cottage, mountains, panorama, homely atmosphere.
Tel: **01874 754407** Mrs Kelleher.
D: £17.00-£17.00 **S:** £17.00-£25.00.
Open: All Year (not Xmas)
Beds: 1D 1T **Baths:** 1 En 1 Pr
ॐ **P** (3) ⅟ ⌷ ✕ ☆ ▥ **V** ⓘ ⊕ ⫶

Erwood 29

National Grid Ref: SO0942

† ◁ Erwood Inn, Wheelwrights' Arms

Trericket Mill Vegetarian Guesthouse, *Erwood, Builth Wells, Powys, LD2 3TQ.*
Actual grid ref: SO112414
Listed C19th watermill in Wye Valley, friendly and informal.
Grades: ETC 2 Star GH
Tel: **01982 560312** Mr Legge.
Fax no: 01982 560768
D: £14.00-£21.00 **S:** £16.00.
Open: All Year (not Xmas)
Beds: 2F 2D 2T **Baths:** 4 En 2 Sh
ॐ **P** (8) ⌷ ✕ ☆ ▥ **V** ⓘ ⊕ ⫶

▲ **Trericket Mill Bunkhouse,** *Erwood, Builth Wells, Powys, LD2 3TQ.*
Actual grid ref: SO112414
Tel: **01982 560312**
Under 18: £8.50 **Adults:** £8.50
Self-catering facilities, Television, Showers, Central heating, Drying room, Cycle store, Parking, Evening meal at 7pm
Brilliant location for river and mountains. Twin and family rooms.

Hafod-y-Gareg, *Erwood, Builth Wells, Powys, LD2 3TQ.*
Actual grid ref: SO107415
Tel: **01982 560400** Mrs McKay.
D: £13.50-£17.50 **S:** £13.50-£17.50.
Open: All Year (not Xmas)
Beds: 1F 2D 1T **Baths:** 3 En
ॐ **P** (6) ⌷ ★ ✕ ☆ ▥ **V** ⓘ ⅋ ⊕ ⫶
Secluded medieval farmhouse in idyllic Welsh hillside locality. Tranquillity personified, a stress free retreat. Rooms overlooking pasture and woodland. Walk the Wye Valley or ancient bridleways. Equidistant from Hay-on-Wye, Brecon Beacons, Builth Wells. The perfect getaway.

The Old Vicarage, *Erwood, Builth Wells, Powys, LD2 3DZ.*
An old vicarage with a difference! There are wonderful views over countryside.
Grades: ETC 3 Star
Tel: **01982 560680**
Mrs Williams.
D: £15.50-£16.00
S: £16.00-£17.00.
Open: All Year
Beds: 1F 1D 1T 1S
Baths: 1 Sh
ॐ (1) **P** ⌷ ★ ✕ ☆ ▥ **V** ⓘ ⅋ ⊕ ⫶

Orchard Cottage, *Erwood, Builth Wells, Powys, LD2 3EZ.*
Actual grid ref: SO096431
C18th tastefully modernised Welsh stone cottage. Gardens overlooking river.
Tel: **01982 560600**
Mr & Mrs Prior.
D: £17.00-£19.50
S: £20.00-£20.00.
Open: All Year (not Xmas)
Beds: 1F 1D 1T
Baths: 1 En 1 Sh
ॐ **P** (6) ⌷ ☆ ▥ **V** ⓘ ⅋ ⊕ ⫶

Aberedw 30

National Grid Ref: SO0847

† ◁ Seven Stars

Court Farm, *Aberedw, Builth Wells, Powys, LD2 3UP.*
Actual grid ref: SO091479
Strictly non-smoking, peaceful, picturesque. Hill-walking, birds and wildlife in abundance.
Tel: **01982 560277**
Mr Davies.
D: £17.00-£19.00
S: £18.00-£20.00.
Open: Easter to Nov
Beds: 2D 1S
Baths: 1 En 1 Pr 1 Sh
⅟ ⌷ ☆ ▥ **V** ⊕ ⫶

Builth Wells 31

National Grid Ref: SO0350

† ◁ Prince Llewelyn, Llanelwedd Arms, Greyhound

Dollynwydd Farm, *Builth Wells, Powys, LD2 3RZ.*
Grades: ETC 2 Star
Tel: **01982 553660** (also fax no)
Mrs Williams.
D: £18.00-£20.00
S: £18.00-£20.00.
Open: All Year (not Xmas)
Beds: 1D 2T 2S
Baths: 1 En 2 Sh
ॐ (14) **P** (6) ⅟ ⌷ ✕ ▥ ⓘ ⅋ ⊕ ⫶
C17th farmhouse lying beneath Eppynt Hills. Superb area for walking, bird-watching within east distance, Brecon Beacons, Elan Valley, Hay-on-Wye, bookshops, very comfortable in quiet area, ample parking, lockup garage for bikes. 1 mile Builth Wells, B4520 first left down farm lane.

The Cedar Guest House, *Hay Road, Builth Wells, Powys, LD2 3AR.*
Built 1880, on A470 backing Wye Valley with good views, good food, parking. **Grades:** ETC 2 Star
Tel: **01982 553356** Mr Morris.
D: £18.00-£20.00 **S:** £27.50-£30.00.
Open: All Year
Beds: 1F 1D 3T 2S
Baths: 5 En 2 Sh
🛇 🅿 (10) ⊬ 🗖 🛌 🗙 🔥 🎐 Ⅲ Ⅴ 🛉 ⊁ ♻

Woodlands, *Hay Road, Builth Wells, Powys, LD2 3BP.*
Actual grid ref: SO049513
Impressive Edwardian house, with ensuite facilities with secluded parking.
Grades: AA 4 Diamond
Tel: **01982 552354** (also fax no)
Mrs Nicholls.
D: £18.00-£20.00 **S:** £22.00-£25.00.
Open: All Year (not Xmas)
Beds: 4T **Baths:** 4 En
🅿 (4) ⊬ 🗖 🎐 Ⅲ & Ⅴ 🛉 ⊁ ♻

The Owls, *40 High Street, Builth Wells, Powys, LD2 3AB.*
Actual grid ref: SO041510
Convenient High Street location, close to showground, owls everywhere.
Tel: **01982 552518** Mrs Turner.
Fax no: 01982 553867
D: £14.00-£16.50 **S:** £14.00-£25.00.
Open: All Year
Beds: 1F 2D 2T 1S **Baths:** 5 En 1 Pr
🛇 🅿 (8) 🗖 🗙 🎐 Ⅲ Ⅴ 🛉 ⊁ ♻

Bron Wye, *Church Street, Builth Wells, Powys, LD2 3BS.*
Actual grid ref: SO039512
Christian family-run guest house.
Overlooking River Wye.
Tel: **01982 553587** Mrs Wiltshire.
D: £17.00-£17.00 **S:** £17.00-£17.00.
Open: All Year
Beds: 1F 2D 1T 2S **Baths:** 6 En
🛇 🅿 (7) ⊬ 🗖 🛌 🎐 Ⅲ Ⅴ 🛉 ⊁ ♻

Cilmery 32

National Grid Ref: SO0051

🍽 🍺 Prince Llewelyn

Llewelyn Leisure Park, *Cilmery, Builth Wells, Powys, LD2 3NU.*
Actual grid ref: SO003514
Jacuzzi, snooker, views, hospitality, inn; cows, sheep; self-catering, camping.
Tel: **01982 552838** Mr Johnson.
Fax no: 01982 551090
D: £16.00-£20.00 **S:** £18.00-£22.00.
Open: All Year
Beds: 2F 1S **Baths:** 2 Sh
🛇 🅿 (7) 🗖 🛌 🗙 🎐 Ⅲ & Ⅴ 🛉 ⊁ ♻

Planning a longer
stay? Always ask for
any special rates.

Cwmbach (Builth Wells) 33

National Grid Ref: SO0254

Rhydfelin, *Cwmbach, Builth Wells, Powys, LD2 3RT.*
1725 cosy stone guest house, restaurant, bar and tea garden.
Grades: ETC 3 Star
Tel: **01982 552493** Moyes.
D: £19.00-£22.00 **S:** £26.00-£44.00.
Open: All Year (not Xmas)
Beds: 1F 2D 1T
Baths: 1 En 2 Sh
🛇 🅿 (12) ⊬ 🗖 🗙 🔥 🎐 Ⅲ Ⅴ 🛉 ♻

Newbridge on Wye 34

National Grid Ref: SO0158

Lluest Newydd, *Llysdinam, Newbridge on Wye, Llandrindod Wells, Powys, LD1 6NA.*
Luxury remote farmhouse. Ideal for walking and birdwatching. Elan Valley close by.
Grades: ETC 4 Star, AA 4 Diamond
Tel: **01597 860435** (also fax no)
Mrs Burton.
D: £18.00-£22.00 **S:** £22.00-£26.00.
Open: All Year
Beds: 1F 1T 2D
Baths: 2 En 1 Pr
🛇 🅿 (6) ⊬ 🗖 🗙 🎐 Ⅲ Ⅴ 🛉 ⊁ ♻

Disserth 35

National Grid Ref: SO0358

🍽 🍺 Drover's Arms

Disserth Mill, *Disserth, Builth Wells, Powys, LD2 3TN.*
Actual grid ref: SO040551
A sun trap by a stream.
Tel: **01982 553217**
Mrs Worts.
D: £17.00-£20.00
S: £18.00-£20.00.
Open: Easter to Oct
Beds: 1T 1S
Baths: 1 En
🛇 🅿 (4) 🗖 🛌 🎐 Ⅲ Ⅴ 🛉 ⊁ ♻

Howey 36

National Grid Ref: SO0558

🍽 🍺 Three Wells, Drover's Arms, Ty Gwyn, Royal Oak, Stables

Holly Farm, *Howey, Llandrindod Wells, Powys, LD1 5PP.*
Actual grid ref: SO050589
Comfortable old farmhouse, dates back to Tudor times, bedrooms have lovely views of countryside.
Grades: ETC 3 Star Farm, AA 4 Diamond
Tel: **01597 822402**
Mrs Jones.
D: £20.00-£25.00
S: £24.00-£26.00.
Open: All Year (not Xmas)
Beds: 1F 2D 2T
Baths: 3 En 2 Sh
🛇 🅿 (6) 🗖 🗙 🎐 Ⅲ Ⅴ 🛉 ⊁ ♻

S = Price range for a single
person in a room

The Three Wells Farm, *Chapel Road, Howey, Llandrindod Wells, Powys, LD1 5PB.*
Three Wells is a hidden gem in the heart of Wales.
Grades: AA 4 Diamond
Tel: **01597 824427** Mr Roobottom.
Fax no: 01597 822484
D: £19.00-£28.00 **S:** £25.00-£30.00.
Open: All Year
Beds: 8D 5T 1S **Baths:** 14 En
🛇 (8) 🅿 (4) ⊬ 🗖 🎐 Ⅲ Ⅴ 🛉 ⊁ ♻

Western Route to Machynlleth

Llanwrtyd Wells is a pretty spa town, developed in the eighteenth century around the sulphur spring named Ffynon Droellwyd. Mr Green at The Neuadd Arms is the organiser of the world famous 'Man v. Horse' race.

Strata Florida Abbey is the very impressive ruin of a twelfth-century Cistercian foundation. Although a victim of the Dissolution, there is a fair amount to see, including a great Norman arch at the western end.

At **Devil's Bridge** three stone bridges, the earliest reputedly built by the Knights Templars, are set against the stunning backdrop of the Mynach Falls.

It was at **Machynlleth** in 1404 that Owain Glyndwr, leader of the resistance to English rule, summoned a parliament and proclaimed himself Prince of Wales. The Parliament House contains themed displays. The town also hosts the Celtica exhibition, with a reconstructioin Celtic settlement and audio-visual displays. The Y Tabernacl building houses a cultural centre which includes the Wales Museum of Modern Art.

Llanyre 37

National Grid Ref: SO0462

⚑ Bell Inn

***Highbury Farm**, Llanyre,
Llandrindod Wells, Powys, LD1 6EA.*
Actual grid ref: SO044628
Peaceful location with short farm
trail. Laundry room. Excellent
food.
Grades: ETC 3 Star
Tel: **01597 822716** (also fax no)
Mrs Evans.
D: £18.00-£21.00 **S:** £21.00-£24.00.
Open: Mar to Nov
Beds: 1F 2D **Baths:** 2 En 1 Pr
🛇 (1) 🅿 (3) ﬞ⍾ 🖳 🛏 ✕ 🕭 🖩 ♥ 🎗 ✦
🚲

***Greenglades**, Llanyre, Llandrindod
Wells, Powys, LD1 6EA.*
Beautiful country house in tranquil
setting near village inn.
Grades: ETC 4 Star
Tel: **01597 822950** Jones.
D: £18.00-£22.00 **S:** £20.00-£24.00.
Open: All Year (not Xmas)
Beds: 1F 1D 1T **Baths:** 2 En
🛇 🅿 (3) ﬞ⍾ 🖳 🛏 🕭 🖩 ♥ ✦ 🚲

Llandrindod Wells 38

National Grid Ref: SO0561

⚑ Bell Inn, Builders Arms, Greenway Manor,
Llanerch Inn, Three Wells, Drovers Arms

***Greylands**, High Street,
Llandrindod Wells, Powys, LD1 6AG.*
Handsome Victorian townhouse.
Surrounded by beautiful country-
side. Secure cycle storage.
Tel: **01597 822253**
Mrs MacDonald.
D: £16.00-£19.00 **S:** £17.00-£20.00.
Open: All Year
Beds: 1F 2D 1T 3S
Baths: 6 En 1 Sh
🛇 🅿 (5) 🖳 🛏 ✕ 🕭 🖩 ♥ 🎗 ✦ 🚲

***Builders Arms**, Crossgates,
Llandrindod Wells, Powys, LD1 6RB.*
Family run village inn. Garden,
patio, large car park.
Grades: ETC 2 Star
Tel: **01597 851235**
D: £17.50-£17.50
S: £19.50-£19.50.
Open: All Year
Beds: 1D 1T
Baths: 1 En
🛇 🅿 ﬞ⍾ 🛏 ✕ 🕭 🖩 ♥ 🎗 🚲

***Charis**, Pentrosfa, Llandrindod
Wells, Powys, LD1 5NG.*
Edwardian house on edge of
Llandrindod Wells in quiet residen-
tial road.
Tel: **01597 824732** (also fax no)
Mrs Gimson.
D: £17.00-£19.00 **S:** £25.00.
Open: All Year (not Xmas)
Beds: 1F 2D 1T
Baths: 2 En 1 Pr
🛇 🅿 (3) ﬞ⍾ 🖳 🛏 🕭 🖩 ♥ 🎗

***Drovers Arms,**
Llandrindod Wells, Powys, LD1 5PT.*
Quiet location, owner-run, great
food, own beer, real fire.
Grades: ETC 2 Star
Tel: **01597 822508**
Mrs Day.
Fax no: 01597 822711
D: £20.00-£25.00 **S:** £30.00-£30.00.
Open: All Year (not Xmas/
New Year)
Beds: 2D 1T **Baths:** 3 En
🛇 (8) 🅿 (3) ﬞ⍾ 🖳 ✕ 🕭 🖩 ♥ 🎗 ✦ 🚲

Llanwrthwl 39

National Grid Ref: SN9763

⚑ Vulcan Arms

***Dyffryn Farm,**
Llanwrthwl, Llandrindod Wells,
Powys, LD1 6NU.*
Actual grid ref: SN972645
Idyllically situated above the Upper
Wye valley, near the Elan Lakes.
Tel: **01597 811017**
Mrs Tyler.
Fax no: 01597 810609
D: £20.00-£22.00
S: £20.00-£22.00.
Open: Mar to Oct
Beds: 1D 1T 1S
Baths: 1 En 1 Pr 1 Sh
🛇 (5) 🅿 (6) ﬞ⍾ 🖳 🛏 ✕ 🕭 🖩 ♥ ✦ 🚲

Rhayader 40

National Grid Ref: SN9768

⚑ Bear's Head, Crown, Triangle

***Liverpool House,**
East House, Rhayader, Powys,
LD6 5EA.*
Grades: ETC 2 Star
Tel: **01597 810706**
Mrs Griffiths.
Fax no: 01597 810964
D: £15.50-£17.00
S: £18.00-£22.00.
Open: All Year (not Xmas)
Beds: 2F 5D 1S
Baths: 7 En 1 Sh
🛇 🅿 (8) 🖳 🛏 🕭 🖩 ♥ 🎗 ✦ 🚲
Excellent accommodation either in
main house or annexe. Very close
to the beautiful Elan Valley
Reservoirs in an area suitable for
bird watching, walking, cycling.
Ideally central for touring Mid
Wales. Groups welcome. Cream
teas, Welsh teas and snacks
available.

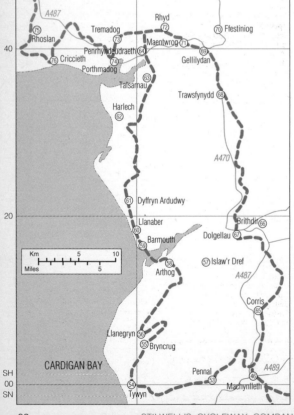

60

40

20

Km 5 10

Miles 5

CARDIGAN BAY

A487

A470

A487

A489

SH
00
SN

Brynafon Country House Hotel, *South Street, Rhayader, Powys, LD6 5BL.*
Grades: ETC 3 Star, AA 2 Star
Tel: 01597 810735 Mrs Collins.
Fax no: 01597 810111
D: £18.00-£40.00 **S:** £35.00.
Open: All Year
Beds: 1F 11D 4T
Baths: 16 En
🛏🅿✕☐🛉✕🖳🖩&Ⅴ♦∅🚲
A former Victorian workhouse built in 1876, this impressive building is now a comfortable, relaxed, family-run hotel. Set amid glorious hills and mountains near Rhayader and the beautiful Elan Valley with a rare 'Red Kite' feeding centre next door.

Brynteg, *East Street, Rhayader, Powys, LD6 5EA.*
Comfortable Edwardian guest house, overlooking hills and gardens.
Grades: ETC 3 Star B & B
Tel: 01597 810052
Mrs Lawrence.
D: £16.50-£17.00 **S:** £16.00-£17.00.
Open: All Year (not Xmas)
Beds: 2D 1T 1S
Baths: 3 En 1 Pr
🛏🅿(4)☐🛉🖳Ⅴ♦🚲

Beili Neuadd, *Rhayader, Powys, LD6 5NS.*
Actual grid ref: SN994698
Award-winning accommodation in farmhouse - secluded position with stunning views.
Grades: ETC 4 Star
Tel: 01597 810211 (also fax no)
Mrs Edwards.
D: £21.00-£23.00 **S:** £21.00.
Open: All Year (not Xmas)
Beds: 2D 1T 1S
Baths: 2 En 2 Pr
🛏(8)🅿☐🛉✕🖳&Ⅴ♦∅🚲

The Horseshoe Guest House, *Church Street, Rhayader, Powys, LD6 5AT.*
Actual grid ref: SN969680
'Country Style' decor, conservatory with fig and grape vines.
Grades: ETC 3 Star GH
Tel: 01597 810982 (also fax no)
Mrs Stubbs.
D: £18.00-£19.00 **S:** £18.00-£18.00.
Open: All Year (not Xmas)
Beds: 2D 1T 1S
Baths: 2 En 1 Sh
🛏🅿(6)☐🛉✕🖳Ⅴ♦∅🚲

Downfield Farm, *Rhayader, Powys, LD6 5PA.*
Beautifully situated, surrounded by hills and lakes. Also, Red Kite country.
Grades: ETC 2 Star
Tel: 01597 810394
Mrs Price.
D: £17.00-£18.00 **S:** £18.00-£19.00.
Open: Mar to Oct
Beds: 2D 1T
Baths: 2 Sh
🛏🅿(10)☐🛉🖳Ⅴ∅🚲

Gigrin Farm, *South Street, Rhayader, Powys, LD6 5BL.*
Actual grid ref: SN980677
Superb views; working farm, nature trail, feeding red kites everyday.
Tel: 01597 810243 Mrs Powell.
Fax no: 01597 810357
D: £16.00-£17.50 **S:** £17.50-£20.00.
Open: All Year
Beds: 2D **Baths:** 1 Sh
🛏(5)🅿(3)☐🛉🖳Ⅴ

Bryncoed, *Dark Lane, Rhayader, Powys, LD6 5DA.*
Victorian house set in 1/3 acre, originally built for local doctor.
Tel: 01597 811082
D: £14.50-£20.00 **S:** £15.00-£21.00.
Open: All Year
Beds: 3F 2D 2T
Baths: 1 En 2 Pr 1 Sh
🛏🅿(4)☐🛉✕🖳Ⅴ♦∅🚲

Llangurig 41

National Grid Ref: SN9079

🍴🍺 Black Lion, Blue Bell

The Old Vicarage Guest House, *Llangurig, Llanidloes, Powys, SY18 6RN.*
Grades: ETC 2 Star
Tel: 01686 440280 (also fax no) Hartley.
D: £18.00-£22.00 **S:** £25.00-£25.00.
Open: Mar to Nov
Beds: 1F 2D 1T **Baths:** 4 En
🛏(5)🅿(6)☐🛉✕🖳Ⅴ♦∅🚲
The Old Vicarage is a charming Victorian House situated in Llangurig, 1000 ft above sea level, the highest village in Wales. Ideal for visiting the mountains and valleys of Central Wales. Good walking/bird watching (Red Kite Country). Warm welcome guaranteed.

Llanidloes 42

National Grid Ref: SN9584

🍴🍺 Unicorn

Lloyds, *Cambrian Place, Llanidloes, Powys, SY18 6BX.*
Actual grid ref: SN955844
Long-established Victorian hotel in centre of attractive market town.
Grades: ETC 2 Star
Tel: 01686 412284 Mr Lines.
Fax no: 01686 412666
D: £25.00-£25.00 **S:** £19.00-£33.00.
Open: Mar to Jan
Beds: 3D 2T 4S
Baths: 6 En 1 Sh
🛏☐✕🖳Ⅴ∅🚲

S = Price range for a single person in a room

Van 43

National Grid Ref: SN9587

🍴🍺 Star Inn, Red Lion

Esgairmaen, *Van, Llanidloes, Powys, SY18 6NT.*
Actual grid ref: SN925904
Comfortable farmhouse in unspoilt countryside, ideal for waking and bird watching.
Tel: 01686 430272
D: £17.00-£19.00
S: £17.00-£19.00.
Open: Easter to Oct
Beds: 1F 1D
Baths: 2 En
🛏(1)🅿(4)☐🛉✕🖳Ⅴ♦∅

Aberhosan 44

National Grid Ref: SN8097

🍴🍺 Star Inn

Bacheiddon Farm, *Aberhosan, Machynlleth, Powys, SY20 8SG.*
Working farm. Ideal walking, touring area. Close RSPB and MWT.
Tel: 01654 702229
Mrs Lewis.
D: £18.00-£20.00
S: £20.00-£25.00.
Open: May to Oct
Beds: 3D
Baths: 3 En
🛏🅿☐🛉Ⅴ

Darowen 45

National Grid Ref: SH8201

Cefn Farm, *Darowen, Machynlleth, Powys, SY20 8NS.*
Unsurpassable views, good walking. Half hour drive seaside. Open fire, personal service.
Tel: 01650 511336
Mr Lloyd.
D: £20.00 **S:** £20.00.
Open: All Year
Beds: 1F 1D
🛏🅿(3)✕☐🛉🖳&Ⅴ

Machynlleth 46

National Grid Ref: SH7400

🍴🍺 White Lion, Black Lion, Glyndwr Hotel, White Horse, Wynnastay, Skinner's Arms

Maenllwyd, *Newtown Road, Machynlleth, Powys, SY20 8EY.*
Actual grid ref: SH752009
Home from home, within walking distance all amenities, safe parking.
Grades: ETC 3 Star GH, AA 3 Diamond
Tel: 01654 702928 (also fax no)
Mr Vince.
D: £19.00-£22.00
S: £25.00-£25.00.
Open: All Year (not Xmas)
Beds: 1F 4D 3T **Baths:** 8 En
🛏🅿(10)✕☐🛉🖳Ⅴ♦∅🚲

Talbontdrain, *Uwchygarreg, Machynlleth, Powys, SY20 8RR.*
Actual grid ref: SN777959
Tel: **01654 702192** Ms Matthews.
D: £19.00-£21.00 **S:** £16.00-£19.00.
Open: All Year (not Xmas/New Year)
Beds: 1D 1T 2S
Baths: 1 Pr 1 Sh
♿ 🅿 (4) ⊬ ☆ ✗ ⚓ 🏛 🖾 🛇 🍴 ∅ ⚲
Friendly family B&B. We like having children here and are flexible about sleeping arrangements - there's even a barn for adventurous kids! We have dogs, cats and chickens, rivers, mountains and seaside not far away. Safe playing space and fantastic food.

Wynnstay Arms Hotel, *Maengwyn Street, Machynlleth, Powys, SY20 8AE.*
Old coaching inn, in heart of historic market town, in stunning Dovey Valley.
Grades: AA 2 Star, RAC 2 Star
Tel: **01654 702941** Mr Dark.
Fax no: 01654 703884
D: £35.00-£48.00 **S:** £45.00.
Open: All Year
Beds: 3F 9D 5T 6S
Baths: 23 En
♿ 🅿 (36) ⊬ ☆ ✗ ⚓ 🏛 🖾 🛇 🍴 ∅ ⚲

Pay B&Bs by cash or cheque and be prepared to pay up front.

Western Route through Snowdonia

From **Tywyn** you can take a steam train on the Talyllyn Railway to Abergynolwyn.

Barmouth is a pleasant seaside resort where you can find the Ty Gwyn Museum, a museum on the Tudors.

Harlech Castle is a World Heritage Site with a spectacular clifftop location overlooking the sea. Built by Edward I at the time of the conquest of Wales in the late thirteenth century, it was taken by Owain Glyndwr in 1404. The future Henry VII was besieged here for seven years during the Wars of the Roses. The most impressive feature is the gatehouse, with its two huge half-round towers.

Cwmdylluan Forge, *Machynlleth, Powys, SY20 8RZ.*
Actual grid ref: SH764000
Modern riverside bungalow, rooms overlook lovely garden and river.
Grades: ETC 3 Star
Tel: **01654 702684** Hughes.
Fax no: 01654 700133
D: £15.50-£17.50 **S:** £16.50-£18.00.
Open: All Year
Beds: 1D 1T 1S **Baths:** 2 Pr 2 Sh
♿ (5) 🅿 (5) ⊬ ☆ ✗ ⚓ 🏛 🖾 🛇 🍴 ∅ ⚲

Gwelfryn, *6 Green Fields, Machynlleth, Powys, SY20 8DR.*
Quiet but central, fantastic breakfasts, near all tourist attractions.
Grades: ETC 2 Star
Tel: **01654 702532**
D: £17.00-£19.50 **S:** £17.00.
Open: Easter to Oct
Beds: 1D 1T 1S
Baths: 1 En 1 Pr
♿ ⊬ ☆ ☆ ⚓ 🏛 🖾 🛇 ∅ ⚲

Awelon, *Heol Powys, Machynlleth, Powys, SY20 8AY.*
Centrally situated, small, comfortable private house. Warm welcome.
Tel: **01654 702047** Ms Williams.
D: £16.00-£17.00 **S:** £16.00-£17.50.
Open: All Year (not Xmas)
Beds: 1T 1S
Baths: 1 Sh
♿ (2) ⊬ ☆ 🏛 🍴 ∅

Llanwrtyd Wells   47

National Grid Ref: SN8746

🍽 🍺 Stonecroft Inn, New Inn

🔺 **Stonecroft Hostel,** *Dolecoed Road, Llanwrtyd Wells, Powys, LD5 4RA.*
Actual grid ref: SN878467
Tel: **01591 610332 / 01591 610327**
Adults: £8.00

Oakfield House, *Dol-y-coed Road, Llanwrtyd Wells, LD5 4RA.*
Comfortable Edwardian house in Britain's smallest town. Red kite country.
Grades: ETC 3 Star
Tel: **01591 610605**
D: £19.00-£19.00
S: £19.00-£22.00.
Open: Easter to Oct
Beds: 1D 1T 1S
Baths: 2 Sh
♿ (5) 🅿 (1) ⊬ ☆ ⚓ 🏛 🛇 ∅ ⚲

Carlton House Hotel, *Dolycoed Road, Llanwrtyd Wells, Powys, LD5 4SN.*
Edwardian restaurant with rooms. Excellent dining, comfortable rooms, warm welcome.
Tel: **01591 610248** Dr Gilchrist.
Fax no: 01591 610242
D: £30.00-£35.00
S: £30.00-£40.00.
Open: All Year (not Xmas)
Beds: 1F 4D 1T 1S
Baths: 5 En 2 Pr
♿ ☆ ☆ ✗ ⚓ 🏛 🖾 🛇 🍴

Haulwen, *Beulah Road, Llanwrtyd Wells, Powys, LD5 4RF.*
Actual grid ref: SN881468
Small & friendly, comfortable rooms, hairdryers, toiletries, robes, electric radio alarms etc in rooms
Tel: **01591 610449** (also fax no)
D: £15.00-£20.00 **S:** £15.00-£20.00.
Open: All Year
Beds: 1D 1S
Baths: 1 Sh
⊬ ☆ ⚓ 🏛 🛇 🛇 ∅ ⚲

Dolgoch   48

National Grid Ref: SN8056

🔺 **Dolgoch Youth Hostel,** *Dolgoch, Tregaron, Cardiganshire, SY25 6NR.*
Actual grid ref: SH806561
Tel: **01974 298680**
Under 18: £4.75 **Adults:** £6.75
Self-catering facilities, Showers, Shop, Wet weather shelter Limited, Parking, No smoking, WC, Kitchen facilities
Mountain hostel in large farmhouse with gas lighting open fires and no electricity. The Tywi Valley is beautiful, remote, and ideal for birdwatching, trekking by foot or by pony.

Pontrhydfendigaid   49

National Grid Ref: SN7366

Red Lion Hotel,
Pontrhydfendigaid, Ystrad Meurig, Ceredigion, SY25 6BH.
Actual grid ref: SN731666
Friendly riverside country pub/inn with caravan/camping facilities.
Tel: **01974 831232** Mr Earey.
D: £18.50 **S:** £18.50.
Open: All Year
Beds: 1F 1T 2D **Baths:** 4 En
♿ 🅿 (50) ⊬ ☆ ☆ ✗ ⚓ 🏛 🛇 ∅ ⚲

Cwmystwyth   50

National Grid Ref: SN7874

🍽 🍺 Miners' Arms

Tainewyddion Uchaf, *Cwmystwyth, Aberystwyth, Ceredigion, SY23 4AF.*
Situated at over 1000 ft. Panoramic views overlooking the Ystwyth Valley.
Tel: **01974 282672** Mrs Liford.
D: £15.00-£18.00 **S:** £15.00-£18.00.
Open: Easter to End Oct
Beds: 1T 1D 1S **Baths:** 1 En 1 Sh
⊬ ✗ 🏛 ∅ ⚲

Hafod Lodge, *Cwmystwyth, Aberystwyth, Ceredigion, SY23 4AD.*
Actual grid ref: SN784742
Picturesque, peaceful location, ideal for touring river valleys, lakes, mountains and coast.
Tel: **01974 282247** Mrs Davis.
D: £18.50-£24.00 **S:** £18.50-£24.00.
Open: All Year
Beds: 1D 1T **Baths:** 1 En 1 Pr
🅿 (6) ⊬ ☆ ☆ ⚓ 🏛 🖾 🛇 🍴 ∅ ⚲

Devil's Bridge 51

National Grid Ref: SN7376

⏼ ⏼ Hafway Inn

*Mount Pleasant, Devil's Bridge,
Aberystwyth, Ceredigion, SY23 4QY.*
Actual grid ref: SN736769
Lose the crowds amidst stunning
scenery where red kites soar.
Tel: **01970 890219**
Mr & Mrs Connell.
Fax no: 01970 890239
D: £21.00-£23.00 **S:** £21.00-£29.00.
Open: All Year (not Xmas)
Beds: 2D 2T
Baths: 3 En 1 Pr
⏼ (12) ⏼ (4) ⏼⏼⏼⏼⏼⏼⏼⏼⏼⏼⏼

Ponterwyd 52

National Grid Ref: SN7480

▲ *Maesnant, Ponterwyd,
Aberystwyth, Dyfed, SY23 3AG.*
Tel: **020 8421 4648**
Under 18: £5.00 **Adults:** £5.00
Self-catering facilities, Showers,
Lounge, Dining room, Grounds
available for games
*Bungalow and outbuildings set in
wild open country about 5 miles
from village. Located on the slopes
of Plynlimon mountain, overlooking
Nant-y-Moch Reservoir. Ideal base
for youth groups undertaking Duke
of Edinburgh's and similar expedi-
tion training. Local attractions
include Llywernog Mine Museum,
Devil's Bridge and Vale of Rheidol
Railway.*

*The George Borrow Hotel,
Ponterwyd, Aberystwyth,
Ceredigion, SY23 3AD.*
Tel: **01970 890230** Mr & Mrs Wall.
Fax no: 01970 890587
D: £25.00**S:** £25.00.
Open: All Year (not Xmas)
Beds: 2F 3D 2T 2S
Baths: 9 En
⏼ ⏼ (40) ⏼⏼⏼⏼⏼⏼⏼⏼⏼⏼⏼⏼
Famous old hotel set in beautiful
countryside, overlooking Eagle
Falls and the Rheidol Gorge. 3
miles Devils Bridge, 12 miles
Aberystwyth. An ideal centre to
explore mid-Wales. Good fishing,
birdwatching and walking. Home
made food and fine beer, log fires
and a friendly welcome.

Pennal 53

National Grid Ref: SH6900

*Marchlyn, Aberdovey Road,
Pennal, Machynlleth, SY20 9YS.*
Quiet location near Aberdovey on a
Welsh-speaking working farm.
Grades: ETC 2 Star
Tel: **01654 702018**
D: £17.00-£20.00 **S:** £17.00-£20.00.
Open: All Year
Beds: 1F 4D 1T 1S
Baths: 2 En 1 Pr

Tywyn (Aberdovey) 54

National Grid Ref: SH5800

⏼ ⏼ Peniarth Arms, Tredegar Arms

Hendy Farm, Tywyn, LL36 9RU.
Actual grid ref: SH597015
Comfortable farmhouse near farm
and beach. Own halt on Talyllyn
railway.
Grades: ETC 3 Star Farm
Tel: **01654 710457** (also fax no)
Mrs Lloyd-Jones.
D: £18.00-£24.00
S: £22.00-£27.00.
Open: Easter to Oct
Beds: 2D 1T
Baths: 2 En 1 Pr
⏼⏼⏼⏼⏼⏼⏼⏼⏼⏼⏼

*Greenfield Hotel & Restaurant,
High Street, Tywyn, LL36 9AD.*
Small friendly licensed hotel. Close
Talyllyn Steam and Main Railway.
Tel: **01654 710354** (also fax no)
Mrs Jenkins.
D: £16.00-£18.50
S: £17.00-£19.50.
Open: Feb to Dec
Beds: 2F 3D 3T
Baths: 6 Pr 1 Sh
⏼⏼⏼⏼⏼⏼⏼

Bryncrug 55

National Grid Ref: SH6003

*Peniarth Arms, Bryncrug, Tywyn,
Gwynedd, LL36 9PH.*
Cosy village inn, Cader Idris.
Tal-y-llyn railway nearby.
Beautiful scenery.
Grades: ETC 3 Star
Tel: **01654 711505** Mrs Mountford.
Fax no: 01654 712169
D: £17.00-£20.00 **S:** £18.00-£25.00.
Open: All Year (not Xmas/New
Year)
Beds: 4D
Baths: 4 En
⏼ (1) ⏼⏼⏼⏼⏼⏼⏼

*Dolgoch Falls Hotel, Dolgoch,
Bryncrug, Tywyn, Gwynedd,
LL36 9UW.*
Actual grid ref: SH650046
One of Wales' most comfortable
family-run hotels, at foot of mag-
nificent waterfalls and ravine.
Tel: **01654 782258** Mr Lycett.
Fax no: 01654 782209
D: £25.00-£30.00 **S:** £25.00.
Open: Mar to Dec
Beds: 3D 2T 1S
Baths: 4 En 1 Sh
⏼ (12) ⏼ (50) ⏼⏼⏼⏼⏼⏼⏼⏼⏼

All rates are subject
to alteration at the
owners' discretion.

Eastern Route
through Snowdonia

On the eastern route out of
Machynlleth, the **Centre for
Alternative Technology** is a
self-sufficient community
started in the 1970s on the
site of a disused slate quarry,
where you can see renew-
able energy generation
(wind, water and solar power)
in action, as well as organic
gardens and numerous other
attractions.

Dolgellau was the site of a
Quaker community; entry to
the Quaker Heritage Centre is
free. To the north of town, the
Gwynfynydd Gold Centre and
Mine is the only working gold
mine open to the public.

Llanegryn 56

National Grid Ref: SH6005

*Cefn Coch Country Guest House,
Llanegryn, Tywyn, LL36 9SD.*
Actual grid ref: SH592050
Grades: ETC 3 Star
Tel: **01654 712193** (also fax no)
Mrs Sylvester.
D: £22.00-£24.00
S: £22.00-£29.00.
Open: Mar to Oct
Beds: 2D 3T
Baths: 3 En 2 Sh
⏼ (14) ⏼ (11) ⏼⏼⏼⏼⏼⏼⏼⏼⏼
⏼
Cefn Coch, a former coaching inn,
enjoys a beautiful garden with
spectacular views over Dysynni
Valley. An outstanding area for
bird watching, walking, cycling,
golfing. Fresh flowers, excellent
cooking and good wine make for an
enjoyable holiday in peaceful
surroundings.

Islaw'r Dref 57

National Grid Ref: SH6815

▲ *Kings (Dolgellau) Youth
Hostel, Islaw'r Dref, Penmaenpool,
Dolgellau, Gwynedd, LL40 1TB.*
Actual grid ref: SH683161
Tel: **01341 422392**
Under 18: £6.50
Adults: £9.25
Self-catering facilities, Showers,
Shop, Lounge, Dining room,
Drying room, Cycle store, Parking,
No smoking, WC, Kitchen
facilities, Credit cards accepted
*Traditional hostel set in idyllic
wooded valley, with magnificent
views up to Cader Idris and Rhinog
mountain ranges.*

All cycleways are popular: you are well-advised to book ahead

▲ *Caban Cader Idris, Islaw'r Dref, Dolgellau, LL40 1TS.*
Actual grid ref: SH682169
Tel: **01766 762588 / 07887 954301**
Under 18: £4.50
Adults: £4.50
Self-catering facilities, Showers, Central heating, Lounge, Drying room, Parking, No smoking
Ideal group accommodation, sleeps 19, kitchen/dining room, heating, shower, drying room, parking, picnic/BBQ area. Listed former school in secluded wooded valley 3 miles from Dolgellau in Snowdonia National Park. Within walking distance of Cader Idris Range, Cregennen Lake and Mawddach Estuary. Other local activities include: mountain biking, pony trekking, skiing, fishing, beaches.

Arthog 58

National Grid Ref: SH6414

⛱ 🍺 Fairbourne Hotel

Graig Wen Guest House, Arthog, LL39 1BQ.
Grades: ETC 2 Star
Tel: **01341 250900** Mrs Ameson.
Fax no: 01341 250482
D: £17.00-£19.00 **S:** £18.00-£24.00.
Open: All Year
Beds: 1F 4D 1T 1S
Baths: 3 En 2 Sh
🛇 (4) 🅿 (20) ⅋ ☐ ✕ 🚲 🎿 🛏 🖂 & Ⓥ 🛆 ∦ ෯

In 42 acres of woodland leading to Mawddach Estuary. Spectacular view of mountains, estuary, sea from house. Ideal for ramblers, cyclists, climbers, bird watchers. Cader Mountain, lakes, beaches, pony trekking, golf course, fishing, stream trains nearby. Disabled welcome.

D = Price range per person sharing in a double room

Barmouth 59

National Grid Ref: SH6115

⛱ 🍺 Last Inn

Wavecrest Hotel, 8 Marine Parade, Barmouth, North West Wales, LL42 1NA.
Actual grid ref: SH609160
Welcoming and relaxing Which? B&B. Excellent food, wine and whiskey.
Grades: ETC 3 Star, AA 2 Star
Tel: **01341 280330** (also fax no)
Mr & Mrs Jarman.
D: £18.00-£27.00 **S:** £22.00-£37.00.
Open: Easter to Oct
Beds: 2F 3D 1S
Baths: 8 En 1 Pr
🛇 🅿 (2) ⅋ ☐ ✕ 🎿 🛏 🖂 Ⓥ ∦

The Gables, Fford Mynach, Barmouth, Gwynedd, LL42 1RL.
Actual grid ref: SH609166
Victorian house of character lovely position near mountains - warm welcome.
Grades: ETC 2 Star
Tel: **01341 280553**
Mr & Mrs Lewis.
D: £18.00-£20.00 **S:** £18.00-£20.00.
Open: Easter to Nov
Beds: 1F 2D 1S
Baths: 2 En 1 Sh
🛇 🅿 (4) ⅋ ☐ ✕ 🎿 🛏 🖂 Ⓥ 🛆 ∦ ෯

Lawrenny Lodge Hotel, Barmouth, LL42 1SU.
Small quiet family run hotel. Views over harbour and estuary.
Grades: ETC 2 Star
Tel: **01341 280466** Mr Barber.
Fax no: 01341 281551
D: £22.00-£32.00 **S:** £32.00-£32.00.
Open: Mar to Nov
Beds: 1F 4D 2T 1S
Baths: 7 En 1 Sh
🛇 🅿 (9) ☐ ✕ 🎿 🛏 🖂 Ⓥ 🛆 ∦

The Sandpiper, 7 Marine Parade, Barmouth, LL42 1NA.
Sea front accommodation close to station. Parking outside.
Grades: ETC 2 Star
Tel: **01341 280318**
Mr & Mrs Palmer.
D: £14.50-£21.00 **S:** £15.50-£17.00.
Open: Easter to Oct
Beds: 2F 7D 3S
Baths: 6 Pr 2 Sh
🛇 🅿 ☐ 🛏 🖂 & Ⓥ

Min Y Mor Hotel, Marine Promenade, Barmouth, North West Wales, LL42 1HW.
Family run hotel, friendly atmosphere, in a good central position.
Grades: ETC 2 Star
Tel: **01341 280555**
Mr Atkins.
Fax no: 01341 280468
D: £52.00-£60.00 **S:** £52.00-£65.00.
Open: All Year
Beds: 8F 6D 8T 3S
Baths: All En
🛇 🅿 (70) ☐ 🛏 ✕ 🎿 🛏 🖂 Ⓥ 🛆 ∦ ෯

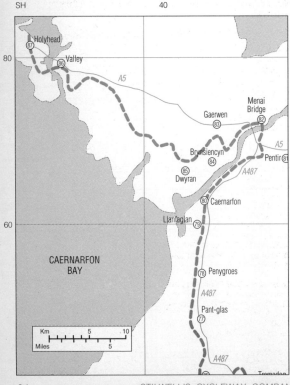

SH   40

80

Holyhead ⑧⑦
Valley ⑧⑥
A5
Gaerwen ⑧③
Menai Bridge ⑧②
A5
Brynsiencyn ⑧④
Pentir ⑧①
A487
Dwyran ⑧⑤
⑧⓪ Caernarfon
Llanfaglan ⑦⑨

60

CAERNARFON BAY

⑦⑧ Penygroes
A487
Pant-glas
⑦⑦
A487
⑦⑥ Tremadog

Km 5 10
Miles 5

Porthmadog to Holyhead

From **Porthmadog** you can take the spectacular narrow-gauge Ffestiniog Railway to Blaenau Ffestiniog, up the route between the old slate mines and the coast. A detour to the southeast of town will bring you to the famous Italianate fantasy village of **Portmeirion**, assembled in the 1920s by Sir Clough Williams-Ellis out of buildings in a myriad styles brought here from different parts of Britain, and elsewhere.

Thirteenth-century **Criccieth Castle** was ruined by Owain Glyndwr in 1404. The ruins yield views across Cardigan Bay to Harlech.

The superlatively well-preserved **Caernarfon Castle**, with its polygonal towers, was built to be the royal seat in conquered Wales by Edward I. It was the scene in 1969 for a made-to-order pseudo-medieval ceremony marking Prince Charles' investiture as Prince of Wales.

At **Bangor**, the cathedral contains the famous sixteenth-century wooden carving, the Mostyn Christ. The main building of the university mirrors the design of the cathedral; the museum and art gallery has a Welsh national flavour; and the renovated Victorian pier gives excellent views of the Menai Suspension Bridge, built by Thomas Telford in 1826.

The reason for the fame of **Llanfairpwllgwyngyllgogerychwyrndrobwll-llantisiliogogogoch** should be self-evident even if this is the first you've ever heard of the place.

Plas Newydd, just beyond Llanfairetc, is an eighteenth-century house in the Gothic style – a rare thing. Designed by James Wyatt, the interior is eclectic; and there is a huge mural by Whistler. The grounds, which include a fine spring garden, yield splendid views to Snowdonia.

If the cycle route has failed to expend all your energy reserves, you can climb the 700-foot Holyhead mountain above **Holyhead**; at the top you will find a large Iron Age hill fort, Caer y Tawr. Below the mountain at South Stack, the Ellin's Tower Seabird Centre offers observation of the abundant bird life on the cliffs.

Tal-Y-Don Hotel, High Street, Barmouth, *LL42 1DL.*
Families welcome. Home cooking, bar meals and good beer.
Tel: **01341 280508** Mrs Davies.
D: £17.00-£20.00 **S:** £20.00-£25.00.
Open: All Year (not Xmas)
Beds: 2F 4D 2T
Baths: 4 En 2 Sh
🛏 🅿 ⅓ 🗗 🗶 ≛ 🎹 Ⅴ 🛉 🐾

Endeavour Guest House, Marine Parade, Barmouth, *LL42 1NA.*
Actual grid ref: SH611159
Sea front location, beach 75 yards, railway station 150 yards.
Tel: **01341 280271**
Mr & Mrs Every.
D: £16.00-£20.00 **S:** £16.00-£16.00.
Open: All Year (not Xmas)
Beds: 7F 1S
Baths: 4 En 1 Sh
🛏 (3) 🅿 (3) 🗗 ≛ 🎹 Ⅴ 🐾 🐾

Llanaber   60

National Grid Ref: SH6017

Llwyndu Farmhouse, Llanaber, Barmouth, Gwynedd, *LL42 1RR.*
Actual grid ref: SH600185
C16th Llwyndu nestles in a spectacular location with panoramic views over Cardigan Bay.
Tel: **01341 280144**
Mrs Thompson.
D: £27.50-£32.00 **S:** £27.50-£32.00.
Open: All Year (not Xmas)
Beds: 2F 4D 1T
Baths: 7 En
🛏 🅿 (10) ⅓ 🗗 🛏 🗶 ≛ 🎹 Ⅴ 🛉 🐾

Dyffryn Ardudwy   61

National Grid Ref: SH5822

🅄 ⬚ Hel y Bryn

Parc yr Onnen, Dyffryn Ardudwy, Gwynedd, *LL44 2DU.*
Actual grid ref: SH592242
Rural setting; superb sea and mountain views by peaceful lane.
Grades: ETC 3 Star
Tel: **01341 247033** Mrs Bethell.
D: £18.00-£20.00 **S:** £20.00-£20.00.
Open: All Year
Beds: 1D 1T **Baths:** 2 En
🛏 🅿 (3) ⅓ 🗗 🛏 🗶 ≛ 🎹 Ⅴ 🛉 🐾 🐾

The Old Farmhouse, Tyddyn Du, Dyffryn Ardudwy, Gwynedd, *LL44 2DW*
Secluded luxury farmhouse; heated pool and hot spa; informal, friendly atmosphere.
Grades: ETC 3 Star
Tel: **01341 242711** Tibbetts.
Fax no: 01341 247881
D: £16.66-£25.00 **S:** £10.00-£30.00.
Open: All Year
Beds: 1F 2D 2T **Baths:** 5 En
🛏 (5) 🅿 (10) ⅓ 🗗 🛏 🗶 ≛ 🎹 Ⅴ 🛉 🐾 🐾

Ystumgwern Hall Farm, Dyffryn Ardudwy, *LL44 2DD.*
C16th luxury farmhouse, barn conversion.
Grades: ETC 4 Star
Tel: **01341 247249** (also fax no)
Mrs Williams.
D: £25.00-£26.00 .**Open:** All Year
Beds: 3F 1D 1T **Baths:** 5 En
🛏 🅿 ⅓ 🗗 🛏 ≛ 🎹 & Ⅴ 🐾 🐾

Harlech   62

National Grid Ref: SH5831

🅄 ⬚ Lion, Victoria

Tyddyn Y Gwynt, Harlech, *LL46 2TH.*
Actual grid ref: SH593298
Perfect setting for peaceful holidays; warm welcome, tourist attractions, mountain scenery, beaches. Car essential.
Grades: ETC 2 Star
Tel: **01766 780298** Mrs Jones.
D: £16.00-£16.00 **S:** £16.00-£18.00.
Open: All Year
Beds: 1F 1D 1T 1S
Baths: 1 Sh
🛏 🅿 (8) 🗗 🛏 ≛ 🎹 Ⅴ 🛉 🐾 🐾

Lion Hotel, Harlech, *LL46 2SG.*
2 bars & restaurant. Double rooms ensuite.
Tel: **01766 780731** Mr Morris.
D: £22.00 **S:** £34.00.
Open: All Year
Beds: 3D 1T 2S
Baths: 5 En 1 Pr
🅿 (3) 🗗 🛏 🗶 ≛ 🎹 Ⅴ

Maes yr Hebog, Heol y Bryn, Harlech, Gwynedd, *LL46 2TU.*
Quality bungalow accommodation, great food, spectacular views, mountains and coast.
Grades: ETC 5 Star
Tel: **01776 780885**
Mr & Mrs Clark.
D: £20.00-£24.00 **S:** £32.00-£42.00.
Open: Easter to Oct
Beds: 2D
Baths: 2 En
🅿 (2) ⅓ 🗗 🗶 ≛ 🎹 Ⅴ 🐾

Gwrach Ynys Country Guest House, *Ynys, Talsarnau, North West Wales, LL47 6TS.*
Grades: ETC 4 Star, AA 4 Diamond
Tel: **01766 780742** Mrs Williams.
Fax no: 01766 781199
D: £23.00-£28.00 **S:** £30.00-£35.00.
Open: March to Nov
Beds: 2F 2D 2T 1S **Baths:** 6 En
🛇 🄿 (8) 🌠 🗏 🛏 🗙 🌣 📖 ♥ 👜 ✦ 🚲
Edwardian country house set in a tranquil rural setting close to the sea and mountains in Snowdonia National Park. High quality, comfortable, non smoking accommodation and good food. Ideally located for walking, bird watching, golf and exploring the numerous castles, railways and attractions.

Castle Cottage Restaurant with Rooms, *Pen Llech, Harlech, LL46 2YL.*
Cosy restaurant with rooms, personal services.
Grades: ETC 3 Star, AA 4 Diamond, RAC 4 Diamond
Tel: **01766 780479** (also fax no)
Mr Roberts.
D: £31.00 **S:** £40.00.
Open: All Year
Beds: 3D 1T 2S **Baths:** 4 Pr 2 Sh
🛇 🌠 🗏 🛏 🗙 🌣 📖 ♥ 👜

Godre'R Graig, *Fford Newydd, Harlech, Gwynedd, LL46 2UD.*
A gracious Edwardian house nestling at the foot of Harlech Castle.
Tel: **01766 780905** (also fax no)
Mr Lynch.
D: £16.00-£18.00 **S:** £16.00-£25.00.
Open: All Year (not Xmas)
Beds: 2F 4D 2T 1S **Baths:** 4 Sh
🛇 🄿 (8) 🗏 🛏 🗙 🌣 📖 & ♥ 👜 ✦ 🚲

Talsarnau 63

National Grid Ref: SH6135

Estuary Motel Y Traeth, *Talsarnau, LL47 6TA.*
Snowdonia National Park, near Portmeirion. All modern ground floor rooms.
Grades: ETC 3 Star, AA 2 Star
Tel: **01766 771155** Mr King.
D: £16.50-£24.50 **S:** £34.50-£34.50.
Open: All Year
Beds: 1F 5D 4T **Baths:** 10 En
🛇 (16) 🄿 (30) 🗏 🛏 🗙 🌣 📖 & ♥ 👜

Penrhyndeudraeth 64

National Grid Ref: SH6139

Wenallt, *Penrhyndeudraeth, Gwynedd, LL48 6PW.*
Award winning guest house near Portmeirion. Lovely views. Ideal touring base.
Grades: ETC 3 Star
Tel: **01766 770321** (also fax no)
Cooper.
D: £22.00-£25.00 **S:** £27.00-£30.00.
Open: All Year (not Xmas/New Year)
Beds: 1T 2D **Baths:** 3 En
🄿 (3) 🌠 🗏 🗙 🌣 📖 ♥ 👜 ✦ 🚲

Corris 65

National Grid Ref: SH7507

▲ **Corris Youth Hostel,** *Old School, Old Road, Corris, Machynlleth, Powys, SY20 9QT.*
Actual grid ref: SH753080
Tel: **01654 761686**
Under 18: £6.50 **Adults:** £9.25
Self-catering facilities, Showers, Laundry facilities, Wet weather shelter, Lounge, Drying room, Security lockers, Cycle store, Parking, Evening meal at 7.00pm, No smoking, Kitchen facilities, Breakfast available
Picturesque former village school, recently renovated, with panoramic views of Corris.

Brithdir 66

National Grid Ref: SH7618

Llwyn Talcen, *Brithdir, Dolgellau, LL40 2RY.*
Grades: ETC 1 Star
Tel: **01341 450276** Mrs Griffiths.
D: £18.00-£20.00 **S:** £18.00-£20.00.
Open: Easter to Oct
Beds: 1D 1S
Baths: 1 En 1 Sh
🛇 (3) 🄿 (3) 🗏 🛏 🗙 🌣 📖 ♥ 👜 ✦ 🚲

Enjoy a holiday/short break at our country house in rhododendron gardens. Mountains on doorstep, yet close to spectacular Mawddach estuary. Ideal for walking, cycle trails, Wales little trains. Log fires, delicious evening dinners. Croeso cynnes; warm welcome.

Dolgellau 67

National Grid Ref: SH7217

🍴 🛏 Cross Foxes, Dylanwad Da, George, Royal Ship, Ivy House, Unicorn

Ivy House, *Finsbury Square, Dolgellau, North West Wales, LL40 1RF.*
Actual grid ref: SH728177
Attractive country town guest house, good home-made food.
Grades: ETC 2 Star GH, AA 3 Diamond
Tel: **01341 422535** Mrs Bamford.
Fax no: 01341 422689
D: £18.50-£24.50 **S:** £23.00-£33.00.
Open: All Year
Beds: 1F 3D 2T **Baths:** 3 En 2 Sh
🛇 🗏 🛏 🗙 🌣 📖 ♥ 👜 ✦ 🚲

All cycleways are popular: you are well-advised to book ahead

---

Tanyfron, *Arran Road, Dolgellau, North West Wales, LL40 2AA.*
Actual grid ref: SH730170
Modernised, former stone farmhouse, beautiful views. Wales in Bloom Winners 1999.
Grades: ETC 3 Star
Tel: **01341 422638**
Mrs Rowlands.
Fax no: 01341 421251
D: £20.00-£22.00.
Open: Feb to Nov
Beds: 1D 2T
Baths: 3 En
🛇 (5) 🄿 (6) 🌠 🗏 🌣 📖 ♥ 👜 ✦ 🚲

Arosfyr Farm, *Penycefn Road, Dolgellau, North West Wales, LL40 2YP.*
Homely friendly, farmhouse, flower, gardens, mountainous, views, self-catering available.
Grades: ETC 2 Star
Tel: **01341 422355** Mrs Skeel Jones.
D: £15.00-£16.50 **S:** £18.00.
Open: All Year
Beds: 1F 1D 1T
Baths: 2 Sh
🛇 🄿 (4) 🗏 🛏 🌣 📖 ♥ 👜 ✦ 🚲

Glyn Farm House, *Dolgellau, LL40 1YA.*
Actual grid ref: SH704178
Bedrooms with views, riverside path to Dolgellau, near organised bicycle track.
Grades: ETC 1 Star
Tel: **01341 422286** Mrs Price.
Fax no: 01341 422105
D: £16.00-£20.00
S: £14.00-£20.00.
Open: Mar to Nov
Beds: 1D 1T
Baths: 1 En 1 Sh
🛇 🄿 (6) 🗏 🛏 🌣 📖 ♥ 👜 ✦ 🚲

Aber Cottage, *Smithfield Street, Dolgellau, Gwynedd, LL40 1DE.*
Cosy market town stone cottage (1811) foot of Cader - comfortable welcoming hospitality.
Tel: **01341 422460**
Mrs Mullin.
D: £18.00-£20.00
S: £18.50-£25.00.
Open: All Year
Beds: 1F 2D 1T 2S
Baths: 2 En 1 Pr 2 Sh
🛇 (5) 🄿 (6) 🗏 🛏 🌣 📖 ♥ 👜 ✦ 🚲

Esgair Wen Newydd, *Garreg Feurig, Llanfachreth Road, Dolgellau, LL40 2YA.*
Actual grid ref: SH736185
Bungalow, mountain views, very quiet. Friendly relaxed atmosphere. High standards.
Grades: ETC 3 Star
Tel: **01341 423952**
Mrs Westwood.
D: £18.00
S: £20.00.
Open: Feb to Nov
Beds: 2D 1T
Baths: 1 Sh
🛇 (3) 🄿 (4) 🌠 🗏 🗙 🌣 📖 ♥ 👜 ✦ 🚲

*Penbryn Croft, Cader Road,
Dolgellau, LL40 1RN.*
Tel: **01341 422815** Ms Dunne.
D: £20.00-£24.00 .
Open: All Year (not Xmas)
Beds: 4T 2D **Baths:** 2 Sh
🛏 🍴 ⬜ ✕ 🎵 Ⅲ. Ⅴ 🛊 ⚡ 🚲
Situated at the foot of Cader Idris
200 yards from Dolgellau town
centre recently refurbished but still
retaining some original features
including oak staircase and mosaic
tiled floors. up to 12 people can be
accommodated and a warm
welcome assured.

*Gwelafon, Caedeintur, Dolgellau,
Gwynedd, North Wales, LL42 2YS.*
Beautiful, high-standard, spacious
house. Panoramic views of town
and mountains.
Grades: ETC 3 Star
Tel: **01341 422634** Mrs Roberts.
D: £20.00-£25.00 **S:** £17.00-£20.00.
Open: March to Oct
Beds: 1D 2S **Baths:** 1 En 1 Sh
🛏 (7) 🅿 (3) 🍴 ⬜ 🎵 Ⅲ. Ⅴ 🛊 ⚡ 🚲

*Bryn Yr Odyn Guest House,
Maescaled, Dolgellau, LL40 1UG.*
Secluded C17th longhouse, 1/2
mile town centre, tour/walking
guidance.
Tel: **01341 423470** Mr Jones.
D: £17.00 **S:** £20.00.
Open: All Year
Beds: 1D 2T **Baths:** 2 Sh
🛏 🅿 (3) 🍴 🐕 🎵 Ⅲ. Ⅴ 🛊 ⚡ 🚲

Trawsfynydd 68

National Grid Ref: SH7035

*Old Mill Farmhouse, Fron Oleu
Farm, Trawsfynydd, Blaenau
Ffestiniog, LL41 4UN.*
Actual grid ref: SH7135
Olde Worlde charm, wonderful
scenery, friendly animals, large
good breakfasts.
Grades: ETC 2 Star Farm
Tel: **01766 540397** (also fax no)
Miss Roberts & Mrs P Osborne.
D: £20.00-£25.00 **S:** £20.00-£25.00.
Open: All Year
Beds: 2F 3D 2T
Baths: 7 En
🛏 🅿 (10) 🍴 🐕 ✕ 🎵 Ⅲ. ♿ Ⅴ 🛊 ⚡
🚲

Gellilydan 69

National Grid Ref: SH6839

🍴 🍺 Bryn Arms

*Tyddyn Du Farm, Gellilydan,
Blaenau Ffestiniog, Gwynedd,
LL41 4RB.*
Actual grid ref: SH691398
Enchanting C17th farmhouse;
deluxe barn suites with jacuzzi,
patio window, gardens etc.
Tel: **01766 590281** Mrs Williams.
D: £20.00-£28.00 .
Open: All Year (not Xmas)
Beds: 3F 1D **Baths:** 3 Pr 2 Sh
🛏 🅿 (8) 🍴 ⬜ 🐕 ✕ 🎵 Ⅲ. ♿ Ⅴ 🛊 ⚡ 🚲

Ffestiniog 70

National Grid Ref: SH7041

▲ **Abbey Arms Hostel, Ffestiniog,
Blaenau Ffestiniog, LL41 4LS.**
Actual grid ref: SH700419
Tel: **01766 762444**
Adults: £12.50
Evening meal available.

Maentwrog 71

National Grid Ref: SH6640

🍴 🍺 Grapes

*The Old Rectory Hotel,
Maentwrog, Blaenau Ffestiniog,
LL41 4HN.*
Actual grid ref: SH665407
Main house/budget annexe, 3 acre
garden. Informal, peaceful.
Tel: **01766 590305** (also fax no)
Ms Herbert.
D: £22.50-£32.50 **S:** £30.00-£45.00.
Open: All Year (not Xmas)
Beds: 2F 6D 2T **Baths:** 10 En
🛏 🅿 ⬜ 🐕 ✕ 🎵 Ⅲ. Ⅴ 🛊 ⚡

Rhyd 72

National Grid Ref: SH6341

🍴 🍺 Brondanw Arms

*Bodlondeb Farm, Rhyd,
Penrhyndeudraeth, LL48 6ST.*
In small rural hamlet near
Ffestiniog Railway, Porthmeirion,
mountains and beaches.
Grades: ETC 2 Star
Tel: **01766 770640**
D: £17.50-£19.50 **S:** £17.50-£19.50.
Open: Easter to Oct
Beds: 1T 2D
🛏 🅿 (2) 🍴 ⬜ ✕ Ⅲ.

Tremadog 73

National Grid Ref: SH5640

*Ty Newydd Guest House, 30
Dublin Street, Tremadog,
Porthmadog, Gwynedd, LL49 9RH.*
Close to the Ffestiniog Railway,
Porthmeirion and many other
attractions.
Grades: ETC 2 Star
Tel: **01766 512553**
D: £18.50-£21.00 **S:** £28.50-£31.00.
Open: All Year (not Xmas/New
Year)
Beds: 1F 1T 2D **Baths:** 1 Sh
🛏 🅿 (6) ⬜ 🎵 Ⅲ. Ⅴ 🛊 🚲

Porthmadog 74

National Grid Ref: SH5638

🍴 🍺 Ship

*35 Madog Street, Porthmadog,
LL49 9BU.*
Modern terraced house.
Tel: **01766 512843** Mrs Skellern.
D: £14.00-£15.00 **S:** £14.00-£15.00.
Open: All Year (not Xmas)
Beds: 1F 1D 1T 1S **Baths:** 2 Sh
🛏 (3) ⬜ 🐕 🎵 Ⅲ. Ⅴ

*Llwyn Derw, Morfa Bychan Road,
Porthmadog, LL49 9UR.*
Period house, own grounds, town
centre 1 km, beach 2 km.
Tel: **01766 513869**
D: £18.00-£23.00 **S:** £21.00-£26.00.
Open: Easter to Oct
Beds: 1F 1D
Baths: 1 En
🛏 (3) 🅿 (3) 🍴 ⬜ 🎵 Ⅲ. Ⅴ 🛊 ⚡ 🚲

Rhoslan 75

National Grid Ref: SH4841

▲ **Stone Barn Bunkhouse Barn,
Tyddyn Morthwyl, Rhoslan,
Criccieth, Gwynedd, LL52 0NF.**
Tel: **01766 522115**
Under 18: £5.00 **Adults:** £5.00
Self-catering facilities, Showers,
Parking
*Sleeping platform for 12, wood
burner stove. Shared facilities with
campsite.*

Criccieth 76

National Grid Ref: SH4938

🍴 🍺 Poachers, Prince Of Wales, Moelwyn

*Mor Heli Guest House, Min Y
Mor, Criccieth, LL52 0EF.*
Tel: **01766 522802**
Fax no: 01766 522878
D: £18.00S: £18.00.
Open: All Year (not Xmas)
Beds: 2F 2D 1T
Baths: 5 Pr
🛏 🅿 ⬜ 🐕 🎵 Ⅲ. 🛊 ⚡
Situated on sea front overlooking
100 miles of coastline. All bed-
rooms sea views, full ensuite facili-
ties, colour TV and hospitality
trays. Recommended by guests
since 1972.

*Bron Rhiw Hotel, Caernarfon
Road, Criccieth, LL52 0AP.*
Cosy, comfortable non-smoking
hotel; a truly warm welcome awaits
you.
Grades: ETC 2 Star Hotel
Tel: **01766 522257** Ms Woodhouse
& Ms S C Williams.
D: £20.00-£22.50 **S:** £20.00-£22.50.
Open: Mar to Nov
Beds: 7D 1T 1F
Baths: 7 En 2 Pr
🛏 🅿 (4) 🍴 ⬜ 🐕 ✕ 🎵 Ⅲ. Ⅴ 🛊 ⚡ 🚲

*Min y Gaer Hotel, Porthmadog
Road, Criccieth, North West Wales,
LL52 0HP.*
Actual grid ref: SH502382
Comfortable hotel with delightful
coastal views. Ideal for touring
Snowdonia.
Grades: ETC 2 Star Hotel,
AA 4 Diamond, RAC 4 Diamond
Tel: **01766 522151**
Fax no: 01766 523540
D: £22.00-£25.00 **S:** £22.00-£22.00.
Open: Easter to Oct
Beds: 3F 4D 2T 1S
Baths: 10 En
🛏 🅿 (12) 🍴 ⬜ 🐕 🎵 Ⅲ. Ⅴ ⚡ 🚲

Craig y Mor Guest House, West
Parade, Criccieth, *LL52 0EN.*
Tastefully upgraded Victorian
house overlooking sea into
Tremadoc Bay.
Grades: ETC 3 Star GH
Tel: 01766 522830 Mr Williamson.
D: £20.00-£21.00 **S:** £20.00.
Open: Mar to Oct
Beds: 4F 2D
Baths: 6 En
🛇 🅿 (6) 🗆 🛏 ♨ 🎏 🗤 ⚡

*Muriau, Criccieth, North West
Wales, LL52 0RS.*
C17th gentleman's residence,
secluded garden.
Tel: 01766 522337 Mrs Neville.
D: £16.50-£21.00 **S:** £16.50-£21.00.
Open: Mar to Oct
Beds: 3D 2T
Baths: 3 En 1 Sh
🛇 (12) 🅿 (6) ⚡🗆🛏♨🎏🗤🛡🏵

*Y Rhoslyn, 8 Marine Terrace,
Criccieth, North West Wales,
LL52 0EF.*
Comfortable seafront guest house
in unspoilt seaside town, close to
beach, castle.
Tel: 01766 522685
D: £13.50-£18.00 **S:** £16.00-£25.00.
Open: Feb to Nov
Beds: 2F 2D 1T 1S
Baths: 2 En 1 Sh
🛇⚡🗆🛏✕♨🎏🗤🛡

Pant-glas 77

National Grid Ref: SH4747

*Hen Ysgol Old School Pant-glas,
Bwlch Derwin, Pant-glas,
Garndolbenmaen, LL51 9EQ.*
Actual grid ref: SH456474
Beautiful mid-C19th Welsh not
country school. Perfectly situated
for the attractions of Snowdonia.
Grades: ETC 2 Star
Tel: 01286 660701 Gibbins.
D: £17.00-£20.00 **S:** £20.00-£25.00.
Open: All year
Beds: 2F 1D 1T
Baths: 1 En 1 Sh
🛇 🅿 (6) ⚡🗆🛏✕♨🎏🗤🛡🔥🗤⚡
🏵

Penygroes 78

National Grid Ref: SH4753

🍴 ◁ Bryn Eisteddfod

*Lleuar Fawr, Penygroes,
Caernarfon, Gwynedd, LL54 6PB.*
Actual grid ref: SH455520
Peaceful location, substantial farm-
house breakfast, comfortable bed-
rooms. Warm Welsh welcome.
Grades: ETC 3 Star
Tel: 01286 660268 (also fax no)
Mrs Lloyd Jones.
D: £18.00-£20.00 **S:** £25.00-£25.00.
Open: All Year (not Xmas)
Beds: 1D 1T
Baths: 2 En
🛇🅿⚡🗆🛏♨🗤🛡🏵

Llanfaglan 79

National Grid Ref: SH4760

🍴 ◁ The Harp

*The White House, Llanfaglan,
Caernarfon, LL54 5RA.*
Actual grid ref: SH457597
Quiet, isolated country house.
Magnificent views to mountains
and sea.
Grades: ETC 3 Star
Tel: 01286 673003
Mr Bayles.
D: £19.50-£21.50 **S:** £25.50.
Open: Mar to Nov
Beds: 2D 2T
Baths: 3 En 1 Pr
🛇 🅿 (8) 🗆 🛏 ♨ 🎏 🗤 ⚡ 🏵

Caernarfon 80

National Grid Ref: SH477627

🍴 ◁ Black Boy, Harp Inn, Newborough Arms

▲ *Totters, Plas Porth Yr Aur,
2 High Street, Caernarfon,
Gwynedd, LL55 1RN.*
Tel: 01286 672963
Under 18: £10.00 **Adults:** £10.00
Self-catering facilities, Television,
Showers, Central heating, Wet
weather shelter, Lounge, Dining
room, Games room, Drying room,
Security lockers, Cycle store,
Parking, No smoking
*Trotters is situated within historic
walled town of Caernarfon, only
100m from the castle and 20m from
the sea. Caernarfon has plenty of
pubs and restaurant and acts as a
perfect base for exploring
Snowdonia and Anglesey.*

*Menai View Guest House &
Restaurant, North Road,
Caernarfon, North Wales, LL55 1BD.*
Close to Caernarfon Castle, over-
looking Menai Straights .
Lounge/bar and restaurant.
Spa-bath.
Grades: ETC 3 Star,
AA 3 Diamonds
Tel: 01286 674602 (also fax no)
D: £17.50-£22.50
S: £22.50-£27.00.
Open: All Year (not Xmas/
New Year)
Beds: 3F 2T 4D
Baths: All En
🛇🗆🛏✕♨🎏🗤🛡⚡🏵

*Prince of Wales Hotel, Bangor
Street, Caernarfon, LL55 1AR.*
Town location, perfect stopover en-
route for Ireland's ferries or explor-
ing Snowdonia.
Grades: ETC 2 Star
Tel: 01286 673367 Ms Parry.
Fax no: 01286 676610
D: £19.00-£32.00
S: £19.00-£32.00.
Open: All Year (not Xmas)
Beds: 2F 8D 7T 4S
Baths: 19 En 2 Sh
🛇🅿 (6)🗆🛏✕♨🎏🗤🛡⚡🏵

*Marianfa, St David's Road,
Caernarfon, Gwynedd, LL55 1EL.*
Ideal base touring Snowdonia, Llyn
Peninsula, Anglesey, Llandudno,
Conwy valley.
Grades: ETC 3 Star
Tel: 01286 675589 Mrs Ashcroft.
Fax no: 01286 673689
D: £16.00-£22.00 **S:** £17.00-£25.00.
Open: All Year
Beds: 2F 1D 1T 1S
Baths: 4 En 1 Pr
🛇 (10) 🅿 (5) ⚡🗆♨🎏🗤🗤

*Cadnant Valley Caravan Park,
Llanberis Road, Caernarfon,
Gwynedd, LL55 2DF.*
Clean comfortable and friendly
house, 0.25 mile from Caernarfon
town.
Tel: 01286 673196 Mrs Noon.
D: £15.00-£15.00 **S:** £15.00-£15.00.
Open: Easter to Sep
Beds: 1D 1T **Baths:** 1 Sh
🅿 (4)🗆♨🎏🗤

Pentir 81

National Grid Ref: SH5667

🍴 ◁ Yaynol Arms

*Rainbow Court Guest House,
Village Square, Pentir, Bangor,
LL57 4UY.*
Actual grid ref: SH574670
1999 award-winning guest
house/restaurant. Mountains,
attractions, peace, friendly.
Tel: 01248 353099 (also fax no)
Mrs Lorrimer Riley.
D: £16.00-£20.00 **S:** £16.00-£27.00.
Open: All Year (not Xmas)
Beds: 1F 1D 1T 1S
Baths: 1 En 1 Pr 1 Sh
🛇🅿 (3)⚡🗆✕♨🎏🗤🛡

Menai Bridge 82

National Grid Ref: SH5572

🍴 ◁ Penrhos Arms

*Wern Farm Guest House,
Pentraeth Road, Menai Bridge,
Anglesey, LL59 5RR.*
Great hospitality. Hearty breakfasts
and everything you could possibly
need for a relaxing holiday.
Tel: 01248 712421 (also fax no)
Mr & Mrs Brayshaw.
D: £21.00-£27.00 **S:** £25.00-£50.00.
Open: Feb to Nov
Beds: 2F 1T **Baths:** 1 En 1 Sh
🛇🅿⚡🗆♨🎏🗤🛡⚡🏵

High season,
bank holidays and
special events mean
low availability
everywhere.

Gaerwen 83

National Grid Ref: SH4771

▶ ⚑ Penrhos Arms, Sailors Return

Benlas, Llandaniel, Gaerwen, Anglesey, LL60 6HB.
Actual grid ref: SH499710
Pretty cottage, quiet country road, superb views to Snowdonia.
Tel: **01248 421543** Mrs Taylor.
D: £18.00-£20.00 **S:** £20.00-£20.00.
Open: Easter to Oct
Beds: 2D
Baths: 1 Sh
🛇 🅿 (3) ⊬ 🛏 ♨ ▥ Ⓥ ⚡ ⊶

Brynsiencyn 84

National Grid Ref: SH4867

▶ ⚑ Penrhos Arms

Fron Guest House, Brynsiencyn, Llanfairpwllgwyngyll, Anglesey, LL61 6TX.
Traditional high class accommodation with magnificent views of Snowdonia.
Grades: ETC 3 Star W.T.B
Tel: **01248 430310** (also fax no)
Mr Geldard.
D: £16.00-£17.50 **S:** £16.50-£18.00.
Open: Easter to Sept 30
Beds: 3D
Baths: 1 En 1 Sh
🅿 (4) ⊬ 🖵 ♨ ▥ Ⓥ ⊶

Dwyran 85

National Grid Ref: SH4466

Tal-y-Foel, Dwyran, Llanfairpwllgwyngyll, LL61 6LQ.
Grades: ETC 4 Star
Tel: **01248 430377**
Fax no: 01248 430977
D: £25.00-£25.00 **S:** £25.00-£30.00.
Open: All Year (not Xmas/ New Year)
Beds: 2F 2T
Baths: 4 En
🛇 🅿 🖵 🛏 ♨ ▥ ⅋ Ⓥ ⅋ ⊶
Isle of Anglesey, spectacular waterfront location overlooking Snowdonia. Wales Tourist Board 4 star farm B&B, Taste of Wales and Welcome Host awards, en-suite bedrooms, some whirlpool baths. Many facilities, birdwatching, walking, fishing. Friendly BHS Riding Centre, horse livery, riding courses.

Valley 86

National Grid Ref: SH2979

Valley Hotel, London Road, Valley, Holyhead, Anglesey, LL65 3DU.
Superior ensuite accommodation and pub situated 4 miles from ferry.
Grades: RAC 3 Diamond
Tel: **01407 740203** Snape.
D: £25.00-£49.50 **S:** £37.50-£37.50.
Open: All Year
Beds: 2F 9T 4D 5S
Baths: 18 En 1 Sh
🛇 🅿 (40) 🖵 🛏 ✕ ♨ ▥ Ⓥ ⚡

Holyhead 87

National Grid Ref: SH2482

▶ ⚑ Valley Hotel, Boat House, Kings Arms, Crown

Wavecrest, 93 Newry Road, Holyhead, Anglesey, LL65 1HU.
Actual grid ref: SH248828
Ideal ferry stopover for Ireland; close to the South Stack.
Grades: ETC 3 Star,
AA 3 Diamond
Tel: **01407 763637** Mr Hiltunen.
Fax no: 01407 764862
D: £16.00-£20.00 **S:** £18.00-£20.00.
Open: All Year (not Xmas)
Beds: 3F 1D 1S
Baths: 2 En 1 Pr 1 Sh
🛇 🅿 (4) ⊬ 🖵 🛏 ✕ ♨ ▥ Ⓥ ⚡ ⊶

Bryn Awel, Edmund Street, Holyhead, Anglesey, LL65 1SA.
Victorian house. 10 minutes town, 10 minutes ferries. Home cooking.
Grades: ETC 2 Stars
Tel: **01407 762948** Mrs Jones.
D: £15.50-£16.00 **S:** £18.00-£20.00.
Open: All Year
Beds: 1F 1D 1T 1S
🛇 🅿 (6) 🖵 🛏 ✕ ♨ ▥ Ⓥ ⊶

Monravon Guest House, Port-y-felin Road, Holyhead, LL65 1PL.
Family-run B&B, 3 minutes to ferry/train terminals. Adjacent to park & beach.
Grades: ETC 3 Star GH
Tel: **01407 762944** (also fax no)
D: £15.00-£18.50 .
Open: All Year (not Xmas)
Beds: 3F 3D 3T
Baths: 9 En
🅿 ⊬ 🖵 ♨ ▥ ⅋ Ⓥ ⊶

D = Price range per person sharing in a double room

Hendre, Porth y Felin Road, Holyhead, Anglesey, LL65 1AH.
Large detached house in its own grounds facing park. All rooms individually designed.
Tel: **01407 762929** (also fax no)
D: £20.00-£22.50
S: £25.00-£30.00.
Open: All Year
Beds: 2D 1T
Baths: 3 En
🛇 🅿 (6) ⊬ 🖵 🛏 ♨ ▥ Ⓥ ⅋ ⊶

Roselea, 26 Holborn Road, Holyhead, Anglesey, LL65 2AT.
Homely family-run B&B - warm welcome guaranteed to our visitors. 2 mins from ferries.
Tel: **01407 764391** (also fax no)
Mrs Foxley.
D: £16.00-£20.00
S: £20.00.
Open: All Year (not Xmas)
Beds: 1D 1T
Baths: 1 Sh
🛇 ⊬ 🖵 ♨ ▥ Ⓥ ⅋ ⊶

Tasma, 31 Walthew Avenue, Holyhead, Anglesey, LL65 1AG.
Comfortable accommodation. Conveniently situated for ferries, railway, beaches and shops.
Tel: **01407 762291**
Mrs Jones.
D: £17.00-£17.00
S: £20.00-£17.00.
Open: All Year (not Xmas)
Beds: 2F
Baths: 2 Sh
🛇 🅿 (1) ⊬ 🖵 🛏 ✕ ♨ ▥ Ⓥ ⅋ ⊶

Order your

packed lunches the

evening before you

need them.

Not at breakfast!

Sustrans Sea to Sea (C2C)

The **Sea to Sea** cycle route is both a section of the new National Cycle Network and an award-winning leisure route. 140 miles long, it starts on the Cumbrian west coast at Workington or Whitehaven, proceeds through the northern Lake District via Keswick to Penrith, and continues through eastern Cumbria to Allenheads in Northumberland; and then through the north of County Durham to Consett, from where it heads either to Newcastle and Tynemouth or to Sunderland. The route is clearly signposted by blue direction signs bearing a cycle silhouette and the legend 'C2C'.

The indispensable **official route map and guide** for the Sea to Sea cycle route is available from Sustrans, 35 King Street, Bristol BS1 4DZ, tel 0117-926 8893, fax 0117-929 4173, @ £5.99 (+ £1.50 p&p).

Maps: Ordnance Survey 1:50,000 Landranger series: 86, 87, 88, 89, 90, 91; and for the Penrith-Carlisle link, 85

Trains: The Intercity west coast main line goes to Carlisle, from where you can connect to Workington, Whitehaven or Penrith; or to Langwathby via the famous scenic Leeds-Settle-Carlisle Railway. The Intercity east coast main line goes to Newcastle, from where you can connect to Tynemouth or Sunderland.

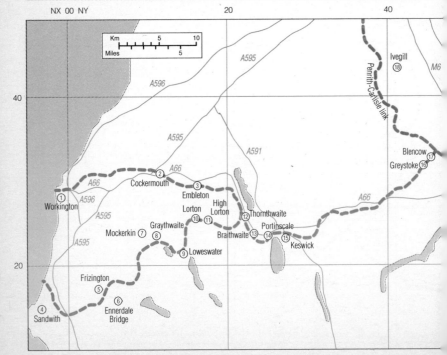

Workington or Whitehaven to Braithwaite

From the mid-nineteenth to mid-twentieth century, **Workington** was a major centre of the iron and steel industry, its particular success due to the fact that Henry Bessemer's steelmaking process depended on a supply of phosphorous free ores, in which this area is rich. The Helena Thompson Museum houses a display of costumes and embroidery. The first stretch of the way takes you up the Derwent Valley to Cockermouth, where the Wordsworth House is the birthplace of the region's most famous son. Elsewhere, the Printing House offers a myriad different types of printing press, and you can tour Jenning's Brewery on the banks of the Cocker. From here you head into the **Lake District National Park**, and on to Wythorp Woods, where you cycle down the west bank of **Bassenthwaite Lake**, with the imposing mass of **Skiddaw** towering above the opposite side, and on to Braithwaite. **Whitehaven** lies to the north of St Bees Head, a Heritage Coast with sandstone cliffs and nature reserves for the important bird life it supports. The town has been through a number of incarnations - harbour for St Bees Priory, major tobacco port, during which time the many Georgian buildings went up, and then coal and shipbuilding centre. The initial stage of the southern route takes you east by way of Cleator Moor to Kirkland, from where you ascend to the edge of the National Park. Here you ride northwards to the northwestern end of **Loweswater**, where you cycle down the northeast bank and then downstream alongside the River Cocker to Low Lorton, from where you ascend into Whinlatter Forest and then descend (steeply) to Thornthwaite, where you turn south to **Braithwaite**.

Workington   1

National Grid Ref: NX9927

🍴 🍺 Ye Old Sportsman

Fernleigh House, 15 High Seaton, Workington, Cumbria, CA14 1PE.
Georgian house, lovely garden, warm and friendly welcome, Excellent breakfasts.
Tel: **01900 605811**
Ms Bewsher.
D: £17.00-£45.00 **S:** £17.00-£17.00.
Open: All Year
Beds: 1F 2T 1S
🛇 🅿 🖵 🛏 🚿 🔟 ☑ ⓘ ✦ ♿

Silverdale, 17 Banklands, Workington, Cumbria, CA14 3EL.
Large Victorian private house.
Near start C2C cycleway and lakes.
Tel: **01900 61887**
Mrs Hardy.
D: £11.00-£13.50 **S:** £12.50-£15.00.
Open: All Year (not Xmas)
Beds: 2T 2S
Baths: 2 Sh
🛇 🖵 🛏 🚿 🔟 ☑

D = Price range per person sharing in a double room

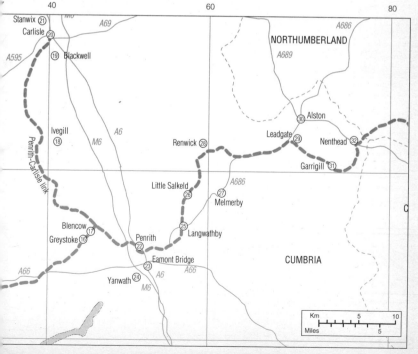

Cockermouth 2

National Grid Ref: NY1230

🍴 🍺 Black Bull, Brown Cow, Bitter End, Old Post House, Shepherds Hotel

▲ **Cockermouth Youth Hostel,**
*Double Mills, Cockermouth,
Cumbria, CA13 0DS.*
Actual grid ref: NY118298
Tel: **01900 822561**
Under 18: £5.75 **Adults:** £8.50
Self-catering facilities, Showers,
Wet weather facilities, Lounge,
Drying room, Cycle store, Parking,
Evening meal at 7.00pm, No smoking, WC, Kitchen facilities, Credit
cards accepted
*Simple accommodation in restored
C17th watermill, convenient for
northern and western fells and
Cumbrian coastline.*

The Rook Guest House,
*9 Castlegate, Cockermouth,
Cumbria, CA13 9EU.*
Actual grid ref: NY122307
Cosy C17th town house. Spiral
staircase. Convenient for all
amenities.
Tel: **01900 828496** Mrs Waters.
D: £16.00-£18.00 **S:** £20.00-£20.00.
Open: All Year (not Xmas)
Beds: 2D 1T
Baths: 1 En 1 Pr 1 Sh
🛏 (5) ⊬ ⊡ 🖢 🎹 Ⅵ ⅋ ♿

Shepherds Hotel, *Egremont Road,
Cockermouth, Cumbria, CA13 0QX.*
Modern hotel with views towards
Lake District, close to gem town of
Cockermouth.
Tel: **01900 822673** (also fax no)
Campbell.
D: £18.75-£20.00 **S:** £37.50-£40.00.
Open: All Year (not Xmas)
Beds: 4D 9T
Baths: 13 En
🛏 🅿 (99) ⊬ ⊡ ✕ 🖢 🎹 ♿ Ⅵ ⅋ ♿

Albany House, *Wordsworth
Terrace, Cockermouth, Cumbria,
CA13 9AH.*
Beautiful Victorian guest house,
stripped pine doors and a warm
welcome.
Tel: **01900 825630** Mr Nichol.
D: £16.00-£16.00 **S:** £16.00-£16.00.
Open: All Year
Beds: 1F 2D 2T 2S
Baths: 1 Pr 1 Sh
🛏 ⊬ ⊡ 🛏 🖢 🎹 Ⅵ ⅋ ♿

Benson Court Cottage, *10 St
Helen's Street, Cockermouth,
Cumbria, CA13 9HX.*
Town centre 1727 cottage.
Commercial/tourist guests
welcome. Generous breakfasts.
Tel: **01900 822303** Mrs Townley.
D: £15.00-£20.00 **S:** £15.00-£22.00.
Open: All Year
Beds: 1F 1D
🛏 (6) ⊬ ⊡ 🖢 🎹 Ⅵ ⅋ ♿

Embleton 3

National Grid Ref: NY1630

🍴 🍺 Wheatsheaf Inn

Orchard House, *Embleton,
Cockermouth, Cumbria, CA13 9XP.*
Detached Edwardian country house
with 3/4 acre garden. Mountain
views.
Tel: **017687 76347** (also fax no)
Mrs Newton.
D: £18.00-£20.00 **S:** £20.00-£25.00.
Open: All Year
Beds: 2D **Baths:** 2 En
🛏 (7) 🅿 (8) ⊬ ⊡ 🛏 🖢 🎹 Ⅵ ⅋ ♿

Lambfoot House, *Embleton,
Cockermouth, Cumbria, CA13 9XL.*
Actual grid ref: NY164303
Relax in elegant and spacious
ensuite rooms, lounge or
conservatory.
Tel: **017687 76424**
Mr & Mrs Holden.
Fax no: 017687 76721
D: £22.00-£23.00 **S:** £22.00-£23.00.
Open: All Year
Beds: 1D 1T 1S
Baths: 3 En
🅿 (5) ⊬ ⊡ 🖢 🎹 Ⅵ ⅋ ♿

Sandwith 4

National Grid Ref: NX9614

🍴 🍺 Lowther Arms

▲ **Tarn Flatt Camping Barn,**
*Tarnflat Hall, Sandwith,
Whitehaven, Cumbria, CA28 9UX.*
Actual grid ref: NX947146
Tel: **017687 72645 Adults:** £3.35
*Situated on St Bees Head overlooking Scottish coastline and the Isle
of Man. RSPB seabird reserve and
lighthouse nearby. ADVANCE
BOOKING ESSENTIAL.*

The Old Granary, *Spout Howse,
Sandwith, Whitehaven, Cumbria,
CA28 9UG.*
Actual grid ref: NX964147
Tastefully converted barn on C2C
route and Coast to Coast path.
Tel: **01946 692097** Mrs Buchanan.
D: £17.00 **S:** £16.00.
Open: All Year
Beds: 1F 1D 1T
Baths: 2 En
🛏 🅿 (2) ⊡ 🛏 🖢 Ⅵ ⅋ ♿

Frizington 5

National Grid Ref: NY0317

14 Lingley Fields, *Frizington,
Cumbria, CA26 3RU.*
Village house set in cottage-style
garden, choice of breakfast.
Tel: **01946 811779** Mrs Hall.
D: £16.00-£20.00 **S:** £16.00-£20.00.
Open: All Year
Beds: 1F 1T
Baths: 1 En 1 Sh
🛏 ⊡ ⊬ ✕ 🖢 🎹 Ⅵ ⅋ ♿

Ennerdale Bridge 6

National Grid Ref: NY0715

🍴 🍺 Shepherds Arms

The Shepherds Arms Hotel,
*Ennerdale Bridge, Cleator,
Cumbria, CA23 3AR.*
Small friendly hotel in the Lake
District National Park which has
been completely refurbished.
Grades: ETC 2 Star
Tel: **01946 861249** (also fax no)
Mr Stanfield.
D: £28.00-£28.00
S: £30.00-£35.00.
Open: All Year
Beds: 1F 3D 3T 1S
Baths: 6 En 2 Pr
🛏 🅿 (6) ⊡ 🛏 🖢 🎹 Ⅵ ⅋ ♿

Mockerkin

National Grid Ref: NY0923

▲ **Swallow Camping Barn,**
*Waterend, Mockerkin,
Cockermouth, Cumbria, CA13 0S*
Actual grid ref: NY116226
Tel: **017687 72645**
Adults: £3.35
*In picturesque valley of
Loweswater, on a 200-acre working farm. Permits for fishing and
boat hire on Loweswater availab
ADVANCE BOOKING ESSENTIAL.*

Graythwaite

National Grid Ref: NY1123

Low Graythwaite Hall,
*Graythwaite, Ulverston, Cumbria
LA12 8AZ.*
Historic statesman's house, old
panelling, fine furnishings, open
log fires.
Grades: ETC 4 Diamond
Tel: **015395 31676** (also fax no)
D: £22.00-£30.00
S: £25.00-£30.00.
Open: 1st Feb to 2nd Jan
Beds: 1F 1T 1D
Baths: 2 En
🛏 🅿 (20) ⊡ 🛏 ✕ 🖢 🎹 Ⅵ ⅋ ♿

Loweswater

National Grid Ref: NY1420

🍴 🍺 Wheatsheaf, Kirkstile

Askhill Farm, *Loweswater,
Cockermouth, Cumbria, CA13 0SU.*
Beef and sheep rearing farm, qui
valley, Loweswater. Ideal countr
walking area.
Grades: ETC 3 Diamond
Tel: **01946 861640**
Mrs Vickers.
D: £18.00-£20.00
S: £19.00-£21.00.
Open: Easter to Oct
Beds: 1F 1D
Baths: 1 Sh
🛏 🅿 (3) ⊬ ⊡ 🛏 🖢 🎹 Ⅵ ⅋ ♿

rook Farm, *Loweswater,
ockermouth, Cumbria, CA13 0RP.*
omfortable, quiet, working farm-
ouse. Good food, open fire, pretty
arden.
el: 01900 85606 (also fax no)
rs Hayton.
: £20.00-£21.00 **S:** £20.00-£21.00.
pen: May to Nov
eds: 1F 1D **Baths:** 1 Sh
▸ 🄿 (3) ⊬⬛ 🛏 ✕ ♨ 🕎 🇻 ⓘ ✦

raythwaite, *Loweswater,
ockermouth, Cumbria, CA13 0SU.*
ctual grid ref: NY115232
ovely home half mile off road in
evated position at northern end of
oweswater.
el: 01946 861555 Mrs Beebe.
ax no: 01946 862300
: £17.00-£18.00 **S:** £17.00-£20.00.
pen: All Year (not Xmas)
eds: 1D 1T 1S
aths: 1 Sh
🄿 (4) ⊬⬛ ✕ ♨ 🕎 🇻 ⓘ ✦ ✦ ⚲

orton 10

ational Grid Ref: NY1525

■ The Wheatsheaf

e Old Vicarage, *Church Lane,
rton, Cockermouth, Cumbria,
'3 9UN.*
egant Victorian country house
th stunning views, wooded
unds, log fires.
ades: AA 4 Diamond
: 01900 85656 (also fax no)
Humphreys.
£22.00-£32.00 **S:** £22.00-£30.00.
en: All Year (not Xmas)
ds: 5D 3T
ths: 8 En
🄿 (10) ⊬⬛ ♨ 🕎 🇻 ⓘ ✦ ⚲

gg End Farm, *Rogerscale,
rton Vale, Cockermouth,
mbria, CA13 0RG.*
autiful views, ideal situation for
king. Quiet, working, family
n.
: 01900 85658 Mrs Steel.
£20.00-£18.00 **S:** £20.00.
en: All Year
ds: 1F 1D 2T
ths: 3 Sh
🄿 ⊬⬛ 🛏 ✕ ✦ ⚲

gh Lorton 11

ional Grid Ref: NY1625

Wheatsheaf Inn

Brook, *Whinlatter Pass, High
ton, Cockermouth, Cumbria,
9TX.*
en slate bungalow, designed by
ers. Pine ceilings. Oak floors.
01900 85333 Mrs Roberts.
£16.50-£17.50 **S:** £16.50-£17.50.
en: All Year
ds: 3D
ths: 1 Sh
) 🄿 (2) ⊬⬛ 🛏 ✕ ♨ 🕎 🇻 ⓘ ✦ ⚲

Thornthwaite 12

National Grid Ref: NY2225

Thwaite Howe Hotel,
*Thornthwaite, Keswick, Cumbria,
CA12 5SA.*
Grades: ETC 2 Star, AA 2 Star,
RAC 2 Star
Tel: 017687 78281
Mr & Mrs Marshall.
D: £28.00-£35.00.
S: £48.00-£58.00.
Open: Mar to Oct
Beds: 5D 3T 1F 1S
Baths: 8 En
▸ (12) 🄿 (10) ⬛ 🛏 ✕ ♨ 🕎 🇻 ⓘ ✦
Beautiful small country house hotel
backing on to Thornthwaite Forest
with views over Derwent Valley to
Skiddaw, Dod and Latrigg
mountains. Midway between
Bassenthwaite lake and Derwent
Water. Tranquil and romantic
atmosphere. Good food and
excellent rooms.

Braithwaite 13

National Grid Ref: NY2323

🍴 🍺 Royal Oak, Middle Ruddings Hotel,
Coledale Inn

Coledale Inn, *Braithwaite,
Keswick, Cumbria, CA12 5TN.*
Georgian inn with spectacular
mountain views. Situated in peace-
ful countryside village.
Grades: ETC 3 Diamond
Tel: 017687 78272
Mr Mawdsley.
D: £22.00-£30.00
S: £17.00-£25.00.
Open: All Year
Beds: 5F 1T 5D 1S
Baths: 12 En
▸ 🄿 (15) ⬛ 🛏 ✕ ♨ 🕎 ♿ 🇻 ✦

Cottage In The Wood Hotel,
*Whinlatter Pass, Braithwaite,
Keswick, Cumbria, CA12 5TW.*
Actual grid ref: NY213245
Superb location in the Whinlatter
Forest Park. Wonderful views.
Tel: 017687 78409
Mrs Littlefair.
Fax no: 017687 78064
D: £25.00-£33.00
S: £25.00-£47.00.
Open: Mar to Nov
Beds: 3F 3D 1T
Baths: 7 En
▸ 🄿 (15) ⊬⬛ 🛏 ✕ ♨ 🕎 ♿ 🇻 ✦
⚲

Bringing children with

you? Always ask for

any special rates.

Portinscale 14

National Grid Ref: NY2523

🍴 🍺 Farmers Arms, Swinside Inn

Skiddaw Croft, *Portinscale,
Keswick, Cumbria, CA12 5RD.*
Actual grid ref: NY251235
Tel: 017687 72321 (also fax no)
Downer.
D: £20.00-£25.00 **S:** £20.00-£25.00.
Open: All Year
Beds: 1F 1T 2D 2S **Baths:** 4 En 1 Sh
▸ 🄿 (6) ⊬⬛ 🛏 ♨ 🕎 🇻 ⓘ ✦ ⚲
Comfortable & friendly B&B in
charming village. Easy walk to
Keswick (15 mins) Splendid lake &
mountain views. Health & hearty
breakfasts. Vegetarians welcome.
Good base for hill & water sports
(marina 5 mins).

Rickerby Grange, *Portinscale,
Keswick, Cumbria, CA12 5RH.*
Set within own garden, private
parking. In the pretty village of
Portinscale.
Grades: ETC 4 Diamond,
AA 4 Diamond, RAC 4 Diamond,
Sparkling
Tel: 017687 72344 Mrs Bradley.
D: £28.00-£30.00 **S:** £28.00-£30.00.
Open: All Year
Beds: 3F 9D 2S **Baths:** 14 En
▸ (5) 🄿 (14) ⊬⬛ 🛏 ♨ 🕎 🇻 ⓘ
✦ ⚲

Thirnbeck Guest House,
*Portinscale, Keswick, Cumbria,
CA12 5RD.*
Comfortable Georgian guest house
with fine views over Derwent
water.
Grades: AA 3 Diamond
Tel: 017687 72869 Savage.
D: £23.00-£23.00 **S:** £23.00-£23.00.
Open: All Year (not Xmas)
Beds: 4D 1T 1S **Baths:** 5 En 1 Pr
▸ (4) 🄿 (4) ⊬⬛ 🛏 ♨ 🕎 🇻 ⓘ ✦ ⚲

Keswick 15

National Grid Ref: NY2623

🍴 🍺 Packhouse, Packhouse Covet, Sun Inn, Four
In Hand, Twa Dogs, Chaucer House, George
Hotel, Kitchin's Cellar Bar, Skiddaw Hotel, Dog
& Gun, Golden Lion, Farmers Arms, Pheasant,
Bank, Wild Strawberry

▲ **Keswick Youth Hostel**, *Station
Rd, Keswick, Cumbria, CA12 5LH.*
Actual grid ref: NY267235
Tel: 017687 72484
Under 18: £7.75 **Adults:** £11.00
Self-catering facilities, Television,
Showers, Laundry facilities,
Lounge, Dining room, Drying
room, Cycle store, Evening meal at
7.00pm, Kitchen facilities,
Breakfast available, Credit cards
accepted
*Standing above the River Greta,
this hostel is ideally placed in
Keswick - the northern hub of the
Lake District - for superb views
across the park to Skiddaw.*

Braithwaite to Penrith

Two miles beyond **Braithwaite** you come to Portinscale, a village fringed by woodland on the banks of **Derwent Water**. From Nichol End, just off your road into the village, there is a boat service on this attractive lake. From Portinscale the route takes you into **Keswick**, the principal (and very popular) town of the northern Lake District. The town has been a major tourist centre since Victorian times, and its buildings date mostly from this period. Attractions include the Cumberland Pencil Museum, harking back to the days when Borrowdale graphite was the draughtsman's favourite substance; the *Beatrix Potter's Lake District* multimedia experience; and the Museum and Art Gallery, most notable for its manuscript collection featuring Wordsworth, Southey et al. Your road east from Keswick takes you (steeply) past Castlerigg Stone Circle, a neolithic site whose fantastic location sets it apart from those in Wiltshire. From here it's on to Threlkeld, below **Blencathra**, and then Troutbeck, before leaving the National Park and heading on to Greystoke and Little Blencow. From here you can make a detour to Hutton-in-the-Forest, a magnificent house built around a thirteenth-century tower, with an attractive eighteenth-century walled garden. From Little Blencow you come to **Penrith**, an attractive old town built of red sandstone, as is its ruined fourteenth-century castle. From Penrith there is a link route via Skelton, Stockdalewath on the Roe Beck and Dalston in the Caldew Valley to **Carlisle**, where you can join the *Sustrans Carlisle-Inverness* route.

Spooney Green, *Spooney Green Lane, Keswick, Cumbria, CA12 4PJ.*
Tel: **017687 72601** Ms Wallace.
D: £20.00-£25.00 **S:** £25.00-£40.00.
Open: All Year
Beds: 1T 1D
Baths: 1 En 1Private
🛇 🅿 (5) ⅌ 🗇 🖬 ✕ 🍴 🎢 📖 ♥ 🐾
Only 15 minutes' walk into Keswick yet on the foothills of Skiddaw, Spooney Green provides a relaxing country retreat. All rooms have extensive views of the western fells. The large wildlife garden includes woodland, wetland and flower meadow.

Chaucer House Hotel,
Derwentwater Place, Keswick, Cumbria, CA12 4DR.
Grades: RAC 2 Star
Tel: **017687 72318** Mr Pechartscheck
Fax no: 017687 75551
D: £30.00-£40.00 **S:** £30.00-£40.00.
Open: Feb to Dec
Beds: 4F 9D 12T 8S
Baths: 29 En 4 Pr
🛇 🅿 🗇 🎢 ✕ 🍴 📖 🚲 ♥ 🐾
Lakeland hospitality at its best. Quiet setting, surrounded by spectacular mountains. Close to theatre, market place and lake. Renowned for a relaxed informal atmosphere and excellent freshly prepared food. Friendly, professional staff always available to help you enjoy your stay, plan tours and walks.

Sunnyside Guest House,
25 Southey Street, Keswick, Cumbria, CA12 4EF.
Grades: ETC 4 Diamond, AA 4 Diamond, RAC 4 Diamond
Tel: **017687 72446**
Mr & Mrs Newton.
Fax no: 017687 74447
D: £19.00**S:** £24.00.
Open: All Year (not Xmas)
Beds: 1F 4D 1T 1S
Baths: 5 En 2 Sh
🛇 🅿 (7) ⅌ 🗇 🎢 🍴 📖 �V ♥ ✦
This recently refurbished Victorian building is situated just five minutes walk from the town centre and ten minutes walk from the lake, yet provides quiet and comfortable accommodation throughout. Relaxing guest lounge with views of Skiddaw.

Brookfield, *Penrith Road, Keswick, Cumbria, CA12 4LJ.*
Tel: **017687 72867** Mr Gregory.
D: £16.00-£20.00 **S:** £16.00-£20.00.
Open: All Year
Beds: 2F 2D
Baths: 4 En
🛇 🅿 (4) ⅌ 🗇 🎢 ✕ 🍴 📖 �V ♥ ✦ 🐾
A warm welcome awaits you at this family-run Victorian guest house. Walking distance to the historic stone circle. Ample street parking. Some rooms with a view of Latrigg. Local information books and videos. Walking boots welcome. Family discounts.

Watendlath, *15 Acorn Street, Keswick, Cumbria, CA12 4EA.*
Grades: ETC 3 Diamond
Tel: **017687 74165**
D: £17.00-£20.00 .
Open: All Year
Beds: 2F 2D **Baths:** 3 En 1 Sh
🛇 🗇 🖬 �V ♥ 🐾
Just a few mins from Keswick town centre, Watendlath is a quiet and relaxed retreat, small, tasteful and renowned for its superb traditional English breakfasts. The attractive rooms have everything to make your holiday a home-from-home experience.

Berkeley Guest House, *The Heads, Keswick, Cumbria, CA12 5ER.*
Grades: ETC 4 Diamond
Tel: **017687 74222** Mrs Crompton
D: £17.00-£24.00 **S:** £20.00-£20.00
Open: Jan to Dec
Beds: 1F 2D 1T 1S
Baths: 3 En 2 Sh
🛇 (3) ⅌ 🗇 🎢 🖬 🖬 �V ♥ ✦ 🐾
Friendly relaxed guest house with superb mountain views from each comfortable room. Situated on a quiet road on the edge of town, close to the lake, an ideal base for walking or water sports. Delicious breakfast choice and warm welcome assured.

Badgers Wood Guest House, *30 Stanger Street, Keswick, Cumbria, CA12 5JU.*
All rooms have mountain views in this outstanding guest house.
Grades: ETC 4 Diamond, AA 4 Diamond
Tel: **017687 72621** Ms Godfrey.
D: £18.00-£22.00 **S:** £18.00.
Open: All Year (not Xmas)
Beds: 3D 1T 2S
Baths: 4 En 1 Sh
⅌ 🗇 🖬 🖬 �V ♥ 🐾

Claremont House, *Chestnut Hill, Keswick, Cumbria, CA12 4LT.*
Grades: AA 4 Diamond
Tel: **017687 72089** Werfel.
D: £21.00-£25.00 .
Open: Easter to Nov
Beds: 3D 1T
Baths: 4 En
🛇 (12) 🅿 (5) ⅌ 🗇 🎢 🖬 🖬 �V ♥ ✦ 🐾
Claremont House, built about 150 years ago as a lodge house to the Fieldside estate, stands elevated about one mile from Keswick centre. Fine accommodation in pleasant surroundings, all tastes catered for with our substantial breakfasts.

All rates are subject to alteration at the owners' discretion

Lairbeck Hotel, *Vicarage Hill, Keswick, Cumbria, CA12 5QB.*
Secluded setting, superb mountain views. Spacious parking. No single supplements.
Grades: ETC 2 Star, Silver, AA 2 Star, RAC 2 Star
Tel: **017687 73373** Mr Coy.
Fax no: 017687 73144
D: £30.00-£38.00 **S:** £30.00-£38.00.
Open: Mar to Jan
Beds: 1F 8D 1T 4S
Baths: 14 En
⛼ (5) 🅿 (16) ⊬ ❑ ✕ ⚚ ⅢⅢ Ⓥ 🛇 ∦

Lynwood House, *35 Helvellyn Street, Keswick, Cumbria, CA12 4EP.*
Victorian-style with modern comforts. Traditional or home-made organic breakfasts.
Grades: ETC 4 Diamond, Silver
Tel: **017687 72398** Mr Picken.
D: £17.00-£20.50 **S:** £18.50-£23.00.
Open: All Year
Beds: 1F 2D 1S
Baths: 1 En
⛼ (3) ⊬ ❑ ⚚ ⅢⅢ Ⓥ 🛇 ∦ ⫘

The Paddock Guest House,
Wordsworth Street, Keswick, Cumbria, CA12 4HU.
Delightful 1800s residence. Close to town, lake, parks and Fells.
Grades: ETC 4 Diamond
Tel: **017687 72510**
D: £19.00-£21.00 **S:** £25.00-£40.00.
Open: All Year (not Xmas)
Beds: 1F 1T 4D
Baths: All En
⛼ 🅿 (5) ⊬ ❑ ⊷ ⚚ ⅢⅢ Ⓥ 🛇 ∦ ⫘

Clarence House, *14 Eskin Street, Keswick, Cumbria, CA12 4DQ.*
Lovely detached Victorian house, excellent ensuite accommodation. Cleanliness guaranteed. No smoking.
Tel: **017687 73186**
Mr & Mrs Robertson.
Fax no: 017687 72317
D: £20.00-£28.00 **S:** £20.00-£28.00.
Open: All Year (not Xmas)
Beds: 1F 4D 3T 1S
Baths: 8 Pr
⛼ (5) ⊬ ❑ ⚚ ⅢⅢ Ⓥ

Glendale Guest House, *7 Eskin Street, Keswick, Cumbria, CA12 4DH.*
Victorian house, mountain views, close to the town and lake.
Tel: **017687 73562** Mr Lankester.
D: £16.00-£20.00 **S:** £16.00-£20.00.
Open: All Year
Beds: 1F 2T 2D 1S
Baths: 3 En 2 Sh
⛼ ⊬ ❑ ⚚ ⅢⅢ Ⓥ 🛇 ⫘

Hawcliffe House, *30 Eskin Street, Keswick, Cumbria, CA12 4DG.*
Warm welcome assured. Short walk to lake and town centre.
Tel: **017687 73250** McConnell.
D: £16.00-£18.00 **S:** £16.00-£18.00.
Open: All Year
Beds: 1T 2D 2S
Baths: 2 Sh
⊬ ❑ ⊷ ⚚ ⅢⅢ Ⓥ 🛇 ∦

Tamara Guest House, *10 Stanger Street, Keswick, Cumbria, CA12 5JU.*
Cosy house, minute walk from town centre with private parking.
Tel: **017687 72913**
Miss Dussoye.
D: £16.00-£18.00 **S:** £16.00-£18.00.
Open: All Year
Beds: 1T 3D
Baths: 1 Sh
⛼ 🅿 (4) ⊬ ❑ ✕ ⚚ ⅢⅢ Ⓥ 🛇

High Hill Farm, *High Hill, Keswick, Cumbria, CA12 5NY.*
Modernised former farmhouse, special breaks, available all year, lovely views.
Tel: **017687 74793** Ms Davies.
D: £18.00-£19.00 .
Open: All Year
Beds: 2D 1T
Baths: 3 En
🅿 (3) ⊬ ❑ ⚚ ⅢⅢ Ⓥ ∦ ⫘

The Queens Hotel, *Main Street, Keswick, Cumbria, CA12 5JF.*
Comfortable, traditional Lake District hotel.
Grades: ETC 3 Star, RAC 3 Star
Tel: **017687 73333**
Fax no: 017687 71144
D: £30.00-£44.00 **S:** £30.00-£44.00.
Open: All Year (not Xmas)
Beds: 10F 20D 5S
Baths: 35 En
⛼ 🅿 ❑ ✕ ⚚ ⅢⅢ Ⓥ ∦

Dalkeith House, *1 Leonards Street, Keswick, Cumbria, CA12 4EJ.*
Clean, comfortable and friendly accommodation. Quiet area close to town.
Tel: **017687 72696** (also fax no)
Mr & Mrs Marsden.
D: £18.00-£22.00 **S:** £18.00-£22.00.
Open: All Year (not Xmas/New Year)
Beds: 4D 1T 1S 1F
Baths: 4 En 3 Sh
⛼ ⊬ ❑ ✕ ⚚ ⅢⅢ Ⓥ 🛇 ∦ ⫘

Century House, *17 Church Street, Keswick, Cumbria, CA12 4DT.*
Warm, friendly guesthouse - the house of many returns.
Tel: **017687 72843** (also fax no)
D: £17.50-£19.50 **S:** £17.50-£19.50.
Open: All Year (not Xmas/New Year)
Beds: 1F 1T 3D
Baths: 4 En 1 Pr
⛼ ⊬ ❑ ⚚ ⅢⅢ Ⓥ 🛇 ∦ ⫘

Derwentdale Guest Hotel, *8 Blencathra Street, Keswick, Cumbria, CA12 4HP.*
Friendly, family-run guest house close to lake and parks.
Grades: ETC 3 Diamond
Tel: **017687 74187** (also fax no)
Mrs Riding.
D: £17.50-£21.00 **S:** £17.50-£18.00.
Open: All Year
Beds: 3D 1T 2S
Baths: 2 En 3 Pr
⛼ ⊬ ❑ ✕ ⚚ ⅢⅢ Ⓥ 🛇 ⫘

Greenside, *48 St John Street, Keswick, Cumbria, CA12 5AG.*
Listed building in conservation area. Views, vegetarian and snack making facilities.
Tel: **017687 74491** Mrs Dalkins.
D: £15.00-£17.00 **S:** £25.00-£30.00.
Open: All Year
Beds: 1D 1T
Baths: 2 En
⛼ (12) 🅿 (2) ⊬ ❑ ⚚ ⅢⅢ Ⓥ 🛇 ∦

Sandon Guest House, *13 Southey Street, Keswick, Cumbria, CA12 4EG.*
Victorian guest house conveniently situated close to lake and theatre.
Grades: ETC 3 diamond
Tel: **017687 73648**
D: £18.00-£21.00 **S:** £18.00-£21.00.
Open: All Year (not Xmas)
Beds: 2T 2D 2S
Baths: 4 En 1 Sh
⛼ ⊬ ❑ ✕ ⚚ ⅢⅢ Ⓥ 🛇 ∦ ⫘

Cumbria House, *1 Derwentwater Place, Ambleside Road, Keswick, Cumbria, CA12 4DR.*
Ideal base for a Lakeland holiday - quiet, 3 minutes from centre of Keswick.
Tel: **017687 73171** (also fax no)
Mr Colam.
D: £18.00-£23.50 **S:** £18.00-£23.50.
Open: Feb to Nov
Beds: 1F 3D 2T 3S
Baths: 4 En 2 Sh
⛼ 🅿 (7) ❑ ✕ ⚚ ⅢⅢ Ⓥ 🛇 ∦

Portland House, *19 Leonard Street, Keswick, Cumbria, CA12 4EL.*
Comfortable and quiet Edwardian house, short walk from town centre.
Tel: **017687 74230**
D: £20.00-£20.00 **S:** £20.00-£20.00.
Open: All Year (not Xmas)
Beds: 1F 2D 1T 1S
Baths: 5 En
⛼ (3) 🅿 (3) ⊬ ❑ ⊷ ⚚ ⅢⅢ 🦽 Ⓥ 🛇 ⫘

Avondale, *20 Southey Street, Keswick, Cumbria, CA12 4EF.*
Actual grid ref: NY268233
Quality accommodation; great breakfasts & close to all amenities.
Tel: **Freephone 0800 0286831** Mr Williams.
Fax no: 017687 75431
D: £19.75-£21.50 **S:** £19.75-£21.50.
Open: All Year (not Xmas)
Beds: 4D 1T 1S
Baths: 6 En
⛼ (12) ⊬ ❑ ⚚ ⅢⅢ Ⓥ 🛇

Beckside, *5 Wordsworth Street, Keswick, Cumbria, CA12 4HU.*
Quality ensuite accommodation. Hearty breakfasts. Close to all amenities.
Tel: **017687 73093**
Mr & Mrs Helling.
D: £15.00-£19.50 **S:** £22.00.
Open: All Year (not Xmas)
Beds: 1F 2D 1T
Baths: 4 En
⊬ ❑ ✕ ⚚ ⅢⅢ Ⓥ 🛇 ∦ ⫘

Penrith to Consett

The route out of **Penrith** heads northeastwards to **Langwathby** in the Eden Valley, and on to **Little Salkeld**. Close to here stand Long Meg and Her Daughters, a late neolithic stone circle - Long Meg herself stands 18 feet high and is named from her eerily humanoid profile. From here you head onto Viol Moor, from where you make the climb to **Hartside**, where there is a cafe during the summer months with a spectacular panorama. There is a great deal of up-and-down in the route through the Pennines, which takes you to **Garrigill** on the River South Tyne, on to **Nenthead** and up to Black Hill on the county boundary, the highest point on the route. From here you descend through Northumberland over Coalcleugh Moor and Allendale Common to **Alienheads**. Now you enter County Durham and follow the Rookhope Burn stream down to **Rookhope**, from where there is a brief steep climb to the start of the Waskerley Way, a reclaimed railway path, which you follow down to **Consett**.

Glaramara Guest House, 9 Acorn Street, Keswick, Cumbria, CA12 4EA.
Actual grid ref: NY269232
Cosy family B&B. Good food, central, bike hire, C2C storage/holiday stabling.
Tel: **017687 73216** (also fax no)
Mrs Harbage (BHSII).
D: £17.00-£22.00 **S:** £17.00-£25.00.
Open: All Year
Beds: 1F 1D 1T 1S
Baths: 2 Pr 2 Sh
🛏 🅿 (3) ⅍ 🗂 ⊁ 📖 Ⅴ ⓣ

Daresfield, Chestnut Hill, Keswick, Cumbria, CA12 4LS.
Actual grid ref: NY279236
Homely accommodation - good views.
Tel: **017687 72531** Mrs Spencer.
D: £16.00-£18.00 **S:** £16.00-£18.00.
Open: All Year (not Xmas)
Beds: 1F 1D 1S **Baths:** 1 Sh
🛏 🅿 (3) ⅍ 🗂 🗙 ⊁ 📖 Ⅴ ⓣ ⚲ ⚲

Foye House, 23 Eskin Street, Keswick, Cumbria, CA12 4DQ.
Foye house is a well-appointed, small, friendly Victorian guest house.
Tel: **017687 73288**
Mr & Mrs Sharpe.
D: £19.00-£21.00 **S:** £16.00-£17.00.
Open: All Year
Beds: 1F 2D 1T 2S
Baths: 4 Pr 2 Sh
🛏 (5) ⅍ 🗂 ⊁ 📖 Ⅴ ⚲

Hall Garth, 37 Blencathra Street, Keswick, Cumbria, CA12 4HX.
Select family-run and non-smoking guest house in quiet, yet convenient location.
Tel: **017687 72627** Mrs Baker.
D: £18.00-£22.00 **S:** £17.00.
Open: All Year **Beds:** 1F 3D 1T
Baths: 2 En 1 Pr 2 Sh
🛏 ⅍ 🗂 🗙 ⊁ 📖 Ⅴ ⓣ ⚲ ⚲

Hunters Way, 4 Eskin Street, Keswick, Cumbria, CA12 4DH.
Spacious comfortable ensuite rooms, close to Keswick Centre and countryside.
Tel: **017687 72324**
D: £20.00-£23.00 **S:** £17.00-£20.00.
Open: All Year (not Xmas)
Beds: 3D 1T 2S **Baths:** 4 En 1 Sh
🛏 (6) ⅍ 🗂 🗙 ⊁ 📖 Ⅴ ⓣ ⚲

Melbreak House, 29 Church Street, Keswick, Cumbria, CA12 4DX.
Close to town centre. Arrive a guest - leave as a friend.
Tel: **017687 73398** Ms Hardman.
D: £18.75-£21.50 .
Open: All Year
Beds: 4F 6D
Baths: 10 En
🛏 ⅍ 🗂 🗙 ⊁ 📖 Ⅴ ⚲

Greystoke House, 9 Leonard Street, Keswick, Cumbria, CA12 4EL.
Traditional Lakeland town house. Two minutes walk from the heart of the town.
Tel: **017687 72603**
Mrs Harbage.
D: £19.00-£20.00
S: £16.00-£17.00.
Open: All Year
Beds: 4D 2S
Baths: 4 En 2 Sh
🛏 ⅍ 🗂 📖 Ⅴ ⓣ ⚲ ⚲

Greystoke 16

National Grid Ref: NY4430

🍴 ⅎ Clickham Inn, Boot & Shoe

Orchard Cottage, Church Road, Greystoke, Penrith, Cumbria, CA11 0TW.
Comfortable peaceful bedrooms overlooking gardens. M6 junction 40 just 4 1/2 miles.
Tel: **017684 83264**
Mrs Theakston.
Fax no: 017684 80015
D: £22.00 **S:** £22.00.
Open: All Year
Beds: 1F 1D
Baths: 1 En 1 Pr
🛏 🅿 (3) ⅍ 🗂 📖 & Ⅴ ⓣ ⚲ ⚲

Lattendales Farm, Greystoke, Penrith, Cumbria, CA11 0UE.
Actual grid ref: NY436307
Comfortable farmhouse in pleasant quiet village.
Tel: **017684 83474**
Mrs Ashburner.
D: £16.00-£17.00 **S:** £17.00-£18.00.
Open: Mar to Oct
Beds: 2D 1T
Baths: 1 Sh
🛏 (1) 🅿 (5) ⅍ 🗂 🗙 📖 ⚲ ⚲

Blencow 17

National Grid Ref: NY4532

🍴 ⅎ Crown Inn

Little Blencow Farm, Blencow, Penrith, Cumbria, CA11 0DG.
Working farm in small village. Comfortable home with friendly welcome.
Tel: **017684 83338**
Mrs Fawcett.
Fax no: 017684 83054
D: £16.00-£18.00
S: £16.00-£18.00.
Open: All Year (not Xmas)
Beds: 1F 1D 1T
Baths: 1 Pr 1 Sh
🛏 🅿 (4) ⅍ 🗂 🗙 📖 Ⅴ ⓣ ⚲ ⚲

Ivegill 18

National Grid Ref: NY4143

🍴 ⅎ White Quay, Crown Inn

Streethead Farm, Ivegill, Carlisle, Cumbria, CA4 0NG.
Distant hills, real fires, homebaking, convenient for Lakes or Scotland.
Tel: **016974 73327** (also fax no)
Mrs Wilson.
D: £20.00-£22.00
S: £22.00-£25.00.
Open: All Year (not Xmas)
Beds: 2D
Baths: 2 En
🛏 (7) 🅿 (2) 🗂 📖 Ⅴ ⓣ ⚲ ⚲

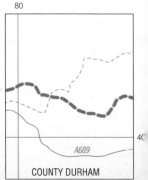

80

A689

40

COUNTY DURHAM

Croft End Hurst, *Ivegill, Carlisle, Cumbria, CA4 0NL.*
Rural bungalow situated midway between J41/42 of M6.
Grades: ETC 3 Diamond
Tel: **017684 84362** Mrs Nichol.
D: £17.00-£19.00 **S:** £17.00.
Open: All Year
Beds: 1D 1T
Baths: 1 Sh
🛇 (1) 🅿 (4) ⊬ 🗖 🖳 🖳 ⅍ Ⓥ ⚡ ♻

Blackwell 19

National Grid Ref: NY4053

🏠 🍴 Black Lion, Old Tote, White Quey

Blackwell Farm, *Lowry Street, Blackwell, Carlisle, Cumbria, CA2 4SH.*
Warm and comfortable family farm close to M6 junction 42.
Grades: AA 3 Diamonds
Tel: **01228 524073**
Ms Westmorland.
D: £18.00-£18.00
S: £20.00-£20.00.
Open: All Year (not Xmas)
Beds: 1F 1D
🛇 🅿 (4) 🗖 🏌 🖳 🖳 Ⓥ ♻

D = Price range per person sharing in a double room

All details shown
are as supplied
by B&B owners in
Autumn 2000.

Carlisle 20

National Grid Ref: NY3955

🏠 🍴 Metal Bridge Inn, The Beehive, Mary's Pantry, Crown & Thistle, Coach & Horses, Golden Fleece, Black Lion

▲ **Carlisle Youth Hostel,**
University of Northumbria, The Old Brewery Residences, Bridge Lane, Caldewgate, Carlisle, Cumbria, CA2 5SR.
Actual grid ref: NY394560
Tel: **01228 597352**
Under 18: £8.75 **Adults:** £13.00
Self-catering facilities, Showers, Cycle store, Parking, Facilities for disabled people, No smoking, WC, Kitchen facilities
University accommodation in an award-winning conversion of the former Theakston's brewery. Single study bedrooms with shared kitchen and bathroom in flats for up to 7 people.

Howard Lodge, *90 Warwick Road, Carlisle, Cumbria, CA1 1JU.*
Actual grid ref: NY407558
Grades: ETC 4 Diamond,
AA 3 Diamond
Tel: **01228 529842** Mr Hendrie.
D: £15.00-£25.00 **S:** £20.00-£30.00.
Open: All Year
Beds: 2F 1D 2T 1S **Baths:** 6 En 1 Sh
🛇 🅿 (6) 🗖 🏌 🗙 🖳 🖳 Ⓥ 🛈 ♻
Friendly family-run guest house in comfortable Victorian town house in conservation area. Spacious rooms all fully ensuite with satellite TV, welcome tray, hairdryer and clock radio. Large breakfasts. 5 minutes' walk from station and city centre. Evening meals by prior arrangement. Private car park.

Craighead, *6 Hartington Place, Carlisle, Cumbria, CA1 1HL.*
Actual grid ref: NY405559
Grades: ETC 3 Diamond
Tel: **01228 596767** Mrs Smith.
D: £17.00 **S:** £16.00.
Open: All Year (not Xmas)
Beds: 1F 2D 1T 1S
Baths: 1 En 2 Sh
🛇 🗖 🏌 🖳 🖳 Ⓥ ♻
You will receive a warm welcome at Craighead, a Grade II Listed spacious Victorian town house with comfortable rooms and original features. CTV, tea/coffee tray in all rooms. Minutes' walk to city centre bus and rail stations and all amenities. Friendly personal service.

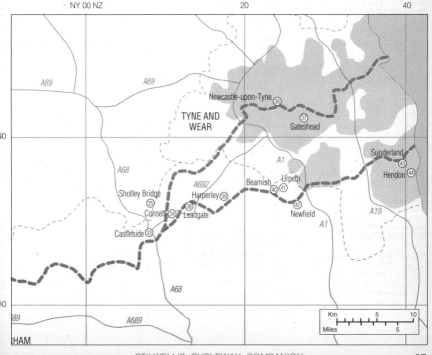

Angus Hotel & Almonds Bistro, 14 Scotland Road, Stanwix, Carlisle, Cumbria, CA3 9DG.
Actual grid ref: NY400571
Grades: AA 4 Diamond
Tel: **01228 523546** Mr Webster.
Fax no: 01228 531895
D: £20.00-£27.00 **S:** £26.00-£42.00.
Open: All Year
Beds: 4F 3D 4T 3S
Baths: 11 En 3 Sh
Victorian town house, foundations on Hadrian's Wall. Excellent food, Les Routiers Awards, local cheeses, home baked bread. Genuine warm welcome from owners. Licensed, draught beer, lounge, meeting room, internet cafe, direct dial telephones, secure garaging. Group rates for cyclists available.

Cherry Grove, 87 Petteril Street, Carlisle, Cumbria, CA1 2AW.
Lovely red brick building close to golf club and town.
Grades: AA 3 Diamond
Tel: **01228 541942** Mrs Houghton.
D: £17.50-£20.00 **S:** £20.00-£30.00.
Open: All Year
Beds: 3F 2D **Baths:** 5 En

Avondale, 3 St Aidans Road, Carlisle, Cumbria, CA1 1LT.
Attractive comfortable Edwardian house. Quiet central position convenient M6 J43.
Grades: ETC 4 Diamond
Tel: **01228 523012** (also fax no)
Mr & Mrs Hayes.
D: £20.00-£20.00 **S:** £20.00-£40.00.
Open: All Year (not Xmas)
Beds: 1D 2T **Baths:** 1 En 1 Pr

Dalroc, 411 Warwick Road, Carlisle, Cumbria, CA1 2RZ.
Small friendly house. Midway city centre and M6 motorway.
Tel: **01228 542805**
Mrs Irving.
D: £16.00-£16.00 **S:** £16.00-£16.00.
Open: All Year (not Xmas/New Year)
Beds: 1T 1D 1S

Chatsworth Guest House, 22 Chatsworth Square, Carlisle, Cumbria, CA1 1HF.
City centre Grade II Listed building, close to all amenities.
Grades: ETC 3 Diamond
Tel: **01228 524023** (also fax no)
Mrs Mackin.
D: £19.00-£22.00 **S:** £25.00-£25.00.
Open: All Year (not Xmas)
Beds: 1F 1D 2T 1S
Baths: 5 En

Kingstown Hotel, 246 Kingstown Road, Carlisle, CA3 0DE.
Grades: AA 3 Diamond
Tel: **01228 515292** (also fax no)
Mrs Marshall.
D: £23.50 **S:** £35.00-£40.00.
Open: All Year
Beds: 1F 4D 2T
Baths: 7 En
Just off the M6 (Jct. 44) we are a licensed hotel providing high-quality accommodation. You will find a friendly and relaxed atmosphere, freshly-prepared cuisine and fine wine at reasonable prices. A good base to explore Cumbria, Northumbria, Lake District, Scotland

Corner House Hotel & Bar, 4 Grey Street, Carlisle, CA1 2JP.
Grades: ETC 3 Diamond
Tel: **01228 533239**
Mrs Anderson.
Fax no: 01228 546628
D: £17.50-£22.00
S: £20.00-£30.00.
Open: All Year
Beds: 3F 4D 4T 3S
Baths: All En
Refurbished family run hotel. All rooms ensuite, colour TV, phones, tea/coffee, radio, toiletries etc. Cosy bar, Sky TV lounge, games room, easy access city centre, bus/train. Base for golf, walking, cycling, touring the Lakes, Roman Wall, Carlisle/Settle line etc.

Ashleigh House, 46 Victoria Place, Carlisle, Cumbria, CA1 1EX.
Beautifully decorated town house. Two minutes from city centre.
Grades: ETC 4 Diamond
Tel: **01228 521631** Mr Davies.
D: £19.00-£22.50 **S:** £25.00-£30.00.
Open: All Year (not Xmas/New Year)
Beds: 3F 1T 2D 1S
Baths: 7 En

Cornerways Guest House, 107 Warwick Road, Carlisle, Cumbria, CA1 1EA.
Large Victorian town house.
Grades: ETC 4 Diamond
Tel: **01228 521733** Mrs Fisher.
D: £14.00-£18.00 **S:** £16.00-£18.00.
Open: All Year (not Xmas)
Beds: 2F 1D 4T 3S
Baths: 3 En 2 Sh

Consett to Tynemonth or Sunderland

From Consett the northern route passes close to the impressively complete Derwentcote Steel Furnace (just beyond **Hamsterley**), a remnant of the Industrial Revolution; and follows the Derwent to the Tyne, which it crosses into **Newcastle**. The capital of the Northeast was built on coal and shipbuilding, rising to a position of importance in the nineteenth century. Sights from the earlier centuries of the city's history include the twelfth-century castle from which it gets its name, and the cathedral, notable for its fifteenth-century lantern tower. The Laing Gallery is the region's foremost art gallery, including a major display of British art. Newcastle's material icon is the Tyne Bridge, the great steel arch whose famous daughter spans Sydney Harbour. You get a view of the bridge to your left as the cycle route crosses the Tyne into Gateshead over the Swing Bridge. From here you head east to **Jarrow**, famed for the 1936 hunger march, where you cross the Tyne again through the pedestrian tunnel, and reach the North Sea at **Tynemouth**

The southern route out of Consett takes you to **Stanley**, and the Beamish Museum beyond. This is a large open-air re-creation of early twentieth-century life in the region, including tours of a reopened drift mine, a period High Street, a train station and a farmyard with rare old breeds of cattle and sheep. The Consett and Sunderland Railway Path takes you to **Chester-le-Street** and **Washington**, where the Old Hall was the ancestral home of the family of the eponymous founder of a certain country. There is also an Arts Centre; and the Washington Wildfowl and Wetlands Centre is east of town. The cycle route east crosses the River Wear over a footbridge to the village of Cox Green and leads into **Sunderland**, another old shipbuilding town. Here you cross back over the Wear into Monkwearmouth, and reach the North Sea by Roker Pier.

Courtfield Guest House,
169 Warwick Road, Carlisle,
Cumbria, CA1 1LP.
Short walk to historic city centre.
Close to M6, J43.
Grades: ETC 4 Diamond
Tel: 01228 522767
Mrs Dawes.
D: £18.00-£22.00 **S:** £25.00.
Open: All Year (not Xmas)
Beds: 1F 2D 2T
Baths: 5 En
⏰ 🅿 (4) ⊬ ❑ 👜 📖 Ⓥ ♿

East View Guest House,
110 Warwick Road, Carlisle,
Cumbria, CA1 1JU.
Actual grid ref: NY407560
10 minutes' walking distance from
city centre, railway station and
restaurants.
Grades: ETC 3 Diamond,
AA 3 Diamond, RAC 3 Diamond
Tel: 01228 522112 (also fax no)
Mrs Glease.
D: £18.00-£20.00 **S:** £20.00-£25.00.
Open: All Year (not Xmas)
Beds: 3F 2D 1T 1S
Baths: 7 En
⏰ 🅿 (4) ⊬ ❑ 👜 📖 Ⓥ ♿

Cambro House, 173 Warwick
Road, Carlisle, Cumbria, CA1 1LP.
Grades: AA 3 Diamond
Tel: 01228 543094 (also fax no)
Mr & Mrs Mawson.
D: £17.00-£20.00 **S:** £20.00-£25.00.
Open: All Year
Beds: 2D 1T
Baths: 3 En
🅿 (2) ⊬ ❑ 👜 📖 Ⓥ ♿
Guests can expect warm hospitality
and friendly service at this attrac-
tively decorated and well-main-
tained guest house. Each ensuite
bedroom includes TV, clock, radio,
hairdryer and welcome tray.
Private off-road parking available,
non-smoking, close to golf course.

Stanwix   21

National Grid Ref: NY3957

🏨 🍺 Cumbria Park Hotel

No. 1, 1 Etterby Street, Stanwix,
Carlisle, Cumbria, CA3 9JB.
Homely accommodation in easy
reach of Hadrian's Wall &
Scotland lakes.
Grades: ETC 3 Diamond
Tel: 01228 547285
Ms Nixon.
D: £17.00-£20.00
S: £17.00-£20.00.
Open: All Year (not Xmas/New
Year)
Beds: 1D 2S
⏰ (4) 🅿 (1) ⊬ ❑ ✕ 👜 📖 Ⓥ ♿

D = Price range per person
sharing in a double room

Penrith   22

National Grid Ref: NY5130

🏨 🍺 Royal Hotel, Lowther Arms, Glen Cottage,
Dog & Duck, Gloucester Arms, Cross Keys,
Agricultural Hotel, Beacon Bank, Herdwick Inn,
Beehive Inn

▲ *Corney House, 1 Corney*
Place, Penrith, Cumbria, CA11 7PY.
Actual grid ref: NY515303
Tel: 01768 867627
Under 18: £8.00 **Adults:** £10.00
Self-catering facilities, Television,
Showers, Central heating, Laundry
facilities, Lounge, Dining room,
Cycle store, Evening meal by
arrangement, Facilities for disabled
people, No smoking
Listed Georgian townhouse.
Friendly welcome. Interestingly
located. Private unit available.

Norcroft Guest House, Graham
Street, Penrith, Cumbria, CA11 9LQ.
Grades: ETC 3 Diamond,
RAC 4 Diamond
Tel: 01768 862365 (also fax no)
Mrs Jackson.
D: £19.50-£21.50 **S:** £21.50.
Open: All Year
Beds: 2F 2D 4T 1S
Baths: 9 En
⏰ 🅿 (9) ⊬ ❑ ✕ 👜 📖 ♿ Ⓥ ♿
Charming Victorian house with
relaxed friendly atmosphere ideal
centre or stop over (M6 junction 40
just 10 mins away) for English
lakes or Scottish borders. Enjoy our
hearty Cumbria food or 5 mins'
walk to town centre for alterna-
tives. Ample private parking.

Blue Swallow, 11 Victoria Road,
Penrith, Cumbria, CA11 8HR.
Victorian town house situated in
lovely market town of Penrith.
Grades: ETC 3 Diamond
Tel: 01768 866335 (also fax no)
Mrs Hughes.
D: £17.00-£20.00 **S:** £22.00-£27.00.
Open: All Year (not Xmas)
Beds: 1F 2D 2T
Baths: 3 En 1 Sh
⏰ 🅿 (5) ❑ 👜 📖 Ⓥ ♿

Brooklands Guest House,
2 Portland Place, Penrith,
Cumbria, CA11 7QN.
Grades: AA 4 Diamonds,
RAC 4 Diamonds
Tel: 01768 863395
Fax no: 01768 864895
D: £18.00-£22.50 **S:** £20.00-£22.00.
Open: All Year
Beds: 1F 2S 3D/T
Baths: 2 Sh, 3 En
⏰ 🅿 (1) ❑ 🔥 👜 📖 Ⓥ ♿
A fine Victorian town house just
100 m, from the town centre, built
in 1874 retaining many of the origi-
nal features, with spacious rooms
tastefully decorated to a very high
standard. Home-from-home com-
forts; a very friendly atmosphere
awaits you.

Albany House, 5 Portland Place,
Penrith, Cumbria, CA11 7QN.
Friendly, comfortable Victorian
house, good breakfast, town centre
M6 5 minutes.
Grades: ETC 3 Diamond
Tel: 01768 863072 (also fax no)
Mrs Blundell.
D: £17.50-£25.00 **S:** £20.00-£27.50.
Open: All Year
Beds: 4F 1D
Baths: 2 En 2 Sh
⏰ 🅿 (1) ❑ 👜 📖 Ⓥ ♿

Grosvenor House, 3 Lonsdale
Terrace, Meeting House Lane,
Penrith, Cumbria, CA11 7TS.
Large comfortable town house con-
venient for lakes and fells.
Tel: 01768 863813 Mrs Fitzpatrick.
D: £14.00-£18.00 **S:** £20.00-£20.00.
Open: Easter to Nov
Beds: 1D 2T
Baths: 1 Sh
⏰ ⊬ ❑ 🔥 👜 ♿

Makalolo, Barco Avenue, Penrith,
Cumbria, CA11 8LU.
Spacious modern house, beamed
lounge, conservatory, views of
Lakeland hills. Local Authority
Approved.
Tel: 01768 891519 Mr Dawson.
D: £17.00-£20.00 **S:** £25.00-£28.00.
Open: All Year
Beds: 1T 1E
Baths: 1 En 1 Pr
🅿 (6) ⊬ ❑ ✕ 👜 📖 Ⓥ ♿

Caledonia Guest House, 8 Victoria
Road, Penrith, Cumbria, CA11 8HR.
Comfortable family-run Victorian
house close to all amenities.
Tel: 01768 864482
Mrs Land.
D: £18.00-£20.00 **S:** £25.00-£30.00.
Open: All Year
Beds: 1F 2D 3T
Baths: 4 En 2 Pr
⏰ 🅿 (5) ⊬ ❑ 👜 📖 Ⓥ ♿

The White House, 94 Lowther
Street, Penrith, Cumbria, CA11 7UW.
Lovely renovated Victorian home,
ensuite facilities, splendid break-
fast, friendly atmosphere.
Tel: 01768 892106
D: £20.00-£24.00
S: £25.00-£30.00.
Open: All Year
Beds: 1T 1D
Baths: 2 En
⏰ ⊬ ❑ 👜 📖 Ⓥ ♿

Keepers Cottage, Brougham,
Penrith, Cumbria, CA10 2DE.
Beamed period cottage in rural set-
ting. Heated indoor swimming
pool.
Grades: ETC 3 Diamond
Tel: 01768 865280 (also fax no)
D: £20.00-£24.50
S: £24.50-£30.00.
Open: All Year
Beds: 1F 1T 1D
Baths: 3 En
🅿 (4) ⊬ ❑ 🔥 👜 📖 Ⓥ ♿

Roundthorn Country House,
Beacon Edge, Penrith, Cumbria,
CA11 8SJ.
Beautiful Georgian mansion with
spectacular views of the surround-
ing area.
Grades: ETC 4 Diamond, Silver
Tel: **01768 863952**
Carruthers.
Fax no: 01768 864100
D: £25.00-£31.50
S: £37.50-£45.00.
Open: All Year
Beds: 1F 1T 8D
Baths: 10 En
⛄ 🅿 🏠 🛇 🖵 🛇 🗙 🚿 🛏 📺 🅥 🛈 ⚡ 🚲

The Friarage, *Friargate, Penrith,*
Cumbria, CA11 7XR.
Clean, comfortable historical
house, town centre. Ideal
North/South, East/West travellers.
Tel: **01768 863635** (also fax no)
Mrs Clark.
D: £15.00-£20.00
S: £17.00-£18.00.
Open: Mar to Oct
Beds: 1F 1D 1T 1S
Baths: 1 En 2 Sh
⛄ 🅿 (3) 🖵 🛏 📺 🅥 ⚡ 🚲

Beacon Bank Hotel, *Beacon Edge,*
Penrith, Cumbria, CA11 7BD.
Beacon Bank is a beautiful
Victorian house in an acre of land-
scaped gardens.
Tel: **01768 862633**
Mrs Black.
D: £25.00-£30.00 **S:** £35.00-£35.00.
Open: All Year
Beds: 2F 4D 2T
Baths: 8 En
⛄ 🅿 (10) 🛇 🖵 🗙 🛏 📺 🅥 🚲

Cumrew, *Graham Street, Penrith,*
Cumbria, CA11 9LG.
Home from home B&B 5 minutes'
walk from town centre.
Tel: **01768 867923** (also fax no)
Mrs Ablewhite.
D: £15.00-£16.00
S: £15.00-£16.00.
Open: Mar to Oct
Beds: 1D 1S
Baths: 1 Sh
⛄ (5) 🅿 (1) 🛇 🖵 🛏 📺 🅥 🛈 🚲

Eamont Bridge 23

National Grid Ref: NY5228

🛏 🍺 Beehive Inn

River View, *6 Lowther Glen,*
Eamont Bridge, Penrith, Cumbria,
CA10 2BP.
Beautiful riverside bungalow near
Lake Ullswater. Comfortable beds,
good breakfasts.
Tel: **01768 864405**
Mrs O'Neil.
D: £18.00-£22.00
S: £20.00-£22.00.
Open: All Year
Beds: 1T 2D 2S
Baths: 1 En
⛄ 🅿 (4) 🖵 🛏 🛏 🖵 🛇 🅥 🛈 ⚡ 🚲

Yanwath 24

National Grid Ref: NY5128

🛏 🍺 Yanwath Gate Inn

Yanwath Gate Farm, *Yanwath,*
Penrith, Cumbria, CA10 2LF.
Comfortable C17th farmhouse,
good food, near a pub.
Tel: **01768 864459**
Mr & Mrs Donnelly.
D: £17.00-£20.00 **S:** £17.00-£20.00.
Open: All Year
Beds: 1F 1D
Baths: 2 En
⛄ 🅿 (9) 🛇 🖵 🖵 🛈 ⚡

Langwathby 25

National Grid Ref: NY5733

▲ *Hay Loft B&B Bunkhouse,*
Langwathby Hall, Langwathby,
Penrith, Cumbria, CA10 1PD.
Actual grid ref: NY568338
Tel: **01768 881771 Adults:** £11.50
Evening meal available.

Little Salkeld 26

National Grid Ref: NY5636

🛏 🍺 Shepher's Inn

Bank House Farm and Stables,
Bankhouse, Little Salkeld, Penrith,
Cumbria, CA10 1NN.
Converted barns on stable yard.
Village location in Eden Valley.
Tel: **01768 881257**
D: £20.00-£30.00 **S:** £25.00-£30.00.
Open: All Year
Beds: 3F 3T 3D
Baths: 6 En 3 Sh
⛄ 🅿 (20) 🖵 🛏 🛏 📺 ⚡ 🚲

Melmerby 27

National Grid Ref: NY6137

🛏 🍺 Shepherds Inn

Gale Hall Farm, *Melmerby,*
Penrith, Cumbria, CA10 1HN.
Actual grid ref: NY6236
Large comfortable farmhouse near
Pennines and Lake District.
Tel: **01768 881254**
Mrs Toppin.
D: £15.00-£15.00 **S:** £15.00-£15.00.
Open: Jun to Nov
Beds: 1F 1T 1S
Baths: 1 Sh
⛄ 🅿 (3) 🖵 🛏 🛈 🚲

Many rates vary
according to season -
the lowest only are
shown here

Renwick 28

National Grid Ref: NY5943

Scalehouse Farm, *Scalehouses,*
Renwick, Penrith, Cumbria,
CA10 1JY.
Actual grid ref: NY588451
Old farmhouse with period
features, open fires and beams,
tastefully renovated.
Tel: **01768 896493** (also fax no)
D: £14.00-£18.00 **S:** £16.00-£20.00.
Open: All Year (not Xmas)
Beds: 2D 1T **Baths:** 1 Pr 1 Sh
⛄ 🅿 (6) 🛇 🖵 🗙 🛏 📺 🅥 🛈 ⚡ 🚲

Leadgate 29

National Grid Ref: NY7043

🛏 🍺 Angel Inn

Brownside House, *Leadgate,*
Alston, Cumbria, CA9 3EL.
Actual grid ref: NY707441
Grades: ETC 3 Diamond
Tel: **01434 382169** (also fax no)
Mrs Le Marie.
D: £18.00-£18.00 **S:** £18.00-£18.00.
Open: All Year
Beds: 1D 2T 1S
Baths: 1 Sh
⛄ 🅿 (4) 🛇 🖵 🛏 🗙 🛏 📺 🅥 🛈 ⚡ 🚲
A warm welcome awaits you at this
peaceful house set in the country
with superb views. Situated in the
unspoilt North Pennines near
Alston. Ideal centre for visiting
Hadrian's Wall, Lake District,
Northumberland.

Alston 30

National Grid Ref: NY7146

🛏 🍺 Blue Bell Inn, Angel Inn, Turks Head,
Crown

▲ *Alston Youth Hostel, The Firs,*
Alston, Cumbria, CA9 3RW.
Actual grid ref: NY717461
Tel: **01434 381509**
Under 18: £6.50 **Adults:** £9.25
Self-catering facilities, Showers,
Lounge, Dining room, Drying
room, Cycle store, Parking,
Evening meal at 7.00pm, No smok-
ing, WC, Kitchen facilities,
Breakfast available, Credit cards
accepted
Purpose-built hostel overlooking
River South Tyne, on outskirts of
Alston, the highest market town in
England.

Nentholme, *The Butts, Alston,*
Cumbria, CA9 3JQ.
Actual grid ref: NY719467
Quiet location, 1 min walk to town,
C2C and walkers welcome.
Tel: **01434 381523** (also fax no)
Mrs Thompson.
D: £17.00-£20.00 **S:** £22.00-£25.00.
Open: All Year
Beds: 2F 3D 3T 1S
Baths: 2 En 1 Sh
⛄ 🅿 (6) 🛇 🖵 🛏 🗙 🛏 📺 🅥 🛈 ⚡ 🚲

Greycroft, Middle Park, The Raise, Alston, Cumbria, CA9 3AR.
Actual grid ref: NY747408
In North Pennines with open views south to Crossfell. 1 mile historic town Alston.
Tel: **01434 381383** (also fax no)
Mrs Dent.
D: £18.00-£22.00 **S:** £20.00-£24.00.
Open: All Year (not Xmas)
Beds: 1D 1T
Baths: 2 En
🛇 🅿 (2) ⊬□✗ 👢 🎟 🛆 Ⅴ ✦ ⚲

Garrigill 31

National Grid Ref: NY7441

🍴 🍺 George & Dragon

Ivy House, Garrigill, Alston, Cumbria, CA9 3DU.
Actual grid ref: NY744414
C17th converted farmhouse. Comfortable, friendly atmosphere. Picturesque North Pennines village.
Tel: **01434 382501** Mrs Humble.
Fax no: 01434 382660
D: £17.00-£19.50 **S:** £26.00-£29.00.
Open: All Year
Beds: 2F 1T **Baths:** 3 En
🛇 🅿 (10) ⊬□↖✗ 👢 🎟 Ⅴ 🔒 ✦ ⚲

Nenthead 32

National Grid Ref: NY7843

🍴 🍺 Miners Arms

The Miners Arms, Nenthead, Alston, Cumbria, CA9 3PF.
Friendly family pub. Real ales, real food, real fires.
Tel: **01434 381427** Miss Clark.
D: £15.00-£15.00 **S:** £15.00-£15.00.
Open: All Year
Beds: 2F 2D 2T 2S
🛇 🅿 ⊬□↖✗ 👢 🎟 Ⅴ ✦ ⚲

Mill Cottage Bunkhouse, Nenthead, Alston, Cumbria, CA9 3PD.
Tel: **01434 382771**
D: £12.00-£12.00 **S:** £12.00-£12.00.
Open: All Year
Beds: 2F
🛇 🅿 (4) ⊬✗ 👢 🎟 Ⅴ ✦ ⚲
Bunkhouse in spectacular landscape, part of Nenthead Mines heritage site.

Castleside 33

National Grid Ref: NZ0849

Bee Cottage Farm, Castleside, Consett, Co Durham, DH8 9HW.
Actual grid ref: NZ068453
Ideally situated for Beanish Museum, Durham Cathedral, C2C cycle track and Metro Centre.
Tel: **01207 508224** Mrs Lawson.
D: £22.00-£70.00 **S:** £28.00-£35.00.
Open: All Year
Beds: 4F 3D 2T 1S
Baths: 5 En 2 Sh
🛇 🅿 (20) ⊬□↖✗ 👢 🎟 Ⅴ 🔒

Consett 34

National Grid Ref: NZ1151

▲ *Consett YMCA, Parliament Street, Consett, County Durham, DH8 5DH.*
Tel: **01207 502680**
Under 18: £12.50 **Adults:** £12.50
Television, Showers, Central heating, Lounge, Dining room, Games room, Drying room, Parking, Facilities for disabled people, No smoking
In town centre. Close to C2C route.

Shotley Bridge 35

National Grid Ref: NZ0852

🍴 🍺 Punchbowl, Manor House

Crown & Crossed Swords Hotel, Shotley Bridge, Consett, Co Durham, DH8 0NH.
Historical country hotel and restaurant in small village.
Tel: **01207 502006** Mrs Suddick.
D: £18.00-£23.00 **S:** £20.00-£25.00.
Open: All Year
Beds: 2F 4D 3T 1S
Baths: 4 En 2 Sh
🛇 🅿 (40) □↖✗ 👢 🎟 Ⅴ 🔒 ✦ ⚲

Redwell Hall Farm, Shotley Bridge, Consett, Co Durham, DH8 9TS.
Redwell Hall Farm is situated 1 mile west of A68 in beautiful Derwent Valley.
Tel: **01207 255216** Mrs Ward.
D: £19.50 **S:** £21.00.
Open: All Year
Beds: 1F 1D 1T 1S
Baths: 1 Sh
🛇 🅿 (10) ⊬□↖✗ 👢 🎟 Ⅴ 🔒 ✦ ⚲

Newcastle-upon-Tyne 36

National Grid Ref: NZ2564

🍴 🍺 Prince of Wales

▲ *Newcastle-upon-Tyne Youth Hostel, 107 Jesmond Road, Newcastle-upon-Tyne, NE2 1NJ.*
Actual grid ref: NZ257656
Tel: **0191 281 2570**
Under 18: £7.75 **Adults:** £11.00
Self-catering facilities, Television, Showers, Lounge, Dining room, Cycle store, Parking, Evening meal at 7.00pm, Kitchen facilities, Breakfast available, Credit cards accepted
A large town house conveniently located for the centre of this vibrant city, the regional capital of the North East.

S = Price range for a single person in a room

D = Price range per person sharing in a double room

Chirton House Hotel, 46 Clifton Road, Newcastle-upon-Tyne, NE4 6SH.
Victorian-style house, conveniently situated for city, airport, Northumberland and Durham.
Tel: **0191 273 0407** (also fax no)
Mrs Turnbull.
D: £18.00-£23.00 **S:** £26.00-£36.00.
Open: All Year
Beds: 3F 2D 3T 3S
Baths: 6 En 5 Sh
🛇 🅿 □↖ 👢 🎟 Ⅴ ✦

Gateshead 37

National Grid Ref: NZ2561

🍴 🍺 Nine Pins, The Victoria

Cox Close House, Ravensworth, Gateshead, Tyne & Wear, NE11 0HQ.
Actual grid ref: NZ228600
Unique C16th. Secluded yet near city and tourist attractions.
Tel: **0191 488 7827**
D: £18.00-£22.00
S: £18.00-£22.00.
Open: All Year
Beds: 1F 1D 1T
Baths: 1 En 1 Sh
🛇 🅿 ⊬□↖✗ 👢 🎟 Ⅴ 🔒 ✦ ⚲

Bellevue Guest House, 31-33 Belle Vue Bank, Low Fell, Gateshead, Tyne & Wear, NE9 6BQ.
Victorian terrace, centrally located for Metro Centre, Newcastle stadium, Beamish Museum.
Tel: **0191 487 8805**
Mr Wallace.
D: £18.00-£20.00 **S:** £18.00-£28.00.
Open: All Year
Beds: 1F 1D 2T 2S
Baths: 2 En 1 Sh
🛇 🅿 □✗ 👢 🎟 🛆 Ⅴ ✦ ⚲

Leadgate 38

National Grid Ref: NZ1251

🍴 🍺 Jolly Droviers

Low Brooms Farm, Consett, County Durham, DH8 7SR.
Actual grid ref: NZ136515
Farmhouse with panoramic view. Base for Durham. Newcastle C2C route.
Grades: ETC 2 Daimond
Tel: **01207 500594** (also fax no)
Mrs Turnbull.
D: £18.00-£23.00 **S:** £19.50-£18.50.
Open: All Year (not Xmas/New Year)
Beds: 1F 1T
🛇 🅿 □↖ 👢 🎟 Ⅴ 🔒 ✦ ⚲

Harperley 39

National Grid Ref: NZ1753

⊯ ⊯ Harperley Hotel

Bushblades Farm, Harperley, Stanley, County Durham, DH9 9UA.
Actual grid ref: NZ1653
Georgian farmhouse, rural setting, close Beamish Museum and Durham City.
Grades: ETC 3 Diamond
Tel: 01207 232722 Mrs Gibson.
D: £17.00-£19.50 **S:** £20.00-£25.00.
Open: All Year (not Xmas)
Beds: 2D 1T
Baths: 1 En 2 Sh
🛏 (12) 🅿 (4) 🖵 🏃 🎹 🕭 Ⅴ ✄ ↝

Beamish 40

National Grid Ref: NZ2253

⊯ ⊯ Beamish Mary Inn

No Place House, Beamish, Stanley, Co Durham, DH9 0QH.
Converted co-operative store, close to Beamish Museum. Friendly warm welcome.
Grades: ETC 2 Diamond
Tel: 0191 370 0891
Mrs Wood.
D: £18.50-£20.00 **S:** £22.00-£25.00.
Open: All Year
Beds: 2D 1T
Baths: 2 En 1 Sh
🛏 (3) 🅿 (5) 🖵 🏃 🎹 Ⅴ ✄

Urpeth 41

National Grid Ref: NZ2554

The Coach House, High Urpeth, Beamish, Stanley, Co Durham, DH9 0SE.
Country hamlet location, near Durham City, Beamish, Metro Centre & A1(M).
Grades: ETC 4 Diamond
Tel: 0191 370 0309 Mrs Foreman.
Fax no: 0191 370 0046
D: £20.00-£22.50 **S:** £25.00-£30.00.
Open: All Year
Beds: 1F 1T 1D
Baths: 1 En 2 Pr
🛏 🅿 (6) 🖵 🏃 ✗ 🎹 Ⅴ ✄ ↝

Newfield 42

National Grid Ref: NZ2452

⊯ ⊯ Highwayman

Malling House, 1 Oakdale Terrace, Newfield, Chester-le-Street, County Durham, DH2 2SU.
Heather, your host, has extensive knowledge of area and attractions.
Grades: ETC 3 Diamond
Tel: 0191 370 2571
Ms Rippon.
Fax no: 0191 370 1391
D: £36.00-£46.00 **S:** £20.00-£26.00.
Open: All Year
Beds: 1F 1T 1S
🛏 🅿 (3) 🖵 🎹 Ⅴ ✄ ↝

Sunderland 43

National Grid Ref: NZ3957

Braeside Guest House, 26 Western Hill, Beside University, Sunderland, Tyne & Wear, SR2 7PH.
Grades: ETC 2 Diamond
Tel: **0191 565 4801**
Fax no: 0191 552 4198
D: £15.00-£17.50 **S:** £18.00-£23.00.
Open: Jan to Nov
Beds: 2T 1D **Baths:** 1En 1Sh
🛏 (12) 🅿 🖵 🎹 Ⅴ ↝
Experience our unique theme rooms, hearty northern breakfasts . The delights of Sunderland indoor shopping mail, recently doubled in size and Northumbria's beautiful countryside. We arrange golf at the top courses and tennis coaching and matches at Puma international centre.

Hendon 44

National Grid Ref: NZ3956

Acorn Guest House, 10 Mowbray Road, Hendon, Sunderland, Tyne & Wear, SR2 8EN.
Situated near town centre Mowbray Park and all local amenities.
Grades: ETC 2 Diamond
Tel: **0191 514 2170** Morrison.
D: £15.00-£15.00 **S:** £16.00-£16.00.
Open: All Year
Beds: 3F 5T 1D
🛏 🅿 (9) 🖵 🏃 ✗ 🎹 Ⅴ ↝

Sustrans

Sustrans - it stands for sustainable transport - is a charity working on practical projects to encourage people to walk and cycle more, so as to reduce motor traffic and its adverse effects.

National Cycle Network

The National Cycle Network is a safe, attractive, high-quality network for cyclists and a major new amenity for walkers and people with disabilities.

It was officially opened in June 2000, with work continuing throughout the year. It offers 5000 miles of continuous routes, including traffic-free and traffic-calmed sections, and minor roads. The routes run right through urban centres and reach all parts of the UK, providing safe links to work, to schools, to friends and family, to shops and stations. This is the first stage of a larger network which will eventually pass within 2 miles of half the population.

Safe Routes to Schools

Safe Routes to Schools is a project to enable and encourage children to cycle and walk to school by improving street design, calming traffic, creating traffic-free spaces and linking with the National Cycle Network.

Sustrans Information Service

Sustrans publish and stock a range of maps, leaflets, information sheets and technical publications. For a free catalogue with further information about Sustrans and the National Cycle Network, and details on how to become a supporter, please contact the Sustrans Information Service, PO Box 21, Bristol BS99 2HA, tel 0117-929 0888, or surf the Web and visit us at **www.sustrans.org.uk**.

Sustrans Severn & Thames

The **Severn & Thames Cycle Route** is a new section of the developing National Cycle Network, running on traffic-free paths and traffic-calmed roads through 140 miles of the South of England, following the Severn from the ancient city of Gloucester before turning inland at Bristol, visiting beautiful Bath and traversing northern Wiltshire with its prehistoric sites to finish at Newbury in Berkshire. An extension of the route from Newbury to Reading is currently at the planning stage. The route connects to the **West Country Way** in Bristol and Bath and the **Welsh National Cycle Route** via the Severn Bridge; it also intersects with the **Wiltshire Cycleway** and the **Round Berkshire Cycle Route**. It is clearly signposted by blue direction signs with a cycle silhouette, numbered 41 from Gloucester to the Severn Bridge and 4 from the Severn Bridge to Newbury.

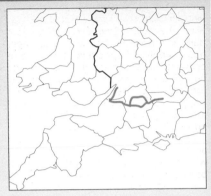

The route south from **Gloucester** strikes out across the Severn flood plain before running for a short distance along the Gloucester and Sharpness Canal towpath after Frampton on Severn. After **Slimbridge**, **Berkeley** and Oldbury-on-Severn, the junction to the Severn Bridge is at Elberton, before you cycle on, with views of the two Severn Bridges to your right, towards **Avonmouth**, Bristol's port. Here you cross the Avon on a cyclepath alongside the M5 to reach Pill, and head along the traffic-free path up the Avon Gorge. This takes you through the Avon Gorge Nature Reserve and under Brunel's Clifton Suspension Bridge before you reach **Bristol** city centre. From here you follow the traffic-free Bristol and Bath Railway Path, the first Sustrans project (shared with the West Country Way), to historic **Bath**, and the Kennet and Avon Canal towpath to lovely **Bradford-on-Avon**. Here the route through Wiltshire divides into two: the northern route through **Corsham**, **Chippenham** and **Calne** heads up into the Marlborough Downs and close by the neolithic

sites of Avebury before reaching Marlborough and taking the Grand Avenue through ancient Savernake Forest to join up with the southern branch. The southern route continues along the Kennet and Avon Canal towpath past the edge of **Trowbridge**, and descends alongside the 'staircase' of 29 locks at Caen Hill to **Devizes** before heading through the Vale of Pewsey to Wootton Rivers and joining up with the northern branch before **Great Bedwyn**. The final stretch of the way follows the Kennet and Avon Canal through the sleepy Berkshire villages of **Hungerford** and **Kintbury** into the Thames Valley to reach **Newbury**.

The indispensable **official route map and guide** for the route is available from Sustrans, 35 King Street, Bristol BS1 4DZ, tel 0117-926 8893, fax 0117-929 4173, @ £5.99 (+ £2.00 p&p).

Maps: Ordnance Survey 1:50,000 Landranger series: 162, 172, 173, 174

Trains: Bristol, Bath, Gloucester, Chippenham and Newbury are served by main line train services; there are connections to several other places on or near to the route.

Gloucester   1

National Grid Ref: SO8318

🍴 🍺 Beacon Hotel, King Edward, Linden Tree, Tall Ship, White Smiths

***Georgian Guest House**, 85 Bristol Road, Gloucester, GL1 5SN.*
Part-Georgian terraced house, 15 minutes walk city centre.
Grades: ETC 1 Diamond
Tel: **01452 413286** (also fax no)
Nash.
D: £14.50-£16.50 **S:** £14.50-£15.50.
Open: All Year
Beds: 4F 3T 2S **Baths:** 5 En 1 Sh
🛌 🅿 (3) 🖵 🏃 🖳 🛏 Ⅲ Ⅴ 🐾

***Gemini Guest House**, 83a Innsworth Lane, Longlevens, Gloucester, GL2 0TT.*
Friendly, family-run guest house, 2 miles from M5/jct 11.
Tel: **01452 415849** Mrs Burby.
D: £15.00-£18.00 **S:** £16.00-£18.00.
Open: All Year (not Xmas/New Year)
Beds: 1F 1D 1T 1S **Baths:** 1 Sh
🛌 (7) 🅿 (6) ⚡ 🖵 🛏 Ⅲ Ⅴ

D = Price range per person sharing in a double room

S = Price range for a single person in a room

***The Chestnuts**, 9 Brunswick Square, Gloucester, GL1 1UG.*
Located in Gloucester's finest Georgian square. Close shops, Cathedral Museum and docks.
Grades: ETC 4 Diamond
Tel: **01452 330356** (also fax no)
Mrs Champion.
D: £21.00 **S:** £25.00.
🛌 🅿 (1) 🖵 ✕ 🛏 Ⅲ Ⅴ ⚡ 🐾

Gloucester, important since Roman times, is most notable for its fantastically preserved cathedral, among England's best examples of the Perpendicular style. The tomb of King Edward II (see under Berkeley), with alabaster statue, is largely responsible for the wealth on which the most magnificent parts of the cathedral were built, as it became a place of pilgrimage. The city also has a wealth of specialist museums, many of them converted warehouses in the redundant docks. The most notable are the National Waterways Museum, recording the heyday of the country's canal network, and the Regiments of Gloucestershire Museum, much more interesting than it sounds thanks to its empathetic approach.

At **Slimbridge**, the Wildfowl and Wetlands Trust offers access to a large variety of birdlife all year round, as in winter migratory Arctic birds arrive. The centre is particularly notable for its large numbers of flamingos.

Slimbridge 2

National Grid Ref: SO7303

▲ *Slimbridge Youth Hostel, Shepherd's Patch, Slimbridge, Gloucester, GL2 7BP.*
Actual grid ref: ST730043
Tel: 01453 890275
Under 18: £6.90
Adults: £10.00
Self-catering facilities, Showers, Shop, Laundry facilities, Lounge, Games room, Drying room, Cycle store, Parking, Evening meal at 7.00pm, No smoking, Kitchen facilities, Breakfast available, Credit cards accepted
Purpose-built youth hostel, with its own pond & wildfowl collection, next to the Sharpness Canal and Sir Peter Scott's famous wildfowl reserve.

Order your packed lunches the *evening before* you need them. Not at breakfast!

Rotherfield House Hotel, 5 Horton Road, Gloucester, GL1 3PX.
Immaculate, extended detached Victorian property. Friendly atmosphere, excellent choice food.
Tel: **01452 410500**
Mr Eacott.
D: £22.00-£25.00
S: £24.00-£36.00.
Open: All Year
Beds: 2F 3D 1T 7S
Baths: 4 En 2 Pr
🛏 🅿 (9) 🗶 ✕ 🏠 ♿ ⬛ 🖊 🚲

High season, bank holidays and special events mean low availability *everywhere*.

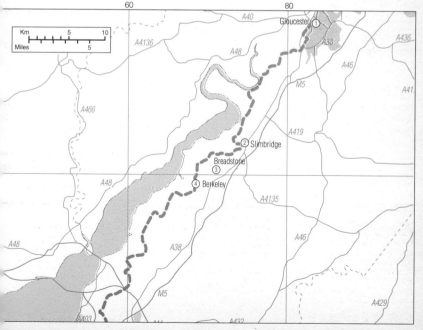

Breadstone 3

National Grid Ref: SO7100

|●| ⌂ Prince of Wales, Salmon Inn

Green Acres Farm Guest House,
Breadstone, Berkeley, Glos,
GL13 9HF.
Tel: **01453 810348** Ms Evans.
Fax no: 01453 810799
D: £23.50-£26.00 **S:** £24.50-£26.50.
Open: All Year
Beds: 2T 2D 2S **Baths:** 6 En
🅿 ⅏ ⏁ ⛤ 🛏 ♨ 📖, Ⅴ
C12th Berkeley Castle. Gloucester
Waterway Museum, Docklands,
wild fowl and wetlands, Bath,
Wales, Forest of Dean, Cotswolds,
Bristol. Tranquil setting in large
garden overlooking Welsh Hills
and Cotswolds. Full English
breakfast. Clean and comfortable
our promise.

Berkeley 4

National Grid Ref: ST6899

|●| ⌂ Black Horse North Nibley, Stage Coach

Pickwick Farm, *Berkeley, Glos,*
GL13 9EU.
Ensuite annexe room overlooks
large garden, views to Cotswolds,
golf nearby.
Grades: ETC 3 Diamond
Tel: **01453 810241** Mrs Jordan.
D: £18.00-£20.00 **S:** £18.00-£19.00.
Open: All Year (not Xmas)
Beds: 1F 1D 1T
Baths: 1 En 1 Sh
⛤ (2) 🅿 (4) ⅏ ⏁ 🛏 ♨ 📖, Ⅴ ⅌ ⚲

Bristol Clifton 5

National Grid Ref: ST5674

Downs View Guest House,
38 Upper Belgrave Road, Clifton,
Bristol, BS8 2XN.
Centrally situated. Overlooking
Durdham Down. Near Zoo and
Clifton Suspension Bridge.
Grades: ETC 3 Diamond
Tel: **0117 973 7046** Ms Cox.
Fax no: 0117 973 8169
D: £22.50-£27.50 **S:** £30.00-£35.00.
Open: All Year (not Xmas)
Beds: 2F 4D 3T 6S
Baths: 7 En 2 Sh
⛤ ⏁ 🛏 ♨ 📖, Ⅴ

Bristol Bedminster 6

National Grid Ref: ST5771

Maison George, *10 Greville Road,*
Southville, Bristol, BS3 1LL.
Large Victorian townhouse within
walking distance of city centre.
Grades: ETC 2 Diamond
Tel: **0117 963 9416** Mr Evans.
Fax no: 0117 953 5760
D: £20.00-£30.00 **S:** £20.00-£30.00.
Open: All Year
Beds: 1F 1D 2T 1S **Baths:** 2 Sh
⛤ ⅏ ⏁ 🛏 ♨ 📖, Ⅴ

S = Price range for a single
person in a room

Bristol Central 7

National Grid Ref: ST6075

▲ **Bristol Youth Hostel,** *Hayman*
House, 14 Narrow Quay, Bristol,
BS1 4QA.
Actual grid ref: ST586725
Tel: **0117 922 1659**
Under 18: £8.50 **Adults:** £12.50
Self-catering facilities, Television,
Showers, Laundry facilities,
Lounge, Games room, Cycle store,
Evening meal at 6.00-7.00pm,
Kitchen facilities, Breakfast
available, Luggage store, Credit
cards accepted
With views over the waterways, this
hostel has been sympathetically
and imaginatively restored to
create a relaxing yet cosmopolitan
atmosphere.

Bristol Cotham 8

National Grid Ref: ST5874

Arches Hotel, *132 Cotham Brow,*
Cotham, Bristol, BS6 6AE.
Actual grid ref: ST588745
Friendly, non-smoking city centre
hotel, close to shops and
restaurants.
Grades: ETC 3 Diamond
Tel: **0117 924 7398** (also fax no)
Mr Lambert.
D: £21.50-£25.50 **S:** £24.50-£37.00
Open: All Year (not Xmas)
Beds: 3F 2D 1T 3S
Baths: 4 En 2 Sh
⛤ (6) ⅏ ⏁ 🛏 ♨ 📖, Ⅴ ⅌

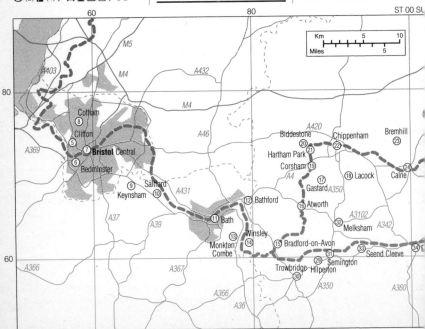

Berkeley Castle is a medieval castle set in Elizabethan gardens. It is most famous as the scene of the murder in 1327 of Edward II, who, unpopular with the barons on account of his homosexuality and the advancement he granted first to Piers Gaveston and then to Hugh le Despenser, was deposed by his wife Queen Isabel with Roger de Mortimer. Read about it in Christopher Marlowe's play. You can visit the room where the deed was done (it involved a red-hot poker). Thereafter, his body was denied burial in both Bristol and Malmesbury, and Gloucester reaped the rewards in later years.

For **Bristol** and **Bath** see under the *Sustrans West Country Way*.

Bath 11

National Grid Ref: ST7464

🍴 🍺 Royal Oak, Dolphin, Wheelwrights Arms, Old Crown, Huntsman, George, Devonshire Arms, Sportsman, Waldergrave Arms, Bear, Park Tavern, Rose & Crown, Weston Walk, Boathouse, Lambridge Harvester, Green Park Station, Saracen's Head, Hop Pole

▲ **Bath Youth Hostel,** *Bathwick Hill, Bath, Somerset, BA2 6JZ.*
Actual grid ref: ST766644
Tel: **01225 465674**
Under 18: £7.75 **Adults:** £11.00
Self-catering facilities, Television, Showers, Lounge, Drying room, Security lockers, Cycle store, Evening meal at 6.00 to 8.00pm, Kitchen facilities, Breakfast available, Credit cards accepted
Handsome Italianate mansion, set in beautiful, secluded gardens, with views of historic city and surrounding hills.

Blairgowrie House, *55 Wellsway, Bath, BA2 4RT.*
Fine late Victorian Residence operating as a privately owned family-run guest house.
Grades: AA 4 Diamond
Tel: **01225 332266**
Mr Roberts.
Fax no: 01225 484535
D: £27.50-£30.00 .
Open: All Year
Beds: 1T 2D
Baths: 2 En 1 Pr
🛏 🄿 🍴 🖵 🕯 🛅 💷 Ⅴ ⚡ 🚲

Keynsham 9

National Grid Ref: ST6568

🍴 🍺 The Talbot

Fiorita, *91 Bath Road, Keynsham, Bristol, BS31 1SR.*
Warm welcome, comfortable family home midway between Bristol and Bath.
Tel: **0117 986 3738** (also fax no)
Mrs Poulter.
D: £14.50-£16.00 **S:** £16.00-£18.00
Open: Jan to Dec
Beds: 1D 1T **Baths:** 1 En 1 Sh
🛏 🄿 (4) 🖵 🕯 🛅 💷 Ⅴ ⚡ 🚲

Saltford 10

National Grid Ref: ST6866

Long Reach House Hotel,
321 Bath Rd, Saltford, Bristol, BS31 1TJ.
Gracious house standing in 2 acres midway between Bath and Bristol.
Grades: ETC 2 Star
Tel: **01225 400500**
Fax no: 01225 400700
D: £22.50-£45.00
S: £45.00-£50.00
Open: All Year
Beds: 2F 7T 7D 2S
Baths: 18 En
🛏 🄿 🍴 🖵 🛉 ✗ 🍴 🛅 💷 🛅 Ⅴ 🕯 ⚡

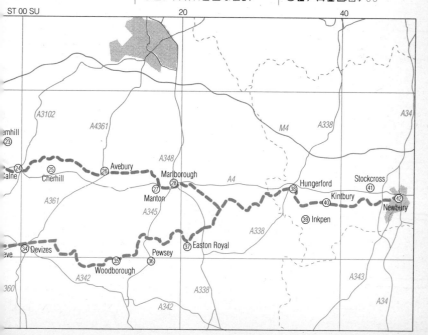

Bailbrook Lodge, *35-37 London Road West, Bath, BA1 7HZ.*
Grades: ETC 3 Diamond, AA 3 Diamond
Tel: 01225 859090 Mrs Sexton.
Fax no: 01225 852299
D: £30.00-£40.00 **S:** £39.00-£50.00.
Open: All Year
Beds: 4F 4D 4T
Baths: 12 En
⚡ ⌴ (14) ⅍ ⌷ ✕ ⋔ 🖳 ▥ ▨ Ⅴ ❀ ⨠
A warm welcome is assured at Bailbrook Lodge, an imposing Georgian house set in its own gardens. The elegant period bedrooms (some four posters) offer ensuite facilities, TV and hospitality trays. Private parking. 1.5 miles from Bath centre. Close to M4.

3 Thomas Street, *Walcot, Bath, Somerset, BA1 5NW.*
Charming Georgian house convenient to all city amenities and shops.
Grades: ETC 3 Diamond
Tel: 01225 789540 Ms Saunders.
D: £20.00-£22.50 **S:** £20.00-£22.50.
Open: All Year (not Xmas)
Beds: 2T
Baths: 1 En 1 Sh
⅍ ⌷ ⋤ 🖳 Ⅴ

Sarnia, *19 Combe Park, Weston, Bath, BA1 3NR.*
Actual grid ref: ST730656
Grades: AA 4 Diamond
Tel: 01225 424159
Mr & Mrs Fradley.
Fax no: 01225 337689
D: £25.00-£32.50
S: £30.00-£40.00.
Open: All Year (not Xmas/New Year)
Beds: 1F 1D 1T
Baths: 2 En 1 Pr
⚡ ⌴ (3) ⅍ ⌷ ⋤ 🖳 Ⅴ ▨ ❀ ⨠
Superb bed & breakfast in large Victorian home, easy reach of town centre. Spacious bedrooms, private facilities, newly decorated, attractively furnished. Breakfast in sunny dining room, English, Continental and vegetarian menus, home made jams, marmalades, comfortable lounge, secluded garden, private parking & children welcome.

Koryu B&B, *7 Pulteney Gardens, Bath, Somerset, BA2 4HG.*
Tel: **01225 337642** (also fax no)
Mrs Shimizu.
D: £22.00-£25.00
S: £22.00-£25.00.
Open: All Year
Beds: 1F 2D 2T 2S
Baths: 5 En 2 Sh
⚡ ⌴ (2) ⅍ ⌷ ✕ ⋤ 🖳 Ⅴ ⨠
Completely renovated Victorian home run by a young Japanese lady, extremely clean, delicious breakfasts with wide menu, beautiful linens; a bright, cheerful and welcoming house. Abbey and Roman baths 5 mins, gorgeous Kennet and Avon canal 2 mins.

Wentworth House Hotel, *106 Bloomfield Road, Bath, BA2 2AP.*
Grades: AA 2 Star, RAC 4 Diamond Sparkling
Tel: 01225 339193
Mrs Boyle.
Fax no: 01225 310460
D: £25.00-£47.50 **S:** £40.00-£60.00.
Open: All Year
Beds: 2F 12D 2T 2S
Baths: 17 En 1 Pr
⚡ ⌴ (5) ⌷ ✕ ⋔ ⋤ 🖳 ▨ ▣ ❀ ⨠
A Victorian mansion 15 minutes' walk from the city. Quiet location with large garden and car park. Heated swimming pool, licensed restaurant and cocktail bar. Golf and walks nearby. Lovely rooms, some with four-poster beds and conservatories.

Wellsway Guest House, *51 Wellsway, Bath, BA2 4RS.*
Edwardian house near Alexandra Park. Easy walks to city centre.
Grades: ETC 2 Diamond
Tel: 01225 423434
Mrs Strong.
D: £18.00-£20.00 **S:** £20.00-£20.00.
Open: All Year
Beds: 1F 1D 1T 1S
Baths: 4 Sh
⚡ ⌴ (4) ⌷ ⋔ 🖳 ❀ ⨠

Marlborough House, *1 Marlborough Lane, Bath, BA1 2NQ.*
Grades: ETC 4 Diamond, AA 4 Diamond
Tel: 01225 318175 Dunlop.
Fax no: 01225 466127
D: £32.50-£47.50.
S: £45.00-£75.00.
Open: All Year
Beds: 2F 1T 3D 1S
Baths: 7 En
⚡ ⌴ ⅍ ⌷ ✕ ⋔ ⋤ 🖳 ▨ ▣ ❀ ⨠
An enchanting Victorian small hotel in the heart of Georgian Bath, exquisitely furnished, but run in a friendly and informal style. Specialising in organic vegetarian world cuisine. Our central location, gorgeous rooms, and unique menu make Marlborough House truly special.

Cranleigh, *159 Newbridge Hill, Bath, N E Somerset, BA1 3PX.*
Grades: AA 4 Diamonds
Tel: 01225 310197
Mr Poole.
Fax no: 01225 423143
D: £33.00-£40.00 **S:** £45.00-£55.00.
Open: All Year (not Xmas)
Beds: 3F 2T 4D
Baths: 8 En
⚡ ⌴ (5) ⅍ ⌷ ⋤ 🖳 Ⅴ ❀
Charming Victorian house a short distance from the city centre. Spacious bedrooms, most with country views, offer comfort and quality. Imaginative breakfasts served in elegant dining room include fresh fruit salad and scrambled eggs with smoked salmon.

Dene Villa, *5 Newbridge Hill, Bath, BA1 3PW.*
Victorian family-run guest house, a warm welcome is assured.
Tel: 01225 427676
Mrs Surry.
Fax no: 01225 482684
D: £20.00-£22.50 **S:** £19.00-£22.00
Open: All Year
Beds: 1F 1D 1T 1S
Baths: 3 En
⚡ ⌴ (3) ⌷ (4) ⌷ ⋤ 🖳 Ⅴ ❀ ⨠

The Old Red House, *37 Newbridge Road, Bath, BA1 3HE.*
A romantic Victorian gingerbread house with stained glass windows, comfortable bedrooms, superbly cooked breakfasts.
Grades: AA 3 Diamond
Tel: 01225 330464
Fax no: 01225 331661
D: £22.00-£33.50 **S:** £30.00-£45.00
Open: Mar to Dec
Beds: 1F 4D 1T 1S
Baths: 3 En 1 Pr 1 Sh
⚡ ⌴ (4) ⌷ (4) ⅍ ⌷ ⋔ 🖳 Ⅴ ❀

The Albany Guest House, *24 Crescent Gardens, Bath, BA1 2NB.*
Grades: ETC 4 Diamond, Silver
Tel: 01225 313339
Mrs Wotley.
D: £17.00-£25.00 **S:** £22.00-£25.00
Open: All Year (not Xmas/New Year)
Beds: 2D 1T 2S
Baths: 1 En 1 Sh
⚡ ⌴ (5) ⌷ (3) ⅍ ⌷ ⋤ 🖳 Ⅴ
Jan & Bryan assure you of a warm welcome in their Victorian home. Only five minutes walk to the city centre - Roman Baths, Abbey, Royal Crescent etc. Delicious English or vegetarian breakfast. Imaginatively decorated rooms and first class service.

Flaxley Villa, *9 Newbridge Hill, Bath, BA1 3PW.*
Comfortable Victorian house near Royal Crescent. 15 minute walk to centre.
Grades: ETC 3 Diamond
Tel: 01225 313237
Mrs Cooper.
D: £20.00-£25.00
S: £18.00-£36.00.
Open: All Year
Beds: 3D 1T 1S
Baths: 3 En
⚡ ⌴ (5) ⌷ ⋤ 🖳 Ⅴ ⨠

14 Raby Place, *Bathwick Hill, Bath, Somerset, BA2 4EH.*
Charming Georgian terraced house with beautiful interior rooms.
Grades: ETC 4 Diamond
Tel: 01225 465120
Mrs Guy.
Fax no: 01225 465283
D: £22.50-£25.00
S: £25.00-£35.00.
Open: All Year
Beds: 1F 2D 1T 1S
Baths: 3 En 2 Pr
⚡ ⅍ ⌷ ⋤ 🖳 Ⅴ ❀ ⨠

Bradford on Avon centres on an arched stone bridge over the Avon, and also features a tithe barn and the ancient Saxon Church of St Laurence.

Corsham Court is a sixteenth-century house, purchased in the late eighteenth century by Paul Methuen, and extensively developed over the following decades by Nash and Bellamy. It now houses an extensive art collection including Michelangelo, Caravaggio, Rubens and Reynolds. There is also a landscaped garden by Brown and Repton. The village itself has weavers' cottages and a Brunel railway tunnel.

Just before **Calne**, Bowood House is a Georgian mansion partly designed by Robert Adam. It was here that Joseph Priestly discovered oxygen in 1774. The house is set in a magnificent landscaped garden designed by 'Capability' Brown, notable for its Rhododendron gardens.

orres House, 172 Newbridge oad, Bath, BA1 3LE.
. warm welcome, comfortable bed nd big breakfast awaits you.
rades: ETC 3 Diamond
el: **01225 427698** Jones.
: £20.00-£25.00 **S:** £30.00-£35.00.
pen: All Year
eds: 2F 1T 2D
aths: 5 En
 ▣ (5) ⊬ ❏ ⚲ ▥ Ⓥ

herry Tree Villa, 7 Newbridge ill, Bath, Somerset, BA1 3PW.
nall friendly Victorian home 1 ile from city centre.
rades: ETC 3 Diamond
el: **01225 331671**
s Goddard.
: £18.00-£24.00
 £20.00-£30.00.
pen: All Year (not Xmas/ ew Year)
eds: 1F 1D 1S
aths: 1 Sh
 (4) ▣ ❏ ⚲ ▥ Ⓥ ⚡ ⚙

2 Crescent Gardens, Upper istol Road, Bath, BA1 2NA.
eautiful B&B in the heart of Bath. arm welcome.
rades: ETC 4 Diamond
el: **01225 331186** Mr Bez.
 £19.00-£25.00 **S:** £19.00-£25.00.
pen: All Year (not Xmas/ ew Year)
eds: 1F 3T 3D
aths: 3 En 1 Sh
 ❏ ⚲ ▥ Ⓥ

ove Lodge, 11 Lambridge , Bath, 6BJ.
egant, Georgian villa, large ooms with views.
l: **01225 310860** Miles.
x no: 01225 429630
 £25.00-£30.00 **S:** £30.00-£35.00.
en: All Year (not Xmas/New ar)
ds: 1F 1T 2D 1S
ths: 3 Pr
 (6) ⊬ ❏ ⚲ ▥ Ⓥ ⓘ ⚙

Ashley House, 8 Pulteney Gardens, Bath, BA2 4HG.
Actual grid ref: ST757646
Comfortable Victorian house level walk to attractions/ stations.
Grades: ETC 3 Diamond
Tel: **01225 425027** Mrs Pharo.
D: £23.00-£33.00 **S:** £25.00-£30.00.
Open: All Year
Beds: 1F 4D 1T 1S
Baths: 5 Pr 2 Sh
 ➹ ⊬ ❏ ⚲ ▥ Ⓥ ⓘ

Westerlea, 87 Greenway Lane, Bath, BA2 4LN.
Georgian style house, large gardens, friendly, ensuite accommodation, cars garaged.
Grades: ETC 4 Diamond
Tel: **01225 311543** (also fax no)
D: £27.50-£37.50
S: £45.00-£65.00.
Open: All Year (not Xmas)
Beds: 2D
Baths: 2 En
 ➹ (12) ▣ (2) ⊬ ❏ ⟊ ⚲ ▥ Ⓥ ⚡ ⚙

Georgian Guest House, 34 Henrietta Street, Bath, BA2 6LR.
Situated just 2 mins' walk to city centre in a peaceful location.
Grades: ETC 3 Diamond
Tel: **01225 424103**
Mr Kingwell.
Fax no: 01225 425279
D: £30.00-£35.00 **S:** £30.00-£50.00.
Open: All Year (not Xmas)
Beds: 7D 2T 2S
Baths: 7 En 1 Sh
 ➹ ⊬ ❏ ⚲ ▥ Ⓥ ⚙

The Terrace Guest House, 3 Pulteney Terrace, Bath, BA2 4HJ.
Mid-terrace house, 7 minutes from city centre and railway station.
Tel: **01225 316578**
Mrs Gould.
D: £16.00-£17.50 **S:** £18.00-£20.00.
Open: All Year (not Xmas)
Beds: 1D 1T
Baths: 1 Sh
 ➹ (6) ❏ ⚲ ▥ Ⓥ ⚙

Joanna House, 5 Pulteney Avenue, Bath, BA2 4HH.
City centre Victorian house near railway, Kennet and Avon canal.
Tel: **01225 335246**
Mr House.
D: £16.00-£19.00
S: £15.00-£18.00.
Open: All Year
Beds: 1F 1D 1T 1S
 ➹ ⊬ ❏ ⚲ ▥ Ⓥ

Brinsley Sheridan Guest House, 95 Wellsway, Bearflat, Bath, BA2 4RU.
Lovely friendly guest house only short walk from city centre.
Tel: **01225 429562**
Fax no: 01225 429616
D: £17.50-£25.00
S: £17.50-£30.00.
Open: All Year
Beds: 1F 2D 1T
Baths: 1 En 1 Pr 2 Sh
 ➹ ⊬ ❏ ⚲ ▥ Ⓥ ⚙

Kinlet Guest House, 99 Wellsway, Bath, BA2 4RA.
Actual grid ref: ST745636
Home from home. Friendly, comfortable, easy walk into the city.
Tel: **01225 420268** (also fax no)
Mrs Bennett.
D: £19.00-£20.00
S: £22.00-£27.00.
Open: All Year
Beds: 1F 1D 1S
Baths: 1 Sh
 ➹ ⊬ ❏ ⚲ ▥ Ⓥ ⓘ ⚡ ⚙

Cairngorm, 3 Gloucester Road, Lower Swainswick, Bath, BA1 7BH.
Charming detached home with beautiful views over city and countryside.
Tel: **01225 429004** Mrs Biggs.
D: £16.50-£20.00 **S:** £18.00.
Open: All Year (not Xmas)
Beds: 2D 1T
Baths: 3 En
 ➹ (2) ▣ (3) ⊬ ❏ ▥ ⚬ Ⓥ ⚡ ⚙

Glan y Dwr, 14 Newbridge Hill, Bath, BA1 3PU.
Personal attention to ensure you have a comfortable stay in Bath.
Tel: **01225 317521**
Mr Kones.
D: £16.00-£24.00 **S:** £18.00-£35.00.
Open: All Year
Beds: 2D 1T 3S
Baths: 1 En 1 Pr 1 Sh
 ➹ (11) ▣ (3) ⊬ ⟊ ⚲ ▥ ⚬ Ⓥ ⚡ ⚙

Cedar Lodge, 13 Lambridge London Road, Bath, BA1 6BJ.
Come, stay, enjoy. Welcoming, comfortable, lovely, well-placed period house.
Tel: **01225 423468**
Mr & Mrs Beckett.
D: £25.00 **S:** £30.00.
Open: All Year
Beds: 1T 2D
Baths: 2 En 1 Pr
 ➹ (10) ▣ (6) ⊬ ❏ ⚲ ▥ Ⓥ ⚡ ⚙

At **Avebury** stands a large neolithic stone circle; nearby are Silbury Hill, Europe's largest man-made prehistoric mound, and West Kennet Long Barrow, a burial complex dating from the fourth millennium BC.

Marlborough has the widest high street in England, with a fine display of Georgian buildings and half-timbered cottages.

Devizes has a number of pretty old coaching inns, Elizabethan houses and an originally Norman church. The town's superb museum specialises in prehistoric finds, including from Avebury and Stonehenge.

Newbury was the site of two battles of the Civil War, one of which (1643) is commemorated by the Falkland Memorial.

Bathford   12

National Grid Ref: ST7966

|◑| ⬚ The Crown

Bridge Cottage, *Northfield End, Ashley Road, Bathford, Bath, BA1 7TT.*
Pretty cottage with lovely gardens. Village location near Bath city.
Tel: **01225 852399**
Mrs Bright.
D: £20.00-£27.50 **S:** £25.00-£40.00.
Open: All Year (not Xmas)
Beds: 2D 1T
Baths: 2 Pr
⛺ ⓟ ⼂◻ ⼍ ⼐ ⼞ 🛋 ⅓ Ⓥ

Garston Cottage, *Ashley Road, Bathford, Bath, N E Somerset, BA1 7TT .*
Country cottage, 2 miles from Bath, courtyard garden with jacuzzi.
Tel: **01225 852510**
Ms Smart.
Fax no: 01225 852793
D: £20.00-£25.00
S: £25.00-£30.00.
Open: All Year
Beds: 1F 1D 1T
Baths: 3 En
⛺ ⓟ (2) ⼂◻ ⼍ ⼐ 🛋 ⼗ 🚲

Monkton Combe   13

National Grid Ref: ST7762

|◑| ⬚ Wheelwrights Arms

The Manor House, *Monkton Combe, Bath, BA2 7HD.*
Restful rambling medieval manor by millstream in Area of Outstanding Natural Beauty.
Grades: ETC 3 Diamond
Tel: **01225 723128**
Mrs Hartley.
Fax no: 01225 722972
D: £22.50-£35.00
S: £30.00-£35.00.
Open: All Year
Beds: 2F 5D 1T
Baths: 8 En
⛺ ⓟ (12) ◻ ⼍ ⼀ ✕ ⼐ 🛋 ⅓ Ⓥ ⼗ 🚲

Winsley   14

National Grid Ref: ST7961

|◑| ⬚ Seven Stars

Conifers, *4 King Alfred Way, Winsley, Bradford-on-Avon, Wilts, BA15 2NG.*
Quiet area, pleasant outlook, friendly atmosphere, convenient Bath, lovely walks.
Grades: ETC 2 Diamond
Tel: **01225 722482** Mrs Kettley.
D: £17.00-£18.00 **S:** £18.00-£20.00.
Open: All Year
Beds: 1T 1D
Baths: 1 Sh
⛺ ⓟ ⼂◻ ⼍ ⼐ 🛋 Ⓥ ⅓ 🚲

3 Corners, *Cottles Lane, Winsley, Bradford-on-Avon, Wilts, BA15 2HJ.*
House in quiet village edge location, attractive rooms and gardens.
Tel: **01225 865380** Mrs Cole.
D: £22.50-£25.00 **S:** £26.00-£30.00.
Open: All Year (not Xmas)
Beds: 1F 1D
Baths: 1 En 1 Pr
⛺ ⓟ (4) ⼂◻ ✕ ⼐ 🛋 Ⓥ 🛋 ⅓ 🚲

Serendipity, *19 Bradford Road, Winsley, Bradford-on-Avon, Wilts, BA15 2HW.*
Bungalow with beautiful gardens, badgers feeding nightly, ground floor room available.
Grades: ETC 4 Diamond
Tel: **01225 722380**
Mrs Shepherd.
Fax no: 01225 723451
D: £21.00-£22.50 **S:** £30.00-£40.00.
Open: All Year
Beds: 1F 1D 1S
Baths: 3 En
⛺ ⓟ (5) ⼂◻ ⼐ 🛋 ⅓ Ⓥ 🛋 ⅓ 🚲

Bringing children with you? Always ask for any special rates.

Bradford-on-Avon   15

National Grid Ref: ST8261

|◑| ⬚ Barge, Bear, Beehive, Cross Guns, Hop Pole, King's Arms, New Inn, Plough, Seven Stars, Three Horseshoes

Chard's Barn, *Leigh Grove, Bradford-on-Avon, Wilts, BA15 2RF.*
Tel: **01225 863461**
Mr & Mrs Stickney.
D: £20.00-£23.00 **S:** £20.00-£20.00
Open: All Year (not Xmas)
Beds: 1D 1T 1S
Baths: 2 En 1 Pr
⛺ ⓟ (4) ⼂◻ ⼍ ⼐ 🛋 ⅓ Ⓥ 🚲
Quiet C17th barn in unspoilt countryside with lovely gardens, view and walks. All ground floor, individually styled bedrooms, choice of breakfasts. Historic town and golf course, one mile. Close - Bath, Castle Combe, Longleat. Easy for Salisbury Plain and Stonehenge.

The Locks, *265 Trowbridge Road, Bradford-on-Avon, Wilts, BA15 1UA.*
Adjoining canal tow path. Ideal walking/cycling 7/8 mile town centre.
Tel: **01225 863358** Mrs Benjamin
D: £17.50-£20.00 **S:** £20.00-£30.00
Open: All Year
Beds: 1F 2T
Baths: 1 En 1 Pr 1 Sh
⛺ (3) ⓟ (6) ⼂◻ ⼐ 🛋 Ⓥ ⅓ 🚲

Great Ashley Farm, *Ashley Lane, Bradford-on-Avon, Wilts, BA15 2PP.*
Actual grid ref: ST813619
Delightful rooms. Great hospitality. Delicious breakfast. Colour brochure. Silver award.
Grades: ETC 4 Diamond
Tel: **01225 864563** (also fax no)
Mrs Rawlings.
D: £20.00-£24.00 **S:** £25.00-£45.00
Open: All Year (not Xmas)
Beds: 1F 2D
Baths: 3 En
⛺ ⓟ ⼂◻ ⼐ 🛋 Ⓥ 🛋 ⅓ 🚲

Springfields, *182a Great Ashley, Bradford on Avon, Wilts, BA15 2PP.*
Unique ground-level ensuite double room with adjoining dining-room/lounge. Peaceful countryside setting.
Grades: ETC 3 Diamond
Tel: **01225 866125** Ms Rawlings.
D: £20.00-£22.50 **S:** £30.00-£35.00
Open: All Year
Beds: 1D
Baths: 1En
⼂◻ ✕ ⼐ Ⓥ

Avonvilla, *Avoncliff, Bradford-on-Avon, Wilts, BA15 2HD.*
Superb canal and riverside setting. Free parking and fishing. Excellent walking.
Tel: **01225 863867** Mrs Mumford
D: £17.00-£17.00 **S:** £20.00-£20.00
Open: All Year
Beds: 1D 1T 1S
⛺ (5) ⓟ ⼂◻ ⼐ 🛋 Ⓥ 🚲

Atworth 16

National Grid Ref: ST8665

|o| ◁ Golden Fleece, White Hart

Kings Stile Cottage, 153 Bath Road, Atworth, Melksham, Wiltshire, SN12 8JR.
Cottage in village location. Convenient for Bath, Bradford-on-Avon, NT properties. Delicious breakfasts.
Tel: **01225 706202** (also fax no)
Mr & Mrs Hughes.
D: £18.00-£20.00 **S:** £20.00-£25.00.
Open: All Year
Beds: 1T 1D
🛉 🖾 (2) ⊬⚡ ♨ ⅲ Ⅵ ⓐ ∮ ⚲

Church Farm, Atworth, Melksham, Wilts, SN12 8JA.
Working dairy farm, large garden. Easy access Bath, Lacock, Bradford-on-Avon.
Tel: **01225 702215** Mrs Hole.
D: £17.50-£20.00 **S:** £20.00-£25.00.
Open: Easter to Oct
Beds: 1F 1D **Baths:** 1 Sh
🛉 🖾 (4) ⚡ ♨ ⅲ Ⅵ

Gastard 17

National Grid Ref: ST8868

|o| ◁ George

Heatherly Cottage, Ladbrook Lane, Gastard, Corsham, Wilts, SN13 9PE.
C17th cottage set in quiet location with large garden. Guests have separate wing.
Grades: ETC 4 Diamond
Tel: **01249 701402** Mrs Daniel.
Fax no: 01249 701412
D: £23.00-£25.00 **S:** £27.00-£30.00.
Open: All Year (not Xmas/New Year)
Beds: 1T 2D
Baths: 3 En
🛉 (10) 🖾 (8) ⊬⚡ ♨ ⅲ Ⅵ ∮ ⚲

Lacock 18

National Grid Ref: ST9168

|o| ◁ George, Red Lion, Carpenters' Arms, Angel

The Old Rectory, Lacock, Chippenham, Wilts, SN15 2JZ.
Grades: ETC 4 Diamond
Tel: **01249 730335** Mrs Sexton.
Fax no: 01249 730166
D: £22.50-£25.00 **S:** £25.00-£27.50.
Open: All Year
Beds: 1F 1D 1T
Baths: 3 En
🛉 🖾 (6) ⊬⚡ ♨ ⅲ Ⅵ ⓐ ∮ ⚲
Superb Gothic Victorian architecture, set in 8 acres of grounds and gardens, many original features and 4 poster beds. Excellent pubs a stroll away in famous Lacock location for tourists and businessmen, M4 (J17), close by. Bath 12 miles, London 2 hours. Recomm in 'Off the Beaten Track'.

Lacock Pottery, The Tan Yard, Lacock, Chippenham, Wilts, SN15 2LB.
Beautiful, comfortable, working pottery, medieval village.
Grades: ETC 4 Diamond
Tel: **01249 730266** Mrs McDowell.
Fax no: 01249 730948
D: £29.50-£39.50 **S:** £37.00-£59.00.
Open: All Year (not Xmas/New Year)
Beds: 1T 2D
Baths: 1 En 1 Sh 1 Pr
🛉 🖾 (6) ⊬⚡ ♨ ⅲ Ⅵ ∮ ⚲

Corsham 19

National Grid Ref: ST8670

|o| ◁ White Horse Inn, Hare & Hounds, Harp and Crown, George

Thurlestone Lodge, 13 Prospect, Corsham, Wilts, SN13 9AD.
Elegant Victorian home set in landscaped gardens, close to town centre.
Tel: **01249 713397**
Mrs Ogilvie-Robb.
D: £21.00-£24.00 **S:** £30.00-£40.00.
Open: All Year (not Xmas/New Year)
Beds: 1T 1D **Baths:** 1 En 1 Pr
🛉 🖾 (5) ♨ ⅲ Ⅵ ∮ ⚲

Bellwood, 45 Pickwick, Corsham, Wilts, SN13 0HX.
Actual grid ref: ST863706
Charming 1708 cottage (adjacent to owners), pubs nearby, Bath 8 miles.
Tel: **01249 713434** Mrs Elliott.
D: £20.00-£22.00 **S:** £22.00-£25.00.
Open: All Year
Beds: 2T 1S
Baths: 1 Pr 1 Sh
🛉 (2) 🖾 (4) ⊬⚡ ♨ ⅲ Ⅵ ⓐ ∮ ⚲

Biddestone 20

National Grid Ref: ST8673

|o| ◁ White Horse

Home Place, Biddestone, Chippenham, Wiltshire, SN14 7DG.
End of farmhouse, on village green. Opposite duck pond.
Grades: ETC 2 Diamond
Tel: **01249 712928** Ms Hall.
D: £15.00-£17.50 **S:** £15.00-£17.50.
Open: All Year
Beds: 1F 1T 1S **Baths:** 1 Sh
🛉 🖾 (2) ⊬⚡ ♨ ⅲ Ⅵ ∮ ⚲

Home Farm, Biddestone, Chippenham, Wilts, SN14 7DQ.
Listed C17th farmhouse working farm, picturesque village. Stroll to pubs.
Tel: **01249 714475**
Mr & Mrs Smith.
Fax no: 01249 701488
D: £20.00-£22.50 **S:** £25.00-£30.00.
Open: All Year (not Xmas)
Beds: 2F 1D **Baths:** 2 En 1 Pr
🛉 🖾 (4) ⊬⚡ ♨ ⅲ Ⅵ ⓐ ∮ ⚲

Hartham Park 21

National Grid Ref: ST8672

Church Farm, Hartham Park, Corsham, Wiltshire, SN13 0PU.
Actual grid ref: ST861715
Cotswold farmhouse in rural location, stunning views, quiet and peaceful.
Grades: ETC 4 Diamond,
AA 4 Diamond
Tel: **01249 715180** Mrs Jones.
Fax no: 01249 715572
D: £20.00-£25.00 **S:** £20.00-£22.00.
Open: All Year (not Xmas/New Year)
Beds: 1F 1D 1S
Baths: 2 En 1 Pr
🛉 (1) 🖾 (6) ⊬⚡ ♨ ⅲ Ⅵ ∮ ⚲

Chippenham 22

National Grid Ref: ST9173

|o| ◁ Biddestone Arms, Rowden Arms, Three Crowns, Wellesley Arms, White Horse

Bramleys, 73 Marshfield Road, Chippenham, Wilts, SN15 1JR.
Large Victorian house, Grade II Listed.
Grades: ETC 1 Diamond
Tel: **01249 653770** Mrs Swatton.
D: £18.00-£20.00 **S:** £17.00-£19.00.
Open: All Year
Beds: 1F 3T 1S
Baths: 1 Pr 1 Sh
🛉 🖾 (4) ⊬⚡ ♨ ⅲ Ⅵ ⓐ ∮ ⚲

Frogwell House, 132 Hungerdown Lane, Chippenham, Wilts, SN14 0BD.
Family-run C19th stone-built house providing comfortable accommodation.
Grades: ETC 4 Diamond
Tel: **01249 650328** (also fax no)
Mrs Burgess.
D: £19.00-£20.00 **S:** £25.00-£28.00.
Open: All Year
Beds: 1F 1D 2T 1S
Baths: 2 En 1 Sh
🛉 🖾 (6) ⊬⚡ ♨ ✕ ♨ ⅲ Ⅵ ∮ ⚲

Bremhill 23

National Grid Ref: ST9773

|o| ◁ George

Lowbridge Farm, Bremhill, Calne, Wilts, SN11 9HE.
Old thatched farmhouse. Varied stock. Scenic views. Places to visit.
Tel: **01249 815889**
Miss Sinden.
D: £23.00-£23.00 **S:** £23.00-£23.00.
Open: All Year
Beds: 1F 1D 1T
Baths: 1 Sh
🛉 🖾 (8) ⊬⚡ ♨ ✕ ♨ ⅲ Ⅵ ∮ ⚲

S = Price range for a single person in a room

Calne 24

National Grid Ref: ST9971

|♦| ◀ Black Horse

Lower Sands Farm, Low Lane, Calne, Wilts, SN11 8TR.
Old farmhouse, v. quiet homely and friendly. Good breakfast, large garden.
Grades: ETC 1 Diamond
Tel: **01249 812402**
Mrs Henly.
D: £17.00-£18.00
S: £17.00-£18.00.
Open: All Year (not Xmas)
Beds: 1D 1T 1S
Baths: 1 Sh
🅿 (10) 🛏 ♨ 🏠 Ⅴ ≮ ↻

Cherhill 25

National Grid Ref: SU0370

Poachers Croft, Yatesbury Hill, Cherhill, Calne, Wilts, SN11 8XY.
Lovely country B&B below white horse. Area of Outstanding Natural Beauty.
Grades: ETC 3 Diamond
Tel: **01249 812587**
Mrs Trafford.
D: £25.00-£30.00 S: £25.00.
Open: All Year
Beds: 1F
☒ 🅿 (6) 🛏 🐾 ♨ 🏠 ⓖ Ⅴ ≮ ↻

Avebury 26

National Grid Ref: SU1069

|♦| ◀ Waggon & Horses, Red Lion

6 Beckhampton Road, Avebury, Marlborough, Wilts, SN8 1QT.
Nearby Avebury Stone Circle, Ridgeway Walk, Silbury Hill, bus route.
Tel: **01672 539588**
Mrs Dixon.
D: £16.00-£20.00 S: £25.00-£30.00.
Open: All Year (not Xmas)
Beds: 1D 1T
Baths: 1 Sh
☒ 🅿 (6) 🛏 ♨ 🏠 Ⅴ ⅰ ≮

Manton 27

National Grid Ref: SU1768

|♦| ◀ Oddfellows Arms

Sunrise Farm, Manton, Marlborough, Wilts, SN8 4HL.
Actual grid ref: SU168682
Peacefully located approximately 1 mile from Marlborough. Friendly, comfortable, relaxing atmosphere.
Grades: ETC 3 Diamond
Tel: **01672 512878** (also fax no)
Mrs Couzens.
D: £19.00-£20.00 S: £19.00-£25.00.
Open: March to Oct
Beds: 1D 2T
Baths: 2 Pr
☒ (14) 🅿 (3) ≮ 🛏 ♨ 🏠 Ⅴ ⅰ ↻

Marlborough 28

National Grid Ref: SU1869

|♦| ◀ Bear, Roebuck, Sun, Oddfellows Arms

Browns Farm, Marlborough, Wilts, SN8 4ND.
Actual grid ref: SU198678
Peaceful farmhouse on edge of Savernake Forest. Overlooking open farmland.
Tel: **01672 515129**
Mrs Crockford.
D: £16.00-£20.00 S: £20.00-£25.00.
Open: All Year
Beds: 1F 1T 2D
Baths: 1 En 1 Sh
☒ 🅿 (6) ≮ 🛏 🐾 ♨ 🏠 Ⅴ ⅰ ↻

Beam End, 67 George Lane, Marlborough, Wilts, SN8 4BY.
Peaceful detached house, every comfort, good centre for touring Wiltshire.
Grades: ETC 3 Diamond
Tel: **01672 515048** (also fax no)
Mrs Drew.
D: £20.00-£27.50
S: £20.00-£30.00.
Open: All Year (not Xmas)
Beds: 1T 2S
Baths: 1 En 1 Sh
🅿 (3) ≮ 🛏 ♨ 🏠 Ⅴ ≮

54 George Lane, Marlborough, Wiltshire, SN8 4BY.
Near town centre. Detached house. Large garden. Non smokers only.
Tel: **01672 512579**
Mr & Mrs Young.
D: £17.00 S: £17.00.
Open: All Year (not Xmas/ New Year)
Beds: 1T 2S
Baths: 1 Sh
🅿 (3) ≮ ♨ 🏠 Ⅴ ≮

West View, Barnfield, Marlborough, Wiltshire, SN8 2AX.
Delightful peaceful, rural home, close to town. Ideal walkers, cyclists.
Grades: ETC 3 Diamond
Tel: **01672 515583**
Maggie Trevelyan-Hall.
Fax no: 01672 519014
D: £20.00-£25.00
S: £35.00-£45.00.
Open: All Year
Beds: 1F 3D
Baths: 2 Pr 1 Sh
☒ 🅿 (3) ≮ 🛏 🐾 ✕ ♨ 🏠 ⓖ Ⅴ ⅰ ≮ ↻

Cartref, 63 George Lane, Marlborough, Wilts, SN8 4BY.
Actual grid ref: SU1969
Family home near town centre. Ideal for Avebury, Savernake, Wiltshire Downs.
Tel: **01672 512771**
Mrs Harrison.
D: £18.00-£18.00 S: £20.00-£20.00.
Open: All Year (not Xmas)
Beds: 1F 1D 1T
Baths: 1 Sh
☒ (6) 🅿 (2) 🐾 🏠 ⅰ ≮ ↻

Hilperton 29

National Grid Ref: ST8759

|♦| ◀ Lion and Fiddle

62b Paxcroft Cottages, Devizes Road, Hilperton, Trowbridge, Wiltshire, BA14 6JB.
Lovely garden with far reaching views overlooking the Wiltshire downs.
Grades: ETC 3 Diamond
Tel: **01225 765838** Styles.
D: £20.00-£22.00 S: £20.00-£22.00.
Open: All Year (not Xmas)
Beds: 1F 1T 1D
Baths: 2 En 1 Pr
☒ 🅿 (6) ≮ 🛏 ✕ ♨ 🏠 Ⅴ ⅰ ≮

Trowbridge 30

National Grid Ref: ST8557

|♦| ◀ Lion and Fiddle, Hungerford Arms

44 Wingfield Road, Trowbridge, Wilts, BA14 9ED.
Fine Victorian house. 'Home from home'.
Tel: **01225 761455**
Mr & Mrs Dobbin.
D: £20.00.
Open: All Year
Beds: 1F 1D 1T 1S
☒ 🛏 🐾 ✕ ♨ 🏠 ⓖ Ⅴ ⅰ

Semington 31

National Grid Ref: ST8960

|♦| ◀ Linnet, Somerset Arms, Lamb on the Strand

New House Farm, Littleton, Semington, Trowbridge, Wilts, BA14 6LF.
Actual grid ref: ST910600
Victorian former farmhouse, open countryside, lovely gardens, good touring centre.
Grades: ETC 3 Diamond
Tel: **01380 870349** Mrs Ball.
D: £20.00-£20.00 S: £25.00-£25.00.
Open: All Year
Beds: 2D 1T **Baths:** 3 En
☒ 🅿 (10) ≮ 🛏 ✕ ♨ 🏠 ⓖ Ⅴ

Brook House, Semington, Trowbridge, Wilts, BA14 6JR.
Georgian house, large grounds. Convenient for Bath, Stonehenge and canal.
Tel: **01380 870232** Mrs Bruges.
Fax no: 01380 871431
D: £19.00-£25.00 S: £25.00-£25.00.
Open: Feb to Nov
Beds: 1F 1D 1T
Baths: 1 En 1 Sh
☒ 🅿 ≮ 🛏 🐾 ♨ 🏠 Ⅴ ≮ ↻

Pay B&Bs by cash or cheque and be prepared to pay up front.

Melksham 32

National Grid Ref: ST9063

⊯ ◁ Kings Arms, Barge Inn, West End Inn

Craycroft, 402 The Spa, Spa Road, Melksham, Wilts, SN12 6QL.
Georgian Spa house, Grade II Listed, offering a warm welcome, comfortable accommodation.
Tel: **01225 707984**
Mrs Pavey.
D: £16.00-£20.00 **S:** £17.00-£21.00.
Open: All Year
Beds: 1F 1D 1T 1S
Baths: 2 En 1 Sh
 🛏 🅿 (6) ⅋ ❑ ★ 📖 Ⅴ ⅋

Seend Cleeve 33

National Grid Ref: ST9261

⊯ ◁ Barge Inn

Rew Farm, Seend Cleeve, Melksham, Wiltshire, SN12 6PS.
Working dairy farm. Few minutes walk to Kennet and Avon Canal.
Grades: ETC 3 Diamond
Tel: **01380 828289**
Newman.
D: £20.00-£20.00
S: £25.00-£25.00.
Open: All Year (not Xmas/ New Year)
Beds: 1T
 🛏 🅿 (2) ⅋ ❑ 📖 Ⅴ ⅋ ふ

Devizes 34

National Grid Ref: SU0061

⊯ ◁ Barge, Bell, Bridge, Bear, Black Swan, Churchill, George & Dragon, Royal Oak, Stage Post, Moonrakers, Elm Tree, Four Seasons, Owl

Lower Foxhangers Farm, Rowde, Devizes, Wilts, SN10 1SS.
Grades: ETC 3 Diamond
Tel: **01380 828254** (also fax no)
Mr & Mrs Fletcher.
D: £20.00-£22.00
S: £22.00-£25.00.
Open: May to Oct
Beds: 2D 1T
Baths: 1 Pr 2 En
 🛏 🅿 (4) ⅋ ❑ ★ 📖 Ⅴ ⅋ ふ
Relax with pleasant dreams in our rural retreat amid the Wiltshire countryside. Roam the canal towpaths and see the gaily painted narrow boats as they lazily glide through the rippling water or climb the unrivalled flight of Caen Hill Locks.

Craven House, Station Road, Devizes, Wilts, SN10 1BZ.
Victorian house 50 yards from centre for restaurants and pubs.
Tel: **01380 723514**
Mrs Shaw.
D: £20.00 **S:** £20.00.
Open: All Year
Beds: 1F 1D 2T
Baths: 2 En 1 Pr 1 Sh
 🛏 ❑ ✕ 📖 Ⅴ ⅋ ふ

Asta, 66 Downlands Road, Devizes, Wilts, SN10 5EF.
Comfortable, modern house in quiet road, 15 minutes from town centre.
Tel: **01380 722546**
Mrs Milne-Day.
D: £16.00 **S:** £16.00.
Open: All Year
Beds: 1D 2S **Baths:** 1 Sh
 🛏 🅿 (2) ❑ ★ ✕ 📖

Glenholme Guest House, 77 Nursteed Road, Devizes, Wilts, SN10 3AJ.
Friendly, comfortable house. Warm welcome. Lovely historic town.
Tel: **01380 723187** Mrs Bishop.
D: £18.00-£18.00 **S:** £20.00-£20.00.
Open: All Year
Beds: 1F 1T
Baths: 1 Sh
 🛏 🅿 ❑ ★ ✕ 📖 Ⅴ

Gate House, Wick Lane, Devizes, Wilts, SN10 5DW.
Large house and garden, not on main road. Bath/Salisbury 25 miles.
Tel: **01380 725283** Mrs Stratton.
Fax no: 01380 722382
D: £20.00-£20.00 **S:** £22.50-£22.50.
Open: All Year (not Xmas)
Beds: 1D 1T 1S
Baths: 1 En 1 Sh
 🅿 (6) ⅋ ❑ 📖 Ⅴ ⅋ ふ

The Chestnuts, Potterne Road, Devizes, Wiltshire, SN10 5DD.
Actual grid ref: SU006608
Good base for Bath, Salisbury, Stonehenge, Avebury and Kennet & Avon Canal.
Tel: **01380 724532** Mrs Mortimer.
D: £20.00-£25.00 **S:** £25.00-£25.00.
Open: All Year (not Xmas)
Beds: 1F 1T
Baths: 2 En
 🛏 🅿 (2) ⅋ ❑ 📖 Ⅴ ⅋ ふ

Woodborough 35

National Grid Ref: SU1159

⊯ ◁ Barge Inn, Seven Stars

St Cross, Woodborough, Pewsey, Wilts, SN9 5PL.
Pewsey Vale - heart of crop circles, beautiful countryside, Kennet & Avon Canal 8 mins' walk.
Tel: **01672 851346** (also fax no)
Mrs Gore.
D: £25.00-£35.00 .
Open: All Year **Beds:** 1D 1T
Baths: 1 Sh
 🛏 (6) 🅿 (1) ⅋ ❑ ★ ⅋ ふ

Planning a longer stay? Always ask for any special rates.

Well Cottage, Honey Street, Woodborough, Pewsey, Wilts, SN9 5PS.
Warm welcome awaits at our picturesque cottage. Amidst outstanding countryside.
Grades: ETC 3 Diamond
Tel: **01672 851577**
Mrs Trowbridge.
D: £18.00-£23.00
S: £28.00-£36.00.
Open: All Year
Beds: 2D 1T
Baths: 3 En
 🛏 🅿 (4) ⅋ ❑ ★ ✕ 📖 Ⅴ ⅋ ふ

Pewsey 36

National Grid Ref: SU1660

⊯ ◁ French Horn

Old Dairy House, Sharcott, Pewsey, Wilts, SN9 5PA.
Thatched dairy house in four acres. Pewsey 1 mile.
Grades: ETC 4 Diamond
Tel: **01672 562287**
Mr & Mrs Stone.
D: £30.00-£30.00
S: £35.00-£35.00.
Open: All Year

Easton Royal 37

National Grid Ref: SU2060

⊯ ◁ Royal Oak, Three Horseshoes

Follets, Easton Royal, Pewsey, Wilts, SN9 5LZ.
Convenient for Kennet & Avon canal. Stonehenge and Avebury.
Grades: ETC 4 Diamond
Tel: **01672 810619** (also fax no)
Mrs Landless.
D: £22.50-£25.00
S: £30.00-£35.00.
Open: All Year (not Xmas/ New Year)
Beds: 2D 1T
Baths: 3 En
 🛏 🅿 (6) ⅋ ❑ ✕ 📖 & Ⅴ ⅋ ふ

Hungerford 38

National Grid Ref: SU3368

⊯ ◁ Just Williams, John O'Gaunt, Plume Of Feathers

Wilton House, 33 High Street, Hungerford, Berks, RG17 0NF.
Elegant ensuite bedrooms in classic, historic English town house predating 1450.
Grades: ETC 4 Diamond
Tel: **01488 684228**
Mrs Welfare.
Fax no: 01488 685037
D: £25.00-£27.50
S: £35.00-£38.00.
Open: All Year (not Xmas)
Beds: 1D 1T
Baths: 2 En
 🛏 (8) 🅿 (3) ⅋ ❑ 📖 Ⅴ ⅋

Alderborne, *33 Bourne Vale,*
Hungerford, Berkshire, RG17 0LL.
Actual grid ref: SU333682
Modern detached family house
overlooking open country. Walking
distance shops.
Grades: ETC 4 Diamond
Tel: **01488 683228**
Mr & Mrs Honeybone.
D: £17.50-£18.50
S: £17.50-£22.50.
Open: All Year (not Xmas)
Beds: 2T 1S
Baths: 1 Pr 1 Sh
ॐ (5) 🅿 (3) ⊬ ❏ 🔥 🍴 ▥ Ⓥ ∮ ♻

Wasing, *35 Sanden Close,*
Hungerford, Berkshire, RG17 0LA.
Warm welcome to the home of ex
farmers. 3 miles M4.
Tel: **01488 684127**
Mrs Smalley.
D: £16.00-£17.00
S: £17.00-£18.00.
Open: All Year (not Xmas)
Beds: 1D 1T 1S
Baths: 1 En 1 Sh
ॐ 🅿 ❏ 🍴 ▥ Ⓥ ∮ ♻

15 Sanden Close, *Hungerford,*
Berks, RG17 0LA.
Semi-detached bungalow in quiet
close. Short walk to shops and
station.
Tel: **01488 682583**
Mrs Hook.
D: £15.00-£16.00
S: £17.00-£18.00.
Open: All Year (not Xmas)
Beds: 1D 1S
Baths: 1 Sh
ॐ (5) 🅿 (3) ⊬ ❏ ▥.

Inkpen   39

National Grid Ref: SU3764

Beacon House, *Bell Lane, Upper*
Green, Inkpen, Hungerford, Berks,
RG17 9QJ.
Actual grid ref: SU368634
Visit our 1930s country home on
Berks/Wilts/Hants border. Lovely
countryside.
Grades: AA 3 Diamond
Tel: **01488 668640**
Mr & Mrs Cave.
D: £22.00
S: £22.00.
Open: All Year
Beds: 1T 2S
Baths: 2 Sh
ॐ 🅿 (6) ❏ 🍴 ✕ 🍴 ▥ Ⓥ 🏛 ∮ ♻

Kintbury   40

National Grid Ref: SU3866

🍴 🍺 Crown & Garter

The Forbury, *Crossways,*
Kintbury, Hungerford, Berks,
RG17 9SU.
Extended C17th cottage. Lovely
position facing south, overlooking
own woodlands.
Tel: **01488 658377**
Mr Cubitt.
D: £22.50-£27.50
S: £22.50-£25.00.
Open: All Year (not Xmas)
Beds: 1F
Baths: 1 Pr 1 Sh
ॐ 🅿 (10) ❏ 🍴 ✕ 🍴 ▥ Ⓥ 🏛 ∮ ♻

Stockcross   41

National Grid Ref: SU4368

🍴 🍺 Lord Lyon

79 Glebe Lane, *Stockcross,*
Newbury, Berks, RG19 8AD.
Spacious detached Edwardian
house. Easy reach of Chievely
Interchange/Newbury.
Tel: **01635 203321**
Mr & Mrs Tipple.
D: £25.00-£25.00 **S:** £25.00-£25.00.
Open: All Year
Beds: 1F 1T **Baths:** 1 Sh
ॐ 🅿 (5) ⊬ ❏ 🍴 🔥 🍴 ▥ Ⓥ ∮

Newbury   42

National Grid Ref: SU4767

🍴 🍺 Lord Lyon, Red Lion, Gun Inn

15 Shaw Road, *Newbury, Berks,*
RG14 1HG.
Late Georgian terraced house near
town centre, rail and canal.
Tel: **01635 44962** Mrs Curtis.
D: £17.00-£18.00 **S:** £17.00-£18.00.
Open: All Year
Beds: 1D, 1T **Baths:** 1 Sh
ॐ 🅿 ⊬ ❏ 🔥 ▥ 🏛 ∮ ♻

Laurel House, *157 Andover Road,*
Newbury, RG14 6NB.
A warm welcome awaits you in our
delightful Georgian house.
Tel: **01635 35931**
Mr & Mrs Dixon.
D: £18.00 **S:** £18.00.
Open: All Year (not Xmas)
Beds: 1D 1T **Baths:** 1 Sh
🅿 (2) ⊬ ❏ 🍴 ▥ Ⓥ ♻

STILWELL'S NATIONAL TRAIL COMPANION

46 Long Distance Footpaths • Where to Stay • Where to Eat

Other guides may show you where to walk, **Stilwell's National Trail Companion** shows your where to stay and eat. The perfect companion guide for the British Isles' famous national trails and long distance footpaths, Stilwell's make pre-planning your accommodation easy. It lists B&Bs, hostels, campsites and pubs - in the order they appear along the routes - and includes such vital information as maps, grid references and distance from the path; Tourist Board ratings; the availability of vehicle pick-up, drying facilities and packed lunches. So whether you walk a trail in stages at weekends or in one continuous journey, you'll never be stuck at the end of the day for a hot meal or a great place to sleep.

Enjoy the beauty and adventure of Britain's – and Ireland's – long distance trails with **Stilwell's National Trail Companion**.

Paths in England

Cleveland Way & Tabular Hills Link – Coast to Coast Path – Cotswald Way – Cumbria Way – Dales Way – Essex Way – Greensand Way – Hadrian's Wall – Heart of England Way – Hereward Way – Icknield Way – Macmillan Way – North Downs Way – Oxfordshire Way – Peddars Way and Norfolk Coastal Path – Pennine Way – Ribble Way – The Ridgeway – Shropshire Way – South Downs Way – South West Coast Path – Staffordshire Way – Tarka Trail – Thames Path – Two Moors Way - Vanguard Way - Viking Way – Wayfarer's Walk – Wealdway – Wessex Ridgeway – Wolds Way

Paths in Ireland

Beara Way – Dingle Way – Kerry Way – Ulster Way – Western Way – Wicklow Way

Paths in Scotland

Fife Coastal Walk – Southern Upland Way – Speyside Way – West Highland Way

Paths in Wales

Cambrian Way – Glyndwr's Way – Offa's Dyke Path – Pembrokeshire Coast Path – Wye Valley Walk

£9.95 from all good bookstores (ISBN 1-900861-25-9) or £10.95 (inc p&p) from Stilwell Publishing Ltd, 59 Charlotte Road, London EC2A 3QW (020 7739 7179)

Sustrans West Country Way

The **West Country Way** is a recently-opened section of the new National Cycle Network, running on traffic-free paths and traffic-calmed roads from Padstow in Cornwall to Bristol, linking many historic towns in Devon and Somerset and passing through a great deal of this beautiful region's varied countryside, from the open heather-clad elevations of Bodmin Moor and Exmoor to the lowland of the Somerset Levels with its network of canals, which abruptly gives rise to the Mendip Hills. The route is clearly signposted by blue direction signs with a cycle silhouette and the number 3 in a red rectangle. The total distance is 230 miles.

The indispensable **official route map and guide** for the West Country Way is available from Sustrans, 35 King Street, Bristol BS1 4DZ, tel 0117-926 8893, fax 0117-929 4173, @ £5.99 (+ £1.50 p&p).

Maps: Ordnance Survey 1:50,000 Landranger series: 172, 180, 181, 182, 190, 193, 200, 201

Trains: Bristol and Bath are main termini on the Intercity network; Bodmin, Tiverton, Taunton and Bridgwater are main line stations, as is Exeter, from where you can connect to Barnstaple.

Padstow to Camelford

The typical pretty Cornish fishing port of **Padstow** sits enclosed from the Atlantic Ocean by the Camel Estuary. Here you will find the fifteenth-century Church of St Petroc, the Celtic monk who founded the town in the sixth century. The route takes you up the estuary to Wadebridge and then follows the river upstream. From the village of **Dunmere** you can make a detour into Bodmin, the historic county town. Here you will find *another* Church of St Petroc, with an elaborate twelfth-century carved font, and Bodmin Jail, a notorious nineteenth-century death row. Bodmin Town Museum covers archaeology of the town as well as Bodmin Moor. From Dunmere the route follows the Camel Trail through Dunmere Wood before turning off to **Blisland**. Here you head north along quiet roads through the western reaches of **Bodmin Moor**, passing close to remains of some of the Bronze Age settlements which are scattered over the moor. As you near the Camelford turning, you can see rising away to your right Rough Tor, the moor's second highest peak, one of the eroded granite outcrops which make the landscape of Bodmin Moor and Dartmoor so dramatic. There is a designated detour to Camelford, one of the many sole authentic locations of King Arthur's court of Camelot.

Padstow   1

National Grid Ref: SW9175

🍴 🍺 Golden Lion, Old Customs House, London Inn, Ring of Bells

Hemingford House, 21 Grenville Road, Padstow, Cornwall, *PL28 8EX.* Comfortable relaxed style. Hearty breakfast. 10 minutes walk to harbour. Welcome.
Tel: **01841 532806** (also fax no) Mr Tamblin.
D: £22.50-£27.50 **S:** £25.00-£30.00.
Open: All Year
Beds: 1T 2D **Baths:** 1 En 1 Pr 1 Sh
🛏 (12) 🅿 (1) ⅍ ▢ ⚡ ➶ 🛎 🖳 Ⅴ 🛢 ⅍ ♻

Mother Ivey Cottage, Trevose Head, Padstow, Cornwall, PL28 8SL.
Actual grid ref: SW859763
Tel: **01841 520329** (also fax no)
Mrs Woosnam Mills.
D: £22.50 **S:** £25.00.
Open: Easter to Oct
Beds: 2T **Baths:** 2 En
🛏 (6) 🅿 ▢ ➶ ✕ 🛎 Ⅴ 🛢 ⅍ ♻
Traditionally-built Cornish clifftop house with stunning sea views, overlooking Trevose Head with a beach below. The area is renowned for swimming, fishing, surfing and walking. A championship golf course - Trevose - is nearby. The Cornwall Coastal Path is adjacent.

D = Price range per person sharing in a double room

Khandalla, Sarahs Lane, Padstow, Cornwall, PL28 8EL.
Traditional bed and breakfast in elegant surroundings with estuary views.
Tel: **01841 532961** Mrs Hair.
D: £20.00-£25.00 **S:** £20.00-£40.00.
Open: All Year
Beds: 1D 1S
Baths: 2 En 1 Sh
🛏 🅿 (3) ⅍ ▢ ➶ 🛎 🖳 Ⅴ 🛢 ⅍

Althea Library B&B, 27 High Street, Padstow, Cornwall, *PL28 8BB*. Converted library, short walk from harbour, old part of town.
Grades: ETC 4 Diamond, Silver
Tel: **01841 532717**
D: £24.00-£30.00 **S:** £27.00-£60.00.
Open: All Year (not Xmas)
Beds: 2D 1T
Baths: 3 En
🅿 (3) ⊬🖵📺🎱📺Ⅴ🚲

St Issey 2

National Grid Ref: SW9271

🍴🍺 Ring of Bells

Trevorrick Farm, St Issey, Wadebridge, Cornwall, *PL27 7QH*. Near Camel Trail and Padstow, centrally situated in North Cornwall for touring.
Grades: ETC 3 Diamond
Tel: **01841 540574** (also fax no) Mr Mealing.
D: £18.00-£25.00 **S:** £27.00-£36.00.
Open: All Year (not Xmas)
Beds: 1F 1D 1T
Baths: 3 En
🛏🅿 (6) ⊬🖵🐾🎱📺Ⅴ

S = Price range for a single person in a room

Bringing children with you? Always ask for any special rates.

Wadebridge 3

National Grid Ref: SW9872

🍴🍺 Earl of St Vincent, The Ship

Little Pound, Bodieve, Wadebridge, Cornwall, *PL27 6EG*. Quiet hamlet, terraced gardens to stream, close to Camel Trail.
Tel: **01208 814449** Mrs Crook.
D: £16.00-£20.00 **S:** £16.00-£22.00.
Open: All Year (not Xmas)
Beds: 1D 1T 1S
Baths: 1 En 1 Sh
🛏 (3) 🅿 (4) ⊬🖵🎱📺Ⅴ🚲

Trevanion House, Trevanion Road, Wadebridge, Cornwall, *PL27 7JY*.
C18th house, casual bookings welcome, specialist holidays for adults with learning disability.
Tel: **01208 814903** Mrs Todd.
Fax no: 01208 816268
D: £19.00-£21.00 **S:** £20.00-£22.00.
Open: All Year
Beds: 10T 5S
Baths: 13 Pr 2 Sh
🛏 (5) 🅿 (8) ⊬🖵🗙🎱📺Ⅳ📺Ⅴ🛡🚲

West Park House, 106 Egloshale Rd, Wadebridge, Cornwall, *PL27 7AG*
Welcome to West Park House, ideally placed to visit and explore Cornwall.
Tel: **01208 813279** Mrs Bishop.
D: £22.50-£28.50 **S:** £18.00-£28.00.
Open: Mar to Dec
Beds: 1D 2T 1S
Baths: 2 En 1 Pr 1 Sh
🛏 (14) 🅿 (4) ⊬🖵🗙🎱📺Ⅴ🛡🚲

Bodmin 4

National Grid Ref: SX0667

🍴🍺 Borough Arms, Halfway House, St Benet's Abbey, Crown Inn, Lanivet Arms, Hole In The Wall, Weavers

Wilbury Guest House, Fletchers Bridge, Bodmin, Cornwall, *PL30 4AN*. Wilbury - beautiful spacious house situated 1 mile from Bodmin. Dogs welcome.
Tel: **01208 74001** Mrs Harrison.
D: £15.00-£15.00 **S:** £15.00.
Open: All Year
Beds: 1F 2T 1S **Baths:** 1 Sh
🛏🅿 (6) ⊬🖵🐾🗙🎱🛡🚲

Planning a longer stay? Always ask for any special rates.

SR 00 SS   20

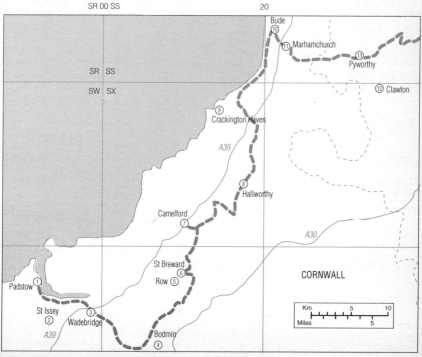

Camelford to Exmoor

The route now leads to the coast at Millook, where there is some steep up-and-down cycling over the clifftops before the descent to Widemouth Bay with its wonderful sandy beach, and the ride into **Bude**, a noted surfing centre. From here you strike out eastwards through Marhamchurch and come into Devon, arriving at the village of Bridgerule on the Tamar. Then it's on to Sheepwash in the Torridge Valley, where you turn north. The way now runs along a former railway line - this stretch is shared with the Tarka Trail, named after Henry Williamson's classic 1927 novel, *Tarka the Otter* - to **Bideford**, on the Torridge Estuary. Here you will find a fourteenth-century bridge and a statue commemorating Charles Kingsley, who wrote the historical romance *Westward Ho!*, set in the town (the eponymous nearby coastal resort was named after the book). Now it's down the Torridge Estuary and up the Taw Estuary to Barnstaple, where John Gay, who wrote *The Beggar's Opera*, went to school at St Anne's Chapel, which can be visited. Then you head inland and on to Bratton Fleming, from where it's a climb into **Exmoor National Park.** The route ascends swiftly to Mole's Chamber, atop the lonely high grass and heather plateau, before turning southeastwards along a particularly stupendous section of road which runs along the Devon-Somerset border. You would be very lucky to see some of Exmoor's indigenous red deer, the largest wild animal native to England; the magnificent views, however, are guaranteed.

Row 5

National Grid Ref: SX0976

Tarny Guest House, Row, St Breward, Bodmin, Cornwall, PL30 4LW.
Warm welcome, large luxury rooms, magnificent views, acres of private gardens with woodside waterfalls.
Tel: **01208 850583** Mrs Turner.
D: £17.00-£22.00 S: £18.00-£25.00
Open: All Year (not Xmas)
Beds: 2F 1D 1T **Baths:** 2 En 1 Sh
ᐃ 🅿 (8) ⊬ ☐ 🖳 🏛 🛒 V ⅰ ⊸

St Breward 6

National Grid Ref: SX0977

⑩ ⊈ The Old Inn

Treswallock Farm, St Breward, Bodmin, Cornwall, PL30 4PL.
Beef and sheep farm on peaceful location of Bodmin Moor.
Tel: **01208 850255** (also fax no)
D: £17.50-£17.50
S: £18.00-£18.00.
Open: May to Oct
Beds: 1D 1S **Baths:** 1 Sh
ᐃ 🅿 ⊬ ☐ 🛒 🏛 🖳 V ⅰ ⊸

D = Price range per person sharing in a double room

Pay B&Bs by cash or cheque and be prepared to pay up front.

Camelford 7

National Grid Ref: SX1083

⑩ ⊈ Masons' Arms, Darlington Inn, Bridge, Osiers

Masons Arms, Market Place, Camelford, Cornwall, PL32 9PD.
C18th public house in the centre of Camelford.
Tel: **01840 213309**
Mr Connolly.
D: £17.50-£17.50 S: £17.50-£17.50.
Open: All Year
Beds: 1F 2D 1T 1S
Baths: 2 Sh
ᐃ 🅿 (2) ☐ 🛒 🗙 🏛 🖳 V ⅰ ⊸

Trenarth, Victoria Road, Camelford, Cornwall, PL32 9XE.
Actual grid ref: SX1184
Friendly comfortable country home, open views.
Tel: **01840 213295** Mrs Hopkins.
D: £15.00-£17.00 S: £15.00-£17.00.
Open: All Year
Beds: 1F 1D 1S
Baths: 1 En 1 Sh
ᐃ (2) 🅿 (4) ⊬ ☐ 🛒 🏛 🖳 & V ⊸ ⊸

Hallworthy 8

National Grid Ref: SX1887

Wilsey Down Hotel, Hallworthy, Camelford, Cornwall, PL32 9SH.
Warm welcome, friendly hotel, views over Bodmin Moor, near to coast.
Tel: **01840 261205** Bremdon.
D: £18.00-£24.00 S: £15.00-£18.00.
Open: All Year
Beds: 1F 2T 2D
Baths: 2 En 1 Pr 1 Sh
ᐃ 🅿 (50) ☐ 🗙 🏛 V ⊸

Crackington Haven 9

National Grid Ref: SX1496

⑩ ⊈ Coombe Barton Inn

Venn Park Farm, Crackington Haven, Bude, Cornwall, EX23 0LB.
Tel: **01840 230159** (also fax no)
Ms Wilson.
D: £18.00-£20.00 S: £20.00-£22.00.
Open: All Year
Beds: 1F 2D
Baths: 2 En 1 Pr
ᐃ 🅿 ⊬ ☐ 🛒 🗙 🏛 🖳 V ⅰ ⊸ ⊸
Relaxation opportunity.
Modernised farmhouse with extensive sea, countryside views.
Ensuite, family bedrooms, colour TV. Coastal/moorland walks, fishing, golfing & cycling easily accessible. Participation farm/natural environmental tasks arrangeable. Close picturesque Boscastle/Crackington Beach. Traditionally cooked food, vegetarian option.

Hallagather, Crackington Haven, Bude, Cornwall, EX23 0LA.
Actual grid ref: SX146956
Ancient farmhouse, warm, welcoming. Substantial buffet style breakfast. Spectacular scenery.
Grades: ETC 4 Diamond, AA 4 Diamonds
Tel: **01840 230 276** Mrs Anthony.
Fax no: 01840 230 449
D: £17.50-£24.00 S: £18.00-£26.00.
Open: Feb to Nov
Beds: 1F 1D 1S **Baths:** 4 En
ᐃ (11) 🅿 (6) ⊬ ☐ 🛒 🏛 🖳 V ⅰ ⊸

The Grid Reference beneath the location heading is for the village or town - *not* for individual houses, which are shown (where supplied) in each entry itself.

Bude 10

National Grid Ref: SS2106

🍴 🍺 Crooklets, Sportsman, Preston Gate, Bencoolen Inn, Inn On The Green, Falcon Inn, Kings Arms

Marhamrise Guest House,
50 Kings Hill, Bude, Cornwall,
EX23 8QH.
Beautiful views. Gardens. Ground floor bedrooms. Plenty good home cooking.
Tel: **01288 354713** Mrs Thornton.
D: £15.00-£17.00 **S:** £15.00-£18.00.
Open: May to Sept
Beds: 1F 2D 1S
Baths: 1 En 2 Sh
🛏 (3) ⓟ (5) 🗔 ✗ 🍖 🚵 🎏 & Ⓥ 📷 ⚡ ♿

Sunrise Guest House, 6 Burn View, Bude, Cornwall, *EX23 8BY.*
Grades: ETC 4 Diamond
Tel: **01288 353214** Mr Masters.
D: £18.00-£23.00 **S:** £18.00-£25.00.
Open: Feb to Nov
Beds: 1F 3D 1T 1S
Baths: 6 En
🛏 (3) ⓟ (2) ✂ 🗔 🍖 🚵 & Ⓥ 📷 ⚡ ♿
'The general standards are high and many of the features are delightful. The hospitality of the owners and the cleanliness experienced count for a lot.' (English Tourist Board Assessment) Come see for yourselves! Centrally located. All rooms ensuite.

St Merryn, *Coastview, Bude, Cornwall, EX23 8AG.*
Tel: **01288 352058** Miss Abbot.
Fax no: 01288 359050
D: £14.00-£16.00 **S:** £20.00-£25.00.
Open: All Year
Beds: 1F 1D 1T 1S **Baths:** 2 Sh
🛏 ⓟ (4) ✂ 🗔 🍖 🚵 🎏 & Ⓥ 📷 ⚡ ♿
A large dormer bungalow with good sized ground floor bedrooms each having vanity unit with hot/cold water, colour TV with remote and tea/coffee making facilities situated on A3072 approximately 500 yards from A39 Atlantic highway, off-road parking.

Link's Side Guest House, *Burn View, Bude, Cornwall, EX23 8BY.*
Victoria house town centre, beaches, path, overlooking golf course.
Grades: ETC 4 Diamond
Tel: **01288 352410**
Mr & Mrs Dockrill.
D: £16.00-£21.00 **S:** £16.00-£21.00.
Open: All Year
Beds: 1F 4D 1T 1S
Baths: 5 En 1 Sh
🛏 ✂ 🗔 🍖 🚵 🎏 & Ⓥ 📷 ⚡ ♿

Pay B&Bs by cash or cheque and be prepared to pay up front.

Laundry Cottage, *Higher Wharf, Bude, Cornwall, EX23 8LW.*
Tel: **01288 353560** Mrs Noakes.
D: £17.00-£21.00 **S:** £17.00-£21.00.
Open: All Year (not Xmas)
Beds: 1D 1T
Baths: 1 Sh 1 Pr
🛏 (10) ⓟ (2) 🗔 🍖 🚵 Ⓥ 📷 ⚡ ♿
Grade II Listed cottage in two acres of garden on historic Bude canal. Secluded yet only a few minutes' walk from town centre, restaurants, coastal path, beach, cycle routes etc. Rooms overlook garden and canal. Quiet, many extras, private parking.

Meadow View, *Kings Hill Close, Bude, Cornwall, EX23 8RR.*
A large house 400 yds from canal. Room overlooks garden and fields.
Tel: **01288 355095** Mrs Shepherd.
D: £15.00-£16.00 **S:** £15.00-£16.00.
Open: All Year
Beds: 1D
Baths: 1 Pr
✂ 🗔 🍖 🚵 Ⓥ ⚡ ♿

Raetor, *Stratton Road, Bude, Cornwall, EX23 8AQ.*
Modern detached house situated on the main road. Bude one mile.
Tel: **01288 354128** Barnard.
D: £15.00-£15.00 **S:** £15.00-£15.00.
Open: All Year
Beds: 1D 1T 1S
Baths: 1 Sh
ⓟ (2) 🗔 🍖 🚵 Ⓥ ♿

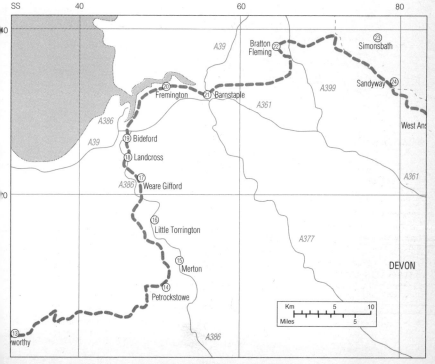

Kisauni, 4 Downs View, Bude, Cornwall, EX23 8RF.
Bright, airy Victorian house. 2 minutes beach. Romantic four poster bed. Home cooking.
Tel: **01288 352653** Mrs Kimpton.
D: £14.00-£16.00 **S:** £14.00-£16.00.
Open: All Year (not Xmas)
Beds: 2F 1D 1T 1S
Baths: 3 En 3 Sh
🛇 🅿 (5) ⬅ ♀ ⊁ ✕ ⚲ ⚐ ⑤ 🗆 ≉ ⁄

Pencarrol Guest House, 21 Downs View, Bude, Cornwall, EX23 8RF.
Pencarrol overlooks Bude's 18-hole golf course and offers comfortable B&B accommodation.
Tel: **01288 352478**
Mr & Mrs Payne.
D: £17.00-£19.00 **S:** £15.00-£22.00.
Open: All Year (not Xmas)
Beds: 1F 3D 1T 2S
Baths: 3 En 1 Pr 3 Sh
⊁ 🗆 ⚲ ⊞ ⑤ ⁄

Marhamchurch   11

National Grid Ref: SS2203

🍴 🍺 Bullers Arms

Hilton Farm House, Marhamchurch, Bude, Cornwall, EX23 0HE.
Actual grid ref: SX232033
Tel: **01288 361521** (also fax no)
Mr & Mrs Goodman.
D: £16.00-£25.00 **S:** £20.00-£24.00.
Open: All Year
Beds: 1F 1D 1S **Baths:** 2 En 1 Pr
🛇 🅿 (18) 🗆 ⬅ ♀ ⊁ ⚲ ⑤ ⓘ ⁄ ♻
C16th Hilton Farmhouse is set in 25 acres with panoramic views of countryside and sea, heated swimming pool (80f) and jacuzzi for guests' use only. Pub/restaurant ten minutes walk. Ideal location for making the most of Devon and Cornwall.

Floraldene, Marhamchurch, Bude, Cornwall, EX23 0HE.
Actual grid ref: SS225036
Lovely and peaceful character cottage in picturesque village of Marhamchurch.
Tel: **01288 361118** Mrs Sibley.
D: £12.00-£16.00 **S:** £16.00-£18.00.
Open: All Year (not Xmas)
Beds: 2D 1T **Baths:** 1 En
🛇 🅿 (2) 🗆 ♀ ⚐ ⓘ ⁄ ♻

Clawton   12

National Grid Ref: SX3599

Churchtown House, Clawton, Holsworthy, Devon, EX22 6PS.
Actual grid ref: SX347993
An elegant part-Georgian C17th farmhouse with a friendly atmosphere.
Tel: **01409 271467** Mrs Farrow.
D: £16.00-£18.00 **S:** £16.00.
Open: All Year
Beds: 1F 1D 1T **Baths:** 1 En 1 Sh
🛇 🅿 (6) ✕ ⚲ ⊞ ⑤ ⓘ ♻

Pay B&Bs by cash or cheque and be prepared to pay up front.

Pyworthy   13

National Grid Ref: SS3103

🍴 🍺 Molesworth Arms

Leworthy Farm, Pyworthy, Holsworthy, Devon, EX22 6SJ.
Tel: **01409 259469** Mrs Jennings.
D: £22.00-£25.00 **S:** £30.00-£40.00.
Open: All Year
Beds: 1F 1T 2D
Baths: 3 En 1 Pr
🛇 🅿 (8) ⊁ 🗆 ✕ ⚲ ⓘ ⁄ ♻
North Cornish Coast 20 minutes. Georgian farmhouse in tranquil, unspoilt location. Lawned gardens, orchard, wildlife haven and fishing lake. Fresh flowers, pretty bone china, fresh milk, hearty breakfasts. Homely atmosphere. Peaceful lounge. Exquisitely decorated with pictures, plates and china throughout.

Little Knowle Farm, Pyworthy, Holsworthy, Devon, EX22 6JY.
Actual grid ref: SX323028
Friendly relaxed farmhouse, home cooking, children welcome.
Tel: **01409 254642** Mrs Aston.
D: £16.00-£17.50 **S:** £16.00-£17.50.
Open: Easter to Oct
Beds: 1D 1T
Baths: 1 Sh
🛇 🅿 (3) 🗆 ✕ ⚲ ⑤ ⁄ ♻

Petrockstowe   14

National Grid Ref: SS5109

🍴 🍺 The Laurels Inn

Aish Villa, Petrockstowe, Okehampton, Devon, EX20 3HL.
Actual grid ref: SS514089
Peaceful location, superb views, ideal for visiting Dartmoor, Exmoor, coast.
Tel: **01837 810581**
Ms Gordon.
D: £17.00-£17.00 **S:** £17.00-£17.00.
Open: All Year
Beds: 1F 1T 1D
Baths: 1 Sh
🛇 🅿 (4) ⊁ 🗆 ⚲ ⊞ ⚐ ⑤ ⁄ ♻

All cycleways are popular: you are well-advised to book ahead

---

Merton   15

National Grid Ref: SS5212

🍴 🍺 Bull & Dragon

Richmond House, New Road (A386), Merton, Okehampton, Devon, EX20 3EG.
Tel: **01805 603258** Mrs Wickett.
D: £15.00-£15.00 **S:** £15.00-£15.00.
Open: All Year
Beds: 3F 1T 2D
Baths: 1 Sh
🛇 (5) 🅿 (4) 🗆 ♀ ⊁ ✕ ⚲ ⑤ ⓘ ⁄ ♻
Country house within easy reach of beach, moors, gardens, Tarka Trail. Evening meal optional. H.C. in all bedrooms.

Little Torrington   16

National Grid Ref: SS4916

Smytham Holiday Park, Little Torrington, Torrington, Devon, EX38 8PU.
C17th manor house, beautiful tranquil grounds. Outdoor heated pool.
Tel: **01805 622110** Mr Bland.
D: £20.00-£30.00 **S:** £24.00-£36.00.
Open: All Year (not Xmas/New Year)
Beds: 4D 3T **Baths:** 5 En 1 Sh
🛇 🅿 ⊁ 🗆 ♀ ✕ ⚲ ⊞ ⚐ ⑤ ⓘ ⁄ ♻

Weare Giffard   17

National Grid Ref: SS4721

▲ *Sea Lock Camping Barn & Tent Site, Vale Cottage, 7 Annery Kiln, Weare Giffard, Bideford, Devon EX39 5JE.*
Tel: **01237 477705 / 07866 026194**
Under 18: £5.00 **Adults:** £5.00
Self-catering facilities, Showers, Parking, Facilities for disabled people
Newly converted barn, offering basic accommodation, in beautiful, tranquil wooded valley overlooking River Torridge, between Bideford and Torrington. Private access to Tarka Trail (NCN 3) and conservation area. Superb walking, cycling, canoeing, fishing, birdwatching. Pubs/shops within 2.5 miles. Book individual beds/family rooms (sharing facilities) or sole use.

Landcross   18

National Grid Ref: SS4623

Sunset Hotel, Landcross, Bideford, Devon, EX39 5JA.
Actual grid ref: SS461239
Small country hotel. Peaceful location overlooking spectacular scenery and Tarka Trail.
Grades: ETC 3 Diamond,
AA 3 Diamond
Tel: **01237 472962** Mrs Lamb.
D: £27.00-£30.00 **S:** £36.00-£40.00.
Open: Easter to Nov
Beds: 2F 2D 2T **Baths:** 4 En
🅿 (8) ⊁ 🗆 ✕ ⚲ ⊞ ⚐ ⑤ ⓘ ♻

Bideford 19

National Grid Ref: SS4526

⊯ ⊈ Tanton's Hotel, Farmers Arms, Crab & Ale, Royal Hotel, Swan Inn, Joiners' Arms, Hunters' Inn, Sunset Hotel

The Mount Hotel, *Northdown Road, Bideford, Devon, EX39 3LP.*
Actual grid ref: SS449269
Grades: AA 4 Diamond
Tel: **01237 473748**
Mr & Mrs Laugharne.
D: £23.00-£25.00 **S:** £25.00-£33.00.
Open: Jan to Dec
Beds: 1F 3D 1T 2S
Baths: 7 En
🛇🅿(4)🗲🗖🚾🛋🕭ᬐ🖤🛆🚲🏍
Charming Georgian licensed guest house only 5 minutes' walk to town centre, private lounge for guests' use, all rooms ensuite, attractive garden, car parking for guests. Convenient for touring N Devon coastline, Clovelly, Lundy, Exmoor and Dartmoor. No smoking.

Fremington 20

National Grid Ref: SS5132

⊯ ⊈ New Inn, Boat House

Lower Yelland Farm, *Yelland Road, Fremington, Barnstaple, Devon, EX31 3EN.*
Tel: **01271 860101** (also fax no)
Mr Day.
D: £20.00-£20.00 **S:** £20.00-£20.00.
Open: All Year (not Xmas/New Year)
Beds: 1T 2D
Baths: 3 En
🛇🅿(6)🗖🏹🛋🚾ᬐ🖤🛆🚲
North Devon Coast beautifully situated period house on Taw Estuary. Ideal touring centre, Instow beach/marina approximately 1 mile, Bideford, Barnstaple 4.5 miles. Several golf courses in the vicinity. Adjacent to bird sanctuary. Private off road parking.

Barnstaple 21

National Grid Ref: SS5633

⊯ ⊈ Windsor Arms, Williams Arms, Rolle Quay Inn, North Country Inn, Pyne Arms, Ring O'Bells, Chichester Arms

Crossways, *Braunton Road, Barnstaple, Devon, EX31 1JY.*
Actual grid ref: SS555333
Detached house - town & Tarka Trail 150 yards, bicycle hire.
Tel: **01271 379120**
Mr & Mrs Tyson.
D: £15.00 **S:** £17.00.
Open: All Year
Beds: 1F 1D 1T
Baths: 2 Pr 1 Sh
🛇🅿(6)🗲🗖🗙🛋🚾ᬐ🖤🛆🚲

Mount Sandford, *Landkey Road, Barnstaple, Devon, EX32 0HL.*
Georgian house in 1.5 acres gardens. 2 double, 1 twin, all ensuite.
Tel: **01271 342354** Mrs White.
D: £18.00-£22.00 **S:** £20.00.
Open: All Year (not Xmas)
Beds: 1F 1D 1T
Baths: 3 En
🛇(3)🅿(3)🗲🗖🛋🚾ᬐ🖤🛆🚲🏍

Bratton Fleming 22

National Grid Ref: SS6437

⊯ ⊈ Black Venus

Haxton Down Farm, *Bratton Fleming, Barnstaple, Devon, EX32 7JL.*
Peaceful working farm in central position. Warm welcome, good food.
Tel: **01598 710275**
Mrs Burge.
D: £17.00-£20.00
S: £18.00-£20.00.
Open: Easter to Nov
Beds: 1F 1D
Baths: 2 En
🛇🅿(3)🗖🏹🗙🛋🚾ᬐ🖤🛆🚲🏍

Simonsbath 23

National Grid Ref: SS7739

Emmett's Grange Farm, *Simonsbath, Minehead, Somerset, TA24 7LD.*
Tel: **01643 831138** (also fax no)
Barlow.
D: £28.00-£35.00 **S:** £33.00-£40.00.
Open: All Year (not Xmas/New Year)
Beds: 1T 2D
🛇🅿🗲🏹🗙🛋🚾ᬐ🖤🛆🚲🏍
Emmett's Grange provides and oasis of friendly civilisation within its own 900 acres amidst the stunning wild and rugged Exmoor National Park. Luxurious B&B with moorland views. Guests' own elegant drawing room. Gourmet food available and many local pubs. Fully licensed.

Sandyway 24

National Grid Ref: SS7933

Barkham, *Sandy, Exmoor, Devon, EX36 3LU.*
Actual grid ref: SS787337
Tucked away in hidden valley in the heart of Exmoor.
Grades: ETC 4 Diamond, AA 4 Diamond
Tel: **01643 831370** (also fax no)
Mrs Adie.
D: £23.00-£30.00 .
Open: All Year (not Xmas)
Beds: 2D 1T
Baths: 1 En 1 Sh
🛇(12)🅿(6)🗲🗖🗙🚾ᬐ🖤🛆🚲

Bringing children with you? Always ask for any special rates.

West Anstey 25

National Grid Ref: SS8527

Jubilee House, *Highaton Farm, West Anstey, South Molton, Devon, EX36 3PJ.*
Actual grid ref: SS844254
Grades: ETC 4 Diamond
Tel: **01398 341312** Mrs Denton.
Fax no: 01398 341323
D: £19.50-£22.50
S: £19.50-£19.50.
Open: All Year
Beds: 2D 3S
Baths: 2 Sh
ॐ **P** (4) ⅍⊡ⅺⓧ₤▥Ⅵ₤↯௸
Elegant farmhouse, close edge
Exmoor National Park, situated on
Two Moors Way. Peaceful
surroundings, easily accessible,
great atmosphere. Large lounge
(with log fire), dining room
available for guests, local
produce/home preserves. Bill is an
international chef. Patio/BBQ/
badminton areas, therapeutic hot
tub spa.

East Anstey 26

National Grid Ref: SS8626

Threadneedle, *East Anstey, Tiverton, Devon, EX16 9JH.*
Built in the style of a Devon
Longhouse, set in three acres, close
Dulverton.
Grades: ETC 3 Diamond
Tel: **01398 341598**
Mr & Mrs Webb.
D: £23.00-£25.00
S: £23.00-£25.00.
Open: All Year
Beds: 1D 1T
Baths: 2 En
ॐ **P** (10) ⅍⊡ⅺ₤▥Ⅵ₤↯௸

Hawkridge 27

National Grid Ref: SS8530

East Hollowcombe Farm,
Hawkridge, Dulverton, Somerset, TA22 9QL.
Working farm, beautiful scenery,
ideal stopover for Two Moors
Way.
Tel: **01398 341622** Floyd.
D: £17.00-£18.00 **S:** £17.00-£18.00.
Open: Easter to Oct
Beds: 1F 1D 1S **Baths:** 1 Sh
ॐ **P** (8) ⊡ⅺ ⓧ ₤ ▥ Ⅵ ₤ ↯

Dulverton 28

National Grid Ref: SS9128

|●| ⧉ Tarr Farm Inn, Bridge, Lion Hotel, White Horse, Rock Inn, Badger's Holt, Lowtrow Cross Inn

Highercombe Farm, *Dulverton, Somerset, TA22 9PT.*
Grades: ETC 4 Diamond, Silver
Tel: **01398 323616** (also fax no)
Mrs Humphrey.
D: £20.00 **S:** £28.00.
Open: Mar to Nov
Beds: 2D 1T
Baths: 3 En
ॐ (6) **P** ⊡ⅺⓧ₤▥Ⅵ₤↯
On the very edge of expansive
moorland, you will find our wel-
coming farmhouse home. All
ensuite rooms beautifully co-ordi-
nated, overlooking our 450 acres of
working farm. Wonderful farmer's
breakfasts, optional evening meals.
A quiet and relaxing place to stay.

D = Price range per person
sharing in a double room

Exmoor to Bridgwater

You eventually descend (steeply) to **Dulverton**, a pretty
village where the National Park Visitors' Centre is located. From
here you head down the Barle Valley to Brushford, where you
leave Exmoor and head on to Morebath and Bampton. Cycling
south from here you pass near to Knightshayes Court, a
Victorian Gothic house with gardens divided into formal
sections themed by scent or colour, before reaching **Tiverton**.
The route now strikes out east along the Grand Western Canal,
through Halberton and Sampford Peverell, crossing into
Somerset and heading on to the county town, **Taunton**, in the
heart of cider country. Taunton Castle was the scene of two
fatal trials, that of the royal pretender Perkin Warbeck at the end
of the fifteenth century; and the 'bloody assizes' of 1685, where
the infamous Judge Jeffries ordered the executions of the Duke
of Monmouth and his followers, who had attempted to seize the
throne of England from James II. From Taunton you head
northwards to **Bridgwater**, close to where the battle of
Sedgemoor, fought in 1685, brought the Monmouth Rebellion to
an end.

Springfield Farm, *Ashwick Lane, Dulverton, Somerset, TA22 9QD.*
Actual grid ref: SS878308
Magnificent moorland/woodland
views. 1.5 miles to Tarr Steps.
Comfortable farmhouse with good
food. **Grades:** ETC 4 Diamond
Tel: **01398 323722** Mrs Vellacott.
D: £20.00-£23.00 **S:** £25.00-£35.00.
Open: Easter to Nov
Beds: 2D 1T **Baths:** 2 En 1 Pr
ॐ (3) **P** (3) ⅍⊡ⅺⓧ₤▥Ⅵ₤↯௸

Winsbere House, *64 Battleton, Dulverton, Somerset, TA22 9HU.*
Delightful private house. Lovely
country views. Excellent location
touring Exmoor.
Grades: ETC 3 Diamonds
Tel: **01398 323278** Mrs Rawle.
D: £17.00-£23.50 **S:** £20.00-£20.00.
Open: All Year (not Xmas/New
Year)
Beds: 1T 2D **Baths:** 2 En 1 Sh
ॐ (8) **P** (3) ⅍⊡₤▥Ⅵ₤↯௸

Town Mills, *Dulverton, Somerset, TA22 9HB.*
Mill house. Full breakfast served in
bedroom, some with log fires.
Tel: **01398 323124**
Mrs Buckingham.
D: £18.50-£25.00 **S:** £22.00-£38.00.
Open: All Year
Beds: 4D 1T **Baths:** 3 Pr 2 Sh
ॐ **P** (5) ⊡₤▥Ⅵ

Bampton 29

National Grid Ref: SS9522

|●| ⧉ Masons Arms, Seahorse

Manor Mill House, *Bampton, Devon, EX16 9LP.*
Welcoming C17th home in historic
Bampton. Ideal base, close to
Exmoor.
Grades: ETC 4 Diamond, Silver
Tel: **01398 332211** Mrs Ayres.
Fax no: 01398 332009
D: £21.00-£24.00 .
Open: All Year
Beds: 2D 1T **Baths:** 3 En
P (20) ⅍⊡₤▥Ⅵ↯௸

Tiverton 30

National Grid Ref: SS9512

|●| ⧉ Exeter Inn, Twyford Inn, Trout Inn, Seahorse, Anchor, White Ball

Lodgehill Farm Hotel, *Tiverton, Devon, EX16 5PA.*
Actual grid ref: SS946111
Good parking, tranquil setting on
A396, 1 mile south of Tiverton,
with Dartmoor, Exmoor.
Grades: ETC 3 Diamond,
AA 3 Diamond, RAC 3 Diamond
Tel: **01884 251200**
Mr & Mrs Reader.
Fax no: 01884 242090
D: £23.00-£27.50 **S:** £25.00-£29.50.
Open: All Year
Beds: 2F 2D 2T 3S **Baths:** 9 En
ॐ **P** (12) ⊡ⅺⓧ₤▥Ⅵ₤↯௸

Angel Guest House, 13 St Peter Street, Tiverton, Devon, EX16 6NU.
Town centre: Georgian house, large cycle shed, ideal touring centre.
Tel: **01884 253392**
Mr & Mrs Evans.
Fax no: 01884 251154
D: £16.00-£18.00 **S:** £16.00-£18.00
Open: All Year
Beds: 2F 3D 1T 1S
Baths: 3 Pr 2 Sh
⑤ 🅿 (4) 🖵 🛒 🛏 🎟 ⒱ 🚲

Hill Cottage, Cove, Tiverton, Devon, EX16 7RN.
Stress-free and calming countryside location. The silence is deafening.
Tel: **01884 256978** Mrs Harris.
D: £20.00-£20.00 **S:** £20.00-£25.00
Open: All Year (not Xmas)
Beds: 1D 1T **Baths:** 1 Sh
🅿 (4) 🗶 🖵 🗙 🛏 🎟 ⒱ 🚲

Uplowman 31

National Grid Ref: ST0115

🍴 🍺 Globe

Hill Farm, Uplowman, Tiverton, Devon, EX16 7PE.
15th century Devon longhouse quiet working farm. Tennis court games room.
Tel: **01884 820388** Branton.
D: £17.00-£18.00 **S:** £17.00-£18.00
Open: All Year
Beds: 3D 1S
⑤ 🅿 (6) 🖵 🗙 🛏 🎟 ⒜ 🍴 🚲

D = Price range per person sharing in a double room

All rates are subject to alteration at the owners' discretion.

Greenham 32

National Grid Ref: ST0720

🍴 🍺 Globe Inn

Greenham Hall, Greenham, Wellington, Somerset, TA21 0JJ.
Actual grid ref: ST076202
Impressive Victorian turreted house with informal friendly atmosphere. Central location in beautiful countryside.
Tel: **01823 672603** Mrs Ayre.
Fax no: 01823 672307
D: £21.00-£21.00 **S:** £27.00-£32.00.
Open: All Year
Beds: 1F 3D 2T 1S
Baths: 4 En 1 Pr 2 Sh
⑤ 🅿 (10) 🖵 🛒 🛏 🎟 ⒱ 🍴

Staplegrove 33

National Grid Ref: ST2126

🍴 🍺 Cross Keys

Yallands Farmhouse, Staplegrove, Taunton, Somerset, TA2 6PZ.
Actual grid ref: ST209259
A warm welcome is assured at our beautiful C16th house.
Grades: ETC 4 Diamond
Tel: **01823 278979** Mr & Mrs Kirk.
Fax no: 0870 284 9194
D: £26.50-£27.50 **S:** £29.00-£33.00.
Open: All Year
Beds: 1F 2D 1T 2S
Baths: 6 En
⑤ 🅿 (6) 🖵 🛒 🛏 🎟 ⒱ 🚲

Taunton 34

National Grid Ref: ST2324

🍴 🍺 Square & Compass, Greyhound Inn, Cross Keys, Pen & Quill, King's Arms, Old Inn, Merry Monk, Cavalier

The Old Mill, Bishops Hull, Taunton, Somerset, TA1 5AB.
Tel: **01823 289732** (also fax no)
Mr & Mrs Slipper.
D: £22.00-£24.00
S: £30.00-£35.00.
Open: All Year (not Xmas)
Beds: 2D
Baths: 1 En 1 Pr
🅿 🗶 🖵 🛏 🎟 ⒱ 🛗
Grade ll. Listed former Corn mill retaining many original workings and beamed ceilings, in lovely riverside setting. A warm welcome awaits you, delightful bedrooms with extensive breakfast menu and large waterside terrace. Exmoor and coast 35 minutes. packed lunches available.

Hillview Guest House, Bishop's Hull, Taunton, Somerset, TA1 5EG.
Spacious accommodation, warm and friendly atmosphere in attractive village near Taunton.
Grades: ETC 3 Diamond
Tel: **01823 275510** (also fax no)
Mr Morgan.
D: £17.50-£22.50 **S:** £17.50-£25.00.
Open: All Year
Beds: 2F 1D 1T 1S
Baths: 2 En 3 Sh
⑤ 🅿 (6) 🗶 🖵 🛒 🛏 🎟 🍴 ⒱ 🚲

Blorenge Guest House, 57 Staplegrove Road, Taunton, Somerset, TA1 1DL.
We are situated within 10 mins of all Taunton's amenities.
Tel: **01823 283005**
Mr Painter.
D: £20.00-£35.00 **S:** £26.00-£40.00.
Open: All Year
Beds: 3F 9D 5T 7S
Baths: 17 En 2 Sh
⑤ 🅿 (18) 🖵 🛒 🗙 🛏 🎟 ⒱ 🚲

Creech St Michael 35

National Grid Ref: ST2625

🍴 🍺 Riverside Inn, Rising Sun

Creechbarn, Vicarage Lane, Creech St Michael, Taunton, TA3 5PP.
Actual grid ref: ST276253
Converted longbarn in rural location. Quiet. 3 mins M5 J25.
Grades: AA 4 Diamond
Tel: **01823 443955** Humphreys.
Fax no: 01823 443509
D: £20.00-£22.00
S: £20.00-£29.00.
Open: All Year (not Xmas/New Year)
Beds: 1T 2D
Baths: 1 En
⑤ 🅿 (4) 🖵 🛒 🗙 🛏 🎟 ⒱ 🍴 🚲

Bridgwater to the Mendips

From here it's east to **Glastonbury**, a small town more redolent with mythology of various kinds than anywhere in England. The towering ruins of the Benedictine abbey are all that remain of one of Britain's earliest Christian foundations. According to legend it was founded by Christ himself, brought here as a child by Joseph of Arimathea, who later returned with the Holy Grail and stuck his staff into the ground, which sprouted spontaneously into a thorn tree. The Glastonbury Thorn, in the abbey grounds, is descended from that original. Nearby

Glastonbury Tor is said to be the Isle of Avalon, where King Arthur was brought after being mortally wounded in battle - the tomb of Arthur and Guinevere lies in the abbey grounds. Allegedly. From Glastonbury the route passes through the pancake-flat Somerset Levels to **Wells**, where stands one of England's most magnificent cathedrals, renowned for the ornately carved west front. Northwest of Wells you come to **Wookey Hole**, a striking group of caves, before ascending onto the limestone ridge of the Mendip Hills; after cycling along the ridge as far as **Charterhouse** you turn east to **East Harptree** and **Hinton Blewett**.

Thorn Falcon   36

National Grid Ref: ST2723

⊨ ⊲ Hope Inn, Tudor Hotel, Quantock Gateway, Malt Shovel Inn, Kings Head

Lower Farm, Thorn Falcon, Taunton, Somerset, TA3 5NR.
Picturesque 15th century thatched farmhouse, log fires, peaceful location, 3 miles Taunton.
Grades: AA 4 Diamond
Tel: **01823 443549** (also fax no)
Mrs Titman.
D: £23.00-£25.00 **S:** £30.00.
Open: All Year (not Xmas)
Beds: 1F 1D 1T
Baths: 1 En 1 Pr
🛏 🅿 (10) ⊬ ☐ ✗ Ⅲ. 🛢 🖉 ⚲

North Petherton   37

National Grid Ref: ST2832

⊨ ⊲ Maypole Inn

Quantock View House, Bridgwater Road, North Petherton, Bridgwater, Somerset, TA6 6PR.
Actual grid ref: ST301342
Central for Cheddar, Wells, Glastonbury, the Quantocks and the sea.
Grades: ETC 3 Diamond, AA 3 Diamond
Tel: **01278 663309**
Mr & Mrs George.
D: £16.00-£20.00 **S:** £18.00-£24.00.
Open: All Year
Beds: 2F 1D 1T
Baths: 3 En 1 Pr
🛏 🅿 (8) ⊬ ☐ ✗ Ⅲ. Ⅵ 🛢 🖉 ⚲

Lower Clavelshay Farm, North Petherton, Bridgwater, Somerset, TA6 6PJ.
Actual grid ref: ST255310
Buzzards, badgers and beautiful countryside surround our C17th farmhouse.
Tel: **01278 662347** (also fax no)
Mrs Milverton.
D: £20.00-£23.00 **S:** £23.00-£26.00.
Open: March-Nov
Beds: 1F 2D
Baths: 2 En 1 Pr
🛏 🅿 (4) ⊬ ☐ ✗ Ⅲ. Ⅵ 🖉 ⚲

Bridgwater   38

National Grid Ref: ST3037

⊨ ⊲ Hope Inn, Tudor Hotel, Quantock Gateway, Malt Shovel Inn, Kings Head

The Acorns, 61 Taunton Road, Bridgwater, Somerset, TA6 3LP.
Tel: **01278 445577**
D: £17.50-£20.00.
S: £17.50-£20.00.
Open: All Year (not Xmas)
Beds: 3F 2D 5T 3S
Baths: 5 En 3 Sh
🛏 🅿 (15) ☐ ↑ 🛢 Ⅲ. Ⅵ 🖉
Jill and Ken offer welcoming and friendly hospitality with modern facilities, good breakfast, guest lounge. Large Victorian house overlooking the Bridgwater and Taunton Canal. 1.5 miles from M5. Ideal for touring Somerset and Devon. Please telephone for colour brochure anytime.

Admirals Rest Guest House, 5 Taunton Road, Bridgwater, Somerset, TA6 3LW.
Elegant Victorian house, close to town centre, children welcome.
Grades: ETC 3 Diamond, AA 3 Diamond
Tel: **01278 458580** (also fax no)
Mrs Parker.
D: £17.00-£22.00
S: £18.00-£24.00.
Open: All Year
Beds: 2F 1D 1T
Baths: 3 En 1 Pr
🛏 🅿 (5) ☐ ✗ 🛢 Ⅲ. Ⅵ ⚲

All rooms full and nowhere else to stay? Ask the owner if there's anywhere nearby

---

Wembdon   39

National Grid Ref: ST2837

⊨ ⊲ Quantock Gateway, Malt Shovel

Model Farm, Perry Green, Wembdon, Bridgwater, Somerset, TA5 2BA.
Between Quantocks and Levels. Comfortable Victorian farmhouse in peaceful rural setting.
Grades: ETC 4 Diamond, AA 4 Diamond
Tel: **01278 433999**
Mr & Mrs Wright.
D: £25.00-£30.00 **S:** £35.00-£35.00.
Open: All Year (not Xmas/New Year)
Beds: 1F 1D 1T **Baths:** 3 En
🛏 🅿 ⊬ ☐ ↑ ✗ 🛢 Ⅲ. Ⅵ ⚲

Ash-Wembdon Farm, Hollow Lane, Wembdon, Bridgwater, Somerset, TA5 2BD.
Actual grid ref: ST281381
Enjoy a refreshing and memorable stay at our elegant yet homely farmhouse.
Grades: ETC 4 Diamond, Silver
Tel: **01278 453097** Mrs Rowe.
Fax no: 01278 445856
D: £22.00-£25.00 **S:** £22.00-£28.00.
Open: All Year (not Xmas)
Beds: 2D 1T **Baths:** 2 En 1 Pr
🛏 (10) 🅿 (4) ⊬ ☐ 🛢 Ⅲ. Ⅵ ⚲

Catcott   40

National Grid Ref: ST3939

⊨ ⊲ King William, The Crown

Honeysuckle, King William Road, Catcott, Bridgwater, Somerset, TA7 9HV.
Set in award-winning 'Britain in Bloom' village of Catcott, within easy reach mystic Glastonbury.
Tel: **01278 722890**
Mr & Mrs Scott.
D: £16.00-£20.00 **S:** £18.00-£25.00.
Open: All Year (not Xmas)
Beds: 1D 1T
Baths: 1 En 1 Sh
🛏 (6) 🅿 (3) ⊬ ☐ 🛢 Ⅲ. Ⅵ 🖉 ⚲

Greinton 41

National Grid Ref: ST4136

|◎| ◀ Pipers Inn

West Town Farm, *Greinton, Bridgwater, Somerset, TA7 9BW.*
A friendly atmosphere, a warm welcome and a high standard of hospitality awaits you.
Tel: **01458 210277** Mrs Hunt.
D: £20.00-£24.00 **S:** £25.00-£29.00.
Open: Mar to Sep
Beds: 1D 1T
Baths: 2 En
🛏 (3) 🅿 (2) 🔌 🖵 ♨ 🎥 ⊡ ♂

Street 42

National Grid Ref: ST4836

▲ ***Street Youth Hostel,*** *The Chalet, Ivythorn Hill, Street, Somerset, BA16 0TZ.*
Actual grid ref: ST480345
Tel: **01458 442961**
Under 18: £6.50 **Adults:** £9.25
Self-catering facilities, Wet weather shelter, Lounge, Drying room, Cycle store, Parking, No smoking, WC, Kitchen facilities, Credit cards accepted
Former holiday home for workers at Clarks' shoemakers, this traditional hostel is a Swiss-style chalet looking towards Glastonbury Tor.

Glastonbury 43

National Grid Ref: ST5039

|◎| ◀ Rose & Portcullis, Who'd A Thought It, Mitre, Camelot Inn, Pilgrim's Rest, Lion

Meadow Barn, *Middlewick Farm, Wick Lane, Glastonbury, Somerset, BA6 8JW.*
Grades: ETC 3 Diamond
Tel: **01458 832351** (also fax no)
Mrs Coles.
D: £20.50-£22.00 **S:** £26.00-£30.00.
Open: All Year (not Xmas)
Beds: 2D 1T 1F
Baths: 3 Pr
🛏 🅿 🖵 ✗ 🔌 🖵 & 🎥 🖷 ♨ ♂
Tastefully converted barn, ground floor ensuite accommodation with olde worlde charm and cottage-style decor. Set in award-winning cottage gardens, apple orchards and meadows. Beautiful tranquil countryside. Meadow Barn has a luxury indoor heated swimming pool.

Lottisham Manor, *Glastonbury, Somerset, BA6 8PF.*
Actual grid ref: ST574343
Tel: **01458 850205**
Mrs Barker-Harland.
D: £17.50-£20.00 **S:** £17.50-£17.50.
Open: All Year
Beds: 1D 1T 1S **Baths:** 2 Sh
🛏 🅿 (8) ✗ 🖵 🔌 🖵 🎥 ♨ ♂
C16th manor house. Lovely garden. Hard tennis court. Perfect peace and comfort.

Pippin, *4 Ridgeway Gardens, Glastonbury, Somerset, BA6 8ER.*
Every comfort in peaceful home opposite Chalice Hill. Short walk Tor/town.
Grades: ETC 3 Diamond
Tel: **01458 834262** Mrs Slater.
D: £16.00-£18.00 **S:** £17.00-£20.00.
Open: All Year
Beds: 1D 1T **Baths:** 1 Sh
🛏 🅿 (2) 🖵 🔌 🖵 🎥 ⊡ ♂

Hillclose, *Street Road, Glastonbury, Somerset, BA6 9EG.*
Warm friendly atmosphere, clean rooms, comfortable beds, full English breakfast.
Tel: **01458 831040** (also fax no)
Mr & Mrs Riddle.
D: £16.00-£20.00 **S:** £25.00-£35.00.
Open: All Year (not Xmas)
Beds: 1F 2D 1T
Baths: 2 Sh
🅿 (4) 🖵 🔌 🖵 🎥 ⊡ ♂

Little Orchard, *Ashwell Lane, Glastonbury, Somerset, BA6 8BG.*
Glastonbury, famous for historic Tor, King Arthur, abbey ruins and alternative centre.
Grades: ETC 3 Diamond
Tel: **01458 831620** Mrs Gifford.
D: £16.50-£21.00 **S:** £17.00-£22.00.
Open: All Year
Beds: 1F 1D 1T 2S
Baths: 2Shared
🛏 🅿 ✗ 🖵 🔌 🖵 🎥 ⊡ ♂

Cradlebridge Farm, *Glastonbury, Somerset, BA16 9SD.*
Only by staying here will you appreciate the ambience.
Grades: AA 4 Diamond, RAC 4 Diamond
Tel: **01458 831827** Mrs Tinney.
D: £22.00-£25.00 **S:** £30.00-£30.00.
Open: All Year
Beds: 2F
Baths: 2 Pr
🛏 (3) 🅿 (10) ✗ 🖵 🔌 🖵 & 🎥 ⊡ ♂

Shambhala Healing Centre, *Coursing Batch, Glastonbury, Somerset, BA6 8BH.*
Beautiful house, sacred site on side of the Tor. Healing, massage, great vegetarian food.
Tel: **01458 833081** Nixon.
Fax no: 01458 831797
D: £20.00-£30.00 **S:** £20.00-£25.00.
Open: All Year
Beds: 3D 1T 1S
Baths: 3 Sh
🛏 🅿 ✗ 🖵 ✗ 🔌 🖵 🎥 ⊡

Blake House, *3 Bove Town, Glastonbury, Somerset, BA6 8JE.*
Actual grid ref: ST503390
Lovely welcoming C17th Listed house built of stones from Glastonbury Abbey.
Tel: **01458 831680** Mrs Hankins.
D: £18.00-£20.00 **S:** £22.50-£25.00.
Open: All Year (not Xmas)
Beds: 1D 1T
Baths: 2 En
🅿 (2) ✗ 🖵 🔌 🖵 🎥 ⊡

1 The Gables, *Street Road, Glastonbury, Somerset, BA6 9EG.*
Tea/coffee all rooms. Shower and toilet separate. 1 minute to town.
Tel: **01458 832519** Mrs Stott.
D: £13.00.
Open: Feb to Nov
Beds: 2D 1F 1T
Baths: 1 En 1 Sh
🛏 (8) 🅿 (4) 🔌 🖵 ⊡

North Wootton 44

National Grid Ref: ST5641

|◎| ◀ Crossways Inn

Riverside Grange, *Tanyard Lane, North Wootton, Wells, Somerset, BA4 4AE.*
A charming converted Tannery quietly situated on the River edge.
Grades: AA 5 Diamonds
Tel: **01749 890761** Mrs English.
D: £19.50-£22.00 **S:** £25.00-£29.00.
Open: All Year
Beds: 1D 1T
Baths: 2 Pr
🛏 🅿 (6) 🖵 🔌 🖵 🎥 ⊡ ♂

Coxley 45

National Grid Ref: ST5343

Tynings House, *Coxley, Wells, Somerset, BA5 1RF.*
Grades: AA 4 Diamonds
Tel: **01749 675368** (also fax no)
Ms Parsons.
D: £25.00-£35.00 **S:** £35.00-£45.00.
Open: All Year (not Xmas/New Year)
Beds: 1T 2D
Baths: 3 En 3 Pr
🅿 (10) ✗ 🖵 ✗ 🔌 🖵 🎥 ⊡ ♦ ♂
Tynings House lies on the edge of a small village in the heart of Somerset. It is surrounded by 8 acres of garden and meadow with beautiful views over unspoilt countryside

Wells 46

National Grid Ref: ST5445

|◎| ◀ Burcott Inn, City Arms, Fountain Inn, Pheasant Inn, Sheppey Inn, City Arms, Wooley Hole Inn, Ring O' Bells, New Inn

The Crown at Wells, *Market Place, Wells, Somerset, BA5 2RP.*
Grades: ETC 3 Diamond
Tel: **01749 673457** Sara Hodges.
Fax no: 01749 679792
D: £27.50-£30.00 **S:** £40.00.
Open: All Year
Beds: 4F 5D 4T 2S
Baths: 15 En
🛏 🅿 (10) 🖵 🔌 ✗ 🔌 🖵 🎥 ⊡ ♦
The C15th Crown Inn is situated in the heart of Wells, within a stone's throw of Wells Cathedral and moated Bishop's Palace. Delicious meals, snacks and refreshments available all day. We pride ourselves on a warm and friendly service.

Infield House, *36 Portway, Wells, Somerset,* BA5 2BN.
Grades: AA 4 Diamond
Tel: 01749 670989
D: £21.00-£24.50 **S:** £31.00-£34.50.
Open: All Year
Beds: 2D 1T
Baths: 3 En
🛏 (14) 🅿 (4) ⊬ 🗆 ⊁ ✕ 🔌 🛖 🛏 Ⅶ 🔒 ⚡
Beautifully restored Victorian town house with period furnishing, portraits and decor. A short walk to city centre, cathedral and bishop's palace. Bountiful breakfasts, traditional English or vegetarian. Touring centre for Glastonbury, Cheddar, Bath or walking on Mendip hills. Evening meals by prior arrangement.

17 Priory Road, *Wells, Somerset,* BA5 1SU.
Large Victorian house. Homemade bread and preserves. Few mins' walk shops, cathedral, bus station.
Tel: 01749 677300 Mrs Winter.
D: £17.50-£17.50 **S:** £17.50-£20.00.
Open: All Year (not Xmas)
Beds: 3F 3S
Baths: 2 Sh
🛏 🅿 (5) ⊬ 🗆 🛖 Ⅶ 🚲

Cadgwith House, *Hawkers Lane, Wells, Somerset,* BA5 3JH.
Actual grid ref: ST559462
Delightfully furnished spacious family house, backing onto field. Beautiful bathrooms.
Grades: ETC 4 Diamond
Tel: 01749 677799
Mr & Mrs Pletts.
D: £18.00-£20.00 **S:** £18.00-£25.00.
Open: All Year
Beds: 1F 1D 1T 1S
Baths: 3 En 1 Pr
🛏 🅿 (3) 🗆 ⊁ 🔌 🛖 Ⅶ 🔒 ⚡ 🚲

30 Mary Road, *Wells, Somerset,* BA5 2NF.
Grades: ETC 3 Diamond
Tel: 01749 674031 (also fax no)
Mrs Bailey.
D: £17.50-£18.00 **S:** £17.50-£18.00.
Open: Feb to Nov
Beds: 2D 2S
Baths: 1 Sh
🛏 (3) 🅿 (5) 🗆 🛖 🛏 Ⅶ 🔒 🚲
Small, friendly family home, approx. 10 minutes walk from city centre offering bright modern rooms and a choice of breakfast.

Winsome House, *Portway, Wells, Somerset,* BA5 2NF.
1930 detached house in quiet cul-de-sac 2 mins from cathedral and city centre.
Grades: ETC 3 Diamond
Tel: 01749 679720 (also fax no)
Mrs Lock.
D: £18.00-£20.00 **S:** £20.00-£24.00.
Open: All Year
Beds: 1F 1D 1T
Baths: 1 Sh
🅿 (3) ⊬ 🗆 ✕ 🔌 🛖 Ⅶ 🔒 🚲

The Limes, *29 Chamberlain Street, Wells, Somerset,* BA5 2PQ.
Beautifully restored Victorian town house in the centre of historic Wells.
Tel: 01749 675716
Fax no: 01749 674874
D: £18.00-£20.00 .
Open: All Year (not Xmas)
Beds: 1D 1T
🛏 🅿 (2) ⊬ 🗆 🔌 🛖 Ⅶ 🔒 🚲

D = Price range per person sharing in a double room

Furlong House, *Lorne Place, St Thomas Street, Wells, Somerset,* BA5 2XF.
Georgian house, central Wells, walled gardens, very quiet, ample parking.
Grades: AA 4 Diamond
Tel: 01749 674064 Mr Howard.
D: £20.00-£23.00 **S:** £20.00-£42.00.
Open: All Year (not Xmas)
Beds: 2D 1T
Baths: 2 En 1 Sh
🛏 🅿 (4) ⊬ 🗆 🔌 🛖 Ⅶ ⚡ 🚲

Birdwood House, *Bath Road, Wells, Somerset,* BA5 3DH.
Actual grid ref: ST571468
Beautifully located on the edge of Mendips large Victorian gardens.
Grades: AA 2 Star
Tel: 01749 679250
Mrs Crane.
D: £18.00-£18.00 **S:** £18.00-£18.00.
Open: All Year (not Xmas/ New Year)
Beds: 2D 1S
Baths: 1 Sh
🛏 (5) 🅿 (6) ⊬ 🗆 🔌 🛖 Ⅶ 🔒 ⚡ 🚲

Bekynton House, *7 St Thomas Street, Wells, Somerset,* BA5 2UU.
Three minutes from cathedral, a few more to city restaurants.
Tel: 01749 672222 (also fax no)
Mr & Mrs Gripper.
D: £23.50-£27.00
S: £25.00-£40.00.
Open: All Year (not Xmas)
Beds: 1F 3D 2T
Baths: 4 En 2 Pr
🛏 (7) 🅿 (6) ⊬ 🗆 🔌 🛖 Ⅶ

Ancient Gate House Hotel, *Sadler Street, Wells, Somerset,* BA5 2RR.
Situated on the cathedral green, overlooking West front of cathedral.
Tel: 01749 672029 Mr Rossi.
Fax no: 01749 670319
D: £30.00-£35.00 **S:** £45.00-£50.00.
Open: All Year
Beds: 1F 6D 1T 1S
Baths: 7 En 1 Sh
🛏 🅿 🗆 ⊁ ✕ 🔌 🛖 Ⅶ

Wookey Hole 47

National Grid Ref: ST5347

🍴 🍺 Wooley Hole Inn, Ring O' Bells, New Inn

Broadleys, *21 Wells Road, Wookey Hole, Wells, Somerset,* BA5 1DN.
Actual grid ref: ST533470
Large detached house situated between Wells and Wookey Hole with panoramic countryside views.
Grades: ETC 4 Diamond, Silver, AA 4 Diamond
Tel: 01749 674746 (also fax no)
Mrs Milton.
D: £18.50-£20.00
S: £25.00-£35.00.
Open: All Year (not Xmas)
Beds: 3D
Baths: 2 En 1 Pr
🛏 (10) 🅿 (4) ⊬ 🗆 🔌 🛖 Ⅶ ⚡ 🚲

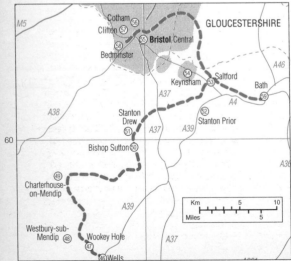

Westbury-sub-Mendip 48

National Grid Ref: ST5048

⋈ ⍟ Westbury Inn

Lana Hollow Farm, The Hollow, Westbury-sub-Mendip, Wells, Somerset, BA5 1HH.
Tel: **01749 870635**
D: £20.00-£22.00
S: £22.00-£25.00.
Open: All Year (not Xmas/New Year)
Beds: 1T 2D
Baths: 3 En
🖢 🅿 (3) ⬦⍟ 🛏 📺 ▦ Ⓥ ⚹ ♻
Modern farmhouse accommodation on working farm. Gently elevated site offering beautiful views over the moors and Somerset. Lovely comfortable family home. Breakfast room for sole guest use, breakfast served at separate tables. Full English breakfast and a varied menu. (Quiet location.)

Charterhouse-on-Mendip 49

National Grid Ref: ST5055

⍟ New Inn

Warren Farm, Charterhouse-on-Mendip, Blagdon, Bristol, BS40 7XR.
1000 acre sheep farm on the Mendips near Cheddar Gorge.
Tel: **01761 462674**
Mrs Small.
D: £17.00-£17.00
S: £17.00-£17.00.
Open: Jan to Dec
Beds: 1F 1D 1S
Baths: 1 Sh
🖢 🅿 (20) ⬦⍟ 🛏 📺 ▦ Ⓥ ⚹ ♻

Bishop Sutton 50

National Grid Ref: ST5859

⋈ ⍟ Ring Of Bells, Red Lion, Pony and Trap

Centaur, Ham Lane, Bishop Sutton, Bristol, BS39 5TZ.
Actual grid ref: ST585598
Comfortable house, peaceful location, within easy reach Bath, Bristol, Wells, Cheddar.
Grades: ETC 3 Diamond
Tel: **01275 332321** Mrs Warden.
D: £18.00-£19.50 **S:** £16.00-£20.50.
Open: Mar to Oct
Beds: 1F 1T 1S
Baths: 1 En 2 Sh
🖢 🅿 (4) ⍟ 🛏 📺 Ⓥ 🛈 ⚹ ♻

Stanton Drew 51

National Grid Ref: ST5963

⋈ ⍟ Druids Arms

Auden House, Stanton Drew, Bristol, BS39 4DJ.
Actual grid ref: ST598623
Large modern house in attractive village, stone circles, historic toll house.
Tel: **01275 332232** (also fax no)
Mrs Smart.
D: £15.00-£17.50 **S:** £17.50-£17.50.
Open: All Year (not Xmas)
Beds: 2F 1D 1T 1S **Baths:** 1 En
🖢 🅿 (6) ⬦⍟ 🛏 📺 ▦ Ⓥ 🛈 ⚹ ♻

Valley Farm, Sandy Lane, Stanton Drew, Bristol, BS39 4EL.
Modern farmhouse, quiet location, old village with druid stones.
Tel: **01275 332723** Mrs Keel.
D: £19.00-£22.00 **S:** £20.00-£24.00.
Open: All Year (not Xmas)
Beds: 1F 2D **Baths:** 3 En
🖢 🅿 (4) ⬦⍟ 🛏 📺 & Ⓥ 🛈 ⚹

Stanton Prior 52

National Grid Ref: ST6762

⋈ ⍟ Wheatsheaf

Poplar Farm, Stanton Prior, Bath, BA2 9HX.
Spacious C17th farmhouse. Family-run farm. Idyllic village setting.
Grades: ETC 3 Diamond,
AA 3 Diamond
Tel: **01761 470382** (also fax no)
Mrs Hardwick.
D: £20.00-£27.00 **S:** £20.00-£30.00.
Open: All Year (not Xmas)
Beds: 1F 1D 1T
Baths: 2 En
🖢 (4) 🅿 (6) ⬦⍟ 📺 ⚹

Saltford 53

National Grid Ref: ST6866

Long Reach House Hotel, 321 Bath Road, Saltford, Bristol, BS31 1TJ.
Gracious house standing in 2 acres midway between Bath and Bristol.
Grades: ETC 2 Star
Tel: **01225 400500**
Fax no: 01225 400700
D: £22.50-£45.00
S: £45.00-£50.00.
Open: All Year
Beds: 2F 7T 7D 2S
Baths: 18 En
🖢 🅿 ⬦⍟ 🛏 ✕ 🛏 📺 & Ⓥ 🛈 ⚹

Pay B&Bs by cash or cheque and be prepared to pay up front.

Bristol (see over for Bath)

The rest of the way takes you through the hilly country of North Somerset to Saltford, where you join the Bristol and Bath Railway Path and turn towards **Bristol**, the capital city of the West Country. A county in its own right from 1373 until 1974, this status was withdrawn with the creation of the short-lived County of Avon, and reinstated in 1996. Before the rapid industrial development of the Midlands and North of England during the nineteenth century, Bristol was England's second city. It was from here that John Cabot made the first European voyage to North America, setting foot on Newfoundland in 1497 - the Cabot Tower in Brandon Hill Park gives panoramic views in all directions. St Mary Redcliffe, Elizabeth I's favourite church, is an outstanding perpendicular-style edifice with a famous nineteenth-century spire. In the seventeenth and eighteenth centuries the city's shady wealth came from the slave trade, as the principal port shipping West African captives to America before this mantle of shame passed to Liverpool. Bristol is most notable for the engineering achievements of Isambard Kingdom Brunel, whose original railway line from London Paddington still operates into Temple Meads Station - the terminus is a surviving Brunel design. Brunel was also responsible for the SS Great Britain, the first large iron passenger ship in the world, which stands in the dry dock; and outstandingly the Clifton Suspension Bridge, magnificently spanning the Avon Gorge west of town. Nowadays the city has a thriving black community; the St Paul's Carnival in early July is Bristol's answer to London's Notting Hill Carnival. The redeveloped quayside has two Arts Centres, the Watershed and the Arnolfini.

Bath

From Saltford an alternative route takes you to the small and lovely city of **Bath**, a World Heritage Site which boasts the stately Georgian houses of the Royal Crescent, the fifteenth-century perpendicular Bath Abbey, with its airy stone vault, and the Roman baths, still fed by a hot spring, covered by a Victorian pillared complex. Part of the Roman complex was a temple to Sulis Minerva, a deity combined from the Roman Minerva and Sul, the local Celtic god of the spa.

Keynsham 54

National Grid Ref: ST6568

🍴 🍺 The Talbot

Fiorita, 91 Bath Road, Keynsham, Bristol, BS31 1SR.
Warm welcome, comfortable family home midway between Bristol and Bath.
Tel: **0117 986 3738** (also fax no)
Mrs Poulter.
D: £14.50-£16.00 **S:** £16.00-£18.00.
Open: Jan to Dec
Beds: 1D 1T
Baths: 1 En 1 Sh
🛇 🄿 (4) ⅏ 🗆 🛏 🔥 🎹 Ⓥ ⚡ ⚲

Bristol Central 55

National Grid Ref: ST6075

▲ *Bristol Youth Hostel, Hayman House, 14 Narrow Quay, Bristol, BS1 4QA.*
Actual grid ref: ST586725
Tel: **0117 922 1659**
Under 18: £8.50 **Adults:** £12.50
Self-catering facilities, Television, Showers, Laundry facilities, Lounge, Games room, Cycle store, Evening meal at 6.00-7.00pm, Kitchen facilities, Breakfast available, Luggage store, Credit cards accepted
With views over the waterways, this hostel has been sympathetically and imaginatively restored to create a relaxing yet cosmopolitan atmosphere.

S = Price range for a single person in a room

Bristol Cotham 56

National Grid Ref: ST5874

Arches Hotel, 132 Cotham Brow, Cotham, Bristol, BS6 6AE.
Actual grid ref: ST588745
Friendly, non-smoking city centre hotel, close to shops and restaurants. **Grades:** ETC 3 Diamond
Tel: **0117 924 7398** (also fax no)
Mr Lambert.
D: £21.50-£25.50 **S:** £24.50-£37.00.
Open: All Year (not Xmas)
Beds: 3F 2D 1T 3S
Baths: 4 En 2 Sh
🛇 (6) ⅏ 🗆 🛏 🔥 🎹 Ⓥ ⚡

Bristol Clifton 57

National Grid Ref: ST5674

Downs View Guest House, 38 Upper Belgrave Road, Clifton, Bristol, BS8 2XN.
Centrally situated. Overlooking Durdham Down. Near Zoo and Clifton Suspension Bridge.
Grades: ETC 3 Diamond
Tel: **0117 973 7046** Ms Cox.
Fax no: 0117 973 8169
D: £22.50-£27.50 **S:** £30.00-£35.00.
Open: All Year (not Xmas)
Beds: 2F 4D 3T 6S **Baths:** 7 En 2 Sh
🛇 🗆 🛏 🔥 🎹 Ⓥ

Bristol Bedminster 58

National Grid Ref: ST5771

Maison George, 10 Greville Road, Southville, Bristol, BS3 1LL.
Large Victorian townhouse within walking distance of city centre.
Grades: ETC 2 Diamond
Tel: **0117 963 9416** Mr Evans.
Fax no: 0117 953 5760
D: £20.00-£30.00 **S:** £20.00-£30.00.
Open: All Year
Beds: 1F 1D 2T 1S **Baths:** 2 Sh
🛇 ⅏ 🗆 🛏 🔥 🎹 Ⓥ

Bath 59

National Grid Ref: ST7464

🍴 🍺 Royal Oak, Dolphin, Wheelwrights Arms, Old Crown, Huntsman, George, Devonshire Arms, Sportsman, Waldergrave Arms, Bear, Park Tavern, Rose & Crown, Weston Walk, Boathouse, Lambridge Harvester,

▲ *Bath Youth Hostel, Bathwick Hill, Bath, Somerset, BA2 6JZ.*
Actual grid ref: ST766644
Tel: **01225 465674**
Under 18: £7.75
Adults: £11.00
Self-catering facilities, Television, Showers, Shop, Laundry facilities, Lounge, Drying room, Security lockers, Cycle store, Evening meal at 6.00 to 8.00pm, Kitchen facilities, Breakfast available, Credit cards accepted
Handsome Italianate mansion, set in beautiful, secluded gardens, with views of historic city and surrounding hills.

Bailbrook Lodge, 35-37 London Road West, Bath, BA1 7HZ.
Grades: ETC 3 Diamond, AA 3 Diamond
Tel: **01225 859090** Mrs Sexton.
Fax no: 01225 852299
D: £30.00-£40.00 **S:** £39.00-£50.00
Open: All Year
Beds: 4F 4D 4T
Baths: 12 En
🛇 🄿 (14) ⅏ 🗆 🗡 🛏 🔥 🎹 Ⓥ ⚡ ⚲
A warm welcome is assured at Bailbrook Lodge, an imposing Georgian House set it its own gardens. The elegant period bedrooms (some four posters) offer ensuite facilities, TV and hospitality trays. Private parking. 1.5 miles from Bath centre. Close to M4.

Sarnia, 19 Combe Park, Weston, Bath, BA1 3NR.
Actual grid ref: ST730656
Grades: AA 4 Diamond
Tel: **01225 424159**
Mr & Mrs Fradley.
Fax no: 01225 337689
D: £25.00-£32.50
S: £30.00-£40.00.
Open: All Year (not Xmas/New Year)
Beds: 1F 1D 1T
Baths: 2 En 1 Pr
🛇 🄿 (3) ⅏ 🗆 🛏 🔥 🎹 Ⓥ 🕯 ⚡ ⚲
Superb bed & breakfast in large Victorian home, easy reach of town centre. Spacious bedrooms, private facilities, newly decorated, attractively furnished. Breakfast in sunny dining room, English, Continental and vegetarian menus, home made jams, marmalades, comfortable lounge, secluded garden, private parking & children welcome.

Dene Villa, 5 Newbridge Hill, Bath, BA1 3PW.
Victorian family-run guest house, warm welcome is assured.
Tel: **01225 427676**
Mrs Surry.
Fax no: 01225 482684
D: £20.00-£22.50
S: £19.00-£22.00.
Open: All Year
Beds: 1F 1D 1T 1S
Baths: 3 En
🛇 (3) 🄿 (4) 🔥 🎹 Ⓥ ⚡ ⚲

Koryu B&B, 7 Pulteney Gardens, Bath, Somerset, BA2 4HG.
Tel: **01225 337642** (also fax no)
Mrs Shimizu.
D: £22.00-£25.00
S: £22.00-£25.00.
Open: All Year
Beds: 1F 2D 2T 2S
Baths: 5 En 2 Sh
🛇 🄿 (2) ⅏ 🗆 🗡 🔥 🎹 Ⓥ ⚲
Completely renovated Victorian home run by a young Japanese lady, extremely clean, delicious breakfasts with wide menu, beautiful linens; a bright, cheerful and welcoming house. Abbey and Roman baths 5 mins, gorgeous Kennet and Avon canal 2 mins.

Wentworth House Hotel, *106 Bloomfield Road, Bath, BA2 2AP.*
Grades: AA 2 Star, RAC 4 Diamond Sparkling
Tel: 01225 339193 Mrs Boyle.
Fax no: 01225 310460
D: £25.00-£47.50 **S:** £40.00-£60.00.
Open: All Year
Beds: 2F 12D 2T 2S
Baths: 17 En 1 Pr
🛏 (5) 🅿 (20) 🖵 🕇 ✕ 🎍 🎹 �🛢 🖂 ✦ ♿

A Victorian mansion 15 minutes' walk from the city. Quiet location with large garden and car park. Heated swimming pool, licensed restaurant and cocktail bar. Golf and walks nearby. Lovely rooms, some with four-poster beds and conservatories.

Blairgowrie House, *55 Wellsway, Bath, BA2 4RT.*
Fine late Victorian Residence operating as a privately owned family-run guest house.
Grades: AA 4 Diamond
Tel: 01225 332266 Mr Roberts.
Fax no: 01225 484535
D: £27.50-£30.00 .
Open: All Year
Beds: 1T 2D
Baths: 2 En 1 Pr
🛏 🅿 ✘ 🖵 🎍 🎹 Ⓥ ✦ ♿

Marlborough House, *1 Marlborough Lane, Bath, BA1 2NQ.*
Grades: ETC 4 Diamond, AA 4 Diamond
Tel: 01225 318175 Dunlop.
Fax no: 01225 466127
D: £32.50-£47.50
S: £45.00-£75.00.
Open: All Year
Beds: 2F 1T 3D 1S
Baths: 7 En
🛏 🅿 ✘ 🖵 🕇 ✕ 🎍 🎹 Ⓥ ⓘ ✦ ♿

An enchanting Victorian small hotel in the heart of Georgian Bath, exquisitely furnished, but run in a friendly and informal style. Specialising in organic vegetarian world cuisine. Our central location, gorgeous rooms, and unique menu make Marlborough House truly special.

Cranleigh, *159 Newbridge Hill, Bath, N E Somerset, BA1 3PX.*
Grades: AA 4 Diamonds
Tel: 01225 310197
Mr Poole.
Fax no: 01225 423143
D: £33.00-£40.00
S: £45.00-£55.00.
Open: All Year (not Xmas)
Beds: 3F 2T 4D
Baths: 8 En
🛏 (5) 🅿 (5) ✘ 🖵 🎍 🎹 Ⓥ ✦

Charming Victorian house a short distance from the city centre. Spacious bedrooms, most with country views, offer comfort and quality. Imaginative breakfasts served in elegant dining room include fresh fruit salad and scrambled eggs with smoked salmon.

The Old Red House, *37 Newbridge Road, Bath, BA1 3HE.*
A romantic Victorian gingerbread house with stained glass windows, comfortable bedrooms, superbly cooked breakfasts.
Grades: AA 3 Diamond
Tel: 01225 330464
Fax no: 01225 331661
D: £22.00-£33.00
S: £30.00-£45.00.
Open: Mar to Dec
Beds: 1F 4D 1T 1S
Baths: 3 En 1 Pr 1 Sh
🛏 (4) 🅿 (4) ✘ 🖵 🕇 🎍 🎹 Ⓥ ♿

The Albany Guest House, *24 Crescent Gardens, Bath, BA1 2NB.*
Grades: ETC 4 Diamond, Silver
Tel: 01225 313339
Mrs Wotley.
D: £17.00-£25.00 **S:** £22.00-£25.00.
Open: All Year (not Xmas/New Year)
Beds: 2D 1T 2S
Baths: 1 En 1 Sh
🛏 (5) 🅿 (3) ✘ 🖵 🎍 🎹 Ⓥ

Jan & Bryan assure you of a warm welcome to their Victorian home. Only five minutes walk to the city centre - Roman Baths, Abbey, Royal Crescent etc. Delicious English or vegetarian breakfast. Imaginatively decorated rooms and first class service.

3 Thomas Street, *Walcot, Bath, Somerset, BA1 5NW.*
Charming Georgian house convenient to all city amenities and shops.
Grades: ETC 3 Diamond
Tel: 01225 789540 Ms Saunders.
D: £20.00-£22.50 **S:** £20.00-£22.50.
Open: All Year (not Xmas)
Beds: 2T
Baths: 1 En 1 Sh
✘ 🖵 🎍 🎹 Ⓥ

Wellsway Guest House, *51 Wellsway, Bath, BA2 4RS.*
Edwardian house near Alexandra Park. Easy walks to city centre.
Grades: ETC 2 Diamond
Tel: 01225 423434
Mrs Strong.
D: £18.00-£20.00
S: £20.00-£20.00.
Open: All Year
Beds: 1F 1D 1T 1S
Baths: 4 Sh
🛏 🅿 (4) 🖵 🕇 🎹 ✦ ♿

Flaxley Villa, *9 Newbridge Hill, Bath, BA1 3PW.*
Comfortable Victorian house near Royal Crescent. 15 minute walk to centre.
Grades: ETC 3 Diamond
Tel: 01225 313237
Mrs Cooper.
D: £20.00-£25.00
S: £18.00-£36.00.
Open: All Year
Beds: 3D 1T 1S
Baths: 3 En
🛏 🅿 (5) 🖵 🎍 🎹 Ⓥ ♿

14 Raby Place, *Bathwick Hill, Bath, Somerset, BA2 4EH.*
Charming Georgian terraced house with beautiful interior rooms.
Grades: ETC 4 Diamond
Tel: 01225 465120 Mrs Guy.
Fax no: 01225 465283
D: £22.50-£25.00 **S:** £25.00-£35.00.
Open: All Year
Beds: 1F 2D 1T 1S
Baths: 3 En 2 Pr
🛏 ✘ 🖵 🎍 🎹 Ⓥ ♿

Forres House, *172 Newbridge Road, Bath, BA1 3LE.*
A warm welcome, comfortable bed and big breakfast awaits you.
Grades: ETC 3 Diamond
Tel: 01225 427698 Jones.
D: £20.00-£25.00 **S:** £30.00-£35.00.
Open: All Year
Beds: 2F 1T 2D
Baths: 5 En
🛏 🅿 (5) ✘ 🖵 🎍 🎹 Ⓥ

Cherry Tree Villa, *7 Newbridge Hill, Bath, Somerset, BA1 3PW.*
Small friendly Victorian home 1 mile from city centre.
Grades: ETC 3 Diamond
Tel: 01225 331671 Ms Goddard.
D: £18.00-£24.00 **S:** £20.00-£30.00.
Open: All Year (not Xmas/New Year)
Beds: 1F 1D 1S
Baths: 1 Sh
🛏 (4) 🅿 🖵 🎍 🎹 Ⓥ ✦ ♿

No 2 Crescent Gardens, *Upper Bristol Road, Bath, BA1 2NA.*
Beautiful B&B in the heart of Bath. Warm welcome.
Grades: ETC 4 Diamond
Tel: 01225 331186 Mr Bez.
D: £19.00-£25.00 **S:** £19.00-£25.00.
Open: All Year (not Xmas/New Year)
Beds: 1F 3T 3D
Baths: 3 En 1 Sh
✘ 🖵 🎍 🎹 Ⓥ

Grove Lodge, *11 Lambridge , Bath, BA1 6BJ.*
Elegant, Georgian villa, large rooms with views.
Tel: 01225 310860 Miles.
Fax no: 01225 429630
D: £25.00-£30.00 **S:** £30.00-£35.00.
Open: All Year (not Xmas/New Year)
Beds: 1F 1T 2D 1S
Baths: 3 Pr
🛏 (6) ✘ 🖵 🎍 🎹 Ⓥ ⓘ ♿

Ashley House, *8 Pulteney Gardens, Bath, BA2 4HG.*
Actual grid ref: ST757646
Comfortable Victorian house, level walk to attractions/stations.
Grades: ETC 3 Diamond
Tel: 01225 425027
Mrs Pharo.
D: £23.00-£33.00 **S:** £25.00-£30.00.
Open: All Year
Beds: 1F 4D 1T 1S
Baths: 5 Pr 2 Sh
🛏 ✘ 🖵 🎍 🎹 Ⓥ ⓘ

Westerlea, *87 Greenway Lane,*
Bath, BA2 4LN.
Georgian style house, large
gardens, friendly, ensuite
accommodation, cars garaged.
Grades: ETC 4 Diamond
Tel: 01225 311543 (also fax no)
D: £27.50-£37.50 **S:** £45.00-£65.00.
Open: All Year (not Xmas)
Beds: 2D
Baths: 2 En
✥ (12) 🅿 (2) ⌿ 🗆 ⅓ 🏃 🖢 🎹 ⚲ 🚲

Georgian Guest House,
34 Henrietta Street, Bath, BA2 6LR.
Situated just 2 mins' walk to city
centre in a peaceful location.
Grades: ETC 3 Diamond
Tel: 01225 424103 Mr Kingwell.
Fax no: 01225 425279
D: £30.00-£35.00 **S:** £30.00-£50.00.
Open: All Year (not Xmas)
Beds: 7D 2T 2S
Baths: 7 En 1 Sh
✥ ⌿ 🗆 🖢 🎹 �v 🚲

The Terrace Guest House,
3 Pulteney Terrace, Bath, BA2 4HJ.
Mid-terrace house, 7 minutes from
city centre and railway station.
Tel: 01225 316578 Mrs Gould.
D: £16.00-£17.50 **S:** £18.00-£20.00.
Open: All Year (not Xmas)
Beds: 1D 1T
Baths: 1 Sh
✥ (6) 🗆 🖢 🎹 �v ⚲ 🚲

Joanna House, *5 Pulteney Avenue,*
Bath, BA2 4HH.
City centre Victorian house near
railway, Kennet and Avon canal.
Tel: 01225 335246 Mr House.
D: £16.00-£19.00 **S:** £15.00-£18.00.
Open: All Year
Beds: 1F 1D 1T 1S
✥ ⌿ 🗆 🖢 🎹 �v

Brinsley Sheridan Guest House,
95 Wellsway, Bearflat, Bath,
BA2 4RU.
Lovely friendly guest house only
short walk from city centre.
Tel: 01225 429562
Fax no: 01225 429616
D: £17.50-£25.00 **S:** £17.50-£30.00.
Open: All Year
Beds: 1F 2D 1T
Baths: 1 En 1 Pr 2 Sh
✥ ⌿ 🗆 🖢 🎹 �v 🚲

Kinlet Guest House, *99 Wellsway,*
Bath, BA2 4RA.
Actual grid ref: ST745636
Home from home. Friendly,
comfortable, easy walk into the
city.
Tel: 01225 420268 (also fax no)
Mrs Bennett.
D: £19.00-£20.00 **S:** £22.00-£27.00.
Open: All Year
Beds: 1F 1D 1S
Baths: 1 Sh
✥ ⌿ 🗆 🖢 🎹 �v 🖊 ⚲ 🚲

Cairngorm, *3 Gloucester Road,*
Lower Swainswick, Bath, BA1 7BH.
Charming detached home with
beautiful views over city and
countryside.
Tel: 01225 429004
Mrs Biggs.
D: £16.50-£20.00 **S:** £18.00.
Open: All Year (not Xmas)
Beds: 2D 1T
Baths: 3 En
✥ (2) 🅿 (3) ⌿ 🗆 🖢 🎹 ⅗ �v ⚲ 🚲

Glan y Dwr, *14 Newbridge Hill,*
Bath, BA1 3PU.
Personal attention to ensure you
have a comfortable stay in Bath.
Tel: 01225 317521
D: £16.00-£24.00 **S:** £18.00-£35.00
Open: All Year
Beds: 2D 1T 3S
Baths: 1 En 1 Pr 1 Sh
✥ (11) 🅿 (3) ⌿ ⅓ 🖢 🎹 ⅗ �v ⚲ 🚲

Cedar Lodge, *13 Lambridge*
London Road, Bath, BA1 6BJ.
Come, stay, enjoy. Welcoming,
comfortable lovely, well-placed
period house.
Tel: 01225 423468
Mr & Mrs Beckett.
D: £25.00 **S:** £30.00.
Open: All Year
Beds: 1T 2D
Baths: 2 En 1 Pr
✥ (10) 🅿 (6) ⌿ 🗆 🖢 🎹 �v ⚲ 🚲

BRITAIN: BED & BREAKFAST

The essential guide to B&Bs in England, Scotland & Wales

The Bed & Breakfast is one of the great British institutions. Like Fish & Chips, it's known by people around the world. But you don't have to be a tourist to enjoy this traditional accommodation. Whether you're travelling, on holiday, away on business or just escaping from it all, the B&B is a great value alternative to expensive hotels and a world away from camping and caravanning.

Stilwell's Britain: Bed & Breakfast 2001 is the most comprehensive guide of its kind, containing over 7,750 entries listed by country, county and location, in England, Scotland and Wales. Each entry includes room rates, facilities, Tourist Board grades and a brief description of the B&B and its location and surroundings.

Stilwell's Britain: Bed & Breakfast 2001: The indispensable guide to great value accommodation:

Private houses, country halls, farms, cottages, inns, small hotels and guest houses

Over 7,750 entries
Average price £19 per person per night
All official grades shown
Local maps
Pubs serving hot evening meals shown
Tourist Information Centres listed
Handy size for easy packing

£9.95 from all good bookstores (ISBN 1-900861-22-4) or £11.95 (inc p&p) from Stilwell Publishing, 59 Charlotte Road, London EC2A 3QW (020 7739 7179)

Sustrans White Rose Cycle Route

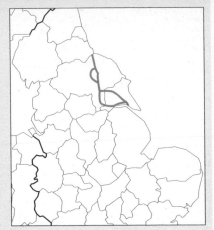

The **White Rose Cycle Route** is a new section of the developing National Cycle Network, running on traffic-free paths and traffic-calmed roads through 120 miles of the varied landscape of eastern Yorkshire from the Humber to the Tees, skirting the North York Moors National Park towards the northern end. It links three of Yorkshire's major cities – from Hull it takes two alternative routes to York before heading north to Middlesbrough – whilst avoiding the industrial west of the region. At the southern end of the route you can join the **Hull to Harwich Cycle Route**. The route is clearly signposted by blue direction signs with a cycle silhouette and the number 65 in a red rectangle (the northern alternative route from Hull to York is 66).

The route west out of **Hull** skirts the southern end of the gentle limestone Yorkshire Wolds before joining the Trans Pennine Trail at Laxton. This pioneering new project is the first British multi-purpose long distance route, catering for cyclists, walkers, horseriders and people with disabilities; it is also a section of the E8 European Long Distance Path (Kerry to Istanbul). After you have followed the TPT through the market towns of **Howden** and **Selby**, a railway path leads to **York**. The alternative route to York, the National Cycle Network's very own Route 66, crosses the Wolds and visits a chain of picturesque Yorkshire market towns – **Beverley, Market Weighton, Pocklington** and **Stamford Bridge**. A leisurely, level stretch takes you through the Vale of York to **Easingwold**, before you wend your way through the lower-lying hills of the heather-clad North York Moors and the villages of **Coxwold, Kilburn, Sutton-under-Whitestonecliffe** and **Cowesby**. An alternative route from Easingwold leads through the villages of Helperby and Dalton to the small market town of **Thirsk**, before rejoining the main route. Now you undertake the somewhat steeper climb over Osmotherley Moor and descent to Cod Beck Reservoir and then **Swainby**. From here it's a more-or-less gentle descent through Hutton Rudby, Maltby and Stainton, and into central **Middlesbrough**.

The indispensable **official route map and guide** for the route is available from Sustrans, 35 King Street, Bristol BS1 4DZ, tel 0117-926 8893, fax 0117-929 4173, @ £5.99 (+ £2.00 p&p).

Maps: Ordnance Survey 1:50,000 Landranger series: 93, 99, 100, 105, 106, 107

Trains: Hull, York, Middlesbrough, Selby and Beverley are all served by main line train services, as are Thirsk and Northallerton, both of which have link routes to the main route.

Hull   1

National Grid Ref: TA0929

🍴 🍺 Hanorth Arms, The Zoological

Allandra Hotel, *5 Park Avenue, Hull, HU5 3EN.*
Grades: ETC 2 Diamond
Tel: **01482 493349** Fax: 01482 492680
D: £19.50-£19.50 **S:** £26.00-£26.00.
Open: All Year
Beds: 2F 1T 7D **Baths:** 10 En
🛇 🅿 (5) 🖵 ❅ ✕ 🍴 🎱 🎥 ⚲
Charming Victorian town house hotel, family run, close to all amenities. Delightfully situated, convenient universities and town centre opposite pleasant parking. All rooms ensuite.

Beck House , *628 Beverley High Road, Hull, HU6 7LL.*
Traditional town house, B&B, fine accommodation, close to university etc.
Tel: **01482 445468** Mrs Aylwin.
D: £19.00-£22.00 **S:** £19.00-£22.00.
Open: All Year
Beds: 3D 3S
Baths: 1 En 1 Sh
🛇 🅿 (4) 🖵 🎱 🎥 ⚲

D = Price range per person sharing in a double room

S = Price range for a single person in a room

The Tree Guest House, *132 Sunny Bank, Spring Bank West, Hull, HU3 1LE.*
Close to the city centre and universities. Special rates available.
Tel: **01482 448822**
Fax no: 01482 442911
D: £15.00-£18.00 **S:** £10.00-£24.00.
Open: All Year
Beds: 1F 3D 3S **Baths:** 3 En 2 Sh
🛇 🅿 🖵 ❅ 🎱 🎥 ♿ 🎥

Marlborough Hotel, 232 Spring Bank, Hull, HU3 1LU.
Family run, near city centre.
Tel: **01482 224479** (also fax no)
Mr Norman.
D: £17.00 **S:** £17.00.
Open: All Year
Beds: 2 F 2D 7T 5S
Baths: 3 Sh
ॐ ᴾ (10) ⌷ ⼧ ✗ Ⅲℬ.

Hessle 2

National Grid Ref: TA0326

⊯ ⊲ Country Park Inn, The Hase

Redcliffe House, Redcliffe Road, Hessle, E Yorks, HU13 0HA.
Beautifully appointed, riverside location close to Humber Bridge, Hull, Beverley.
Grades: ETC 4 Diamond
Tel: **01482 648655** Skiba.
D: £20.00-£20.00
S: £20.00-£35.00.
Open: All Year
Beds: 2D 2T 1S
Baths: 4 En 1 Sh
ॐ ᴾ (6) ⌷ ⽥ Ⅲℬ. Ⅴ ⅰ ⼁ ⼯ ᴔ

D = Price range per person

sharing in a double room

North Ferriby 3

National Grid Ref: SE9826

B&B at 103, 103 Ferriby High Road, North Ferriby, East Yorks, HU14 3LA.
Comfortable house, large garden, overlooking river near Humber Bridge and Hull.
Grades: ETC 3 Diamond
Tel: **01482 633637** Mrs Simpson.
D: £15.00-£15.00 **S:** £15.00-£15.00.
Open: All Year
Beds: 1D 1T 1S **Baths:** 1 Sh
ॐ (7) ᴾ (2) ⼁⌷ ⼧ ✗ ⽥ Ⅲℬ. Ⅴ ⅰ ⼁ ᴔ

Selby 4

National Grid Ref: SE6132

⊯ ⊲ Londesborough, Grey Horse

Hazeldene Guest House, 32-34 Brook Street, Selby, N. Yorks, YO8 4AR.
Attractive period house, featuring spacious ensuite rooms, market town location.
Grades: ETC 2 Diamond,
AA 2 Diamond
Tel: **01757 704809** Mr Leake.
Fax no: 01757 709300
D: £18.00-£22.00 **S:** £21.00-£30.00.
Open: All Year (not Xmas)
Beds: 3D 3T 2S **Baths:** 4 En 2 Sh
ॐ (12) ᴾ (5) ⼁⌷ ⽥ Ⅲℬ. Ⅴ ⼁ ᴔ

Kingston-upon-Hull is the major port of the Humber (see under *Sustrans Hull to Harwich* for further information).

Howden Minster is a large thirteenth to fifteenth-century church, the tower and nave imposingly intact, the choir and chapter house atmospherically ruined.

Beverley, county town of the East Riding of Yorkshire, is an attractive historic market town with elegant Georgian houses and cobbled streets, most famous for its minster. A cathedral in every respect but the lack of an episcopal seat, this formidable edifice was built over the course of several centuries up to the fifteenth, when it was completed by Hawksmoor's splendid west front, whose twin towers crown the views from miles around.

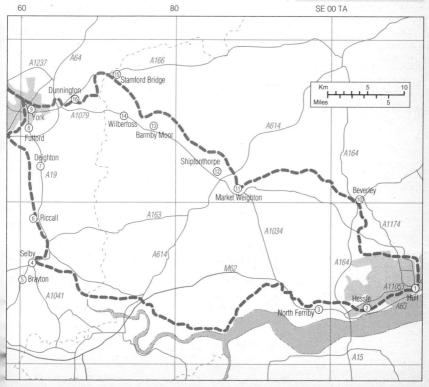

Brayton 5

National Grid Ref: SE6030

West Cottage, Mill Lane, Brayton, Selby, N. Yorks, YO8 9LB.
Small family-run B&B set in a delightful cottage garden with grass tennis court.
Tel: **01757 213318** (also fax no) Mrs Fletcher.
D: £20.00S: £25.00.
Open: All Year
Beds: 1F 1T
Baths: 2 En
♿ (12) �🅿 (5) �🍽 🛏 🖤 🎵 🅥

Riccall 6

National Grid Ref: SE6237

🍽 🍺 Grey Mare, Hare & Hounds, Drovers

South Newlands Farm, Selby Road, Riccall, York, YO19 6QR.
Friendly people, comfortable beds, ample fresh cooked food. Well located.
Grades: ETC 3 Diamond
Tel: **01757 248203** Mrs Swann.
Fax no: 01757 249450
D: £18.00-£20.00 **S:** £20.00-£22.00.
Open: All Year
Beds: 1F 1D 1T
Baths: 2 En
♿ (3) 🅿 🍽 🛏 🔥 ✕ 🎵 🖤 ⚿ 🅥 🅰 ✦
🐾

Deighton (York) 7

National Grid Ref: SE6244

🍽 🍺 White Swan

Grimston House, Deighton, York, YO19 6HB.
Tel: **01904 728328**
Fax no: 01904720093
D: £48.00-£50.00
S: £30.00-£32.00.
Open: All Year
Beds: 1F 1T 5D
Baths: 5 En
♿ 🅿 🍽 🛏 🔥 🎵 🖤 🅥 ✦ 🐾
Built in the 1930s, Grimston House is an attractive place standing within a walled garden. Easy reach of York and on good bus route. Good local pub with bar meals.

Fulford 8

National Grid Ref: SE6149

🍽 🍺 Saddle, Plough

The Old Registry, 12 Main Street, Fulford, York, YO10 4PQ.
Family-run period house. Easy access to York and University.
Tel: **01904 628136**
Mr Beckett.
D: £17.00-£25.00
S: £17.00-£25.00.
Open: All Year (not Xmas)
Beds: 2D 1T 2S
Baths: 4 En
♿ 🅿 (6) 🍽 🛏 🎵 🖤 🅥

Alfreda Guest House, 61 Heslington Lane, Fulford, York, YO10 4HN.
Edwardian residence, large grounds. Car park security lighting/camera.
Tel: **01904 631698**
Mr Bentley.
Fax no: 01904 211215
D: £22.00-£27.00
S: £25.00-£50.00.
Open: All Year (not Xmas)
Beds: 4F 3D 3T
Baths: 8 En 2 Sh
♿ 🅿 🍽 🔥 🛏 🎵 🖤 🅰 ✦ 🐾

York 9

National Grid Ref: SE5951

🍽 🍺 BoothamTavern, Churchill's, Cross Keys, Doormouse, Elliott's, Exhibition, Four Alls, Gimcrack, Golden Slipper, Grange Hotel, Haxby Court, Hole In The Wall, Mason's Arms, Ye Olde Punch Bowl, Plough, Plunkett's, Royal Oak, Rubicon, Shoulder Of Mutton, Tankard, Tom Cobley's, Wagon & Horses, Walnut Tree, Windmill, York Arms

🔺 *York International Youth Hostel, Water End, Clifton, York, YO30 6LP.*
Actual grid ref: SE589528
Tel: **01904 653147**
Under 18: £11.50
Adults: £15.50
Self-catering facilities, Television, Licensed bar, Laundry facilities, Lounge, Games room, Cycle store, Parking, Evening meal at 5.30-7.30pm, Kitchen facilities, Breakfast available, Luggage store, Credit cards accepted
Comfortable Victorian house with spacious grounds in a peaceful location just a walk along the river from the city. The hostel has its own restaurant.

🔺 *York Youth Hotel, 11/17 Bishophill Senior, York, YO1 6EF.*
Actual grid ref: SE601515
Tel: **01904 625904**
Under 18: £11.00 **Adults:** £12.00
Self-catering facilities, Television, Showers, Licensed bar, Central heating, Shop, Laundry facilities, Lounge, Dining room, Games room, Drying room, Cycle store, Parking, Evening meal at for groups only, No smoking
Large Georgian house in city centre location.

🔺 *The Racecourse Centre, Tadcaster Road, York, YO24.*
Tel: **01904 636553**
Under 18: £17.50 **Adults:** £18.50
Television, Showers, Central heating, Lounge, Dining room, Games room, Grounds available for games, Security lockers, Cycle store, Parking, Evening meal at 6pm, Facilities for disabled people
Easily accessible by road and rail, the centre provides excellent value budget accommodation for groups of all ages throughout the year. 134 beds in single, twin and family rooms. Cafeteria style dining room and a large recreation room suitable for receptions, meetings and leisure. Excellent coach/car parking. GROUPS ONLY.

🔺 *Micklegate House Youth Hotel, 88-90 Micklegate, York, YO1 6JX.*
Tel: **01904 627720**
Under 18: £9.00 **Adults:** £9.00
Self-catering facilities, Television, Showers, Licensed bar, Central heating, Shop, Laundry facilities, Lounge, Dining room, Games room, Drying room, Security lockers, Cycle store, Evening meal at
1752 Georgian mansion, located in the heart of medieval York.

The city of **York** has a rich cultural history dating back through centuries. From the ashes of Roman Eboracum came Anglo-Saxon Eoforwic; but it was Viking Jorvik that gave the city its modern name. At the excellent Jorvik Viking Centre you can take a train back through time and visit a street reconstructed for all the senses, complete with Viking chatter and smells (yes, really). It is striking that the reconstruction is situated immediately next to the specific excavation on which it is based. Among the city's numerous other sights is the National Railway Museum, part heavy-duty array of locomotives, part reconstruction of life on railways past. This includes Queen Victoria's carriage, from which the new-fangled electric lights were stripped out by royal command – but the electric bell for summoning of servants somehow escaped censure. York Minster is the largest European medieval cathedral and the largest Gothic building in Britain. Its superb range of stained glass is impressive for the Big – the Great East Window is the world's largest intact medieval window – and for the Old – dating from as far back as the thirteenth century.

The Hazelwood, *24-25 Portland Street, Gillygate, York,* YO31 7EH.
Grades: ETC 4 Diamond, AA 4 Diamond, RAC 4 Diamond
Tel: **01904 626548**
McNabb.
Fax no: 01904 628032
D: £32.50-£45.00 **S:** £35.00-£80.00.
Open: All Year
Beds: 2F 8D 3T 1S
Baths: 14 En
⚅ (8) 🅿 (10) ⤩ ⬛ ♨ Ⅲ ⓥ
Situated in the very heart of York in an extremely quiet residential area only 400 yards from York Minster & with its own car park, an elegant Victorian townhouse with individually styled ensuite bedrooms. Wide choice of quality breakfasts including vegetarian and croissants and Danish pastries. Non-smoking.

Barrington House, *15 Nunthorpe Avenue, Scarcroft Road, York,* YO23 1PF.
Lovely guesthouse near city centre, racecourse, station, theatres, parking.
Grades: ETC 3 Diamond
Tel: **01904 634539**
D: £17.00-£22.00 **S:** £17.00-£22.00.
Open: All Year (not Xmas/New Year)
Beds: 2F 2T 2D 1S
Baths: 7 En
⚅ ⬛ ♨ Ⅲ & ⓥ ⊶

Holly Lodge, *206 Fulford Road, York,* YO10 4DD.
Grades: ETC 4 Diamond, AA 4 Diamond, RAC 4 Diamond
Tel: **01904 646005**
Mr Gallagher.
D: £29.00-£34.00 **S:** £48.00-£58.00.
Open: All Year
Beds: 1F 3D 1T
Baths: 5 En 5 Pr
⚅ (7) 🅿 ⤩ ⬛ ♨ Ⅲ ⓥ ⊶
Ideally located 10 mins' riverside walk from the centre, convenient for all York's amenities. This fine Georgian building, with comfortable rooms, walled garden and car park, offers a warm welcome. Booking recommended. Located on A19,1.5 miles towards the city from A19/A64 intersection.

Ascot House, *80 East Parade, Heworth, York,* YO31 7YH.
Grades: ETC 4 Diamond
Tel: **01904 426826** Mrs Wood.
Fax no: 01904 431077
D: £21.00-£25.00 **S:** £20.00-£24.00.
Open: All Year (not Xmas)
Beds: 3F 8D 3T 1S
Baths: 12 En 1 Pr 1 Sh
⚅ 🅿 (14) ⬛ ⊁ ♨ Ⅲ ⓥ ⊶
A family-run Victorian villa, built in 1869, with rooms of character and many four-poster or canopy beds. Superb English breakfasts. Fifteen minutes' walk to Jorvik Viking Centre, Castle Museum or York Minster. Residential licence, sauna, private enclosed car park.

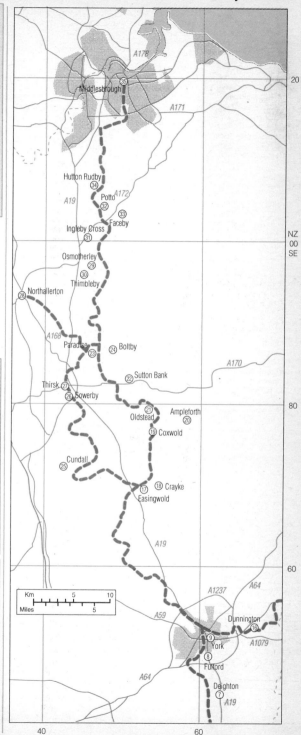

Midway House Hotel, *145 Fulford Road, York, YO10 4HG.*
Grades: ETC 3 Diamond
Tel: **01904 659272** (also fax no)
Armitage.
D: £18.00–£33.00
S: £18.00–£35.00.
Open: All Year
Beds: 4F 8D 1T 1S
Baths: 12 En 2 Sh
🛇 🅿 (14) ⅍🖵 🏃 ▥ �V ⚓ ⅌
Built in 1897, an elegant late-Victorian detached villa close to the city centre, university and minutes from York's bypass. We are totally non-smoking with an informal, friendly atmosphere. Large on-site private garden & secluded gardens.

Cumbria House, *2 Vyner Street, Haxby Road, York, YO31 8HS.*
Beautifully decorated family-run guest house. Private car park. Ideal for city centre & all attractions.
Grades: ETC 3 Diamond,
AA 3 Diamond
Tel: **01904 636817** Mrs Clark.
D: £19.00–£25.00 **S:** £20.00–£25.00.
Open: All Year
Beds: 2F 2D 1T 1S
Baths: 2 En 4 Sh
🛇 🅿 (5) 🖵 🛴 ▥ �V

Feversham Lodge International Guest House, *1 Feversham Crescent, York, YO31 8HQ.*
Grades: ETC 3 Diamond
Tel: **01904 623882** (also fax no)
Mr & Mrs Lutyens-Humfrey.
D: £20.00–£32.00
S: £25.00.
Open: All Year
Beds: 2F 5D 2T 1S
Baths: 7 En 1 Pr 2 Sh
🛇 🅿 (9) ⅍🖵 🛴 ▥ �V
A former C19th Methodist manse with lovely ensuite rooms, including 'Laura Ashley' style honeymoon room with four poster or canopy bed; still retains characteristic original features. York Minster views; fresh home cooked delicious breakfast served. Winter short breaks OK. Japanese/Chinese/Italian/French spoken.

Nunmill House, *85 Bishopthorpe Road, York, YO23 1NX.*
Grades: ETC 4 Diamond,
AA 4 Diamond
Tel: **01904 634047**
Mr & Mrs Whitbourn-Hammond.
Fax no: 01904 655879
D: £25.00–£30.00
S: £4500.00.
Open: Feb to Nov
Beds: 1F 6D 1T
Baths: 7 En 1 Pr
🛇 🅿 (6) ⅍🖵 🛴 ▥ �V ⚓ ⅌
Splendid Victorian house, lovingly furnished & smoke-free, for those looking for comfortable yet affordable accommodation. Easy walk to all attractions. SAE for brochure.

Bowen House, *4 Gladstone Street, Huntington Road, York, YO31 8RF.*
Grades: ETC 3 Diamond
Tel: **01904 636881** Mrs Wood.
Fax no: 01904 338700
D: £18.50–£24.00 **S:** £23.00–£28.00.
Open: All Year (not Xmas)
Beds: 1F 2D 1T 1S
Baths: 2 En 1 Sh
🛇 🅿 (4) ⅍🖵 🏃 🛴 ▥ �V
Small, family-run, Victorian guest house with period furnishings throughout. Excellent traditional and vegetarian breakfasts with free-range eggs and home made preserves. Short stroll to York city centre. Private car park. Non-smoking in all rooms. Brochure available.

Grange Lodge, *52 Bootham Crescent, Bootham, York, YO30 7AH.*
Lovely family-run guest house.
Grades: ETC 1 Diamond
Tel: **01904 621137** Mrs Robinson.
D: £16.00–£22.00 **S:** £18.00–£20.00.
Open: All Year
Beds: 2F 3D 1T 1S
Baths: 1 En 5 Pr 2 Sh
🛇 🅿 🗙 ▥.

Wold View House Hotel, *171-175 Haxby Road, York, YO31 8JL.*
Tel: **01904 632061** (also fax no)
Mr & Mrs Wheeldon.
D: £19.00–£26.00 **S:** £19.00–£26.00.
Open: All Year (not Xmas/New Year)
Beds: 2F 2T 10D 3S **Baths:** 17 En
🛇 🅿 (1) 🖵 🗙 🏃 🛴 ▥ ⅌
Turn of the century hotel, tea and coffee facilities, clock radio alarms, all ensuite, cosy licensed bar, evening meals available, 15 minutes walk York Minster. Handy for touring Moors and East Coast. Near Sustrans cycle track.

Ashbourne House, *139 Fulford Road, York, YO10 4HG.*
Friendly family run Victorian establishment. Providing the highest of standards.
Grades: ETC 4 Diamond,
AA 4 Diamond, RAC 4 Diamond
Tel: **01904 639912**
Mr & Mrs Minns.
Fax no: 01904 631332
D: £20.00–£30.00 **S:** £34.00–£40.00.
Open: All Year (not Xmas/New Year)
Beds: 2F 2T 3D **Baths:** 6 En 1 Pr
🛇 🅿 (6) ⅍🖵 🛴 ▥ �V

St Raphael Guest House, *44 Queen Annes Road, Bootham, York, YO30 7AF.*
Family-run mock Tudor guest house, tastefully decorated.
Grades: ETC 2 Diamond,
AA 2 Diamond, RAC 2 Diamond
Tel: **01904 645028** Mrs Foster.
Fax no: 01904 658788
D: £19.00–£25.00 **S:** £21.00.
Open: All Year
Beds: 3F 2D 1T 2S
Baths: All En
🛇 🅿 (2) 🖵 🏃 🛴 ▥ �V 🛴

Ivy House Farm, *Kexby, York, YO41 5LQ.*
C19th farmhouse, central for York, East Coast, Dales, Herriot country.
Grades: AA 3 Diamond,
RAC 3 Diamond
Tel: **01904 489368** Mrs Daniel.
D: £16.00–£20.00 **S:** £20.00–£22.00.
Open: All Year (not Xmas)
Beds: 1F 1D 1T 1S
Baths: 2 En 1 Sh
🛇 🅿 (10) 🖵 🛴 ▥ �V 🛴

Park View Guest House, *34 Grosvenor Terrace, Bootham, York, YO30 7AG.*
Victorian town house close to centre. Front rooms have views of Minster. **Grades:** ETC 3 Diamond
Tel: **01904 620437** (also fax no)
Mrs Ashton.
D: £22.00–£25.00 **S:** £25.00–£30.00.
Open: All Year (not Xmas)
Beds: 1F 3D 2T 1S **Baths:** 5 En 1 Pr
🛇 ⅍🖵 🛴 ▥ �V

Bay Tree Guest House, *92 Bishopthorpe Rd, York, YO23 1JS.*
Tastefully decorated Victorian town house, ten minutes walk from attractions.
Grades: ETC 3 Diamond
Tel: **01904 659462** (also fax no)
Mr Ridley.
D: £21.00–£24.00 **S:** £22.00–£22.00.
Open: all year (not Xmas)
Beds: 1F 1D 1T 2S
Baths: 2 En 1 Sh
🛇 (1) ⅍🖵 🏃 🛴 ▥ �V 🛴

Georgian Guest House, *35 Bootham, York, YO30 7BT.*
Quality city centre accommodation with car park.
Grades: ETC 3 Diamond,
AA 3 Diamond, RAC 3 Diamond
Tel: **01904 622874** Mr Semple.
Fax no: 01904 635379
D: £18.00–£28.00 **S:** £18.00–£35.00.
Open: All Year (not Xmas)
Beds: 2F 7D 2T 2S
Baths: 11 En 2 Sh
🛇 (5) 🅿 (8) ⅍🖵 🛴 ▥ �V 🛴

Cornmill Lodge, *120 Haxby Road, York, YO31 8JP.*
Vegetarian/vegan guest house. 15 mins' walk York Minster.
Grades: ETC 3 Diamond,
AA 3 Diamond
Tel: **01904 620566** (also fax no)
Mrs Williams.
D: £20.00–£26.00 **S:** £20.00–£26.00.
Open: All Year
Beds: 2D 1T/F 1S **Baths:** 3 En 1 Pr
🛇 🅿 (4) ⅍🖵 🛴 ▥ �V

Newton Guest House, *Neville Street, Haxby Road, York, YO31 8NP.*
Few minutes walk from city. Friendly family run. Non smoking.
Grades: ETC 3 Diamond
Tel: **01904 635627** Mrs Tindall.
D: £19.00–£22.00 **S:** £20.00–£25.00.
Open: All Year (not Xmas)
Beds: 1F 2D 1T 1S **Baths:** 4 En 1 Pr
🛇 🅿 (5) ⅍🖵 🛴 ▥ �V 🛴

Kismet Guest House, 147 Haxby Road, York, YO31 8JW.
Close to city centre, friendly welcome, substantial breakfast. Cleanliness foremost.
Tel: **01904 621056**
Chamberlain & N Summers.
D: £25.00-£30.00
S: £20.00-£25.00.
Open: All Year
Beds: 1F 1T 4D
Baths: 1S
🛇 🅿 (6) ⚡☐✗🍴🎿🚾ⅤＩＩ🚲

Northholme Guest House, 114 Shipton Road, York, YO30 5RN.
Grades: ETC 3 Diamond
Tel: **01904 639132** Liddle.
D: £14.50-£19.00
S: £17.00-£24.00.
Open: All Year (not Xmas)
Beds: 1F 1D 2T 1S
Baths: 3 En 1 Sh
🛇 🅿 (4) ⚡☐🎿🚾Ⅴ⚡🚲
Our family run detached home, in a semi-rural setting, is convenient for York city centre and the ring road. We have comfortable, spacious, ensuite rooms with colour TV and welcome tray. Private parking.

Heworth Court Hotel, 76 Heworth Green, York, YO31 7TQ.
Established recommended hotel. Ample parking, York Minster within 1 mile
Grades: ETC 2 Star, AA 2 Star, RAC 2 Star
Tel: **01904 425156** Mr Smith.
D: £30.00-£52.50 **S:** £46.00-£65.00.
Open: All Year
Beds: 2F 5T 10D 8S
Baths: 25 En
🛇 🅿 (25) ⚡☐✗🍴🚾ⅤＩ

Chimney's Bed and Breakfast, 18 Bootham Cresent, York, YO30 7AH.
Beautiful olde-worlde house, 5 minutes walk from York Minster/city walls.
Grades: ETC 3 Diamond
Tel: **01904 644334**
D: £18.00-£25.00 **S:** £18.00-£25.00.
Open: All Year
Beds: 2T 2D 1S
🛇 (10) ⚡🚾🎿🚲

Bishopgarth Guest House, 3 Southlands Road, Bishopthorpe Road, York, YO23 1NP.
Grades: ETC 3 Diamond
Tel: **01904 635220** Mrs Spreckley.
D: £15.00-£23.00 **S:** £20.00-£46.00.
Open: All Year (not Xmas/New Year)
Beds: 2F 2D 1T
Baths: 5 En 2 Sh
🛇 ⚡☐✗🎿🚾Ⅴ🚲
In a quiet Victorian terrace, just ten minutes pleasant walk from York's historic heart, Bishopgarth offers comfort, cleanliness and excellent home cooking (evening meals available in the winter), unfailing courtesy and a warm Yorkshire welcome from the locally born resident owners.

Sagar B&B The Bungalow, Kexby, York, YO41 5LA.
A modern bungalow, four miles east of York on A1079.
Tel: **01759 380247** Mrs Sagar.
D: £18.00-£18.00 **S:** £20.00-£20.00.
Open: All Year (not Xmas)
Beds: 1D 1T
Baths: 2 En
🛇 🅿 (2) ☐🎿🚾Ⅴ⚡

The Bentley Hotel, 25 Grosvenor Terrace, Bootham, York, YO30 7AG.
Victorian town house overlooking York Minster with personal attention and home-from-home hospitality.
Grades: ETC 4 Diamond
Tel: **01904 644313** (also fax no)
Mr Lefebve.
D: £20.00-£27.00 **S:** £25.00-£30.00.
Open: Feb to Dec
Beds: 3D 1T 2S
Baths: 4 En 1 Sh
🛇 (10) 🅿 (1) ⚡☐🎿🚾Ⅴ🚲

Abbeyfields Guest House, 19 Bootham Terrace, York, YO30 7DH.
Lovely Listed Victorian guest house 5 minutes walk from city centre.
Grades: ETC 3 Diamond
Tel: **01904 636471** (also fax no)
Mr Martin.
D: £24.00-£26.00 **S:** £30.00-£33.00.
Open: Feb to Jan
Beds: 5D 1T 3S
Baths: 8 En 1 Pr
🛇 (12) 🅿 (4) ⚡☐🎿🚾Ⅴ

The Racecourse Centre, Tadcaster Road, York, YO24 1QG.
Superior budget accommodation for groups only. Minimum of 10 people.
Tel: **01904 636553** Mr Patmore.
Fax no: 01904 612815
D: £17.50-£19.50 **S:** £17.50-£24.50.
Open: All Year
Beds: 23F 12T 8S
Baths: 7 Sh
🛇 🅿 (40) ☐✗🚾🚸♿Ⅰ

Chelmsford Place Guest House, 85 Fulford Road, York, YO10 4BD.
Victorian house, 300 yards from river, 5 mins walk to centre.
Grades: ETC 3 Diamond
Tel: **01904 624491**
D: £17.00-£24.00 **S:** £17.00-£38.00.
Open: All Year
Beds: 2F 3D 2T 1S
Baths: 6 En 1 Sh
🛇 🅿 ☐🎿🚾Ⅴ🚲

Ashbury Hotel, 103 The Mount, York, YO24 1AX.
Elegant refurbished Victorian townhouse, close to city centre. Ensuite facilities.
Grades: ETC 3 Diamond
Tel: **01904 647339** (also fax no)
Mrs Richardson.
D: £20.00-£27.50 **S:** £15.00-£25.00.
Open: All Year (not Xmas)
Beds: 1F 3D 1T
Baths: 5 Pr 🛇 🅿 ☐⚡🎿🚾Ⅴ🚲

City Guest House, 68 Monkgate, York, YO31 7PF.
Five minutes' walk to Minster, car park, excellent value.
Tel: **01904 622483**
Mr & Mrs Robinson.
D: £20.00-£27.00
S: £20.00-£27.00.
Open: All Year (not Xmas)
Beds: 1F 4D 1T 1S
Baths: 6 En 1 Pr
🛇 (5) 🅿 (5) ⚡☐🎿🚾Ⅴ

Dairy Guest House, 3 Scarcroft Road, York, YO23 1ND.
Beautiful appointed Victorian house. Tasteful in many ways!
Tel: **01904 639367**
Mr Hunt.
D: £20.00-£25.00 **S:** £30.00-£40.00.
Open: Feb to Dec
Beds: 2F 2D 1T
Baths: 2 Pr 1 Sh
🛇 ⚡🐾🍴🎿🚾♿Ⅴ

The Beckett, 58 Bootham Crescent, Bootham, York, YO30 7AH.
Large Victorian house in city centre near Minster. Great breakfast.
Tel: **01904 644728**
Mrs Brown.
Fax no: 01904 639915
D: £25.00-£27.50 **S:** £23.00-£26.00.
Open: All Year
Beds: 1F 3D 2T 1S
Baths: 5 En 1 Pr 1 Sh
🛇 🅿 ⚡☐🎿🚾Ⅴ

The Hollies, 141 Fulford Road, York, YO10 4HG.
Distinctive Edwardian residence, recently refurbished to provide quality accommodation.
Tel: **01904 634279**
Mrs Wise.
Fax no: 01904 625435
D: £18.00-£28.00
S: £18.00-£27.00.
Open: All Year
Beds: 1F 3D 1S
Baths: 3 En 2 Sh
🛇 (5) 🅿 (5) ⚡☐🎿♿Ⅴ🚲

Foss Bank Guest House, 16 Huntington Road, York, YO31 8RB.
Small family-run Victorian house, 5 minutes walk from York Minster.
Tel: **01904 635548**
D: £17.00-£20.00
S: £18.50-£22.00.
Open: Feb to Dec
Beds: 3D 1T 2S
Baths: 2 En 2 Sh
🛇 🅿 (5) ⚡☐🎿🚾Ⅴ⚡🚲

Gables Guest House, 50 Bootham Crescent, York, YO30 7AH.
Valerie Lapworth extends a warm welcome to our home & historic city.
Tel: **01904 624381** (also fax no)
D: £18.00-£27.00
S: £18.00-£28.00.
Open: All Year
Beds: 1F 2D 2T 1S
Baths: 4 En 2 Sh
🛇 🅿 ☐🐾✗🎿🚾ⅤＩ⚡🚲

Bank House, *9 Southlands Road,*
York, YO23 1NP.
5 minutes' walk to the city centre.
Comfortable Victorian house. Race
course nearby.
Tel: **01904 627803** Mr Farrell.
D: £16.00-£22.00 **S:** £20.00.
Open: All Year
Beds: 7F 2D 2T 3S
Baths: 1 En 7 Pr 7 Sh
⚒ ⅏ ❑ ⅍ ✕ ⚲ 🛏 Ⅶ ⚲ ⚲

Bronte Guesthouse, *22 Grosvenor*
Terrace, Bootham, York, YO30 7AG.
Family-run Victorian guest house,
quietly but conveniently situated
from the historic centre.
Tel: **01904 621066**
Fax no: 01904 653434
D: £23.00-£30.00 **S:** £25.00-£35.00.
Open: All Year (not Xmas)
Beds: 1F 1D 1T 2S
Baths: 5 En
⚒ 🅿 (1) ❑ ⚲ 🛏 Ⅶ ⚲ ⚲

Victoria Villa, *72 Heslington Road,*
York, YO10 5AU.
The Victorian villa guest house is a
beautiful Victorian town house.
Tel: **01904 631647**
D: £15.00-£20.00 **S:** £16.00-£25.00.
Open: All Year
Beds: 1F 3D 1T 1S
Baths: 2 Sh
⚒ 🅿 (1) ❑ 🛏 ⚲ Ⅶ Ⅴ ⚲

York Lodge Guest House,
64 Bootham Crescent, Bootham,
York, YO30 7AH.
Comfortable, relaxing accommoda-
tion, friendly service.
Tel: **01904 654289**
Mr Moore.
D: £20.00-£22.00 **S:** £20.00-£20.00.
Open: All Year
Beds: 2F 3D 2T 1S
Baths: 4 En 2 Sh
⚒ ❑ ⚲ Ⅶ Ⅴ

Dalescroft Guest House,
10 Southlands Road, Bishopthorpe
Road, York, YO23 1NP.
Warm welcome in family-run guest
house, 10 mins from city & race
course.
Tel: **01904 626801**
Mrs Blower.
D: £14.00-£22.00 **S:** £15.00-£20.00.
Open: All Year
Beds: 1F 2D 2T 1S
Baths: 2 En 1 Pr
⚒ ⅏ ❑ 🛏 ✕ ⚲ Ⅶ Ⅴ ⚲

Tower Guest House, *2 Feversham*
Crescent, Wiggington Road, York,
YO31 8HQ.
Friendly family-run guest house,
10 mins walk to city centre, full
English breakfast.
Tel: **01904 655571**
D: £20.00-£25.00
S: £22.00-£30.00.
Open: All Year
Beds: 1F 3D 1T 1S
Baths: 6 En
⚒ 🅿 (6) ⅏ ❑ ✕ ⚲ Ⅶ Ⅴ ⚲ ⚲

Beverley   10

National Grid Ref: TA0440

⚒ ⚲ Rose & Crown, Mokescroft Inn, Hayride,
Queens Head

▲ **Beverley Friary Youth Hostel,**
The Friary, Friar's Lane, Beverley,
East Yorkshire, HU17 0DF.
Actual grid ref: TA038393
Tel: **01482 881751**
Under 18: £5.75 **Adults:** £8.50
Showers, Shop, Lounge, Games
room, Drying room, Cycle store,
Parking, Evening meal at 7.00pm,
Kitchen facilities, Breakfast avail-
able, Credit cards accepted
Restored Dominican friary men-
tioned in the Canterbury Tales and
next to Beverley Minster.

Number One, *1 Woodlands,*
Beverley, E. Yorks, HU17 8BT.
Victorian house, home cooking,
open fires, library, lovely gardens.
Tel: **01482 862752** Mrs King.
D: £18.00-£22.00 **S:** £19.50-£29.00.
Open: All Year
Beds: 1D 1T 1S
Baths: 1 En 1 Sh
⚒ 🅿 (1) ⅏ ❑ 🛏 ✕ ⚲ Ⅶ Ⅴ ⚲ ⚲

Eastgate Guest House, *7 Eastgate,*
Beverley, E. Yorks, HU17 0DR.
Family-run Victorian guest house
close to Beverley Minster and army
museum.
Tel: **01482 868464** Ms Anderson.
Fax no: 01482 871899
D: £15.00-£25.00 **S:** £20.00-£35.00.
Open: All Year (not Xmas)
Beds: 7F 3D 3T 5S
Baths: 7 Pr 3 Sh
⚒ ❑ 🛏 ⚲

All cycleways are
popular: you are
well-advised to
book ahead

Market Weighton   11

National Grid Ref: SE8741

⚒ ⚲ Black Horse

The Gables, *38 Londesborough Rd,*
Market Weighton, York, YO43 3HS.
Actual grid ref: SE877423
Friendly, comfortable, quiet
country house.
Tel: **01430 872255**
Mr & Mrs Reeson.
D: £16.00 **S:** £16.00.
Open: All Year (not Xmas)
Beds: 1D 1T 1S **Baths:** 1 Sh
⚒ 🅿 (5) ❑ 🛏 ⚲ Ⅶ Ⅴ ⚲ ⅏

Shiptonthorpe   12

National Grid Ref: SE8543

⚒ ⚲ Crown, Black Horse, Ship

Robeanne House Farm & Stables,
Driffield Lane, Shiptonthorpe,
York, YO43 3PW.
Tel: **01430 873312** (also fax no)
Mrs Wilson.
D: £20.00-£40.00 **S:** £20.00-£25.00.
Open: All Year
Beds: 3F 2D 1T
Baths: 6 En
⚒ 🅿 (10) ❑ 🛏 ✕ ⚲ Ⅶ Ⅴ ⅏ ⚲
Comfortable family house,large
spacious rooms countryside views.
Good food warm welcome, within
easy reach of York, the Yorkshire
coast, Moors and Dales. Local
walking, gliding, racing, Castle
Howard and much more.

Barmby Moor   13

National Grid Ref: SE7748

⚒ ⚲ Wellington Oak

Alder Carr House, *York Road,*
Barmby Moor, York, YO42 4HU.
Georgian style house set in 10
acres. Well positioned for historic
Beverley and coast.
Tel: **01759 380566** Mrs Steel.
D: £17.00-£20.00 **S:** £20.00-£22.00.
Open: All Year (not Xmas)
Beds: 1F 2D **Baths:** 2 En 1 Pr
⚒ 🅿 (10) ❑ ⚲ Ⅶ Ⅴ

The lovely village of **Coxwold** is most famous as the home
and burial place of Laurence Sterne, author of Tristram Shandy,
a novel whose literary self-consciousness seemed merely
quirky in the eighteenth century but was later recognised as a
major forerunner of the twentieth-century novel. Shandy Hall,
his home, is now a dedicated museum publicising itself as 'the
Medieval House where the Modern Novel was born'.

Thirsk was made famous as James Herriot's 'Darrowby', the
fictional setting of his Yorkshire veterinary tales. The James
Herriot Visitor Centre will be a must for enthusiasts.

In **Middlesbrough** you can visit the Captain Cook Birthplace
Museum; several other museums and galleries; and Ormesby
Hall, a Georgian mansion notable for its decoration, particularly
the plasterwork.

Wilberfoss 14

National Grid Ref: SE7351

🍴 🍺 Gold Cup

Cuckoo Nest Farm, *Wilberfoss, York, YO41 5NL.*
Red brick traditional house, park and ride nearby for York.
Grades: ETC 3 Diamond
Tel: 01759 380365 Liversidge.
D: £20.00-£25.00 **S:** £23.00.
Open: All Year (not Xmas)
Beds: 1T 1D
Baths: 1 Pr
🛇 🄿 ⅍ ❑ 🎄 🛏 🗮 📷 Ⓥ

Stamford Bridge 15

National Grid Ref: SE7155

🍴 🍺 Goldcup Inn

High Catton Grange, *Stamford Bridge, York, YO41 1EP.*
Grades: ETC 4 Diamond
Tel: 01759 371374 (also fax no)
Ms Foster.
D: £19.00-£23.00
S: £28.00-£35.00.
Open: All Year (not Xmas/New Year)
Beds: 1F 1D
Baths: 1 En 1 Pr
🛇 🄿 (6) ❑ 🎄 🛏 🗮 📷 Ⓥ 🛢
A warm welcome awaits you at this C18th farmhouse in peaceful rural location. With ample parking, only 7 miles from historic York. Bedrooms are prettily furnished with colour TV. Cosy lounge, elegant dining room, good English breakfasts. Also self catering cottage available.

Dunnington 16

National Grid Ref: SE6652

🍴 🍺 Windmill Inn, Cross Keys

Brookland House, *Hull Road, Dunnington, York, YO19 5LW.*
Private detached house, country area. Wholesome breakfast, home-made preserves.
Tel: 01904 489548
Mrs Foster.
D: £16.00-£18.00
S: £17.00-£19.00.
Open: Mar to Dec
Beds: 1D 1T 1S
Baths: 1 Sh
🛇 (5) 🄿 (3) ⅍ ❑ 🗮 📷 Ⓥ ক

Moonlight Cottage, *8 Greencroft Court, Dunnington, York, YO19 5QJ.*
Comfortable and quiet. Convenient to York Moors, dales, castle, Howard Coast.
Tel: 01904 489369 (also fax no)
Mrs McNab.
D: £15.00-£17.00 .
Open: All Year
Beds: 1D
Baths: 1 En
🛇 🄿 (2) ⅍ ❑ 🗮 📷 Ⓥ

Easingwold 17

National Grid Ref: SE5369

🍴 🍺 Carlton, Falconberg

Yeoman's Course House, *Thornton Hill, Easingwold, York, YO61 3PY.*
Set in an elevated position overlooking the beautiful vale of York.
Grades: ETC 2 Diamond
Tel: 01347 868126
Mr & Mrs Addy.
Fax no: 01347 868129
D: £18.50-£19.50 **S:** £18.50-£19.50.
Open: Easter to Oct
Beds: 1T 2D
🛇 (12) 🄿 (8) ⅍ ❑ 🛏 🗮 📷 Ⓥ ⚡ ক

Garbutts Ghyll, *Thornton Hill, Easingwold, York, YO61 3PZ.*
Family-run B&B on a working farm in its own valley with panoramic views.
Tel: 01347 868644 Mrs Glaister.
Fax no: 01347 868133
D: £20.00-£25.00 **S:** £18.00-£20.00.
Open: Easter to Nov
Beds: 1D 1T
Baths: 1 En
🛇 🄿 ⅍ ❑ 🎄 🛏 🗮 📷 Ⓥ ⚡ ক

Crayke 18

National Grid Ref: SE5670

🍴 🍺 Durham Ox

The Hermitage, *Crayke, York, YO61 4TB.*
Actual grid ref: SE562707
Grades: ETC 3 Diamond
Tel: 01347 821635
Mr Moverley.
D: £26.00-£27.00 **S:** £26.00-£27.00.
Open: All Year
Beds: 1D 2T
Baths: 1 En 1 Sh
🛇 🄿 (4) ❑ 🛏 🗮 📷 Ⓥ ⚡ ক
Located on edge of small pretty village, stone-built house set in large garden; quiet setting with magnificent view in Area of Outstanding Natural Beauty, handy for York North York Moors, Wolds and Dales. Two miles from A19.

Coxwold 19

National Grid Ref: SE5377

🍴 🍺 Abbey Inn, Black Swan, Fauconberg Arms

Dale Croft, *Main Street, Coxwold, York, YO61 4AB.*
Dale Croft is a C17th old worldly cottage; large gardens.
Tel: 01347 868356
Mr & Mrs Richardson.
D: £17.00-£20.00
S: £18.50-£20.00.
Open: All Year (not Xmas/New Year)
Beds: 1F 1D 1T
Baths: 1 Sh
🛇 🄿 (5) ❑ 🎄 🛏 🗮 📷 Ⓥ

Ampleforth 20

National Grid Ref: SE5878

🍴 🍺 Abbey In, White Horse, White Swan, Wombwell Arms, Rydale Lodge

Carr House Farm, *Shallowdale, Ampleforth, York, YO62 4ED.*
Idyllic C16th farmhouse, romantic 4 poster bedrooms, internationally recommended, Heartbeat countryside.
Grades: ETC 3 Diamond
Tel: 01347 868526
Mrs Lupton.
D: £20.00**S:** £20.00.
Open: All Year (not Xmas)
Beds: 3D
Baths: 3 En
🛇 (7) 🄿 (5) ⅍ ❑ 🛏 🗮 📷 Ⓥ ⚡ ক

Spring Cottage, *Ampleforth, York, YO62 4DA.*
Magnificent views over Ryedale; close to Heartbeat and Herriot Country.
Grades: ETC 3 Diamond
Tel: 01439 788579 (also fax no)
Mr Benson.
D: £20.00-£22.00
S: £20.00-£22.00.
Open: All Year
Beds: 1F 1D
Baths: 2 En
🛇 🄿 (4) ⅍ ❑ 🎄 🛏 🗮 📷 Ⓥ ⚡ ক

Oldstead 21

National Grid Ref: SE5280

🍴 🍺 Abbey Inn

Oldstead Grange, *Oldstead, York, YO61 4BJ.*
Actual grid ref: SE523793
Beautiful quiet situation amidst our fields, woods and valleys. Traditional C17th features.
Tel: 01347 868634
Mrs Banks.
D: £24.00-£27.50
S: £28.00-£32.00.
Open: All Year
Beds: 1F 1D 1T
Baths: 3 En
🛇 🄿 (3) ⅍ ❑ 🗮 📷 Ⓥ ⚡ ক

Sutton Bank 22

National Grid Ref: SE5182

🍴 🍺 Hambleton Inn, Hare Inn

Cote Faw, *Hambleton Cottages, Sutton Bank, Thirsk, N. Yorks, YO7 2EZ.*
Actual grid ref: SE522830
Comfortable cottage in National Park, central for visiting North Yorkshire.
Tel: 01845 597363
Mrs Jeffray.
D: £16.00-£17.00 **S:** £16.00-£17.00.
Open: All Year (not Xmas)
Beds: 1F 1D 1S
Baths: 1 Sh
🛇 🄿 (3) ❑ 🛏 🗮 📷 Ⓥ ⚡ ক

High House Farm, *Sutton Bank, Thirsk, N. Yorks, YO7 2HA.*
Actual grid ref: SE523830
Family-run dairy farm set in open countryside in a tranquil part of W Yorks.
Tel: **01845 597557** Mrs Hope.
D: £20.00-£25.00 **S:** £22.00-£26.00.
Open: Easter to Nov
Beds: 1F 1D **Baths:** 1 Sh
🛇 🅿 (6) 🗔 ✕ 👗 Ⅲ. Ⅴ 🛡 🥢 🚲

Paradise   23

National Grid Ref: SE4687

High Paradise Farm, *Boltby, Thirsk, N Yorks, YO7 2HT.*
Set between the forest and the moors in Herriot Country.
Grades: ETC 3 Diamond
Tel: **01845 537235**
Mr & Mrs Skilbeck.
Fax no: 01845 537033
D: £20.00-£20.00 **S:** £23.00-£23.00.
Open: All Year
Beds: 1F 1T 1D **Baths:** 3 En
🛇 🅿 🕇 ✕ 👗 Ⅲ. ♿ Ⅴ 🥢 🚲

Boltby   24

National Grid Ref: SE4986

🍴 🍺 Carpenters' Arms, Whitstoncliffe Hotel, Hambleton Inn

Willow Tree Cottage, *Boltby, Thirsk, N. Yorkshire, YO7 2DY.*
Actual grid ref: SE492865
Large luxurious room with kitch-enette. Quiet hillside village, spectacular views.
Tel: **01845 537406** Townsend.
Fax no: 01845 537073
D: £22.00-£30.00 **S:** £30.00-£38.00.
Open: All Year (not Xmas)
Beds: 1F
Baths: 1 En
🛇 (5) 🅿 (2) 🥢 🗔 🕇 ✕ 👗 Ⅲ. Ⅴ 🛡
🚲

Low Paradise Farm, *Boltby, Thirsk, N. Yorks, YO7 2HS.*
Actual grid ref: SE502882
Warm welcome. Hill walking, cycling and Herriot Museum nearby.
Tel: **01845 537253** Mrs Todd.
D: £17.00-£18.00 **S:** £20.00-£20.00.
Open: March to Nov
Beds: 1D 2T
Baths: 1 Sh
🛇 (6) 🅿 (7) 🥢 🗔 🕇 ✕ 👗 Ⅲ. Ⅴ 🛡 🥢
🚲

Town Pasture Farm, *Boltby, Thirsk, N. Yorks, YO7 2DY.*
Actual grid ref: SE494866
Comfortable farmhouse in beautiful village, central for Yorkshire Dales.
Grades: ETC 3 Diamond
Tel: **01845 537298** Mrs Fountain.
D: £17.50-£19.50 **S:** £18.50-£20.00.
Open: All Year (not Xmas)
Beds: 1F 1T **Baths:** 2 En
🛇 🅿 (3) 🗔 🕇 ✕ 👗 Ⅲ. Ⅴ 🛡 🥢 🚲

Cundall   25

National Grid Ref: SE4272

🍴 🍺 Farmers' Inn

Lodge Farm, *Cundall, York, YO61 2RN.*
Actual grid ref: SE421732
A Georgian farmhouse by River Swale offering accommodation in own private suite.
Tel: **01423 360203** (also fax no)
Mrs Barker.
D: £20.00-£25.00 **S:** £30.00-£36.00.
Open: Mar to Nov
Beds: 1D **Baths:** 1 En
🛇 (2) 🅿 (2) 🥢 🗔 ✕ 👗 Ⅲ. Ⅴ 🥢 🚲

Sowerby   26

National Grid Ref: SE4281

The Old Manor House, *27 Front Street, Sowerby, Thirsk, N. Yorks, YO7 1JQ.*
Restored C15th manor house. Guest suites overlooking gardens or village green.
Tel: **01845 526642** Mr Jackson.
Fax no: 01845 526568
D: £20.00 **S:** £35.00.
Open: All Year (not Xmas)
Beds: 1F 1D **Baths:** 2 En
🛇 🅿 🥢 🗔 👗 Ⅲ. Ⅴ 🛡 🥢

Thirsk   27

National Grid Ref: SE4282

🍴 🍺 Hambleton Inn, Hare Inn, Dog & Gun, Carpenters' Arms, Whitstoncliffe Hotel, Old Oak Tree, Golden Fleece, Darrowby Inn, Black Swan, Carpenters' Arms, Shepparas Table, George

8a The Conifers, Ingramgate, *Thirsk, N. Yorks, YO7 1DD.*
Beautiful Dower House built in 1850. 5 mins walk from market place.
Tel: **01845 522179** Mrs Lee.
D: £15.00-£15.00 **S:** £15.00-£15.00.
Open: Jan to Dec
Beds: 1F 1D 1S
Baths: 1 Sh
🛇 🅿 (3) 🗔 🕇 👗 Ⅲ. Ⅴ 🥢 🚲

Lavender House, *27 Kirkgate, Thirsk, N. Yorks, YO7 1PL.*
Base for touring Dales and Moors, next door to James Herriot Centre.
Tel: **01845 522224** Mrs Dodds.
D: £17.00-£17.00 **S:** £17.00-£20.00.
Open: All Year (not Xmas)
Beds: 2F 1S
Baths: 2 Sh
🛇 🅿 (3) 🥢 🗔 🕇 ✕ 👗 Ⅲ. Ⅴ 🥢

Station House, *Station Road, Thirsk, N. Yorks, YO7 4LS.*
Old station master's house retaining character of railways. Ideal base for touring Dales & Moors.
Tel: **01845 522063** Mrs Jones.
D: £17.00 **S:** £21.00.
Open: Easter to Oct
Beds: 1F 1D **Baths:** 2 En
🛇 🅿 (6) 🥢 🗔 🕇 👗 Ⅲ. Ⅴ 🛡 🥢 🚲

Laburnham House, *31 Topcliff Rd, Thirsk, N. Yorks, YO7 1RX.*
Spacious detached house, tastefully furnished with antiques and in the traditional manner.
Tel: **01845 524120** Mrs Ogleby.
D: £19.00-£21.00 **S:** £25.00-£35.00.
Open: Easter to Nov
Beds: 1F 1D 1T
Baths: 2 En 1 Pr
🛇 (5) 🅿 (3) 🥢 🗔 👗 Ⅲ. Ⅴ 🥢 🚲

Hambleton House, *78 St James Green, Thirsk, N Yorks, YO7 1AJ.*
Restored Victorian house (though parts date back to 1683) overlooking the green.
Tel: **01845 525532**
Mr & Mrs Boumer.
D: £16.00-£20.00 **S:** £18.00-£25.00.
Open: Easter to Oct
Beds: 2D 1T **Baths:** 2 En 1 Pr
🛇 (10) 🥢 🗔 👗 Ⅲ. Ⅴ 🥢 🚲

Northallerton   28

National Grid Ref: SE3794

🍴 🍺 Bassetts, Black Swan, Golden Lion, Pepper Mill, New Inn

Porch House, *68 High Street, Northallerton, N. Yorks, DL7 8EG.*
Built 1584 original fireplaces and beams between Yorkshire Dales and Moors.
Grades: ETC 4 Diamond, Silver, AA 4 Diamond
Tel: **01609 779831**
Barrow.
Fax no: 01609 778603
D: £24.50-£26.00
S: £33.00-£35.00.
Open: All year (not Xmas)
Beds: 4D 2T
Baths: 6 En
🛇 (12) 🅿 (6) 🥢 🗔 👗 Ⅲ. Ⅴ

Honeypots, *4 Pennine View, Northallerton, DL7 8HP.*
Well-recommended guest house (visitors love it!) decorated to extremely high standard.
Tel: **01609 777264**
D: £18.00-£20.00
S: £18.00-£20.00.
Open: All Year (not Xmas/New Year)
Beds: 1T
Baths: 1P
🛇 (12) 🅿 (1) 🥢 🗔 ✕ 👗 Ⅲ. Ⅴ 🛡 🥢

Alverton Guest House, *26 South Parade, Northallerton, N. Yorks, DL7 8SG.*
Actual grid ref: SE367934
Modernised Victorian town house convenient for all the county town facilities.
Tel: **01609 776207** (also fax no)
Mr Longley.
D: £18.00-£19.50
S: £17.50-£24.00.
Open: All Year (not Xmas)
Beds: 1F 1D 1T 2S
Baths: 3 En 1 Sh
🛇 🅿 (4) 🗔 👗 Ⅲ. Ⅴ 🛡 🥢 🚲

Osmotherley   29

National Grid Ref: SE4597

▲ *Osmotherley Youth Hostel,*
Cote Ghyll, Osmotherley,
Northallerton, North Yorkshire,
DL6 3AH.
Actual grid ref: SE461981
Tel: **01609 883575**
Under 18: £6.90 **Adults:** £10.00
Self-catering facilities, Television,
Showers, Laundry facilities, Wet
weather shelter, Lounge, Games
room, Drying room, Cycle store,
Parking, Evening meal at 7.00pm,
No smoking, WC, Kitchen facili-
ties, Breakfast available, Credit
cards accepted
Surrounded by woodland, the youth
hostel is fully modernised with
excellent facilities, right on the
edge of the North York Moors
National Park.

Thimbleby   30

National Grid Ref: SE4495

|●| ◀ Golden Lion

Stonehaven, Thimbleby,
Osmotherly, Northallerton, DL6 3PY.
Comfortable farmhouse, super view,
lovely walks, good beds and good
food. **Grades:** ETC 3 Diamond
Tel: **01609 883689** Mrs Shepherd.
D: £18.00-£20.00 **S:** £20.00-£22.00.
Open: Easter to Nov
Beds: 1D 1T **Baths:** 1 Pr
🛏 (1) 🅿 (3) ⊬◻ 🛏 🖤 Ⅶ 🕯 ⚡ ⚲

Ingleby Cross   31

National Grid Ref: NZ4500

|●| ◀ Black Horse, Blue Bell

North York Moors Adventure Ctr,
Park House, Ingleby Cross,
Northallerton, N. Yorks, DL6 3PE.
Actual grid ref: SE453995
Park House, traditional sandstone
farmhouse set in The National Park.
Tel: **01609 882571** (also fax no)
Mr Bennett. **D:** £15.00 **S:** £15.00.
Open: Easter to Oct
Beds: 3F 1D 3T **Baths:** 2 Sh
🛏 (1) 🅿 (20) ◻ 🛏 ✗ 🛏 🖤 Ⅶ 🕯 ⚡ ⚲

Blue Bell Inn, Ingleby Cross,
Northallerton, N. Yorks, DL6 3NF.
Family run, real ales, coal fire,
quiet annexed accommodation.
Tel: **01609 882272**
Mrs Kinsella.
D: £20.00-£20.00
S: £20.00-£20.00.
Open: All Year
Beds: 4F 1D 4T
Baths: 5 En
🛏 🅿 (20) ◻ ✗ 🛏 🖤 Ⅶ 🕯 ⚲

Potto   32

National Grid Ref: NZ4703

Dog & Gun Country Inn, Potto,
Northallerton, DL6 3HQ.
Tel: **01642 700232**
D: £20.00-£25.00
S: £25.00-£30.00.
Open: All Year
Beds: 2F 2T 2D
Baths: 5 En
🛏 🅿 (30) ◻ ✗ 🛏 🖤 Ⅶ 🕯 ⚲
Traditional country inn situated
beside North Yorkshire Moors
National Park. Warm friendly
welcome, excellent cuisine and
accommodation. Ideal touring base
close to Teeside, Darlington,
Northallerton, Thirsk.
Approximately 25 miles from
Whitby, Durham City, Yorkshire
Dales, City of York, Ripon,
Harrogate.

Faceby   33

National Grid Ref: NZ4903

Four Wynds, Whorl Hill, Faceby,
Middlesbrough, TS9 7BZ.
Actual grid ref: NZ487033
Small holding in beautiful
countryside. Located off A172
between Swainby/Faceby.
Grades: ETC 3 Diamond
Tel: **01642 701315**
Mr Barnfather.
D: £18.00-£20.00.
S: £18.00-£20.00.
Open: All Year
Beds: 1F 1D 1T
Baths: 1 En 1 Sh
🛏 🅿 (8) ◻ 🛏 ✗ 🛏 🖤 Ⅶ 🕯 ⚡ ⚲

Hutton Rudby   34

National Grid Ref: NZ4606

|●| ◀ Bay Horse

Greenview, 13 Eastside, Hutton
Rudby, Yarm, N Yorks, TS15 0DB.
Tel: **01642 701739**
Mrs Ashton.
D: £18.00-£18.00
S: £18.00.
Open: All Year
Beds: 1D 1T
Baths: 2 En
🛏 (3) ⊬◻ 🛏 🖤 Ⅶ ⚲
Overlooking the village green at
Hutton Rudby, Greenview offers
you a delightful stay bordering the
National Park in North Yorkshire.
Rooms have showers, comfortable
beds, with a hearty breakfast. Ideal
for Coast to Coast, Cleveland Way
and new cycle route.

Middlesbrough   35

National Grid Ref: NZ5118

|●| ◀ Highfield

White House Hotel, 311 Marton
Road, Middlesbrough, TS4 2HG.
Family run, close to centre, good
English breakfast, car parking.
Tel: **01642 244531**
D: £15.00-£17.50
S: £18.50-£22.00.
Open: All Year
Beds: 2F 2D 6T 5S
Baths: 4 En 3 Sh
🛏 ◻ 🛏 🛏 🖤 Ⅶ

Many rates vary

according to season -

the lowest only are

shown here

Round Berkshire Cycle Route

The **Round Berkshire Cycle Route** is a 140-mile circular route around the county of Berkshire, which has been deliberately routed along minor roads wherever possible. It starts and finishes in Reading, and runs anticlockwise around the whole of the county.

A detailed **guide leaflet** to the route is available free from Bracknell Forest Borough Council, Leisure Services, Edward Elgar House, Skimped Hill Lane, Bracknell, Berkshire RG12 1LR, tel 01344 354107. The route is signposted by blue direction signs with a cycle silhouette on a green outline map of Berkshire.

Maps: Ordnance Survey 1:50,000 Landranger series: 174, 175

Trains: Reading, Maidenhead and Slough (from where there is a connection to Windsor) are on the main line out of London. There are connections to Newbury, Hungerford, Bracknell and many other places on or near the route.

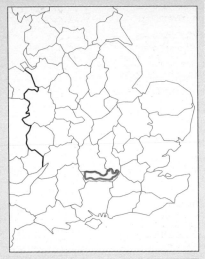

Reading to Tidmarsh

Reading, the county town of Berkshire, lies where the River Kennet joins the Thames, and is economically one of the most important towns of the Thames Valley. It is largely nineteenth-century redbrick, and has a thriving commercial town centre. In medieval times there was a Benedictine abbey, founded in the twelfth century, of which a few ruins remain. The town also has a good museum, which houses the finds from the Roman town at Silchester in Hampshire, and a good theatre, the Hexagon. This is where Oscar Wilde spent two years in prison, after which he wrote the *Ballad of Reading Gaol*. Cycling west from the south bank of the Thames at Caversham Bridge, you leave town after Tilehurst station, and reach the village of **Tidmarsh.** A short detour north at this point leads to the small Thameside town of **Pangbourne**, used by the artist Ernest Shepard as the setting for his illustrations to *The Wind in the Willows*, whose author, Kenneth Grahame, lived here.

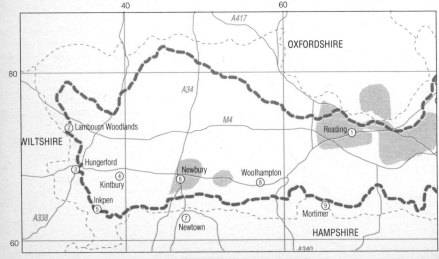

Reading 1

National Grid Ref: SU7173

🍴🍺 Clifton Arms, Horse & Jockey, Unicorn, ~ed Lion, Grouse & Claret, Rose & Thistle, ~weeney & Todd, Queen's Head

~reystoke Guest House,
~0 Greystoke Road, Caversham,
~eading, Berks, RG4 5EL.
~rivate home in quiet road, TV & ~ea/coffee making in lounge.
~rades: ETC 3 Diamond
~el: **0118 947 5784** Mrs Tyler.
~: £25.00-£30.00 **S:** £28.00-£35.00.
~pen: All Year (not Xmas)
~eds: 1D 2S
~aths: 1 Sh
🛏 (3) �🚫🍳🗄🕯🛁🖾Ⅴ✂🚲

~ Hilda's, 24 Castle Crescent,
~eading, Berkshire, RG1 6AG.
~uiet Victorian home near town ~entre, all rooms have colour TVs ~ fridges.
~el: **0118 961 0329**
~r & Mrs Hubbard.
~ax no: 0118 954 2585
~: £19.00-£24.00 **S:** £20.00-£27.00.
~pen: All Year
~eds: 3F 2T
~aths: 3 Sh
🛏 (1) 🅿✂🍳🕯🛁🖾Ⅴ✂🚲

~ittisham Guest House,
~3 Tilehurst Road, Reading, Berks,
~30 2JL.
~uiet central location in a restored ~dwardian home. High standards at ~ensible prices.
~rades: ETC 3 Diamond
~el: **0118 956 9483**
~r Harding.
~ : £20.00-£27.50 **S:** £26.00-£35.00.
~pen: All Year
~eds: 2D 1T 2S
~aths: 3 En 2 Sh
~🅿✂🍳🕯🛁🖾Ⅴ✂🚲

Abadair House, *46 Redlands Road,*
Reading, Berks, RG1 5HE.
Family run guest house close to railway and town centre.
Grades: ETC 2 Diamond
Tel: **0118 986 3792** (also fax no)
Mrs Clifford.
D: £30.00 **S:** £30.00-£35.00.
Open: All Year
Beds: 3T 6S
Baths: 8 En 1 Sh
🛏 🅿 (6) ✂🍳🗄🕯🛁🖾Ⅴ

Lambourn Woodlands 2

National Grid Ref: SU3175

🍴🍺 Hare and Hound

Lodge Down, *Lambourn,*
Hungerford, Berks, RG17 7BJ.
Tel: **01672 540304** (also fax no)
Mrs Cook.
D: £22.50 **S:** £30.00.
Open: All Year
Beds: 1F 2D 2T
Baths: 3 En
🛏🅿🗄🕯🛁🖾Ⅴ🖾✂
Magnificent house with spacious rooms and extensive garden with woodland and cross country course in the grounds overlooking horse training gallops and wonderful views of the Downs, looking towards the Ridgeway, the centre of Dick Francis country.

All rooms full and
nowhere else to stay?
Ask the owner if
there's anywhere
nearby

Hungerford 3

National Grid Ref: SU3368

🍴🍺 Just Williams, John O'Gaunt, Plume Of Feathers

Wilton House, *33 High Street,*
Hungerford, Berks, RG17 0NF.
Elegant ensuite bedrooms in classic, historic English town house predating 1450.
Grades: ETC 4 Diamond
Tel: **01488 684228** Mrs Welfare.
Fax no: 01488 685037
D: £25.00-£27.50 **S:** £35.00-£38.00.
Open: All Year (not Xmas)
Beds: 1D 1T **Baths:** 2 En
🛏 (8) 🅿 (3) ✂🍳🕯🛁🖾Ⅴ🖾✂

Tidmarsh to Hungerford

After Tidmarsh you pass into the **North Wessex Downs** with the villages of Upper Basildon and Aldworth, where you will find the Four Points pub, from where you can head onto an alternative route along **the Ridgeway**, an ancient path along which lie numerous Iron Age forts. Near the point where you join the Ridgeway is the site of the Battle of Ashdown. In 871, the Saxons of Wessex won a resounding victory, under Alfred the Great (then the brother of King Aethelred I), in their campaign against the invasion of England by the Danes – only to be crushed by them at Merton (now in South London) shortly afterwards. After Aldworth you come to Compton, East and West Ilsley and Farnborough, and then down off the downs to the village of **Great Shefford** on the banks of the River Lambourn, which you follow upstream to **Lambourn** town, Berkshire's horseracing centre. After Lambourn it's south until you hit Ermine Street, the lesser of two Roman roads of that name, which runs from Silchester to Gloucester. After a brief stretch you turn right, cross the M4 and head on to **Hungerford**, on the River Kennet. At the Wharf you can view the **Kennet and Avon Canal**, constructed in 1774 and recently restored.

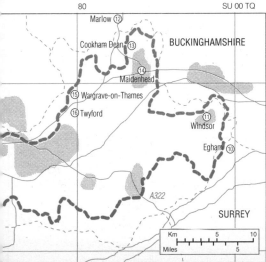

Hungerford to Finchampstead Ridges

Heading across Hungerford Common, the route takes you to the foot of **Walbury Hill**, the highest chalk hill in England. If you fancy a challenge, the view from the top is worth the climb, along quiet lanes. Otherwise, the route takes you around the hill and then eastwards on to **Newbury**, site of two battles in the Civil War, one of which (1643) is commemorated by the Falkland Memorial, close to the route on the way into town. The next stretch takes in two sites of legendary importance to the anti-nuclear movement, **Greenham Common**, just outside Newbury, former site of American Cruise Missiles and the resultant women's peace camp during the 1980s, and **Aldermaston**, site of the Atomic Weapons Research Establishment and of annual CND marches in the 1950s and 60s. Then it's into the coniferous woodland around Mortimer. A short detour over the Hampshire boundary takes you to the site of the Roman town of Calleva Atrebatum, at **Silchester**. This was the capital of the Atrebates tribe in the third and fourth centuries, and the site includes the walls, still up to 13 feet high in places, an amphitheatre, the foundations of a forum and the earliest known Christian church in Britain. After Mortimer it's across the Rivers Loddon and Blackwater near to Swallowfield Park, a seventeenth-century country house, and on to Wellingtonia Avenue, from where you can take a short detour to the viewpoint over the Blackwater Valley at Finchampstead Ridges.

Alderborne, 33 Bourne Vale, Hungerford, Berkshire, RG17 0LL.
Actual grid ref: SU333682
Modern detached family house overlooking open country. Walking distance shops.
Grades: ETC 4 Diamond
Tel: **01488 683228**
Mr & Mrs Honeybone.
D: £17.50-£18.50 **S:** £17.50-£22.50.
Open: All Year (not Xmas)
Beds: 2T 1S
Baths: 1 Pr 1 Sh
⚡ (5) 🅿 (3) ✂🔲 ♨ 🛏 🎢 🖳 Ⓥ ⚡ ♻

Wasing, 35 Sanden Close, Hungerford, Berkshire, RG17 0LA.
Warm welcome to the home of ex farmers. 3 miles M4.
Tel: **01488 684127** Mrs Smalley.
D: £16.00-£17.00 **S:** £17.00-£18.00.
Open: All Year (not Xmas)
Beds: 1D 1T 1S **Baths:** 1 En 1 Sh
⚡🅿🔲♨🖳Ⓥ ⚡♻

15 Sanden Close, Hungerford, Berks, RG17 0LA.
Semi-detached bungalow in quiet close. Short walk to shops and station.
Tel: **01488 682583** Mrs Hook.
D: £15.00-£16.00 **S:** £17.00-£18.00.
Open: All Year (not Xmas)
Beds: 1D 1S **Baths:** 1 Sh
⚡ (5) 🅿 (3) ✂🔲🖳.

Kintbury 4

National Grid Ref: SU3866

🍽 ⚫ Crown & Garter

The Forbury, Crossways, Kintbury, Hungerford, Berks, RG17 9SU.
Extended C17th cottage. Lovely position facing south, overlooking own woodlands.
Tel: **01488 658377** Mr Cubitt.
D: £22.50-£27.50 **S:** £22.50-£25.00.
Open: All Year (not Xmas)
Beds: 1F **Baths:** 1 Pr 1 Sh
⚡🅿 (10) 🔲🛏🗙♨🖳Ⓥ⚡♻

S = Price range for a single person in a room

Inkpen 5

National Grid Ref: SU3764

Beacon House, Bell Lane, Upper Green, Inkpen, Hungerford, Berks, RG17 9QJ.
Actual grid ref: SU368634
Visit our 1930s country home on Berks/Wilts/Hants border. Lovely countryside.
Grades: AA 3 Diamond
Tel: **01488 668640**
Mr & Mrs Cave.
D: £22.00 **S:** £22.00.
Open: All Year
Beds: 1T 2S **Baths:** 2 Sh
⚡🅿 (6) 🔲🛏🗙♨🖳Ⓥⓘ⚡♻

Newbury 6

National Grid Ref: SU4767

🍽 ⚫ Lord Lyon, Red Lion, Gun Inn

15 Shaw Road, Newbury, Berks, RG14 1HG.
Late Georgian terraced house near town centre, rail and canal.
Tel: **01635 44962** Mrs Curtis.
D: £17.00-£18.00 **S:** £17.00-£18.00.
Open: All Year
Beds: 1D, 1T **Baths:** 1 Sh
⚡🅿✂🔲♨🖳Ⓥⓘ⚡♻

Laurel House, 157 Andover Road, Newbury, RG14 6NB.
A warm welcome awaits you in our delightful Georgian house.
Tel: **01635 35931** Mr & Mrs Dixon
D: £18.00 **S:** £18.00.
Open: All Year (not Xmas)
Beds: 1D 1T **Baths:** 1 Sh
🅿 (2) ✂🔲♨🖳Ⓥ♻

Newtown (Newbury)

National Grid Ref: SU4763

🍽 ⚫ Swan Inn, Carpenters Arms

White Cottage, Newtown, Newbury Berks, RG20 9AP.
Delightful semi-rural cottage on the edge of Watership Down.
Grades: ETC 3 Diamond
Tel: **01635 43097** (also fax no)
Mrs Meiklejohn.
D: £22.00-£25.00
S: £25.00-£30.00.
Open: All Year (not Xmas)
Beds: 1D 1T 1S
Baths: 1 Sh
⚡ (3) 🅿✂🔲🛏♨🖳Ⓥ♻

Woolhampton

National Grid Ref: SU5766

🍽 ⚫ Rowbarge Inn, Angel Inn

Bridge Cottage, Station Road, Woolhampton, Reading, Berks, RG7 5SF.
Beautiful 300-year-old riverside home with secluded cottage garden
Tel: **01189 713138**
Mrs Thornely.
Fax no: 01189 714331
D: £26.00-£26.00
S: £24.00.
Open: All Year (not Xmas)
Beds: 1D 1T 3S
Baths: 2 En 1 Sh
⚡🅿🔲♨🖳Ⓥ⚡♻

All rates are subject to alteration at the owners' discretion.

Mortimer 9

National Grid Ref: SU6564

◀ ◖ Red Lion

5 The Avenue, Mortimer, Reading, Berks, RG7 3QU.
Large garden; quiet location; Mortimer Station 1 mile; rural location.
Tel: 0118 933 3166
Mrs Keast.
D: £20.00
S: £20.00.
Open: All Year
Beds: 3F 2D 1S
Baths: 1 En 1 Sh
☐ (2) ☐ (8) ☐ ✝ ✕ ☰ ▥ & ▣ ▤ ✦ ♿

Egham 10

National Grid Ref: TQ0071

◀ ◖ Happy Man, The Beehive

The Old Parsonage, 2 Parsonage Road, Englefield Green, Egham, Surrey, TW20 0JW.
Actual grid ref: SU995709
Georgian parsonage, traditionally furnished, old fashioned gardens. 30 minutes from London.
Tel: 01784 436706 (also fax no)
Mr & Mrs Clark.
D: £25.00-£40.00
S: £35.00-£55.00.
Open: All Year (not Xmas)
Beds: 1F 2D 2T 1S
Baths: 3 En 1 Sh
☐ ▣ (6) ⧾ ☐ ✝ ✕ ☰ ▥ ▣ ♿

Windsor 11

National Grid Ref: SU9676

◀ ◖ The Mitre, Bexley Arms, The Trooper, Nags Head, The Queen, Windsor Lad, George Inn, Vansitart Arms, Crow's Nest, Red Lion, White Horse, Hungry Horse

▲ Windsor Youth Hostel, Edgeworth House, Mill Lane, Windsor, Berks, SL4 5JE.
Actual grid ref: SU955770
Tel: 01753 861710
Under 18: £7.75
Adults: £11.00
Self-catering facilities, Television, Showers, Laundry facilities, Lounge, Drying room, Cycle store, Parking cars only, Kitchen facilities, Breakfast available, Luggage store, Credit cards accepted
Queen Anne residence in the old Clewer village quarter on the outskirts of historic Windsor.

Jean's, 1 Stovell Road, Windsor, Berks, SL4 5JB.
Actual grid ref: SU958771
Grades: ETC 2 Diamond
Tel: 01753 852055 Ms Sumner.
Fax no: 01753 842932
D: £22.50-£25.00
S: £40.00-£40.00.
Open: All Year
Beds: 1D 1T
Baths: 2 En
▣ (2) ⧾ ☐ ✝ ☰ ▥ & ▣ ▣
Quiet comfortable self-contained ground floor flat comprising 2 ensuite bedrooms which share a large lounge. 100 yds river and leisure centre, 7 mins' walk to castle, town centre and railway stations, 4 mins to buses.

Langton House, 46 Alma Road, Windsor, Berks, SL4 3HA.
Victorian house, quiet tree-lined road, 5 minutes walk to town and castle.
Tel: 01753 858299
Mrs Fogg.
D: £30.00-£32.50 S: £50.00.
Open: All Year (not Xmas)
Beds: 2D 1T
Baths: 2 En 1 Pr
▣ (2) ⧾ ☐ ☰ ▥ ▣ ♿

All details shown are as supplied by B&B owners in Autumn 2000.

D = Price range per person sharing in a double room

62 Queens Road, Windsor, Berks, SL4 3BH.
Actual grid ref: SU964761
Excellent reputation, quiet, convenient, ground floor rooms. Largest family room available.
Tel: 01753 866036 (also fax no)
Mrs Hughes.
D: £20.00-£25.00 S: £30.00-£35.00.
Open: All Year
Beds: 1F 1T
Baths: 2 Pr
☐ ▣ (1) ⧾ ☐ ☰ ▥ & ▣ ✦ ♿

Elansey, 65 Clifton Rise, Windsor, Berks, SL4 5SX.
Modern, quiet, comfortable house. Garden, patio, excellent breakfasts, highly recommended.
Tel: 01753 864438 Mrs Forbutt.
D: £20.00-£25.00 S: £20.00-£26.00.
Open: All Year (not Xmas)
Beds: 1D 1T 1S
Baths: 1 En 1 Sh
▣ (3) ☐ ☰ ▥ ▣

The Andrews, 77 Whitehorse Road, Windsor, Berks, SL4 4PG.
Modern, comfortable private house.
Tel: 01753 866803 Mrs Andrews.
D: £18.00-£20.00 S: £23.00-£25.00.
Open: All Year (not Xmas)
Beds: 1D 2T
Baths: 2 Sh
☐ (5) ▣ (3) ⧾ ☐ ▥ ♿

Finchampstead Ridges to Windsor

Cycling northeast you go around the southern perimeter of Bracknell, via Caesar's Camp, an Iron Age hill fort in Bracknell Forest, and then through woodland and parkland and across the Virginia Water beechlands into **Windsor Great Park**, a large tract of formal parkland replete with grazing deer. The route takes you through the Savill Gardens, and a short detour will bring you to the viewpoint at Snow Hill, by the 'Copper Horse' statue of George III. North of the Great Park you arrive at Old Windsor, from where a short detour east into Surrey will take you to **Runnymede**, the riverside meadow where in 1215 King John relinquished the absolute power of the monarchy with his signature on the Magna Carta. Here also stands the memorial to John F Kennedy. Sticking to the route, you hit the Thames at Datchet, and cycle along the north bank to **Eton**, where you can visit the red-brick Tudor buildings of *that* school, and then cross the river into **Windsor**. This town is dominated by the renowned castle, now restored after the great fire of 1992, whose most notable features are St George's Chapel, one of the most impressive examples of the Perpendicular style in England, and the State Apartments, which house, among other treasures, a large collection of pictures, including a tryptych of Charles I by Van Dyck and works by Canaletto, Holbein, Rubens, Rembrandt, Reynolds and Hogarth, as well as drawings by Leonardo and Michaelangelo.

Chasela, *30 Convent Road, Windsor, Berks, SL4 3RB.*
Modern semi-detached near M4, M40, M25. Castle 1 mile and Legoland.
Grades: ETC 3 Diamond
Tel: **01753 860410**
Mrs Williams.
D: £22.00-£24.00
S: £22.00-£24.00.
Open: All Year
Beds: 1T 1S
Baths: 1 Sh
🛏 (12) 🅿 (5) ⅋☐🐾🛁☕Ⅲ.Ⅴ

The Laurells, *22 Dedworth Road, Windsor, Berks, SL4 5AY.*
Pretty Victorian house 3/4 mile town centre. Heathrow 20 minutes.
Tel: **01753 855821**
Mrs Joyce.
D: £20.00 **S:** £25.00.
Open: All Year (not Xmas)
Beds: 2T
🛏 (5) ⅋☐🛁☕Ⅲ.Ⅴ⅍ 🚲

2 Benning Close, St Leonards Park, *Windsor, Berks, SL4 4YS.*
A modern detached house set in a quiet residential area.
Tel: **01753 852294**
Mrs Hume.
D: £20.00-£20.00 **S:** £25.00-£25.00.
Open: All Year (not Xmas/New Year)
Beds: 1F 1D 1S
🛏 🅿 (2) ⅋☐🛁☕Ⅲ.&.Ⅴ⅍ ⅍

12 Parsonage Lane, *Windsor, Berks, SL4 5EN.*
Tastefully furnished detached private house. Quiet location. Parking. Lovely gardens.
Tel: **01753 868052** (also fax no)
Mr & Mrs Riddle.
D: £25.00-£35.00
S: £32.00-£35.00.
Open: All Year
Beds: 1D 1S
Baths: 1 Sh
🛏 🅿 (4) ⅋☐🐾🛁☕Ⅲ.Ⅴ⅍ 🚲

Marlow 12

National Grid Ref: SU8586

🍴 🍺 Hare & Hounds, Three Horseshoes, Osbourne Arms, Clayton Arms, Royal Oak

Merrie Hollow, *Seymour Court Hill, Marlow, Bucks, SL7 3DE.*
Actual grid ref: SU840889
Grades: ETC 3 Diamond
Tel: **01628 485663** (also fax no)
Mr Wells.
D: £20.00-£25.00
S: £25.00-£35.00.
Open: All Year
Beds: 1D 1T
Baths: 1 Sh
🛏 🅿 (4) ⅋☐🐾✕🛁☕Ⅲ.Ⅴ⅍ ⅍
Secluded quiet country cottage in large garden 150 yds off B482 Marlow to Stokenchurch road, easy access to M4 & M25, 35 mins from Heathrow & Oxford, private off-road car parking.

Sneppen House, *Henley Road, Marlow, Bucks, SL7 2DF.*
Within walking distance of town centre and river. Breakfast menu choice. Pub food nearby.
Grades: ETC 4 Diamond
Tel: **01628 485227**
Mr Norris.
D: £22.50-£22.50
S: £30.00-£30.00.
Open: All Year
Beds: 1D 1T
Baths: 1 Sh
🛏 (2) 🅿 (3) ☐🛁☕Ⅲ.Ⅴ⅍ 🚲

Acha Pani, *Bovingdon Green, Marlow, Bucks, SL7 2JL.*
Actual grid ref: SU836869
Quiet location, easy access Thames Foothpath, Chilterns, Windsor, London, Heathrow.
Grades: ETC 2 Diamond
Tel: **01628 483435** (also fax no)
Mrs Cowling.
D: £17.00-£18.00
S: £17.00-£18.00.
Open: All Year
Beds: 1D 1T 1S
Baths: 1 En 1 Sh
🛏 (10) 🅿 (3) ☐🐾✕🛁☕Ⅲ.Ⅴ🛈⅍ 🚲

Sunnyside, *Munday Dean, Marlow, Bucks, SL7 3BU.*
Comfortable, friendly, family home in Area of Outstanding Natural Beauty.
Tel: **01628 485701**
Mrs O'Connor.
D: £17.50-£17.50
S: £20.00-£20.00.
Open: All Year
Beds: 2D 1T
Baths: 1 Sh
🛏 🅿 (5) ⅋☐&. 🚲

29 Oaktree Road, *Marlow, Bucks, SL7 3ED.*
Friendly and efficiently run Bed & Breakfast. Convenient M4, M48 and M25.
Tel: **01628 472145** Mr Lasenby.
D: £25.00-£27.50 **S:** £28.00-£30.00.
Open: All Year (not Xmas)
Beds: 5F 2T
Baths: 1 En
🅿 (2) ⅋☐🐾🛁☕Ⅲ.Ⅴ⅍ 🚲

Cookham Dean 13

National Grid Ref: SU8684

🍴 🍺 Checkers

Cartlands Cottage, *King's Lane, Cookham Dean, Maidenhead, Berks, SL6 9AY.*
Self-contained guest room in garden. Rural, very quiet.
Tel: **01628 482196**
Mr & Mrs Parkes.
D: £22.00-£25.00
S: £23.50-£26.00.
Open: All Year
Beds: 1F
Baths: 1 Pr
🛏 🅿 (2) ☐🛁☕Ⅲ.Ⅴ

Windsor to Reading

At **Maidenhead**, the 128-foot brick arches - the largest in the world - of the railway bridge show that Brunel could do both kinds of bridge, Bristol's suspension bridge at Clifton being his famous example of the other kind. **Cookham** was home to the artist Stanley Spencer, whose painting of Cookham Bridge is in London's Tate Gallery. The village has a gallery of his work, as well as a slightly odd fifteenth-century church tower with both a clock and a sundial. The viewpoint at Winter Hill yields a panorama onto the Chilterns in Buckinghamshire. The final stretch of the route takes you through some lovely Thames Valley countryside, and then by way of **Wargrave** and **Twyford** back into Reading.

Maidenhead 14

National Grid Ref: SU8781

🍴 🍺 Boulter's Lock Inn, Thames Hotel, Kingswood Hotel, Windsor Castle, Pond House, Hare & Hounds

Sheephouse Manor, *Sheephouse Road, Maidenhead, Berks, SL6 8HJ.*
Actual grid ref: SU8878
Charming C16th farmhouse, with health suite and jacuzzi. Beautiful grounds.
Grades: ETC 3 Diamond
Tel: **01628 776902** Mrs Street.
Fax no: 01628 625138
D: £28.00-£30.00
S: £40.00-£45.00.
Open: All Year (not Xmas)
Beds: 1D 1T 3S
Baths: 5 En
🛏 🅿 (7) ☐🐾🛁☕Ⅲ.Ⅴ⅍

Laburnham Guest House, *31 Laburnham Road, Maidenhead, Berks, SL6 4DB.*
Actual grid ref: SU881808
Fine Edwardian house, near town centre, station and M4 motorway.
Tel: **01628 676748** (also fax no)
Mrs Stevens.
D: £23.00-£25.00
S: £35.00-£40.00.
Open: All Year (not Xmas)
Beds: 1F 2D 1T 1S
Baths: 5 En
🛏 🅿 (5) ⅋☐🛁☕Ⅲ.Ⅴ 🚲

Clifton Guest House, 21 Craufurd Rise, Maidenhead, Berks, SL6 7LR.
Family-run guest house. 10 mins from town centre. Easy access London M4/M25/M40.
Grades: ETC 3 Diamond, RAC 3 Diamond
Tel: **01628 623572** (also fax no)
Mr Arora. **D:** £45.00-£60.00 .
Open: All Year
Beds: 2F 5D 5T 3S
Baths: 8 En 1 Pr 4 Sh
⛺🅿🗆✕🎂🛏&Ⓥ

Copperfields Guest House, 54 Bath Rd, Maidenhead, Berks, SL6 4JY
Comfortable accommodation, near Windsor, Henley, Reading and M4 to London.
Tel: **01628 674941** Mrs Lindsay.
D: £22.50-£25.00 **S:** £30.00-£33.00.
Open: All Year
Beds: 2T 2S **Baths:** 3 Pr
⛺🅿(5)🗆🛏🎂🛏Ⓥ

Wargrave-on-Thames 15

National Grid Ref: SU7978
🍴🍺 The Bull, The Queen Victoria

Windy Brow, 204 Victoria Road, Wargrave-on-Thames, Reading, Berks, RG10 8AJ.
Actual grid ref: SU794788
Victorian detached house, close M4/M40, 1 mile A4, 6 miles Reading and Maidenhead.
Grades: ETC 4 Diamond
Tel: **0118 940 3336** Mrs Carver.
Fax no: 0118 401 1260
D: £25.00-£30.00 **S:** £32.00-£45.00.
Open: All Year (not Xmas/New Year)
Beds: 1D 2T 2S **Baths:** 1 En 2 Sh
⛺🅿(5)✂🗆🛏🎂🛏&Ⓥ🚲

Twyford 16

National Grid Ref: SU7975
🍴🍺 Queen Victoria, La Fontana, Waggon & Horse, The Bull

Somewhere To Stay, c/o Loddon Acres, Bath Road, Twyford, Reading, Berks, RG10 9RU.
Grades: ETC 4 Diamond
Tel: **0118 934 5880** (also fax no)
Fisher.
D: £24.50-£29.00
S: £35.00-£45.00.
Open: All Year
Beds: 1F 1D 1T 1S
Baths: 3 En 1 Pr
⛺🅿(6)✂🗆🛏🎂🛏Ⓥ🌿🐾
Self-contained, modern, detached accommodation with kitchenette and sauna. Situated next to owners' house in beautiful river-fronted 2 acre garden, tennis/canoes available. Rooms ensuite, tastefully decorated with colour TV, tea/coffee, easy access to Reading, Windsor, Maidenhead and Heathrow.

Copper Beeches, Bath Road, Kiln Green, Twyford, Reading, Berks, RG10 9UT.
Quiet house in large gardens with tennis court, warm welcome.
Tel: **0118 940 2929** (also fax no)
Mrs Gorecki.
D: £22.50-£25.00
S: £28.00-£35.00.
Open: All Year
Beds: 3F 4T 1D 1S
Baths: 1 En 3 Sh
⛺(3)🅿(14)🗆🎂🛏Ⓥ🌿

Chesham House, 79 Wargrave Road, Twyford, Reading, Berks, RG10 9PE.
Windsor 20 minutes by car or rail, to London 30 minutes.
Tel: **0118 932 0428**
Mr & Mrs Ferguson.
D: £30.00-£50.00 **S:** £27.50.
Open: Mar to Dec
Beds: 1D 1T
Baths: 2 En
⛺(7)🅿(3)🗆🎂🛏Ⓥ

The Hermitage, 63 London Road, Twyford, Reading, Berks, RG10 9EJ.
Elegant period house, village centre, close mainline railway, London 40 mins.
Tel: **0118 934 0004** (also fax no)
Mrs Barker.
D: £26.00-£30.00 **S:** £35.00-£48.00.
Open: All Year (not Xmas)
Beds: 2D 3T
Baths: 3 En 1 Sh
🅿(6)✂🗆🎂🛏Ⓥ

Order your
packed lunches the
evening before you
need them.
Not at breakfast!

Cheshire Cycleway

The 135-mile **Cheshire Cycleway** takes you through the whole range of the county's scenery, from plain and parkland to the edge of the Pennine moors, and also gives a taste of Cheshire's urban landscape: the circular route has the historic towns of Chester and Macclesfield at either pole, and is sprinkled with castles and country houses.

A detailed **guide leaflet** to the cycleway route, which includes a list of cycle repair/hire shops on or near to the route, is available from Cheshire County Council, Tourism and Marketing Unit, 4 Hillyards Court, Chester Business Park, Wrexham Road, Chester CH4 9RD, tel 01244 603107, @ 60p (+20p p&p). The route is signposted by blue Cheshire Cycleway direction signs with a cycle silhouette, only in a clockwise direction as described above.

Maps: Ordnance Survey 1:50,000 Landranger series: 117, 118.

Major **railway** termini along the route are Chester, Crewe, Macclesfield and Wilmslow, north east of Knutsford. Many other places

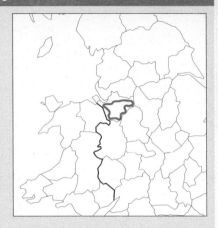

are served by local trains.

If you would like advice or help with planning the cycleway, **Byways Bike Breaks** specialise in cycling holidays in Cheshire. They can be contacted at 25 Mayville Road, Liverpool L18 0HG, tel 0151-722 8050.

Chester

The route begins in **Chester**, the county town with a fortress history. The largest fortified town of Roman Britain, in medieval times it was the centre of the Plantagenets' military campaigns against Wales, and boasts the most complete medieval and Roman city wall in Britain - two miles long with seven gates. Landmarks along the wall include the fifteenth-century King Charles Tower, from which

Charles I watched the defeat of the royalist side in the battle of Rowton Moor, and the Water Tower, which contains a display on the city's history. Other features of the city are the cathedral, containing architectural vestiges from the eleventh to the sixteenth centuries, including the intersecting stone arches of the 'crown of stone' and a cloistered garden; and the half-excavated Roman Amphitheatre, the largest in Britain, its estimated capacity of 7000 even greater than that in Caerleon.

Chester   1

National Grid Ref: SJ4066

|¶| ◄▣ Bromfield Arms, Faulkner Arms, Spinning Wheel, Chester Bells, Plough, Red Lion, King's Head, Eversley Hotel, Royal Oak, Swan Inn, Wetherspoons, Cavendish, Glynne Arms, Miller's Kitchen, Town Crier, Halfway House

▲ **Chester Youth Hostel,** *Hough Green House, 40 Hough Green, Chester, CH4 8HD.*
Actual grid ref: SJ397651
Tel: **01244 680056**
Under 18: £7.75 **Adults:** £11.00
Self-catering facilities, Television, Showers, Shop, Laundry facilities, Lounge, Drying room, Security lockers, Parking, Evening meal at 6.00-7.30pm, Kitchen facilities, Credit cards accepted
Barely a mile from the city centre, this Victorian house and mews has comfortable accommodation for both families and singles.

Dee Heights Guest House, 23 City Walls, Chester, CH1 1SB.
Tel: **01244 350386**
Mrs Willis.
D: £20.00-£24.00 **S:** £30.00-£35.00.
Open: All Year
Beds: 1D
Baths: 1 Pr
⚘⌂☐♨▥.Ⅴ♿
A charming riverside house situated on the Roman walls overlooking the River Dee and Old Dee Bridge. Fresh flowers and magnificent river views. Studio bed-sitting room with French window opening onto south facing balcony. Three minutes from city centre.

D = Price range per person

sharing in a double room

*Aplas Guest House, 106 Brook
Street, Chester, Cheshire, CH1 3DU.*
Tel: **01244 312401** Mr Aplas.
D: £13.00-£17.50 .
Open: All Year
Beds: 1F 4D 2T
Baths: 5 En, 2 Sh
🛇 (3) 🅿 (7) ⌺ 🐾 🖫 �𝗩 ⨉
We are a family run guest house,
under the personal supervision of
Patricia and Michael Aplas. We are
ideally located for historic Chester.
10 minutes walk to city centre, 5
minutes walk to railway/bus sta-
tion. Parking and room only rates
available.

The Grid Reference
beneath the location
heading is for the
village or town - *not*
for individual houses,
which are shown
(where supplied) in
each entry itself.

---

*Grosvenor Place Guest House, 2-4
Grosvenor Place, Chester, CH1 2DE.*
City centre guest house; proprietor:
Alma Wood.
Tel: **01244 324455** Mrs Wood.
Fax no: 01244 400225
D: £18.00-£22.00 **S:** £20.00-£25.00.
Open: All Year (not Xmas)
Beds: 2F 3D 2T 3S
Baths: 4 En 2 Sh
🛇 🅿 ⌺ 🐾 🖫 🖫 ⟨𝗩⟩ ⨉ ⨶

*Stone Villa, 3 Stone Place, Hoole,
Chester, CH2 3NR.*
A haven of quiet relaxation with
individual attention and warm hos-
pitality.
Grades: RAC 4 Diamond,
Sparkling Diamond Award
Tel: **01244 345014** Mr Pow.
D: £25.00-£28.00 **S:** £25.00-£32.00.
Open: All Year (not Xmas)
Beds: 1F 6D 2T 1S
Baths: 9 En 1 Pr
🛇 🅿 (10) ⨯ ⌺ 🐾 🖫 & ᵭ ⨉ ⨶

*Castle House, 23 Castle Street,
Chester, CH1 2DS.*
Pre-1580 Tudor house, plus
Georgian front (1738).
Grades: ETC 3 Diamond
Tel: **01244 350354** Mr Marl.
D: £24.00-£25.00 **S:** £38.00-£38.00.
Open: All Year
Beds: 1F 1D 1T 2S
Baths: 3 En 1 Sh
🛇 🅿 ⌺ 🐾 🖫 🖫 ⟨𝗩⟩ ⨉

*Homeleigh, 14 Hough Green,
Chester, CH4 8JG.*
Family-run Victorian house, 10
minutes walk from city centre.
Grades: ETC 3 Diamond
Tel: **01244 676761**
Mr & Mrs Smith.
Fax no: 01244 679977
D: £18.00-£20.00 **S:** £20.00-£22.00.
Open: All Year (not Xmas)
Beds: 1F 4D 2T 2S
Baths: 9 En
🛇 🅿 (10) ⌺ 🐾 🖫 🖫 ⟨𝗩⟩ ⨶

*Buckingham House, 38 Hough
Green, Chester, Cheshire, CH4 8JQ.*
Well appointed rooms. Near city
centre and race course. Excellent
value.
Grades: ETC 3 Diamond
Tel: **01244 678885** (also fax no)
Ms Langmead.
D: £17.00-£23.00 **S:** £22.00-£38.00.
Open: All Year
Beds: 3F 1D **Baths:** 4 En
🛇 🅿 (8) ⌺ 🐾 🖫 🖫 ⟨𝗩⟩ ᵭ ⨶

Planning a longer
stay? Always ask for
any special rates.

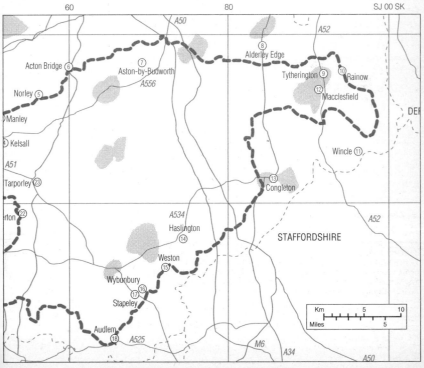

Ba Ba Guest House, 65 Hoole Road, Hoole, Chester, Cheshire, CH2 3NJ.
Family run B&B in Victorian town house, birth place of Leonard Cheshire.
Tel: **01244 315047**
Mrs Smith.
Fax no: 01244 315046
D: £20.00-£25.00 **S:** £25.00-£30.00.
Open: All Year (not Xmas/New Year)
Beds: 3F 2D/T
Baths: 4 En 1 Pr
🛏 🅿 (5) ⌿ 🖵 🛋 📖 Ⓥ

Mitchells Of Chester, Green Gables House, 28 Hough Green, Chester, Cheshire, CH4 8JQ.
Victorian residence with tall ceilings, sweeping staircase and antique furniture.
Grades: ETC 4 Diamond, Silver
Tel: **01244 679004**
Mrs Mitchell.
Fax no: 01244 659567
D: £24.00-£28.00 **S:** £30.00-£40.00.
Open: All Year (not Xmas)
Beds: 1F 1D 1T 1S
Baths: 7 En
🛏 🅿 (5) ⌿ 🖵 🛋 📖 Ⓥ 🚲

Laurels, 14 Selkirk Road, Curzon Park, Chester, CH4 8AH.
Lovely family home near racecourse; best residential area, very quiet.
Tel: **01244 679682** Mrs Roberts.
D: £18.50-£19.50 **S:** £18.50-£19.50.
Open: All Year (not Xmas)
Beds: 1F 2D 1T 1S
Baths: 1 En 1 Pr
🛏 🅿 (3) 🖵 🛋 📖 Ⓥ

Devonia, 33-35 Hoole Road, Chester, CH2 3NH.
Large Victorian family-run guest house. Same owner for 35 years.
Tel: **01244 322236**
Fax no: 01244 401511
D: £17.50-£20.00
S: £25.00-£30.00.
Open: All Year
Beds: 4F 2D 2T 2S
Baths: 1 En 3 Sh
🛏 🅿 (20) ⌿ 🖵 🛌 🛋 📖 Ⓥ 🍴 ⌿

Littleton 2

National Grid Ref: SJ4466

🍴 🍺 The Plough

Firbank, 64 Tarvin Road, Littleton, Chester, CH3 7DF.
Traditional Victorian house, warm welcome, extensive gardens, two miles Chester.
Tel: **01244 335644**
Mrs Shambler.
Fax no: 01244 332068
D: £20.00-£27.50
S: £25.00-£30.00.
Open: All Year (not Xmas)
Beds: 1D 1T
Baths: 2 En
🅿 (2) 🖵 🛋 📖 Ⓥ

Manley 3

National Grid Ref: SJ5071

🍴 🍺 The Goshawk, White Lion

Rangeway Bank Farm, Manley, Warrington, Cheshire, WA6 9EF.
Actual grid ref: SJ517717
Friendly traditional farmhouse in quiet countryside adjacent to Delamere Forest.
Tel: **01928 740236**
Challoner.
Fax no: 01928 740703
D: £20.00-£25.00 **S:** £22.00-£25.00.
Open: All Year (not Xmas)
Beds: 1F 1D 1T
Baths: 2 En 1 Sh
🛏 🅿 (6) ⌿ 🖵 🛌 🛋 📖 Ⓥ 🍴 🚲

Kelsall 4

National Grid Ref: SJ5268

🍴 🍺 Morris Dancer, The Boot

Northwood Hall, Dog Lane, Kelsall, Chester, Cheshire, CW6 0RP.
Elegant Victorian farmhouse with cobblestone courtyard. All rooms traditionally appointed.
Tel: **01829 752569**
Mr & Mrs Nock.
Fax no: 01829 751157
D: £21.50-£23.50 **S:** £27.50.
Open: All Year (not Xmas)
Beds: 2D
Baths: 2 En
🛏 🅿 (6) ⌿ 🖵 🛋 📖 Ⓥ 🍴 🚲

Pay B&Bs by cash or cheque and be prepared to pay up front.

All rates are subject to alteration at the owners' discretion.

Norley 5

National Grid Ref: SJ5672

🍴 🍺 Carriers Inn

Wicken Tree Farm, Blakemere Lane, Norley, Warrington, Cheshire, WA6 6NW.
High quality self-contained accommodation and B&B, surrounded by Delamere Forest.
Tel: **01928 788355** Mr Appleton.
D: £23.50-£25.00 **S:** £23.50-£31.00.
Open: All Year
Beds: 1F 5D 7T 3S
Baths: 6 En 1 Pr 2 Sh
🛏 🅿 (14) ⌿ 🖵 🛌 🛋 📖 ♿ Ⓥ 🍴 🚲

Acton Bridge 6

National Grid Ref: SJ5975

🍴 🍺 Maypole, Hazel Pear

Manor Farm, Cliff Road, Acton Bridge, Northwich, Cheshire, CW8 3QP.
Actual grid ref: SJ586766
Peaceful, elegantly furnished traditional country house. Large garden and views.
Grades: ETC 4 Diamond
Tel: **01606 853181** Mrs Campbell.
D: £20.00-£25.00 **S:** £20.00-£25.00.
Open: All Year (not Xmas)
Beds: 1F 1T 1S
Baths: 1 En 2 Pr
🛏 (1) 🅿 (10) ⌿ 🖵 🛌 🛋 📖 Ⓥ 🍴 🚲

Chester to Knutsford

Attractions along the first stretch of the route after Chester include the Mouldsworth Motor Museum, a collection of vintage vehicles which, despite its name, also contains some early bicycles; and Delamere Forest Park, 4000 acres of woodland, with waymarked walks and cycling trails for if you fancy a diversion from the serious business of the cycleway itself. From here you strike out across the Cheshire Plain, and can admire the half-timbered cottages of the village of Great Budworth before reaching the town of **Knutsford.** *Canute's Ford*, where the Danish king crossed the Lily Stream in the early eleventh century, was important in medieval times for its market and coaching inns, but the modern town dates largely from the eighteenth century, and was the model for Elizabeth Gaskell's *Cranford* in the nineteenth. In more recent times, nearby Knutsford Heath was the scene of a memorable confrontation during the 1997 election campaign, between Martin Bell, who became Independent Member of Parliament, and Christine Hamilton, as she leapt heroically but vainly to the defence of her errant husband, Neil, the discredited sitting MP.

Knutsford to Audlem

After Knutsford it's a gradual climb to Alderley Edge, a sandstone ridge inhabited by a legendary wizard, around **Macclesfield**, historically important for its silk production, and towards the edge of the **Peak District National Park**. Attractions along the way include two National Trust properties, a fifteenth-century water mill at Nether Alderley, and Hare Hill Gardens, a Victorian woodland garden and walled garden; and Prestbury, a village notable for its nineteenth-century weaver's cottages. A little way off the route is Tegg's Nose Country Park, where the gritstone hill provides a magnificent panorama in every direction, and then comes the most remote part of the cycleway, as you head towards the village of Wildboarclough inside the White Peak. After this the route takes you back down off the Peak; across the Macclesfield Canal you come to Galsworth Hall, a Tudor house set in beautiful grounds. Past Congleton and Alsager you come to Barthomley, another beautiful Cheshire village with half-timbered cottages and a seventeenth-century pub, the White Lion. The route bypasses Nantwich, famous for its timber-framed Tudor buildings and the fourteenth-century Church of St Mary, after Crewe, famous for its railway junction, and takes you to Audlem, which boasts another fourteenth-century church and stands upon the Shropshire Union Canal, with a succession of locks.

Aston-by-Budworth   7

National Grid Ref: SJ6976

🍴 🍺 The Red Lion

Clock Cottage, *Hield Lane, Aston-by-Budworth, Northwich, Cheshire,* CW9 6LP.
Lovely C17th thatched country cottage, beautiful country garden, wooded countryside.
Tel: **01606 891271**
Mrs Tanner-Betts.
D: £17.50-£20.00.
S: £17.50-£20.00.
Open: All Year (not Xmas)
Beds: 1T 2S **Baths:** 1 Sh
🛇 (2) 🅿 (4) ⊬ 🖵 🌡 🖿 Ⓥ ♻ 🚲

Alderley Edge   8

National Grid Ref: SJ8478

🍴 🍺 Prospect House Hotel, Oakwood, Bird In Hand, Frozen Mop, Plough & Flail, Kings Arms

Trafford House Farm, *Beswicks Lane, Row of Trees, Alderley Edge, Wilmslow, Cheshire,* SK9 7SN.
Trafford House Farm is situated in quiet rural location, but with easy access.
Tel: **01625 582160**
Mr & Mrs Blackmore.
Fax no: 01625 584968
D: £15.00-£15.00
S: £20.00-£20.00.
Open: All Year
Beds: 1F 1T 1S
Baths: 2 Sh
🛇 🅿 (10) ⊬ 🖵 🏋 🗙 🌡 🖿 Ⓥ ♻
🚲

Planning a longer
stay? Always ask for
any special rates.

Bringing children with

you? Always ask for

any special rates.

Tytherington   9

National Grid Ref: SJ9175

🍴 🍺 Cock & Pheasant

Moorhayes House Hotel, *27 Manchester Road, Tytherington, Macclesfield, Cheshire,* SK10 2JJ.
Actual grid ref: SJ915752
Warm welcome comfortable home, attractive garden, 0.5 mile from Macclesfield.
Tel: **01625 433228** (also fax no)
Helen Wood.
D: £24.00-£29.00
S: £28.00-£45.00.
Open: All Year (not Xmas)
Beds: 1F 4D 2T 1S
Baths: 7 En 1 Sh
🛇 🅿 (14) 🖵 🏋 🌡 🖿 Ⓥ ♻ 🚲

Rainow   10

National Grid Ref: SJ9576

🍴 🍺 Rising Sun, Robin Hood

The Tower House, *Tower Hill, Rainow, Macclesfield, Cheshire,* SK10 5TX.
Luxury accommodation in carefully restored C16th farmhouse. Superb breakfasts.
Tel: **01625 438022** (also fax no)
Mrs Buckley.
D: £25.00-£25.00
S: £25.00-£35.00.
Open: All Year
Beds: 2T 1S
Baths: 1 Pr
🛇 🅿 (4) ⊬ 🖵 🌡 🖿 Ⓥ ♻ 🚲

Wincle   11

National Grid Ref: SJ9566

🍴 🍺 Ship Inn

Hill Top Farm, *Wincle, Macclesfield, Cheshire,* SK11 0QH.
Actual grid ref: SJ959662
Peaceful, comfortable farmhouse accommodation, set in beautiful countryside. Lovely walks.
Tel: **01260 227257**
Mrs Brocklehurst.
D: £18.00-£20.00 **S:** £20.00-£22.00.
Open: All Year (not Xmas)
Beds: 2T 1D
Baths: 2 En 1 Pr
🛇 🅿 (4) ⊬ 🖵 🏋 🗙 🌡 🖿 Ⓥ ♻ 🚲

Macclesfield   12

National Grid Ref: SJ9173

Penrose Guest House, *56 Birtles Road, Whirley, Macclesfield, Cheshire,* SK10 3JQ.
Central for Wilmslow, Prestbury, Macclesfield. Close intercity trains, motorway, airport.
Tel: **01625 615323**
Fax no: 01625 432284
D: £20.00
S: £20.00.
Open: All Year
Beds: 1T 2S
🛇 (4) 🅿 (6) ⊬ 🖵 🌡 🖿 Ⓥ

High season,
bank holidays and
special events mean
low availability
everywhere.

Audlem to Chester

Two more villages worth a look along the route are Wrenbury and Marbury, before you arrive at **Malpas**, an historic market town with half-timbered buildings, Georgian houses and coaching inns. The town is also the place to sample the range of salty Cheshire cheeses, on sale everywhere. Notable places along the home strait of the cycleway are Stretton Mill, a working water mill that has been restored, and two castles - Peckforton Castle, built in the mid-nineteenth century medievalist revival for Lord Tollemache, and by contrast the ruins of the very genuinely medieval Beeston Castle, dating from the thirteenth century and set romantically against glorious views over the Cheshire Plain. From here you ride parallel to the Shropshire Union Canal back into **Chester**.

Congleton 13

National Grid Ref: SJ8663

⊯ ⊲ Lamb Inn, Bull's Head Hotel, Brown Cow Inn, Edgerton Arms, Brownlow Inn

The Lamb Inn, *3 Blake Street, Congleton, Cheshire,* CW12 4DS.
Central location convenient for Cheshire country houses and attractions.
Tel: **01260 272731** Mr Kelly.
D: £16.00-£20.00 **S:** £18.00-£24.00
Open: All Year
Beds: 1F 2D 2T 1S
Baths: 3 En 3 Sh
🛏 🅿 (40) ⬚ ⼪ 📻 🛒 🎞 Ⓥ ⼗

8 Cloud View, *Congleton, Cheshire,* CW12 3TP.
Lovely family home, edge of countryside, good views.
Tel: **01260 276048** Mrs Stewart.
D: £18.00-£20.00
S: £19.00-£20.00.
Open: All Year (not Xmas)
Beds: 1D 1S **Baths:** 1 En 1 Sh
🛏 🅿 (1) ⼭ ⬚ ✕ 🛒 🎞 Ⓥ

D = Price range per person sharing in a double room

Cuttleford Farm, *Newcastle Road, Astbury, Congleton, Cheshire,* CW12 4SD.
16th Century farmhouse - working farm close to National Trust House.
Tel: **01260 272499** Mrs Downs.
D: £20.00-£25.00 .
Open: All Year
Beds: 2D 1T **Baths:** 1 En 1 Sh
🛏 🅿 ⼭ ⬚ 📻 🛒 🎞 Ⓥ

Loachbrook Farm, *Sandbach Road, Congleton, Cheshire,* CW12 4TE.
Actual grid ref: SJ833630
C17th working farm close to M6 and many attractions.
Tel: **01260 273318** Mrs Dale.
D: £17.50-£19.00 **S:** £18.50-£20.00.
Open: All Year (not Xmas)
Beds: 1D 1T 1S **Baths:** 1 Sh
🛏 (5) 🅿 (4) ⼭ ⬚ 🛒 🎞 Ⓥ ⼗

Haslington 14

National Grid Ref: SJ7355

Ferndale House, *Gutterscroft, Haslington, Crewe, Cheshire,* CW1 5RJ.
Victorian home, large rooms, excellent food, secure parking, convenient M6.
Tel: **01270 584048** Docherty.
D: £20.00-£23.50 **S:** £20.00-£20.00.
Open: All Year
🛏 🅿 (7) ⼭ ⬚ ✕ 🛒 🎞 Ⓥ 🛉

Weston (Crewe) 15

National Grid Ref: SJ7352

⊯ ⊲ White Lion Inn

Snape Farm, *Snape Lane, Weston, Crewe, Cheshire,* CW2 5NB.
Actual grid ref: SJ743518
Warm comfortable Victorian farmhouse in quiet location near Junction 16 M6.
Tel: **01270 820208** (also fax no)
Mrs Williamson.
D: £18.00-£20.00 **S:** £20.00-£28.00.
Open: All Year (not Xmas)
Beds: 3F 1D 2T
Baths: 1 En 1 Pr 1 Sh
🛏 🅿 (6) ⼭ ⬚ 📻 ✕ 🛒 🎞 Ⓥ ⼗

Wybunbury 16

National Grid Ref: SJ6949

⊯ ⊲ Swan

Lea Farm, *Wrinehill Road, Wybunbury, Nantwich, Cheshire,* CW5 7HS.
Charming farmhouse set in landscaped gardens where peacocks roam.
Grades: AA 3 Diamond
Tel: **01270 841429** (also fax no)
Mrs Callwood.
D: £18.00 **S:** £21.00.
Open: All Year (not Xmas)
Beds: 1F 1D 1T
Baths: 2 Pr 1 Sh
🛏 🅿 (22) ⬚ 📻 ✕ 🛒 Ⓥ 🛉 ⼗

S = Price range for a single person in a room

Stapeley 17

National Grid Ref: SJ6749

⊯ ⊲ Globe

York Cottage, *82 Broad Lane, Stapeley, Nantwich, Cheshire,* CW5 7QL.
Comfortable detached rural cottage, with garden, 2 miles from Nantwich.
Tel: **01270 629829**
Mrs Orford.
Fax no: 01270 625404
D: £18.00-£20.00 **S:** £18.00-£22.00.
Open: All Year
Beds: 2D 1F
Baths: 1 Sh
🛏 🅿 (3) ⼭ ⬚ 📻 🛒 🎞 Ⓥ 🛉 ⼤ ⼗

Audlem 18

National Grid Ref: SJ6643

⊯ ⊲ Lord Cumbermere

Little Heath Farm, *Audlem, Crewe, Cheshire,* CW3 0HE.
Warm traditionally furnished oak beamed farmhouse in canal side village of Audlem.
Grades: AA 3 Diamond
Tel: **01270 811324** (also fax no)
Mrs Bennion.
D: £18.00-£24.00 **S:** £22.00-£26.00.
Open: All Year (not Xmas/New Year)
Beds: 1D 1T 1F
Baths: 1 Pr 1 Sh
🛏 🅿 (3) ⼭ ⬚ 📻 ✕ 🛒 🎞 Ⓥ 🛉 ⼗

Malpas 19

National Grid Ref: SJ4847

Farm Ground Cottage, *Edge, Malpas, Cheshire,* SY14 8LE.
Peaceful, comfortable Victorian Cottage in rural surroundings. Excellent touring base.
Tel: **01948 820333**
D: £19.50-£21.00 **S:** £20.00-£22.00.
Open: All Year (not Xmas)
Beds: 1D
Baths: 1 Pr
🅿 (2) ⼭ ⬚ 📻 ✕ 🛒 🎞 Ⓥ 🛉 ⼤ ⼗

High season, bank holidays and special events mean low availability *everywhere.*

Tilston 20

National Grid Ref: SJ4551

⍾ ◖ Carden Arms

Tilston Lodge, *Tilston, Malpas, Cheshire, SY14 7DR.*
Handsome country house with spacious grounds. Luxuriously equipped quiet bedrooms.
Grades: AA 5 Diamond
Tel: **01829 250223** Mrs Ritchie.
Fax no: 01829 250223
D: £33.00-£35.00 **S:** £43.00-£45.00.
Open: All Year (not Xmas/New Year)
Beds: 1T 1D **Baths:** 2 En
⛄ 🅿 (10) ⍀ ☐ 🛒 🎢 Ⅲ Ⅴ ⓘ ✦ ♻

Broxton 21

National Grid Ref: SJ4754

⍾ ◖ Frog Manor

Frogg Manor Hotel, *Fullers Moor, Nantwich Road, Broxton, Chester, CH3 9JH.*
Not far from the madding crowd, a superb Georgian manor house.
Tel: **01829 782629**
D: £45.00-£72.50 **S:** £60.00-£100.00
Open: All Year
Beds: 6D **Baths:** 6 En
⛄ (4) 🅿 (40) ⍀ ☐ 🐾 ✕ 🛒 Ⅲ Ⅴ ⓘ ✦ ♻

Tiverton 22

National Grid Ref: SJ5460

⍾ ◖ Red Lion

The Gables, *Tiverton, Tarporley, Cheshire, CW6 9NH.*
Beautiful country cottage set amidst almost 1/2 acre of gardens.
Tel: **01829 733028** Mr Wilson.
Fax no: 01829 733399
D: £17.50-£19.00 **S:** £25.00-£35.00.
Open: All Year
Beds: 3D **Baths:** 1 Sh
⛄ 🅿 (8) ⍀ ☐ 🐾 🛒 Ⅲ Ⅴ ♻

Tarporley 23

National Grid Ref: SJ5462

Foresters Arms, *92 High Street, Tarporley, Cheshire, CW6 0AX.*
A traditional country inn offering fine ales and comfortable rooms.
Grades: ETC 3 Diamond
Tel: **01829 733151**
Fax no: 01829 730020
D: £18.00-£22.50 **S:** £18.00-£22.50.
Open: All Year (not Xmas/New Year)
Beds: 4T 1D
Baths: 1 En 1 Sh
⛄ (10) 🅿 (20) ☐ 🛒 Ⅲ Ⅴ ⓘ ✦ ♻

Hatton Heath 24

National Grid Ref: SJ4561

⍾ ◖ Grosvenor Arms

Golborne Manor, *Platts Lane, Hatton Heath, Chester, Cheshire, CH3 9AN.*
Beautifully decorated 19th century manor house with glorious views and garden.
Grades: ETC 4 Diamond
Tel: **01829 770310** Mrs Ikin.
Fax no: 01829 770370
D: £58.00-£68.00 **S:** £28.00-£38.00.
Open: All Year
Beds: 1F 1T 1D
Baths: 3 En
⛄ 🅿 (6) ⍀ ☐ ✕ 🛒 Ⅲ Ⅴ ⓘ ✦ ♻

Please respect
a B&B's wishes
regarding children,
animals & smoking.

Cumbria Cycleway

The **Cumbria Cycleway** is a mammoth 260-mile circular route around the perimeter of the County of Cumbria, from moorland and wooded river valleys inland to a long stretch along the coast, from Morecambe Bay to the Solway Firth. It completely avoids the Lakes (see the *Sustrans Sea to Sea (C2C)* route for a route through the Lake District), and as such takes you to parts of the county not frequented by visitors. The route is clearly waymarked in both directions by brown 'Cumbria' direction signs with a cycle silhouette, and there is no designated start/finish. The description that follows takes the route clockwise from Carlisle.

A detailed **guide leaflet** to the cycleway route, which includes a list of cycle repair/hire shops on or near to the route, is available free from West Cumbria Cycleway Network, Groundwork West Cumbria, Crowgarth House, 48 High Street, Cleator Moor, Cumbria CA25 5AA, tel 01946 813677 and a **guide book**, *The Cumbria Cycleway* by Roy Walker and Ron Jarvis (ISBN 1 852841 06 0) is published by Cicerone Press and available from the publishers at 2 Police Square, Milnthorpe, Cumbria LA7 7PY, tel 01539 562069, @ £6.99 (+75p p&p).

Maps: Ordnance Survey 1:50,000 Landranger series: 85, 86, 89, 90, 91, 96, 97, 98

The major **railway** termini are Carlisle, Oxenholme (near Kendal) and Penrith. There is also the famous scenic Leeds-Settle-Carlisle Railway, which stops at Garsdale, Kirkby Stephen and Appleby-in-Westmorland, and other local services.

Carlisle   1

National Grid Ref: NY3955

|⊙| ◁ Metal Bridge Inn, The Beehive, Mary's Pantry, Crown & Thistle, Coach & Horses, Golden Fleece, Black Lion

▲ *Carlisle Youth Hostel,*
University of Northumbria, The
Old Brewery Residences, Bridge
Lane, Caldewgate, Carlisle,
Cumbria, CA2 5SR.
Actual grid ref: NY394560
Tel: **01228 597352**
Under 18: £8.75 **Adults:** £13.00
Self-catering facilities, Showers, Cycle store, Parking, Facilities for disabled people, No smoking, WC, Kitchen facilities
University accommodation in an award-winning conversion of the former Theakston's brewery. Single study bedrooms with shared kitchen and bathroom in flats for up to 7 people.

Pay B&Bs by cash or cheque and be prepared to pay up front.

Howard Lodge, 90 Warwick Road,
Carlisle, Cumbria, CA1 1JU.
Actual grid ref: NY407558
Grades: ETC 4 Diamond,
AA 3 Diamond
Tel: **01228 529842**
Mr Hendrie.
D: £15.00-£25.00
S: £20.00-£30.00.
Open: All Year
Beds: 2F 1D 2T 1S
Baths: 6 En 1 Sh
🛇 🅿 (6) 🔲 ⭢ ✕ 🖄 🕭 🛋 Ⅴ 👜 🐾
Friendly family-run guest house in comfortable Victorian town house in conservation area. Spacious rooms all fully ensuite with satellite TV, welcome tray, hairdryer and clock radio. Large breakfasts. 5 minutes' walk from station and city centre. Evening meals by prior arrangement. Private car park.

Craighead, 6 Hartington Place,
Carlisle, Cumbria, CA1 1HL.
Actual grid ref: NY405559
Grades: ETC 3 Diamond
Tel: **01228 596767**
Mrs Smith.
D: £17.00 **S:** £16.00.
Open: All Year (not Xmas)
Beds: 1F 2D 1T 1S
Baths: 1 En 2 Sh
🛇 🔲 ⭢ 🖄 🕭 🛋 Ⅴ 👜 🐾
You will receive a warm welcome at Craighead, a Grade II Listed spacious Victorian town house with comfortable rooms and original features. CTV, tea/coffee tray in all rooms. Minutes' walk to city centre bus and rail stations and all amenities. Friendly personal service.

Cherry Grove, 87 Petteril Street,
Carlisle, Cumbria, CA1 2AW.
Lovely red brick building close to golf club and town.
Grades: AA 3 Diamond
Tel: **01228 541942**
Mr & Mrs Houghton.
D: £17.50-£20.00
S: £20.00-£30.00.
Open: All Year
Beds: 3F 2D
Baths: 5 En
🛇 🅿 (3) 🖄 🔲 ⭢ 🖄 🕭 🛋 Ⅴ 👜 🐾

Angus Hotel & Almonds Bistro,
14 Scotland Road, Stanwix,
Carlisle, Cumbria, CA3 9DG.
Actual grid ref: NY400571
Grades: AA 4 Diamond
Tel: **01228 523546**
Mr Webster.
Fax no: 01228 531895
D: £20.00-£27.00
S: £26.00-£42.00.
Open: All Year
Beds: 4F 3D 4T 3S
Baths: 11 En 3 Sh
🛏🅿(6)🛇🗢↑✕🕴🖥🔟📖⬩⚡🚲
Victorian town house, foundations
on Hadrian's Wall. Excellent food,
Les Routiers Awards, local
cheeses, home baked bread.
Genuine warm welcome from
owners. Licensed, draught beer,
lounge, meeting room, internet
cafe, direct dial telephones, secure
garaging. Group rates for cyclists
available.

Avondale, 3 St Aidans Road,
Carlisle, Cumbria, CA1 1LT.
Attractive comfortable Edwardian
house. Quiet central position
convenient M6 J43.
Grades: ETC 4 Diamond
Tel: **01228 523012** (also fax no)
Mr & Mrs Hayes.
D: £20.00-£20.00
S: £20.00-£40.00.
Open: All Year (not Xmas)
Beds: 1D 2T
Baths: 1 En 1 Pr
🛏🅿(3)🛇🗢✕🕴🖥🔟📖⚡🚲

Carlisle

As a border city, **Carlisle**, the county town, was for
centuries the focus of tribal struggles: the original settlement of
Celtic Britons was subdued by the Roman Empire to build an
outpost for the construction of Hadrian's Wall, and later attempts
of Anglo-Saxons, Scots and Danes to prevail ended with the
Norman takeover. However, the Scots never quite gave up, and
captured the town for a brief period during the Jacobite
rebellion of 1745. The notable remains of these struggles are the
eleventh- to twelfth-century city walls and the Castle, built by the
Norman King William Rufus, with many later additions, where
Mary Queen of Scots was kept prisoner by Elizabeth I in 1568,
and Scottish prisoners of war were accommodated after the
crushing of the Jacobite rebellion. Carlisle Cathedral, built in red
sandstone, was begun by the same king, completed by Henry I
and desecrated by Cromwell's men five hundred years later.
Two Romanesque arches remain from the original building, set
against the Gothic East Window; there is also a treasury housing
important objects from the city's ecclesiastical heritage.

All rooms full and
nowhere else to stay?
Ask the owner if
there's anywhere
nearby

Dalroc, 411 Warwick Road,
Carlisle, Cumbria, CA1 2RZ.
Small friendly house. Midway city
centre and M6 motorway.
Tel: **01228 542805**
Mrs Irving.
D: £16.00-£16.00
S: £16.00-£16.00.
Open: All Year (not Xmas/New
Year)
Beds: 1T 1D 1S
🛏(7)🅿🗢✕🕴🖥🔟📖⚡🚲

Kingstown Hotel, 246 Kingstown
Road, Carlisle, CA3 0DE.
Grades: AA 3 Diamond
Tel: **01228 515292** (also fax no)
Mrs Marshall.
D: £23.50
S: £35.00-£40.00.
Open: All Year
Beds: 1F 4D 2T
Baths: 7 En
🛏🅿(14)🗢↑✕🕴🖥🔟♿🔟⚡🚲
Just off the M6 (Jct. 44) we are a
licensed hotel providing high-qual-
ity accommodation. You will find a
friendly and relaxed atmosphere,
freshly-prepared cuisine and fine
wine at reasonable prices. A good
base to explore Cumbria,
Northumbria, Lake District,
Scotland

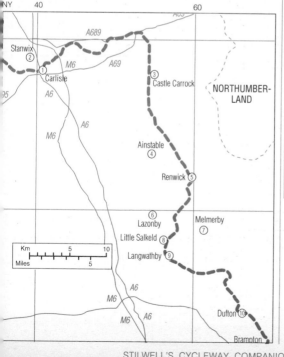

High season,
bank holidays and
special events mean
low availability
everywhere.

Chatsworth Guest House, 22
*Chatsworth Square, Carlisle,
Cumbria, CA1 1HF.*
City centre Grade II Listed building, close to all amenities.
Grades: ETC 3 Diamond
Tel: **01228 524023** (also fax no)
Mrs Mackin.
D: £19.00-£22.00 **S:** £25.00-£25.00.
Open: All Year (not Xmas)
Beds: 1F 1D 2T 1S
Baths: 5 En ⛄🛏️🅿️ (2) 🗝️🚪🛗📺 Ⓥ

All cycleways are
popular: you are
well-advised to
book ahead

D = Price range per person
sharing in a double room

Corner House Hotel & Bar, 4
Grey Street, Carlisle, CA1 2JP.
Grades: ETC 3 Diamond
Tel: **01228 533239** Mrs Anderson.
Fax no: 01228 546628
D: £17.50-£22.00 **S:** £20.00-£30.00.
Open: All Year
Beds: 3F 4D 4T 3S **Baths:** All En
⛄🚪🛏️❌🛗📺🛗♿Ⓥ🐾☂️🚲
Refurbished family run hotel. All
rooms ensuite, colour TV, phones,
tea/coffee, radio, toiletries etc.
Cosy bar, Sky TV lounge, games
room, easy access city centre,
bus/train. Base for golf, walking,
cycling, touring the Lakes, Roman
Wall, Carlisle/Settle line etc.

Ashleigh House, 46 *Victoria
Place, Carlisle, Cumbria, CA1 1EX.*
Beautifully decorated town house.
Two minutes from city centre.
Grades: ETC 4 Diamond
Tel: **01228 521631** Mr Davies.
D: £19.00-£22.50 **S:** £25.00-£30.00.
Open: All Year (not Xmas/
New Year)
Beds: 3F 1T 2D 1S
Baths: 7 En
⛄ (5) 🚪🛗📺Ⓥ

Cornerways Guest House, 107
*Warwick Road, Carlisle, Cumbria,
CA1 1EA.*
Large Victorian town house.
Grades: ETC 4 Diamond
Tel: **01228 521733** Mrs Fisher.
D: £14.00-£18.00 **S:** £16.00-£18.00.
Open: All Year (not Xmas)
Beds: 2F 1D 4T 3S
Baths: 3 En 2 Sh
⛄🅿️ (4) 🚪🐾❌🗝️🛗Ⓥ🐾☂️

Courtfield Guest House, 169
*Warwick Road, Carlisle, Cumbria,
CA1 1LP.*
Short walk to historic city centre.
Close to M6, J43.
Grades: ETC 4 Diamond
Tel: **01228 522767**
Mrs Dawes.
D: £18.00-£22.00 **S:** £25.00.
Open: All Year (not Xmas)
Beds: 1F 2D 2T
Baths: 5 En
⛄🅿️ (4) 🗝️🚪🛗📺Ⓥ☂️

East View Guest House, 110
*Warwick Road, Carlisle, Cumbria,
CA1 1JU.*
Actual grid ref: NY407560
10 minutes' walking distance from
city centre, railway station and
restaurants.
Grades: ETC 3 Diamond,
AA 3 Diamond, RAC 3 Diamond
Tel: **01228 522112** (also fax no)
Mrs Glease.
D: £18.00-£20.00
S: £20.00-£25.00.
Open: All Year (not Xmas)
Beds: 3F 2D 1T 1S
Baths: 7 En
⛄🅿️ (4) 🗝️🚪🛗📺Ⓥ♿☂️

The Grid Reference
beneath the location
heading is for the
village or town - *not*
for individual houses,
which are shown
(where supplied) in
each entry itself.

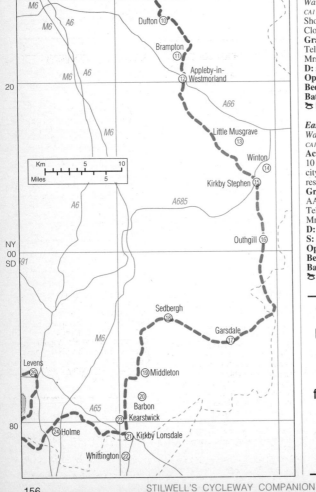

Carlisle to the Eden Valley

Out of Carlisle you ride east, via Rickerby Park, to **Brampton**, within reach of a number of buildings of historic interest, including a section of Hadrian's Wall. Then it's south, passing Talkin Tarn Country Park, and down the foothills of the northern Pennines, through a string of villages whose names evidence this region's eclectic ancient history - Celtic (Castle Carrock, Cumrew), Anglo-Saxon (Newbiggin, Croglin), Scandinavian (Glassonby) - into the gentle Eden Valley. Here stand **Long Meg and Her Daughters**, a late neolithic stone circle - Long Meg herself stands 18 feet high and is named from her eerily humanoid profile. A little way off the route are the red sandstone town of **Penrith** and the ruins of Brougham Castle with its Britanno-Roman graveyard. **Appleby-in-Westmorland**, former county town of old Westmorland, has a castle with a Norman keep, a twelfth-century church and an annual gypsy Horse Fair. Crossing the Eden at Appleby, the route heads for **Kirkby Stephen**, where there is a thirteenth-century church. You now follow the Eden to its source on the edge of the **Yorkshire Dales National Park**, briefly leaving Cumbria.

Cambro House, 173 Warwick Road, Carlisle, Cumbria, CA1 1LP.
Grades: AA 3 Diamond
Tel: **01228 543094** (also fax no)
Mr & Mrs Mawson.
D: £17.00-£20.00 **S:** £20.00-£25.00.
Open: All Year
Beds: 2D 1T
Baths: 3 En
🅿 (2) ⅋ 🗖 🛋 🍴 Ⅷ Ⅵ 🔒 ∦ ⚲ 🚲
Guests can expect warm hospitality and friendly service at this attractively decorated and well-maintained guest house. Each ensuite bedroom includes TV, clock, radio, hairdryer and welcome tray. Private off-road parking available, non-smoking, close to golf course.

Stanwix 2
National Grid Ref: NY3957

🍴 🍺 Cumbria Park Hotel

No. 1, 1 Etterby Street, Stanwix, Carlisle, Cumbria, CA3 9JB.
Homely accommodation in easy reach of Hadrian's Wall & Scotland lakes.
Grades: ETC 3 Diamond
Tel: **01228 547285** Ms Nixon.
D: £17.00-£20.00 **S:** £17.00-£20.00.
Open: All Year (not Xmas/New Year)
Beds: 1D 2S
🖙 (4) 🅿 (1) ⅋ 🗖 ✗ 🛋 🍴 Ⅷ 🔒 ∦ 🚲

S = Price range for a single person in a room

D = Price range per person sharing in a double room

Castle Carrock 3
National Grid Ref: NY5455

🍴 🍺 The Bluebell

Gelt Hall Farm, Castle Carrock, Carlisle, Cumbria, CA4 9LT.
Near Hadrian's Wall, Scottish border, Gretna Green. Scenic walks all around, looks onto Pennines.
Grades: AA 3 Diamond
Tel: **01228 670260** Ms Robinson.
D: £15.00-£16.50 **S:** £16.00-£17.00.
Open: All Year
Beds: 1F 1D 1T
Baths: 2 Sh
🖙 🅿 ⅋ 🗖 🍴 🍴 🚲

Ainstable 4
National Grid Ref: NY5346

🍴 🍺 Fox & Pheasant, New Crown

▲ *Eden Valley Centre, Ainstable, Carlisle, Cumbria, CA4 9QA.*
Actual grid ref: NY529463
Tel: **01768 896202**
Under 18: £8.00 **Adults:** £8.00
Self-catering facilities, Television, Showers, Central heating, Wet weather shelter, Lounge, Dining room, Grounds available for games, Drying room, Cycle store, Parking, Evening meal at 6pm, No smoking
Near Cumbria cycle way, Eden Way and River Eden.

Bell House, Ainstable, Carlisle, Cumbria, CA4 9RE.
Set in the Eden Valley. Explore the Lakes, Hadrian's Wall.
Grades: ETC 4 Diamond
Tel: **01768 896255** Ms Robinson.
D: £20.00-£22.50 **S:** £20.00-£22.50.
Open: All Year (not Xmas/New Year)
Beds: 1D **Baths:** 1 En
🖙 🅿 (1) ⅋ 🗖 🍴 🛋 🍴 Ⅷ Ⅵ ∦ 🚲

Renwick 5
National Grid Ref: NY5943

Scalehouse Farm, Scalehouses, Renwick, Penrith, Cumbria, CA10 1JY.
Actual grid ref: NY588451
Old farmhouse with period features, open fires and beams, tastefully renovated.
Tel: **01768 896493** (also fax no)
D: £14.00-£18.00 **S:** £16.00-£20.00.
Open: All Year (not Xmas)
Beds: 2D 1T
Baths: 1 Pr 1 Sh
🖙 🅿 (6) ⅋ 🗖 🛋 🍴 Ⅷ Ⅵ 🔒 ∦ 🚲

Lazonby 6
National Grid Ref: NY5439

🍴 🍺 Midland hotel, Joiners Arms

Harlea, Lazonby, Penrith, Cumbria, CA10 1BX.
Tel: **01768 897055** Mrs Blaylock.
D: £20.00-£21.00 **S:** £25.00-£25.00.
Open: All Year (not Xmas/New Year)
🖙 (11) 🅿 ⅋ 🗖 🛋 🍴 🛋 Ⅷ Ⅵ ∦ 🚲
Refurbished 19th Century Coach House with panoramic views of the Pennines and Eden Valley. Overlooks the famous Carlisle/Settle Railway line. Ideal for walkers, twitchers, rail enthusiasts and those seeking peace and quiet in comfort and style.

Melmerby 7
National Grid Ref: NY6137

🍴 🍺 Shepherds Inn

Gale Hall Farm, Melmerby, Penrith, Cumbria, CA10 1HN.
Actual grid ref: NY6236
Large comfortable farmhouse near Pennines and Lake District.
Tel: **01768 881254** Mrs Toppin.
D: £15.00-£15.00 **S:** £15.00-£15.00.
Open: Jun to Nov
Beds: 1F 1T 1S **Baths:** 1 Sh
🖙 🅿 (3) 🗖 🍴 🔒 🚲

Bringing children with you? Always ask for any special rates.

Little Salkeld 8

National Grid Ref: NY5636

|●| ◀Shepher's Inn

Bankhouse Farm and Stables,
Bankhouse, Little Salkeld, Penrith,
Cumbria, CA10 1NN.
Converted barns on stable yard.
Village location in Eden Valley.
Tel: **01768 881257**
D: £20.00-£30.00 S: £25.00-£30.00
Open: All Year
Beds: 3F 3T 3D
Baths: 6 En 3 Sh
ৰ 🅿 (20) 🖵 ★ 🖾 🔟 ৬ Ⅴ ▮ ≠ ⊶

Langwathby 9

National Grid Ref: NY5733

▲ **Hay Loft B&B Bunkhouse,**
Langwathby Hall, Langwathby,
Penrith, Cumbria, CA10 1PD.
Actual grid ref: NY568338
Tel: **01768 881771**
Adults: £11.50
Evening meal available.

Dufton 10

National Grid Ref: NY6825

|●| ◀Stag Inn

▲ **Dufton Youth Hostel,**
Redstones, Dufton, Appleby-in-
Westmorland, Cumbria, CA16 6DB.
Actual grid ref: NY688251
Tel: **017683 51236**
Under 18: £6.50 **Adults:** £9.25
Showers, Shop, Lounge, Dining
room 2, Drying room, Parking,
Evening meal at 7.00pm, No
smoking, Kitchen facilities,
Breakfast available, Luggage store,
Credit cards accepted
Large stone-built house with log
fire in attractive C18th village
surrounded by fine scenery of the
Eden Valley.

Sycamore House, *Dufton,*
Appleby-in-Westmorland,
Cumbria, CA16 6DB.
Listed cottage, cosy living room,
close to pub and shop.
Tel: **017683 51296**
Mrs O'Halloran.
D: £18.00-£20.00 S: £17.00-£20.00
Open: Easter to Dec
Beds: 1D 1T 2S
Baths: 1 En 1 Sh
ৰ 🅿 (2) 🖵 ★ 🖾 🔟 Ⅴ ▮ ≠ ⊶

Pay B&Bs by cash or
cheque and be prepared
to pay up front.

Eden Valley to Ulverston

From here it's through Garsdale to Sedbergh, and along the River Lune to **Kirkby Lonsdale**, where you can find the fourteenth-century stone Devil's Bridge, a thirteenth-century church and the famous view over the Lune Valley painted by Turner and idealised by Ruskin. Now you ride west along a stretch shared with the *Lancashire Cycleway*, to **Hutton Roof**, a hilltop hamlet commanding magnificent views, and then over Farleton Fell, and hit the coast at **Arnside**. You will now be at or near the coast for the rest of the way. Attractions along the next stretch include the Elizabethan Levens Hall, with the world-famous topiary gardens designed by Guillaume Beaumont (1694), a collection of Jacobean furniture and the earliest example of English patchwork. After Grange-over-Sands, **Cartmel** boasts two remainders of a twelfth-century priory which stood here until Henry VIII's Dissolution: St Mary's Church, with its many medieval tombs, and the Priory Gatehouse, now home to an art gallery. The next stage is through woodland via Cark and Greenodd to **Ulverston**, where three important figures from local history are represented in their different ways - the martial Sir John Barrow, secretary of the admiralty, by the Hoad Monument, fashioned after the design of the Eddystone Lighthouse, the pacific George Fox, the Quaker, whose home was Swarthmoor Hall, and the fantastic Stan Laurel, by the Laurel and Hardy Museum, attached to a cinema devoted to L & H's work.

Brampton (Appleby) 11

National Grid Ref: NY6723

|●| ◀New Inn, Drove Inn, White Lion

Sunray, *Brampton, Appleby-in-*
Westmorland, Cumbria, CA16 6JS.
Modern bungalow. Guest rooms
overlook Pennines, comfortable,
welcoming, good breakfast.
Tel: **017683 52905** Mrs Tinkler.
D: £15.00-£20.00 S: £18.00-£20.00.
Open: Easter to Oct
Beds: 2D **Baths:** 1 En

Appleby-in-Westmorland 12

National Grid Ref: NY6820

|●| ◀Royal Oak, Crown & Cushion

Limnerslease, *Bongate, Appleby-*
in-Westmorland, Cumbria, CA16 6UE.
Family-run guest house 10 mins
town centre. Lovely golf course &
many walks.
Tel: **017683 51578** Mrs Coward.
D: £17.00-£17.00 .
Open: All Year (not Xmas)
Beds: 2D 1T
Baths: 1 Pr 1 Sh
ৰ (13) 🅿 (3) 🖵 ★ 🖾 🔟 Ⅴ ▮ ≠ ⊶

Wemyss House, *48 Boroughgate,*
Appleby-in-Westmorland, Cumbria,
CA16 6XG.
Actual grid ref: NY684203
Georgian house in small country
town.
Tel: **017683 51494** Mrs Hirst.
D: £17.00-£17.00 S: £17.00-£17.00.
Open: Easter to Oct
Beds: 1D 1T 1S **Baths:** 2 Sh
ৰ 🅿 (2) 🖵 🖾 🔟 Ⅴ ≠ ⊶

Church View, *Bongate, Appleby-*
in-Westmorland, Cumbria,
CA16 6UN.
C18th character house, near old
coaching inn and town facilities.
Tel: **017683 51792** (also fax no)
Mrs Kemp.
D: £16.00-£18.00 S: £18.00-£20.00.
Open: All Year (not Xmas)
Beds: 1F 1D 1S
Baths: 1 Sh
ৰ (5) 🅿 (4) ⚡ 🖵 🔟 ≠ ⊶

Bongate House, *Appleby-in-*
Westmorland, Cumbria, CA16 6UE.
Actual grid ref: NY687202
This large Georgian guest house is
in an acre of secluded gardens.
Tel: **017683 51245** Mrs Dayson.
Fax no: 017683 51423
D: £18.50-£21.00 S: £18.50-£28.00.
Open: Mar to Nov
Beds: 1F 3D 3T 1S
Baths: 5 En
ৰ (5) 🅿 (8) 🖵 ★ ✕ 🖾 🔟 Ⅴ ▮ ≠
⊶

Little Musgrave 13

National Grid Ref: NY7513

Smithfield Barn, *Little Musgrave,*
Kirkby Stephen, Cumbria, CA17 4PG.
Modern barn conversion. Tranquil
setting. beautiful views over
unspoilt countryside.
Tel: **017683 41002** Hodgson.
D: £19.00-£19.00 S: £19.00-£19.00.
Open: All Year
Beds: 2D
Baths: 1 En 1 Pr
ৰ 🅿 ⚡ 🖵 ★ ✕ 🖾 🔟 Ⅴ ▮ ≠ ⊶

Winton 14

National Grid Ref: NY7811

|⊶| ⊕ Bay Horse Inn

South View Farm, Winton, Kirkby Stephen, Cumbria, CA17 4HS.
Lovely farmhouse situated in quiet village, easy access to the Lakes and Dales.
Tel: **017683 71120**
Mrs Marston.
D: £15.00-£15.00 **S:** £15.00-£15.00.
Open: All Year
Beds: 1F 1D 1S
🛏 🅿 (2) 🗖 ⵏ ✕ ⚓ 🆑 🔽 🛇 ⵏ ✗

Kirkby Stephen 15

National Grid Ref: NY7708

|⊶| ⊕ King's Arms, Old Forge, Pennine Hotel

▲ *Kirkby Stephen Youth Hostel, Fletcher Hill, Market Street, Kirkby Stephen, Cumbria, CA17 7QQ.*
Actual grid ref: NY774085
Tel: **017683 71793**
Under 18: £6.90
Adults: £10.00
Self-catering facilities, Showers, Laundry facilities, Lounge, Dining room, Cycle store, Parking, Evening meal at 7.00pm, No smoking, WC, Kitchen facilities, Breakfast available, Luggage store, Credit cards accepted
Attractive converted chapel, just south of the town square in this interesting old market town in the Upper Eden Valley.

The Old Coach House, Faraday Road, Kirkby Stephen, Cumbria, CA17 4QL.
Quiet comfortable C18th coach house close to town centre.
Tel: **017683 71582**
Mrs Rome.
D: £17.00-£19.00 **S:** £17.00-£22.00.
Open: All Year
Beds: 1D 1T 1S
Baths: 1 En 1 Sh
🛏 (5) ⵏ 🗖 ⚓ 🆑 🔽 🛇 ⵏ ✗

Cold Keld Guided Walking Holidays, Fell End, Kirkby Stephen, Cumbria, CA17 4LN.
Actual grid ref: SD729998
Guided walking holidays.
Delectable dining. Suit all abilities.
Singles welcome.
Tel: **015396 23273** (also fax no)
Mr & Mrs Trimmer.
D: £20.00-£30.00
S: £20.00-£30.00.
Open: All Year (not Xmas/New Year)
Beds: 1F 3D 1T 2S
Baths: 7 En
🛏 🅿 (12) ⵏ 🗖 ⵏ ⚓ 🆑 🔽 🛇 ⵏ ✗

Lyndhurst, 46 South Road, Kirkby Stephen, Cumbria, CA17 4SN.
Actual grid ref: NY772078
A warm welcome to a delightful Victorian home. Lovely breakfast.
Tel: **017683 71448**
Mrs Bell.
D: £16.00-£20.00 **S:** £20.00-£22.50.
Open: All Year (not Xmas/New Year)
Beds: 1D 2T
Baths: 1 Pr 1 Sh
🛏 🅿 (3) ⵏ 🗖 ⵏ ✕ ⚓ 🆑 🔽 🛇 ⵏ ✗

Lockholme, 48 South Road, Kirkby Stephen, Cumbria, CA17 4SN.
Friendly Victorian home with antique furnishings and king-sized beds.
Tel: **017683 71321** Mrs Graham.
D: £16.00-£18.00 **S:** £16.00-£22.00.
Open: All Year (not Xmas)
Beds: 1F 1T 1D 1S
Baths: 2 En 1 Sh
🛏 🅿 (4) ⵏ 🗖 ⵏ ⚓ 🆑 🔽 🛇 ⵏ ✗

Outhgill 16

National Grid Ref: NY7801

Faraday Cottage, Outhgill, Kirkby Stephen, Cumbria, CA17 4JU.
Historic cottage. Heart of Mallerstang Valley, walkers' paradise.
Tel: **017683 72351**
Mrs Porter.
D: £15.00-£15.00
S: £15.00-£15.00.
Open: All Year (not Xmas/New Year)
Beds: 1T 1D
Baths: 1 Sh
🛏 🅿 (2) ⵏ 🗖 ⵏ ✕ ⚓ 🆑 🔽 🛇 ⵏ ✗

All rooms full and nowhere else to stay? Ask the owner if there's anywhere nearby

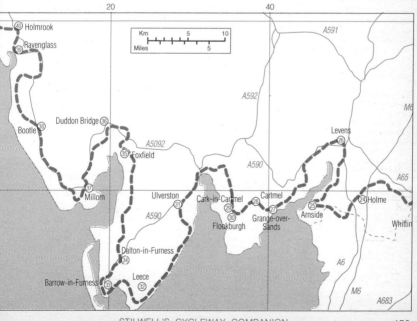

Ulverston to Ravenglass

The road out of Ulverston is largely along-side the beach, overlooking Morecambe Bay, scientifically important for the wading birds it supports. **Barrow-in-Furness** is the biggest town in Cumbria outside Carlisle, and sits at the opposite end of the cycleway and of the county, both in position and in character. This is the Furness Peninsula, the industrial power-house of old North Lancashire, the skyline dominated by the cranes of the shipyards. The town was built on the iron industry and is nowadays famous for Trident. The pre-industrial era is represented by Furness Abbey, the romantic sandstone ruin of a magnificent twelfth-century Cistercian foundation which was accorded the dubious honour of being the first large abbey earmarked for the scrapheap by Henry VIII. The next stage takes you north through several villages called Something-in-Furness and then off the Peninsula at **Duddon Bridge** and back into old Cumberland, as you follow the Duddon Estuary south along the opposite side to **Millom**. Then through a stretch of coast within the Lake District National Park by way of **Bootle** and **Waberthwaite** to **Ravenglass**, where if you wish you can take time out with a trip inland through Eskdale on the old narrow-gauge railway.

Garsdale 17
National Grid Ref: SD7389

|●| ⚐ Dalesman, Red Lion, Bull Hotel

Farfield Country Guest House, *Garsdale Road, Garsdale, Sedbergh, Cumbria, LA10 5JN.*
Actual grid ref: SD677919
Quietly located amongst some of the finest walking country in the Yorkshire Dales.
Tel: **015396 20537**
Mr & Mrs Wilson.
D: £19.00-£24.00 **S:** £20.00-£21.00.
Open: All Year
Beds: 1F 4D 1T 1S
Baths: 4 En 1 Pr 2 Sh
🛏 🅿 (12) ⠝ ⬜ ✗ ♨ 🎮 � 🛈 ∦ 🚲

Sedbergh 18
National Grid Ref: SD6592

|●| ⚐ Dalesman Inn, Cross Keys, Red Lion, Bull Hotel

Stable Antiques, *15 Back Lane, Sedbergh, Cumbria, LA10 5AQ.*
Actual grid ref: SD659921
C18th wheelwright's cottage with wonderful views of Howgill Fells.
Grades: ETC 2 Diamond
Tel: **015396 20251**
Miss Thurlby.
D: £18.00-£19.00 **S:** £18.00-£19.00.
Open: All Year
Beds: 1D 1T
Baths: 1 Sh
🛏 (10) ⬜ ♨ ♨ 🎮 ⬜V 🛈 ∦

Holmecroft, *Station Road, Sedbergh, Cumbria, LA10 5DW.*
Actual grid ref: SD650919
Recommended by 'Which' Good Bed and Breakfast Guide.
Grades: ETC 3 Diamond
Tel: **015396 20754** (also fax no)
Mrs Sharrocks.
D: £19.00-£19.00
S: £19.00-£19.00.
Open: All Year (not Xmas)
Beds: 1D 1T 1S
Baths: 1 Sh
🛏 🅿 (6) ⠝ ⬜ ♨ 🎮 ⬜V 🛈 ∦ ♨

Sun Lea, *Joss Lane, Sedbergh, Cumbria, LA10 5AS.*
Large Victorian family house near town centre run by walkers.
Tel: **015396 20828**
Mr & Mrs Ramsden.
D: £18.00-£20.00 **S:** £18.00-£20.00.
Open: All Year (not Xmas/New Year)
Beds: 2D 1T
Baths: 2 En 1 Sh
🛏 🅿 (3) ⠝ ⬜ ♨ 🎮 ⬜V 🛈 ∦ ♨

Marshall House, *Main Street, Sedbergh, Cumbria, LA10 5BL.*
Which? recommended Dales town house situated under the magnificent Howgill Fells.
Tel: **015396 21053** Mrs Kerry.
D: £22.00-£27.00 **S:** £35.00-£45.00.
Open: All Year (not Xmas)
Beds: 1D 2T **Baths:** 2 En 1 Pr
🛏 (12) 🅿 (5) ⬜ ♨ 🎮 ⬜V 🛈 ∦ ♨

Middleton 19
National Grid Ref: SD6286

|●| ⚐ Swan Inn

Tossbeck Farm, *Middleton, Carnforth, Lancashire, LA6 2LZ.*
A friendly welcome awaits you at Tossbeck, mixed farm in unspoilt Lune Valley.
Tel: **015242 76214**
D: £17.00-£19.00 **S:** £22.00-£25.00.
Open: Easter to Oct
Beds: 1F 1D
Baths: 1 En 1Private
🛏 🅿 (2) ⠝ ⬜ ♨ ♨ 🎮 ⬜V 🚲

Order your
packed lunches the
evening before you
need them.
Not at breakfast!

Barbon 20
National Grid Ref: SD6282

|●| ⚐ Barbon Inn

Kemps Hill, *Moorthwaite Lane, Barbon, Kirkby Lonsdale, Carnforth, LA6 2LP.*
Ideally situated between the Lake District and Yorkshire Dales.
Tel: **015242 76233**
Fax no: 015242 76544
D: £20.00-£20.00
S: £30.00-£30.00.
Open: All Year
Beds: 2D
Baths: 2 En
🅿 ⠝ ⬜ ♨ ✗ ♨ 🎮 ⬜V 🛈 ∦ ♨

Kirkby Lonsdale 21
National Grid Ref: SD6178

|●| ⚐ Kings Arms, Sun Inn, Lunesdale Arms, Swan Inn, Orange Tree, Snooty Fox

Wyck House, *4 Main Street, Kirkby Lonsdale, Carnforth, Lancs, LA6 2AE.*
A Victorian town house situated 50 yards from the market square.
Tel: **015242 71953** (also fax no)
Bradley.
D: £20.00-£22.50
S: £18.50-£30.00.
Open: All Year (except 2 weeks)
Beds: 1F 1T 2D 2S
Baths: 3 En 1 Sh
🛏 🅿 (3) ⠝ ⬜ ♨ 🎮 ⬜V 🛈 ∦ ♨

9 Mill Brow House, *Kirkby Lonsdale, Carnforth, Lancs, LA6 2AT.*
Actual grid ref: SD612786
Wonderful views of river, shops/pubs nearby, holiday apartment available.
Tel: **015242 71615** (also fax no)
Mrs Nicholson.
D: £18.00-£21.00
S: £20.00-£25.00.
Open: Easter to Oct
Beds: 1D 1T
Baths: 2 Sh
🛏 🅿 (2) ⠝ ♨ 🎮 ⬜V ♨

Whittington 22

National Grid Ref: SD6076

🍴 🍺 Dragon's Head

The Dragon's Head, *Main Street, Whittington, Carnforth, LA6 2NY.*
Small country pub in Lune valley 2 miles west of Kirkby Lonsdale B6254.
Tel: **015242 72383**
D: £20.00-£25.00 **S:** £20.00-£25.00.
Open: All Year
Beds: 1F 1D 1S
Baths: 1 Sh
🛏 (5) 🅿 (10) 🗗 🕇 ✕ 🛔 🖳 🛇 ⊶

S = Price range for a single
person in a room

NX 00 NY

⑱ Maryport

㊼ Workington

㊻ High Harrington

㊺ Moresby

Sandwith
㊹

St Bees
㊸ ㊷ Egremont
㊶ Thornhill

Km 5 10
Miles 5
A595

⑳ H

All details shown
are as supplied
by B&B owners in
Autumn 2000.

Kearstwick 23

National Grid Ref: SD6080

🍴 🍺 Courtyard, Snooty Fox, Orange Tree

Kearstwick House, *Kearstwick, Kirkby Lonsdale, Carnforth, LA6 2EA.*
Elegant Edwardian Country House on edge of historic Kirkby Lonsdale.
Tel: **015242 72398**
D: £20.00-£22.50 **S:** £25.00-£30.00.
Open: All Year (not Xmas/ New Year)
Beds: 1T 1D
Baths: 1 Pr 1 Sh
🛏 (12) 🅿 (3) 🗗 🕇 ✕ 🛔 🖳 🛇 🛉 ⊶

Holme 24

National Grid Ref: SD5279

🍴 🍺 Smithy Inn

Marwin House, *Duke Street, Holme, Carnforth, Cumbria, LA6 1PY.*
Gateway to Lake District, Yorkshire Dales. M6 (J36) 5 minutes.
Grades: ETC 2 Diamond
Tel: **01524 781144** (also fax no)
D: £16.00-£18.00 **S:** £17.00-£19.00.
Open: All Year
Beds: 1F 1T
Baths: 1 Sh
🛏 🅿 (3) ⅏ 🗗 🛔 🖳 🛇 🛉 ⊶

Arnside 25

National Grid Ref: SD4578

🍴 🍺 The Albion

🔺 ***Arnside Youth Hostel,*** *Oakfield Lodge, Redhills Road, Arnside, Carnforth, Lancashire, LA5 0AT.*
Actual grid ref: SD452783
Tel: **01524 761781**
Under 18: £6.90 **Adults:** £10.00
Self-catering facilities, Television, Showers, Laundry facilities, Lounge, Games room, Drying room, Cycle store, Parking, Evening meal at 7.00pm, WC, Kitchen facilities, Breakfast available, Credit cards accepted
A few minutes' walk from the shore with views across Morecambe Bay to the Lakeland Fells. A mellow stone house on the edge of a coastal village on the Kent estuary. RSPB reserve nearby.

Please don't camp
on *anyone's* land
without first obtaining
their permission.

Willowfield Hotel, *The Promenade, Arnside, Carnforth, Lancs, LA5 0AD.*
Actual grid ref: SD455785
Non-smoking family-run hotel in superb estuary-side location.
Grades: ETC 4 Diamond, AA 4 Diamond, RAC 4 Diamond
Tel: **01524 761354** Mr Kerr.
D: £26.00-£28.00 **S:** £25.00-£42.00.
Open: All Year
Beds: 2F 3D 3T 2S
Baths: 8 En 1 Pr 2 Sh
🛏 🅿 (8) ⅏ 🗗 ✕ 🛔 🖳 🛇 🛉 ⊶

Stonegate, *The Promenade, Arnside, Carnforth, Lancs, LA5 0AA.*
Actual grid ref: SD455786
Stonegate offers comfort & relaxation in AONB overlooking tidal estuary with panoramic views.
Tel: **01524 762560** (also fax no)
D: £19.50-£22.50 **S:** £22.00-£25.00.
Open: All Year
Beds: 2D 1T 1S **Baths:** 2 En 1 Pr
🛏 (8) ⅏ 🗗 🕇 🛔 🖳 🛇 🛉 ⊶

Levens 26

National Grid Ref: SD4886

🍴 🍺 Blue Bell, Gilpin Bridge, Hare & Hounds, Stricklands Arms, Kendal Arms, The Station, The Castle, The Plough, The Union, Ye Olde Fleece, The Wheatsheaf, Castle Inn, Punch Bowl, The Moon, The Watermill, Brown Horse

Glen Robin, *Church Road, Levens, Kendal, Cumbria, LA8 8PS.*
Beautiful house with lovely views, delicious breakfasts, peace and quiet.
Tel: **015395 60369** (also fax no)
D: £16.00-£20.00 **S:** £16.00-£20.00.
Open: All Year (not Xmas)
Beds: 1D 1T 1S **Baths:** 1 Sh
🛏 (3) 🅿 (3) ⅏ 🗗 🛔 🖳 🛇 🛉 ⊶

Grange-over-Sands 27

National Grid Ref: SD4077

🍴 🍺 Lindale Inn, Commodore Hotel, Kents Bank Hotel, Hard Crag Hotel

Grangeways, *6 Morecambe Bank, Grange-over-Sands, Cumbria, LA11 6DX.*
Quiet location overlooking Morecambe Bay. Ideal base for Lake District.
Tel: **015395 35329** (also fax no)
Mr & Mrs Campbell.
D: £18.00-£20.00 **S:** £18.00-£20.00.
Open: Easter to Nov
Beds: 1F 1D 1T 1S **Baths:** 1 Sh
🛏 (6) 🅿 (2) ⅏ 🗗 🕇 ✕ 🛔 🖳 🛇 🛉

Please respect
a B&B's wishes
regarding children,
animals & smoking.

---

*Cartmel Fell, High Tarn Green,
Grange-over-Sands, Cumbria,
LA11 6NE.*
Warm welcome in quiet country
setting, ideal for touring, walking
and cycling.
Tel: **015395 52314** (also fax no)
D: £18.00-£22.00 .
Open: All Year (not Xmas)
Beds: 1F 1D
Baths: 1 En
🛇🄿➡️🆆✕🛆🎄Ⅵ🛈🖋️

*The Laurels B&B, Berriedale
Terrace, Lindale Road, Grange-
over-Sands, Cumbria, LA11 6ER.*
Actual grid ref: SD416783
Relax and enjoy the friendly
atmosphere of our elegant
Victorian villa.
Tel: **015395 35919** (also fax no)
D: £20.00-£25.00
S: £25.00-£27.00.
Open: All Year
Beds: 2T 1D
Baths: 3 En
🄿(3)✂️➡️✕🛆🎄Ⅵ🛈🖋️🚲

Always telephone
to get directions to
the B&B - you will
save time!

Cartmel 28

National Grid Ref: SD3878

🍴🍺 Caverdish Arms, Royal Oak, Kings Arms

*Bank Court Cottage, The Square,
Cartmel, Grange-over-Sands,
Cumbria, LA11 6QB.*
Grades: ETC 3 Diamond
Tel: **015395 36593** (also fax no)
Mrs Lawson.
D: £18.50-£25.00 **S:** £18.50.
Open: All Year (not Xmas)
Beds: 1D 1T
Baths: 1 Sh
🛇✂️➡️🆆✕🛆🎄Ⅵ🛈🚲
We offer a warm welcome to our
pretty character cottage in a quiet
courtyard off the village square.
Beams, log fires, home grown
vegetables and fruit, free range
eggs from our own hens. Lovely
views of Cartmel Park and
racecourse.

Cark-in-Cartmel 29

National Grid Ref: SD3676

🍴🍺 Engine Inn

*Eeabank House, 123 Station Road,
Cark-in-Cartmel, Grange-over-
Sands, Cumbria, LA11 7NY.*
C17th coaching house inn, licensed
bar, log fires, Old England is here.
Tel: **015395 58156** (also fax no)
Mr Reece.
D: £16.50-£24.00 **S:** £16.50-£24.00.
Open: All Year
Beds: 2D 1T
Baths: 2 En 1 Pr
➡️🆆✕🛆🎄Ⅵ

D = Price range per person
sharing in a double room

All rooms full and
nowhere else to stay?
Ask the owner if
there's anywhere
nearby

Flookburgh 30

National Grid Ref: SD3675

🍴🍺 Rose & Crown

*Fieldhead Farm House,
Flookburgh, Grange-over-Sands,
Cumbria, LA11 7LN.*
A C17th farmhouse on edge of
ancient fishing village.
Tel: **015395 58651**
D: £17.00-£20.00 **S:** £17.00-£20.00.
Open: All Year
Beds: 2D 1S 1T 1F
Baths: 1 Sh
🛇🄿(3)✂️➡️✕🛆🎄Ⅵ🛈🖋️🚲

Ulverston 31

National Grid Ref: SD2878

🍴🍺 Rose & Crown, Pier Castle, Farmers Arms

*Sefton House , Queen Street,
Ulverston, Cumbria, LA12 7AF.*
Georgian town house in the busy
market town of Ulverston.
Tel: **01229 582190** Mrs Glaister.
Fax no: 01229 581773
D: £20.00-£22.50 **S:** £27.50-£30.00.
Open: All Year (not Xmas)
Beds: 1F 1D 1S 1T
Baths: 4 En
🛇🄿(15)➡️🛆🎄Ⅵ🛈🖋️🚲

*Rock House, 1 Alexander Road,
Ulverston, Cumbria, LA12 0DE.*
Actual grid ref: SD287779
Large family rooms. Convenient to
railway/bus station/town centre.
Grades: ETC 4 Diamond
Tel: **01229 586879** Mr Ramsay.
D: £20.00-£20.00 **S:** £20.00-£20.00.
Open: March to October
Beds: 3F 1S
Baths: 1 Sh
🛇✂️➡️✕🛆🎄Ⅵ🛈🖋️

Leece 32

National Grid Ref: SD2469

*Winander, Leece, Ulverston,
Cumbria, LA12 0QP.*
Converted barn in quiet village
location in Lake District Peninsula.
Tel: **01229 822353** Mr Cockshott.
D: £18.00-£23.00
S: £21.00-£26.00.
Open: All Year (not Xmas)
Beds: 1T 1D
Baths: 1 Pr 1 Sh
🛇(5)🄿(3)✂️➡️✕🛆🎄Ⅵ🛈🖋️🚲

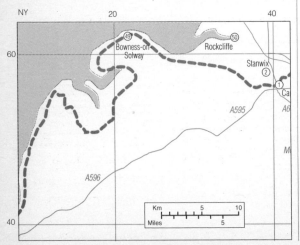

Ravenglass to Carlisle

Sellafield will interest anyone on the nuclear trail from Barrow, and after **Egremont**, which offers the ruins of a Norman castle, the route passes **St Bees Head**, with its sandstone cliffs. The final stretch of coast, north-eastwards towards the Solway Firth, takes you through a series of towns reflecting the industrial history of the region: **Whitehaven** has been through a number of incarnations - harbour for St Bees Priory, major tobacco port, during which time the many Georgian buildings went up, and then coal and shipbuilding centre; **Workington** and **Maryport** are major nineteenth-century centres of the iron industry. A different side of Victoriana is reflected in **Silloth**, a planned town and resort. After this there is another Cistercian abbey at **Abbeytown** and then an idyllic section with magnificent views across the **Solway Firth**. Another historic site is the Roman fort at **Burgh-by-Sands**, before you cycle back into Carlisle.

arrow-in-Furness   33

ational Grid Ref: SD1969

🍴 Brown Cow

len Garth Hotel, 359 Abbey oad, Barrow-in-Furness, umbria, LA13 9JY.
el: **01229 825374**
ax no: 01229 811744
: £27.45-£34.95
: £49.90-£59.90.
pen: All Year
eds: 2F 1T 5D 7S
aths: 15 En
🛏 🄿 (15) ⊬ 🗆 ✕ 🎄 🎘 📖 Ⅵ ♿ ⚵
eautiful Victorian mansion with iendly service. All rooms well ppointed, ensuite with satellite elevision. popular restaurant rving à la carte and bistro menus ily. comfortable relaxing lounge. ccasions and parties catered for. rfect wedding venue and pretty wn and gazebo for photos.

Barrie House, 179 Abbey Road, Barrow-in-Furness, Cumbria, LA14 5JP.
Actual grid ref: SD203702
Victorian home among trees and roses. Nearby lakes and sea.
Tel: **01229 825507** (also fax no)
Mrs Maitland.
D: £16.00-£20.00
S: £16.00-£20.00.
Open: All Year (not Xmas)
Beds: 1F 1D 4T 5S
Baths: 4 En 3 Sh
🛏 ⊬ 🗆 🐾 🎄 🎘 📖 Ⅵ 🛈 ♿ ⚵

Dalton-in-Furness   34

National Grid Ref: SD2374

🍴 🍺 Black Dog Inn

Black Dog Inn, Holmes Green, Broughton Road, Dalton-in-Furness, Cumbria, LA15 8JP.
Actual grid ref: SD233761
A cosy, beamed coaching inn with open fires, a friendly atmosphere.
Tel: **01229 462561**
Mr Taylor.
Fax no: 01229 468036
D: £15.00-£17.50
S: £12.50-£20.00.
Open: All Year
Beds: 3D 3S
Baths: 3 En 2 Pr 1 Sh
🛏 (1) 🄿 (30) ⊬ 🗆 🐾 ✕ 🎄 Ⅵ ♿ ⚵

Foxfield   35

National Grid Ref: SD2185

🍴 🍺 Prince of Wales

Woodhouse, Foxfield, Broughton-in-Furness, Cumbria, LA20 6BT.
Charming C17th farmhouse, superb views, 3 acres of private grounds.
Tel: **01229 716086** Mrs Corkill.
Fax no: 01229 716644
D: £19.00-£22.00 **S:** £30.00-£30.00.
Open: All Year
Beds: 1F 1D
Baths: 2 En
🛏 🄿 🐾 ✕ 🎄 🎘 📖 Ⅵ ♿ ⚵

Duddon Bridge   36

National Grid Ref: SD1988

🍴 🍺 High Cross Inn

The Dower House, High Duddon, Duddon Bridge, Broughton in Furness, Cumbria, LA20 6ET.
Actual grid ref: SD196882
Delightful Victorian country house offering a warm and friendly welcome. Comfortable bedrooms.
Tel: **01229 716279** (also fax no)
Mrs Nichols.
D: £20.00-£25.00
S: £25.00-£27.00.
Open: All Year (not Xmas/ New Year)
Beds: 1F 2D 1T 1S
Baths: 1 En 3 Pr
🛏 🄿 (8) 🗆 ✕ 🎄 🎘 📖 Ⅵ 🛈 ♿ ⚵

Bringing children with you? Always ask for any special rates.

Millom   37

National Grid Ref: SD1780

▲ *Duddon Estuary, Borwick Rails, Millom, Cumbria, LA18 4JU.*
Tel: **01229 773937**
Under 18: £5.75 **Adults:** £8.50
Self-catering facilities, Showers, Laundry facilities, Lounge, Parking, Facilities for disabled people, No smoking, Kitchen facilities
The hostel overlooks the estuary, and has fine views in all directions. Handy for the RSPB reserve.

Bootle   38

National Grid Ref: SD1188

The Stables, Bootle, Millom, Cumbria, LA19 5TJ.
Spacious accommodation, lovely views, two rivers, mountains, fells. Home-cooking.
Tel: **01229 718644** Mrs Light.
D: £16.00-£18.50 **S:** £17.50-£25.00.
Open: All Year
Beds: 1F 2D **Baths:** 2 En 1 Sh
🛏 🄿 (6) 🗆 🐾 ✕ 🎄 🎘 📖 Ⅵ 🛈 ♿ ⚵

Ravenglass   39

National Grid Ref: SD0896

🍴 🍺 Ratty Arms, Brown Cow

Muncaster Country Guest House, Ravenglass, Cumbria, CA18 1RD.
Actual grid ref: SD098967
Grades: RAC 3 Diamond
Tel: **01229 717693** (also fax no)
Mr Putnam.
D: £20.00-£24.00 **S:** £22.00-£28.00.
Open: Mar to Oct
Beds: 1F 3D 2T 3S
Baths: 2 En 2 Sh
🛏 (1) 🄿 (16) ⊬ 🗆 🐾 🎄 🎘 📖 ♿ Ⅵ 🛈 ♿ ⚵
A very comfortable and welcoming country guest house adjoining Muncaster estate and open countryside. Easy access to miniature railway, Eskdale and Wasdale. Walkers welcome. Children and dogs accepted. Hearty breakfasts.

Pay B&Bs by cash or cheque and be prepared to pay up front.

Holmrook   40

National Grid Ref: SD0799

⚓ ⚑ Lulwidge Arms, Bridge Inn

Hill Farm, *Holmrook, Cumbria,*
CA19 1UG.
Working farm; beautiful views
overlooking River Irt and Wasdale
Fells.
Tel: **019467 24217** Mrs Leak.
D: £14.00 **S:** £14.00.
Open: All Year (not Xmas)
Beds: 2F 1D
Baths: 2 Sh
🛏 🅿 🏧 ⌂ 🍴 🛁 Ⅲ, Ⅴ 🖊 ⚡ ♿

Thornhill   41

National Grid Ref: NY0108

⚓ ⚑ Royal Oak

The Old Vicarage Guest House,
Thornhill, Egremont, Cumbria,
CA22 2NY.
C19th vicarage of character, within
easy reach fells & lakes.
Grades: ETC 3 Diamond
Tel: **01946 841577** Mrs Graham.
D: £15.00-£17.00 **S:** £15.00-£17.00.
Open: All Year (not Xmas)
Beds: 3F
Baths: 2 Sh
🛏 🅿 (6) ⌂ 🏧 🛁 Ⅲ, Ⅴ ♿

Egremont   42

National Grid Ref: NY0110

⚓ ⚑ White Mare, Oddfellows

Ghyll Farm Guest House,
Egremont, Cumbria, CA22 2UA.
Tel: **01946 822256** Mrs Holliday.
D: £14.00-£14.00 **S:** £14.00-£14.00.
Open: All Year (not Xmas)
Beds: 2T 2S
Baths: 2 Sh
🛏 🅿 (6) ⌂ 🏧 🛁 Ⅲ, Ⅴ 🖊 ♿
Comfortable clean friendly farmhouse. Good breakfast, private off-
road parking. Try a fishing holiday
on River Irt at Holmrook and catch
salmon and sea trout. Reasonable
rates; while the men fish, the ladies
can visit our beautiful lakes etc.

Far Head of Haile, *Haile,*
Egremont, CA22 2PE.
Actual grid ref: NY042093
Explore the quieter Western lakes,
mountains and coast. Between
Ennerdale and Wastwater.
Tel: **01946 841205** Mr Greening.
D: £15.00-£18.50 **S:** £15.50-£21.00.
Open: All Year
Beds: 1F 2D 5S
Baths: 1 En 3 Sh
🛏 🅿 (12) ⌨ ⌂ 🏧 Ⅲ, Ⅴ 🖊 ⚡ ♿

S = Price range for a single

person in a room

St Bees   43

National Grid Ref: NX9711

⚓ ⚑ Queens Head, Manor House, Oddfellows

Tomlin Guest House, *1 Tomlin*
House, St Bees, Cumbria, *CA27 0EN.*
Actual grid ref: NX963118
Comfortable Victorian house con-
venient to beach and St Bees Head.
Tel: **01946 822284**
Mrs Whitehead.
Fax no: 01946 824243
D: £15.00-£18.00 **S:** £18.00-£18.00.
Open: All Year (not Xmas)
Beds: 1F 2D 1T 0S
Baths: 2 En 2 Sh
🛏 🅿 (2) ⌨ ⌂ 🏧 🛁 Ⅲ, Ⅴ 🖊 ♿

Stonehouse Farm, *Main Street,*
St Bees, Cumbria, CA27 0DE.
Actual grid ref: NX972119
Modern Georgian farmhouse in
centre of village, next to railway
station.
Grades: ETC 3 Diamond
Tel: **01946 822224**
Mrs Smith.
D: £16.00-£20.00 **S:** £20.00-£20.00.
Open: All Year (not Xmas)
Beds: 1F 2D 2T 1S
Baths: 4 En 1 Sh
🛏 🅿 (20) ⌂ 🏧 🛁 Ⅲ, Ⅴ 🖊 ♿

Fairladies Barn Guest House,
Main Street, St Bees, CA27 0AD.
Large converted barn located in
centre of seaside village.
Tel: **01946 822718**
Mrs Carr.
D: £16.00-£16.00 **S:** £16.00-£16.00.
Open: All Year
Beds: 6D 2T 1S
Baths: 3 En 2 Sh
🛏 🅿 (10) ⌂ 🏧 Ⅲ, Ⅴ 🖊 ♿

Outrigg House, *St Bees, Cumbria,*
CA27 0AN.
Georgian guest house of unique
character located in village centre.
Tel: **01956 822348** (also fax no)
Mrs Moffat.
D: £16.00-£16.00
S: £16.00-£16.00.
Open: All Year (not Xmas)
Beds: 1F 1T 1S
Baths: 1 Sh
🛏 🅿 (2) ⌨ ⌂ 🏧 ♿ ♿

Sandwith   44

National Grid Ref: NX9614

⚓ ⚑ Lowther Arms

🔺 **Tarn Flatt Camping Barn,**
Tarnflat Hall, Sandwith,
Whitehaven, Cumbria, CA28 9UX.
Actual grid ref: NX947146
Tel: **017687 72645**
Adults: £3.35
Situated on St Bees Head overlook-
ing Scottish coastline and the Isle
of Man. RSPB seabird reserve and
lighthouse nearby. ADVANCE
BOOKING ESSENTIAL.

The Old Granary, *Spout Howse,*
Sandwith, Whitehaven, Cumbria,
CA28 9UG.
Actual grid ref: NX964147
Tastefully converted barn on C2C
route and Coast to Coast path.
Tel: **01946 692097** Mrs Buchanan.
D: £17.00**S:** £16.00.
Open: All Year
Beds: 1F 1D 1T
Baths: 2 En
🛏 🅿 (2) ⌂ 🏧 🛁 Ⅴ 🖊 ⚡ ♿

Moresby   45

National Grid Ref: NX9921

⚓ ⚑ Moresby Hall, Howgate Inn

Moresby Hall, *Moresby,*
Whitehaven, Cumbria, CA28 6PJ.
Tel: **01946 696317** Mrs Saxon.
Fax no: 01946 692666
D: £22.50-£32.50 **S:** £25.00-£35.00
Open: All Year
Beds: 1F 1T 2D
Baths: 2 En 2 Pr
🛏 (10) 🅿 (6) ⌨ ⌂ 🏧 ✗ 🛁 Ⅲ, Ⅴ 🖊 ♿
♿
A Grade I Listed character build-
ing. Spacious and well equipped
rooms. Semi-rural location and 2
acres of walled gardens. Lakes,
fells, cultural & tourist locations.
Delicious food in an elegant set-
ting. Licensed. A warm welcome to
our relaxing family home.

High Harrington   46

National Grid Ref: NY0025

⚓ ⚑ Galoping Horse

Riversleigh Guest House, *39*
Primrose Terrace, High
Harrington, Workington, Cumbria
CA14 5PS.
Riverside house overlooking
gardens, 5 mins from station and
marina.
Tel: **01946 830267**
Mrs Davies.
D: £15.00-£20.00
S: £15.00-£20.00.
Open: All Year
Beds: 1F 1T 1D
Baths: 2 En 1 Pr
🛏 (5) 🅿 (8) ⌨ ⌂ 🏧 🛁 Ⅲ, Ⅴ 🖊 ⚡ ♿

Workington   47

National Grid Ref: NX9927

⚓ ⚑ Ye Old Sportsman

Fernleigh House, *15 High Seaton*
Workington, Cumbria, CA14 1PE.
Georgian house, lovely garden,
warm and friendly welcome,
Excellent breakfasts.
Tel: **01900 605811**
Ms Bewsher.
D: £17.00-£45.00
S: £17.00-£17.00.
Open: All Year
Beds: 1F 2T 1S
🛏 🅿 🏧 🛁 Ⅲ, Ⅴ 🖊 ⚡ ♿

Silverdale, *17 Banklands,*
Workington, Cumbria, CA14 3EL.
Large Victorian private house.
Near start C2C cycleway and lakes.
Tel: **01900 61887** Mrs Hardy.
D: £11.00-£13.50 **S:** £12.50-£15.00.
Open: All Year (not Xmas)
Beds: 2T 2S
Baths: 2 Sh
🛏🏻🔥🛆🖿🔄Ⓥ

Maryport 48

National Grid Ref: NY0336

🍴🍺 Retreat Hotel

The Retreat Hotel, *Birkby,*
Maryport, Cumbria, CA15 6RG.
Former Victorian sea captain's resi-
dence with large walled garden to
rear.
Tel: **01900 814056**
Mr & Mrs Geissler.
D: £23.50-£26.00 **S:** £33.50-£38.50.
Open: All Year (not Xmas)
Beds: 2D 1T
Baths: 3 En
🏳(12)🖵✗🛆🖿Ⓥ🛡🔄🌂

Bowness-on-Solway 49

National Grid Ref: NY2262

🍴🍺 Kings Arms

Maia Lodge, *Bowness-on-Solway,*
Wigton, Cumbria, CA7 5BH.
Actual grid ref: NY225627
Panoramic views of Solway Firth
and Scottish Borders. End of
Hadrian's Wall.
Grades: ETC 3 Diamond
Tel: **016973 51955** Mrs Chettle.
D: £17.00-£20.00 **S:** £20.00-£20.00.
Open: All Year (not Xmas)
Beds: 1F 1D 1T **Baths:** 2 Sh
🛏(5)🅿(4)⊬🖵✗🛆🖿Ⓥ🛡🌂

The Old Rectory, *Bowness-on-*
Solway, Carlisle, Cumbria, CA75AF.
Actual grid ref: NY224626
Fully ensuite old rectory at end of
Hadrian's Wall. www.wallsend.net
Grades: ETC 4 Diamond
Tel: **016973 51055**
Mr & Mrs Knowles.
D: £20.00-£25.00 **S:** £20.00-£25.00.
Open: All Year (not Xmas)
Beds: 1F 2D 1S **Baths:** 4 En
🛏(5)🅿(6)⊬🖵✗🛆🖿Ⓥ🔄🌂

Rockcliffe 50

National Grid Ref: NY3561

🍴🍺 Metal Bridge Inn

Metal Bridge House, *Metal*
Bridge, Rockcliffe, Carlisle,
Cumbria, CA6 4HG.
Actual grid ref: NY356649
In country, close to M6/A74,
quality accommodation, friendly
welcome.
Tel: **01228 674695**
Mr Rae.
D: £16.00-£18.00
S: £20.00-£22.00.
Open: All Year (not Xmas)
Beds: 1D 2T
Baths: 1 Sh
🛏🅿(6)⊬🐕🛆🖿Ⓥ🔄🌂

Pay B&Bs by cash or
cheque and be prepared
to pay up front.

Essex Cycle Route

Essex provides good cycling country, as it is relatively flat, whilst offering a gentle agrarian beauty away from its ugly south end, which the cycle route avoids. The **Essex Cycle Route** consists of a large circuit around the interior of the county, with a 'spur' out east to the port of Harwich. Directed along quiet roads and not signposted, it is only a recommended tour, and you can devise your own alternatives at any point. The designated route can be cycled in either direction and you can start anywhere; for no particular reason, the description that follows takes the circuit clockwise from Coggeshall, east of Braintree, and finishes with the section to Harwich.

A detailed **guide booklet** to the cycleway route, which includes a list of cycle repair/hire shops on or near to the route, is available from Essex Tourism, Essex County Planning Department, County Hall, Chelmsford, Essex CM1 1LF, tel 01245 437548, @ £1.00 (inc p&p).

Maps: Ordnance Survey 1:50,000 Landranger series: 154, 155, 167, 168, 169

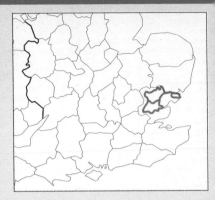

Essex is well-connected by **train** to London and to Eastern and Central England. Major railway termini are Chelmsford, Colchester and Harwich. London also connects to Stansted Airport, Stansted Mountfitchet, Elsenham, Newport and Audley End (for Saffron Walden). There are connections to many other places on or near the route.

Coggeshall to Maldon

Coggeshall is a medieval town on the banks of the Blackwater, one of Essex's major rivers, with the remains of a Cistercian Abbey nearby. In contrast with the Abbey ruins, there are two excellently preserved historic buildings: the Grange Barn is a 120-foot timber-framed barn constructed in 1140 to serve the Abbey, and is the oldest of its kind in Europe. It houses a display of historic farm wagons. Paycocke's is a merchant's house from the turn of the sixteenth century with rich panelling and wood carving, and a display of lace. On to **Cressing**, with more medieval timber-framed barns at nearby 'Cressing Temple', and **Terling**. From here there is an alternative route via **Pleshey**, where

you will find a Norman castle earthwork, and **Great Clanfield**, whose twelfth-century church is a Grade I Listed building with a mural of the Madonna and Child; connecting up to the eastern side of the circuit between Hatfield Broad Oak and Takeley. From Terling proceed to **Maldon**, on the Blackwater Estuary. This ancient town, with an attractive High Street, is famous for a battle fought here in 991, at which Viking invaders defeated the local East Saxons, told of in an early Anglo-Saxon poem, *The Battle of Maldon*. The millennium of the battle was commemorated by the *Maldon Embroidery*, made by local people in 1991. It celebrates the town's history and is on display in the Moot Hall. Also worth a look is the Hythe Quay with its Thames sailing barges.

Coggeshall 1	Kelvedon 2	Messing
National Grid Ref: TL8522	National Grid Ref: TL8518	National Grid Ref: TL8918
⋈ ⬛ Woolpack Inn	⋈ ⬛ Sun Inn	
White Heather Guest House, *19 Colchester Road, Coggeshall, Colchester, Essex, CO6 1RP.* **Actual grid ref:** TL859228 Modern, family-run guest house, overlooking farmland. Tel: **01376 563004** Mrs Shaw. **D:** £22.00-£22.50 **S:** £22.00-£25.00. **Open:** All Year (not Xmas) **Beds:** 2D 2S **Baths:** 2 En 1 Sh P (8) ⑂ ☐ ♨ ▥ Ⓥ	**Highfields Farm,** *Kelvedon, Colchester, Essex, CO5 9BJ.* Farmhouse in quiet countryside location, convenient for A12 and London. **Grades:** ETC 3 Diamond Tel: **01376 570334** (also fax no) Mrs Bunting. **D:** £22.00-£22.00 **S:** £22.00-£24.00. **Open:** All Year **Beds:** 1D 2T **Baths:** 2 En 1 Pr ♿ P (4) ⑂ ☐ ⌗ ♨ ▥ Ⓥ ✦ ⚲	**Crispin's,** *The Street, Messing, Colchester, Essex, CO5 9TR.* Candle-lit Elizabethan restaurant with beamed rooms, lounge and secluded garden. Tel: **01621 815868** **D:** £24.75-£24.75 **S:** £30.00-£30.00. **Open:** All Year **Beds:** 1F 1D **Baths:** 2 En

Braintree 4

National Grid Ref: TL7623

The Old House Guesthouse, 11 Bradford Street, Braintree, Essex, CM7 9AS.
Actual grid ref: TL760238
Family-run, C16th guest house within walking distance town centre.
Tel: **01376 550457**
Mrs Hughes.
Fax no: 01376 343863
D: £19.00-£30.00
S: £23.00-£30.00.
Open: All Year
Beds: 2F 5D 1T
Baths: 6 Pr 2 Sh
🛏 🅿 (10) ⚲ 🗇 ✗ �£ 🎢 ♨ 🔽 🛗 🍵

Felsted 5

National Grid Ref: TL6720

🍴 🍺 Flitch Of Bacon, The Chequers, The Swan, Three Horseshoes

Yarrow, Felsted, Great Dunmow, Essex, CM6 3HD.
Actual grid ref: TL668206
Please see website
www.yarrow.ic24.net.
Tel: **01371 820878** (also fax no)
Mr & Mrs Bellingham Smith.
D: £17.00
S: £18.00.
Open: All Year
Beds: 1D 1T 1S
Baths: 1 En 1 Sh
🛏 🅿 (6) ⚲ 🗇 �£ 🎢 🔽 ♨

Great Dunmow 6

National Grid Ref: TL6221

🍴 🍺 Flitch of Bacon

Homelye Farm, Homelye Chase, Braintree Road, Great Dunmow, Essex, CM6 3AW.
Actual grid ref: TL6522
Good quality motel-style accommodation close to Stansted Airport.
Grades: ETC 4 Diamond, AA 4 Diamond
Tel: **01371 872127**
Mrs Pickford.
Fax no: 01371 876428
D: £25.00 **S:** £25.00-£30.00.
Open: All Year
Beds: 1F 3D 2T 3S **Baths:** 9 En
🛏 🅿 (9) ⚲ 🗇 �£ 🎢 🔽 ♨

Margaret Roding 7

National Grid Ref: TL5912

Greys, Ongar Road, Margaret Roding, Great Dunmow, Essex, CM6 1QR.
Actual grid ref: TL605112
Old beamed cottage, pleasantly situated amidst our farmland tiny village.
Grades: ETC 3 Diamond, AA 3 Diamond
Tel: **01245 231509**
Mrs Matthews.
D: £22.00**S:** £23.00.
Open: All Year (not Xmas)
Beds: 2D 1T
Baths: 1 Sh
🛏 (10) 🅿 (3) ⚲ 🗇 🎢 ♨ 🍵

High Easter 8

National Grid Ref: TL6214

The Cock & Bell, The Street, High Easter, Chelmsford, Essex, CM1 4QW.
C14th former coaching inn - operating as charming guest house.
Tel: **01245 231296** Steel.
D: £19.50-£24.50 **S:** £22.50-£27.50.
Open: All Year (not Xmas/New Year)
Beds: 2D 1F 1S
Baths: 2 En 1 Sh
🅿 🗇 ✗ �£ 🎢 🔽 🍵 ♨

Terling 9

National Grid Ref: TL7614

🍴 🍺 Square & Compass

Old Bakery, Waltham Road, Terling, Chelmsford, Essex, CM3 2QR.
Converted bakery in quiet unspoilt village on the Essex Way.
Grades: ETC 4 Diamond
Tel: **01245 233363**
Mrs Lewis.
D: £22.50-£25.00 **S:** £22.50-£25.00.
Open: All Year
Beds: 1T 1D
Baths: 2 En
🛏 (10) 🅿 (2) ⚲ 🗇 �£ 🎢 ♿ 🔽 🍵

D = Price range per person sharing in a double room

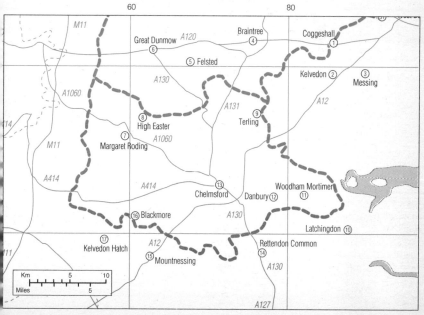

Latchingdon 10

National Grid Ref: TL8800

⚑ 🍴 Red Lion, Black Lion

Neptune Cafe Motel, Burnham Road, Latchingdon, Chelmsford, Essex, CM3 6EX.
Grades: ETC 2 Diamond,
AA 2 Diamond
Tel: 01621 740770 Mr Lloyd.
D: £17.50 **S:** £25.00.
Open: All Year
Beds: 4F 4D 2T 10S
Baths: 10 En 2 Pr 1 Sh
🛏 🅿 (40) ⚄ 🗖 📺 🛆 📖 🗓 🕎 🎗 🐾
Cafe motel, luxury chalets adjoining. Close to boating and fishing areas, golfing and horse riding close by. Lovely rural setting with grand views.

Woodham Mortimer 11

National Grid Ref: TL8104

⚑ 🍴 Hurdlemakers' Arms

Little Owls, Post Office Road, Woodham Mortimer, Maldon, Essex, CM9 6ST.
Grades: ETC 3 Diamond
Tel: 01245 224355 (also fax no)
Mrs Bush.
D: £20.00-£25.00 **S:** £25.00-£30.00.
Open: All Year
Beds: 1F 1T 1D
Baths: 2 Sh
🛏 🅿 (10) ⚄ 🗖 🛆 ✗ 📺 📖 🗓 🕎 🎗 🐾
Panoramic views over surrounding countryside. Private indoor swimming pool.

Danbury 12

National Grid Ref: TL7705

⚑ 🍴 The Bell, Griffin Inn, The Cricketers

Southways, Copt Hill, Danbury, Chelmsford, Essex, CM3 4NN.
House with large attractive garden adjoining National Trust common land.
Grades: ETC 3 Diamond
Tel: 01245 223428
Mrs Deavin.
D: £19.00-£20.00
S: £20.00-£20.00.
Open: All Year
Beds: 2T
Baths: 1 Sh
🛏 🅿 (2) 🗖 📺 🛆 📖 🗓

**High season,
bank holidays and
special events mean
low availability
everywhere.**

Chelmsford 13

National Grid Ref: TL7006

⚑ 🍴 Black Bull, White Hart Pub, Springfield Arms

Aquila B&B, 11 Daffodil Way, Springfield, Chelmsford, Essex, CM1 6XB.
B&B, frequent buses to Chelmsford. London 35 mins by train.
Grades: ETC 2 Diamond
Tel: 01245 465274
D: £19.50-£24.50
S: £19.50-£24.50.
Open: All Year
Beds: 1D 1T 1S
🅿 (3) 🗖 🛆 📖 🗓

Aarandale, 9 Roxwell Road, Chelmsford, Essex, CM1 2LY.
Large Victorian house close to Chelmsford town centre and park.
Tel: 01245 251713 (also fax no)
Mrs Perera.
D: £20.00-£22.00
S: £22.00-£32.00.
Open: All Year
Beds: 1F 1T 4S
Baths: 1 En 1 Sh
🅿 (6) 🗖 ✗ 🛆 📖 🗓 🕎 🐾

Rettendon Common 14

National Grid Ref: TQ7796

⚑ 🍴 Bell, Wheatsheaf, Hawk

Crossways, Main Road, Rettendon Common, Chelmsford, Essex, CM3 8DY.
Actual grid ref: TQ764982
Secluded home set well back from A130, dual carriageway.
Grades: ETC 3 Diamond
Tel: 01245 400539
Mr Graham.
Fax no: 01245 400127
D: £20.00-£20.00
S: £20.00-£25.00.
Open: All Year (not Xmas)
Beds: 1T
Baths: 1 Pr
🅿 (3) ⚄ 🗖 🛆 📖 🗓 🕎 🎗 🐾

Mountnessing 15

National Grid Ref: TQ6297

⚑ 🍴 George & Dragon, Prince of Wales, Plough

Millers, Thoby Lane, Mountnessing, Brentwood, Essex, CM15 0TD.
Beautiful house and garden overlooking countryside close to A12, 10 mins M25.
Tel: 01277 354595
Mrs Stacey.
D: £25.00-£25.00
S: £30.00-£30.00.
Open: All Year
Beds: 1F 2T
Baths: 1 Pr
🛏 🅿 ⚄ 🗖 🛆 📖 🗓

Blackmore 16

National Grid Ref: TL6001

⚑ 🍴 The Bull

Little Lampetts, Hay Green Lane, Blackmore, Ingatestone, Essex, CM4 0QE.
Secluded period house; easy access to M25 mainline stations towns.
Tel: 01277 822030 Mrs Porter.
D: £22.50-£25.00 **S:** £25.00-£27.50.
Open: All Year
Beds: 2T
Baths: 1 Pr
🅿 (5) ⚄ 🗖 🛆 ✗ 🛆 📖 🗓 🕎 🎗 🐾

Kelvedon Hatch 17

National Grid Ref: TQ5799

⚑ 🍴 Dog & Partridge, Eagle

57 Great Fox Meadow, Kelvedon Hatch, Brentwood, Essex, CM15 0AX.
Homely, friendly, clean, comfortable, overlooking farmlands. 4 miles from Brentwood and Ongar.
Tel: 01277 374659 Mrs Maguire.
D: £16.00-£21.00 **S:** £16.00-£21.00.
Open: All Year (not Xmas)
Beds: 1D 1S
Baths: 1 Sh
🛏 (3) 🅿 (2) ⚄ 🗖 🛆 📖 🗓

Henham 18

National Grid Ref: TL5428

⚑ 🍴 The Crown, The Cock

Roblin, Carters Lane, Henham, Bishop's Stortford, Herts, CM22 6AQ.
Family home, large garden, lovely country village quiet setting.
Tel: 01279 850370 (also fax no)
Mrs Burgess.
D: £20.00-£20.00 **S:** £22.50-£22.50.
Open: April to Nov
Beds: 1D 1T
Baths: 1 Sh
🛏 (8) ⚄ 🗖 🛆 📖 🗓 🎗 🐾

Bacons Cottage, Crow Street, Henham, Bishops Stortford, Herts, CM22 6AG.
Thatched cottage in picturesque setting near Stansted Airport, charming village.
Tel: 01279 850754 Mrs Philpot.
D: £16.00-£18.00 **S:** £18.00-£22.00.
Open: All Year (not Xmas)
Beds: 1D 1S
Baths: 1 En
🅿 (1) ⚄ 🛆 📖 🗓

**Please respect
a B&B's wishes
regarding children,
animals & smoking.**

Maldon to Saffron Walden

From Maldon the route takes you south to **Purleigh**, where George Washington's great-grandfather was the local vicar, and then after East Hanningfield you can take a slight detour to the Royal Horticultural Society's Garden at Hyde Hall, a 24-acre hilltop garden with rose walks and waterfalls, as well as a small plant centre and a cafeteria. Around **Hanningfield Reservoir**, which offers sail-boarding, fishing and a nature trail, it's on to **Ingatestone**, where stands Ingatestone Hall, a redbrick Tudor mansion with 11 acres of grounds including a lake. On to the village of **Greensted**, where the Log Church is the oldest wooden church in the world, and then you turn north, through a string of medieval villages and near to the National Trust-owned **Hatfield Forest**, where there is a nature trail and lake. After this you pass close to **Stansted Airport**, whose magnificent terminal building was designed by Norman Foster. You are now into the relative high ground of the chalk uplands of northwestern Essex. Between **Broxted** and **Thaxted** the route veers out into a loop that takes in the pretty villages of Clavering, Arkesden and Wendens Ambo and the town of **Saffron Walden**. Here you will find an art gallery, a museum, the Sun Inn, embellished with plasterwork decoration, and a maze on the town's common. Nearby stands **Audley End House**. This imposing mansion was built on the foundations of a Benedictine Abbey in the early seventeenth century for Thomas Howard, Lord Treasurer to King James I (who described it as 'too large for a King but might do for a Lord Treasurer'), but the interior was largely remodelled by Robert Adam in the eighteenth century. It has a splendid Renaissance facade and a garden landscaped by 'Capability' Brown.

Arkesden 19

National Grid Ref: TL4834

¶ ◀ Axe & Compass

Parsonage Farm, Arkesden, Saffron Walden, Essex, CB11 4HB.
Victorian farmhouse on arable farm in centre of award-winning village.
Tel: **01799 550306** Mrs Forster.
D: £17.50-£25.00 **S:** £25.00-£25.00
Open: All Year (not Xmas)
Beds: 2D 1T
Baths: 2 En 1 Sh
ॐ ▣ (5) ⊬◻ ♁ ♨ ▥ Ⅴ ৯

Saffron Walden 20

National Grid Ref: TL5438

¶ ◀ Crown, Eight Bells, Rose & Crown, White Hart

▲ *Saffron Walden Youth Hostel,* 1 Myddylton Place, Saffron Walden, Essex, CB10 1BB.
Actual grid ref: TL535386
Tel: **01799 523117**
Under 18: £6.50 **Adults:** £9.25
Lounge, Dining room, Drying room, Evening meal at 7.00pm, No smoking, Breakfast available, Credit cards accepted
500-year-old oak-beamed former maltings with oak beams and uneven floors, and courtyard garden, a stone's throw from the town centre.

S = Price range for a single person in a room

Rowley Hill Lodge, Little Walden Road, Saffron Walden, Essex, CB10 1UZ.
Actual grid ref: TL542407
C19th farm lodge thoughtfully enlarged. Both bedrooms with baths & power showers.
Grades: ETC 4 Diamond
Tel: **01799 525975**
Mr & Mrs Haslam.
Fax no: 01799 516622
D: £24.00
S: £28.00.
Open: All Year (not Xmas)
Beds: 1D 1T
Baths: 2 Pr
ॐ ▣ (4) ◻ ♨ ▥ Ⅴ ৶

Archway Guest House, Church Street, Saffron Walden, Essex, CB10 1JW.
Unique house decorated with antiques, toys and rock & pop memorabilia.
Grades: ETC 4 Diamond
Tel: **01799 501500**
Miles.
D: £25.00-£30.00 **S:** £30.00-£40.00.
Open: All Year
Beds: 1F 2D 2T 1S
Baths: 3 En 1 Pr 1 Sh
ॐ ▣ (3) ◻ ♁ ♨ ▥ Ⅴ ৯

Ashleigh House, 7 Farmadine Grove, Saffron Walden, Essex, CB11 3DR.
Pleasant house close to town centre. Comfortable rooms. Quiet location.
Grades: ETC 4 Diamond
Tel: **01799 513611**
Mrs Gilder.
D: £18.00-£19.00 **S:** £20.00-£24.00.
Open: All Year
Beds: 1D 1T 2S
Baths: 1 Pr 1 Sh
ॐ (6) ▣ (5) ⊬◻ ♁ ♨ ▥ Ⅴ ৶ ৯

---

10 Victoria Avenue, Saffron Walden, Essex, CB11 3AE.
Detached house, one hundred years old. Lock up for bicycles. On street parking.
Grades: ETC 2 Diamond
Tel: **01799 525923**
Mrs Gilder.
D: £16.00-£16.00 **S:** £16.00-£16.00.
Open: All Year
Beds: 1T 3S
Baths: 1 Sh
ॐ ⊬◻ ♁ ♨ ▥ Ⅴ ৶ ৯

1 Gunters Cottages, Thaxted Road, Saffron Walden, Essex, CB10 2UT.
Quiet comfortable accommodation. Indoor heated swimming pool. Friendly welcome.
Tel: **01799 522091**
Mrs Goddard.
D: £19.50 **S:** £25.00.
Open: All Year (not Xmas)
Beds: 1D
Baths: 1 Pr
▣ (4) ⊬◻ ♁ ♨ ▥ Ⅴ ৯

Great Chesterford 21

National Grid Ref: TL5042

¶ ◀ The Plough

White Gates, School Street, Great Chesterford, Saffron Walden, Essex, CB10 1PH.
C18th timber framed cottage in heart of historic village.
Grades: ETC 4 Diamond
Tel: **01799 530249**
Mrs Mortimer.
D: £19.00-£25.00
S: £23.00-£25.00.
Open: All Year
Beds: 1F 1T 1S
Baths: 1 En 1 Sh
ॐ ▣ (3) ⊬◻ ♁ ♨ ▥ Ⅴ ৯

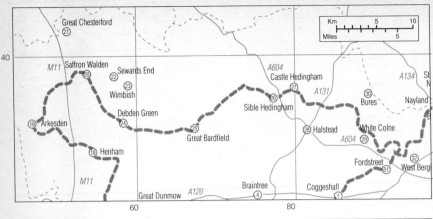

Sewards End 22

National Grid Ref: TL5638

Tipswains, Cole End, Sewards End, Saffron Walden, Essex, CB10 2LJ.
Beautiful Listed C17th thatched cottage situated in 1-acre garden surrounded by farmland.
Tel: **01799 523911** Mrs Dighton.
D: £20.00-£25.00 **S:** £25.00-£28.00.
Open: All Year (not Xmas)
Beds: 2D
Baths: 2 Pr
🛏 (1) 🅿 (5) ⌿ 🛏 🏃 🎹 Ⅴ ▮ ⌿ ♻

Wimbish 23

National Grid Ref: TL5837

🍴 🍺 White Hart

Newdegate House, Howlett End, Wimbish, Saffron Walden, Essex, CB10 2XW.
Warm welcome, convenient for Duxford War Museum, Cambridge, Stansted Airport.
Grades: ETC 4 Diamond, Silver
Tel: **01799 599748** (also fax no)
Mr & Mrs Haigh.
D: £17.00-£20.00 **S:** £24.00-£29.50.
Open: All Year (not Xmas)
Beds: 1D 1T
Baths: 1 En 1 Pr
🛏 (10) 🅿 (10) ⌿ 🛏 🏃 🎹 Ⅴ ▮ ⌿ ♻

Debden Green 24

National Grid Ref: TL5732

Wigmores Farm, Debden Green, Saffron Walden, Essex, CB11 3LX.
Situated in beautiful open countryside near Thaxted and Saffron Walden.
Tel: **01371 830050**
Mr & Mrs Worth.
D: £19.00-£24.00 **S:** £24.00-£24.00.
Open: All Year (not Xmas)
Beds: 1F 2D 1T
Baths: 2 Sh
🛏 🅿 (10) 🛏 🐾 ✗ 🏃 🎹 Ⅴ ⌿ ♻

Great Bardfield 25

National Grid Ref: TL6730

🍴 🍺 The Vine

Bucks House, Vine Street, Great Bardfield, Braintree, Essex, CM7 4SR.
Actual grid ref: TL676305
Beautiful C16th house, great breakfasts, warm welcome. Conservation village centre.
Tel: **01371 810519** Mrs Turner.
Fax no: 01371 811175
D: £20.00-£25.00 **S:** £25.00-£25.00.
Open: All Year (not Xmas)
Beds: 2D 1T
Baths: 3 En 1 Pr
🛏 ⌿ 🛏 🐾 🏃 🎹 Ⅴ ▮ ⌿ ♻

Sible Hedingham 26

National Grid Ref: TL7734

🍴 🍺 Bell Castle, Wjite Horse

Hedingham Antiques, 100 Swan Street, Sible Hedingham, Halstead, Essex, CO9 3HP.
Actual grid ref: TL783341
Victorian house and shop combined in centre of busy village.
Grades: ETC 3 Diamond
Tel: **01787 460360** Mrs Patterson.
Fax no: 01787 469109
D: £20.00-£20.00 **S:** £22.50-£22.50.
Open: All Year (not Xmas)
Beds: 1D 2T
Baths: 3 En
🛏 🅿 (4) 🛏 🏃 🎹 Ⅴ ♻

Order your packed lunches the *evening before* you need them.
Not at breakfast!

All details shown are as supplied by B&B owners in Autumn 2000.

Castle Hedingham 27

National Grid Ref: TL7835

🍴 🍺 The Bell, White Hart

▲ *Castle Hedingham Youth Hostel, 7 Falcon Square, Castle Hedingham, Halstead, Essex, CO9 3BU.*
Actual grid ref: TL786355
Tel: **01787 460799**
Under 18: £6.90 **Adults:** £10.00
Self-catering facilities, Television, Showers, Wet weather shelter, Lounge, Drying room, Cycle store, Evening meal at 7.00pm, No smoking, WC, Kitchen facilities, Breakfast available, Credit cards accepted
C16th building with modern annexe and large lawned garden, close by the Norman Castle and half-timbered houses of this medieval town.

Fishers, 36 St James Street, Castle Hedingham, Halstead, Essex, CO9 3EW.
Actual grid ref: TL787355
Peaceful stay overlooking lovely garden. Excellent for touring Essex/Suffolk border.
Tel: **01787 460382** (also fax no)
Mrs Hutchings.
D: £20.00-£25.00
S: £25.00-£30.00.
Open: All Year (not Xmas)
Beds: 1T
Baths: 1 Pr
🛏 (8) 🅿 (1) ⌿ 🛏 🏃 🎹 Ⅴ ♻

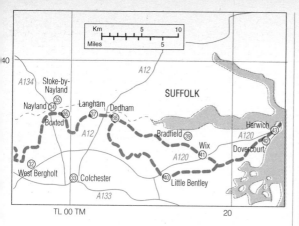

TL 00 TM   20

Saffron Walden to Fordham

Southeast of Saffron Walden you will find an interesting architecturally-eclectic church at **Debden**, before coming to **Thaxted**. Originating in Saxon times, the town has many medieval half-timbered buildings, including the Guildhall, which stands as evidence of the town's prosperity based historically on the cutlery industry. You are now on the long eastwards stretch of the route, which takes you through a series of attractive villages - Great Bardfield, Finchingfield and **Castle Hedingham**, where the well-preserved Norman castle keep is set in grounds with a formal canal and woodland walks. From here you continue east to **Fordham**, from where you can head south, cross the River Colne and proceed to **Coggeshall**; or continue into the eastern 'spur' to **Harwich**. A detour into **Colchester** will enable you to take in some of the rich store of architectural remains on offer in Britain's oldest town. (See under *Sustrans Hull to Harwich*.)

Halstead   28

National Grid Ref: TL8130

⌖ ⌑ The Bull

Mill House, The Causeway, Halstead, Essex, CO9 1ET.
Listed town house in the market town, private parking, brochure available.
Grades: ETC 4 Diamond
Tel: **01787 474451**
Mr & Mrs Stuckey.
Fax no: 01787 473893
D: £24.00-£25.00
S: £30.00-£48.00.
Open: All Year (not Xmas)
⌖ (12) ⊞ (18) ⌁ ⛶ ⍟ ▥ ▣ ⚲ ⚘

The Woodman Inn, Colchester Road, Halstead, Essex, CO9 2DY.
Comfortable mock-Tudor public house.
Tel: **01787 476218** (also fax no)
Mr Redsell.
D: £18.00-£18.00 **S:** £18.00-£18.00
Open: All Year
Beds: 1F 1D 1T 1S **Baths:** 1 Sh
⌖ ⊞ (12) ⍟ ✕ ⛶ ▥ ▣

White Colne   29

National Grid Ref: TL8729

Larkswood, 32 Colchester Road, White Colne, Colchester, Essex, CO6 2PN.
Pretty chalet bungalow in Colne Valley west of Colchester.
Grades: ETC 3 Diamond
Tel: **01787 224362** Mr Fewster.
D: £17.50-£19.00
S: £25.00-£25.00
Open: All Year
Beds: 1T **Baths:** 1 En
⊞ (2) ⍟ ⛶ ▥ ▣

D = Price range per person

sharing in a double room

Bures   30

National Grid Ref: TL9034

⌖ ⌑ Eight Bells, The Swan

Queens House Guest House, Church Square, Bures, Suffolk, CO8 5AB.
Actual grid ref: TL906341
Former C17th coaching inn in beautiful Stour Valley, Constable country.
Tel: **01787 227760** Mr Arnold.
Fax no: 01787 227082
D: £24.00-£28.00 **S:** £28.00-£32.00.
Open: All Year (not Xmas)
Beds: 1F 2D 2T
Baths: 4 En 1 Pr
⌖ ⊞ (4) ⍟ ⌁ ✕ ⛶ ▥ ▣ ⚲ ⚘

Swan House, Bridge Street, Bures, Suffolk, CO8 5AD.
Actual grid ref: TL905340
Great welcome awaits you at a beautiful, spacious, riverside home in the Stour Valley.
Tel: **01787 228098** (also fax no)
Mrs Tweed.
D: £20.00-£22.00 **S:** £22.00-£25.00.
Open: All Year
Beds: 1F 1D 1S **Baths:** 2 Pr
⌖ (1) ⊞ (2) ⌁ ⛶ ⍟ ▥ ▣ ⚲ ⚘

Fordstreet   31

National Grid Ref: TL9226

⌖ ⌑ Coopers Arms, Queen's Head, Shoulder of Mutton

Old House, Fordstreet, Aldham, Colchester, Essex, CO6 3PH.
Actual grid ref: TL920270
Fascinating Grade II Listed C14th hall house - oak beams, log fires, large garden.
Grades: ETC 3 Diamond
Tel: **01206 240456** (also fax no)
Mrs Mitchell.
D: £20.00-£25.00 **S:** £27.50.
Open: All Year
Beds: 1F 1T 1S **Baths:** 1 En 2 Pr
⌖ ⊞ (6) ⍟ ⛶ ▥ ▣ ⚲ ⚘

West Bergholt   32

National Grid Ref: TL9627

⌖ ⌑ Queens Head, White Hart, Treble Tile

The Old Post House, 10 Colchester Road, West Bergholt, Colchester, Essex, CO6 3JG.
Actual grid ref: TL9527
Large Victorian private house, warm welcome, quiet secluded garden.
Grades: ETC 3 Diamond
Tel: **01206 240379** Mrs Brown.
Fax no: 01206 243301
D: £20.00-£25.00 **S:** £20.00.
Open: All Year
Beds: 1F 1D 1T **Baths:** 1 En 1 Sh
⌖ (1) ⊞ (3) ⛶ ⍟ ▥ ▣ ⚲ ⚘

S = Price range for a single

person in a room

Colchester 33

National Grid Ref: TL9925

🍴 🍺 Forresters, George, Siege House, Red Lion, Roverstye, Peveril Hotel

Salisbury Hotel, 112 Butt Road, Colchester, Essex, CO3 3DL.
Grades: AA 2 Diamond
Tel: 01206 508508
Fax no: 01206 797265
D: £25.00-£35.00 **S:** £30.00-£40.00.
Open: All Year
Beds: 2F 4T 3D 3S
Baths: All En
🛇 🅿 🗆 🗙 🕭 🎟 🚾 🛈 🛗
Situated in the historical garrison town of Colchester and within easy reach of 3 cathedral cities. Despite being in the centre of town this pub has a relaxed and informal atmosphere. The in-house bar and restaurant serve delicious and innovative meals

St John's Guest House, 330 Ipswich Road, Colchester, Essex, CO4 4ET.
Well situated close to town, convenient for A12 and A120 Harwich.
Tel: **01206 852288** Mrs Knight.
D: £20.00-£25.00 **S:** £26.00-£45.00.
Open: All Year
Beds: 2F 2D 2T 2S
Baths: 5 En 3 Sh
🛇 🅿 (10) 🗲 🗆 🕭 🎟 🚾 🛈 🍴

11a Lincoln Way, Colchester, Essex, CO1 2RL.
Friendly, comfortable modern house in quiet residential area, five minutes' walk from town centre.
Tel: **01206 867192**
Mr & Mrs Edwards.
Fax no: 01206 799993
D: £18.00-£20.00
S: £18.00-£22.00.
Open: All Year
Beds: 1T 1S
Baths: 1 Sh
🛇 (4) 🅿 (1) 🗲 🗆 🕈 🗙 🕭 🎟 🚾 🛈 🍴

Peveril Hotel, 51 North Hill, Colchester, Essex, CO1 1PY.
Town centre holiday accommodation. Superb food, near castle.
Tel: **01206 574001** (also fax no)
D: £27.00-£45.00 **S:** £27.00-£45.00.
Open: All Year (not Xmas)
Beds: 4F 6D 2T 5S
Baths: 6 En 4 Sh
🛇 🅿 (10) 🗆 🕈 🗙 🕭 🎟 🚾 🛈 🍴

8 Broadmead Road, Parsons Heath, Colchester, Essex, CO4 3HB.
Friendly family home, quiet residential area. 10 mins bus/car from town centre.
Tel: **01206 861818** (also fax no)
Mr & Mrs Smith.
D: £18.50-£18.50 **S:** £25.00-£25.00.
Open: All Year
Beds: 1D
Baths: 1 Sh
🅿 🗲 🗆 🗙 🕭 🎟 🚾 🛈

Nayland 34

National Grid Ref: TL9734

🍴 🍺 The Lion, White Hart

Gladwins Farm, Harpers Hill, Nayland, Colchester, Essex, CO6 4NU.
Actual grid ref: TL961347
Grades: ETC 4 Diamond
Tel: 01206 262261 Mrs Dossor.
Fax no: 01206 263001
D: £28.00-£30.00 **S:** £25.00-£30.00.
Open: All Year (not Xmas)
Beds: 2D 1S
Baths: 2 En 1 Pr
🛇 (8) 🅿 (14) 🗲 🗆 🗙 🕭 🎟 🚾 🛈 🍴

Traditional Suffolk farmhouse B&B with ensuite rooms, in 22 acres of beautiful rolling Constable country, or choose a self-catering cottage. Heated indoor pool, sauna, aromatherapy suite, hard tennis court, fishing lake, children's playground. Pets welcome. Colour brochure from resident owners.

Hill House, Gravel Hill, Nayland, Colchester, Essex, CO6 4JB.
Actual grid ref: TL975345
C16th beamed hall house on edge of historic Constable village.
Tel: **01206 262782** Mrs Heigham.
D: £20.00-£26.00 **S:** £22.00-£25.00.
Open: All Year (not Xmas)
Beds: 1D 1T 1S
Baths: 1 En 2 Pr
🛇 (8) 🅿 (6) 🗲 🗆 🕭 🎟 🚾 🛈 🍴

Bringing children with you? Always ask for any special rates.

Stoke-by-Nayland 35

National Grid Ref: TL9836

🍴 🍺 The Angel

Thorington Hall, Stoke-by-Nayland, Colchester, Essex, CO6 4SS.
Beautiful C17th house belonging to the National Trust.
Tel: **01206 337329** Mrs Wollaston.
D: £20.00-£22.00 **S:** £28.00-£28.00.
Open: Easter to Sep
Beds: 1F 1D 1T 1S
Baths: 1 Sh
🛇 🅿 (4) 🕈 🍴

Ryegate House, Stoke-by-Nayland, Colchester, Essex, CO6 4RA.
Actual grid ref: TL986366
In pleasant village setting. Warm welcome, fine food, restful rooms.
Tel: **01206 263679** Mrs Geater.
D: £20.00-£24.00
S: £28.00-£34.00.
Open: All Year (not Xmas)
Beds: 2D 1T **Baths:** 3 En
🛇 (12) 🅿 (5) 🗲 🗆 🕈 🕭 🎟 🚾 🛈

Boxted 36

National Grid Ref: TL9933

Round Hill House, Parsonage Hill, Boxted, Colchester, Essex, CO4 5ST.
Actual grid ref: TM001334
Stands on a low hill overlooking pastures where cattle graze.
Grades: ETC 4 Diamond
Tel: **01206 272392** (also fax no)
D: £22.50-£26.00 **S:** £30.00-£35.00.
Open: All Year
Beds: 1F 1D 1T **Baths:** 2 En 1 Pr
🛇 🅿 (6) 🗆 🕈 🗙 🕭 🎟 🚾 🛈 🍴 🍷

Langham 37

National Grid Ref: TM0233

🍴 🍺 Shepherd & Dog

Oak Apple Farm, Greyhound Hill, Langham, Colchester, Essex, CO4 5QF.
Actual grid ref: TM023320
Comfortable farmhouse tastefully decorated with large attractive garden.
Grades: ETC 4 Diamond
Tel: **01206 272234** Mrs Helliwell.
D: £22.00 **S:** £22.00.
Open: All Year (not Xmas)
Beds: 2T 1S **Baths:** 1 Sh
🛇 🅿 (6) 🗆 🕭 🎟 🚾 🛈 🍴 🍷

Fordham to Harwich

The village of **Dedham** boasts an immaculate neo-classical row of houses, and a church where one of the pews is decorated in memory of the Apollo 11 moon landing. Just over the border in Suffolk, **Flatford Mill** has become dedicated to the memory of the painter John Constable, whose painting *The Hay Wain* featured the original mill, on the site of which the present Victorian building stands. The route to Harwich runs along two alternative ways - the northern way goes through **Manningtree** and **Mistley**, the southern through **Ardleigh**, where there are a number of buildings of historic interest, and some other villages. The northern way is likely to be the more crowded, particularly during summer. **Harwich** is a major ferry port to the European mainland, and can be used to link the Essex Cycle Route with Continental cycling tours.

Dedham 38

National Grid Ref: TM0533

🍴 🍺 Marlborough Head

Mays Barn Farm, Mays Lane, Dedham, Colchester, Essex, CO7 6EW.
Actual grid ref: TM0531
A comfortable well-furnished old house with wonderful views of Dedham Vale.
Grades: ETC 4 Diamond
Tel: **01206 323191** Mrs Freeman.
D: £20.00-£22.00 **S:** £25.00-£30.00.
Open: All Year
Beds: 1D 1T
Baths: 1 En 1 Pr
🗶 (12) 🅿 (3) ⊬ 🖵 🛓 🎟 ⚡ 🚲

Bradfield 39

National Grid Ref: TM1430

🍴 🍺 Village Maid

Emsworth House, Ship Hill, Bradfield, Manningtree, Essex, CO11 2UP.
Set in a large beautiful garden with stunning views over the estuary.
Tel: **01255 870860** Mrs Linton.
D: £19.00-£25.00 **S:** £27.00-£36.00.
Open: All Year
Beds: 1F 2D 1T
Baths: 1 En 2 Sh
🗶 🅿 (10) 🖵 🐾 ✗ 🛓 🎟 🆅 ⓘ ⚡ 🚲

Little Bentley 40

National Grid Ref: TM1125

🍴 🍺 Bricklayers Arms

Bentley Manor, Little Bentley, Colchester, Essex, CO7 8SE.
C15th manor house, close to Colchester, 15 mins port of Harwich.
Tel: **01206 250622** Mrs Dyson.
Fax no: 01206 251820
D: £20.00-£22.00 **S:** £24.00-£26.00.
Open: All Year
Beds: 1F 1S 1T
Baths: 2 En
🗶 🅿 ⊬ 🖵 🛓 🎟 🆅 ⚡ 🚲

Wix 41

National Grid Ref: TM1628

🍴 🍺 Village Maid

Dairy House Farm, Bradfield Road, Wix, Manningtree, Essex, CO11 2SR.
Spacious quality, rural accommodation. A really relaxing place to stay.
Grades: ETC 4 Diamond, Gold
Tel: **01255 870322** Mrs Whitworth.
Fax no: 01255 870186
D: £18.50-£20.00 **S:** £26.00-£26.00.
Open: All Year (not Xmas)
Beds: 1D 2T
Baths: 2 En 1 Pr
🗶 (12) 🅿 (4) 🖵 🛓 🎟 🆅 ⓘ 🚲

Dovercourt 42

National Grid Ref: TM2531

🍴 🍺 Royal Oak Inn

Dudley Guest House, 34 Cliff Road, Dovercourt, Harwich, Essex, CO12 3PP.
Family-run Victorian house. Railway/buses short walk. Pubs, restaurants, shops, banks close by.
Grades: ETC 2 Diamond
Tel: **01255 504927**
Mr Rackham.
D: £14.00-£18.00
S: £18.00-£22.00.
Open: All Year
Beds: 1F 1D 1T 1S
Baths: 1 En 2 Sh
🗶 🅿 (4) ⊬ 🖵 🛓 🎟 🆅 🚲

Harwich 43

National Grid Ref: TM2431

🍴 🍺 The Royal Oak

Tudor Rose, 124 Fronks Road, Dovercourt, Harwich, CO12 4EQ.
Harwich international port. Seafront, railway 5 minutes. London 1 hour.
Tel: **01255 552398**
D: £17.50-£17.50
S: £20.00-£30.00.
Open: May to Aug
🗶 🅿 (2) ⊬ 🖵 🛓 🎟 🆅 ⚡ 🚲

Icknield Way

The great prehistoric track that runs from Dorset to The Wash along Southern England's chalk ridgeway is the most ancient road still in use in Europe. Although the name applied historically to the whole section from the Thames to the north coast of Norfolk, the present **Icknield Way** runs from the northern end of the Ridgeway National Trail in Buckinghamshire to the starting point, on Norfolk's southern border, of the Peddars Way, another National Trail. Passing through Buckinghamshire, Bedfordshire, Hertfordshire, Cambridgeshire, Essex and Suffolk, it is now a Regional Recreational Route created, primarily for walkers, by the Countryside Commission on the basis of work done by the Icknield Way Association. A little over 100 miles long, the route is waymarked by a distinctive flint axe emblem. **Note:** Cyclists should follow the route designed for horseriders. This frequently diverges from the walkers' route, which follows many footpaths open only to walkers. Wherever the two are different, follow the waymarks and signposts marked 'Riders' Route'.

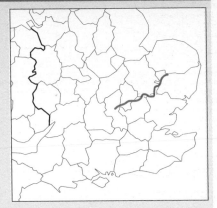

Guides: *The Icknield Way Path – A Guide for Horseriders, Cyclists and Others* by Elizabeth Barrett (ISBN 0 951601 12 1), published by Wimpole Books and available from the publishers at Pip's Peace, Kenton, Stowmarket, Suffolk IP14 6JS, tel 01728 860429, @ £4.50 (inc p&p), describes the riders' route, which cyclists should follow. This guide takes the route in reverse from the above description. It finishes at Luton, so you should also get hold of a copy of *The Icknield Way – A Walkers' Guide* (ISBN 0 952181 90 8), published by the Icknield Way Association and available from the Ramblers' Association National Office, 1/5 Wandsworth Road, London SW8 2XX, tel 020-7339 8500, @ £4.50 (+ 70p p&p). This guide has excellent material on the flora and fauna, archaeology and geology of the path.

Maps: Ordnance Survey 1:50,000 Landranger series: 144, 153, 154, 155, 165, 166

Trains: Tring, about 4 miles from Ivinghoe Beacon, is served by trains from London, as is Luton. Letchworth and Baldock are on the line between London and Cambridge. Newmarket is on the line between Cambridge and Ipswich. Thetford, about 6 miles from Knettishall Heath, is on the line between Cambridge and Norwich.

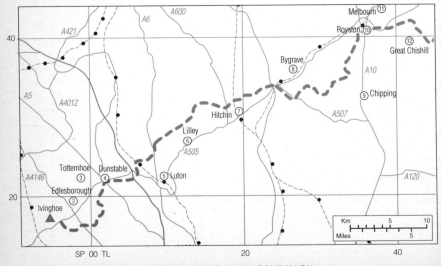

vinghoe 1

National Grid Ref: SP9416

🏠 *Ivinghoe Youth Hostel, The Old Brewery House, High Street, vinghoe, Leighton Buzzard, LU7 9EP*
ctual grid ref: SP945161
el: **01296 668251**
nder 18: £6.90 **Adults:** £10.00
elf-catering facilities, Television, howers, Lounge, Drying room, ycle store, Parking, Evening meal t 7.00pm, Kitchen facilities, reakfast available
eorgian mansion, once home of a ocal brewer, next to village church Chilterns' Area of Outstanding atural Beauty.

All cycleways are popular: you are well-advised to book ahead

---

Pay B&Bs by cash or cheque and be prepared to pay up front.

Edlesborough 2

National Grid Ref: SP9719

🍴 🍺 The Golden Rule

Ridgeway End, 5 Ivinghoe Way, Edlesborough, Dunstable, Beds, LU6 2EL.
Actual grid ref: SP975183
Pretty bungalow in private road, surrounded by fields and views of the Chiltern Hills.
Tel: **01525 220405** (also fax no)
Mrs Lloyd.
D: £20.00-£22.00 **S:** £22.00-£24.00.
Open: All Year (not Xmas)
Beds: 1D 1T
Baths: 1 En
🏃 (2) 🅿 (3) ✄ 🗆 🔌 🛏 Ⓥ 🗎 ⚡ ♻

Totternhoe 3

National Grid Ref: SP9821

🍴 🍺 Old Farm Inn, Cross Keys

Country Cottage, 5 Brightwell Avenue, Totternhoe, Dunstable, Beds, LU6 1QT.
Actual grid ref: SP994210
Quiet village house in countryside with views of Dunstable Downs.
Tel: **01582 601287** (also fax no)
Mrs Mardell.
D: £25.00-£25.00 **S:** £25.00-£25.00.
Open: All Year (not Xmas)
Beds: 1T 1D 1S
Baths: 2 En 1Shared
🏃 🅿 (3) ✄ 🗆 🔌 🛏 Ⓥ 🗎 ⚡

Many rates vary according to season - the lowest only are shown here

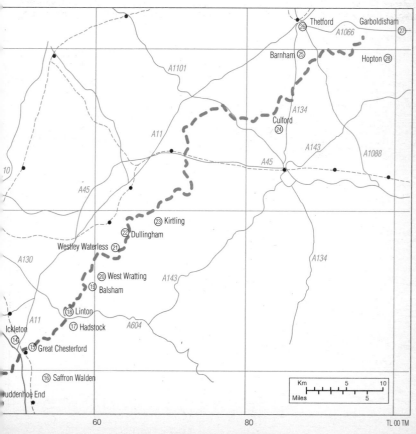

Ivinghoe Beacon to Baldock

The official start of the Icknield Way is at **Ivinghoe Beacon**, a hill with an ancient fort, which yields good views. Close by is Pitstone Windmill, the oldest in England (seventeenth century). Crossing into Bedfordshire, the route passes near **Whipsnade Wild Animal Park**, which you can tour by steam train, as well as on foot; and crosses the **Dustable Downs Country Park**, where there are several Neolithic burial mounds. From here you go through the towns of **Dunstable** and **Luton**. Luton Museum exhibits archaeological finds from the Icknield Way. Into Hertfordshire, and you reach **Telegraph Hill**, one of a series of such hills in a line from London to Great Yarmouth, named from the communication stations, which signalled using a system of shutters on the roof, of the Napoleonic Wars. The views from the hill are excellent. North of Tingley Wood is the Knocking Hoe long barrow, and a nearby National Nature Reserve. You head through the village of **Ickleford**, north of Hitchin, to reach **Letchworth**, an early 'garden city'. From here you pass to the north of **Baldock**, a town important in Iron Age and Roman times and developed by the Knights Templars. There are some fine Georgian buildings.

Dunstable 4

National Grid Ref: TL0121

|◎| ◁| Sugar Loaf

***Regent House Guest House**, 79a High Street North, Dunstable, Beds, LU6 1JF.*
Dunstable town centre, close to MI.
Tel: **01582 660196**
Mr Woodhouse.
D: £17.00-£17.00 **S:** £20.00-£20.00.
Open: All Year
Beds: 5T 5S 1F
Baths: 4 En
⌂ 🅿 (6) ⊟ ↑ ≜ ▥ Ⅴ ⓵ ⌀

Luton 5

National Grid Ref: TL0921

|◎| ◁| Wigmore Arms, O'Shea's

***Stockwood Hotel**, 41-43 Stockwood Crescent, Luton, Beds, LU1 3SS.*
Actual grid ref: TL090206
Tudor-style town centre premises, near M1, airport, golf course.
Tel: **01582 721000** Mr Blanchard.
D: £20.00**S:** £25.00.
Open: All Year (not Xmas)
Beds: 1F 2D 6T 9S
Baths: 4 Pr 3 Sh
⌂ 🅿 (14) ⊟ ✕ ▥,

***Belzayne**, 70 Lalleford Road, Luton, Beds, LU2 9JH.*
Modern semi, close to London bus stop. Old fashioned hospitality.
Tel: **01582 736591** (also fax no)
Mrs Bell.
D: £12.00-£14.00 **S:** £18.00.
Open: All Year (not Xmas)
Beds: 1F 2T
Baths: 2 Sh
⌂ (7) 🅿 (5) ≜ ▥, Ⅴ

Lilley 6

National Grid Ref: TL1126

|◎| ◁| Lilley Arms

***Lilley Arms**, West Street, Lilley, Luton, Beds, LU2 8LN.*
Early C18th coaching inn.
Tel: **01462 768371** Mrs Brown.
D: £20.00-£30.00 .
Open: All Year
Beds: 1F 1D 3T **Baths:** 3En 1 Sh
⌂ 🅿 ⊬ ⊟ ✕ ≜ ▥, Ⅴ ⓵ ⌀

Hitchin 7

National Grid Ref: TL1828

***Firs Hotel**, 83 Bedford Road, Hitchin, Herts, SG5 2TY.*
Comfortable hotel with relaxed informal atmosphere. Excellent rail/road links and car parking.
Grades: RAC Star
Tel: **01462 422322** Girgenti.
Fax no: 01462 432051
D: £26.00-£30.00 **S:** £37.50-£50.00.
Open: All Year
Beds: 3F 3D 8T 16S **Baths:** 30 En
⌂ 🅿 (30) ⊬ ⊟ ↑ ✕ ≜ ▥, Ⅴ ⓵ ⌀

Bygrave 8

National Grid Ref: TL2636

|◎| ◁| Bushel & Strike, Rose & Crown, Engine

***Bygrave B&B**, 59 Ashwell Road, Bygrave, Baldock, Hertfordshire, SG7 5DY.*
Friendly family home, rural location. Guests' room, use of garden.
Tel: **01462 894749** Mrs Spaul.
D: £22.00-£25.00 **S:** £22.00-£25.00.
Open: All Year (not Xmas)
Beds: 2D 2T 1S **Baths:** 2 En 1 Sh
⌂ 🅿 (5) ⊬ ⊟ ≜ ▥, Ⅴ ⌀

Chipping 9

National Grid Ref: TL3532

|◎| ◁| Countryman Inn

***Ashford Cottage**, Chipping, Buntingford, Herts, SG9 0PG.*
Elizabethan thatched cottage, acre of gardens, heavily timbered.
Tel: **01763 274163**
Mr & Mrs Kenyon.
Fax no: 01763 271655
D: £22.50-£22.50 **S:** £22.50-£22.50
Open: All Year
Beds: 1D 2S
Baths: 1 Sh
⌂ 🅿 (6) ⊬ ⊟ ✕ ≜ ▥, Ⅴ ⓵ ⌀ ⌀

Royston 10

National Grid Ref: TL3541

|◎| ◁| Jockey Inn, White Bear Lodge, Green Man

***Jockey Inn**, 31-33 Baldock Street, Royston, Herts, SG8 5BD.*
Traditional public house, real ales. Comfortable rooms - ensuite/cable TV. Hearty breakfast.
Tel: **01763 243377**
D: £26.50-£28.50 **S:** £29.95-£34.00
Open: All Year
Beds: 3T 1F
Baths: 5 En
⌂ (8) 🅿 (5) ⊟ ✕ ≜ ▥, Ⅴ ⌀

Melbourn 11

National Grid Ref: TL3844

|◎| ◁| The Star, Black Horse, The Chequers

***The Carlings**, Melbourn, Royston, SG8 6DX.*
Luxurious rooms in delightful secluded setting. Separate entrance, conservatory gardens.
Tel: **01763 260686** Mrs Howard.
Fax no: 01763 261988
D: £22.00-£22.00 **S:** £30.00-£35.00
Open: All Year (not Xmas)
Beds: 1D 1T **Baths:** 2 En
⌂ 🅿 (3) ⊬ ⊟ ↑ ≜ ▥, ⟁ Ⅴ ⌀ ⌀

Great Chishill 12

National Grid Ref: TL4238

|◎| ◁| The Pleasant

***Hall Farm**, Great Chishill, Royston, Cambridgeshire, SG8 8SH.*
Grades: ETC 4 Diamond
Tel: **01763 838263** (also fax no)
Mrs Wiseman.
D: £20.00-£30.00 **S:** £30.00-£35.00
Open: All Year
Beds: 1F 1T 1D
Baths: 1 En 1 Sh
⌂ 🅿 (4) ⊬ ⊟ ↑ ≜ Ⅴ ⓵ ⌀
Beautiful manor house in secluded gardens on the edge of this pretty hilltop village, 11 miles south of Cambridge, wonderful views and footpaths. Duxford Air Museum 4 miles. Good local food. Working arable farm. Comfortable new beds.

Baldock to Gazeley

After **Ashwell**, an interesting village with a museum on local archaeological finds, the route enters Cambridgeshire and continues along Ashwell Street, a probably Roman road which may well be based on a stretch of the original Icknield Way, to reach **Melbourn**. Here you turn south before continuing eastwards to cross the River Cam into the northwestern corner of Essex, and the village of **Great Chesterford**, which was once a walled Roman town. Back in Cambridgeshire, the village of **Linton** has numerous sixteenth- and seventeenth-century houses, and a garden zoo. At **Balsham**, the county's highest point, there is a fascinating medieval church, which has a thirteenth-century bell tower, and a three-hundred-year-old musical manuscript on display. Crossing the ancient Fleam Dyke, you cycle up green hedged Fox Lane before wending your way through a string of villages to **Woodditton**, from where there are two routes to **Herringswell** in Suffolk. The northern alternative takes you via **Newmarket**, the famous horseracing centre, where you can visit the National Stud and the National Horseracing Museum, and **Chippenham**, with nearby Chippenham Park. The southern route leads over quieter roads through **Cheveley** and **Gazeley**, with its tower mill.

Duddenhoe End   13

National Grid Ref: TL4636

🍽 🍺 Axe and Compass

Rockells Farm, Duddenhoe End, *affron Walden, Essex, CB11 4UY.*
Georgian farmhouse with lake view.
Grades: ETC 4 Diamond
Tel: **01763 838053**
Mrs Westerhuis.
: £20.00-£25.00 **S:** £20.00-£25.00.
Open: All Year (not Xmas/New Year)
Beds: 1F 1T 1S
Baths: 3 En
🛇 🅿 (4) 🗖 ✕ 🍴 🛏 & 🖂 🛡 ∦ 🐾

ckleton   14

National Grid Ref: TL4843

🍽 🍺 Red Lion

ew Inn House, 10 Brookhampton *treet, Ickleton, Duxford, Cambs, B10 1SP.*
Tel: **01799 530463** Mrs Fletcher.
Fax no: 01799 531499
: £15.00-£19.00 **S:** £25.00-£30.00.
Open: All Year (not Xmas)
Beds: 1D 1T **Baths:** 1 Sh
🛇 (5) 🅿 (6) ✕ 🗖 🛏 🖂 🛡
Traditional beamed property combining comfortable modern facilities with historic charm. Luxury guest shower room. Good breakfasts. Small rural village, 3 miles Duxford Imperial War Museum. Handy for Cambridge and Saffron Walden. 2 miles M11.

Many rates vary according to season - the lowest only are shown here

Great Chesterford   15

National Grid Ref: TL5042

🍽 🍺 The Plough

White Gates, School Street, Great Chesterford, Saffron Walden, Essex, CB10 1PH.
C18th timber framed cottage in heart of historic village.
Grades: ETC 4 Diamond
Tel: **01799 530249** Mrs Mortimer.
D: £19.00-£25.00 **S:** £23.00-£25.00.
Open: All Year
Beds: 1F 1T 1S
Baths: 1 En 1 Sh
🛇 🅿 (3) ✕ 🗖 🛏 🖂 🛡 🐾

Saffron Walden   16

National Grid Ref: TL5438

🍽 🍺 Crown, Eight Bells, Rose & Crown

🔺 *Saffron Walden Youth Hostel*, 1 Myddylton Place, Saffron Walden, Essex, CB10 1BB.
Actual grid ref: TL535386
Tel: **01799 523117**
Under 18: £6.50 **Adults:** £9.25
Lounge, Dining room, Drying room, Evening meal at 7.00pm, No smoking, Breakfast available, Credit cards accepted
500-year-old oak-beamed former maltings with oak beams and uneven floors, and courtyard garden, a stone's throw from the town centre.

Rowley Hill Lodge, Little Walden Road, Saffron Walden, Essex, CB10 1UZ.
Actual grid ref: TL542407
C19th farm lodge thoughtfully enlarged. Both bedrooms with baths & power showers.
Grades: ETC 4 Diamond
Tel: **01799 525975** Mrs Haslam.
Fax no: 01799 516622
D: £24.00 **S:** £28.00.
Open: All Year (not Xmas)
Beds: 1D 1T **Baths:** 2 Pr
🛇 🅿 (4) 🗖 🛏 🖂 🛡 ∦

All details shown are as supplied by B&B owners in Autumn 2000.

Gazeley to Knettishall Heath

You are now in the open heath of **the Breckland**. The way through Suffolk leads to **Icklingham**, one of whose two churches is medieval and thatched and whose mill is recorded in the Domesday Book; nearby **West Stow Country Park** has a reconstructed Saxon village, accurately based on excavation work. The route takes you around the west and north of the **King's Forest**, planted from 1935 to celebrate the silver jubilee of George V, to **Euston**, not the London station but a village close to Euston Hall, an attractive eighteenth-century house and grounds with lakes, open to the public on Thursdays. The earlier house was a favourite haunt of the seventeenth-century diarist John Evelyn. From Euston it's on to **Knettishall Heath Country Park**, on the banks of the Little Ouse.

Archway Guest House, *Church Street, Saffron Walden, Essex, CB10 1JW.*
Unique house decorated with antiques, toys and rock & pop memorabilia.
Grades: ETC 4 Diamond
Tel: 01799 501500 Miles.
D: £25.00-£30.00 **S:** £30.00-£40.00.
Open: All Year
Beds: 1F 2D 2T 1S
Baths: 3 En 1 Pr 1 Sh
🛏 🅿 (3) ❑ ⊩ 🎴 ▥ Ⓥ ⌖

Ashleigh House, *7 Farmadine Grove, Saffron Walden, Essex, CB11 3DR.*
Pleasant house close to town centre. Comfortable rooms. Quiet location.
Grades: ETC 4 Diamond
Tel: 01799 513611 Mrs Gilder.
D: £18.00-£19.00 **S:** £20.00-£24.00.
Open: All Year
Beds: 1D 1T 2S **Baths:** 1 Pr 1 Sh
🛏 (6) 🅿 (5) ⌿ ❑ 🎴 ▥ Ⓥ ⌖ ⌖

10 Victoria Avenue, *Saffron Walden, Essex, CB11 3AE.*
Detached house, one hundred years old. Lock up for bicycles. On street parking. **Grades:** ETC 2 Diamond
Tel: 01799 525923 Mrs Gilder.
D: £16.00-£16.00 **S:** £16.00-£16.00.
Open: All Year
Beds: 1T 3S **Baths:** 1 Sh
🛏 ⌿ ❑ 🎴 ▥ Ⓥ ⌖ ⌖

1 Gunters Cottages, *Thaxted Road, Saffron Walden, Essex, CB10 2UT.*
Quiet comfortable accommodation. Indoor heated swimming pool. Friendly welcome.
Tel: 01799 522091 Mrs Goddard.
D: £19.50 **S:** £25.00.
Open: All Year (not Xmas)
Beds: 1D
Baths: 1 Pr
🅿 (4) ⌿ ❑ 🎴 ▥ Ⓥ ⌖

Hadstock   17

National Grid Ref: TL5544

⊩ 🍴 Kings Head

Yardleys, *Orchard Pightle, Hadstock, Cambridge, CB1 6PQ.*
Grades: ETC 4 Diamond
Tel: 01223 891822 (also fax no)
Mrs Ludgate.
D: £22.00-£25.00 **S:** £25.00-£32.00.
Open: All Year (not Xmas/New Year)
Beds: 2T 1D
Baths: 1 En 2 Pr
🛏 🅿 (5) ⌿ ❑ Ⅹ 🎴 ▥ Ⓥ ⌖
Peace and quiet in pretty village only 20 minutes Cambridge, 10 minutes Saffron Walden. Warm welcome and excellent breakfasts in comfortable home with guest lounge, garden and conservatory. Convenient for M11, Duxford, Newmarket, Stansted and Harwich. E.M by arrangement or good local restaurants.

Linton   18

National Grid Ref: TL5646

⊩ 🍴 Crown, Dog & Duck

Cantilena, *4 Harefield Rise, Linton, Cambridge, CB1 6LS.*
Spacious bungalow, quiet cul-de-sac, edge of historic village. Cambridge, 9 miles.
Tel: 01223 892988 (also fax no)
Mr & Mrs Clarkson.
D: £18.00-£20.00
S: £18.00-£25.00.
Open: All Year
Beds: 1F 1D 1T
Baths: 1 Sh
🛏 🅿 (3) ⌿ ❑ 🎴 ▥ ⅄ Ⓥ ⌖ ⌖

Linton Heights, *36 Wheatsheaf Way, Linton, Cambridge, Cambs, CB1 6XB.*
Actual grid ref: TL573475
Comfortable, friendly home, sharing lounge, convenient Duxford, Cambridge, Newmarket, Saffron Walden, Bury.
Tel: 01223 892516
Mr & Mrs Peake.
D: £17.00-£20.00
S: £17.00-£20.00.
Open: All Year (not Xmas)
Beds: 1T 1S
Baths: 1 Sh
🛏 (6) 🅿 (2) ⌿ ❑ 🎴 ▥ Ⓥ ⌖ ⌖

Balsham   19

National Grid Ref: TL5849

The Garden End, *10 West Wratting Road, Balsham, Cambridge, CB1 6DX.*
Actual grid ref: TL587506
Self-contained ground floor suite - children / pets welcome all year.
Tel: 01223 894021 (also fax no)
Mrs Greenaway.
D: £18.00-£18.00
S: £20.00.
Open: All Year
Beds: 1F
Baths: 1 En 1 Pr
🛏 🅿 (2) ⌿ ❑ ⊩ Ⅹ 🎴 ▥ ⅄ Ⓥ ⌖ ⌖

West Wratting   20

National Grid Ref: TL5951

⊩ 🍴 The Chesnut

The Old Bakery, *West Wratting, Cambridge, CB1 5LU.*
Period cottage situated in quiet village with nice garden.
Tel: 01223 290492
Mr & Mrs Denny.
Fax no: 01223 290845
D: £22.50 **S:** £22.50.
Open: All Year
Beds: 2T 3D
Baths: 1 En 1 Pr
🛏 🅿 (2) ❑ 🎴 ▥ Ⓥ ⌖ ⌖

Westley Waterless   21

National Grid Ref: TL6256

⊩ 🍴 Kings Head

Westley House, *Westley Waterless, Newmarket, Suffolk, CB8 0RQ.*
C18th Georgian country home in quiet rural area 5 miles from Newmarket.
Tel: 01638 508112
Mrs Galpin.
Fax no: 01638 508113
D: £22.50-£24.00
S: £24.00-£25.00.
Open: All Year
Beds: 2T 2S
Baths: 2 Sh
🛏 (4) 🅿 (6) ❑ ⊩ Ⅹ ▥ ⌖ ⌖

Dullingham   22

National Grid Ref: TL6257

The Old School, *Dullingham, Newmarket, Suffolk, CB8 9XF.*
Attractive conversion, spacious rooms, delightful village, nearby pub serves food.
Tel: 01638 507813
Mrs Andrews.
Fax no: 01638 507022
D: £23.00-£25.00 .
Open: All Year
Beds: 1D
Baths: 1 En
🛏 🅿 (2) ⌿ 🎴 ▥ Ⓥ ⌖ ⌖

Kirtling   23

National Grid Ref: TL6858

⊩ 🍴 Rain Deer

Hill Farm Guest House, *Kirtling, Newmarket, Suffolk, CB8 9HQ.*
Grades: ETC 3 Diamond, AA 3 Diamond
Tel: 01638 730253 (also fax no)
Mrs Benley.
D: £25.00-£50.00
S: £25.00-£25.00.
Open: All Year
Beds: 1D 1T 1S
Baths: 2 En 1 Pr
🅿 (5) ❑ ⊩ Ⅹ 🎴 ▥ ⌖ ⌖ ⌖
Delightful farm house in rural setting.

Culford   2

National Grid Ref: TL8369

⊩ 🍴 Woolpack, Linden Tree

47 Benyon Gardens, *Culford, Bur St Edmunds, Suffolk, IP28 6EA.*
A modern bungalow overlooking fields and quietly situated.
Tel: 01284 728763
Mrs Townsend.
D: £16.00-£32.00
S: £18.00-£18.00.
Open: All Year (not Xmas/New Year)
🅿 (4) ⌿ ❑ ▥ ⌖

Barnham 25

National Grid Ref: TL8779

🍴 🍺 Grafton Arms, Dolphin

East Farm, Barnham, Thetford, Norfolk, IP24 2PB.
Come & stay in large welcoming farmhouse and enjoy the farm countryside.
Grades: ETC 4 Diamond
Tel: **01842 890231** Mrs Heading.
D: £20.00-£22.50 **S:** £23.00-£25.00.
Open: All Year (not Xmas)
Beds: 1D 1T **Baths:** 2 En
🛇 🅿 (6) ⏰ ☐ ♨ 🎍 🛏 Ⅲ, Ⅵ 🛍 🚲

Thetford 26

National Grid Ref: TL8783

🍴 🍺 Black Horse, Anchor Hotel

43 Magdalen Street, Thetford, Thetford, Norfolk, IP24 2BP.
House built in 1575 close to town centre.
Tel: **01842 764564** Mrs Findlay.
D: £36.00-£36.00 **S:** £18.00-£18.00.
Open: All Year (not Xmas/New Year)
Beds: 2T 1S **Baths:** 1 Sh
🛇 🅿 (1) ☐ 🎍 Ⅲ, Ⅵ 🛍 🚲

Garboldisham 27

National Grid Ref: TM0081

🍴 🍺 The Fox, White Horse

Ingleneuk Lodge, Hopton Road, Garboldisham, Diss, Norfolk, IP22 2RQ.
Actual grid ref: TM002801
Pretty rural location with all rooms overlooking partly wooded grounds.
Tel: **01953 681541**
Mr & Mrs Stone.
Fax no: 01953 681638
D: £27.50-£27.50 **S:** £33.00-£33.00.
Open: All Year
Beds: 3D 3T 1S 1F
Baths: 8 En
🛇 🅿 (15) ☐ 🐾 🎍 Ⅲ, & Ⅵ 🛍 🚲

D = Price range per person sharing in a double room

Hopton 28

National Grid Ref: TL9978

🍴 🍺 The Fox

Holly Bank, High Street, Hopton, Diss, IP22 2QX.
Converted 1960s public house, guests' lounge, comfortable bedrooms. Sauna available at extra cost.
Tel: **01953 688147** (also fax no)
Mr & Mrs Tomlinson.
D: £17.50-£17.50 **S:** £20.00-£20.00.
Open: All Year
Beds: 2D 1T
Baths: 1 Sh
🛇 🅿 (8) ⏰ ☐ 🎍 🛏 Ⅲ, Ⅵ 🚲

Lancashire Cycleway

At 250 miles, the **Lancashire Cycleway** is one of the longer county cycle routes, and really consists of two circular routes, around the northern and southern halves of the county, together forming a great figure of eight, linking up at the Ribble Valley town of Whalley. The north end of the northern circle links up with the *Cumbria Cycleway* - those with bags of energy and more time can undertake the two cycleways together to make a massive 500-mile tour of the beautiful northwest corner of England. The Lancashire route is signposted with blue cycle silhouette signs with a letter 'N' for the northern circle or 'S' for the southern circle, and can be cycled in either direction, but the County Council recommend cycling clockwise, to beat the prevailing southwesterly wind. The description that follows takes the route clockwise around the northern circle and then clockwise around the southern circle, starting and finishing both sections in Whalley.

A detailed **guide booklet** to the cycleway route is available free from the County Public Relations Officer, PO Box 78, County Hall, Preston PR1 8XJ, tel 01772 263521. In addition, over 200 attractions in the county are list-

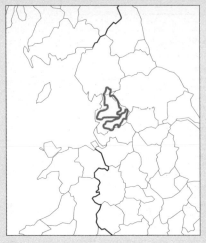

ed in a free leaflet, 'Great Days Out in Lancashire', available from the same address.

Maps: Ordnance Survey 1:50,000 Landranger series: 97, 98, 102, 103, 108, 109

Trains: Whalley is served by trains from Manchester and elsewhere. Numerous places on or near the route are served by the rail network.

Hurst Green　　　　1

National Grid Ref: SD6838

🍽 🍺 The Shireburn

Shireburn Arms Hotel, *Whalley Road, Hurst Green, Clitheroe, Lancs, BB6 9QJ.*
A warm friendly welcome, excellent inn and restaurant, unrivalled views.
Grades: ETC 2 Star, AA 2 Star
Tel: 01254 826518 Alcock.
Fax no: 01254 826208
D: £32.50-£42.50
S: £45.00-£65.00
Open: All Year
Beds: 1S 2F 12D 3T
Baths: 18 En
🛏 🅿 (50) 🗲 🛏 🛏 ✗ 🍴 ⬛ ♿ 👤 ⚡ 🚲

High season,
bank holidays and
special events mean
low availability
everywhere.

Ribchester　　　　2

National Grid Ref: SD6435

🍽 🍺 Hall's Arms, Punch Bowl, Black Bull, White Bull

New House Farm, *Preston Road, Ribchester, Preston, Lancs, PR3 3XL.*
Actual grid ref: SD648354
Old renovated farmhouse, rare breeds.
Tel: 01254 878954
Bamber.
D: £18.00-£22.00
S: £22.00-£25.00
Open: All Year
Beds: 1F 1D 1T
Baths: 3 En
🛏 (4) 🅿 (8) 🗲 🛏 🛏 🍴 ⬛ 👤 ⚡ 🚲

Smithy Farm, *Huntingdon Hall Lane, Dutton, Ribchester, Preston, Lancs, PR3 2ZT.*
Unspoilt countryside 15 mins M6. Friendly hospitality, children half price.
Tel: 01254 878250
Jackson.
D: £12.50-£12.50 **S:** £18.00-£18.00.
Open: Mar to Nov
Beds: 1F 1D 1T
Baths: 1 Sh
🛏 🅿 🛏 🛏 ✗ 🍴 👤 ⚡ 🚲

Longridge　　　　3

National Grid Ref: SD6037

🍽 🍺 Alston Arms, White Bull, Heathcotes

14 Whittingham Road, *Longridge, Preston, Lancs, PR3 2AA.*
Homely, hearty breakfasts, scenic area, walking, sports, shopping, motorway accessibility.
Tel: 01772 783992
Morley.
D: £18.00-£18.00
S: £18.00-£18.00.
Open: All Year
Beds: 1F 1T 1S
Baths: 1 Sh
🛏 🅿 (4) 🛏 🛏 ⬛ 👤

Jenkinsons Farmhouse, *Longridge, Alston, Preston, Lancs, PR3 3BD.*
Set in idyllic countryside. Perfect stopover from London to Scotland.
Grades: AA 4 Diamond
Tel: 01772 782624
Mrs Ibison.
D: £20.00
S: £23.50.
Open: All Year (not Xmas)
Beds: 2D 3T 1S
Baths: 4 Sh
🛏 (12) 🅿 (10) 🗲 🛏 🛏 🍴 ⬛ 👤 ⚡

S = Price range for a single person in a room

Goosnargh 4

National Grid Ref: SD5536

¶⚫ Green Man, The Grapes

Isles Field Barn, Syke House Lane, Goosnargh, Preston, Lancs, PR3 2EN.
Actual grid ref: SD561398
Spacious accommodation surrounded by beautiful countryside. Hearty breakfast, friendly welcome.
Tel: **01995 640398** Mr McHugh.
D: £19.00-£19.00 **S:** £19.00-£19.00.
Open: All Year
Beds: 1F 1D 1T
Baths: 3 En
🛇 🅿 (6) 🖵 🛌 🚵 🆚 ✦ ♻

1 Willow Grove, Goosnargh, Preston, PR3 2DE.
Private house, village location, close to M6, M55, Blackpool, Lancaster.
Tel: **01772 865455**
Mrs Dewhurst.
D: £15.00-£15.00
S: £15.00-£15.00.
Open: All Year (not Xmas)
Beds: 1D 1T 1S
Baths: 1 Sh
🛇 ✕ 🖵 🛌 🚵 🆚 ✦ ♻

All rooms full and nowhere else to stay? Ask the owner if there's anywhere nearby

---

All rates are subject to alteration at the owners' discretion.

Bilsborrow 5

National Grid Ref: SD5139

¶⚫ Roebuck Inn

Olde Duncombe House, Garstang Road, Bilsborrow, Preston, Lancs, PR3 0RE.
Traditional cottage-style family run bed & breakfast offering a high standard of accommodation.
Tel: **01995 640336** Mr Bolton.
D: £22.50-£25.00 **S:** £35.00-£39.50.
Open: All Year
Beds: 1F 5D 1T 2S
Baths: 9 En
🛇 🅿 (2) 🖵 🛌 🚵 🆚 ♻

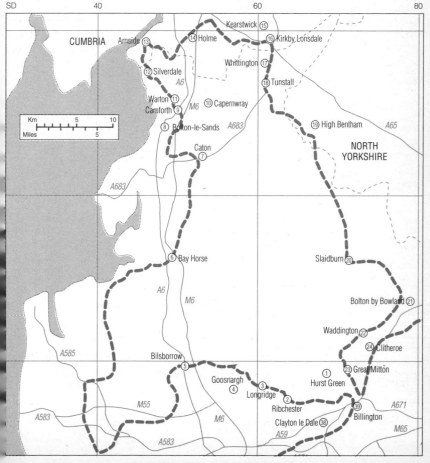

Bay Horse 6

National Grid Ref: SD4953

🍴 🍺 Bay Horse Hotel, Manor Inn

Stanley Lodge Farmhouse,
Cockerham Road, Bay Horse,
Lancaster, Lancs., LA2 0HE.
Rural area, Lancaster canal nearby.
Lakes, Yorkshire Dales, golfing,
horse riding nearby.
Grades: ETC 3 Diamond
Tel: 01524 791863
D: £18.00-£20.00 **S:** £18.00-£20.00.
Open: All Year (not Xmas/
New Year)
Beds: 1F 2D **Baths:** 1 Sh
🛏 🅿 (4) 🖵 🛏 ⚑ 🏌 📖 Ⅴ 🛉 🌡 ♿ ⛟

Saltoke South, *Bay Horse,*
Galgate, Lancaster, LA2 0HL.
A beautiful old stone family home
set in open countryside.
Tel: 01524 752313 Robin.
D: £15.00-£20.00 **S:** £20.00.
Open: All Year (not Xmas)
Beds: 1D 1T **Baths:** 1 Sh
🛏 🅿 (6) 🖵 🛏 ⚑ 🏌 📖 Ⅴ 🌡 ⛟

Caton 7

National Grid Ref: SD5364

Kilcredan, *14 Brookhouse Road,*
Caton, Lancaster, Lancashire,
LA2 9QT.
Friendly welcome set in the Lune
Valley. Ideal for walking.
Grades: ETC 1 Diamond
Tel: 01524 770271 Miss Beattie.
D: £18.00-£18.00 **S:** £18.00-£18.00.
Open: All Year
Beds: 1F 1D 1T 1S
Baths: 1 En 1 Sh
🛏 🅿 (3) 🖵 🛏 ⚑ 🏌 📖 Ⅴ 🛉 🌡 ♿ ⛟

Bolton le Sands 8

National Grid Ref: SD4868

🍴 🍺 Robin Hood, Railway Inn

Row-Bar, *4 Whin Grove, Bolton-*
le-Sands, Carnforth, Lancs, LA5 8DD.
Actual grid ref: SD482752
Friendly family-run private home
close to M6 and Lakes.
Tel: 01524 735369 Udall.
D: £16.00-£16.00 **S:** £20.00.
Open: All Year (not Xmas)
Beds: 2D
Baths: 2 En
🛏 🅿 (2) 🖵 🏌 📖 Ⅴ

Carnforth 9

National Grid Ref: SD4970

🍴 🍺 Malt Shovel, George Washington, County
Hotel

Galley Hall Farm, *Shore Road,*
Carnforth, Lancashire, LA5 9HZ.
C17th farm house, lovely coastal
and Lakeland views and friendly
welcome.
Grades: ETC 4 Diamond
Tel: 01524 732544
Casson.
D: £18.00-£18.00 **S:** £18.00-£18.00.
Open: All Year (not Xmas/
New Year)
Beds: 1T 1D 1S
Baths: 1 Sh
🖵 🛏 ⚑ 🏌 📖 Ⅴ ⛟

D = Price range per person
sharing in a double room

Order your
packed lunches the
evening before you
need them.
Not at breakfast!

Capernwray 10

National Grid Ref: SD5371

Capernwray House, *Capernwray,*
Carnforth, Lancs, LA6 1AE.
Beautiful country house.
Panoramic views. Tastefully
decorated throughout. Close Lakes,
Dales, Lancaster.
Grades: ETC 4 Diamond, Silver
Tel: 01524 732363 (also fax no)
Mrs Smith.
D: £21.00-£23.00
S: £30.00-£30.00.
Open: All Year (not Xmas)
Beds: 2D 1T 1S
Baths: 3 En 1 Sh
🛏 (5) 🅿 (8) 🖵 🏌 ✕ ⚑ 🏌 📖 Ⅴ 🛉 🌡 ♿ ⛟

Whalley to Wrea Green

Whalley nestles in the beautiful Ribble Valley, where
wooded lanes form the backdrop to countless
picturesque villages. Traces of all aspects of the history
of the Red Rose County can be found here - the ruined
abbey recalling the Dissolution in the sixteenth century,
the railway viaduct a reminder of the county's
nineteenth-century history, when it was at the core of the
Industrial Revolution. Proceeding west, the route hits the
Ribble at **Ribchester**, where the Museum of Roman
Antiquities tells of the town's history as a Roman fort,
and the many weavers' cottages bear witness to
Lancashire's historic textile industry. After the villages of
Inglewhite and **Bilsborrow** you ride down into **the
Fylde**, the plain of Western Lancashire north of the
Ribble. Here you pass through the old market town of
Kirkham, another textile town which made sails for the
Royal Navy, and the archetypal picturesque Fylde village
of **Wrea Green**.

Warton 11

National Grid Ref: SD5072

🍴 🍺 Malt Shovel, George Washington

Cotestone Farm, *Sand Lane, Warton, Carnforth, Lancs, LA5 9NH.*
Near Leighton Moss RSPB Reserve, Lancaster/Morecambe, Lakes & Dales.
Grades: ETC 3 Diamond
Tel: **01524 732418** Close.
D: £16.00-£16.00 **S:** £17.00-£17.00.
Open: All Year (not Xmas)
Beds: 1F 1D 1T 1S
Baths: 2 Sh
🛌 🅿 (4) 🗆 🛏 🚲 🎰 Ⓥ ⚡ 🐾

Silverdale 12

National Grid Ref: SD4675

🍴 🍺 The Ship

The Limes Village Guest House, *23 Stanklet Road, Silverdale, Carnforth, Lancs, LA5 0TF.*
A lovely Victorian house. Very comfortable. Excellent food.
Tel: **01524 701454** (also fax no)
Mrs Livesey.
D: £20.00-£22.00 .
Open: All Year
Beds: 1F 1D 1T
Baths: 3 Pr
🛌 🅿 (3) ⚡ 🗆 🗙 🚲 🎰 Ⓥ ⚡ 🐾

Arnside 13

National Grid Ref: SD4578

🍴 🍺 The Albion

🔺 ***Arnside Youth Hostel,*** *Oakfield Lodge, Redhills Road, Arnside, Carnforth, Lancashire, LA5 0AT.*
Actual grid ref: SD452783
Tel: **01524 761781**
Under 18: £6.90 **Adults:** £10.00
Self-catering facilities, Television, Showers, Laundry facilities, Lounge, Games room, Drying room, Cycle store, Parking, Evening meal at 7.00pm, WC, Kitchen facilities, Breakfast available, Credit cards accepted
A few minutes' walk from the shore with views across Morecambe Bay to the Lakeland Fells. A mellow stone house on the edge of a coastal village on the Kent estuary. RSPB reserve nearby.

All rates are subject to alteration at the owners' discretion.

S = Price range for a single person in a room

Willowfield Hotel, *The Promenade, Arnside, Carnforth, Lancs, LA5 0AD.*
Actual grid ref: SD455785
Non-smoking family-run hotel in superb estuary-side location.
Grades: ETC 4 Diamond, AA 4 Diamond, RAC 4 Diamond
Tel: **01524 761354**
Mr Kerr.
D: £26.00-£28.00 **S:** £25.00-£42.00.
Open: All Year
Beds: 2F 3D 3T 2S
Baths: 8 En 1 Pr 2 Sh
🛌 🅿 (8) ⚡ 🗆 🗙 🚲 🎰 Ⓥ 🍴 ⚡ 🐾

Stonegate, *The Promenade, Arnside, Carnforth, Lancs, LA5 0AA.*
Actual grid ref: SD455786
Stonegate offers comfort & relaxation in AONB overlooking tidal estuary with panoramic views.
Tel: **01524 762560** (also fax no)
D: £19.50-£22.50 **S:** £22.00-£25.00.
Open: All Year
Beds: 2D 1T 1S
Baths: 2 En 1 Pr
🛌 🅿 (8) ⚡ 🗆 🛏 🚲 🎰 Ⓥ 🍴 ⚡ 🐾

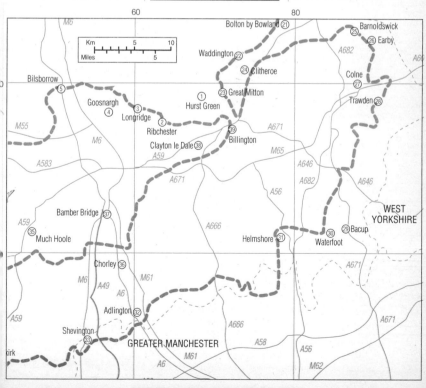

Holme 14

National Grid Ref: SD5279

⌘⌖ Smithy Inn

Marwin House, Duke Street, Holme, Carnforth, Cumbria, LA6 1PY.
Gateway to Lake District, Yorkshire Dales. M6 (J36) 5 minutes.
Grades: ETC 2 Diamond
Tel: **01524 781144** (also fax no)
D: £16.00-£18.00
S: £17.00-£19.00.
Open: All Year
Beds: 1F 1T
Baths: 1 Sh
⇗ ₽ (3) ⅍ ♉ ⚓ Ⅲ. Ⅴ ᵻ ⟋ ᨏ

Kearstwick 15

National Grid Ref: SD6080

⌘⌖ Courtyard, Snooty Fox, Orange Tree

Kearstwick House, Kearstwick , Kirkby Lonsdale, Carnforth, LA6 2EA.
Elegant Edwardian Country House on edge of historic Kirkby Lonsdale.
Tel: **015242 72398**
D: £20.00-£22.50
S: £25.00-£30.00.
Open: All Year (not Xmas/New Year)
Beds: 1T 1D
Baths: 1 Pr 1 Sh
⇗ (12) ₽ (3) ♉ ↑ ✕ ⚓ Ⅲ. Ⅴ ᨏ

Kirkby Lonsdale 16

National Grid Ref: SD6178

⌘⌖ Kings Arms, Sun Inn, Lunesdale Arms, Swan Inn, Orange Tree, Snooty Fox

Wyck House, 4 Main Street, Kirkby Lonsdale, Carnforth, Lancs, LA6 2AE.
A Victorian town house situated 50 yards from the market square.
Tel: **015242 71953** (also fax no)
Bradley.
D: £20.00-£22.50
S: £18.50-£30.00.
Open: All Year (except 2 weeks)
Beds: 1F 1T 2D 2S
Baths: 3 En 1 Sh
⇗ ₽ (3) ⅍ ♉ ⚓ Ⅲ. Ⅴ ᵻ ⟋

9 Mill Brow House, Kirkby Lonsdale, Carnforth, Lancs, LA6 2AT.
Actual grid ref: SD612786
Wonderful views of river, shops/pubs nearby, holiday apartment available.
Tel: **015242 71615** (also fax no)
Mrs Nicholson.
D: £18.00-£21.00
S: £20.00-£25.00.
Open: Easter to Oct
Beds: 1D 1T
Baths: 2 Sh
⇗ ₽ (2) ⅍ ♉ ⚓ Ⅲ. Ⅴ ᨏ

Whittington 17

National Grid Ref: SD6076

⌘⌖ Dragon's Head

The Dragon's Head, Main Street, Whittington, Carnforth, LA6 2NY.
Small country pub in Lune valley 2 miles west of Kirkby Lonsdale B6254.
Tel: **015242 72383**
D: £20.00-£25.00.
S: £20.00-£25.00.
Open: All Year
Beds: 1F 1D 1S
Baths: 1 Sh
⇗ (5) ₽ (10) ♉ ↑ ✕ ⚓ Ⅲ. Ⅴ ᨏ

Tunstall 18

National Grid Ref: SD6073

⌘⌖ Lunesdale Arms

Barnfield Farm, Tunstall, Kirkby Lonsdale, Carnforth, Lancs, LA6 2QP.
Actual grid ref: SD607736
1702 family farmhouse on a 200 acre working farm.
Tel: **015242 74284** (also fax no)
Mrs Stephenson.
D: £16.00**S:** £17.50.
Open: All Year (not Xmas)
Beds: 1F/T 1D
Baths: 2 Sh
⇗ ₽ ⅍ ♉ ⚓ Ⅲ. Ⅴ ᵻ ⟋ ᨏ

High Bentham 19

National Grid Ref: SD6669

⌘⌖ Punch Bowl

Fowgill Park Farm, High Bentham, Lancaster, LA2 7AH.
Beamed farmhouse enjoying panoramic views, close to caves and waterfalls.
Grades: ETC 4 Diamond
Tel: **015242 61630**
Mrs Metcalfe.
D: £19.00-£22.00 .
Open: Easter to Oct
Beds: 1D 1T
Baths: 2 En
⇗ ₽ (4) ⅍ ♉ ↑ ✕ ⚓ Ⅲ. Ⅴ ᵻ ᨏ

Slaidburn 20

National Grid Ref: SD7152

▲ *Slaidburn Youth Hostel, King's House, Slaidburn, Clitheroe, Lancashire, BB7 3ER.*
Actual grid ref: SD711523
Tel: **01200 446656**
Under 18: £6.50
Adults: £9.25
Self-catering facilities, Television, Showers, Shop, Lounge, Drying room, Parking, No smoking, WC, Kitchen facilities
Basic village accommodation for walkers and cyclists in the middle of the Forest of Bowland. The hostel is a C17th former inn, with log fires as well as central heating.

Wrea Green to the Lancaster Canal

Cycling north through the Fylde, you cross the River Wyre, and pass by the old marsh village of **Pilling** before crossing the **Lancaster Canal**. A possible detour here takes you to the lovely old port at **Glasson Dock**, from where you may wish to follow the River Lune Path north as an alternative to the designated route of the cycleway, rejoining it north of Lancaster. Either way, the county town is well worth a look. **Lancaster** boasts many elegant Georgian buildings, testament to its shadily prosperous period as a major port in the slave trade; the town's roots go back way beyond then to Roman Britain. Landmarks include Lancaster Castle, whose Norman keep overlooking the Lune presides over a crown court and the county's Shire Hall, the Priory Church of St Mary, a former Benedictine foundation notable for its Saxon doorway, the seventeenth-century Judges' Lodging (now a museum) and the grounds of the Ashton Memorial, sporting a butterfly and palm house.

Bolton by Bowland 21

National Grid Ref: SD7849

Middle Flass Lodge, Settle Road, Bolton by Bowland, Clitheroe, Yorkshire, BB7 4NY.
Idyllic countryside location. Chef prepared cuisine. Cosy rooms. Friendly welcome.
Grades: ETC 4 Diamond, AA 4 Diamond
Tel: **01200 447259** Mrs Simpson.
Fax no: 01200 447300
D: £22.00-£30.00 **S:** £27.00-£35.00.
Open: All Year
Beds: 1F 2D 2T **Baths:** 5 En suite
⇗ ₽ (24) ⅍ ♉ ✕ ⚓ Ⅲ. Ⅴ ᵻ ⟋ ᨏ

D = Price range per person sharing in a double room

Waddington 22

National Grid Ref: SD7243

🏨 ⬥ Moorcock Inn, Duke of York

Moorcock Inn, *Slaidburn Road, Waddington, Clitheroe, Lancs, BB7 3AA.*
A warm welcome awaits at this friendly country inn.
Grades: ETC 2 Star
Tel: **01200 422333** Fillary.
D: £30.00-£35.00 **S:** £38.00-£42.00.
Open: All Year
Beds: 3D 8T
Baths: 11 Pr
🛏 🅿 (150) 🗖 🛏 ✕ 🏋 🛏 ▥ Ⅴ ⬥ ⌇

Waddington Arms, *Clitheroe Road, Waddington, Clitheroe, Lancs, BB7 3HP.*
Traditional country inn, real beer, real food, real bedrooms.
Tel: **01200 423262** Warburton.
D: £25.00-£35.00 **S:** £35.00-£45.00.
Open: All Year
Beds: 4D 2T **Baths:** 6 En
🛏 🅿 (50) ⌿ 🗖 🛏 ✕ 🏋 🛏 ▥ Ⅴ ⬥ ⌇
⌂

Great Mitton 23

National Grid Ref: SD7138

Aspinall Arms Hotel, *Great Mitton, Clitheroe, Lancs, BB7 9PQ.*
Actual grid ref: SD718388
Originally the ferryman's house, the Aspinall Arms dates back to coach and horses times.
Tel: **01254 826223** Mr Morrell.
D: £22.50-£22.50 **S:** £30.00-£30.00.
Open: All Year
Beds: 2D 1S
Baths: 3 En
🅿 (50) 🗖 🛏 🛏 ▥ Ⅴ ⬥ ⌇ ⌂

Clitheroe 24

National Grid Ref: SD7441

🏨 ⬥ Swan With Two Necks, Edisford Bridge Inn, Edisford Inn, Old Post House

Selborne House, *Back Commons, Clitheroe, Lancs, BB7 2DX.*
Detached house on quiet lane giving peace and tranquillity.
Excellent for walking, birdwatching, fishing.
Grades: ETC 3 Diamond
Tel: **01200 423571** (also fax no) Barnes.
D: £18.50-£20.00
S: £21.00-£22.50.
Open: All Year
Beds: 1F 2D 1T
Baths: 4 En
🛏 (1) 🅿 (4) 🗖 🛏 ✕ 🏋 🛏 ▥ Ⅴ ⬥ ⌇ ⌂

S = Price range for a single person in a room

All details shown
are as supplied
by B&B owners in
Autumn 2000.

Brooklands, *9 Pendle Road, Clitheroe, Lancs, BB7 1JQ.*
Actual grid ref: SD750414
A warm welcome. Detached comfortable Victorian home. Town centre nearby.
Grades: ETC 3 Diamond
Tel: **01200 422797** (also fax no) Lord.
D: £16.00-£19.50 **S:** £17.00-£22.00.
Open: All Year
Beds: 1D 2T
Baths: 1 En 1 Sh
🛏 🅿 (5) 🗖 🛏 🏋 🛏 ▥ Ⅴ ⬥ ⌇ ⌂

Barnoldswick 25

National Grid Ref: SD8746

🏨 ⬥ Fosters Arms, Fanny Grey, Milano's

Foster's House, *203 Gisburn Road, Barnoldswick, Lancs, BB18 5JU.*
A warm welcome awaits at our beautiful home from home.
Grades: ETC 2 Diamond
Tel: **01282 850718**
Mr & Mrs Edwards.
D: £20.00-£20.00
S: £20.00-£20.00.
Open: All Year
Beds: 2D 2T
Baths: 3 En 1 Sh
🛏 🅿 (4) 🗖 🛏 🏋 🛏 ▥ Ⅴ ⬥ ⌇ ⌂

Earby 26

National Grid Ref: SD9046

▲ **Earby Youth Hostel,** *Glen Cottage, Birch Hall Lane, Earby, Colne, Lancashire, BB8 6JX.*
Actual grid ref: SD915468
Tel: **01282 842349**
Under 18: £6.50 **Adults:** £9.25
Self-catering facilities, Showers, Lounge 2, Dining room, Drying room, Cycle store, Parking, No smoking, WC, Kitchen facilities, Credit cards accepted
Attractive cottage with own picturesque garden and waterfall, on NE outskirts of Earby. Convenient for Pendle.

Colne 27

National Grid Ref: SD8940

🏨 ⬥ Hare & Hounds, White Bear

Wickets, *148 Keighley Road, Colne, Lancs, BB8 0PJ.*
Edwardian family home overlooking open countryside, comfortable and attractive bedrooms.
Grades: ETC 4 Diamond
Tel: **01282 862002** Mrs Etherington
Fax no: 01282 859675
D: £18.00-£21.00 **S:** £18.00-£22.00.
Open: All Year (not Xmas)
Beds: 1D 1T 1S
Baths: 1 En 1 Pr 1 Sh
🛏 (11) 🅿 (1) ⌿ 🛏 🏋 🛏 ▥ Ⅴ ⬥ ⌇

Pay B&Bs by cash or
cheque and be prepared
to pay up front.

The Lancaster Canal to Whalley

From here you ride north through **Carnforth**, which offers railway enthusiasts the Steamtown Railway Museum, to the small coastal village of **Silverdale**, and then over the county boundary to **Arnside** in Cumbria; the headland between Silverdale and Arnside, overlooking Morecambe Bay, is a designated Area of Outstanding Natural Beauty. The next stretch, as far as Kirkby Lonsdale, is also part of the *Cumbria Cycleway*, and takes you over Farleton Fell to **Hutton Roof**, with its panoramic views. **Kirkby Lonsdale** is famous for the Devil's Bridge, as well as 'Ruskin's View', behind St Mary's Church. From here it is south through the wooded Lune Valley, and then the beautiful gritstone moorland of the **Forest of Bowland**, another designated Area of Outstanding Natural Beauty which belonged historically to the old rival, Yorkshire. The village of **Slaidburn** offers welcome refreshment at the thirteenth-century Hark and Bounty Inn; after this the route takes you through the old Ribble Valley villages of **Sawley**, with its twelfth-century abbey ruins, and **Waddington**, back to Whalley.

Bringing children with
you? Always ask for
any special rates.

---

*Higher Wanless Farm, Red Lane,
Colne, Lancs, BB8 7JP.*
Beautifully situated, canalside,
lovely walking, ideal for business
people, Mill, shops etc.
Tel: **01282 865301**
Mitson.
Fax no: 01282 865823
D: £20.00-£24.00 **S:** £20.00-£24.00.
Open: Jan to Nov
Beds: 1F 1T 1S
Baths: 1 En 1 Sh
⌂ (3) **P** (4) ⌨ ⌁ ⬚ ▥ **V** 🛈 ⚡ 🚲

Trawden   28

National Grid Ref: SD9138

🍴 ⌁ Sun Inn

*Middle Beardshaw Head Farm,
Trawden, Colne, Lancs, BB8 8PP.*
Actual grid ref: SD895395
C18th beamed farmhouse in
picturesque setting of woodland,
pools and meadows.
Tel: **01282 865257**
Mrs Mann.
D: £18.50-£20.00
S: £18.50-£20.00.
Open: All Year (not Xmas)
Beds: 1F 2D 3S
Baths: 1 En 1 Sh
⌂ **P** (10) ⌨ ✕ ⌁ ⬚ ▥ **V** 🛈 ⚡ 🚲

Bacup   29

National Grid Ref: SD8622

🍴 ⌁ Rose & Bowl, The Crown, Mario's

*Pasture Bottom Farm, Bacup,
Lancs, OL13 0UZ.*
Comfortable farmhouse bed &
breakfast in a quiet rural area on a
working beef farm.
Grades: ETC 3 Diamond
Tel: **01706 873790** (also fax no)
Isherwood.
D: £15.00-£16.00 **S:** £15.00-£16.00.
Open: All Year (not Xmas)
Beds: 1D 2T
Baths: 2 En 1 Pr 1 Sh
⌂ **P** (4) ⌨ ⌁ ⌨ ✕ ⌁ ⌁ ⬚ **V** 🛈 ⚡

Waterfoot   30

National Grid Ref: SD8322

*729 Bacup Road, Waterfoot,
Rossendale, Lancs, BB4 7EU.*
In the heart of the picturesque
Rossendale Valley. Food everyday.
Tel: **01706 214493** Stannard.
Fax no: 01706 215371
D: £23.50-£30.00 **S:** £25.00-£35.00.
Open: All Year
Beds: 1F 5D 2T 5S
Baths: 13 En
⌂ **P** (10) ⌨ ⌁ ✕ ⌁ ⬚ ▥ **V** 🛈 ⚡ 🚲

Planning a longer
stay? Always ask for
any special rates.

D = Price range per person
sharing in a double room

Helmshore   31

National Grid Ref: SD7821

🍴 ⌁ White Horse

*The Willows, 41 Cherrytree Way,
Helmshore, Rossendale, Lancs,
BB4 4JZ.*
The Willows - warm welcome
awaits, beautiful views, swimming
pool.
Grades: ETC 4 Diamond
Tel: **01706 212698** Mrs Tod.
D: £18.00-£22.00 .
Open: All Year (not Xmas)
Beds: 2D
Baths: 2 En
⌂ **P** (2) ⌨ ⌨ ⌁ ⬚ ▥ **V** 🛈 ⚡ 🚲

Adlington   32

National Grid Ref: SD6013

🍴 ⌁ The Millstone

*Briarfield House, Bolton Road,
Anderton, Adlington, Chorley,
Lancs, PR6 9HW.*
In own grounds, beautiful views
over open countryside. Private
parking.
Tel: **01257 480105** Mrs Baldwin.
D: £17.50 **S:** £20.00.
Open: All Year
Beds: 1D 2T
Baths: 2 En 1 Pr
⌂ ⌨ ⌨ ⌁ ⬚ ▥ **V**

The Southern Circle

The northeastern half of the southern circle
is a demanding up-and-down ride through the
Lancashire Pennines. **Clitheroe** is a busy
market town with a twelfth-century Castle
keep. From here the route takes you around
Pendle Hill; here in 1652 George Fox had the
vision that led him to found the Society of
Friends. **Downham** is an English village as
archetypal as Castle Combe (see the *Wiltshire
Cycleway*), but here church, pub, village
green and stocks sit astride a hilltop. Now the
route takes you to **Barnoldswick**, and around
Colne, Nelson and Burnley - you are at the
eastern end of Lancashire's central belt of
industrial towns. Wycoller Country Park in the
Forest of Trawden offers welcome respite;
Towneley Hall, on the route around Burnley, is
a fourteenth century house hosting an art
gallery and museum with collections of
eighteenth and nineteenth century paintings
and decorative arts, and a natural history

centre with an aquarium.
Now it's south, by Rawtenstall, Haslingden
and Ramsbottom. The Peel Tower at
Holcombe commemorates Sir Robert Peel;
Turton Tower, by **Chapeltown**, is a medieval
tower that was extended over the centuries
into a country house: it has a local history
museum and nine acres of woodland
gardens. The next stretch descends off the
West Pennine Moors onto the West Lancashire
Plain, skirting the north of Greater Manchester
and crossing the Leeds and Liverpool Canal a
number of times. The beautiful Lever Park is
on the edge of Lower Rivington Reservoir;
Beacon Country Park, east of Skelmersdale,
affords splendid views in all directions. The
route now rounds **Ormskirk** and heads
northwards, taking you near the Wildfowl and
Wetland Centre at Martin Mere. The final
stretch back into **Whalley** takes you south of
Leyland and between Preston and Blackburn;
attractions along the way include fifteenth-
century houses at Rufford and Hoghton.

Shevington 33

National Grid Ref: SD5408

🍴 🍺 The Hartwood, Seaview Inn

Wilden, *11a Miles Lane, Shevington,*
Wigan, Lancashire, WN6 8EB.
Large bungalow. Secluded large gardens. 1 mile M6. Off road parking.
Grades: ETC 3 Diamond
Tel: **01257 251516** Axon.
D: £17.50-£20.00 **S:** £17.50-£20.00.
Open: All Year (not Xmas/New Year)
Beds: 1T 2D **Baths:** 1 En 1 Sh
🅿 (5) ⌇⏻🗙 🕯 🛏 ♿ 🅥 🌠 ⭗

Ormskirk 34

National Grid Ref: SD4108

🍴 🍺 Briars Hall Hotel, Ship Inn

The Meadows, *New Sutch Farm,*
Sutch Lane, Ormskirk, Lancashire,
L40 4BU.
Beautiful C17th farmhouse. Ground
floor guest rooms. Excellent
breakfasts.
Grades: ETC 4 Diamond
Tel: **01704 894048**
D: £17.50 **S:** £19.50.
Open: All Year (not Xmas)
Beds: 2D 1S **Baths:** 2 En 1 Pr
⏻ 🛏 ♿ & 🅥 🌠 ⭗

Much Hoole 35

National Grid Ref: SD4723

🍴 🍺 Black Horse

The Barn Guest House, *204*
Liverpool Old Road, Much Hoole,
Preston, Lancs., PR4 4QB.
Semi rural location off the A59
between Preston and Southport.
Grades: ETC 3 Diamond
Tel: **01772 612654** Gabbott.
D: £20.00-£22.50 **S:** £25.00-£27.50.
Open: All Year (not Xmas/New Year)
Beds: 1F 1T 1S **Baths:** 2 Sh
🕭 🅿 (3) ⏻ 🛏 🕯 ♿ 🅥

Chorley 36

National Grid Ref: SD5817

🍴 🍺 The Hartwood, Seaview Inn

Crowtress Cottage Guest House,
190 Preston Road, Chorley,
Lancashire, PR6 7AZ.
C18th country cottage complemented with Lancashire hospitality.
Grades: ETC 3 Diamond
Tel: **01257 269380** Wrenall.
D: £20.00-£30.00 **S:** £25.00.
Open: All Year
Beds: 1D 1T 1S **Baths:** 1 En 1 Sh

The Roost, *81 Pall Mall, Chorley,*
Lancs, PR7 3LT.
Late Victorian, homely atmosphere.
Five mins' walk market, town centre.
Tel: **01257 263856**
Mr & Mrs Edelston.
D: £18.00-£18.00 **S:** £20.00-£20.00.
Open: All Year
Beds: 1T
Baths: 1 Sh
⌇⏻🗙 🕯 🛏 ♿ 🅥 ⭗

Bamber Bridge 37

National Grid Ref: SD5626

🍴 🍺 Hob Inn

Anvil Guest House, *321 Station*
Road, Bamber Bridge, Preston,
Lancs, PR5 6EE.
Actual grid ref: SD564254
Comfortable, friendly, near junct.
M6, M61, M65. Central heating,
TV lounge.
Tel: **01772 339022** Arkwright.
D: £13.50-£13.50 **S:** £15.00-£15.00.
Open: All Year (not Xmas)
Beds: 2F 4D 3T
Baths: 2 Sh
🕭 ⏻ 🕯 ♿ 🅥

Clayton Le Dale 38

National Grid Ref: SD6733

🍴 🍺 Royal Oak, The Traders

2 Rose Cottage, *Longsight Road ,*
Clayton le Dale, Blackburn, Lancs,
BB1 9EX.
Picturesque cottage, gateway to
Ribble Valley. Comfortable, fully
equipped rooms.
Tel: **01254 813223** Adderley.
Fax no: 01254 813831
D: £19.00 **S:** £23.00.
Open: All Year
Beds: 1F 1D 2T
Baths: 3 En 1 Pr
🕭 🅿 (4) ⏻ 🛏 🕯 ♿ 🅥 🔒 🌠 ⭗

Billington 39

National Grid Ref: SD7235

Rosebury, *51 Pasturelands Drive,*
Billington, Clitheroe, Lancs,
BB7 9LW.
Quality family accommodation,
guest rooms overlook the beautiful
Ribble Valley.
Grades: ETC 3 Diamond
Tel: **01254 822658** Hamer.
D: £20.00-£22.50 **S:** £20.00-£22.50.
Open: All Year (not Xmas/New
Year)
Beds: 1F 1T **Baths:** 2 Sh
🕭 🅿 ⌇⏻🛏🗙 🕯 ♿ 🅥 ⭗

D = Price range per
person sharing in a
double room

Leicestershire County Cycle Route

The **Leicestershire County Cycle Route** is a 140-mile circular tour, which goes in an anticlockwise direction around the inside of the perimeter of most of Leicestershire, and through the middle of the County of Rutland, starting and finishing at Rutland Water. It is routed along quiet country lanes and tracks, almost completely avoiding main roads, through gentle terrain without rigorous climbs.

A detailed **guide leaflet** to the route is available from Leicestershire County Council, Environmental Management, Department of Planning & Transportation, County Hall, Glenfield, Leicester, LE3 8RJ, tel 0116-265 7091. Cycle hire is available from Rutland Water Cycling at Whitwell and at Normanton, tel 01780 86705.

Maps: Ordnance Survey 1:50,000 Landranger series: 128, 129, 130, 140, 141

The major **railway** termini are at Oakham, Stamford, Melton Mowbray, Leicester, Loughborough, Hinckley and Market Harborough.

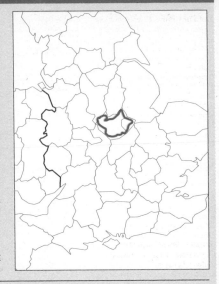

Rutland Water to Belvoir Castle

From Whitwell, on the banks of Rutland Water, you cycle north through the gentle Rutland countryside, and the villages of **Exton**, where the ruins of the early seventeenth-century Old Hall of Exton Park can be seen beyond the village church, Greetham and Thistleton. This stretch runs close to the Viking Way (see Stilwell's *National Trail Companion*), named from the history of this area as part of the Danelaw, ruled by the invaders that the kings of Wessex and England failed to keep at bay.

Through Thistleton Gap, where three counties meet, you take the Bronze Age track called Sewstern Lane into Leicestershire, and follow it north along the border with Lincolnshire before turning west towards **Buckminster**, and then north through a string of old farming villages to **Belvoir Castle**. On the site of a Norman castle, the present extravagant edifice was built in the mid-seventeenth century and rebuilt in 1816. It contains an impressive collection of tapestries and paintings, including Holbein's portrait of Henry VIII, and a garden with seventeenth-century sculptures.

Exton   1

National Grid Ref: SK9211

📧 ⬛ Fox & Hounds

Fox & Hounds, *Exton, Oakham, Rutland, LE15 8AP.*
Country inn overlooking village green. 2 miles Rutland Water, half mile Bransdale Gardens.
Tel: **01572 812403** D Hillier.
D: £20.00-£22.00 **S:** £22.00-£24.00
Open: All Year (not Xmas/New Year)
Beds: 1D 1T 1S
🛏 (8) 🅿 (20) 🐾 ✗ 📺 🛆

D = Price range per person sharing in a double room

Hall Farm, *Cottesmore Road, Exton, Oakham, Rutland, LE15 8AN.*
Close to Rutland Water and Geoff Hamiltons Barnsdale TV gardens.
Grades: ETC 3 Diamond
Tel: **01572 812271**
Mr & Mrs Williamson.
D: £17.50-£22.00
S: £20.00-£24.50.
Open: All Year (not Xmas)
Beds: 1F 1D 1T
Baths: 1 En 2 Sh
🛏 🅿 (6) ✂ 🗗 🐾 🔔 📺 Ⓥ ✈ 🚲

Cottesmore 2

National Grid Ref: SK9013

Sun Inn

The Tithe Barn, *Clatterpot Lane, Cottesmore, Oakham, Rutland, LE15 7DW.*
Comfortable, spacious, ensuite rooms with a wealth of original features.
Grades: ETC 3 Diamond
Tel: **01572 813591**
D: £18.00-£24.00
S: £20.00-£35.00.
Open: All Year
Beds: 2F 1D 1T
Baths: 3 En 1 Pr
🛇 (1) 🅿 (6) ⬚↜□🖘🛆 🕮 🖳 🔽 🛈

South Witham 3

National Grid Ref: SK9219

Blue Cow

Rose Cottage,
7 High Street, South Witham, Grantham, Lincs, NG33 5QB.
Actual grid ref: SK929192
C18th stone cottage in two acres midway between Stamford/Grantham/Rutland Water.
Tel: **01572 767757**
Mrs Van Kimmenade.
Fax no: 01572 767199
D: £22.50-£25.00
S: £25.00-£25.00.
Open: All Year
Beds: 1F 1D 1T 2S
Baths: 3 En
🛇 🅿 (6) ⬚↜□🖘🗶🛆 🕮 ♿ 🔽 ⚡ ⊶

Stainby 4

National Grid Ref: SK9022

The Old Blue Dog, *Colsterworth Road, Stainby, Grantham, Lincs, NG33 5QT.*
Beautiful stone residence in lovely rural countryside.
Leicestershire/Lincolnshire border.
Tel: **01476 861010** Mrs Jones.
Fax no: 01476 861645
D: £25.00-£25.00 **S:** £25.00-£25.00.
Open: All Year **Beds:** 1F 1D
🛇 🅿 (7) ⬚↜🖘🗶🛆 🕮 🔽 🛈 ⚡ ⊶

Skillington 5

National Grid Ref: SK8925

Cross Swords

Sproxton Lodge, *Skillington, Grantham, Lincs, NG33 5HJ.*
Quiet family farm alongside Viking way. Everyone welcome.
Tel: **01476 860307** Mrs Whatton.
D: £17.00-£18.00 **S:** £17.00-£18.00.
Open: All Year (not Xmas)
Beds: 1F 1D 1S **Baths:** 1 En 1 Sh
🛇 (5) 🅿 (4) ⬚↜□🗶🛆 🕮 🔽 🛈 ⚡ ⊶

Redmile 6

National Grid Ref: SK7935

Peacock Farm & Restaurant, & Guest House, *Redmile, Vale of Belvoir, Nottingham, NG13 0GQ.*
Great atmosphere, great food.
Tel: **01949 842475** Miss Need.
Fax no: 01949 843127
D: £26.00 **S:** £38.00.
Open: All Year
Beds: 5F 2D 2T 1S **Baths:** 6 Pr 1 Sh
🛇 🅿 (20) □🖘🛆 🕮 🔽

Barnstone 7

National Grid Ref: SK7335

Barnstone Olde House, *Barnstone, Nottingham, NG13 9JP.*
Central for Newark, Grantham, Nottingham. Landscaped garden, rustic charm, beautiful view.
Grades: ETC 3 Diamond
Tel: **01949 860456** (also fax no)
Mrs Baker.
D: £20.00-£25.00 **S:** £22.50-£30.00.
Open: All Year (not Xmas)
Beds: 2D 1T
Baths: 2 En
🛇 🅿 (4) ⬚↜□🖘🗶🛆 🕮 🔽 🛈 ⚡ ⊶

Long Clawson 8

National Grid Ref: SK7227

Elms Farm, *52 East End, Long Clawson, Melton Mowbray, Leics, LE14 4NG.*
Warm comfortable old farmhouse village setting in Vale of Belvoir.
Tel: **01664 822395** Mrs Whittard.
Fax no: 01664 823399
D: £17.00-£21.00 **S:** £18.00-£26.00.
Open: All Year (not Xmas)
Beds: 1F 1D 1S
Baths: 1 En 1 Sh
🛇 🅿 (4) ⬚↜□🗶🛆 🕮 🔽 🛈 ⚡ ⊶

S = Price range for a single person in a room

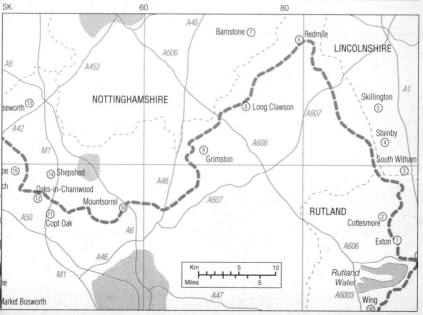

Please respect a B&B's wishes regarding children, animals & smoking.

Grimston 9

National Grid Ref: SK6821

⁍ Black Horse

Gorse House, Main Street, Grimston, Melton Mowbray, Leicestershire, LE14 3BZ.
Grades: ETC 4 Diamond
Tel: **01664 813537** (also fax no)
Mr & Mrs Cowdell.
D: £20.00-£25.00
S: £20.00-£25.00.
Open: All Year
Beds: 1F 1T 1D
Baths: 2 En 1 Sh
⛄ (12) ₱ (4) ⊁⌷ 🛏 ▥. ▨ ⋔ ♣ ⚙
Extended 17th Century cottage, well furnished attractive garden, in quiet conservation village. two miles from A46 convenient Leicester, Nottingham and East Midlands Airport. Good restaurant and pub within 100 yards. Beautiful countryside for walking, riding (stables available) and touring.

Mountsorrel 10

National Grid Ref: SK5814

⁍ Quorndon Fox

Barley Loft Guest House, 33a Hawcliffe Road, Mountsorrel, Loughborough, Leics, LE12 7AQ.
Tel: **01509 413514** Mrs Pegg.
D: £17.50-£19.00 **S:** £18.00-£20.00.
Open: All Year
Beds: 2F 1D 1T 2S
Baths: 2 Sh
⛄ ₱ (12) ⌷ 🛏 🛏 ▥ & ▨ ⚙
Spacious bungalow close to A6 between Leicester and Loughborough. Quiet, rural location, riverside walks, local historical attractions. Comfortable base for working away from home. Guests' fridge, microwave, toaster. Traditional hearty breakfast. Suitable for disabled. Excellent local supermarket, pubs, takeaways, restaurants.

High season, bank holidays and special events mean low availability *everywhere*.

Copt Oak 11

National Grid Ref: SK4813

▲ *Copt Oak Youth Hostel, Whitwick Road, Copt Oak, Markfield, Leicestershire, LE67 9QB.*
Actual grid ref: SK482129
Tel: **01530 242661**
Under 18: £5.75
Adults: £8.50
Self-catering facilities, Showers, Shop, Wet weather shelter, Lounge, Security lockers, Cycle store, Parking, No smoking, Kitchen facilities, Credit cards accepted
Converted schoolhouse in the hills of north west Leicestershire providing basic accommodation. Charnwood Forest is nearby, with superb countryside for walking and cycling.

Oaks in Charnwood 12

National Grid Ref: SK4716

⁍ Ye Olde Bulls Head, Forrest Rock, Jolly Farmers

Lubcloud Farm, Charley Road, Oaks in Charnwood, Loughborough, Leics, LE12 9YA.
Actual grid ref: SK477163
Organic working dairy farm. Peaceful rural location on Charnwood Forest.
Tel: **01509 503204**
Mr & Mrs Newcombe.
Fax no: 01509 651267
D: £20.00-£22.00 **S:** £22.50-£25.00.
Open: All Year
Beds: 1F 2D
Baths: 3 En
⛄ ₱ (10) ⊁⌷ 🛏 ▥. ▨ ⚙

Belvoir Castle to Staunton Harold

Shortly after Belvoir, the route turns southwestwards and runs parallel to the Grantham Canal as far as **Long Clawson**, where Stilton cheese is produced. From here you go on to **Old Dalby**, and then south to Hoby and along the River Wreake as far as **Ratcliffe** on the Wreake. From here the route goes through Sileby and crosses the River Soar into **Mountsorrel**. Then on to **Woodhouse Eaves**, a lovely old village built of the local slate. Here you will find Long Close, a 5-acre landscaped garden with wild flowers and shrubs. From here it's a short (if steepish) ride to Beacon Hill, a Bronze Age hill fort which yields magnificent views. You are now in **Charnwood Forest**, where the craggy hills and ferns make a landscape wilder than most of the county. Cycling north out of Charnwood Forest, you come to **Breedon on the Hill**, where there is an Iron Age hill fort. A detour north from here will take you to the Donington Park motor racing circuit, which stages the British motorcycle Grand Prix every year and hosts an impressive collection of racing cars and motorcycles. Then it's southwest to **Staunton Harold**, with its rare Commonwealth period church.

St Josephs, *Abbey Road, Oaks in Charnwood, Coalville, Leics,* *LE67 4UA.*
Old country house where hosts welcome you to their home.
Tel: **01509 503943** Mrs Havers.
D: £19.00-£19.00 **S:** £19.00-£19.00.
Open: Apr to Oct
Beds: 2T 1S **Baths:** 1 Sh
☺ ₽ (3) ⚡ 🗷 🛏 🏠 🎵 V ≠ ♻

Diseworth 13

National Grid Ref: SK4524

|◎| ⊈ Bull & Swan

Lady Gate Nursery, *47 The Green, Diseworth, Derby, Derbyshire,* *DE74 2QN.*
Close to airport, Donington Park Racing Circuit, exhibition centre, M1/M42.
Tel: **01332 855263** (also fax no)
Mrs Bebbington.
D: £18.00-£25.00 **S:** £20.00-£25.00.
Open: All Year (not Xmas)
Beds: 1T 1D 1S
Baths: 2 Sh
☺ (9) ₽ (5) ⚡ 🗷 🛏 🏠 V ≠ ♻

Shepshed 14

National Grid Ref: SK4719

Croft Guesthouse, *21 Hall Croft, Shepshed , Loughborough, Leicestershire, LE12 9AN.*
Warm family atmosphere, spacious rooms, secure parking - motor bikes, cycles.
Grades: ETC 3 Diamond
Tel: **01509 505657**
Fax no: **08700 522266**
D: £22.00-£25.00 **S:** £30.00-£35.00.
Open: All Year (not Xmas/ New Year)
Beds: 2F 3T 3D 2S
Baths: 5 En 1 Sh
☺ ⚡ 🗷 🛏 🏠 V ♻

Staunton Harold to Foxton

After a brief foray into Derbyshire, and the village of Smisby, you pass near to **Ashby-de-la-Zouch**, which has a striking castle, dating from Norman times to the fifteenth century and ruined in the Civil War, featuring an underground passageway for the non-claustrophobic. From here it's south through **Donisthorpe**, parallel to the River Mease through Measham, and southeastwards along the Ashby Canal from Shackerstone to **Market Bosworth**. From here it's on to Sutton Cheney, which is near to the site of the Battle of Bosworth Field, where the Wars of the Roses came to an end with the death of Richard III and the fall of the House of York at the hands of Henry VII, the first king in the Tudor line. There is a Country Park and Visitor Centre at the battlefield. Now it's on to Barwell and through **Burbage Common and Woods**, the remainder of the medieval Hinckley Forest, and then across the Fosse Way and east towards the locks on the Grand Union Canal at **Foxton**.

Osgathorpe 15

National Grid Ref: SK4219

|◎| ⊈ George & Dragon

The Royal Oak Inn, *20 Main Street, Osgathorpe, Loughborough, Leicestershire, LE12 9TA.*
High standard coaching inn in picturesque countryside. Secured parking.
Grades: ETC 3 Diamond
Tel: **01530 222443** Jacobs.
D: £20.00-£22.50 **S:** £30.00-£35.00.
Open: All Year
Beds: 2T 1D **Baths:** 3 En
☺ ₽ (50) ⚡ 🗷 🛏 🏠 & V 🍴 ≠ ♻

Ashby de la Zouch 16

National Grid Ref: SK3516

|◎| ⊈ Bull & Lion

The Bungalow, *10 Trinity Close, Ashby de la Zouch, Leics, LE65 2GQ.*
Private family home in quiet cul-de-sac, easy access to motorways.
Tel: **01530 560698** Mrs Chapman.
D: £17.50-£18.00
S: £18.00-£18.00.
Open: All Year
Beds: 1D 1T
Baths: 1 Sh
☺ ₽ (3) ⚡ 🗷 ✕ 🛏 🏠 V 🍴

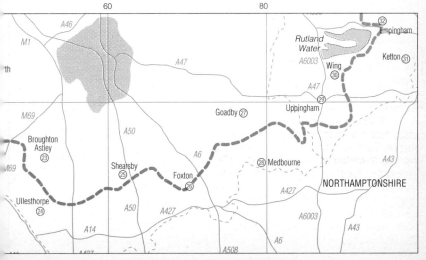

Measham 17

National Grid Ref: SK3312

🍴 🍺 Belper Inn, Hollybush Inn, The Swan

Measham House Farm, *Gallows Lane, Measham, Swadlincote, Derbyshire, DE12 7HD.*
Actual grid ref: SK348125
Grades: ETC 4 Diamond
Tel: 01530 270465 (also fax no)
Mr Lovett.
D: £21.00-£21.00 **S:** £21.00-£21.00.
Open: All Year (not Xmas)
Beds: 1F 2T **Baths:** 3 En 1 Pr
🛇 🅿 (20) ⅍⊑↟≒墨⃣⃣▥Ⅵ⃣🚲
Large Georgian farmhouse on 500 acre working farm close to the heart of the National Forest. Warm welcome, spacious garden, country walks, three ensuite bedrooms.

Laurels Guest House, *17 Ashby Road, Measham, Swadlincote, Derbyshire, DE12 7JR.*
High class accommodation. Rural surroundings. Orchard, pond. Parking. Motorway access.
Grades: ETC 3 Diamond
Tel: 01530 272567 (also fax no)
Mrs Evans.
D: £22.00-£25.00 **S:** £22.00-£25.00.
Open: All Year
Beds: 1D 2T **Baths:** 2 En 1 Pr
🛇 (1) 🅿 (8) ⅍⊑↟≒墨⃣▥Ⅵ⃣🚲

Appleby Magna 18

National Grid Ref: SK3110

🍴 🍺 Black Horse

Ferne Cottage, *5 Black Horse Hill, Appleby Magna, Swadlincote, Derbyshire, DE12 7AQ.*
Grades: ETC 3 Diamond
Tel: 01530 271772 Bird.
Fax no: 01530 270652
D: £17.00-£25.00 **S:** £17.00-£25.00.
Open: All Year (not Xmas)
Beds: 1F 1D 1T 1S
Baths: 1 En 1 Sh
🛇 🅿 (5) ⊑↟墨⃣▥Ⅵ⃣ 🚲
C18th beamed cottage. Homely, friendly, comfortable accommodation in the quiet historic village of Appleby Magna with off road parking. Half a mile from M42 (J11), 20 mins from NEC, Birmingham and East Midlands Airport. Lace making tuition by arrangement.

Appleby Parva 19

National Grid Ref: SK3109

🍴 🍺 Cock Inn

Elms Farm, *Atherstone Road, Appleby Parva, Swadlincote, Leicestershire, DE12 7AG.*
Pleasant farmhouse in rural position within 1.5 miles of M42.
Grades: ETC 3 Diamond
Tel: 01530 270450 Ms Frisby.
D: £20.00-£22.00 **S:** £20.00-£22.00.
Open: All Year (not Xmas)
Beds: 1D 1T 1S **Baths:** 2 En 1 Pr
🛇 (4) 🅿 (4) ⊑↟墨⃣▥Ⅵ⃣🚲

Congerstone 20

National Grid Ref: SK3605

🍴 🍺 Horse & Jockey, Rising Sun

Church House Farm, *Shadows Lane, Congerstone, Nuneaton, Warks, CV13 6NA.*
Former farmhouse convenient Bosworth Battlefield, Mallory Park, Twycross Zoo, motorways.
Tel: 01827 880402 Mrs Martin.
D: £20.00-£20.00 **S:** £19.00-£22.00.
Open: All Year (not Xmas)
Beds: 1D 1T 1S
Baths: 1 En 1 Sh
🛇 (12) 🅿 (6) ⊑↟墨⃣▥Ⅵ⃣🚲

The Old Barn, *Shadows Lane, Congerstone, Nuneaton, Warks, CV13 6NF.*
Beautiful walled garden in quiet location. Good pub food 300 yds.
Tel: 01827 880431 Mrs Savage.
D: £18.00 **S:** £17.00.
Open: All Year (not Xmas)
Beds: 2T 1S
Baths: 1 Pr
🛇 (10) 🅿 (3) ⅍⊑✗墨⃣▥ 🚲

Market Bosworth 21

National Grid Ref: SK4003

Bosworth Firs, *Bosworth Road, Market Bosworth, Nuneaton, Warks, CV13 0DW.*
Comfortable, clean, friendly. Home cooking, varied menu. Attractive decor, furnishings.
Tel: 01455 290727 Mrs Christian.
D: £20.00-£24.00 **S:** £20.00-£30.00.
Open: All Year
Beds: 2D 2T 2S
Baths: 2 En 1 Pr 1 Sh
🛇 🅿 (6) ⅍⊑✗墨⃣▥&Ⅵ⃣🚲

Hinckley 22

National Grid Ref: SP4294

🍴 🍺 Holywell Inn

The Guest House, *45 Priesthills Road, Hinckley, Leics, LE10 1AQ.*
Edwardian period house set in quiet pleasant area of Hinckley.
Grades: ETC 3 Diamond
Tel: 01455 619720 Farmer.
D: £20.00-£20.00 **S:** £22.00-£22.00.
Open: All Year (not Xmas)
Beds: 3T 1S
Baths: 2 Sh 1 En
⅍⊑墨⃣▥Ⅵ⃣🚲

Hollycroft Hotel, *24 Hollycroft, Hinckley, Leics, LE10 0HG.*
Small family run hotel. All rooms ensuite, private car park.
Tel: 01455 637356 (also fax no)
Mrs Hughes.
D: £22.50 **S:** £25.00.
Open: All Year
Beds: 2F 2D 1T
Baths: 5 En
🛇 🅿 (10) ⊑↟≒✗墨⃣&Ⅵ⃣🚲

Foxton to Rutland Water

From here you proceed to **Hallaton**, a typical pretty English village with medieval church, pond and ancient pub on the village green. It is also the site, every Easter, of the centuries-old Hare Pie Scramble and Bottle-Kicking Contest, a permanent home fixture against the nearby village of Medbourne. Then the route takes you through Horninghold and around the **Eye Brook Reservoir**, an important wildfowl site. Back in Rutland, places of interest along the final stretch are the fourteenth-century Bede House at **Lyddington** and the circular maze at **Wing**. **Edith Weston**, on the southern side of Rutland Water, provides access to sailing on England's largest lowland lake. Also available is trout fishing, and many other leisure activities. A detour to the western end of the lake takes you to the nature reserve, and it is not far to **Oakham**, Rutland's county town. **Normanton**, by Edith Weston, has a classical-style church which has now been converted into a museum and juts into the lake.

Broughton Astley 23

National Grid Ref: SP5292

🍴 🍺 White Horse, Bull's Head

The Old Farm House, *Old Mill Road, Broughton Astley, Leicester, Leics, LE9 6PQ.*
Georgian farmhouse, quietly situated in well-serviced village. Good access M1 (J20/21), M69.
Tel: 01455 282254 Mrs Cornelius.
D: £19.00-£23.00 **S:** £19.00-£23.00.
Open: All Year (not Xmas)
Beds: 1D 2T 1S
Baths: 2 Sh
🅿 (6) ⅍⊑墨⃣▥Ⅵ⃣

D = Price range per person
sharing in a double room

Ullesthorpe 24

National Grid Ref: SP5087

🍴 🍺 The Swan

Forge House, College Street,
Ullesthorpe, Lutterworth, Leics,
LE17 5BU.
Excellent accommodation with
attractive gardens. Ideal for busi-
ness and pleasure.
Tel: **01455 202454** (also fax no)
D: £20.00 **S:** £20.00-£25.00.
Open: All Year
Beds: 1D 1T
Baths: 1 En 1 Sh
🛇 (10) 🅿 (3) ⽅⏘✗🍽 🛏🛆 Ⅴ

Shearsby 25

National Grid Ref: SP6290

🍴 🍺 Chandlers' Arms

The Greenway, Knaptoft House
Farm, Bruntingthorpe Road,
Shearsby, Lutterworth, Leics,
LE17 6PR.
Farmhouse B&B at its best. Set
deep in Leicestershire countryside.
Grades: ETC 4 Diamond,
AA 4 Diamond
Tel: **0116 247 8388** (also fax no)
Mr Hutchinson.
D: £21.00-£24.00 **S:** £27.00-£38.00.
Open: All Year (not Xmas/New
Year)
Beds: 2D 1T
Baths: 2 Pr 1 Sh
🛇 (5) 🅿 (5) ⽅⏘🛏🛆 Ⅴ ⫽

Foxton 26

National Grid Ref: SP7089

🍴 🍺 Black Horse

The Old Manse, Swingbridge
Street, Foxton, Market
Harborough, Leics, LE16 7RH.
Period house in conservation vil-
lage. Canals, locks, local inns near-
by.
Grades: ETC 4 Diamond, Silver
Tel: **01858 545456** Mrs Pickering.
D: £22.50 **S:** £32.00.
Open: All Year (not Xmas)
Beds: 3T/D
Baths: 3 En
🛇 🅿 (6) ⽅⏘🛏🛆 Ⅴ 🎯 ⫽ 🚲

Goadby 27

National Grid Ref: SP7598

🍴 🍺 Fox & Hounds

The Hollies, Goadby, Leicester,
LE7 9EE.
Beautiful Listed house in quiet vil-
lage in pretty Leicestershire coun-
tryside.
Grades: ETC 3 Diamond
Tel: **0116 259 8301** Mrs Parr.
Fax no: 0116 259 8491
D: £22.50-£22.50 **S:** £25.00-£25.00.
Open: All Year (not Xmas)
Beds: 1F 1D 1S
Baths: 1 En 1 Sh
🛇 (5) 🅿 (3) ⽅⏘🍴🛏🛆 Ⅴ ⫽

Medbourne 28

National Grid Ref: SP7993

🍴 🍺 Nevill Arms

Medbourne Grange, Nevill Holt,
Medbourne, Market Harborough,
Leics, LE16 8EF.
Actual grid ref: SP816946
Comfortable farmhouse with
breathtaking views; quiet location
& heated pool.
Tel: **01858 565249** Mrs Beaty.
Fax no: 01858 565257
D: £19.00-£22.00 **S:** £19.00-£25.00.
Open: All Year (not Xmas)
Beds: 2D 1T
Baths: 1 Sh 2 En
🛇 🅿 (6) ⽅⏘✗🛏🛆 Ⅴ ⫽ 🚲

Uppingham 29

National Grid Ref: SP8699

🍴 🍺 Vaults

Boundary Farm B&B, Glaston
Road, Uppingham, Oakham,
Rutland, LE15 9PX.
Modern farmhouse in countryside.
5 mins easy walk into Uppingham.
Grades: ETC 4 Diamond
Tel: **01572 822354** (also fax no)
Mrs Scott.
D: £21.00 **S:** £22.00.
Open: Easter to Dec
Beds: 1T 1D
Baths: 2 En
🛇 🅿 (3) ⽅⏘🛏🛆 Ⅴ ⫽ 🚲

Wing 30

National Grid Ref: SK8903

🍴 🍺 Kings Arms

The Kings Arms Inn, Top Street,
Wing, Oakham, Rutland, LE15 8SE.
Grades: ETC 4 Diamond,
AA 4 Diamond
Tel: **01572 737634** Mr Hornsey.
Fax no: 01572 737255
D: £25.00-£50.00 **S:** £35.00-£70.00.
Open: All Year
Beds: 4F 4D 4T 8S
Baths: All En
🛇 🅿 (40) ⽅⏘✗🛏🛆 Ⅴ 🎯 🚲
A 350-year-old family owned
country inn. Peaceful village,
plenty of character throughout. All
rooms decorated and furnished to
very high standard. Fresh cooked
food, ideal base for
walking/cycling/fishing/sailing.
Rutland Water 2 miles.

Ketton 31

National Grid Ref: SK9704

🍴 🍺 Northwick Arms

16 Northwick Road, Ketton,
Stamford, PE9 3SB.
Actual grid ref: SK978043
Split-level stone bungalow. Warm
welcome. Between Rutland Water
and Stamford.
Tel: **01780 721411** Coyne.
D: £16.50-£16.50 **S:** £16.50-£16.50.
Open: Feb to Nov
Beds: 1T 1S **Baths:** 1 Sh
🅿 (1) ⽅⏘🛆 🚲

Empingham 32

National Grid Ref: SK9508

🍴 🍺 White Horse

Little Hoo, Nook Lane,
Empingham, Oakham, Rutland,
LE15 8PT.
Actual grid ref: SK947085
C16th luxury cottage, 2 minutes
from Rutland Water. Barn for dry-
ing clothes.
Tel: **01780 460293** Mr Coxhead.
D: £22.50-£22.50 **S:** £26.00-£26.00.
Open: All Year
Beds: 1F 3T 1S **Baths:** 2 Pr
🛇 (2) 🅿 (10) ⽅⏘🍴✗🛏🛆 Ⅴ ⫽ 🚲

Oxfordshire Cycleway

The **Oxfordshire Cycleway** is a circuit of the county, connected to Oxford, where it starts and finishes. It runs mainly along minor country roads and lanes, and takes in the whole range of the varied scenery Oxfordshire has to offer - the Cotswolds in the west, the Chilterns in the southeast and the Vale of the White Horse south of the Thames, where Britain's most ancient hillside carving lies close to the Ridgeway Path, the most ancient road still in use in Europe. The total distance around the circuit and into and out of Oxford is 178 miles, and the route is clearly signposted in both directions by blue Oxfordshire Cycleway direction signs with a cycle silhouette. The description which follows takes the circuit clockwise.

A detailed **guide booklet** to the cycleway route, which includes a list of cycle repair/hire shops on or near to the route, is available from Countryside Service, Department of Leisure and Arts, Oxfordshire County Council, Holton, Oxford OX33 1QQ, tel 01865 810226, @ £3.20 (+ 50p p&p).

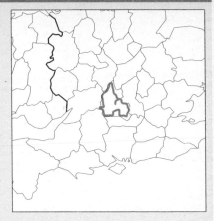

Maps: Ordnance Survey 1:50,000 Landranger series: 151, 163, 164, 165, 174, 175

Trains: Oxford, Didcot and Banbury are the main termini, with connections to other places on or near the route. Goring is a stop on the main line out of London.

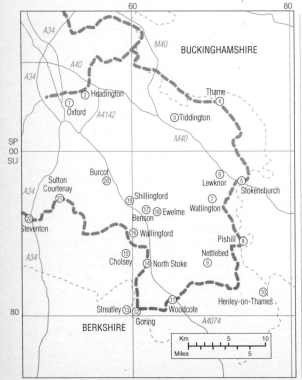

Oxford   1

National Grid Ref: SP5106

🍴 🍺 Carpenters' Arms, Vine, Bear & Ragged Staff, Tree, Marsh Harrier, Prince of Wales, Trout Inn, Old Ale House, Radcliffe Arms, Eight Bells, Fox & Hounds, Boundary House, Ox, Cafe Noir, Squire Basset, Victoria Arms, Duke of Monmouth

▲ *Oxford Backpackers Hostel, 9a Hythe Bridge Street, Oxford, OX1 2EW.*
Tel: **01865 721761 Adults:** £11.00 Self-catering facilities, Television, Showers, Licensed bar, Central heating, Laundry facilities, Wet weather shelter, Lounge, Security lockers, Cycle store
City centre location. Groups welcome. Bar, Internet, kitchen. Great atmosphere.

▲ *New Oxford YHA*, 2a Botley Road, Oxford, OX2 0AB.
Tel: **01865 727275**
Under 18: £13.50 **Adults:** £18.00
Self-catering facilities, Evening meal at 7.00pm, Facilities for disabled people, Breakfast available
Brand new hostel, opening at Easter 2001, and replacing the former hostel in Jack Straw's Lane.

Green Gables, 326 Abingdon Road, Oxford, OX1 4TE.
Actual grid ref: SP518043
Grades: ETC 3 Diamond, AA 3 Diamond
Tel: **01865 725870**
Mr & Mrs Bhella.
Fax no: 01865 723115
D: £25.00-£30.00 **S:** £32.00-£50.00.
Open: All Year (not Xmas/New Year)
Beds: 3F 4D 1T 1S
Baths: 7 En 1 Sh
♿ ❒ (9) ❑ ❄ ⬛ 🖵 & ♉
Characterful detached Edwardian house shielded by trees. Bright spacious rooms with TV & beverage facilities. Ensuite rooms. 1.25 miles to city centre, on bus routes. Ample off-street parking. Direct line phones in rooms and disabled room available.

Pine Castle Hotel, 290 Iffley Road, Oxford, OX4 4AE.
Actual grid ref: SP528048
Close to shops, launderette, post office. Frequent buses. River walks nearby.
Grades: ETC 4 Diamond, AA 4 Diamond
Tel: **01865 241497** Mrs Morris.
Fax no: 01685 727230
D: £32.50-£37.00 **S:** £55.00-£60.00.
Open: All Year (not Xmas)
Beds: 1F 5D 2T **Baths:** 8 En
♿ ❒ (4) ❑ ⬛ 🖵 ♉ ▯

The Bungalow, Cherwell Farm, Mill Lane, Old Marston, Oxford, OX3 0QF.
Actual grid ref: SP523098
Grades: ETC 3 Diamond
Tel: **01865 557171** Mrs Burdon.
D: £21.00-£25.00 **S:** £25.00-£35.00.
Open: Mar to Oct
Beds: 2D 2T
Baths: 2 En 1 Sh
♿ (7) ❒ (6) ❄ ❑ ⬛ 🖵 ♉
Modern bungalow in five acres open countryside, no bus route. 3 miles to city centre.

Gables Guest House, 6 Cumnor Hill, Oxford, Oxfordshire, OX2 9HA.
Award winning detached house with beautiful garden. Close to city.
Grades: ETC 4 Diamond, AA 4 Diamond
Tel: **01865 862153** Mrs Tompkins.
Fax no: 01865 864054
D: £22.00 **S:** £26.00.
Open: All Year (not Xmas)
Beds: 2S 2D 2T **Baths:** 6 En
♿ ❒ (6) ❄ ❑ ⬛ 🖵 ♉

Highfield West, 188 Cumnor Hill, Oxford, OX2 9PJ.
Actual grid ref: SP469042
Comfortable home in residential area, heated outdoor pool in season.
Grades: ETC 3 Diamond
Tel: **01865 863007**
Mr & Mrs Mitchell.
D: £22.50-£28.50 **S:** £26.00-£29.00.
Open: All Year (not Xmas)
Beds: 1F 1D 1T 2S
Baths: 3 En 1 Sh
♿ ❒ (5) ❄ ❑ ❄ ⬛ 🖵 ♉

Sportsview Guest House, 106-110 Abingdon Road, Oxford, OX1 4PX.
Grades: ETC 3 Diamond
Tel: **01865 244268** Mrs Saini.
Fax no: 01865 249270
D: £24.00-£30.00 **S:** £30.00-£50.00.
Open: All Year (not Xmas)
Beds: 5F 6T 3D 6S
Baths: 12 En 12 Pr 2 Sh
♿ (4) ❒ (11) ❄ ❑ ⬛ 🖵 ♉ ⚲
Situated south of the city centre. A few minutes' walk takes you to the towpath and a very pleasant walk to the city & its famous landmarks. On a direct bus route, with easy access to railway & bus stations.

All Seasons Guest House, 63 Windmill Road, Headington, Oxford, Oxfordshire, OX3 7BP.
Comfortable guest house, non-smoking, parking, convenient airports and Brookes University.
Tel: **01865 742215**
Mr & Mrs Melbye.
Fax no: 01865 432691
D: £22.50-£31.00 **S:** £27.00-£45.00.
Open: All Year
Beds: 1T 3D 2S
Baths: 4 En 1 Sh
♿ (6) ❒ (6) ❄ ❑ ⬛ 🖵 ♉ ▯

Acorn Guest House, 260 Iffley Road, Oxford, Oxfordshire, OX4 1SE.
Modern comfort in Victorian house convenient for all local attractions.
Grades: ETC 2 Diamond, AA 2 Diamond, RAC 2 Diamond
Tel: **01865 247998**
Mrs Lewis.
D: £24.00-£27.00
S: £26.00-£29.00.
Open: All Year (not Xmas/New Year)
Beds: 5F 2D 1T 4S
Baths: 1 En, 4 Sh
♿ (9) ❒ (11) ❑ ⬛ 🖵 ♉ ⚡

Oxford

The city of **Oxford** is one of England's architectural treasure houses. The imposing facades, spires and 'quadrangles' (courtyards) of the colleges and other university buildings bear witness to centuries of conspicuous creation. But although the university is a dominant presence, Oxford is also an important commercial city, which has plenty of life of its own away from students and tourists. Of the colleges, Merton is the most beautiful - the Gothic college chapel and the library, which contains centuries-old globes and other trappings of Renaissance scholarship, stand on 'Mob Quad', built in the fourteenth century, which has the eerie atmosphere of a medieval time warp. Magdalen, with its secluded cloisters and the famous tower, is also well worth a visit. Christ Church is big and famous. Also worth a look are Trinity, where the college chapel, the first not built in the Gothic style, was designed by Wren, who also designed the Sheldonian Theatre; and St Catherine's, built in the 1960s in a unique and very distinctive style. Elsewhere, the University Museum is a Pre-Raphaelite gem, its interior constructed around intricate ironwork which plays visually on the dinosaur skeletons, surrounded by statues honouring notable figures of science and philosophy; the adjacent Pitt-Rivers Museum is a fantastic ethnographic collection best known for the shrunken heads from South America. The other major museum is the Ashmolean, the oldest museum in Britain, with a very impressive range of collections; and Christ Church has its own picture gallery, with a collection of Italian art. Away from the university, the city has many interesting pockets, not least the canalside backstreets of Jericho, famous for the Pre-Raphaelite St Barnabas' Church; and don't leave Oxford without trying one or two of its many excellent pubs.

58 St John Street, *Oxford, OX1 2QR.*
Tall Victorian house central to all
colleges, museums and theatres.
Tel: **01865 515454**
Mrs Old.
D: £18.00-£19.00 **S:** £18.00.
Open: All Year
Beds: 1F 1T 1S
Baths: 2 En
🛇 (1) 🗶 🛏 ☑ 🌣 🚲

Chestnuts, *72 Cumnor Hill,
Oxford, OX2 9HU.*
Country house in acre of garden,
1.5 miles from Oxford.
Grades: ETC 3 Diamond
Tel: **01865 863602**
D: £21.00-£24.00 **S:** £24.00-£30.00.
Open: All Year
Beds: 1D 1T
Baths: 1 En 1 Pr
🅿 🗶 🛏 🛋 ☑

Milka's Guest House, *379 Iffley
Road, Oxford, Oxon, OX4 4DP.*
Family run guest house situated
close to Iffley village.
Grades: ETC 3 Diamond
Tel: **01865 778458**
Fax no: 01865 776477
D: £22.50-£27.50
S: £25.00-£35.00.
Open: All Year
Beds: 2D 1S
Baths: 1 En
🛇 (5) 🅿 (5) 🗶 🖵 🛋 ☑ 🚲

Oxford to Wallingford

When you've had your fill of **Oxford**, the cycleway
commences with a leisurely stretch linking you to the county
circuit at **Horton-cum-Studley**, where you turn southeast, to
reach **Worminghall** in Buckinghamshire. A short detour from
here will bring you to Waterperry Gardens, an 83-acre
herbaceous and alpine centre with a Saxon church and a
gallery which exhibits and sells paintings, ceramics and
textiles. From Worminghall it's not far to the pretty small town of
Thame. From here you head south and after Sydenham and
Kingston Blount up into the beautiful wooded countryside of the
Chiltern Hills. An attraction along this stretch of the way is
Stonor Park. This beautiful house in a picturesque setting was
built over centuries and is the ancestral home of a Catholic
family and a notable centre of resistance to Protestant
domination: the martyr Edmund Campion received sanctuary
here before being captured and hanged in 1581. There is a fine
art collection including paintings by Tintoretto and Caracci.
From here it is on to the village of **Bix**. The Fox pub is
recommended. From here a detour is possible to **Henley-on-
Thames**, famous for rowing, and with a wide Georgian High
Street. From Bix it's on to **Goring**, at the southwestern end of
the Chiltern range. From here there is an alternative route (best
attempted only on an all terrain bicycle) along the ancient
Ridgeway Path, from which you can link up to the *Round
Berkshire Cycle Route*. From Goring you go north, parallel to
the Thames, to Crowmarsh Gifford, where you cross the river
into the small town of **Wallingford**.

Lakeside Guest House, *118
Abingdon Road, Oxford,
Oxfordshire, OX1 4PZ.*
Edwardian house overlooking
Thames. One mile Oxford. Next to
park - swimming pool/tennis.
Grades: ETC 3 Diamond
Tel: **01865 244725** (also fax no)
Mrs Shirley.
D: £24.00-£30.00 .
Open: All Year
Beds: 2F 3D 1T **Baths:** 3 En 3 Sh
🛇 🅿 (6) 🗶 🖵 🗙 🛋 ☑ 🚲

5 Galley Field, *Radley Road,
Abington, Oxon, OX14 3RU.*
Detached house in quiet cul-de-sac,
north of the Thames, Abingdon &
A34.
Tel: **01235 521088** Mrs Bird.
D: £16.50-£17.50 **S:** £23.00-£25.00.
Open: Easter to Oct
Beds: 2T 1S **Baths:** 2 Sh
🛇 (12) 🅿 (2) 🗶 🖵 🛋 ☑ 🚲

Arden Lodge, *34 Sunderland
Avenue, Oxford, OX2 8DX.*
Select spacious modern detached
house within easy reach city centre.
Tel: **01865 552076**
Mr & Mrs Price.
D: £24.00-£25.00 **S:** £30.00-£35.00.
Open: All Year (not Xmas)
Beds: 1F 1D 1T 1S
Baths: 4 En
🛇 (3) 🅿 (7) 🗶 🖵 🛋 ☑ 🚲

Walton Guest House, *169 Walton
Street, Oxford, OX1 2HD.*
Most centrally situated guest house
in Oxford. 2 mins bus station
Tel: **01865 52137** Mrs Durrant.
D: £19.00-£25.00 **S:** £19.00-£35.00.
Open: All Year
Beds: 1F 2D 3T 3S
🛇 🖵 🛏 🛋 🛋 ☑ 🛋 🌣

Bravalla Guest House, *242 Iffley
Road, Oxford, Oxfordshire, OX4 1SE.*
Late Victorian home attractively
decorated in Sanderson patterns.
Close city ring road and river.
Tel: **01865 241326** Ms Downes.
Fax no: 01865 250511
D: £23.00-£25.00 **S:** £30.00-£40.00.
Open: All Year (not Xmas)
Beds: 1F 3D 2T 1S
Baths: 6 En
🛇 🅿 (4) 🗶 🖵 🛏 🛋 ☑

Headington 2

National Grid Ref: SP5407

🍴 🍺 White Horse, Cafe Noir

Sandfield House, *19 London Road,
Headington, Oxford, OX3 7RE.*
Fine period house. Direct coaches
to London, Heathrow & Gatwick.
Grades: ETC 4 Diamond
Tel: **01865 762406** (also fax no)
Mrs Anderson.
D: £29.00-£34.00 **S:** £30.00-£34.00.
Open: All Year (not Xmas)
Beds: 2D 2S
Baths: 3 En 1 Pr
🛇 (6) 🅿 (5) 🗶 🖵 🛋 ☑ 🛋

Tiddington 3

National Grid Ref: SP6504

🍴 🍺 Fox Pub

Albury Farm, *Draycott,
Tiddington, Thame, Oxon, OX9 2LX.*
Peaceful open views in quiet loca-
tion, clean, tidy, friendly.
Tel: **01844 339740** (also fax no)
Mrs Ilbery.
D: £20.00-£20.00 **S:** £20.00-£20.00.
Open: All Year
Beds: 1D 1T
Baths: 1 Pr 1 Sh
🅿 (4) 🗶 🖵 🗙 🛋 ☑ 🛋 🌣 🚲

Thame 4

National Grid Ref: SP7005

🍴 🍺 Lion On The Green

Field Farm, *Rycote Lane, Thame,
Oxon, OX9 2HQ.*
Grades: ETC 3 Diamond
Tel: **01844 215428** Mrs Quartly.
D: £20.00-£20.00 **S:** £25.00-£25.00
Open: All Year (not Xmas)
Beds: 2D
Baths: 2 En
🅿 🗶 🖵 🛋 ☑
Comfortable bungalow on working
farm. Pretty garden, countryside
views.

Oakfield, *Thame Park Road, Thame, Oxon, OX9 3PL.*
Grades: ETC 4 Diamond
Tel: 01844 213709
D: £20.00-£25.00 -£27.50.
Open: All Year (not Xmas)
Beds: 1D 2T
Baths: 1 En 1 Sh
⛲ (8) 🅿 (6) ⚲⌷🛏🍴🎕&Ⅴ⚕
⊶
We offer a warm welcome to our lovely farmhouse home, set in 25 acres of grounds - part of our larger 400 acre mixed farm. We have good food comfortable beds and a homely atmosphere. Out in the country, but only 10 minutes walk to town centre.

Stokenchurch 5

National Grid Ref: SU7695

⋈ ⬗ Blue Flag

Gibbons Farm, *Bigmore Lane, Stokenchurch, High Wycombe, Bucks, HP14 3UR.*
Tel: 01494 482385 Mrs McKelvey.
Fax no: 01494 485400
D: £25.00-£30.00 **S:** £25.00-£30.00.
Open: All Year
Beds: 2F 1D 1T 4S
Baths: 6 En 1 Sh
⛲ 🅿 (20) 🍴🎕&Ⅴ⚕⊶
Traditional farm offering accommodation in converted barn. Set in courtyard surrounded by open countryside, this family-run B&B offers a warm and friendly welcome with Marlow and Oxford within half-hour drive, situated within 5 mins of M40, London is easily accessible.

Lewknor 6

National Grid Ref: SU7197

⋈ ⬗ Leathern Bottle

Moorcourt Cottage, *Weston Road, Lewknor, Watlington, Oxfordshire, OX9 5RU.*
Beautiful C15th cottage, open views, very quiet, friendly and comfortable.
Tel: 01844 351419 (also fax no)
Mrs Hodgson.
D: £22.50-£22.50
S: £30.00-£30.00.
Open: All Year
Beds: 1T 1D
Baths: 1 En 1 Pr
🅿 (4) ⌷🍴🎕Ⅴ⚕⊶

> Pay B&Bs by cash or cheque and be prepared to pay up front.

Watlington 7

National Grid Ref: SU6894

Woodgate Orchard Cottage, *Howe Road, Watlington, Oxon, OX9 5EL.*
Actual grid ref: SU691937
Tel: 01491 612675 (also fax no)
Roberts.
D: £25.00-£35.00 **S:** £30.00-£30.00.
Open: All Year
Beds: 1F 1T 1D
Baths: 1 En 1 Pr
⛲🅿(8)⚲⌷✕🎕Ⅴ⚕⊶
Warm welcome, countryside location, comfortable rooms, home-cooking, restful gardens, red kites gliding above. 500m off Ridgeway, convenient for Oxfordshire Way and Cycle Path, Chiltern Way, Thames Path and towns of Oxford, Henley, Reading, Windsor, Heathrow. Oxford Tube bus stop 2 miles away Lewknor - transport arrangements.

Pishill 8

National Grid Ref: SU7289

⋈ ⬗ The Crown

Bank Farm, *Pishill, Henley-on-Thames, Oxon, RG9 6HJ.*
Actual grid ref: SU724898
Quiet comfortable farmhouse, beautiful countryside. Convenient Oxford, London, Windsor.
Grades: ETC 2 Diamond
Tel: 01491 638601 Mrs Lakey.
D: £23.00-£23.00 **S:** £20.00-£23.00.
Open: All Year (not Xmas)
Beds: 1F 1S
Baths: 1 En 1 Sh
⛲🅿(5)⚲⌷🛏🎕Ⅴ⚕⊶

Orchard House, *Pishill, Henley-on-Thames, Oxfordshire, RG9 6HJ.*
Property in Area of Outstanding Natural Beauty surrounded by ancient woodlands.
Tel: 01491 638351 (also fax no)
Mrs Connolly.
D: £25.00-£25.00 **S:** £25.00-£25.00.
Open: All Year
Beds: 2F 1D 1T
Baths: 3 En 1 Pr
⛲🅿⚲⌷🛏✕🎕Ⅴ⚕⊶

Nettlebed 9

National Grid Ref: SU6986

⋈ ⬗ Crown Inn

Park Corner Farm House, *Nettlebed, Henley-on-Thames, Oxon, RG9 6DX.*
Queen Anne farmhouse in AONB between Henley-on-Thames and Oxford.
Tel: 01491 641450 Mrs Rutter.
D: £22.50 **S:** £25.00.
Open: All Year (not Xmas/ New Year)
Beds: 2T 1S
Baths: 1 Sh 1 Pr
⛲🅿(6)⚲🛏🎕Ⅴ⚕⚕

Henley-on-Thames 10

National Grid Ref: SU7682

⋈ ⬗ Anchor, Bottle & Glass, Golden Ball, Rose & Crown

Ledard, *Rotherfield Road, Henley-on-Thames, Oxon, RG9 1NN.*
Actual grid ref: SU761814
Elegant Victorian house and garden within easy reach of Henley.
Tel: 01491 575611
Mrs Howard.
D: £20.00-£20.00 **S:** £20.00-£20.00.
Open: All Year (not Xmas)
Beds: 1F 1D 1T
Baths: 2 Pr
⛲🅿(4)⚲⌷🎕Ⅴ⚕⊶

Alftrudis, *8 Norman Avenue, Henley-on-Thames, Oxon, RG9 1SG.*
Victorian home, quiet cul-de-sac two minutes town centre station, river.
Grades: ETC 4 Diamond
Tel: 01491 573099
Mrs Lambert.
Fax no: 01491 411747
D: £25.00-£30.00 **S:** £40.00-£50.00.
Open: All Year
Beds: 2D 1T
Baths: 2 En 1 Pr
⛲ (8) 🅿 (2) ⚲⌷🎕Ⅴ

4 Coldharbour Close, *Henley-on-Thames, Oxon, RG9 1QP.*
Large sunny bungalow in quiet location; secluded garden with patio.
Grades: ETC 3 Diamond
Tel: 01491 575297 (also fax no)
Mrs Bower.
D: £24.00-£28.00 **S:** £27.00-£30.00.
Open: Easter to Nov
Beds: 1D 1T
Baths: 1 Pr 1 En
⛲🅿(3)⚲⌷✕🎕&Ⅴ⚕

Lenwade, *3 Western Road, Henley-on-Thames, Oxon, RG9 1JL.*
Beautiful Victorian family home, convenient river, restaurants, public transport.
Tel: 01491 573468 (also fax no)
Mrs Williams.
D: £25.00-£27.50
S: £25.00-£27.50.
Open: All Year (not Xmas)
Beds: 2D 1T
Baths: 2 En 1 Pr
⛲🅿(2)⚲⌷🎕Ⅴ⚕⊶

New Lodge, *Henley Park, Henley-on-Thames, Oxon, RG9 6HU.*
Actual grid ref: SU758847
Victorian cottage, Area of Outstanding Natural Beauty. Minimum stay two nights.
Tel: 01491 576340 (also fax no)
Mrs Warner.
D: £19.00-£21.00
S: £24.00-£27.00.
Open: All Year
Beds: 2D
Baths: 1 En 1 Pr
⛲🅿(5)⚲⌷🎕&Ⅴ

Woodcote 11

National Grid Ref: SU6481

⌖ ⊈ Red Lion

The Hedges, *South Stoke Road, Woodcote, Reading, Berks, RG8 0PL.* Peaceful, rural situation, historic Area of Outstanding Natural Beauty.
Grades: ETC 3 Diamond
Tel: **01491 680461**
Mrs Howard-Allen.
D: £17.00-£19.00 **S:** £17.00-£19.00.
Open: All Year (not Xmas)
Beds: 2T 2S **Baths:** 1 Pr 1 Sh
⏲ 🄿 (4) ☐ ⋔ ⏣ ⟟ Ⅷ Ⅴ ⓘ ⨍ ⛾

Goring 12

National Grid Ref: SU6081

⌖ ⊈ Catherine Wheel, John Barleycorn, Miller Of Mansfield, Bull Inn, Perch & Pike

The Catherine Wheel, *Station Rd, Goring, Reading, Berks, RG8 9HB.* Accommodation in a Victorian cottage in riverside village.
Tel: **01491 872379** Mrs Kerr.
D: £20.00 **S:** £25.00. **Open:** All Year
Beds: 2D 1**Baths:** 2 Sh
⏲ ⨼ ☐ ✗ ⏣ ⟟ Ⅴ ⛾

Streatley 13

National Grid Ref: SU5980

⌖ ⊈ The Bull, Catherine Wheel

▲ **Streatley-on-Thames Youth Hostel,** *Hill House, Reading Road, Streatley, Reading, Berks, RG8 9JJ.*
Actual grid ref: SU591806
Tel: **01491 872278**
Under 18: £7.75 **Adults:** £11.00
Self-catering facilities, Television, Showers, Dining room, Drying room, Cycle store, Parking Limited, Evening meal at 7.00pm, No smoking, WC, Kitchen facilities, Breakfast available, Credit cards accepted
Homely Victorian family house, completely refurbished, in a beautiful riverside village.

Pennyfield, *The Coombe, Streatley, Reading, Berkshire, RG8 9QT.* Pretty village house with attractive terraced garden. Friendly welcoming hosts.
Grades: ETC 4 Diamond
Tel: **01491 872048** (also fax no)
D: £22.50-£25.00 **S:** £22.50-£25.00.
Open: All Year (not Xmas/ New Year)
Beds: 1T 2D
Baths: 2 En 1 Sh
🄿 (4) ⨼ ☐ ⏣ ⟟ Ⅴ ⓘ ⨍ ⛾

North Stoke 14

National Grid Ref: SU6186

Footpath Cottage, *The Street, North Stoke, Wallingford, Oxon, OX10 6BJ.* Lovely old cottage, peaceful river village. Warm welcome, excellent food.
Tel: **01491 839763**
Mrs Tanner.
D: £19.00-£20.00
S: £20.00-£20.00.
Open: All Year
Beds: 2D 1S
Baths: 1 En 1 Sh
⏲ ☐ ⋔ ✗ ⏣ ⟟ Ⅴ ⓘ ⨍ ⛾

Cholsey 15

National Grid Ref: SU5886

⌖ ⊈ The Beatle and Wedge

The Well Cottage, *Caps Lane, Cholsey, Wallingford, Oxon, OX10 9HQ.* Delightful cottage with ensuite bedrooms in secluded garden flat.
Tel: **01491 651959**
Alexander.
Fax no: 01491 651675
D: £15.00-£25.00
S: £20.00-£30.00.
Open: All Year
Beds: 2T 1D
Baths: 2 En 1 Pr

Wallingford 16

National Grid Ref: SU6089

⌖ ⊈ Shepherd's Hut, Six Bells, Bell, The Queens Head

Little Gables, *166 Crowmarsh Hill, Wallingford, Oxford, OX10 8BG.*
Actual grid ref: SU623889
Delightfully large private house where a warm welcome awaits you.
Grades: ETC 3 Diamond
Tel: **01491 837834** Mrs Reeves.
Fax no: 01491 834426
D: £25.00-£35.00 **S:** £30.00-£35.00.
Open: All Year
Beds: 2F 2D 3T 1S
Baths: 2 En 1 Pr
⏲ 🄿 ⨼ ☐ ⏣ ⟟ ⅙ Ⅴ ⓘ ⨍ ⛾

Munts Mill, *Castle Lane, Wallingford, Oxfordshire, OX10 0BN.*
Actual grid ref: SU609895
Near town centre on edge of Chilterns - advance booking only.
Tel: **01491 836654** Mrs Broster.
S: £20.00-£25.00.
Open: All Year (not Xmas)
Beds: 2S
⨼ ☐ ⏣ ⟟ Ⅴ ⨍

North Farm, *Shillingford Hill, Wallingford, Oxon, OX10 8NB.*
Actual grid ref: SU586924
Quiet comfortable farmhouse on working farm, close to River Thames.
Tel: **01865 858406**
Mrs Warburton.
Fax no: 01865 858519
D: £24.00-£28.00 **S:** £28.00-£38.00.
Open: All Year (not Xmas)
Beds: 2D 1T
Baths: 1 En 2 Pr
⏲ (8) 🄿 (6) ⨼ ☐ ⏣ ⟟ Ⅴ ⓘ ⨍ ⛾

D = Price range per person sharing in a double room

Wallingford to Lechlade

From here the route takes you west and close to **Didcot**, where there is a railway museum. Between Appelford and Culham you can make a detour to the pretty town of **Abingdon**. There are scant remains of the Benedictine abbey which went the way of all the others under Henry VIII, but there is an impressive Perpendicular church, St Helen's, the seventeenth-century County Hall and many streets with seventeenth- and eighteenth-century houses. Westwards to **Wantage**, birthplace of Alfred the Great, whose statue stands imposingly over the town square. Further westwards, the route passes close to the world-famous prehistoric White Horse hillside carving. By far the oldest of England's chalk carvings, the figure captures in huge bold lines the movement of a galloping horse. The earthworks of Uffington Castle, a fort from the same era, stand atop the hill. From here, where the Ridgeway alternative rejoins the main route, it's north to **Uffington**, and on to **Faringdon**. A short stretch west to Coleshill and then north to **Buscot** brings you close to Buscot Park, a National Trust property with painted pannels and stained glass by Edward Burne-Jones. Just over the border in Gloucestershire is the village of **Lechlade**, built of Cotswold limestone and boasting a church, St Lawrence's, whose spire is celebrated in a poem by Shelley. The village is the highest navigable point of the Thames.

Benson 17

National Grid Ref: SU6191

🍴 🍺 Three Horseshoes, Crown

Fyfield Manor, Brook Street, Benson, Wallingford, Oxon, OX10 6HA.
Medieval dining room. Beautiful water gardens. Essentially a family house.
Tel: **01491 835184** Mrs Brown.
Fax no: 01491 825635
D: £25.00-£25.00 **S:** £30.00-£30.00.
Open: All Year (not Xmas/New Year)
Beds: 1D 1T
Baths: 2 En 1 Pr
🛇 (10) 🅿 (6) ⊬ ⌷ 🌣 🛏 Ⅲ. Ⅴ ⓘ ≠

Ewelme 18

National Grid Ref: SU6491

🍴 🍺 Crown, Shepherds Hut

Fords Farm, Ewelme, Wallingford, Oxon, OX10 6HU.
Picturesque setting in historic village. Warm, friendly atmosphere. Good views.
Grades: ETC 4 Diamond
Tel: **01491 839272**
Miss Edwards.
D: £24.00-£25.00
S: £30.00-£35.00.
Open: All Year
Beds: 1D 2T
Baths: 1 Pr 1 Sh
🅿 (8) ⊬ ⌷ 🌣 Ⅲ. Ⅴ ⌀

May's Farm, Turner's Court, Ewelme, Wallingford, Oxon, OX10 6QF.
Working stock farm. Fabulous views, quiet location, good walking.
Tel: **01491 641294**
Mrs Passmore.
Fax no: 01491 641697
D: £19.00-£22.00
S: £25.00-£30.00.
Open: All Year
Beds: 1F 1T 1S
Baths: 1 En 1 Sh
🛇 🅿 (4) ⊬ ⌷ 🌣 Ⅲ. Ⅴ ≠

Shillingford 19

National Grid Ref: SU5992

🍴 🍺 Six Bells

Marsh House, Court Drive, Shillingford, Wallingford, Oxon, OX10 7ER.
Spacious house in quiet rural surroundings, next to the Thames Path and River Thames.
Tel: **01865 858496** (also fax no)
Nickson.
D: £20.00-£25.00
S: £20.00-£25.00.
Open: All Year (not Xmas)
Beds: 1T 2S
Baths: 2 En 1 Pr
🛇 (8) 🅿 (4) ⊬ ⌷ 🌣 Ⅲ. Ⅴ ⓘ ≠ ⊶

Burcot 20

National Grid Ref: SU5695

Dinckley Court, Burcot, Abingdon, Oxon, OX14 3DP.
Actual grid ref: SU563959
Beautiful Thames riverside coach house, offering luxury ensuite accommodation in 8 acre grounds.
Grades: ETC 4 Diamond,
AA 4 Diamond
Tel: **01865 407763**
Mrs Godfrey.
D: £27.50-£32.50 **S:** £45.00-£55.00.
Open: All Year
Beds: 1D 4T
Baths: 5 Pr
🛇 🅿 (20) ⊬ ⌷ ✕ 🌣 Ⅲ. Ⅴ ⓘ ≠

Sutton Courtenay 21

National Grid Ref: SU5093

🍴 🍺 George & Dragon, The Fish, The Swan

Bekynton House, 7 The Green, Sutton Courtenay, Abingdon, Oxon, OX14 4AE.
Courthouse overlooking village green. Thames and 3 pubs - 5 minutes.
Tel: **01235 848630** Ms Cornwall.
Fax no: 01235 848436
D: £25.00-£28.00 **S:** £25.00-£28.00.
Open: All Year (not Xmas)
Beds: 1D 2T 1S
Baths: 2 Sh
🛇 🅿 (2) ⊬ ⌷ 🌣 Ⅲ. Ⅴ ⓘ ≠ ⊶

Steventon 22

National Grid Ref: SU4691

🍴 🍺 The Fox, The Cherry Tree

Tethers End, Abingdon Road, Steventon, Abingdon, Oxon, OX13 6RW.
Tel: **01235 834015** Ms Miller.
Fax no: 01235 862990
D: £22.00-£25.00 **S:** £25.00-£28.00.
Open: All Year
Beds: 1F 1D **Baths:** 2 En
🛇 🅿 ⊬ ⌷ 🌣 Ⅲ. Ⅴ ⓘ ≠
Comfortable ground floor accommodation, situated on the edge of a peaceful village green. Ideally placed for visiting Oxford, Abingdon, Wantage, historic Ridgeway, Blenheim Palace and Didcot Railway Centre. Caroline and Peter Miller offer you a warm welcome.

East Hanney 23

National Grid Ref: SU4192

Bramley House, Mill Orchard, East Hanney, Wantage, Oxon, OX12 0JH.
Village near Berkshire Downs, Oxford, Cotswolds. Pubs, restaurant serve food.
Tel: **01235 868314**
D: £19.00-£20.00 **S:** £20.00-£22.00.
Open: All Year (not Xmas)
Beds: 2D 1S **Baths:** 1 En 1 Sh
🅿 (3) ⊬ ⌷ 🌣 Ⅲ. Ⅴ

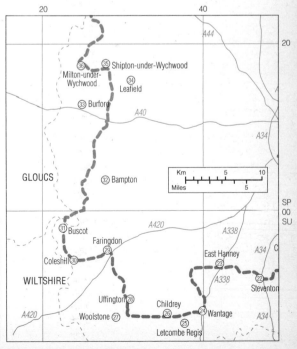

Wantage 24

National Grid Ref: SU4087

The Bell Inn, 38 Market Place, Wantage, Oxon, OX12 8AH.
C16th market town inn. Good beer and home-cooked food in warm friendly atmosphere.
Tel: **01235 763718** (also fax no)
Mrs Williams.
D: £22.50-£27.50
S: £20.00-£35.00.
Open: All Year
Beds: 2F 5D 4T 7S
Baths: 11 En 2 Sh
🛏🍴🗲❌💺🛏️🖵🎧♿

Letcombe Regis 25

National Grid Ref: SU3886

🍴🍺Greyhound, Lamb

Quince Cottage, Letcombe Regis, Wantage, Oxon, OX12 9J.
Large thatched cottage, exposed beams, near Ridgeway, warm family atmosphere.
Tel: **01235 763652**
Mrs Boden.
D: £21.00-£25.00
S: £25.00-£25.00.
Open: All Year
Beds: 1T 1S
Baths: 1 Pr
🛏(1)🅿(2)🗲❌💺🛏️🖵🎧♿🚲

Old Vicarage, Letcombe Regis, Wantage, Oxon, OX12 9JP.
Delightful Victorian home, elegant accommodation, near pub, pretty downland village.
Tel: **01235 765827**
Mrs Barton.
Fax no: 020 8743 8740
D: £22.00-£25.00
S: £22.00-£30.00.
Open: All Year (not Xmas)
Beds: 1D 1T 1S
Baths: 1 En 1 Sh
🛏🅿(2)🗲❌🖵🎧♿🚲

Childrey 26

National Grid Ref: SU3587

🍴🍺The Hatchett

Ridgeway House, West Street, Childrey, Wantage, Oxon, OX12 9UL.
Actual grid ref: SU335873
Luxury, countryside home in quiet Downland village near the Ridgeway.
Tel: **01235 751538** (also fax no)
Mrs Roberts.
D: £20.00-£22.50 **S:** £23.00-£29.00.
Open: All Year
Beds: 1F 1T 1S
Baths: 2 En
🛏🅿(5)🗲❌🛏️🖵🎧♿🚲

Woolstone 27

National Grid Ref: SU2988

🍴🍺White Horse

Hickory House, Woolstone, Faringdon, Oxon, SN7 7QL.
Actual grid ref: SU294877
Tel: **01367 820303**
Mr & Mrs Grist.
Fax no: 01367 820958
D: £19.00-£25.00 **S:** £21.00-£25.00.
Open: All Year (not Xmas)
Beds: 2T **Baths:** 2 En
🛏(12)🅿(2)🗲❌💺🛏️🖵🎧♿🚲
Situated in a delightful picturesque village beneath the White Horse Hill near the Ridgeway, Hickory House offers comfortable accommodation in a recently built self-contained extension. Pub serving food is a minute's walk. Oxford, Bath and the Cotswolds are within easy driving distance.

**S = Price range for a single
person in a room**

Uffington 28

National Grid Ref: SU3089

🍴🍺Fox & Hounds

Norton House, Broad Street, Uffington, Faringdon, Oxon, SN7 7RA.
Actual grid ref: SU305895
Friendly C18th family home in centre of quiet, pretty village.
Tel: **01367 820230** (also fax no)
Mrs Oberman.
D: £20.00-£21.00 **S:** £23.00-£26.00.
Open: All Year (not Xmas)
Beds: 1F 1D 1S
Baths: 2 Pr
🛏🅿(3)🗲❌🛏️🖵🎧♿🚲

The Craven, Uffington, Faringdon, Oxon, SN7 7RD.
C17th thatched, beamed farmhouse/hotel.
Tel: **01367 820449**
Mrs Wadsworth.
D: £20.00 **S:** £25.00.
Open: All Year
Beds: 1F 3D 2T 2S
Baths: 2 Pr 2 Sh
🛏🅿(9)🗲❌💺🛏️♿🎧♿

Faringdon 29

National Grid Ref: SU2895

🍴🍺Fox & Hounds, The Plough

Faringdon Hotel, 1 Market Place, Faringdon, Oxon, SN7 7HL.
Grades: ETC 3 Diamond, AA 2 Star, RAC 2 Star
Tel: **01367 240536**
Fax no: 01367 243250
D: £30.00-£35.00
S: £45.00-£60.00.
Open: All Year
Beds: 3F 14D 1T 3S
Baths: 20 En
🛏🗲❌💺🛏️🖵🎧🚲
Situated near C12th parish church, on site of palace of Alfred the Great.

From Lechlade through the Cotswolds

Back in Oxfordshire, **Kelmscott Manor** (open Wednesdays, April-September), a classic Elizabethan manor, was home to the founder of the Arts and Crafts movement, socialist William Morris, for the last twenty-five years of his life. The house sports decor by Morris' friends in the Pre-Raphaelite movement, including Edward Burne-Jones (who worked on Buscot Park whilst staying here) and Dante Gabriel Rossetti, who had an affair with Morris' wife, Jane. From here you ride north; a detour westwards from Shilton will take you to the Cotswold Wildlife Park. On to **Swinbrook**, on the banks of the Windrush, where the church boasts the Tudor and Stuart Fettiplace

Monuments. A short detour leads to **Burford**, another beautiful village of Cotswold stone with an impressive sloping High Street lined by fourteenth- to sixteenth-century houses. The most interesting feature of the large parish church is tucked away high up in the rafters - a small statue of a pagan deity by a craftsman hedging his bets for the hereafter. The churchyard was the scene in the seventeenth century of the martyrdom of Levellers in Cromwell's army, members of a radical democratic movement shot for refusing to fight in Ireland. North of Swinbrook you come into the ancient **Wychwood** region. You are now in true Cotswold country, where you remain for most of the remaining distance - this lengthy stretch of the cycleway affords the most picturesque landscape.

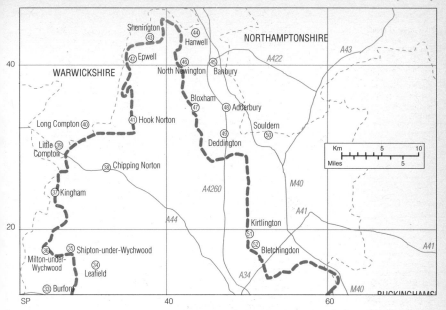

Portwell House Hotel, *Market Place, Faringdon, Oxon, SN7 7HU.*
Relax in the ancient market town of Faringdon within reach of the Cotswolds.
Grades: ETC 1 Star
Tel: **01367 240197** Mr Pakeman.
Fax no: 01367 244330
D: £25.00 **S:** £40.00.
Open: All Year
Beds: 2F 3D 2T 1S **Baths:** 8 En
🛇 (2) 🅿 (4) ⊬ 🗆 ✗ 🛋 🎟 & 🛚 🛈 ⚡ ♻

Coleshill 30

National Grid Ref: SU2393

⏐⏐ ⊲ Radnor Arms

Ashen Copse Farm, *Coleshill, Highworth, Swindon, Wilts, SN6 7PU.*
Farmhouse in beautiful, peaceful countryside.
Tel: **01367 240175** Ms Hoddinott.
D: £21.00-£24.00 **S:** £21.00-£30.00.
Open: All Year (not Xmas)
Beds: 1F 1T 1S **Baths:** 1 Pr 1 Sh
🛇 🅿 (6) ⊬ 🗆 🛋 🛚

Buscot 31

National Grid Ref: SU2397

⏐⏐ ⊲ Trout Inn

Apple Tree House, *Buscot, Faringdon, Oxon, SN7 8DA.*
Old property in National Trust village, 5 mins' walk River Thames, one acre garden.
Grades: ETC 3 Diamond, AA 3 Diamond, RAC 3 Diamond
Tel: **01367 252592** Mrs Reay.
D: £18.00-£22.00 **S:** £23.00-£28.00.
Open: All Year (not Xmas)
Beds: 2D 1T **Baths:** 1 En 2 Pr
🛇 🅿 (10) ⊬ 🗆 🛋 🎟 🛚 ♻

Bampton 32

National Grid Ref: SP3103

⏐⏐ ⊲ Talbot Hotel, Romany Inn

Morar, *Weald Street, Bampton, Oxon, OX18 2HL.*
Actual grid ref: SP312026
Wake to the mouthwatering smell of homemade bread baking.
Tel: **01993 850162** Ms Rouse.
Fax no: 01993 851738
D: £22.50-£25.00 **S:** £22.50-£25.00.
Open: Mar to Dec
Beds: 2D 1T **Baths:** 2 En 1 Pr
🛇 (6) 🅿 (4) ⊬ 🗆 🛋 🎟 🛚 🛈 ⚡ ♻

Burford 33

National Grid Ref: SP2512

⏐⏐ ⊲ Old Bull

The Old Bell Foundry, *45 Witney Street, Burford, Oxon, OX18 4RX.*
Tranquil setting, a short distance from Burford High Street.
Tel: **01993 822234** (also fax no)
Ms Barguss.
D: £24.00-£25.00 .
Open: All Year (not Xmas)
Beds: 1F **Baths:** 1 En
🛇 🅿 (1) ⊬ 🗆 🛋 🎟 🛚 ♻ 🚲

All cycleways are
popular: you are
well-advised to
book ahead

Leafield 34

National Grid Ref: SP3115

⏐⏐ ⊲ The Swan, The Maytime

Langley Farm, *Leafield, Witney, Oxon, OX8 5QD.*
Working farm set in open country 3 miles from Burford.
Grades: ETC 3 Diamond
Tel: **01993 878686** Mrs Greves.
D: £17.50-£20.00 .
Open: May to Oct
Beds: 2D 1T **Baths:** 1 Pr 2 Sh
🛇 (8) 🅿 (8) 🗆 🖪 🛋 🎟 🛚

Pond View, *10 Fairspear Road, Leafield, Witney, Oxon, OX8 5NT.*
Village location handy for visiting Burford, Blenheim Palace and Oxford.
Grades: ETC 3 Diamond
Tel: **01993 878133** Mrs Wiggins.
D: £19.00-£21.00 **S:** £19.00-£21.00.
Open: All Year
Beds: 3D 2S **Baths:** 2 En 2 Sh
🛇 🅿 (4) ⊬ 🗆 🖪 🛋 🎟 🛚 🛈

Shipton-under-Wychwood 35

National Grid Ref: SP2717

⏐⏐ ⊲ Red Horse, Lamb Inn, Crown Hotel

Garden Cottage, *Fiddlers Hill, Shipton-under-Wychwood, Chipping Norton, Oxon, OX7 6DR.*
Attractive stone cottage, country views, quiet, ideal for exploring Cotswolds.
Grades: ETC 3 Diamond
Tel: **01993 830640** Worker.
D: £15.00-£25.00 **S:** £25.00-£35.00.
Open: All Year (not Xmas)
Beds: 1D 1T **Baths:** 2 En
🛇 (8) 🅿 (2) ⊬ 🗆 🛋 🎟 🛚 🛈 ⚡

From the Cotswolds to Oxford

The northernmost point of the route is **Hornton**, from where you turn southwards and head to **Broughton**, where stands Broughton Castle, an Elizabethan mansion surrounded by a moat. It contains splendid pannelling, fireplaces and plaster ceilings. Inhabited by a Parliamentarian in the Civil War, it was captured by the Royalists after the Battle of Edgehill, a few miles away in Warwickshire. There is a display of Civil War arms and armour. From here you can make a detour to visit **Banbury**, the main town of Northern Oxfordshire. The Victorian market cross stands on the site of a medieval original. After Broughton you head south into the **Cherwell Valley**. A detour from **Upper Heyford** leads to Rousham House, a seventeenth-century mansion which served as a Royalist garrison during the Civil War. It has the only surviving landscape garden by William Kent. From Upper Heyford it's an easy ride to Horton-cum-Studley to complete the county circuit, and you can return to Oxford by the route along which you left.

6 Courtlands Road, *Shipton-under-Wychwood, Chipping Norton, Oxon, OX7 6DF.*
Friendly, quiet, comfortable house/garden.
Tel: **01993 830551**
Mr & Mrs Fletcher.
D: £17.50-£22.50
S: £20.00-£25.00.
Open: All Year
Beds: 2D 1T
Baths: 2 En 1 Pr
🛏 (3) �📠 🖵 👤 🏛 Ⓥ 🛍 ≠

S = Price range for a single person in a room

Milton-under-Wychwood 36

National Grid Ref: SP2618

🍴 🍺 Quart Pot, Lamb Inn

Sunset House, *Jubilee Lane, Milton-under-Wychwood, Chipping Norton, Oxfordshire, OX7 6EW.*
Period Cotswold house, charming bedrooms with ensuite private facilities.
Tel: **01993 830581** Mrs Durston.
D: £23.50-£25.00 **S:** £27.50-£30.00.
Open: All Year
Beds: 2D 1T
Baths: 2 En 1 Pr
🛏 (5) �📠 (3) ≠ 🖵 👤 🏛 Ⓥ

Kingham 37

National Grid Ref: SP2524

🍴 🍺 Kings Head

The Old Stores, *Foscot, Kingham, Chipping Norton, Oxon, OX7 6RH.*
Actual grid ref: SP2522
Charming Cotswold stone cottage in lovely rural location, 1.5 miles from Kingham.
Tel: **01608 659844** (also fax no)
D: £18.00-£20.00 **S:** £22.00-£23.00.
Open: Mar to Nov
Beds: 1D
Baths: 1 Pr
📠 (2) ≠ 🖵 👤 🏛 Ⓥ ≠ 🚲

Chipping Norton 38

National Grid Ref: SP3126

🍴 🍺 Blue Boar

The Old Bakehouse, *50 West Street, Chipping Norton, Oxon, OX7 5ER.*
An old bakehouse, warm & friendly atmosphere, near town centre.
Tel: **01608 643441**
Mr & Mrs Cashmore.
D: £22.50-£25.00 **S:** £35.00-£35.00.
Open: All Year (not Xmas/New Year)
Beds: 1F 1D
Baths: 2 En
🛏 (8) 📠 (2) ≠ 🖵 👤 🏛 Ⓥ 🚲

Little Compton 39

National Grid Ref: SP2630

🍴 🍺 Red Lion

Rigside, *Little Compton, Moreton-in-Marsh, Glos, GL56 0RR.*
Lovely landscaped gardens backing onto farmland.
Grades: AA 4 Diamond
Tel: **01608 674128** (also fax no)
Ms Cox.
D: £22.00-£23.00
S: £20.00-£22.00.
Open: All Year
Beds: 2D 1S 1T
Baths: 2 En 1 Sh
🛏 (9) 📠 (6) 🖵 👤 🏛 Ⓥ 🛍 ≠ 🚲

Long Compton 40

National Grid Ref: SP2832

Tallet Barn, *Yerdley Farm, Long Compton, Shipston-on-Stour, Warks, CV36 5LH.*
Comfortable annexed rooms, a warm welcome and a quiet village location.
Grades: ETC 4 Diamond
Tel: **01608 684248**
Mrs Richardson.
Fax no: 01068 684248
D: £20.00-£21.00 **S:** £25.00-£25.00.
Open: All Year
Beds: 1D 1T
Baths: 2 En
🛏 (6) 📠 (2) ≠ 🖵 👤 🏛 Ⓥ ≠

Hook Norton 41

National Grid Ref: SP3533

🍴 🍺 Sun Inn

Symnel, *High St, Hook Norton, Banbury, Oxfordshire, OX15 5NH.*
Real ale brewery, pottery, Roll Right stones. Excellent restaurants wonderful countryside.
Grades: ETC 2 Diamond
Tel: **01608 737547** Mrs Cornelius.
D: £16.00-£16.00 **S:** £16.00-£16.00.
Open: All Year (not Xmas)
Beds: 1D 2T
Baths: 1 Sh
🛏 📠 ≠ 🖵 ✕ 👤 🏛 Ⓥ 🛍 ≠ 🚲

Epwell 42

National Grid Ref: SP3441

🍴 🍺 The Bell

Yarnhill Farm, *Shenington Road, Epwell, Banbury, Oxon, OX15 6JA.*
Peaceful farmhouse; ideally situated for Cotswolds, Stratford upon Avon, Oxford.
Grades: ETC 3 Diamond
Tel: **01295 780250**
D: £18.00-£25.00
S: £18.00-£25.00.
Open: All Year (not Xmas)
Beds: 1D 1T 1S
Baths: 1 Pr 1 Sh
🛏 (8) 📠 (6) ≠ 🖵 👤 🏛 Ⓥ ≠ 🚲

Shenington 43

National Grid Ref: SP3742

🍴 🍺 The Bell Inn

Top Farm House, *Shenington, Banbury, Oxfordshire, OX15 6LZ.*
C18th Horton stone farmhouse set on the edge of village green.
Grades: ETC 3 Diamond
Tel: **01295 670226**
Fax no: 01295 678170
D: £20.00-£25.00 **S:** £25.00-£30.00.
Open: All Year (not Xmas/New Year)
Beds: 1T 2D
Baths: 1Ensuite 1Shared
🛏 📠 (4) ≠ 🖵 👤 🏛 Ⓥ 🛍 ≠ 🚲

Hanwell 44

National Grid Ref: SP4344

￦ ◁ The Bell

The Coach House, Hanwell Castle, Hanwell, Banbury, Oxon, OX17 1HN.
Part of C15th castle in 20 acre garden undergoing restoration.
Tel: **01295 730764**
Mrs Taylor.
D: £18.00-£25.00 **S:** £18.00-£25.00.
Open: Apr to Oct
Beds: 1F 1D 1T
Baths: 3 En
ᗡ (1) ▣ (6) ❐ ⽥ ≛ ⊞ ⟨ ⓥ

Banbury 45

National Grid Ref: SP4540

￦ ◁ Swan Inn, Merto's

Belmont Guest House, 34 Crouch Street, Banbury, Oxon, OX16 9PR.
Family run guest house close to all town amenities.
Tel: **01295 262308**
Mr Raby.
Fax no: 01295 275982
D: £21.00-£22.50 **S:** £25.00-£35.00.
Open: All Year (not Xmas)
Beds: 1F 2D 2T 3S
Baths: 5 Pr 1 Sh
ᗡ (10) ▣ (6) ⣯ ❐ ✕ ≛ ⊞ ⟨ ⓥ ⸜

North Newington 46

National Grid Ref: SP4239

￦ ◁ North Arms

Broughton Grounds Farm, North Newington, Banbury, Oxon, OX15 6AW.
Tel: **01295 730315**
Margaret Taylor.
D: £16.00-£18.00
S: £16.00-£18.00.
Open: All Year (not Xmas)
Beds: 1D 1T 1S
Baths: 1 Sh
ᗡ (2) ▣ (3) ⣯ ❐ ≛ ⓥ ⸪ ⷫ
Enjoy warm hospitality & peaceful surroundings at our C17th stone farmhouse. A working family farm situated on the Broughton Castle estate with beautiful views & walks. New, very comfortable spacious accommodation, log fire in dining room, delicious breakfast & cream teas with home produce.

Bloxham 47

National Grid Ref: SP4236

￦ ◁ Red Lion

Brook Cottage, Little Bridge Road, Bloxham, Banbury, Oxon, OX15 4PU.
Warm welcome to C17th thatched cottage. Personal management by owner. Tel: **01295 721089**
D: £18.50-£18.50 **S:** £18.50-£18.50.
Open: All Year
Beds: 1D 1T 1S **Baths:** 1 En 1 Pr
▣ (4) ⣯ ❐ ≛ ⊞ ⟨ ⓥ ⷫ

Adderbury 48

National Grid Ref: SP4735

Morgans Orchard Restaurant, 9 Twyford Gardens, Twyford, Adderbury, Banbury, Oxon, OX17 3JA.
Award-winning French restaurant with quality B&B within rustic village location.
Tel: **01295 812047** Mr Morgan.
D: £20.00-£25.00 **S:** £27.50-£40.00.
Open: All Year
Beds: 1D 2T 1S
Baths: 1 En 1 Pr 3 Sh
ᗡ ▣ (3) ⣯ ❐ ⽥ ✕ ≛ ⊞ ⟨ ⓥ ⸪ ⸜ ⷫ

Deddington 49

National Grid Ref: SP4631

￦ ◁ The Unicorn

Hill Barn, Milton Gated Road, Deddington, Banbury, Oxon, OX15 0TS.
Converted barn in open country-side, convenient for Oxford, Cotswolds, Warwick, Stratford.
Grades: ETC 2 Diamond
Tel: **01869 338631** Mrs White.
D: £20.00-£25.00 **S:** £25.00-£27.50.
Open: All Year (not Xmas)
Beds: 1F 1D 2T **Baths:** 1 En 1 Sh
ᗡ ▣ (6) ❐ ⽥ ≛ ⊞ ⟨ ⓥ ⷫ

Stonecrop Guest House, Hempton Road, Deddington, Banbury, Oxon, OX15 0QH.
Detached house close to places of interest. A warm welcome.
Grades: ETC 2 Diamond
Tel: **01869 338335**
Fax no: 01869 338505
D: £16.00-£19.00 **S:** £16.00-£19.00.
Open: All Year
Beds: 1F 1D 1T 1S **Baths:** 2 Sh
ᗡ (10) ▣ (6) ❐ ≛ ⊞ ⟨ ⓥ ⸪ ⸜ ⷫ

Souldern 50

National Grid Ref: SP5231

￦ ◁ The Fox

The Fox Inn, Souldern, Bicester, Oxon, OX6 9JN.
Stone inn, restaurant, beautiful village convenient for Oxford, Woodstock, Stratford and Warwick.
Grades: ETC 2 Diamond
Tel: **01869 345284** Mr MacKay.
Fax no: 01869 345667
D: £20.00-£25.00 **S:** £28.00-£35.00.
Open: All Year (not Xmas)
Beds: 3D 1T
Baths: 2 En 1 Sh
ᗡ ▣ (6) ❐ ⽥ ✕ ≛ ⊞ ⟨ ⓥ

Kirtlington 51

National Grid Ref: SP4919

￦ ◁ Oxford Arms

Two Turnpike Cottages, Kirtlington, Oxford, OX5 3HB.
Cotswold stone cottage with pretty gardens in village setting.
Tel: **01869 350706** Mrs Jones.
D: £21.00-£24.00 **S:** £25.00-£25.00.
Open: All Year
Beds: 2D **Baths:** 1 Sh
ᗡ ▣ (2) ⣯ ❐ ⽥ ≛ ⊞ ⟨ ⓥ ⸪ ⸜ ⷫ

Bletchingdon 52

National Grid Ref: SP5018

Stonehouse Farm, Weston Road, Bletchingdon, Kidlington, Oxon, OX5 3EA.
C17th farmhouse set in 560 acres 15 mins from Oxford.
Tel: **01869 350585** Mrs Hedges.
D: £18.00-£22.00 **S:** £20.00-£24.00.
Open: All Year (not Xmas/New Year)
Beds: 1F 1D 1T 1S **Baths:** 2 Sh
ᗡ (12) ▣ (6) ⣯ ❐ ≛ ⓥ

Always telephone to get directions to the B&B - you will save time!

Reivers Cycle Route

The **Reivers Route** is a new path through Northumberland and Cumbria (once briefly crossing the Scottish border) from Tynemouth to Whitehaven. Over 180 miles long, it has been developed by the local authorities in conjunction with Sustrans, who designate it a Regional Route, linking in several places to the National Cycle Network. The route is clearly signposted by blue direction signs bearing a cycle silhouette and the legend 'REIVERS' with the number 10 in a rectangle. It can be cycled as a return path with the **Sea to Sea (C2C)**, to form a giant circle through the whole splendid gamut of England's northern scenery between the North Sea and Irish Sea coasts. Passing through the remote grandeur of Northumberland National Park, the Border Forest Park and Kielder Water, you will take in the historic city of Carlisle before skirting the northern Lake District and continuing to the west coast.

The route takes its name from the Border Reivers, outlaw clans who held anarchic sway between the secure hearts of the kingdoms of England and Scotland, feuding, raiding and rustling each other's cattle through most of the fourteenth, fifteenth and sixteenth centuries, after the Anglo-Scottish Wars over rights to the crown of Scotland left this debatable land virtually ungoverned. Many Reiver family names – Armstrong, Graham, Bell, Robson, Nixon (who says there's no criminal gene?) – survive, as well as lasting contributions to the English vocabulary, notably 'blackmail' and 'bereaved'.

As you experience this wild country, look out for secluded hollows which might have been used to ambush rivals in centuries past.

The indispensable **official route map and guide** for the route is available from Sustrans, 35 King Street, Bristol BS1 4DZ, tel 0117-926 8893, fax 0117-929 4173, @ £4.50 (+ £2.00 p&p).

Maps: Ordnance Survey 1:50,000 Landranger series: 79, 80, 85, 87, 88, 89, 90

Trains: The Intercity west coast main line goes to Carlisle, from where you can connect to Workington or Whitehaven. The Intercity east coast main line goes to Newcastle, from where you can connect to Tynemouth.

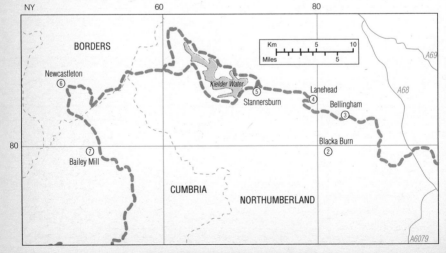

Ponteland 1

National Grid Ref: NZ1673

⚑ Blackbird Inn, The Plough

7 Collingwood Cottages, Limestone Lane, Ponteland, Newcastle-upon-Tyne, NE20 0DD.
Actual grid ref: NZ149732
Quiet informal home in country-side. Lovely views from rooms.
Tel: **01661 825967** Mrs Baxter.
D: £17.50-£17.50 **S:** £20.00-£25.00.
Open: All Year (not Xmas)
Beds: 1F 1D
Baths: 1 Sh
🛇 🄿 (4) ⿻⛌🏠 🛉 ⊞ 🖾 ⚲

Blacka Burn 2

National Grid Ref: NY8278

⚑ Battlesteads Hotel

Hetherington Farm, Blacka Burn, Wark, Hexham, Northd, NE48 3DR.
Actual grid ref: NY824782
Traditional farmhouse in lovely countryside. Ideal walking, touring, warm welcome.
Tel: **01434 230260**
Mrs Nichol.
D: £18.00-£25.00 **S:** £18.00-£25.00.
Open: Easter to Nov
Beds: 4F 1D 1S
Baths: 1 En 1 Pr 1 Sh
🛇 (10) 🄿 (4) 🛉 ⊞ 🖾 ⚶ ⚲

All rooms full and
nowhere else to stay?
Ask the owner if
there's anywhere
nearby

Tynemouth to Bellingham

The route begins in the urban sprawl around **Newcastle-upon-Tyne** (see under *Sustrans Sea to Sea*), heading through **Tynemouth** and **North Shields** before leaving the industrial wasteland behind and striking out west up the Pont Valley through Reiver country. When you reach the village of Matfen you are only two miles north of **Hadrian's Wall**, the biggest single engineering endeavour of the Roman Empire, built by Emperor Hadrian in the Second Century to keep the Caledonian hordes at bay, and now a World Heritage Site. From the stones that remain atop the bleak Northumberland hills you can trace out the line of the wall in your mind's eye, with the milecastles and turrets from which it was patrolled. At **Bellingham**, the gateway to Northumberland National Park, you will find a mark left by the Reiver era in the shape of Black Middens Bastle House, a sixteenth-century fortified farmhouse where livestock were kept safe from raids on the ground floor, and the family upstairs. St Cuthbert's church has a stone-vaulted roof also built to prevent Reiver raids; the Heritage Centre gives an insight into this period and the rest of the town's social history.

Bellingham 3

National Grid Ref: NY8383

⚑ Rose & Crown, Cheviot Hotel

▲ *Bellingham Youth Hostel,*
Woodburn Road, Bellingham, Hexham, Northumberland, NE48 2ED.
Actual grid ref: NY843834
Tel: **01434 220313**
Under 18: £5.75
Adults: £8.50
Self-catering facilities, Showers, Lounge, Cycle store, No smoking, WC, Kitchen facilities
Hostel built of red cedarwood on the Pennine Way, high above the small Borders town of Bellingham. Near Kielder Water (with forest trails and watersports) and Hadrian's Wall.

Lyndale Guest House, Bellingham, Hexham, Northd, NE48 2AW.
Grades: ETC 4 Diamond
Tel: **01434 220361** (also fax no)
Mrs Gaskin.
D: £23.50-£25.00
S: £23.50.
Open: All Year (not Xmas)
Beds: 1F 2D 1T 1S
Baths: 2 En 1 Pr 1 Sh
🛇 🄿 (5) ⿻⛌✗ 🛉 ⊞ & 🖾 ⚶ ⚲
Tour the Borders, good walking, Hadrian's Wall, Pennine Way, Kielder Water or cycle the Reivers Route. Enjoy a welcome break. Relax in our walled garden. Sunlounge with panoramic views. Excellent dinners, choice of breakfasts, quality ground floor ensuites. Special discounts.

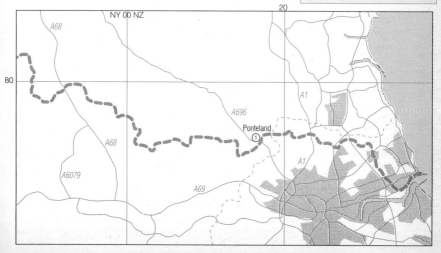

Lanehead 4

National Grid Ref: NY7985

⑪ ◫ The Holly Bush Inn

Ivy Cottage, Lanehead, Tarset,
Hexham, Northumberland, NE48 1NT.
200-year-old cottage with stunning
views over open countryside.
Grades: ETC 3 Diamond
Tel: **01434 240337** (also fax no)
Mrs Holland.
D: £18.00-£20.00 **S:** £18.00-£20.00.
Open: All Year
Beds: 1T 1D
Baths: 1 En 1 Sh
☎ ▣ ⬛ ♨ ▥ ⅋ ⬚ ᵭ

Stannersburn 5

National Grid Ref: NY7287

⑪ ◫ Pheasant Inn

Spring Cottage, Stannersburn,
Hexham, Northumberland,
NE48 1DD.
1 mile Kielder Water. Warm
welcome, good food, beautiful
scenery.
Grades: ETC 3 Diamond
Tel: **01434 240388**
Mr & Mrs Ormesher.
D: £18.00-£21.00 **S:** £18.00-£21.00.
Open: All Year (not Xmas)
Beds: 1F 1D **Baths:** 2 En
☎ ▣ ⬛ ⏻ ♨ ⬛ ▥ ⅋ ᵭ

Bringing children with
you? Always ask for
any special rates.

Bellingham to Whitehaven

Kielder Water and Kielder Forest Park are the largest
man-made reservoir and forest in Europe. As well as the
spectacular scenery, the lake also offers all manner of watersports, and fishing. Close to the Kielder Dam, where the route
reaches the lake, the Kielder Water Exhibition at Tower Knowe
Visitor Centre documents the development of this remote valley
through the ages. At the other end of the lake, **Kielder Castle**,
originally an eighteenth-century hunting lodge, is now the
Forest Park Centre, with information on the work of the Forestry
Commission. Crossing the Scottish border to reach
Newcastleton, you are now in Liddesdale, heart of the Reiver
wildlands, whose story is portrayed in the Liddesdale Trust
Museum. Back in England, following a winding route into the
Lyne Valley, the approach to **Rockcliffe** at the mouth of the
Eden yields views over the Solway Estuary, a renowned wildlife
haven, before you come to Carlisle (see under *Cumbria*
Cycleway) Heading through the northern Lake District, you
pass below the Caldbeck Fells and up the Derwent Valley to
reach **Cockermouth**, before striking out west to the coastal
towns of **Workington** and **Whitehaven** (see under *Sustrans*
Sea to Sea (C2C) for information on these towns).

D = Price range per person
sharing in a double room

Newcastleton 6

National Grid Ref: NY4887

⑪ ◫ Bailey Mill

Bailey Mill, Bailey, Newcastleton,
Roxburghshire, TD9 0TR.
Remote 18th century grain mill by
river. Ideal retreat, jacuzzi, pony
trekking
Tel: **016977 48617**
Mrs Copeland.
Fax no: 016977 48074
D: £20.00-£25.00 **S:** £22.00-£28.00.
Open: All Year
Beds: 4F 6T 3D 4S
Baths: 6 En 4 Pr 6 Sh
☎ ▣ ⏻ ♨ ⬛ ♿ ▥ ⅋ ᵭ

Bailey Mill 7

National Grid Ref: NY5179

▲ *Folly, Bailey Mill, Bailey,*
Newcastleton, Roxburghshire,
TD9 0TR.
Tel: **016977 48617**
Fax no: **016977 48074**
Under 18: £8.00 **Adults:** £10.00
Self-catering facilities, Television,
Showers, Licensed bar, Central
heating, Shop, Laundry facilities,
Wet weather shelter, Lounge,
Dining room, Games room,
Grounds available for games,
Drying room, Cycle store, Parking,
Evening meal available, Facilities
for disabled people
Courtyard Apartments on site;
Pony trekking, jacuzzi, sauna, bar
and mountain bike hire.

Walton 8

National Grid Ref: NY5264

⑪ ◫ Stag, Centurion, Lane End Inn

High Rigg Farm, Walton,
Brampton, Cumbria, CA8 2AZ.
Grades: ETC 3 Diamond
Tel: **016977 2117** Mrs Mounsey.
D: £16.00-£18.00 **S:** £18.00.
Open: All Year (not Xmas)
Beds: 2F
Baths: 1 Pr 1 Sh
☎ ▣ (4) ⅋ ⬛ ⏻ ⬛ ▥ ⅋ ᵭ
A warm welcome to our Listed
beautiful Georgian farmhouse with
breath taking views of the Pennines
& Lake District hills. Comfortable
spacious accommodation, excellent
food, much home produced. A
working dairy sheep farm. Good
parking. Central for visits to
Roman Wall/Lakes.

Low Rigg Farm, Walton,
Brampton, Cumbria, CA8 2DX.
Actual grid ref: NY522651
Comfortable accommodation on a
working farm in beautiful Hadrian's
Wall country. Excellent home
cooking.
Tel: **016977 3233** Mrs Thompson.
D: £15.00-£18.00 **S:** £18.00-£20.00.
Open: All Year (not Xmas)
Beds: 1F
Baths: 1 Sh
☎ ▣ (6) ⬛ ⏻ ✕ ♨ ⬛ ▥ ⬛

Blackford 9

National Grid Ref: NY3962

⑪ ◫ Crown & Thistle, Coach & Horses, Golden
Fleece

Gill Farm, Blackford, Carlisle,
Cumbria, CA6 4EL.
Welcome to our C18th farmhouse
on working farm, set in quiet
peaceful countryside.
Tel: **01228 675326**
Mrs Nicholson.
D: £17.50-£21.00
S: £18.00-£20.00.
Open: All Year
Beds: 1F 1D 1T
Baths: 2 Sh
☎ ▣ (7) ⬛ ⏻ ✕ ♨ ⬛ ▥ ⅋ ᵭ

Westlinton 10

National Grid Ref: NY3964

Lynebank, Westlinton, Carlisle,
Cumbria, CA6 6AA.
Family-run, excellent food, ideal
stop for England/Scotland journey.
Grades: ETC 4 Diamond
Tel: **01228 792820** (also fax no)
Mrs Butler.
D: £18.00-£22.00
S: £20.00-£24.00.
Open: All Year
Beds: 2F 3D 1T 3S
Baths: 9 En
☎ ▣ (15) ⬛ ✕ ♨ ⬛ ▥ ⅋ ᵭ

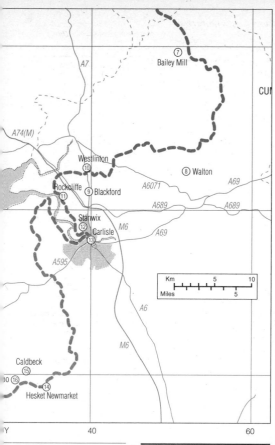

The Grid Reference beneath the location heading is for the village or town - *not* for individual houses, which are shown (where supplied) in each entry itself.

Carlisle 13

National Grid Ref: NY3955

🍴 ◁ Metal Bridge Inn, The Beehive, Mary's Pantry, Crown & Thistle, Coach & Horses, Golden Fleece, Black Lion

▲ *Carlisle Youth Hostel,*
University of Northumbria, The Old Brewery Residences, Bridge Lane, Caldewgate, Carlisle, Cumbria, CA2 5SR.
Actual grid ref: NY394560
Tel: **01228 597352**
Under 18: £8.75 **Adults:** £13.00
Self-catering facilities, Showers, Cycle store, Parking, Facilities for disabled people, No smoking, WC, Kitchen facilities
University accommodation in an award-winning conversion of the former Theakston's brewery. Single study bedrooms with shared kitchen and bathroom in flats for up to 7 people.

Howard Lodge, 90 Warwick Road, Carlisle, Cumbria, CA1 1JU.
Actual grid ref: NY407558
Grades: ETC 4 Diamond, AA 3 Diamond
Tel: **01228 529842** Mr Hendrie.
D: £15.00-£25.00 **S:** £20.00-£30.00.
Open: All Year
Beds: 2F 1D 2T 1S
Baths: 6 En 1 Sh
🛇 🅿 (6) 🖵 🕇 ✕ 🛒 ▥ Ⓥ 🛇 🌣
Friendly family-run guest house in comfortable Victorian town house in conservation area. Spacious rooms all fully ensuite with satellite TV, welcome tray, hairdryer and clock radio. Large breakfasts. 5 minutes' walk from station and city centre. Evening meals by prior arrangement. Private car park.

D = Price range per person sharing in a double room

---

ockcliffe 11

ational Grid Ref: NY3561

◁ Metal Bridge Inn

etal Bridge House, Metal Bridge,
ockcliffe, Carlisle, Cumbria,
6 4HG.
ctual grid ref: NY356649
 country, close to M6/A74,
ality accommodation, friendly
elcome.
el: **01228 674695** Mr Rae.
: £16.00-£18.00 **S:** £20.00-£22.00.
pen: All Year (not Xmas)
eds: 1D 2T
aths: 1 Sh
🅿 (6) 🖵 🕇 🛒 ▥ Ⓥ 🌣 🛇

Please don't camp on *anyone's* land ithout first obtaining their permission.

All details shown are as supplied by B&B owners in Autumn 2000.

Stanwix 12

National Grid Ref: NY3957

🍴 ◁ Cumbria Park Hotel

No. 1, 1 Etterby Street, Stanwix,
Carlisle, Cumbria, CA3 9JB.
Homely accommodation in easy reach of Hadrian's Wall & Scotland lakes.
Grades: ETC 3 Diamond
Tel: **01228 547285**
Ms Nixon.
D: £17.00-£20.00 **S:** £17.00-£20.00.
Open: All Year (not Xmas/ New Year)
Beds: 1D 2S
🛇 (4) 🅿 (1) 🖵 ✕ 🛒 ▥ Ⓥ 🛇 🌣

Always telephone to get directions to the B&B - you will save time!

Craighead, 6 Hartington Place, Carlisle, Cumbria, CA1 1HL.
Actual grid ref: NY405559
Grades: ETC 3 Diamond
Tel: **01228 596767** Mrs Smith.
D: £17.00 **S:** £16.00.
Open: All Year (not Xmas)
Beds: 1F 2D 1T 1S
Baths: 1 En 2 Sh
🛇 🖳 🏋 👗 🛒 ⅧⅢ ⚥ ✓ ♻
You will receive a warm welcome at Craighead, a Grade II Listed spacious Victorian town house with comfortable rooms and original features. CTV, tea/coffee tray in all rooms. Minutes' walk to city centre bus and rail stations and all amenities. Friendly personal service.

Cherry Grove, 87 Petteril Street, Carlisle, Cumbria, CA1 2AW.
Lovely red brick building close to golf club and town.
Grades: AA 3 Diamond
Tel: **01228 541942**
Mr & Mrs Houghton.
D: £17.50-£20.00 **S:** £20.00-£30.00.
Open: All Year
Beds: 3F 2D **Baths:** 5 En
🛇 🖳 (3) ✓ 🖵 🏋 ⅧⅢ Ⅴ ⅰ ✓ ♻

Angus Hotel & Almonds Bistro, 14 Scotland Road, Stanwix, Carlisle, Cumbria, CA3 9DG.
Actual grid ref: NY400571
Grades: AA 4 Diamond
Tel: **01228 523546** Mr Webster.
Fax no: 01228 531895
D: £20.00-£27.00 **S:** £26.00-£42.00.
Open: All Year
Beds: 4F 3D 4T 3S
Baths: 11 En 3 Sh
🛇 🖳 (6) 🖵 🏋 🏋 👗 ⅧⅢ Ⅴ ⅰ ✓ ♻
Victorian town house, foundations on Hadrian's Wall. Excellent food, Les Routiers Awards, local cheeses, home baked bread. Genuine warm welcome from owners. Licensed, draught beer, lounge, meeting room, internet cafe, direct dial telephones, secure garaging. Group rates for cyclists available.

Avondale, 3 St Aidans Road, Carlisle, Cumbria, CA1 1LT.
Attractive comfortable Edwardian house. Quiet central position convenient M6 J43.
Grades: ETC 4 Diamond
Tel: **01228 523012** (also fax no)
Mr & Mrs Hayes.
D: £20.00-£20.00 **S:** £20.00-£40.00.
Open: All Year (not Xmas)
Beds: 1D 2T
Baths: 1 En 1 Pr
🛇 🖳 (3) ✓ 🖵 🏋 👗 ⅧⅢ Ⅴ ⅰ ✓ ♻

Dalroc, 411 Warwick Road, Carlisle, Cumbria, CA1 2RZ.
Small friendly house. Midway city centre and M6 motorway.
Tel: **01228 542805** Mrs Irving.
D: £16.00-£16.00 **S:** £16.00-£16.00.
Open: All Year (not Xmas/New Year)
Beds: 1T 1D 1S
🛇 (7) 🖳 🖵 🏋 👗 ⅧⅢ Ⅴ ⅰ ✓ ♻

Chatsworth Guest House, 22 Chatsworth Square, Carlisle, Cumbria, CA1 1HF.
City centre Grade II Listed building, close to all amenities.
Grades: ETC 3 Diamond
Tel: **01228 524023** (also fax no)
Mrs Mackin.
D: £19.00-£22.00 **S:** £25.00-£25.00.
Open: All Year (not Xmas)
Beds: 1F 1D 2T 1S
Baths: 5 En
🛇 🖳 (2) ✓ 🖵 👗 ⅧⅢ Ⅴ

Kingstown Hotel, 246 Kingstown Road, Carlisle, CA3 0DE.
Grades: AA 3 Diamond
Tel: **01228 515292** (also fax no)
Mrs Marshall.
D: £23.50 **S:** £35.00-£40.00.
Open: All Year
Beds: 1F 4D 2T
Baths: 7 En
🛇 🖳 (14) 🖵 🏋 🏋 👗 ⅧⅢ 🔥 Ⅴ ✓ ♻
Just off the M6 (Jct. 44) we are a licensed hotel providing high-quality accommodation. You will find a friendly and relaxed atmosphere, freshly-prepared cuisine and fine wine at reasonable prices. A good base to explore Cumbria, Northumbria, Lake District, Scotland

Corner House Hotel & Bar, 4 Grey Street, Carlisle, CA1 2JP.
Grades: ETC 3 Diamond
Tel: **01228 533239**
Mrs Anderson.
Fax no: 01228 546628
D: £17.50-£22.00
S: £20.00-£30.00.
Open: All Year
Beds: 3F 4D 4T 3S
Baths: All En
🛇 🖳 🏋 🏋 👗 ⅧⅢ 🔥 Ⅴ ⅰ ✓ ♻
Refurbished family run hotel. All rooms ensuite., colour TV, phones, tea/coffee, radio, toiletries etc. Cosy bar, Sky TV lounge, games room, easy access city centre, bus/train. Base for golf, walking, cycling, touring the Lakes, Roman Wall, Carlisle/ Settle line etc.

All cycleways are popular: you are well-advised to book ahead

---

Ashleigh House, 46 Victoria Place, Carlisle, Cumbria, CA1 1EX.
Beautifully decorated town house. Two minutes from city centre.
Grades: ETC 4 Diamond
Tel: **01228 521631**
Mr Davies.
D: £19.00-£22.50 **S:** £25.00-£30.00.
Open: All Year (not Xmas/New Year)
Beds: 3F 1T 2D 1S
Baths: 7 En
🛇 (5) 🖵 👗 ⅧⅢ Ⅴ

Cornerways Guest House, 107 Warwick Road, Carlisle, Cumbria, CA1 1EA.
Large Victorian town house.
Grades: ETC 4 Diamond
Tel: **01228 521733**
Mrs Fisher.
D: £14.00-£18.00 **S:** £16.00-£18.00
Open: All Year (not Xmas)
Beds: 2F 1D 4T 3S
Baths: 3 En 2 Sh
🛇 🖳 (4) 🖵 🏋 🏋 👗 ⅧⅢ Ⅴ ⅰ ✓ ♻

Courtfield Guest House, 169 Warwick Road, Carlisle, Cumbria, CA1 1LP.
Short walk to historic city centre. Close to M6, J43.
Grades: ETC 4 Diamond
Tel: **01228 522767**
Mrs Dawes.
D: £18.00-£22.00 **S:** £25.00.
Open: All Year (not Xmas)
Beds: 1F 2D 2T
Baths: 5 En
🛇 🖳 (4) ✓ 🖵 👗 ⅧⅢ Ⅴ ♻

East View Guest House, 110 Warwick Road, Carlisle, Cumbria, CA1 1JU.
Actual grid ref: NY407560
10 minutes' walking distance from city centre, railway station and restaurants.
Grades: ETC 3 Diamond, AA 3 Diamond, RAC 3 Diamond
Tel: **01228 522112** (also fax no)
Mrs Glease.
D: £18.00-£20.00 **S:** £20.00-£25.00
Open: All Year (not Xmas)
Beds: 3F 2D 1T 1S
Baths: 7 En
🛇 🖳 (4) ✓ 🖵 👗 ⅧⅢ Ⅴ ✓ ♻

Cambro House, 173 Warwick Road, Carlisle, Cumbria, CA1 1LP.
Grades: AA 3 Diamond
Tel: **01228 543094** (also fax no)
Mr & Mrs Mawson.
D: £17.00-£20.00 **S:** £20.00-£25.00
Open: All Year
Beds: 2D 1T
Baths: 3 En
🖳 (2) ✓ 🖵 👗 ⅧⅢ Ⅴ ⅰ ✓ ♻
Guests can expect warm hospitality and friendly service at this attractively decorated and well-maintained guest house. Each ensuite bedroom includes TV, clock, radio, hairdryer and welcome tray. Private off-road parking available, non-smoking, close to golf course.

Please don't camp

on *anyone's* land

without first obtaining

their permission.

Hesket Newmarket   14

National Grid Ref: NY3338

▲ *Hudscales Camping Barn,*
Hudscales, Hesket Newmarket,
Wigton, Cumbria, CA7 8JZ.
Actual grid ref: NY332375
Tel: **017687 72645**
Adults: £3.35
Part of group of traditional farm
buildings situated at 1,000 ft on
northernmost edge of Lakeland
Fells. ADVANCE BOOKING
ESSENTIAL.

Newlands Grange, Hesket
Newmarket, Caldbeck, Wigton,
Cumbria, CA7 8HP.
Comfortable, oak beamed
farmhouse offering all home
cooking. All welcome.
Tel: **016974 78676**
Mrs Studholme.
D: £16.50-£19.50
S: £16.50-£19.50.
Open: All Year (not Xmas)
Beds: 1F 1D 1T 1S
Baths: 1 En 1 Sh
🛇 🅿 ⛁ 🛏 ✕ 🛋 ▥ 🎬 ▮ ⌇ 🚲

Caldbeck   15

National Grid Ref: NY3239

⋈ ◁ Oddfellow Arm

The Briars, Friar Row, Caldbeck,
Wigton, Cumbria, CA7 8DS.
Actual grid ref: NY3339
In Caldbeck village, right on
Cumbria Way. 2 mins' walk pub.
Grades: ETC 3 Diamond
Tel: **016974 78633** Mrs Coulthard.
D: £18.50-£20.00 **S:** £18.50-£20.00.
Open: All Year (not Xmas)
Beds: 1D 1T 1S
Baths: 1 En 1 Sh
🅿 (4) ⛁ ⛁ 🛏 🛋 ▥ 🎬 ⌇ 🚲

Whelpo   16

National Grid Ref: NY3039

Swaledale Watch, Whelpo,
Caldbeck, Wigton, Cumbria,
CA7 8HQ.
Actual grid ref: NY309397
Enjoy great comfort, excellent
home cooking, warm friendly
farmhouse welcome.
Tel: **016974 78409** (also fax no)
Mrs Savage.
D: £17.50-£20.50
S: £18.50-£25.00.
Open: All Year (not Xmas)
Beds: 2F 2D 1T
Baths: 4 En 1 Pr
🛇 🅿 (10) ⛁ ✕ 🛋 ▥ 🎬 ▮ ⌇ 🚲

D = Price range per person
sharing in a double room

Bassenthwaite   17

National Grid Ref: NY2332

⋈ ◁ Sun Inn

Parkergate, Bassenthwaite,
Keswick, Cumbria, CA12 4QG.
Actual grid ref: NY234303
Wonderful views of mountains and
lake. Cosy. Tranquil and relaxing.
Tel: **017687 76376**
Mr & Mrs Phillips.
Fax no: 017687 76911
D: £18.00-£25.00 **S:** £25.00-£30.00.
Open: All year (not Xmas)
Beds: 1F 2D 1T 1Pr
🛇 (5) 🅿 (4) ⛁ 🛏 ✕ 🛋 ▥ 🎬 ▮ ⌇
🚲

Bassenthwaite Hall Farm,
Bassenthwaite, Keswick, Cumbria,
CA12 4QP.
Charming, olde worlde, farmhouse
- excellent accommodation. By a
stream with ducks!
Tel: **017687 76393** (also fax no)
Mrs Trafford.
D: £16.00-£20.00 **S:** £25.00-£30.00.
Open: All Year
Beds: 1D 1T
Baths: 2 Sh
🛇 (10) 🅿 (4) ⛁ 🛋 ▥ 🎬 ▮ ⌇

Chapel Farm, Bassenthwaite Lake,
Bassenthwaite, Keswick, Cumbria,
CA12 4QH.
Working family farm, friendly
accommodation, good home
cooking.
Tel: **017687 76495** Mrs Fell.
D: £15.00-£17.00 **S:** £15.00-£17.00.
Open: All Year
Beds: 1T 1D
Baths: 1 Sh
🛇 🅿 (3) ⛁ 🛏 ✕ ▮ ⌇ 🚲

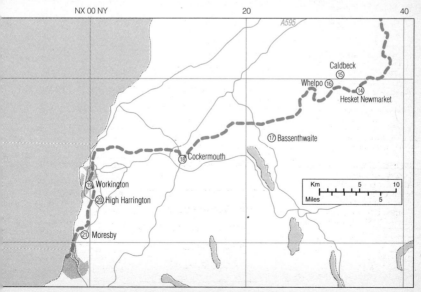

Mirkholme Farm, *Bassenthwaite, Keswick, Cumbria, CA12 4QX.*
Near the Cumbrian Way on the back 'o' Skiddaw. Friendly.
Tel: **016973 71333** Mrs Todd.
D: £16.00-£17.00 **S:** £16.00-£17.00.
Open: All Year
Beds: 1F 1D **Baths:** 1 Sh
🛇 🄿 ☐ ⛏ ✕ ♨ Ⅴ ▮ ∥ ♻

Willow Cottage, *Bassenthwaite, Keswick, Cumbria, CA12 4QP.*
Peaceful village location, log fires, stencilling, patchwork, beams, flagged floors.
Tel: **017687 76440** Mrs Beaty.
D: £20.00-£22.50 **S:** £25.00-£30.00.
Open: All Year (not Xmas)
Beds: 1D 1T **Baths:** 2 En
🄿 (2) ⅙ ♨ Ⅲ. Ⅴ ▮ ∥

Cockermouth 18

National Grid Ref: NY1230

🍴 🍺 Black Bull, Brown Cow, Bitter End, Old Post House, Shepherds Hotel

▲ **Cockermouth Youth Hostel,**
Double Mills, Cockermouth, Cumbria, CA13 0DS.
Actual grid ref: NY118298
Tel: **01900 822561**
Under 18: £5.75 **Adults:** £8.50
Self-catering facilities, Showers, Wet weather shelter, Lounge, Drying room, Cycle store, Parking, Evening meal at 7.00pm, No smoking, WC, Kitchen facilities, Credit cards accepted
Simple accommodation in restored C17th watermill, convenient for northern and western fells and Cumbrian coastline.

The Rook Guest House, *9 Castlegate, Cockermouth, Cumbria, CA13 9EU.*
Actual grid ref: NY122307
Cosy C17th town house. Spiral staircase. Convenient for all amenities.
Tel: **01900 828496** Mrs Waters.
D: £16.00-£18.00 **S:** £20.00-£20.00.
Open: All Year (not Xmas)
Beds: 2D 1T **Baths:** 1 En 1 Pr 1 Sh
🛇 (5) ⅙ ☐ ♨ Ⅲ. Ⅴ ▮ ∥ ♻

Shepherds Hotel, *Egremont Road, Cockermouth, Cumbria, CA13 0QX.*
Modern hotel with views towards Lake District, close to gem town of Cockermouth.
Tel: **01900 822673** (also fax no) Campbell.
D: £18.75-£20.00 **S:** £37.50-£40.00.
Open: All Year (not Xmas)
Beds: 4D 9T
Baths: 13 En
🛇 🄿 (99) ⅙ ☐ ✕ ♨ Ⅲ. ♿ Ⅴ ▮ ∥ ♻

Albany House, *Wordsworth Terrace, Cockermouth, Cumbria, CA13 9AH.*
Beautiful Victorian guest house, stripped pine doors and a warm welcome.
Tel: **01900 825630**
Mr Nichol.
D: £16.00-£16.00 **S:** £16.00-£16.00.
Open: All Year
Beds: 1F 2D 2T 2S
Baths: 1 Pr 1 Sh
🛇 ⅙ ☐ ♨ Ⅲ. Ⅴ ▮ ∥ ♻

Benson Court Cottage, *10 St Helen's Street, Cockermouth, Cumbria, CA13 9HX.*
Town centre 1727 cottage. Commercial/ tourist guests welcome. Generous breakfasts.
Tel: **01900 822303**
Mrs Townley.
D: £15.00-£20.00 **S:** £15.00-£22.00.
Open: All Year
Beds: 1F 1D
🛇 (6) ⅙ ☐ ♨ Ⅲ. Ⅴ ▮ ∥ ♻

Workington 19

National Grid Ref: NX9927

🍴 🍺 Ye Old Sportsman

Fernleigh House, *15 High Seaton, Workington, Cumbria, CA14 1PE.*
Georgian house, lovely garden, warm and friendly welcome, Excellent breakfasts.
Tel: **01900 605811**
Ms Bewsher.
D: £17.00-£45.00 **S:** £17.00-£17.00.
Open: All Year
Beds: 1F 2T 1S
🛇 🄿 ☐ ♨ Ⅲ. Ⅴ ▮ ∥ 🚲

Silverdale, *17 Banklands, Workington, Cumbria, CA14 3EL.*
Large Victorian private house. Near start C2C cycleway and lakes.
Tel: **01900 61887** Mrs Hardy.
D: £11.00-£13.50 **S:** £12.50-£15.00.
Open: All Year (not Xmas)
Beds: 2T 2S
Baths: 2 Sh
🛇 ☐ ⛏ ♨ Ⅲ. Ⅴ

High Harrington 20

National Grid Ref: NY0025

🍴 🍺 Galoping Horse

Riversleigh Guest House, *39 Primrose Terrace, High Harrington, Workington, Cumbria, CA14 5PS.*
Riverside house overlooking gardens, 5 mins from station and marina.
Tel: **01946 830267**
Mrs Davies.
D: £15.00-£20.00 **S:** £15.00-£20.00
Open: All Year
Beds: 1F 1T 1D
Baths: 2 En 1 Pr
🛇 (5) 🄿 (8) ⅙ ☐ ♨ Ⅲ. Ⅴ ▮ ∥ ♻

Moresby 21

National Grid Ref: NX9921

🍴 🍺 Moresby Hall, Howgate Inn

Moresby Hall, *Moresby, Whitehaven, Cumbria, CA28 6PJ.*
Tel: **01946 696317**
Mrs Saxon.
Fax no: 01946 692666
D: £22.50-£32.50
S: £25.00-£35.00.
Open: All Year
Beds: 1F 1T 2D
Baths: 2 En 2 Pr
🛇 (10) 🄿 (6) ⅙ ☐ ✕ ♨ Ⅲ. Ⅴ ▮ ∥ ♻
A Grade I Listed character building. Spacious and well equipped rooms. Semi-rural location and 2 acres of walled gardens. Lakes, fells, cultural & tourist locations. Delicious food in an elegant setting. Licensed. A warm welcome to our relaxing family home.

BRITAIN: BED & BREAKFAST

The essential guide to B&Bs in England, Scotland & Wales

The Bed & Breakfast is one of the great British institutions.
Like Fish & Chips, it's known by people around the world. But
you don't have to be a tourist to enjoy this traditional
accommodation. Whether you're travelling, on holiday, away
on business or just escaping from it all, the B&B is a great
value alternative to expensive hotels and a world away from
camping and caravanning.

Stilwell's Britain: Bed & Breakfast 2001 is the most
comprehensive guide of its kind, containing over 7,750 entries
listed by country, county and location, in England, Scotland
and Wales. Each entry includes room rates, facilities, Tourist
Board grades and a brief description of the B&B and its
location and surroundings.

Stilwell's Britain: Bed & Breakfast 2001: The indispensable
guide to great value accommodation:

Private houses, country halls, farms, cottages, inns, small
hotels and guest houses

Over 7,750 entries
Average price £19 per person per night
All official grades shown
Local maps
Pubs serving hot evening meals shown
Tourist Information Centres listed
Handy size for easy packing

£9.95 from all good bookstores (ISBN 1-900861-22-4) or
£11.95 (inc p&p) from Stilwell Publishing, 59 Charlotte Road,
London EC2A 3QW (020 7739 7179)

South Downs Way

At 96 miles, this route is shorter than many featured in this book. However, designed as a National Trail for walkers, it is routed mainly along a chalk track, which can get muddy, and involves a considerable amount of climbing, so should only really be undertaken on an all terrain bicycle. It runs west along the ridge of the great chalk escarpment of the South Downs, from Eastbourne in East Sussex to Winchester in Hampshire. The views from the path, southwards out to sea and northwards over the Sussex Weald, are stunning.

The route is waymarked along its whole length by the National Trail acorn symbol, and, by virtue of the fact that these walking routes are long-established by comparison with Britain's still relatively nascent cycleways, is very well served by thoroughgoing **guide books**. You will find everything you need (including mapping) in the *National Trail Guide - South Downs Way* by Paul Millmore (ISBN 1 85410 099 8), published by Aurum Press in association with the Countryside Commission and Ordnance Survey @ £10.99. This book includes a list of cycle repair/hire shops on or near to the route; and a general list of facilities available at locations along the way.

Other guides are *Along the South Downs Way to Winchester* by the Society of Sussex Downsmen, available from the RA's National Office at 1/5 Wandsworth Road, London SW8 2XX, tel 020-7339 8500, @ £5.00 (+£1.00 p&p);

A Guide to the South Downs Way by Miles Jebb (ISBN 09 471170 4), published by Constable & Co Ltd @ £10.95;

and *South Downs Way & The Downs Link* by Kev Reynolds (ISBN 1 85284 023 4), published by Cicerone Press and available from the publishers at 2 Police Square, Milnthorpe, Cumbria LA7 7PY, tel 01539 562069, @ £5.99 (+75p p&p).

Maps: Ordnance Survey 1:50,000 Landranger series: 185, 197, 198, 199

Trains: Services from London go to Eastbourne, Lewes and Brighton (all from Victoria) and to Petersfield and Winchester (from Waterloo). Many other places along or near to the route are covered by local services.

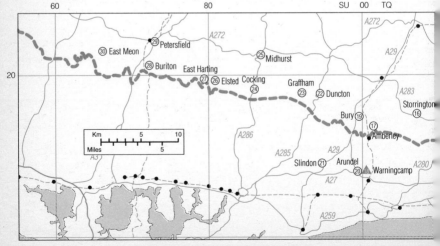

Eastbourne 1

National Grid Ref: TQ5900

🍴🍺 The Marine, Town House, Castle Inn, Lamb Inn, The Beach, The Waterfront, The Pilot, The Alexander

▲ *Eastbourne Youth Hostel,*
East Dean Road, Eastbourne, East Sussex, BN20 8ES.
Actual grid ref: TV588990
Tel: **01323 721081**
Under 18: £6.90 **Adults:** £10.00
Self-catering facilities, Showers, Lounge, Dining room, Drying room, Cycle store, Parking Limited, No smoking, WC, Kitchen facilities, Credit cards accepted
Former golf clubhouse on South Downs, 450 ft above sea level with sweeping views across Eastbourne & Pevensey Bay.

Heatherdene Hotel, 26-28 Elms Avenue, Eastbourne, E. Sussex, BN21 3DN.
Grades: ETC 3 Diamond
Tel: **01323 723598** (also fax no)
Mrs Mockford.
D: £17.00-£45.00 **S:** £16.00-£25.00
Open: All Year
Beds: 1F 4D 8T 3S
Baths: 6 En 3 Sh
🛏🍴🐾✗🍽🌐&♿Ⓥ
You will find good food and comfortable rooms at the Heatherdene. This family-run licensed hotel, set in a pleasant avenue, is close to the sea front and town centre. Train and coach stations are nearby, as are the theatres.

D = Price range per person sharing in a double room

Eastbourne to Alfriston

Eastbourne is a typical English seaside resort, with a three-mile seafront and a Victorian pier. One feature worth a mention is the Trower Gallery and Museum, which exhibits contemporary art. The initial stretch of the way skirts Paradise Wood and climbs gently to the top of the Downs, continuing to the village of **Jevington**. (The alternative route over Beachy Head and the Seven Sisters is for walkers only and cannot be cycled.) A little way off the path beyond Jevington, the Lullington Heath National Nature Reserve can be reached by a bridleway. At **Wilmington**, a little way off the route, stands a ruined Benedictine priory and a twelfth-century church, but more renowned is the ancient hillside carving, the Long Man. This massive representation of a figure bearing a staff in each hand had long faded until the Victorian restoration. It is likely they modified the image so as not to offend the sensibilities of the period (compare the Cerne Giant in Dorset), and as such it was not so much a restoration as a desecration, which begs the question, why did they bother restoring it at all? Close by lies the old smuggling village of **Alfriston** with a number of centuries-old inns and an untouched fourteenth-century church known as 'the cathedral of the Downs', and beyond it the noted viewpoint at Firle Beacon.

Innisfree House, 130a Royal Parade, Eastbourne, East Sussex, BN22 7JY.
Tel: **01323 646777** (also fax no)
Mrs Petrie.
D: £19.00-£20.00 **S:** £25.00-£30.00.
Open: All Year (not Xmas)
Beds: 1F 1D 1T
Baths: 3 En
🛏✗🍴🌐🍽Ⓥ🚲
Small family-run B&B on seafront, close to amenities, refurbished to high standards. Exclusive location with sea views, easy parking on road outside. Motorcycle storage. Stay a day or stay a week, your comfort & praise we aim to seek.

High season,

bank holidays and

special events mean

low availability

everywhere.

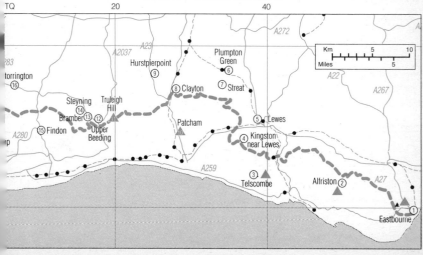

Ambleside Private Hotel, *24 Elms Avenue, Eastbourne, E. Sussex,* BN21 3DN.
Tel: **01323 724991**
Mr Pattenden.
D: £18.00-£18.00
S: £18.00-£25.00.
Open: All Year
Beds: 4D 4T 2S
Baths: 2 Sh 2 En
⌷ ⚲ ✕ ⚲ Ⅲ Ⅴ ∅ ♺
Situated on quiet avenue adjacent to seafront, pier, town centre, theatres, convenient for railway and coach stations. Short distance from South Downs Way, Wealdway. Colour TV in bedrooms. Compliant with environmental and fire regulations.

Sheldon Hotel, *9-11 Burlington Place, Eastbourne, East Sussex,* BN21 4AS.
Situated within a few minutes walk of sea front, theatres. Licensed.
Tel: **01323 724120**
Fax no: 01323 430406
D: £24.00-£27.00
S: £24.00-£27.00.
Open: All Year
Beds: 4F 6T 8D 6S
Baths: 24 En
♺ ▣ ⌷ ⚲ ✕ ⚲ Ⅲ Ⅴ ∅

Camberley Hotel, *27-29 Elms Avenue, Eastbourne, E. Sussex,* BN21 3DN.
Tel: **01323 723789**
D: £18.00-£21.00
S: £18.00-£21.00.
Open: Mar to Oct
Beds: 4F 3D 3T 2S
Baths: 7 En 2 Sh
♺ ▣ (3) ⌷ ✕ ⚲ Ⅴ ▪ ♺
Situated in a pleasant avenue close to town centre, sea front and all amenities. Licensed, ensuite, tea-making, colour TV in bedrooms. English breakfast.

The Manse, *7 Dittons Road, Eastbourne, East Sussex,* BN21 1DW.
Tel: **01323 737851** Mrs Walker.
D: £15.00-£20.00 **S:** £20.00-£25.00.
Open: All Year (not Xmas)
Beds: 1F 2T **Baths:** 2 En 1 Pr
♺ (8) ▣ (1) ⌷ ⚲ Ⅲ Ⅴ ▪ ∅ ♺
Originally a Presbyterian manse, this character house is located in a quiet area yet within 5 minutes' walk of the town centre with its shops, restaurants and theatres. Seafront, South Downs, castles and Downland villages nearby.

Cherry Tree Hotel, *15 Silverdale Rd, Eastbourne, E. Sussex,* BN20 7AJ.
Actual grid ref: TV612982
Award-winning family-run hotel, close to sea front, downlands and theatres.
Grades: ETC 4 Diamond, Silver
Tel: **01323 722406** Mr Henley.
Fax no: 01323 648838
D: £26.00-£33.00 **S:** £26.00-£33.00.
Open: All Year
Beds: 1F 3D 4T 2S
Baths: 10 En
♺ (7) ⌷ ✕ ⚲ Ⅲ Ⅴ ▪

The Grid Reference beneath the location heading is for the village or town - *not* for individual houses, which are shown (where supplied) in each entry itself.

All rates are subject to alteration at the owners' discretion.

Southcroft Hotel, *15 South Cliff Avenue, Eastbourne, E. Sussex,* BN20 7AH.
Actual grid ref: TV609979
Friendly, family-run, non-smoking hotel. Close to Downs, sea and theatre.
Grades: ETC 4 Diamond
Tel: **01323 729071** Mrs Skriczka.
D: £25.00-£28.00 **S:** £25.00-£28.00.
Open: All Year
Beds: 3D 2T 1S **Baths:** 6 En
✗ ⌷ ✕ ⚲ Ⅲ Ⅴ ∅

Edelweiss Hotel, *10-12 Elms Avenue, Eastbourne, E. Sussex,* BN21 3DN.
Central family-run hotel just off sea front. Comfortable and welcoming.
Grades: ETC 3 Diamond
Tel: **01323 732071** (also fax no)
Mr & Mrs Butler.
D: £16.00-£20.00 **S:** £16.00-£25.00.
Open: All Year
Beds: 1F 6D 5T 2S
Baths: 3 En 4 Sh
♺ ⌷ ✕ ⚲ Ⅲ Ⅴ ▪ ∅ ♺

Cromwell Private Hotel, *23 Cavendish Place, Eastbourne, E. Sussex,* BN21 3EJ.
Family run hotel in Victorian town house (1851). Centrally located.
Grades: ETC 4 Diamond
Tel: **01323 725288** (also fax no)
Mr & Mrs Millar.
D: £19.00-£24.00 **S:** £19.00-£23.00.
Open: Easter to Nov
Beds: 2F 3D 3T 3S **Baths:** 5 Pr 2 Sh
♺ ⌷ ✕ ⚲ Ⅲ Ⅴ ▪

Alfriston to Ditchling Beacon

After crossing one of the many English rivers called Ouse into the village of **Southease**, whose church has a circular Saxon tower, a short detour will take you into the pretty town of **Lewes,** site of the 1264 Battle of Lewes between Henry III and Simon de Montfort, and the burning of the Protestant Lewes Martyrs in 1556. Here in the eighteenth century lived the great progressive writer Thomas Paine. Predominantly Georgian, there are older parts including the Norman castle. Several miles after Southease you come to **Ditchling Beacon**, site of an Iron Age fort and close to a Sussex Wildlife Trust nature reserve. A short detour north leads to **Ditchling**, where you will find a house that belonged to Anne of Cleves, who was, for six months in 1540, the fourth wife of Henry VIII, who fell in love with Holbein's portrait of her only to be disappointed with the real thing. I can't imagine she was less disappointed herself, but at least she fared better than Anne Boleyn and Catherine Howard, in that she came out of it with her neck intact (and, indeed, outlived Henry by ten years and Catherine Parr, his last wife, by nine).

Courtlands Hotel, *68 Royal Parade, Eastbourne, E. Sussex,* *BN22 7AQ.*
Seafront position, business/touring base.
Tel: **01323 721068**
D: £20.00-£25.00 **S:** £20.00-£25.00.
Open: All Year
Beds: 3F 2D 1T 2S
Baths: 3 En 1 Pr
⛷ 🅿 (2) ◻ ✕ 🛁 🎺 Ⅴ ₤ ⚕ ✦

La Mer Guest House, *7 Marine Road, Eastbourne, E. Sussex,* *BN22 7AU.*
Just 50 yards from Eastbourne's beautiful seafront and beach easy access to South Downs
Tel: **01323 724926** Mrs Byrne.
D: £18.00-£24.00 **S:** £18.00-£24.00.
Open: May to Sep
Beds: 2D 2T 2S
Baths: 2 En
⛷ (14) 🅿 ◻ ✕ 🛁 🎺 Ⅴ ₤

Channel View Hotel, *57 Royal Parade, Eastbourne, E. Sussex,* *BN22 7AQ.*
A friendly family-run seafront hotel situated opposite the Redoubt Gardens.
Tel: **01323 736730**
Fax no: 01323 644299
D: £17.00-£22.00 **S:** £22.00-£32.00.
Open: All Year (not Xmas)
Beds: 1F 2D 3T 2S
Baths: 4 En 1 Sh
⛷ ◻ 🎺 ✕ 🛁 🎺 Ⅴ

Beachy Rise, *20 Beachy Head Road, Eastbourne, E. Sussex,* *BN20 7QN.*
In Meads village near Beachy Head and sea and university. Ensuite bedrooms.
Tel: **01323 639171**
D: £22.00-£28.00 **S:** £25.00-£29.00.
Open: All Year
Beds: 1F 4D 1T
Baths: 6 En
⛷ (1) ◻ 🛁 🎺 Ⅴ ₤ ⚕ ✦ ⚲

Downland Hotel, *37 Lewes Road, Eastbourne, East Sussex, BN21 2BU.*
Charming small hotel, ideally located for all main amenities and commercial centre.
Tel: **01323 732689**
Fax no: 01323 720321
D: £25.00-£37.50
S: £30.00-£40.00.
Open: All Year
Beds: 2F 7D 2T 1S
Baths: 12 En
🅿 (9) ⚡ ◻ ✕ 🛁 🎺 Ⅴ ₤ ⚕

Pay B&Bs by
cash or cheque and
be prepared to
pay up front.

Alfriston 2

National Grid Ref: TQ5103

🍴 🍺 Wingrove Inn, Ye Olde Smuggler's Inn, The George

🔺 **Alfriston Youth Hostel,** *Frog Firle, Alfriston, Polegate, East Sussex, BN26 5TT.*
Actual grid ref: TQ518019
Tel: **01323 870423**
Under 18: £6.90 **Adults:** £10.00
Self-catering facilities, Showers, Wet weather shelter, Lounge, Drying room, Parking, Evening meal at 6.30pm, WC, Kitchen facilities, Breakfast available, Credit cards accepted
A comfortable Sussex country house dating from 1530, set in Cuckmere Valley with views over river and Litlington.

Meadowbank, *Sloe Lane, Alfriston, East Sussex, BN26 5UR.*
Tel: **01323 870742** Mrs Petch.
D: £20.00-£25.00 **S:** £30.00-£35.00.
Open: All Year (not Xmas/New Year)
Beds: 1T 2D
Baths: 1 En 2 Sh
🅿 (4) ⚡ ◻ 🎺 🛁 🎺 ♿ Ⅴ ⚕ ✦ ⚲
The beautiful private dwelling in tranquil setting, offers views of Cuckmere Valley and South Downs. only 3 minutes walk village centre. Ideal for walkers/cyclists. Private car park. Lovely gardens and conservatory in which to relax. Delicious English breakfast.

Dacres, *Alfriston, Polegate, East Sussex, BN26 5TP.*
Country cottage. Beautiful gardens. Near South Downs Way, Glyndebourne, Seven Sisters.
Tel: **01323 870447**
Mrs Embry.
D: £25.00-£25.00
S: £40.00.
Open: All Year
Beds: 1T
Baths: 1 Pr
🅿 (1) ⚡ ◻ 🛁 🎺 ♿ Ⅴ ⚲

Telscombe 3

National Grid Ref: TQ4003

🔺 **Telscombe Youth Hostel,** *Bank Cottages, Telscombe, Lewes, East Sussex, BN7 3HZ.*
Actual grid ref: TQ405033
Tel: **01273 301357**
Under 18: £6.50
Adults: £9.25
Self-catering facilities, Showers, Lounge, Drying room, Cycle store, Parking By arrangement, No smoking, WC, Kitchen facilities
Three 200-year-old cottages combined into one hostel, next to the Norman church in a small unspoilt village in Sussex Downs Area of Outstanding Natural Beauty.

Order your
packed lunches the
evening before you
need them.
Not at breakfast!

Kingston near Lewes 4

National Grid Ref: TQ3908

🍴 🍺 The Juggs

Settlands, *Wellgreen Lane, Kingston near Lewes, Lewes, E Sussex, BN7 3NP.*
Actual grid ref: TQ398082
Grades: ETC 4 Diamond
Tel: **01273 472295** (also fax no)
Mrs Arlett.
D: £20.00-£25.00 **S:** £25.00-£27.50.
Open: All Year (not Xmas)
Beds: 1D 1T
Baths: 2 Sh
⛷ 🅿 (3) ⚡ ◻ 🛁 🎺 Ⅴ ₤ ⚕ ⚲
Swedish timber-framed house in picturesque down land village. Excellent walking, coast 6 miles. Friendly atmosphere, comfortable accommodation. Historic Lewes, Glyndebourne, ferries nearby.

Lewes 5

National Grid Ref: TQ4110

🍴 🍺 Royal Oak, Pelham Arms, Cock Inn, Steward's Enquiry, King's Head

Sussex Country Accommodation, *Crink House, Barcombe Mills, Lewes, E. Sussex, BN8 5BJ.*
Grades: ETC 4 Diamond, Silver
Tel: **01273 400625** Mrs Gaydon.
D: £25.00-£30.00 **S:** £30.00-£40.00.
Open: All Year (not Xmas)
Beds: 2D 1T
Baths: 3 En
⛷ 🅿 (10) ⚡ ◻ 🛁 🎺 Ⅴ
Victorian farmhouse with panoramic views. Welcoming rural family home, ideal base for exploring Sussex with its wealth of walks and attractions, castles, country houses, gardens, museums. Within reach Brighton, Eastbourne, Glyndebourne - self catering also available.

Many rates vary
according to season -
the lowest only are
shown here

Castle Banks Cottage, *4 Castle Banks, Lewes, E. Sussex, BN7 1UZ.* Beamed cottage, pretty garden, quiet lane, close to castle, shops, restaurants.
Tel: **01273 476291** (also fax no)
Mrs Wigglesworth.
D: £22.50-£22.50
S: £22.50-£30.00.
Open: All Year (not Xmas)
Beds: 1T 1S
Baths: 1 Sh
⛇ ⅍ ⌷ ⚲ ☕ ▥ ⚐ ⌁

Phoenix House, *23 Gundreda Road, Lewes, E Sussex, BN7 1PT.* Comfortable family home - quiet road - 5 minutes to town centre.
Tel: **01273 473250**
Mrs Greene.
D: £17.50-£22.50
S: £25.00-£25.00.
Open: All Year (not Xmas/New Year)
Beds: 1T 1D 1S
Baths: 1 Pr 1 Sh
⛇ ℗ (2) ⅍ ⌷ ⚲ ☕ ▥ ⚐ ⌁ ⚵

Normandy, *37 Houndean Rise, Lewes, East Sussex, BN7 1EQ.* Comfortable room in large detached family house, additional bed available, overlooking South Downs.
Tel: **01273 473853** (also fax no)
Mrs Kemp.
D: £22.00-£25.00 **S:** £30.00-£35.00.
Open: All Year (not Xmas)
Beds: 1D
Baths: 1 Pr
⛇ ⅍ ⌷ ⚲ ☕ ▥ ⌁ ⚵

Plumpton Green 6

National Grid Ref: TQ3616

⋈ ⚐ Winning Post

Farthings, *Station Road, Plumpton Green, Lewes, E. Sussex, BN7 3BY.* **Actual grid ref:** TQ365172
Relaxed, friendly atmosphere in village setting under South Downs.
Tel: **01273 890415**
Mrs Baker.
D: £20.00-£25.00
S: £22.00-£30.00.
Open: All Year (not Xmas)
Beds: 2D 1T
Baths: 1 En 1 Sh
⛇ (11) ℗ (4) ⅍ ⌷ ⋉ ✗ ⚲ ☕ ▥ ⌁

High season,
bank holidays and
special events mean
low availability
everywhere.

Always telephone
to get directions to
the B&B - you will
save time!

Streat 7

National Grid Ref: TQ3515

⋈ ⚐ The Bull

North Acres, *Streat, Hassocks, E. Sussex, BN6 8RX.* Unique Victorian country house in tiny hamlet near South Downs.
Tel: **01273 890278** (also fax no)
Eastwood.
D: £20.00-£20.00
S: £20.00-£25.00.
Open: All Year (not Xmas)
Beds: 2F 2T 1S
Baths: 3 Sh
⛇ ℗ (20) ⅍ ⌷ ⚲ ☕ ▥ ⚐ ⌁ ⚵

Clayton 8

National Grid Ref: TQ3014

⋈ ⚐ Jack & Jill

Dower Cottage, *Underhill Lane, Clayton, Hassocks, W. Sussex, BN6 9PL.* **Actual grid ref:** TQ309136
Tel: **01273 843363** Mrs Bailey.
Fax no: 01273 846503
D: £22.50-£30.00
S: £30.00-£50.00.
Open: All Year (not Xmas)
Beds: 2F 2D 1T 1S
Baths: 2 En 1 Sh
⛇ ℗ (8) ⅍ ⌷ ⚲ ⚐ ⌁ ⚵
Large country house in beautiful location overlooking the Sussex Weald. Ideal for walking, cycling, riding the South Downs yet only 15 mins from Brighton for nightlife. Library for guest use & colour TVs in all rooms. Peace & quiet away from city stress!

Hurstpierpoint 9

National Grid Ref: TQ2816

⋈ ⚐ The Pilgrim, The Goose

Wickham Place, *Wickham Drive, Hurstpierpoint, Hassocks, W. Sussex, BN6 9AP.* Large house in a lovely village just off the A23.
Tel: **01273 832172** Mrs Moore.
D: £22.50-£25.00
S: £30.00-£30.00.
Open: All Year (not Xmas)
Beds: 1D 2T
Baths: 1 Sh
⛇ ℗ (5) ⅍ ⌷ ⋉ ⚲ ☕ ▥

Patcham 10

National Grid Ref: TQ3008

▲ **Brighton Youth Hostel,** *Patcham Place, London Road, Patcham, Brighton, East Sussex, BN1 8YD.*
Actual grid ref: TQ300088
Tel: **01273 556196**
Under 18: £6.90 **Adults:** £10.00
Self-catering facilities, Television, Showers, Laundry facilities, Lounge, Games room, Security lockers, Cycle store, Evening meal at 6.30 to 7.30, Kitchen facilities, Breakfast available, Credit cards accepted
Splendid country house with Queen Anne front, on the edge of Brighton and the South Downs.

Truleigh Hill 11

National Grid Ref: TQ2210

▲ **Truleigh Hill Youth Hostel,** *Tottington Barn, Truleigh Hill, Shoreham-by-Sea, West Sussex, BN43 5FB.*
Actual grid ref: TQ220105
Tel: **01903 813419**
Under 18: £6.90 **Adults:** £10.00
Television, Showers, Showers, Lounge, Dining room, Cycle store, Parking, Evening meal at 7.00pm, No smoking, WC, Credit cards accepted
Modern hostel in the Sussex Downs Area of Outstanding Natural Beauty with conservation project and old dew pond in grounds.

Upper Beeding 12

National Grid Ref: TQ1910

The Rising Sun, *Upper Beeding, Steyning, W. Sussex, BN44 3TQ.* **Actual grid ref:** TQ197097
Tel: **01903 814424** Mr & Mrs Taylor-Mason.
D: £17.00-£17.00 **S:** £20.00-£20.00.
Open: All Year (not Xmas)
Beds: 2D 1T 2S **Baths:** 1 Sh
℗ (20) ⌷ ⋔ ✗ ⚲ ☕ ▥ ⚐ ⌁ ⚵
A delightful Georgian country inn, set amidst the South Downs. Tony & Sue offer a warm welcome, fine selection of real ales and traditional home-cooked food lunctime and evenings. Comfortable rooms, all with wash basin. Renowned full English breakfast.

Please respect
a B&B's wishes
regarding children,
animals & smoking.

Bramber 13

National Grid Ref: TQ1810

Castle Hotel, The Street, Bramber, Steyning, W. Sussex, BN44 3WE.
Actual grid ref: TQ189106
Pretty village, spacious characterful romantic friendly inn.
Tel: **01903 812102**
Mr & Mrs Mitchell.
Fax no: 01903 816711
D: £22.00-£30.00 **S:** £35.00-£40.00.
Open: All Year
Beds: 1F 6D 3T
Baths: 10 En
🛏 🅿 (15) ⅏ ⛌ 🗙 ≟ 🎹 🎖 🛊 🌲 ⅙ 🚲

Steyning 14

National Grid Ref: TQ1711

🍴 🍺 Star Inn, The Fountain, The Chequers

Wappingthorn Farmhouse, Horsham Road, Steyning, West Sussex, BN44 3AA.
Grades: ETC 4 Diamond
Tel: **01903 813236** Mr Shapland.
D: £20.00-£25.00 **S:** £27.50-£35.00.
Open: All Year
Beds: 1F 1T 1D 1S
Baths: 4 En
🛏 🅿 (8) ⅏ ⛌ 🎹
Traditional farmhouse, recently refurbished, set in 2 acres of gardens. Located within our family operated, 300 acre dairy farm. All rooms overlook fields and the South Downs. Includes breakfast. 10 miles Brighton. 8 miles Worthing. Steyning Village 1 mile.

5 Coxham Lane, Steyning, W. Sussex, BN44 3LG.
Comfortable house in quiet lane.
Tel: **01903 812286** Mrs Morrow.
D: £16.00-£16.00 **S:** £16.00-£16.00.
Open: All Year
Beds: 2T 1S
Baths: 1 Sh
🅿 (3) 🎠 ≟ 🎹 🎖 🛊 🌲 🌿

Sheppenstrete House, Sheep Pen Lane, Steyning, W. Sussex, BN44 3GP.
Charming, comfortable period house, hidden just off High Street.
Tel: **01903 813179** Mrs Wood.
Fax no: 01903 814400
D: £25.00-£30.00 **S:** £25.00-£40.00.
Open: All Year (not Xmas)
Beds: 1T 1S
🅿 (1) ⅏ ⛌ 🗙 ≟ 🎹 🎖 🛊 🌿

All rooms full and nowhere else to stay? Ask the owner if there's anywhere nearby

Findon 15

National Grid Ref: TQ1208

🍴 🍺 The Gun, Findon Manor, Black Horse

The Coach House, 41 High Street, Findon, Worthing, West Sussex, BN14 0SU.
Actual grid ref: TQ123084
Village location in South Downs. Excellent walks/cycling. Close to coast.
Tel: **01903 873924** Goble.
D: £19.50-£22.00 **S:** £25.00-£27.50.
Open: All Year
Beds: 1F 1T 1D
Baths: 3 En
🛏 🅿 (3) 🎠 🎠 ≟ 🎹 🎖 🌲

Findon Tower, Cross Lane, Findon, Worthing, W Sussex, BN14 0UG.
Actual grid ref: TQ123083
Elegant Edwardian country house, walking distance excellent village pubs/restaurants.
Tel: **01903 873870**
Mr & Mrs Smith.
D: £25.00-£30.00 **S:** £30.00-£40.00.
Open: All Year (not Xmas)
Beds: 2D 1T 1S
Baths: 3 En
🛏 🅿 (10) ⅏ ≟ 🎹 🎖 🌲 ⅙ 🌿

S = Price range for a single person in a room

D = Price range per person sharing in a double room

Storrington 16

National Grid Ref: TQ0814

🍴 🍺 Anchor Inn, Old Forge, New Moon

Willow Tree Cottage, Washington Road, Storrington, Pulborough, W. Sussex, RH20 4AF.
Actual grid ref: TQ104134
Welcoming, friendly, quiet. All rooms ensuite. Colour TV, tea-making facilities.
Tel: **01903 740835** Mrs Smith.
D: £20.00-£22.50 **S:** £25.00-£30.00.
Open: All Year (not Xmas)
Beds: 2D 1T
Baths: 3 Pr
🛏 🅿 (10) ⅏ ⛌ 🎠 ≟ 🎹 🎖 🌿

No 1, Lime Chase (off Fryern Road), Storrington, Pulborough, W. Sussex, RH20 4LX.
Actual grid ref: TQ089147
Award winning luxury accommodation in secluded village setting. Restaurants close by.
Grades: ETC 5 Diamond, Gold
Tel: **01903 740437** (also fax no)
Mrs Warton.
D: £32.50-£40.00 **S:** £45.00-£55.00.
Open: All Year
Beds: 1T 1D
Baths: 1 En 1 Pr
🛏 (10) 🅿 (5) ⅏ ⛌ 🎹 🎖 & 🛊 🌲 ⅙ 🌿

Ditchling Beacon to Buriton

After Ditchling Beacon you cross into West Sussex and come to **Pyecombe**, before passing Devil's Dyke, a deep valley formed in the Ice Age with an Iron Age fort, en route to **Upper Beeding**, with the Saxon Botolphs Church and a ruined Norman castle at Bramber nearby. A little after this the route joins the road between Worthing and Steyning and juts north before leaving the road and passing close to another Iron Age hill fort, Chanctonbury Ring, which is topped with a coronet of trees. Past Washington, the route leads to the village of **Amberley**, which has a twin-towered castle gatehouse and a number of attractive pubs, before passing between two chalk pits. The village hosts the Chalk Pits Museum, including a narrow-gauge quarry railway. After Amberley and **Houghton**, a detour along a bridleway is possible to **Bignor**, where there is a Roman villa with mosaic floors on show. The way now crosses Stane Street, the Roman route from London to Chichester, and there are magnificent views southwards to Chichester Cathedral and the sea. The next stretch is a long wooded section of the Downs, which takes you to **Cocking**, over **Pen Hill**, around **Beacon Hill** and on to **Harting Hill**, before crossing the border into Hampshire. Queen Elizabeth Country Park, by **Buriton**, is a beautiful woodland area which has an ancient farm with a reconstruction Iron Age settlement.

*Hampers End, Rock Road,
Storrington, Pulborough,
W. Sussex, RH20 3AF.*
Mike and Lorna Cheeseman welcome you to their lovely mellowed country house.
Tel: **01903 742777**
Fax no: 01903 742776
D: £22.50-£27.50 .
Open: All Year (not Xmas)
Beds: 1F 2D 1T
Baths: 3 En 1 Pr
🛇 (10) **P** (6) 🗖 🕿 🗻 🎟 Ⅴ ⚡ ⅋ ⚵

Amberley   17

National Grid Ref: TQ0313

🍴 🍺 The Sportsman, Black Horse

*Bacons, Amberley, Arundel,
W. Sussex, BN18 9NJ.*
Pretty old cottage in the heart of the village.
Tel: **01798 831234** Mrs Jollands.
D: £18.00**S:** £18.00.
Open: All Year (not Xmas)
Beds: 2T
Baths: 1 Sh
🛇 🕿 🎟 ⅋ ⚵

*Woodybanks, Crossgates,
Amberley, Arundel, W. Sussex,
BN18 9NR.*
Actual grid ref: TQ041136
Magnificent elevated views across the beautiful Wildbrooks, situated in picturesque historic Amberley.
Tel: **01798 831295**
Mr & Mrs Hardy.
D: £18.00-£18.00 **S:** £20.00-£25.00.
Open: All Year
Beds: 1D 1T
Baths: 1 Sh
🛇 **P** (2) 🗲🗖 🗻 🎟 ⅋ Ⅴ 🔋 ⅋ ⚵

Pay B&Bs by cash or
cheque and be prepared
to pay up front.

Warningcamp   18

National Grid Ref: TQ0306

▲ *Arundel Youth Hostel,
Warningcamp, Arundel, West
Sussex, BN18 9QY.*
Actual grid ref: TQ032076
Tel: **01903 882204**
Under 18: £7.75 **Adults:** £11.00
Self-catering facilities, Television, Showers, Wet weather shelter, Lounge, Dining room, Games room, Drying room, Cycle store, Parking, Evening meal at 7.00pm, WC, Breakfast available, Credit cards accepted
Georgian building 1.5 miles from ancient town of Arundel, dominated by its castle & the South Downs.

Bury   19

National Grid Ref: TQ0113

🍴 🍺 George & Dragon, The Swan

*Tanglewood, Houghton Lane,
Bury, Pulborough, W Sussex,
RH20 1PD.*
Warm welcome in our comfortable home, with beautiful views of South Downs.
Tel: **01798 831606** (also fax no)
Mrs House.
D: £22.00-£25.00
S: £18.00-£20.00.
Open: All Year
Beds: 1D 1S **Baths:** 1 Sh
P (3) 🗖 🗻 🎟 Ⅴ 🔋 ⅋ ⚵

*Pulborough Eedes Cottage, Bignor
Park Road, Bury Gate, Bury,
Pulborough, W Sussex, RH20 1EZ.*
Actual grid ref: TQ003161
Quiet country house surrounded by farmland, very warm personal welcome.
Grades: ETC 4 Diamond
Tel: **01798 831438**
Fax no: 01798 831942
D: £22.50-£25.00 **S:** £25.00-£30.00.
Open: All Year (not Xmas)
Beds: 1D 2T **Baths:** 1 En 1 Sh
🛇 **P** (10) 🗖 🕿 🗻 🎟 ♿ 🔋 ⚵

*Harkaway, 8 Houghton Lane,
Bury, Pulborough, W. Sussex,
RH20 1PD.*
Actual grid ref: TQ012130
Quiet location beneath South Downs. Full English and vegetarian breakfast.
Tel: **01798 831843**
Mrs Clark.
D: £17.00-£19.00
S: £17.00-£19.00.
Open: All Year
Beds: 1D 2T
Baths: 1 En 1 Sh
🛇 (6) **P** (3) 🗲🗖 🗻 🎟 Ⅴ 🔋 ⅋ ⚵

Arundel   20

National Grid Ref: TQ0106

🍴 🍺 George & Dragon, Six Bells, The Spur, White Hart

*Portreeves Acre, The Causeway,
Arundel, W. Sussex, BN18 9JL.*
Actual grid ref: TQ0207
3 minute from station, castle and town centre.
Tel: **01903 883277**
Mr Rogers.
D: £21.00-£23.00
S: £30.00-£35.00.
Open: All Year (not Xmas/New Year)
Beds: 1F 1D 1T
Baths: 2 En 1 Pr
🛇 (12) **P** (6) 🗖 🕿 🗻 🎟 Ⅴ ⅋ ⚵

Slindon   21

National Grid Ref: SU9608

🍴 🍺 Newburgh Arms

*Mill Lane House, Mill Lane,
Slindon, Arundel, W. Sussex,
BN18 0RP.*
Actual grid ref: SU964084
In peaceful village on South Downs, views to coast.
Grades: ETC 3 Diamond
Tel: **01243 814440**
Mrs Fuente.
Fax no: 01243 814436
D: £22.50-£22.50 **S:** £28.50-£28.50.
Open: All Year
Beds: 2D 1T
Baths: 3 En
🛇 **P** (7) 🗖 🕿 🗙 🗻 🎟 ♿ Ⅴ 🔋 ⅋ ⚵

Duncton   22

National Grid Ref: SU9517

🍴 🍺 Cricketers

*Drifters, Duncton, Petworth,
W. Sussex, GU28 0JZ.*
Quiet comfortable country house - TV - tea & coffee making facilities in rooms.
Grades: ETC 3 Diamond
Tel: **01798 342706** Mrs Folkes.
D: £20.00-£25.00 **S:** £25.00.
Open: All Year (not Xmas)
Beds: 1D 2T 1S
Baths: 1 En 1 Sh
P (3) 🗲🗖 🗙 🗻 🎟 Ⅴ 🔋 ⅋

SU   60

40

A33

A34

A32   A325

Km   5   10

Miles   5

Winchester

Cheriton ③①

A272

Owslebury ③②

A32

③⓪ East Meon

②⑨ Petersfield

②⑧ Buriton   Eas

20

Graffham 23

National Grid Ref: SU9217

⚑ ◖ The Foresters, White Horse

Brook Barn, Selham Road, Graffham, Petworth, W Sussex, GU28 0PU.
Actual grid ref: 19831023
Grades: ETC 4 Diamond, Silver
Tel: **01798 867356**
Mr & Mrs Jollands.
D: £25.00-£25.00
S: £30.00-£30.00.
Open: All Year (not Xmas)
Beds: 1D **Baths:** 1 En
ॐ ▣ (2) **❑ ⌨ ⬥ ▥ ▾ ⚡ ⚓**
Large double bedroom with ensuite bathroom, leads directly to own conservatory and secluded 2-acre garden. Close to South Downs Way, excellent pubs within walking distance, in quiet rural village in beautiful area of Sussex, ideal for a relaxing break.

Cocking 24

National Grid Ref: SU8717

⚑ ◖ Bell Inn

Moonlight Cottage Tea Rooms, Chichester Road, Cocking, Midhurst, W. Sussex, GU29 0HN.
Warm welcome, pretty tea rooms/garden. comfortable bed, excellent breakfast.
Grades: ETC 3 Diamond
Tel: **01730 813336**
Mrs Longland.
D: £20.00-£23.00.
S: £20.00-£23.00.
Open: All Year
Beds: 2D **Baths:** 1 Sh
ॐ ▣ (5) **⬥ ▥ ▾ ⚡**

Midhurst 25

National Grid Ref: SU8821

⚑ ◖ The Wheatsheaf, Half Moon, Bricklayers Arms, The Swan, The Elsted

Oakhurst Cottage, Carron Lane, Midhurst, W. Sussex, GU29 9LF.
Beautiful cottage in lovely surroundings within easy reach of Midhurst amenities.
Grades: ETC 3 Diamond
Tel: **01730 813523**
Mrs Whitmore Jones.
D: £25.00-£30.00
S: £25.00-£30.00.
Open: All Year
Beds: 1D 1T 1S **Baths:** 1 En 1 Sh
ॐ (4) **▣** (2) **❑ ▥ ⚡ ⚓**

All rates are subject to alteration at the owners' discretion.

The Crown Inn, Edinburgh Square, Midhurst, W. Sussex, GU29 9NL.
Actual grid ref: SU887215
C16th character inn, real ales, log fires, home-cooked food.
Tel: **01730 813462** Mr Stevens.
D: £17.50-£20.00 **S:** £20.00-£25.00.
Open: All Year
Beds: 1D 1T 1S
Baths: 1 Sh
⬥ ❑ ⬥ ⌨ ▥ ▾ ⚡ ⚓

Carrondune, Carron Lane, Midhurst, W Sussex, GU29 9LD.
Comfortable old family country house, quiet location, 5 mins town centre.
Tel: **01730 813558** Mrs Beck.
D: £20.00-£25.00 **S:** £25.00-£30.00.
Open: Feb to Nov
Beds: 1D 1T
Baths: 1 Sh
ॐ (5) **▣** (4) **❑ ⬥ ▥ ▾ ⚡ ⚓**

Elsted 26

National Grid Ref: SU8119

⚑ ◖ The Wheatsheaf, Half Moon, Bricklayers Arms, The Swan, The Elsted, Three Horseshoes

Three, Elsted, Midhurst, W Sussex, GU29 0JY.
Oldest house in village (1520).
Pub, cricket ground, church nearby.
Warm welcome.
Tel: **01730 825065**
Mrs Hill.
Fax no: 01730 825496
D: £25.00 **S:** £22.50.
Open: Mar to Nov
Beds: 1D 1T 1S
Baths: 1 Pr 1 Sh

East Harting 27

National Grid Ref: SU7919

⚑ ◖ The Ship, Three Horseshoes, White Hart

Oakwood, Eastfield Lane, East Harting, Petersfield, Hampshire, GU31 5NF.
Actual grid ref: SU802193
Foot of South Downs, beautiful countryside, Chichester, Portsmouth easy reach.
Tel: **01730 825245** Mrs Brightwell.
D: £20.00-£22.50 **S:** £20.00-£25.00.
Open: All Year
Beds: 2T
Baths: 2 Pr
▣ ⬥ ⌨ ✕ ⬥ ▾ ⚓

Buriton 28

National Grid Ref: SU7320

Nursted Farm, Buriton, Petersfield, Hants, GU31 5RW.
Relax in the atmosphere of our 300 year old farmhouse.
Tel: **01730 264278** Mrs Bray.
D: £18.00-£18.00 **S:** £18.00-£18.00.
Open: May to Feb
Beds: 3T **Baths:** 1 Pr 1 Sh
ॐ ▣ ❑ ▥ ⬥ ⚡

Petersfield 29

National Grid Ref: SU7423

⚑ ◖ Harrow Inn, Half Moon, Good Intent, Five Bells

Heath Farmhouse, Sussex Road, Petersfield, Hants, GU31 4HU.
Actual grid ref: SU7522
Georgian farmhouse, lovely views, large garden, quiet surroundings, near town.
Grades: ETC 3 Diamond
Tel: **01730 264709** Mrs Scurfield.
D: £18.00-£20.00 **S:** £20.00-£25.00.
Open: All Year
Beds: 1F 1D 1T **Baths:** 1 En 1 Sh
ॐ ▣ (5) **⬥ ❑ ⬥ ▥ ▾ ⚡ ⚓**

D = Price range per person sharing in a double room

Buriton to Winchester

The meandering path through Hampshire takes you on from **Butser Hill** to **Old Winchester Hill**, where there is an Iron Age fort, a nature reserve and a viewpoint from which you can see to the Isle of Wight in clear weather. After Exton you climb towards another **Beacon Hill**, with superb views over the Meon Valley. The final stretch leads to **Telegraph Hill** and Chilcomb, with its early Saxon church, and into **Winchester**. The ancient capital of the kingdom of Wessex, the end of Saxon hegemony was confirmed here by the coronation of Norman King William the Conqueror, whose son William Rufus is buried in the cathedral, as is Jane Austen. Built over centuries, the cathedral is a hotch-potch of Norman, Gothic and Perpendicular. The city goes back further, evidenced by the Iron Age fort overlooking it and a remaining part of the Roman wall. Other sights include Wolvesey Castle and the City and Westgate Museums.

Heathside, *36 Heath Road East, Petersfield, Hants, GU31 4HR.*
Petersfield pretty market square and shops. 15 minutes walk across heath.
Grades: ETC 3 Diamond
Tel: **01730 262337**
Mrs Cafferata.
D: £20.00-£25.00
S: £22.00-£25.00.
Open: All Year (not Xmas)
Beds: 1T 2S
Baths: 1 En 1 Pr 1 Sh
🄿 (3) ⅊▱ 🛉🎍🏛.Ⅴ. ⅋ ⚲

Ridgefield, *Station Road, Petersfield, Hants, GU32 3DE.*
Actual grid ref: SU743237
Friendly family atmosphere, near town & station; Portsmouth ferries: 20 mins drive.
Grades: ETC 2 Diamond
Tel: **01730 261402**
Mrs West.
D: £20.00-£20.00 **S:** £25.00-£30.00.
Open: All Year (not Xmas)
Beds: 1D 2T
Baths: 2 Sh
🛏🄿 (4) ⅊▱🏛.⅋⅋

Beaumont, *22 Stafford Road, Petersfield, Hampshire, GU32 2JG.*
Warm welcome, comfortable beds, excellent breakfasts with home-made preserves.
Grades: ETC 3 Diamond
Tel: **01730 264744** (also fax no)
Mrs Bewes.
D: £20.00-£20.00 **S:** £20.00-£25.00.
Open: All Year (not Xmas)
Beds: 2T 1S
Baths: 1 Sh
🛏 (12) 🄿 (2) ⅊▱🏛.⅋⚲

East Meon 30

National Grid Ref: SU6822

🍽 🍺 Old George Inn, The Thomas Lord

Drayton Cottage, *East Meon, Petersfield, Hants, GU32 1PW.*
Actual grid ref: SU669232
Luxury country cottage; antiques and oak beams, overlooking glorious countryside.
Tel: **01730 823472** Mrs Rockett.
D: £20.00-£23.00 **S:** £25.00-£25.00.
Open: All Year
Beds: 1D 1T
Baths: 1 En 1 Pr
🄿 (3) ▱🛉🏛.Ⅴ🛉⅋

Coombe Cross House & Stables, *Coombe Road, East Meon, Petersfield, Hants, GU32 1HQ.*
Actual grid ref: SU667210
Early Georgian house on South Downs, beautiful views, tranquil setting.
Tel: **01730 823298** Mrs Bulmer.
Fax no: 01730 823515
D: £25.00 **S:** £30.00.
Open: All Year (not Xmas)
Beds: 1D 2T 1S
Baths: 2 Pr 1 Sh
🛏 (12) 🄿 (10) ▱🛉🏛.Ⅴ🛉⅋

Cheriton 31

National Grid Ref: SU5828

🍽 🍺 Flower Pots

The Garden House, *Cheriton, Alresford, Hampshire, SO24 0QQ.*
Edge of pretty village. Tennis court. Near Cheriton Battle Field. Personal tour by arrangement
Tel: **01962 771352** Mrs Verney.
Fax no: 01962 771667
D: £20.00-£24.00 **S:** £20.00-£24.00.
Open: All Year
Beds: 2T 1D
Baths: 1 Pr 1 Sh
🛏🄿 (4) ⅊▱✕🏛.&Ⅴ⅋⚲

Owslebury 32

National Grid Ref: SU5123

🍽 🍺 Ship Inn

Mays Farmhouse, *Longwood Dean, Owslebury, Winchester, Hants, SO21 1JS.*
Actual grid ref: SU547241
Lovely C16th farmhouse, beautiful countryside; peaceful with good walks.
Tel: **01962 777486** Mrs Ashby.
Fax no: 01962 777747
D: £22.50-£25.00 **S:** £25.00-£30.00.
Open: All Year
Beds: 1F 1D 1T
Baths: 3 Pr
🛏 (7) 🄿 (5) ⅊▱🛌🛉🏛.&Ⅴ⅋

Winchester 33

National Grid Ref: SU4829

🍽 🍺 Roebuck Inn, Queen Inn, Bell Inn, Wykeham Arms, White Horse, Stanmore Hotel, Cart Horse, Plough

▲ **Winchester Youth Hostel,** *The City Mill, 1 Water Lane, Winchester, Hampshire, SO23 8EJ.*
Actual grid ref: SU486293
Tel: **01962 853723**
Under 18: £6.50 **Adults:** £9.25
Showers, Lounge, Cycle store, No smoking, Kitchen facilities, Breakfast available, Credit cards accepted
Charming C18th watermill (NT) straddling the River Itchen at East End of King Alfred's capital, a half mile from the cathedral

The Farrells, *5 Ranelagh Road, Winchester, Hants, SO23 9TA.*
Actual grid ref: SU476287
Grades: ETC 3 Diamond
Tel: **01962 869555** (also fax no)
Mr Farrell.
D: £20.00-£25.00 **S:** £22.00-£22.00.
Open: All Year (not Xmas)
Beds: 1F 1D 1T 1S
Baths: 1 En 1 Pr 2 Sh
🛏 (5) ⅊▱🛉🏛.Ⅴ⅋⚲
Turn of the century Victorian villa, furnished in that style. We are close to the Cathedral and like to share our love of Winchester with our guests.

High season, bank holidays and special events mean low availability *everywhere.*

---

8 Salters Acres, *Winchester, Hants, SO22 5JW.*
Detached family home in large gardens. Breakfast in conservatory, easy access to city centre.
Tel: **01962 856112**
Mr & Mrs Cater.
D: £19.00-£22.50 **S:** £25.00-£30.00.
Open: All Year (not Xmas/New Year)
Beds: 1T 1D 1S
Baths: 1 Pr 1 Sh
🛏 (8) 🄿 (8) ⅊▱🛉🏛.Ⅴ⅋⚲

Sycamores, *4 Bereweeke Close, Winchester, Hants, SO22 6AR.*
Actual grid ref: SU472304
Convenient but peaceful location about 2 km north-west of city centre.
Grades: ETC 3 Diamond
Tel: **01962 867242** Mrs Edwards.
Fax no: 01962 620300
D: £20.00-£20.00 .
Open: All Year
Beds: 2D 1T **Baths:** 3 Pr
🄿 (3) ⅊▱🛉🏛.Ⅴ⚲

85 Christchurch Road, *Winchester, Hants, SO23 9QY.*
Actual grid ref: SU473282
Comfortable detached Victorian family house, convenient base for Hampshire sightseeing.
Grades: ETC 4 Diamond
Tel: **01962 868661** (also fax no)
Mrs Fetherston-Dilke.
D: £25.00-£26.00 **S:** £25.00-£30.00.
Open: All Year
Beds: 1D 1T 1S
Baths: 2 En 1 Sh
🛏🄿 (3) ⅊▱🛉🏛.Ⅴ⅋⚲

St Margaret's, *3 St Michael's Road, Winchester, Hampshire, SO23 9JE.*
Comfortable rooms in Victorian house, close to cathedral and colleges.
Grades: ETC 2 Diamond
Tel: **01962 861450** Mrs Brett.
D: £20.00-£21.00 **S:** £22.00-£22.00.
Open: All Year (not Xmas)
Beds: 1D 1T 2S
Baths: 2 Sh
🛏 (4) 🄿 (1) ⅊▱🛉🏛.Ⅴ⚲

S = Price range for a single person in a room

Rocquaine, *19 Downside Road, Winchester, SO22 5LT.*
Spacious welcoming detached family home in quiet residential area.
Tel: **01962 861426**
Mrs Quick.
D: £18.00-£19.00
S: £20.00-£25.00.
Open: All Year (not Xmas)
Beds: 1D 1T 1S
Baths: 1 Sh
⛄ (8) ₽ (4) ⅙⛌ ♨ �🖩 Ⅶ ⌁ ⚲

32 Hyde Street, *Winchester, Hants, SO23 7DX.*
Actual grid ref: SU481301
Attractive C18th town house, close to city centre.
Tel: **01962 851621**
Mrs Tisdall.
D: £17.00-£18.00 **S:** £26.00-£26.00.
Open: All Year (not Xmas/ New Year)
Beds: 1F 1D
Baths: 1 Sh
⛄⅙⛌ ♨ 🖩 Ⅶ ⚲

Portland House Hotel, *63 Tower Street, Winchester, Hants, SO23 8TA.*
Quiet city centre location a few minutes from major sites.
Grades: ETC 3 Diamond
Tel: **01962 865195**
Mr & Mrs Knight.
D: £22.50-£55.00 **S:** £48.00-£48.00.
Open: All Year (not Xmas/New Year)
Beds: 1F 1T 2D
Baths: 4 En
⛄ (5) ₽ (5) ⛌ ♨ 🖩 Ⅶ

The Lilacs, *1 Harestock Close, off Andover Road North, Winchester, Hants, SO22 6NP.*
Attractive, Georgian-style family home. Comfortable, clean and excellent cuisine.
Tel: **01962 884122** Mrs Pell.
D: £17.50-£18.00 **S:** £22.00-£25.00.
Open: All Year (not Xmas)
Beds: 1D 1T
Baths: 1 Sh
⛄ ₽ (3) ⅙⛌ ♨ 🖩 Ⅶ ▮ ⌁ ⚲

Giffard House Hotel, *50 Christchurch Road, St Cross, Winchester, Hants, SO23 9SU.*
Comfortable Victorian house within ten minutes' walk of the city centre.
Tel: **01962 852628**
Fax no: 01962 856722
D: £25.00-£35.00 **S:** £35.00-£45.00.
Open: All Year
Beds: 1F 6D 2T 5S
Baths: 14 En
⛄ ₽ (14) ⛌ ♨ 🖩 Ⅶ

Shawlands, *46 Kilham Lane, Winchester, Hants, SO22 5QD.*
Actual grid ref: SU456289
Attractive house on edge of Winchester in quiet lane overlooking fields.
Tel: **01962 861166** (also fax no)
Mrs Pollock.
D: £19.00-£22.50 **S:** £27.00-£30.00.
Open: All Year
Beds: 2F 1D 2T **Baths:** 1 Pr 2 Sh
⛄ (5) ₽ (4) ⅙⛌ 🐾 ♨ 🖩 ⅙ Ⅶ ⌁ ⚲

Surrey Cycleway

At 86 miles, the **Surrey Cycleway** is the shortest featured in this book. It is in fact a circular tour of the southeast of the county, over the chalk escarpment that is the North Downs and then through the southern woodlands - steering well clear of London. The route runs anticlockwise and is signposted by brown Surrey Cycleway direction signs with a cycle silhouette; the description that follows starts and finishes at Boxhill and Westhumble Railway Station.

A detailed **guide leaflet** to the cycleway route, which includes a list of cycle repair/hire shops on or near to the route, is available free from the County Cycling Officer, Surrey County Council, Room 314, County Hall, Kingston-upon-Thames KT1 2DY, tel 020-8541 8044.

Maps: Ordnance Survey 1:50,000 Landranger series: 186, 187

Surrey is well-connected by **train** to London and everywhere else in the Southeast. Trains to Boxhill and Westhumble, as well as many other locations, connect to Clapham Junction.

Dorking   1

National Grid Ref: TQ1649

|○| ◑ King's Arms, Old School House, King William, The Bush, Inn on the Green

The Waltons, *5 Rose Hill, Dorking, Surrey, RH4 2EG.*
Listed house in conservation area. Beautiful views and friendly atmosphere.
Tel: **01306 883127** (also fax no)
Mrs Walton.
D: £17.50-£20.00 **S:** £20.00-£32.50.
Open: All Year
Beds: 1F 1D 1T 1S
Baths: 3 Sh
⛌ 🅿 (3) ⅙ ⬛ 🔭 ♨ 🎗 Ⅷ 🗎 🌡 ⚡

Shrub Hill, *3 Calvert Road, Dorking, Surrey, RH4 1LT.*
Actual grid ref: TQ167504
Quiet comfortable family home with excellent views.
Tel: **01306 885229** Mrs Scott Kerr.
D: £25.00-£26.00 **S:** £35.00.
Open: All Year (not Xmas)
Beds: 1T 1S 1D
Baths: 1 Sh 1 En
⛌ (8) 🅿 (2) ⅙ ⬛ 🔭 ♨ 🎗 Ⅷ ⚡ 🚲

Torridon Guest House, *Longfield Road, Dorking, Surrey, RH4 3DF.*
Large chalet bungalow - quiet location.
Grades: ETC 3 Diamond
Tel: **01306 883724** Mrs Short.
Fax no: 01306 880759
D: £23.00-£24.00 **S:** £26.00-£28.00.
Open: All Year
Beds: 1D 1T 1S **Baths:** 1 Sh
⛌ 🅿 (4) ⅙ ⬛ 🔭 ✕ 🎗 Ⅷ 🌡 ⚡ 🚲

D = Price range per person sharing in a double room

Great Bookham   2

National Grid Ref: TQ1354

|○| ◑ Windsor Castle, The Plough

Selworthy, *310 Lower Road, Great Bookham, Leatherhead, Surrey, KT23 4DW.*
Attractive location overlooking Green Belt. Convenient, M25, Gatwick and Heathrow airports.
Tel: **01372 453952** (also fax no)
Mrs Kent.
D: £19.00-£22.00 **S:** £23.00-£26.00.
Open: All Year (not Xmas)
Beds: 1D 1T
Baths: 1 Sh
⛌ (10) 🅿 (4) ⅙ ⬛ 🎗 Ⅷ

Order your packed lunches the *evening before* you need them. Not at breakfast!

S = Price range for a single person in a room

Abinger Common   3

National Grid Ref: TQ1145

|○| ◑ Plough Inn

Park House Farm, *Leith Hill Road, Abinger Common, Dorking, Surrey, RH5 6LW.*
Tel: **01306 730101**
Mr & Mrs Wallis
Fax no: 01306 730643
D: £20.00-£30.00 **S:** £30.00-£50.00.
Open: All Year (not Xmas/New Year)
Beds: 1T 2D **Baths:** 3 En
⛌ (12) 🅿 (10) ⅙ ⬛ 🎗 Ⅷ
Set in 25 acres in an Area of Outstanding Natural Beauty, you are welcome to join us in a large spacious home which provides bright, tastefully decorated rooms, all with excellent views. Easy access to Gatwick and Heathrow.

Pay B&Bs by cash or cheque and be prepared to pay up front.

Holmbury St Mary 4

National Grid Ref: TQ1144

Royal Oak, Parrot Inn, The Volunteer, King's Head

Holmbury St Mary Youth Hostel, Radnor Lane, Holmbury St Mary, Dorking, Surrey, RH5 6NW.
Actual grid ref: TQ104450
Tel: **01306 730777**
Under 18: £6.90 **Adults:** £10.00
Self-catering facilities, Showers, Wet weather shelter, Lounge, Drying room, Cycle store, Evening meal at 7.00pm, No smoking, Kitchen facilities, Breakfast available, Credit cards accepted
Set in its own 5,000 acres of woodland grounds, this purpose-built hostel offers tranquil beauty among the Surrey Hills.

Bulmer Farm, Holmbury St Mary, Dorking, Surrey, RH5 6LG.
Actual grid ref: TQ114441
Quiet modernised C17th farmhouse/barn, large garden, picturesque village, self-catering.
Grades: ETC 4 Diamond
Tel: **01306 730210**
Mrs Hill.
: £22.00-£24.00
: £22.00-£35.00.
Open: All Year
Beds: 3D 5T
Baths: 5 En 2 Sh
(12) P (12) ⊬⊡⊓⚓⚒⊞&♥Ⅴ∮⚲

All rooms full and nowhere else to stay? Ask the owner if there's anywhere nearby

---

Westhumble to Bramley

The first part of the route takes you to **Ranmore Common**; nearby stands **Polesden Lacey**, an elegant Regency house with a collection of furniture, silverware, porcelain and paintings amassed in Edwardian times and a country estate with landscaped walks. Cycling around the White Downs and Hackhurst Downs, you come to **Shere**, an old village whose name means 'clear stream', from the brook that runs through it, and then **Wonersh** and **Bramley**. A detour north will take you to **Guildford**, the county town, noted for its cobbled High Street with Georgian architecture, as well as one or two older buildings - the Guildhall dates from Tudor times but has a Restoration facade with a gilded clock dated 1683. Also on the High Street is Guildford House Gallery, a restored seventeenth-century house displaying pictures and craftwork. There is also a small ruined Norman castle, and the red-brick cathedral dating from 1954. Just outside Guildford to the east is Clandon Park, a house dating from c1730 whose grand Palladian exterior contrasts with the Baroque ceiling of the Marble Hall.

Planning a longer stay? Always ask for any special rates.

West Horsley 5

National Grid Ref: TQ0752

King William IV

Brinford, Off Shere Road, West Horsley, Leatherhead, KT24 6EJ.
Comfortable modern house in peaceful rural location with panoramic views.
Tel: **01483 283636** Mrs Wiltshire.
D: £20.00-£25.00 **S:** £25.00.
Open: All Year
Beds: 1D 1T 1S **Baths:** 1 En 1 Sh
P (4) ⊬⊡⚒⊞Ⅴ⚲

Shere 6

National Grid Ref: TQ0747

White Horse, Prince of Wales

Manor Cottage, Shere, Guildford, Surrey, GU5 9JE.
C16th cottage with old world garden, in centre of beautiful village.
Tel: **01483 202979** Mrs James.
D: £20.00-£20.00 **S:** £20.00-£20.00.
Open: May to Sep
Beds: 1D 1S
Baths: 1 Sh
☎ (5) P ⊬⚒Ⅴ∮⚲

Bringing children with you? Always ask for any special rates.

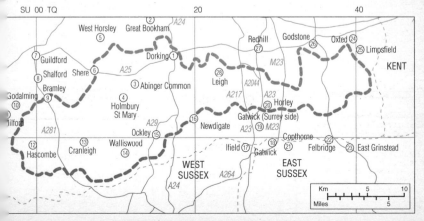

Cherry Trees, Gomshall, Shere, Guildford, Surrey, GU5 9HE.
Actual grid ref: TQ072487
Quiet comfortable house, lovely garden, village foot of North Downs.
Tel: **01483 202288**
Mrs Warren.
D: £25.00 **S:** £25.00-£30.00.
Open: All Year (not Xmas/New Year)
Beds: 2D 3F 1S
Baths: 2 En 1 Sh
🛏 🅿 (4) ⌿ 🗆 🕯 🖢 🞣 & Ⓥ 🛍 ✦ ♉

Guildford 7

National Grid Ref: SU9949

🍴 🍺 King's Head, Jolly Farmer, Hare & Hounds, The Fox, White House, George Abbot, Grantley Arms

Weybrook House, 113 Stoke Road, Guildford, Surrey, GU1 1ET.
Actual grid ref: SU998504
Quiet family B&B. A320 Near town centre/stations. Delicious breakfast.
Tel: **01483 302394**
Mr & Mrs Bourne.
D: £20.00-£22.00 **S:** £28.00-£28.00.
Open: All Year (not Xmas)
Beds: 1F 1D 1S
Baths: 2 Sh
🛏 🗆 🕯 🖢 🞣 Ⓥ 🛍 ✦ ♉

Atkinsons Guest House, 129 Stoke Road, Guildford, Surrey, GU1 1ET.
Small comfortable family-run guest house close to town centre & all local amenities.
Tel: **01483 538260**
Mrs Atkinson.
D: £20.00-£22.50 **S:** £28.00-£45.00.
Open: All Year
Beds: 1D 1T 2S
Baths: 2 En 1 Sh
🛏 (6) 🅿 (2) 🗆 🖢 🞣 Ⓥ ✦ ♉

Westbury Cottage, Waterden Road, Guildford, Surrey, GU1 2AN.
Cottage-style house in large secluded garden, 5 mins town centre, 2 mins station.
Tel: **01483 822602** (also fax no)
Mrs Smythe.
D: £25.00-£25.00
S: £30.00-£30.00.
Open: All Year (not Xmas)
Beds: 1D 2T
Baths: 1 Sh
🛏 (6) 🅿 (3) ⌿ 🗆 🖢 🞣 Ⓥ ✦ ♉

High season,
bank holidays and
special events mean
low availability
everywhere.

---

25 The Chase, Guildford, Surrey, GU2 5UA.
10 minutes to town and station. Easy access to A3.
Tel: **01483 569782**
Mrs Ellis.
S: £16.00-£16.00.
Open: All Year (not Xmas/New Year)
Beds: 2S
⌿ 🗆 🞣

2 Wodeland Avenue, Guildford, GU2 4JX.
Centrally located rooms with panorama. Friendly and modernised family home.
Tel: **01483 451142**
Mrs Hay.
Fax no: 01483 572980
D: £20.00-£22.00
S: £20.00-£25.00.
Open: All Year (not Xmas)
Beds: 1D 1T
Baths: 1 Pr 1 Sh
🛏 (3) 🅿 (3) ⌿ 🗆 🖢 🞣 & Ⓥ ✦ ♉

Quietways, 29 Liddington Hall Drive, Guildford, Surrey, GU3 3AE.
Off A323, quiet cottage, end of cul-de-sac. Lounge, conservatory, pleasant garden.
Tel: **01483 232347**
Mr White.
D: £19.00 **S:** £25.00.
Open: Jan to Nov
Beds: 1D 1T
Baths: 1 En 1 Pr
🅿 (2) ⌿ 🗆 🖢 🞣 & Ⓥ ✦ ♉

Field Villa, Liddington New Road, Guildford, Surrey, GU3 3AH.
Small private B&B in a quiet private road. Friendly welcome awaits.
Tel: **01483 233961**
Mrs Townsend.
Fax no: 01483 234045
D: £19.00-£20.00
S: £19.00-£20.00.
Open: All Year (not Xmas)
Beds: 1D 1T 2S
Baths: 1 Pr 1 Sh
🛏 🅿 (5) ⌿ 🗆 ✗ 🖢 🞣 Ⓥ

Shalford 8

National Grid Ref: TQ0046

🍴 🍺 Sea Horse Pub

The Laurels, 23 Dagden Road, Shalford, Guildford, Surrey, GU4 8DD.
Quiet detached house. Direct access to footpaths. Near Guildford centre.
Tel: **01483 565753**
Mrs Deeks.
D: £20.00-£23.00
S: £22.00-£22.00.
Open: All Year
Beds: 1T 1D
🛏 (6) 🅿 (5) ⌿ 🗆 🕯 ✗ 🖢 🞣 Ⓥ 🛍 ✦ ♉

Bramley 9

National Grid Ref: TQ0044

🍴 🍺 Jolly Farmer, Grantley Arms

Beevers Farm, Chinthurst Lane, Bramley, Guildford, Surrey, GU5 0DR.
Peaceful surroundings, friendly atmosphere, own preserves, honey, eggs, nearby villages.
Grades: ETC 3 Diamond
Tel: **01483 898764** (also fax no)
Mr Cook.
D: £18.00-£25.00 **S:** £30.00.
Open: Easter to Nov
Beds: 1F 2T
Baths: 1 Pr 1 Sh
🛏 🅿 (10) ⌿ 🗆 🖢 🞣 Ⓥ 🛍 ✦

Godalming 10

National Grid Ref: SU9643

🍴 🍺 Inn on the Lake

Sherwood, Ashtead Lane, Godalming, Surrey, GU7 1SY.
We have 4 cats and one Cavalier King Charles Spaniel - we welcome animal lovers.
Tel: **01483 427545** (also fax no)
Mr & Mrs Harrison.
D: £22.50 **S:** £24.00.
Open: All Year
Beds: 1T 2S
Baths: 1 Sh
🛏 (5) 🗆 🖢 🞣 Ⓥ ✦ ♉

Milford 11

National Grid Ref: SU9442

🍴 🍺 The Star, Red Lion

Coturnix House, Rake Lane, Milford, Godalming, Surrey, GU8 5AB.
Modern house, family atmosphere countryside position, easy access road/rail.
Tel: **01483 416897** Mr Bell.
D: £20.00-£20.00 **S:** £20.00-£20.00
Open: All Year
Beds: 1D 1T 1S
Baths: 1 Pr 1 Sh
🛏 (1) 🅿 (6) ⌿ 🗆 🕯 🖢 🞣 Ⓥ ♉

Hascombe 12

National Grid Ref: SU9939

🍴 🍺 White Horse

Hoe Farm, Hoe Lane, Hascombe, Godalming, Surrey, GU8 4JQ.
Actual grid ref: SU997395
Elizabethan farmhouse in tranquil wooded valley, former retreat of Winston Churchill.
Tel: **01483 208222** Mrs Gordon.
Fax no: 01483 208538
D: £25.00-£30.00 **S:** £30.00-£30.00
Open: All Year
Beds: 1F 3D 3T 1S
Baths: 3 Sh
🛏 🅿 (8) ⌿ 🗆 🕯 ✗ 🖢 🞣 Ⓥ 🛍 ✦

Cranleigh 13

National Grid Ref: TQ0638

*The White Hart Hotel, Ewhurst
Road, Cranleigh, Surrey, GU6 7AE.*
Listed coaching inn situated 8.5
miles south of Guildford.
Tel: **01483 268647** Mr Silver.
Fax no: 01483 267154
D: £24.00-£26.00 **S:** £38.00-£42.00.
Open: All Year
Beds: 1F 1S **Baths:** 12 En
ⓢ☐♐★☓⬥📶▣🖊✦🐾

Walliswood 14

National Grid Ref: TQ1137

⑩◗ The Parrot

*Kerne Hus, Walliswood Green
Road, Walliswood, Dorking,
Surrey, RH5 5RD.*
Tel: **01306 627548** Mrs Seller.
D: £22.00-£22.00 **S:** £25.00-£25.00.
Open: All Year (not Xmas/New
Year)
Beds: 1T 1D **Baths:** 1 Sh
ⓢ (2) ☑ (3) ⅌☐⬥📶▣🗄🐾
1930s detached family home set in
1/2 acre of garden. Situated in
small hamlet, west of Ockley and 7
miles north of Horsham. Interesting
houses and gardens in Surrey and
Sussex within easy reach and close
to the Downs for walking.

Ockley 15

National Grid Ref: TQ1439

◗ Parrot Inn

*Hazels, Walliswood, Ockley,
Dorking, Surrey, RH5 5PL.*
Separate suite. Superior accommo-
dation. Beautiful gardens. Relaxed
& peaceful. Convenient airports.
Tel: **01306 627228** Mrs Floud.
D: £20.00-£25.00 **S:** £20.00-£30.00.
Open: All Year
Beds: 1F 1S
Baths: 1 En 1 Sh
ⓢ☑ (2) ⅌☐⬥📶▣✦🐾

Newdigate 16

National Grid Ref: TQ1942

◗ Six Bells, The Star, The Plough, Surrey
Oaks

*Sturtwood Farm, Partridge Lane,
Newdigate, Dorking, Surrey,
RH5 5EE.*
Comfortable welcoming farmhouse
in beautiful wooded countryside.
Many historic properties nearby.
Grades: ETC 3 Diamond
Tel: **01306 631308**
Mrs MacKinnon.
Fax no: 01306 631908
D: £22.50-£25.00 **S:** £30.00-£35.00.
Open: All Year (not Xmas/
New Year)
Beds: 1T 1S 1D **Baths:** 1 En 1 Sh
ⓢ☑ (6) ⅌☐★☓⬥📶▣🐾

Ifield 17

National Grid Ref: TQ2537

⑩◗ The Plough, Royal Oak, The Gate, The
Flight

*Waterhall Country House,
Prestwood Lane, Ifield Wood,
Ifield, Crawley, W Sussex, RH11 0LA.*
Attractive country house set in 28
acres - ideal for Gatwick, bed &
breakfast.
Grades: ETC 3 Diamond
RAC 3 Diamond
Tel: **01293 520002**
Mrs Dawson.
Fax no: 01293 539905
D: £22.50-£22.50
S: £35.00-£35.00.
Open: All Year (not Xmas)
Beds: 4D 3T 1S 2F
Baths: 10 En
ⓢ☑ (25) ⅌☐⬥📶▣

*April Cottage, 10 Langley Lane,
Ifield, Crawley, West Sussex,
RH11 0NA.*
Warm & friendly 200-year-old
house in quiet lane, near pubs,
churches, station, shops.
Tel: **01293 546222** Mrs Pedlow.
Fax no: 01293 518712
D: £22.50-£25.00 -£35.00.
Open: All Year
Beds: 1F 1D 2T
Baths: 2 En 2 Sh
ⓢ (6) ☑ (8) ⅌☐⬥📶▣

D = Price range per person
sharing in a double room

Gatwick 18

National Grid Ref: TQ2740

⑩◗ The Plough, Royal Oak, The Gate, The
Greyhound, Flight Tavern

*Brooklyn Manor Hotel, Bonnetts
Lane, Gatwick, Crawley,
W. Sussex, RH11 0NY.*
Ideal location for Gatwick
overnight stopover. Courtesy
transport & holiday parking.
Grades: ETC 3 Diamond
Tel: **01293 546024**
Mr Davis.
Fax no: 01293 510366
D: £19.50-£26.00 **S:** £32.00-£43.50.
Open: All Year (not Xmas)
Beds: 3F 4D 3T 1S
Baths: 4 En 3 Sh
ⓢ☑⅌☐⬥📶▣🐾

Gatwick (Surrey side) 19

National Grid Ref: TQ2843

⑩◗ Air Balloon, Ye Olde Six Bells, King's
Head

*Melville Lodge Guest House,
15 Brighton Road, Gatwick,
Horley, Surrey, RH6 7HH.*
Edwardian early 1900 house.
Access to coach station and buses.
Grades: ETC 2 Diamond
RAC 2 Diamond
Tel: **01293 784951**
Mr & Mrs Brooks.
Fax no: 01293 785669
D: £19.00-£22.50 **S:** £25.00-£35.00.
Open: All Year
Beds: 1F 3D 2T 1S
Baths: 3 En 2 Sh
ⓢ (1) ☑☐★⬥📶♿▣

Bramley to Westhumble

From Bramley it's southwest to **Godalming**, and then around
Hydon Heath to **Dunsfold** and east, crossing the Wey and Arun
Canal, to Alfold Crossways and then **Ellen's Green**. Shortly
after here there's a link to Leith Hill, the highest point in
Southeast England. Back on the route and cycling east, you are
now in the lush woodland of the south of the county. Near to
Ockley are nature reserves at Wallis Wood and Vann Lake, and
the Hannah Peschar Sculpture Garden, an open-air gallery
which features annual exhibitions of contemporary sculpture,
both figurative and abstract and in all materials. Then it's east
through a string of villages and small towns whose medieval
names bespeak the era when this whole region was covered by
trees - **Newdigate** ('Gate near a new wood'), **Horley**
('Woodland clearing in a horn of land'), **Lingfield** ('Wood-
dwellers' field') - to the eastern end of the route at **Haxted Mill**,
a working mill with old-world milling machinery, which hosts,
from Easter to mid-September, a museum of the history of
milling. The next stretch takes you via **Bletcingley** to **Outwood**,
with another mill and nearby Outwood Common, and then by
way of Woodhatch, Reigate Heath, Betchworth and Brockham
back into the vicinity of **Box Hill**, which it is worth climbing for
the magnificent view, and to the station at Westhumble.

Horley 20

National Grid Ref: TQ2843

🏨 🍺 Air Balloon, Ye Olde Six Bells, King's Head

Yew Tree, 31 Massetts Road, Horley, Surrey, RH6 7DQ.
Tudor style house 1/2 acre gardens, close Gatwick Airport, near town centre.
Grades: ETC 1 Diamond
Tel: **01293 785855** (also fax no)
Mr Stroud.
D: £15.00-£20.00 **S:** £20.00-£25.00.
Open: All Year
Beds: 1F 2D 1T 2S
Baths: 1 En 1 Sh
🛏 (2) 🅿 (10) 🗍 🕭 🛆 🖳

Victoria Lodge Guest House, 161 Victoria Road, Horley, Surrey, RH6 7AS.
Well-located for town centre, BR station, pubs, shops etc. Families welcome.
Tel: **01293 432040**
Mr & Mrs Robson.
Fax no: 01293 432042
D: £19.00-£25.00 **S:** £30.00-£48.00.
Open: All Year
Beds: 2F 2D 2S **Baths:** 2 En 2 Sh
🛏 🅿 (14) 🗡 🗍 🕭 🖳 🖳 ☞

Prinsted Guest House, Oldfield Road, Horley, Surrey, RH6 7EP.
Spacious Victorian house in quiet situation ideal for Gatwick Airport.
Grades: ETC 4 Diamond, AA 3 Diamond, RAC 3 Diamond, Sparkling
Tel: **01293 785233** Mrs Kendall.
Fax no: 01293 820624
D: £22.50-£23.50 **S:** £32.00-£32.00.
Open: All Year (not Xmas)
Beds: 2D 3T 2S
Baths: 6 En 1 Pr
🛏 🅿 (10) 🗍 ☞

Berrens Guest House, 62 Massetts Road, Horley, Surrey, RH6 7DS.
Grades: ETC 2 Diamond
Tel: **01293 786125** (also fax no)
Mr Worham.
D: £19.00-£24.00 **S:** £26.00-£37.00.
Open: All Year (not Xmas/ New Year)
Beds: 1F 2T 1D 2S
🛏 (5) 🅿 (6) 🗡 🗍 🕭 🖳
Comfortable non-smoking Edwardian guest house. 5 minutes drive to Gatwick airport. 40 minutes by train to London Victoria station. Within walking distance shops, banks & restaurants.

Blackberry House, 8 Brighton Road, Horley, Surrey, RH6 7ES.
Attractive house on the main A23. 5 mins' drive Gatwick airport.
Tel: **01293 772447**
D: £18.00-£20.00
S: £26.00-£30.00.
Open: All Year (not Xmas)
Beds: 1D
🅿 (4) 🗡 🗍 🕭 🖳

Logans Guest House, 93 Povey Cross Road, Horley, Surrey, RH6 0AE.
Victorian garden setting, friendly hosts, holiday parking, really nice atmosphere.
Tel: **01293 783363** (also fax no)
D: £20.00-£30.00 **S:** £20.00-£30.00.
Open: All Year
Beds: 2F 3D 4T 2S
Baths: 3 En 1 Pr 2 Sh
🛏 🅿 🗡 🗍 🕆 🗶 🗍 🕭 🛆 🖳 🖳 ✦ ☞

Gorse Cottage, 66 Balcombe Road, Horley, Surrey, RH6 9AY.
Gatwick Airport 2 miles, pretty, detached house in residential area.
Tel: **01293 784402** (also fax no)
D: £17.50-£18.00 .
Open: All Year (not Xmas)
Beds: 1D 1T
🅿 (2) 🗡 🕆 🕭 🖳 🖳

Copthorne 21

National Grid Ref: TQ3139

🏨 🍺 Cherry Tree, Duke's Head

Homesteads, 58 Church Lane, Copthorne, Crawley, W Sussex, RH10 3QF.
Semi detached family home, warm welcome. M23 5 mins, Gatwick 8 mins.
Tel: **01342 713221** Mrs Nixon.
D: £20.00-£20.00 **S:** £20.00-£20.00.
Open: All Year
Beds: 2T
🛏 🅿 (2) 🗡 🗍 🕭 🖳 🖳 🗍 ✦ ☞

Felbridge 22

National Grid Ref: TQ3639

Toads Croak House, 30 Copthorne Road, Felbridge, East Grinstead, W Sussex, RH19 2NS.
Beautiful Sussex cottage-style house, gardens. Gatwick parking. 17th independent year.
Tel: **01342 328524** (also fax no)
D: £18.50-£23.00 **S:** £24.00.
Open: All Year
Beds: 1F 1D 2T 1S
Baths: 2 En 1 Sh
🛏 🅿 (7) 🗡 🗍 🕭 🖳 🖳

East Grinstead 23

National Grid Ref: TQ3938

🏨 🍺 Dorset Arms, Bricklayers Arms, Star Inn

Cranston House, Cranston Road, East Grinstead, W. Sussex, RH19 3HW.
Actual grid ref: TQ397386
Attractive large detached house in residential area. Gatwick 15 minutes.
Grades: ETC 3 Diamond
Tel: **01342 323609** (also fax no)
Mr Linacre.
D: £20.00-£40.00 **S:** £28.00-£40.00.
Open: All Year (not Xmas)
Beds: 1F 1D 1T **Baths:** 1 En
🛏 (6) 🅿 (4) 🗡 🗍 🕆 🕭 🖳 🖳 ✦ ☞

Grinstead Lodge Guest House, London Road, East Grinstead, W Sussex, RH19 1QE.
Friendly, family-run, with ample parking. Open all year round.
Tel: **01342 317222** (also fax no)
D: £22.00-£28.00 **S:** £20.00-£33.00.
Open: All Year
Beds: 1F 4T 2D 2S
Baths: 7 En 1 Sh
🛏 🅿 (8) 🗍 🕭 🖳 🖳 🗍 ☞

Brentridge, 24 Portland Road, East Grinstead, W. Sussex, RH19 4EA.
Beautiful garden, central and quiet. Close to Gatwick, M25 & south coast.
Tel: **01342 322004**
Mrs Greenwood.
Fax no: 01342 324145
D: £18.00-£25.00 **S:** £25.00-£25.00
Open: All Year (not Xmas)
Beds: 2D
Baths: 1 En 1 Sh
🛏 🅿 (1) 🗡 🕭

Oxted 24

National Grid Ref: TQ3852

🏨 🍺 The Oxted, Old Bell, The Crown, The George, The Gurkha, Royal Oak

Pinehurst Grange Guest House, East Hill (Part of A25), Oxted, Surrey, RH8 9AE.
Actual grid ref: TQ393525
Comfortable Victorian ex-farm-house with traditional service and relaxed friendly atmosphere.
Tel: **01883 716413**
Mr Rodgers.
D: £21.00-£21.00
S: £26.00-£26.00.
Open: All Year (not Xmas/ New Year)
Beds: 1D 1T 1S
Baths: 1 Sh
🛏 (5) 🅿 (3) 🗡 🗍 🕭 🖳 🖳 🗍 ✦ ☞

Meads, 23 Granville Road, Oxted, Surrey, RH8 0BX.
Tudor style house on Kent/Surrey border, station to London.
Grades: ETC 4 Diamond
Tel: **01883 730115**
Mrs Holgate.
D: £25.00-£28.00
S: £28.00-£30.00.
Open: All Year
Beds: 1T 1D
Baths: 1 En 1 Pr
🛏 🅿 🗡 🗍 🕭 🖳 🖳 ✦ ☞

Old Forge House, Merle Common, Oxted, Surrey, RH8 0JB.
Actual grid ref: TQ416493
Welcoming family home in rural surroundings. Ten minutes from M25.
Tel: **01883 715969**
Mrs Mills.
D: £18.00-£20.00 **S:** £18.00-£20.00
Open: All Year (not Xmas)
Beds: 1D 1T 1S
Baths: 1 Sh
🛏 🅿 (4) 🗍 🕆 🕭 ✦ ☞

Limpsfield 25

National Grid Ref: TQ4052

🍴 🍺 The George, The Crown, The Gurkha

Arawa, 58 Granville Road,
Limpsfield, Oxted, Surrey, RH8 0BZ.
Actual grid ref: TQ402532
Friendly, comfortable, welcoming.
Lovely garden, excellent breakfast,
good London trains.
Grades: ETC 3 Diamond
Tel: **01883 714104** (also fax no)
Gibbs.
D: £18.00-£30.00
S: £18.00-£30.00.
Open: All Year
Beds: 1F 2T
Baths: 1 En 1 Sh
🛏 🅿 (3) ⏚ 🖵 🛉 ♨ 🍴 ⓥ 🗄 ♦ 🚲

All cycleways are
popular: you are
well-advised to
book ahead

Pay B&Bs by cash or
cheque and be prepared
to pay up front.

Godstone 26

National Grid Ref: TQ3551

🍴 🍺 Coach House

Godstone Hotel, The Green,
Godstone, Surrey, RH9 8DT.
Tel: **01883 742461** (also fax no)
Mr Howe.
D: £27.50 **S:** £39.00.
Open: All Year
Beds: 6D 2T
Baths: 8 Pr
🛏 🅿 🖵 🛉 ✗ ♨ 🍴 ⓥ 🗄 ♦
C16th coaching house, original
features, inglenook fireplaces. Our
restaurant 'The Coach House' is
renowned in the vicinity for superb
cuisine at sensible prices - well
worth a visit. Pre-booking is
highly recommended. Our friendly
staff look forward to welcoming
you.

Redhill 27

National Grid Ref: TQ2750

🍴 🍺 The Sun

Lynwood Guest House, 50 London
Road, Redhill, Surrey, RH1 1LN.
Actual grid ref: TQ280511
Adjacent to a lovely park, within 6
minutes walking from railway sta-
tion, town centre.
Grades: AA 3 Diamond
Tel: **01737 766894** Mrs Trozado.
Fax no: 01737 778253
D: £25.00-£28.00 **S:** £32.00-£35.00.
Open: All Year **Beds:** 4F 2D 1T 2S
Baths: 3 En 6 Pr 1 Sh
🛏 🅿 (8) 🖵 ♨ 🍴 ⓥ ♦

Leigh 28

National Grid Ref: TQ2246

🍴 🍺 The Plough

Barn Cottage, Church Road,
Leigh, Reigate, Surrey, RH2 8RF.
Converted C17th barn, gardens
with swimming pool, 100 yards
from pub, 0.25 hr Gatwick.
Tel: **01306 611347** Mrs Comer.
D: £25.00-£30.00 **S:** £35.00-£35.00.
Open: All Year
Beds: 1D 1T **Baths:** 1 Sh
🛏 🅿 (3) ⏚ 🖵 🛉 ✗ ♨ 🍴 ⓥ 🗄 ♦ 🚲

Wiltshire Cycleway

The **Wiltshire Cycleway** is a 160-mile circular tour of the County of Wiltshire, which takes you from rolling hills to the Salisbury Plain, from prehistoric chalk hillside carvings and Stonehenge to old English villages and towns - Salisbury, Marlborough, Malmesbury and close to Bath, across the border in Somerset. It is signposted in both directions by blue Wiltshire Cycleway direction signs with a cycle silhouette, but is designed to be cycled anticlockwise. NB: There are a number of alternative routes, for which the signposts feature coloured spots; for the route featured in this book follow the plain blue signs.

A detailed **guide leaflet** to the cycleway route is available free from the Director of Environmental Services, Wiltshire County Council, County Hall, Trowbridge, Wiltshire BA14 8JD, tel 01225 713349. A separate factsheet on cycle repair/hire shops is also available free from the same address.

Maps: Ordnance Survey 1:50,000 Landranger series: 172, 173, 174, 183, 184

Trains: Bath, Chippenham and Swindon

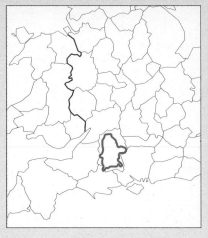

are on the main London (Paddington)-Bristol railway line. Frome, Westbury, Pewsey and Great Bedwyn are on the main London (Paddington)-Penzance line. Salisbury, Tisbury and Gillingham are on the line that runs between London Waterloo and Exeter. Bath, Bradford-on-Avon, Trowbridge, Westbury, Warminster and Salisbury are on the Bristol-Southampton line.

Malmesbury   1

National Grid Ref: ST9387

🍴 🍺 Plough Inn, Wheatsheaf Inn, Old Inn, White Horse, Smoking Dog, Whole Hog, Horse & Groom

Bremilham House, Bremilham Road, Malmesbury, Wilts, SN16 0DQ.
Grades: ETC 3 Diamond
Tel: **01666 822680** Mrs Ball.
D: £17.50-£17.50 **S:** £20.00-£20.00
Open: All Year (not Xmas)
Beds: 2D 1T **Baths:** 2 Sh
🛇 🅿 (3) ⊬ 🗖 🕇 🛒 🎞 🖤 🎗 ♣
Delightful Edwardian cottage set in a mature walled garden in a quiet location on the edge of historic Malmesbury, England's oldest borough. The town, dominated by a stunning Norman Abbey, is central for Bath, Cheltenham, Salisbury and the glorious Cotswolds.

D = Price range per person sharing in a double room

Pay B&Bs by cash or cheque and be prepared to pay up front.

Yatton Keynell   2

National Grid Ref: ST8676

🍴 🍺 Bell Inn, Salutation Inn

Oakfield Farm, Easton Piercy Lane, Yatton Keynell, Chippenham, Wilts, SN14 6JU.
Cotswold stone farmhouse in open countryside. Ideal for Cotswolds, Bath, Stonehenge.
Tel: **01249 782355**
Mrs Read.
Fax no: 01249 783458
D: £20.00-£22.50
S: £25.00-£30.00.
Open: Mar to Oct
Beds: 2D 1T
Baths: 1 En 1 Sh
🛇 🅿 (8) ⊬ 🗖 🛒 🎞 🖤 🎗 ♣

Biddestone   3

National Grid Ref: ST8673

🍴 🍺 White Horse

Home Place, Biddestone, Chippenham, Wiltshire, SN14 7DG.
End of farmhouse, on village green. Opposite duck pond.
Grades: ETC 2 Diamond
Tel: **01249 712928** Ms Hall.
D: £15.00-£17.50 **S:** £15.00-£17.50.
Open: All Year
Beds: 1F 1T 1S
Baths: 1 Sh
🛇 🅿 (2) ⊬ 🗖 🛒 🎞 🖤 🎗 ♣

Home Farm, Biddestone, Chippenham, Wilts, SN14 7DQ.
Listed C17th farmhouse working farm, picturesque village. Stroll to pubs.
Tel: **01249 714475**
Mr & Mrs Smith.
Fax no: 01249 701488
D: £20.00-£22.50 **S:** £25.00-£30.00.
Open: All Year (not Xmas)
Beds: 2F 1D
Baths: 2 En 1 Pr
🛇 🅿 (4) ⊬ 🗖 🛒 🎞 🖤 🎄 ♣

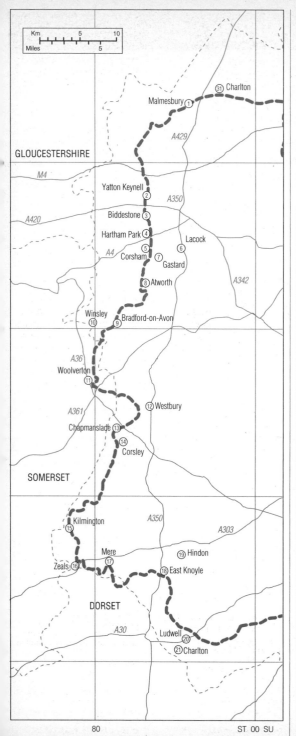

Hartham Park 4

National Grid Ref: ST8672

***Church Farm,** Hartham Park, Corsham, Wiltshire, SN13 0PU.*
Actual grid ref: ST861715
Cotswold farmhouse in rural location, stunning views, quiet and peaceful.
Grades: ETC 4 Diamond,
AA 4 Diamond
Tel: **01249 715180** Mrs Jones.
Fax no: 01249 715572
D: £20.00-£25.00 **S:** £20.00-£22.00.
Open: All Year (not Xmas/New Year)
Beds: 1F 1D 1S **Baths:** 2 En 1 Pr
🛏 (1) 🅿 (6) ✄ ☐ 🛢 ▦ Ⓥ 🛢 ⊬ ♻

Malmesbury to Corsham

   Malmesbury is a small town which breathes English history. Its partially-ruined Romanesque abbey stands on the site of a seventh-century Benedictine foundation which burned down in the eleventh century; the present Norman structure suffered damage at the Dissolution. In the Dark Ages this county lay at the heart of the domain of the West Saxons, a heritage represented in the abbey by the tomb of King Athelstan, the first Saxon to be acknowledged king of all England and the grandson of Alfred the Great of Wessex. In more recent times, the philosopher Thomas Hobbes was born in Malmesbury in 1588. Cycling south west, slightly off the route but well worth a visit is **Castle Combe**, *the* archetypal English village, where the cottages, church and bridge over the brook are built in the same local stone; it was used as the location for Puddleby-in-the-Marsh in the 1967 film of *Dr Dolittle*. Back on the cycleway and **Corsham** boasts weavers' cottages and the Elizabethan Corsham Court, with Capability Brown gardens and a fine art collection containing pictures from Renaissance masters onwards.

Corsham 5

National Grid Ref: ST8670

|⊙| ◫ White Horse Inn, Hare & Hounds, Harp and Crown, George

Thurlestone Lodge, *13 Prospect, Corsham, Wilts, SN13 9AD.*
Elegant Victorian home set in landscaped gardens, close to town centre.
Tel: **01249 713397**
Mrs Ogilvie-Robb.
D: £21.00-£24.00 **S:** £30.00-£40.00.
Open: All Year (not Xmas/New Year)
Beds: 1T 1D
Baths: 1 En 1 Pr
⌂ �ᴘ (5) ⊡ ⴕ ⴕ ⏆ Ⅴ ⋈ ⌖

Bellwood, *45 Pickwick, Corsham, Wilts, SN13 0HX.*
Actual grid ref: ST863706
Charming 1708 cottage (adjacent to owners), pubs nearby, Bath 8 miles.
Tel: **01249 713434** Mrs Elliott.
D: £20.00-£22.00 **S:** £22.00-£25.00.
Open: All Year
Beds: 2T 1S **Baths:** 1 Pr 1 Sh
⌂ (2) ᴘ (4) ⊡ ⴕ ⴕ ⏆ Ⅴ ⋈ ⌖

Lacock 6

National Grid Ref: ST9168

|⊙| ◫ George, Red Lion, Carpenters' Arms, Angel

Lacock Pottery, *The Tan Yard, Lacock, Chippenham, Wilts, SN15 2LB.*
Beautiful, comfortable, working pottery, medieval village.
Grades: ETC 4 Diamond
Tel: **01249 730266** Mrs McDowell.
Fax no: 01249 730948
D: £29.50-£39.50 **S:** £37.00-£59.00.
Open: All Year (not Xmas/New Year)
Beds: 1T 2D **Baths:** 1 En 1 Sh 1 Pr
⌂ ᴘ (6) ⊡ ⴕ ⴕ ⏆ Ⅴ ⋈ ⌖

The Old Rectory, *Lacock, Chippenham, Wilts, SN15 2JZ.*
Grades: ETC 4 Diamond
Tel: **01249 730335** Mrs Sexton.
Fax no: 01249 730166
D: £22.50-£25.00 **S:** £25.00-£27.50.
Open: All Year
Beds: 1F 1D 1T
Baths: 3 En
⌂ ᴘ (6) ⊡ ⴕ ⴕ ⏆ Ⅴ ⋈ ⌖
Superb Gothic Victorian architecture, set in 8 acres of grounds and gardens, many original features and 4 poster beds. Excellent pubs a stroll away in famous Lacock location for tourists and businessmen, M4 (J17), close by. Bath 12 miles, London 2 hours. Recomm in 'Off the Beaten Track'.

Gastard 7

National Grid Ref: ST8868

|⊙| ◫ George

Heatherly Cottage, *Ladbrook Lane, Gastard, Corsham, Wilts, SN13 9PE.*
C17th cottage set in quiet location with large garden. Guests have separate wing.
Grades: ETC 4 Diamond
Tel: **01249 701402**
Mrs Daniel.
Fax no: 01249 701412
D: £23.00-£25.00 **S:** £27.00-£30.00.
Open: All Year (not Xmas/New Year)
Beds: 1T 2D
Baths: 3 En
⌂ (10) ᴘ (8) ⊡ ⴕ ⏆ Ⅴ ⋈ ⌖

Pay B&Bs by cash or cheque and be prepared to pay up front.

Atworth 8

National Grid Ref: ST8665

|⊙| ◫ Golden Fleece, White Hart

Kings Stile Cottage, *153 Bath Road, Atworth, Melksham, Wiltshire, SN12 8JR.*
Cottage in village location. Convenient for Bath, Bradford-on-Avon, NT properties. Delicious breakfasts.
Tel: **01225 706202** (also fax no)
Mr & Mrs Hughes.
D: £18.00-£20.00 **S:** £20.00-£25.00.
Open: All Year **Beds:** 1T 1D
⌂ ᴘ (2) ⊡ ⴕ ⏆ Ⅴ ⋈ ⌖

Church Farm, *Atworth, Melksham, Wilts, SN12 8JA.*
Working dairy farm, large garden. Easy access Bath, Lacock, Bradford-on-Avon.
Tel: **01225 702215** Mrs Hole.
D: £17.50-£20.00 **S:** £20.00-£25.00.
Open: Easter to Oct
Beds: 1F 1D **Baths:** 1 Sh
⌂ ᴘ (4) ⊡ ⴕ ⏆ Ⅴ

Bradford-on-Avon 9

National Grid Ref: ST8261

|⊙| ◫ Barge, Bear, Beehive, Cross Guns, Hop Pole, King's Arms, New Inn, Plough, Seven Stars, Three Horseshoes

Chard's Barn, *Leigh Grove, Bradford-on-Avon, Wilts, BA15 2RF.*
Tel: **01225 863461**
Mr & Mrs Stickney.
D: £20.00-£23.00 **S:** £20.00-£20.00.
Open: All Year (not Xmas)
Beds: 1D 1T 1S **Baths:** 2 En 1 Pr
⌂ ᴘ (4) ⊡ ⴕ ⴕ ⏆ ⌖
Quiet C17th barn in unspoilt countryside with lovely gardens, view and walks. All ground floor, individually styled bedrooms, choice of breakfasts. Historic town and golf course, one mile. Close - Bath, Castle Combe, Longleat. Easy for Salisbury Plain and Stonehenge.

Corsham to Salisbury

Bradford on Avon, another quaint English town, centres on an arched stone bridge over the Avon, and also features a tithe barn and the ancient Saxon Church of St Laurence. From here you may wish to take a detour to **Bath**, which is possible to reach by bicycle along the towpath of the Kennet and Avon Canal (see the *Sustrans* West Country Way). South of Bradford on Avon you pass the ruins of Farleigh Castle and you can find Iford Manor and its famous landscaped garden with mediterranean plants, by Harold Peto. The next stretch takes in a piece of Wiltshire's famous prehistory, as you pass the renowned Westbury White Horse hillside carving - you are now at the west side of Salisbury Plain.

This pocket of the county contains a clutch of stately piles - **Longleat** boasts the bizarre combination of a splendid renaissance manor and a theme park with only one obvious feature in common with the house: its sheer scale - based on an African safari park, it offers a variety of other attractions including the world's longest maze. **Stourhead**, although built on a comparable scale, is more restrained in every respect. Dating from the eighteenth century, the Palladian mansion is accompanied by a famous landscaped garden, whose carefully-orchestrated classical harmony is mirrored in a lake; also here is King Alfred's Tower, a folly offering impressive views. **Stourton House Gardens**, nearby, have a collection of unusual plants. From here it is a beautiful ride around the West Wiltshire Downs towards Salisbury.

The Locks, 265 Trowbridge Road, Bradford-on-Avon, Wilts, *BA15 1UA.* Adjoining canal tow path. Ideal walking/cycling 7/8 mile town centre.
Tel: **01225 863358** Mrs Benjamin.
D: £17.50-£20.00 **S:** £20.00-£30.00.
Open: All Year
Beds: 1F 2T
Baths: 1 En 1 Pr 1 Sh
🛏 (3) 🅿 (6) ⊬⛒🗔📓 🎹 Ⓥ 🌢 ≠ ♿

Great Ashley Farm, Ashley Lane, Bradford-on-Avon, Wilts, *BA15 2PP.*
Actual grid ref: ST813619
Delightful rooms. Great hospitality. Delicious breakfast. Colour brochure. Silver award.
Grades: ETC 4 Diamond
Tel: **01225 864563** (also fax no)
Mrs Rawlings.
D: £20.00-£24.00
S: £25.00-£45.00.
Open: All Year (not Xmas)
Beds: 1F 2D
Baths: 3 En
🛏 🅿 ⊬⛒🗔📓 🎹 Ⓥ 🌢 ≠ ♿

Springfields, 182a Great Ashley, Bradford on Avon, Wilts, *BA15 2PP.*
Unique ground-level ensuite double room with adjoining dining-room/lounge. Peaceful countryside setting.
Grades: ETC 3 Diamond
Tel: **01225 866125**
Ms Rawlings.
D: £20.00-£22.50
S: £30.00-£35.00.
Open: All Year
Beds: 1D
Baths: 1En
⊬⛒🗔✗📓 🎹 Ⓥ

Avonvilla, Avoncliff, Bradford-on-Avon, Wilts, *BA15 2HD.*
Superb canal and riverside setting. Free parking and fishing. Excellent walking.
Tel: **01225 863867**
Mrs Mumford.
D: £17.00-£17.00
S: £20.00-£20.00.
Open: All Year
Beds: 1D 1T 1S
🛏 (5) 🅿 ⊬⛒🗔📓 🎹 Ⓥ ≠

Winsley 10

National Grid Ref: ST7961

🍴 🍺 Seven Stars

Conifers, 4 King Alfred Way, Winsley, Bradford-on-Avon, Wilts, *BA15 2NG.*
Quiet area, pleasant outlook, friendly atmosphere, convenient Bath, lovely walks.
Grades: ETC 2 Diamond
Tel: **01225 722482**
Mrs Kettlety.
D: £17.00-£18.00 **S:** £18.00-£20.00.
Open: All Year
Beds: 1T 1D
Baths: 1 Sh
🛏 🅿 ⊬⛒🗔🐾📓 🎹 Ⓥ ≠ ♿

3 Corners, Cottles Lane, Winsley, Bradford-on-Avon, Wilts, *BA15 2HJ.*
House in quiet village edge location, attractive rooms and gardens.
Tel: **01225 865380** Mrs Cole.
D: £22.50-£25.00 **S:** £26.00-£30.00.
Open: All Year (not Xmas)
Beds: 1F 1D
Baths: 1 En 1 Pr
🛏 🅿 (4) ⊬⛒🗔✗📓 🎹 Ⓥ 🌢 ≠ ♿

Serendipity, 19 Bradford Road, Winsley, Bradford-on-Avon, Wilts, *BA15 2HW.*
Bungalow with beautiful gardens, badgers feeding nightly, ground floor room available.
Grades: ETC 4 Diamond
Tel: **01225 722380** Mrs Shepherd.
Fax no: 01225 723451
D: £21.00-£22.50 **S:** £30.00-£40.00.
Open: All Year
Beds: 1F 1D 1S
Baths: 3 En
🛏 🅿 (5) ⊬⛒🗔📓 ♿ Ⓥ 🌢 ≠ ♿

Woolverton 11

National Grid Ref: ST7854

🍴 🍺 Red Lion

The Old School House, Woolverton, Bath, Somerset, *BA3 6RH.*
Homely accommodation. Converted Victorian school, 10 minutes south of Bath.
Tel: **01373 830200** (also fax no)
Thornton.
D: £20.00-£25.00 **S:** £25.00-£30.00.
Open: All Year (not Xmas/New Year)
Beds: 1F 1T 2D
Baths: Sh
🛏 🅿 ⊬📓 🎹 Ⓥ

Westbury 12

National Grid Ref: ST8650

🍴 🍺 Full Moon

Brokerswood House, Brokerswood, Westbury, Wilts, *BA13 4EH.*
Situated in front of 80 acres of woodland, open to the public.
Tel: **01373 823428**
Mrs Phillips.
D: £15.00-£18.00
S: £15.00-£18.00.
Open: All Year (not Xmas)
Beds: 3F 1D 1T 1S
Baths: 1 En 1 Pr 1 Sh
🛏 (1) 🅿 (6) ⊬⛒🐾📓 Ⓥ 🌢 ≠ ♿

All cycleways are popular: you are well-advised to book ahead

---

Chapmanslade 13

National Grid Ref: ST8348

🍴 🍺 Three Horseshoes

Spinney Farm, Thoulstone, Chapmanslade, Westbury, Wilts, *BA13 4AQ.*
In heart of Wiltshire countryside. Easy reach of Bath, Longleat.
Tel: **01373 832412** Mrs Hoskins.
D: £19.00**S:** £20.00.
Open: All Year
Beds: 1F 1D 1T
Baths: 2 Sh
🛏 🅿 (8) 🗔🐾✗♿📓 🎹 Ⓥ 🌢 ≠ ♿

Corsley 14

National Grid Ref: ST8246

Sturford Mead Farm, Corsley, Warminster, Wilts, *BA12 7QU.*
Farmhouse in Area of Outstanding Natural Beauty close to Longleat.
Grades: ETC 4 Diamond, AA 4 Diamond
Tel: **01373 832213** (also fax no)
Mrs Corp.
D: £22.00-£22.00 **S:** £30.00-£28.00.
Open: All Year
Beds: 1D 2T
Baths: 2 En 1 Pr
🛏 🅿 (6) ⊬⛒🗔📓 🎹 Ⓥ ♿

Kilmington 15

National Grid Ref: ST7736

🍴 🍺 Spread Eagle

The Red Lion Inn, On B3092 (Mere to Frome road), Kilmington, Warminster, Wilts, *BA12 6RP.*
Actual grid ref: ST786354
Unspoilt 15th century traditional inn. Stourhead 1 mile. Comfortable beds, good breakfasts.
Tel: **01985 844263** Mr Gibbs.
D: £17.50-£17.50 **S:** £25.00-£25.00.
Open: All Year (not Xmas/New Year)
Baths: 1 Sh
🛏 (4) 🅿 (25) ⊬🐾♿📓 🎹 Ⓥ ≠ ♿

Zeals 16

National Grid Ref: ST7731

🍴 🍺 White Lion

Cornerways Cottage, Zeals, Longcross, Warminster, Wilts, *BA12 6LL.*
Grades: ETC 4 Diamond
Tel: **01747 840477** (also fax no)
Mr & Mrs Snook.
D: £19.00-£21.00 **S:** £25.00-£25.00.
Open: All Year
Beds: 2D 1T **Baths:** 2 En 1 Pr
🛏 (8) 🅿 (6) ⊬⛒🗔✗♿📓 🎹 Ⓥ 🌢 ≠ ♿
Cornerways is a C18th cottage offering a high standard of accommodation with a lovely 'cottagey' feel, complemented by excellent breakfasts in the old dining room. Stourhead 2 miles, Longleat 4 miles, Bath/Salisbury 25 miles.

Salisbury to Amesbury

Wilton House, just before Salisbury, dates mainly from the seventeenth century, when Inigo Jones rebuilt it after a fire, and includes a fantastic collection of paintings and landscaped parkland with an old English rose garden. **Salisbury** is an historic city most famous for its cathedral, whose 404-foot spire is the tallest in England, and which is also notable for the chapter house, the vaulted cloisters and the library, which contains one of only four existing original copies of the Magna Carta. The secluded Cathedral Close leads into the narrow medieval city streets. Cycling north, **Old Sarum** is the site of an Iron Age fort, and was settled by Romans, Saxons and Normans, and was the original site of the cathedral before it was transferred (including the fabric) to Salisbury. **Amesbury** is where to make the detour to **Stonehenge**, the world-renowned prehistoric enigma at the heart of Salisbury Plain. In fact, because of the remains of several different constructions separated by hundreds of years, the site seems to have been a centre of religious devotion for centuries. The stones of the earlier circle were hewn from a quarry in Wales and transported; the later circle is remarkable for the sheer size of the megaliths, and their construction into sets of two uprights crossed by a lintel.

All rates are subject to alteration at the owners' discretion.

Mere   17

National Grid Ref: ST8132

|O| ◀Talbot Inn, Butt of Sherry, Old Ship

Norwood House, Mere, Warminster, Wilts, BA12 6LA.
Actual grid ref: ST802323
Large ground floor room with French windows onto pleasant garden.
Tel: **01747 860992** (also fax no)
Mrs Tillbrook.
D: £18.00-£18.00 **S:** £22.00-£22.00.
Open: All Year
Beds: 1F 1T **Baths:** 1 En
🛏 🄿 (3) ⛽ 🍴 ⚓ ▥ ♿ 🚲 ⚲

Downleaze, North Street, Mere, Warminster, Wilts, BA12 6HH.
Comfortable red brick house, quiet, close to town centre. Warm welcome. Stourhead - two miles.
Grades: ETC 2 Diamond
Tel: **01747 860876** Mrs Lampard.
D: £16.00-£18.00 **S:** £17.50-£20.00.
Open: All Year (not Xmas/New Year)
Beds: 1D 1T **Baths:** 1 Sh
🛏 (5) 🄿 (6) ⛽ 🍴 ⚓ ▥ Ⓥ

East Knoyle   18

National Grid Ref: ST8830

|O| ◀Fox & Hounds

Moors Farmhouse, East Knoyle, Salisbury, Wilts, SP3 6BU.
Actual grid ref: ST863301
C17th farmhouse suite of large rooms. Naturally beautiful/interesting area.
Tel: **01747 830385** Mrs Reading.
D: £25.00-£25.00 **S:** £25.00-£25.00.
Open: All Year (not Xmas)
Beds: 1T **Baths:** 1 En
🛏 (8) 🄿 (2) ⛽ ⚓ ▥ Ⓥ ⓘ ✦ ⚲

Hindon   19

National Grid Ref: ST9132

Chicklade Lodge, Chicklade, Hindon, Salisbury, Wilts, SP3 5SU.
Charming Victorian cottage. Under 2 hour drive from Heathrow.
Tel: **01747 820389** Mrs Jerram.
D: £20.00-£20.00 **S:** £25.00-£25.00.
Open: All Year
Beds: 2T 1D
Baths: 1 Sh
🛏 (5) 🄿 (4) ⛽ ⚓ 🍴 ✕ ♨ ▥ Ⓥ ⓘ

Ludwell   20

National Grid Ref: ST9122

|O| ◀Rising Sun

Ye Olde Wheelwrights, Birdbush, Ludwell, Shaftesbury, Dorset, SP7 9NH.
Accommodation in separate annexe. Children and families welcome. Hearty breakfast.
Tel: **01747 828955** Dieppe.
D: £17.50-£20.00
S: £20.00-£22.00.
Open: April to October
Beds: 1T 1D
Baths: 1 Sh
🛏 🄿 ⛽ ⚓ ♨ Ⓥ ⚲

All cycleways are popular: you are well-advised to book ahead

---

Charlton (Shaftesbury)   21

National Grid Ref: ST9022

|O| ◀Grove Arms, Talbot

Charnwood Cottage, Charlton, Shaftesbury, Dorset, SP7 9LZ.
Actual grid ref: ST902226
C17th thatched cottage with lovely garden. Good base for touring.
Tel: **01747 828310** (also fax no)
Mr & Mrs Morgan.
D: £18.00-£19.00 **S:** £20.00.
Open: All Year (not Xmas/New Year)
Beds: 1T 1D **Baths:** 1 Sh
🛏 (5) 🄿 (2) ⚓ 🍴 ▥

Coombe Bissett   22

National Grid Ref: SU1026

|O| ◀Fox & Goose, Yew Tree Inn, White Hart, Radnor Arms

Swaynes Firs Farm, Grimsdyke, Coombe Bissett, Salisbury, Wilts, SP5 5RF.
Spacious farmhouse on working farm with horses, cattle, poultry, geese & duck ponds etc.
Grades: ETC 3 Diamond
Tel: **01725 519240** Mr Shering.
D: £20.00-£22.00 **S:** £25.00-£30.00.
Open: All Year (not Xmas)
Beds: 1F 2T
Baths: 3 En
🛏 🄿 (6) ⚓ 🍴 ⚓ ▥ Ⓥ ⚲

Salisbury   23

National Grid Ref: SU1430

|O| ◀Avon Brewery, Barford Inn, Bell Inn, Castle Inn, Fox & Goose, George & Dragon, Grey Fisher, Haunch Of Venison, Hogs Head, Markest Inn, Radnor Arms, Ship, White Hart, White Horse, Wyndham Arms Yew Tree

▲ *Salisbury Youth Hostel, Milford Hill House, Milford Hill, Salisbury, Wiltshire, SP1 2QW.*
Actual grid ref: SU149299
Tel: **01722 327572**
Under 18: £7.75 **Adults:** £11.00
Self-catering facilities, Television, Showers, Laundry facilities, Lounge, Cycle store, Parking, Evening meal at 5.30-7.45pm, Kitchen facilities, Breakfast available, Credit cards accepted
200-year-old Listed building in secluded grounds only a few minutes from the city centre. Enjoy the relaxed atmosphere of the hostel and the well-tended grounds which include a fine old cedar tree.

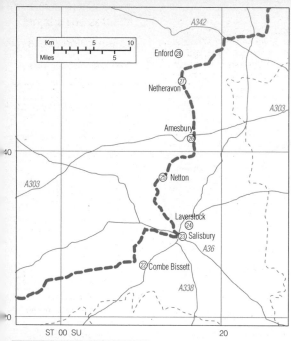

Wyndham Park Lodge,
51 Wyndham Road, Salisbury,
Wilts, SP1 3AB.
Large Victorian house, close to city
centre. Friendly family-run estab-
lishment.
Grades: ETC 4 Diamond
Tel: **01722 416517**
P Legg & S Coppen.
Fax no: 01722 328851
D: £19.00-£21.00 **S:** £26.00-£32.00.
Open: All Year
Beds: 1F 1T 1D 1S
Baths: 4 En
⌂ **P** (3) ⅄ ◻ ♨ ▥ 🔲

Byways House, *31 Fowlers Road,*
Salisbury, Wilts, SP1 2QP.
Attractive Victorian House, quiet,
parking. Fowlers Road opposite
youth hostel.
Grades: ETC 3 Diamond
Tel: **01722 328364**
Mr & Mrs Arthey.
Fax no: 01722 322146
D: £22.50-£39.00 **S:** £30.00-£60.00.
Open: All Year (not Xmas/New
Year)
Beds: 3F 7T 7D 4S
Baths: 19 En 1 Sh
⌂ **P** (15) ⅄ ◻ ♖ ♨ ▥ & 🔲 ⅏ ♣

Cricket Field House Hotel, *Wilton*
Road, Salisbury, Wilts, SP2 7NS.
All rooms ensuite. Ample car park-
ing, Beautiful garden.
Grades: AA 4 Diamond
Tel: **01722 322595** (also fax no)
Mrs James.
D: £30.00-£35.00
S: £40.00-£45.00.
Open: All Year (not Xmas)
Beds: 1F 7D 3T 3S
Baths: 14 En
P (14) ⅄ ◻ ✕ ♨ ▥ & 🔲 ♟

Farthings, *9 Swaynes Close,*
Wyndham Road, Salisbury, Wilts,
SP1 3AE.
Comfortable old house in quiet
street near city centre.
Grades: ETC 3 Diamond
Tel: **01722 330749** (also fax no)
Mrs Rodwell.
D: £20.00-£25.00
S: £20.00.
Open: All Year
Beds: 1D 1T 2S
Baths: 2 En 1 Sh
P (1) ⅄ ◻ ♨ ▥ 🔲 ⅏ ♣

Richburn Guest House, *25*
Estcourt Road, Salisbury, Wilts,
SP1 3AP.
Building over 150 years old - 5
mins walk city centre,10 minutes
Cathedral.
Grades: ETC 3 Diamond
Tel: **01722 325189** (also fax no)
Mrs West.
D: £18.00-£30.00
S: £20.00-£40.00.
Open: All Year (not Xmas/New
Year)
Beds: 1F 1D 1T 1S
Baths: 4 En
⌂ **P** (10) **P** (5) ⅄ ◻ ✕ ♨ ▥ 🔲 ♣

The Old Rectory B&B, *Belle Vue*
Road, Salisbury, Wiltshire, SP1 3YE.
Grades: ETC 4 Diamond
Tel: **01722 502702** Ms Smith.
Fax no: 01722 501135
D: £18.00-£27.00 **S:** £20.00-£40.00.
Open: All Year
Beds: 2T 1D
Baths: 2 En 1 Pr
⌂ (10) **P** (1) ⅄ ◻ ♨ ▥ 🔲 🔒 ⅏ ♣
Welcoming Victorian home, nes-
tled in rich green English garden on
a quiet street. Offering warm hospi-
tality, bright airy bedrooms, quiet
breakfast/sitting room with picture
window and open fire. Short walk
to city centre. Perfect for a quiet
comfortable stay.

Hayburn Wyke Guest House, *72*
Castle Road, Salisbury, Wilts,
SP1 3RL.
Grades: AA 3 Diamond,
RAC 3 Diamond
Tel: **01722 412627**
Mrs Curnow.
D: £20.00-£25.00
S: £29.00-£48.00.
Open: All Year
Beds: 2F 3D 2T
Baths: 4 En 3 Sh
⌂ **P** (7) ◻ ♨ ▥ 🔲 ⅏ ♣
A family run friendly guest house,
Hayburn Wyke is a fine Victorian
house, situated by Victoria Park,
half a mile riverside walk from
Salisbury Cathedral and city centre.
Many places to visit locally,
including Stonehenge, Wilton
House and Old Sarum.

Weaver's Cottage, *37 Bedwin*
Street, Salisbury, Wilts, SP1 3UT.
C15th city centre cottage, cosy,
oak-beamed, 2 minutes market
square & bus station.
Tel: **01722 341812** Mrs Bunce.
D: £15.00-£20.00 **S:** £23.00-£25.00.
Open: All Year (not Xmas)
Beds: 1F 1D **Baths:** 1 Sh
◻ ♨ ▥ 🔲 ♣

Websters, *11 Hartington Road,*
Salisbury, Wilts, SP2 7LG.
Set on the end of a delightfully
colourful terrace with sumptuous
choices for breakfast.
Grades: ETC 4 Diamond, Silver,
RAC 4 Diamond, Sparkling
Tel: **01722 339779** (also fax no)
Mrs Webb.
D: £19.00-£21.00 **S:** £30.00-£34.00.
Open: All Year
Beds: 1D 2T 2S
Baths: 5 En
⌂ (12) **P** (5) ◻ ✕ ♨ ▥ & 🔲

The White Horse Hotel, *38 Castle*
Street, Salisbury, SP1 1BN.
Tel: **01722 327844**
Fax no: 01722 336226
D: £35.00-£50.00 **S:** £27.00-£35.00.
Open: All Year
Beds: 2F 3T 4D
Baths: 1 En 2 Sh
⌂ **P** (9) ◻ ✕ ♨ ▥ 🔒 ♣
Traditional pub/inn offering a
beautiful Cathedral view and only
10 minutes walk. Off side parking.
Comfortable rooms. Home cooked
pub food. Friendly welcoming
service.

Wiltshire Cycleway

Netton 25

National Grid Ref: SU1336

🏨 🍺 Bridge, Black Horse

The Old Bakery, Netton, Salisbury, Wilts, *SP4 6AW.*
Actual grid ref: SU128369
The Old Bakery is a pleasantly modernised former village bakery in the Woodford Valley.
Grades: ETC 3 Diamond
Tel: **01722 782351** Mrs Dunlop.
D: £18.00-£20.00 **S:** £20.00-£25.00.
Open: All Year (not Xmas)
Beds: 1D 1T 1S
Baths: 2 En 1 Pr
🛏 (5) 🅿 (3) 🍴 🔥 🛏 🧺 Ⅴ

Thorntons, Netton, Salisbury, Wilts, *SP4 6AW.*
Tranquil village convenient for Salisbury and Stonehenge. Home cooking a speciality.
Tel: **01722 782535** (also fax no)
Mrs Bridger.
D: £18.00-£20.00 **S:** £20.00-£25.00.
Open: All Year (not Xmas)
Beds: 1F 1D 1S
Baths: 2 Sh
🛏 (5) 🅿 ⌿ 🍴 ✕ 🔥 🧺 🛏 🐾 Ⅴ ✦ 🚲

Avonbank, Netton, Salisbury, Wilts, *SP4 6AW.*
Grades: ETC 3 Diamond
Tel: **01722 782331** Mrs Vincent.
D: £16.00-£20.00 **S:** £20.00-£25.00.
Open: All Year (not Xmas)
Beds: 3F 2T 1D
Baths: 1 En 1 Sh
🛏 🅿 (3) ⌿ 🍴 ✕ 🔥 🧺 🛏 🐾 Ⅴ ✦ 🚲
Comfortable modern house with very pretty garden overlooking water meadow and River Avon. Guests' sitting room. Good breakfast with home-made marmalade and jams. Baby sitting by arrangement. It is possible to obtain day fishing license.

Amesbury 26

National Grid Ref: SU1541

🏨 🍺 New Inn, Rose and Crown

Catkin Lodge, 93 Countess Road, Amesbury, Salisbury, *SP4 7AT.*
The nearest B&B to Stonehenge. Friendly, comfortable and good value.
Grades: AA 3 Diamond
Tel: **01980 624810**
Mr Grace.
Fax no: 01980622139
D: £19.00-£23.00 **S:** £18.00.
Open: All Year
Beds: 2F 1D 1T
Baths: 1 En 1 Sh
🛏 (5) 🅿 (5) ⌿ 🔥 🧺 Ⅴ ✦ 🚲

Castlewood Guest House,
45 Castle Road, Salisbury, Wilts, *SP1 3RH.*
Large Edwardian house tastefully restored throughout, pleasant 10 mins' riverside walk city centre.
Grades: ETC 3 Diamond
Tel: **01722 324809** Mrs Feltham.
Fax no: 01722 421494
D: £20.00-£22.50 **S:** £20.00-£25.00.
Open: All Year
Beds: 3F 1D 1T 1S
Baths: 3 En 2 Sh
🛏 🅿 (4) ⌿ 🍴 ✕ 🔥 Ⅴ

The Old Bakery, 35 Bedwin Street, Salisbury, Wilts, *SP1 3UT.*
C15th house, cosy oak-beamed bedrooms, room only rates also available.
Grades: ETC 2 Diamond
Tel: **01722 320100** Mrs Bunce.
D: £19.00-£26.00 **S:** £23.00-£26.00.
Open: All Year (not Xmas)
Beds: 1F 1D 1T 1S
Baths: 2 En 1 Sh
🛏 🍴 🔥 🧺 Ⅴ ✦ 🚲

Gerrans House, 91 Castle Road, Salisbury, Wilts, *SP1 3RW.*
Comfortable detached home, private facilities and secure parking.
Tel: **01722 334394** Mrs Robins.
Fax no: 01722 332508
D: £20.00-£23.00 **S:** £30.00-£35.00.
Open: Easter to Nov
Beds: 1D 1T
Baths: 2 En
🛏 (7) 🅿 (2) ⌿ 🍴 🔥 🧺 Ⅴ

48 Wyndham Road, Salisbury, Wilts, *SP1 3AB.*
Edwardian home, tastefully restored and furnished with antiques, close to city centre, quiet area.
Tel: **01722 327757** Mrs Jukes.
D: £17.00-£20.00 **S:** £20.00.
Open: All Year (not Xmas)
Beds: 2D 1T **Baths:** 1 En 1 Sh
🛏 ⌿ 🔥 🧺 Ⅴ ✦ 🚲

Leenas Guest House, 50 Castle Road, Salisbury, Wilts, *SP1 3RL.*
Friendly family-run guest house. Pretty bedrooms and delightful public areas.
Tel: **01722 335419** (also fax no)
Mrs Street.
D: £21.00-£24.00 **S:** £22.00-£36.00.
Open: All Year
Beds: 1F 2D 2T 1S **Baths:** 5 En 1 Sh
🛏 🅿 (6) 🍴 🔥 🧺 Ⅴ

Laverstock 24

National Grid Ref: SU1530

The Twitterings, 73 Church Street, Laverstock, Salisbury, Wiltshire, *SP1 1QZ.*
Quiet location. Comfortable self contained rooms. English breakfast a speciality.
Grades: ETC 3 Diamond
Tel: **01722 321760** Mrs Henly.
D: £20.00-£20.00 **S:** £20.00-£25.00.
Open: All Year (not Xmas/New Year)
Beds: 1T 1D **Baths:** 2 En
🛏 🅿 (4) ⌿ 🔥 🧺 🐾 Ⅴ ✦

D = Price range per person sharing in a double room

234 STILWELL'S CYCLEWAY COMPANION

Netheravon 27

National Grid Ref: SU1549

⋈ ◀ Dog and Gun

Paddock House, *High Street, Netheravon, Salisbury, Wiltshire, SP4 9QP.*
Comfortable village house in Netheravon. Close to Stonehenge and Avebury.
Grades: ETC 3 Diamond
Tel: 01980 670401 (also fax no)
Mrs Davis.
D: £18.00-£20.00
S: £18.00-£20.00.
Open: All Year (not Xmas/ New Year)
Beds: 1T 1D
Baths: 1 En 1 Sh
🛏 (3) ✿ (2) ⚡ ⌷ 🎄 📠 Ⅴ ⚡ 🚲

Enford 28

National Grid Ref: SU1351

⋈ ◀ Swan Inn

Enford House, *Enford, Pewsey, Wilts, SN9 6DJ.*
Salisbury Plain. River village, old rectory, beautiful garden, thatched wall.
Grades: ETC 3 Diamond
Tel: 01980 670414
Mr Campbell.
D: £18.00-£18.00 **S:** £20.00-£20.00.
Open: All Year (not Xmas)
Beds: 1D 2T
Baths: 2 Sh
🛏 📠 (5) ✿ ⌷ 🎄 ✗ 🎄 📠 Ⅴ ⚡ 🚲

Marlborough 29

National Grid Ref: SU1869

⋈ ◀ Bear, Roebuck, Sun, Oddfellows Arms

Browns Farm, *Marlborough, Wilts, SN8 4ND.*
Actual grid ref: SU198678
Peaceful farmhouse on edge of Savernake Forest. Overlooking open farmland.
Tel: 01672 515129
Mrs Crockford.
D: £16.00-£20.00
S: £20.00-£25.00.
Open: All Year
Beds: 1F 1T 2D
Baths: 1 En 1 Sh
🛏 📠 (6) ✿ ⌷ 🎄 🎄 📠 Ⅴ 🔒 🚲

Beam End, *67 George Lane, Marlborough, Wilts, SN8 4BY.*
Peaceful detached house, every comfort, good centre for touring Wiltshire.
Grades: ETC 3 Diamond
Tel: 01672 515048 (also fax no)
Mrs Drew.
D: £20.00-£27.50
S: £20.00-£30.00.
Open: All Year (not Xmas)
Beds: 1T 2S
Baths: 1 En 1 Sh
📠 (3) ✿ ⌷ 🎄 📠 Ⅴ 🔒 🚲

54 George Lane, *Marlborough, Wiltshire, SN8 4BY.*
Near town centre. Detached house. Large garden. Non smokers only.
Tel: 01672 512579
Mr & Mrs Young.
D: £17.00 **S:** £17.00.
Open: All Year (not Xmas/New Year)
Beds: 1T 2S
Baths: 1 Sh
📠 (3) ✿ ⚡ 🎄 📠 Ⅴ ⚡

West View, *Barnfield, Marlborough, Wiltshire, SN8 2AX.*
Delightful peaceful, rural home, close to town. Ideal walkers, cyclists.
Grades: ETC 3 Diamond
Tel: 01672 515583
Maggie Trevelyan-Hall.
Fax no: 01672 519014
D: £20.00-£25.00 **S:** £35.00-£45.00.
Open: All Year
Beds: 1F 3D
Baths: 2 Pr 1 Sh
🛏 📠 (3) ✿ ⌷ 🎄 ✗ 🎄 📠 🔓 Ⅴ 🔒 ⚡ 🚲

Cartref, *63 George Lane, Marlborough, Wilts, SN8 4BY.*
Actual grid ref: SU1969
Family home near town centre. Ideal for Avebury, Savernake, Wiltshire Downs.
Tel: 01672 512771 Mrs Harrison.
D: £18.00-£18.00 **S:** £20.00-£20.00.
Open: All Year (not Xmas)
Beds: 1F 1D 1T
Baths: 1 Sh
🛏 (6) 📠 (2) 🎄 📠 🔒 🔒 ⚡ 🚲

Manton 30

National Grid Ref: SU1768

⋈ ◀ Oddfellows Arms

Sunrise Farm, *Manton, Marlborough, Wilts, SN8 4HL.*
Actual grid ref: SU168682
Peacefully located approximately 1 mile from Marlborough. Friendly, comfortable, relaxing atmosphere.
Grades: ETC 3 Diamond
Tel: 01672 512878 (also fax no)
Mrs Couzens.
D: £19.00-£20.00
S: £19.00-£25.00.
Open: March to Oct
Beds: 1D 2T
Baths: 2 Pr
🛏 (14) 📠 (3) ✿ ⌷ 🎄 📠 Ⅴ 🔒 🚲

All rooms full and nowhere else to stay? Ask the owner if there's anywhere nearby

---

Amesbury to Malmesbury

The cycleway now heads north up the east side of Salisbury Plain, through the Vale of Pewsey, back across the Kennet and Avon Canal and into the Marlborough Downs. **Marlborough** has the widest high street in England, with a fine display of Georgian buildings and half-timbered cottages. Back up into the Downs, and a worthwhile detour would be south along **the Ridgeway** National Trail to Avebury, another important prehistoric site. Here stands a stone circle far wider than Stonehenge, though the stones are much smaller and not so consummately finished. Nearby are Silbury Hill, Europe's largest man-made prehistoric mound, and West Kennet Long Barrow, a burial complex dating from the fourth millennium BC. This is probably best attempted only on an all terrain bicycle. Close to the junction of the cycleway with the Ridgeway is **Hackpen Hill**, where you will find another white horse hillside carving and a panoramic viewpoint over Swindon to the Thames Valley. From here it's off the Downs into the final stretch to Malmesbury.

Charlton (Malmesbury) 31

National Grid Ref: ST9588

⋈ ◀ Horse and Groom

Stonehill Farm, *Charlton, Malmesbury, Wilts, SN16 9DY.*
C15th farmhouse on dairy farm, warm welcome, delicious breakfasts.
Grades: ETC 4 Diamond
Tel: 01666 823310 (also fax no)
Mr & Mrs Edwards.
D: £20.00-£25.00 **S:** £20.00-£27.00.
Open: All Year
Beds: 2D 1T **Baths:** 1 En 1 Sh
🛏 📠 (3) ⌷ 🎄 🎄 📠 Ⅴ ⚡

Yorkshire Dales Cycleway

The Yorkshire Dales National Park, the heart of the Pennines, is one of England's most beautiful areas, with rolling moors forming the backdrop to gentle river valleys. The **Yorkshire Dales Cycleway** is a 131-mile tour of the Dales, starting and finishing at Skipton. The route is directed along quiet roads, but some sections are very up-and-down, so a reasonably resilient bike (and cyclist!) is necessary. The cycleway is signposted by rectangular blue direction signs with a cycle silhouette.

A detailed **guide** to the cycleway route (6 route cards), which includes a list of cycle repair/hire shops on or near to the route, is available from the Yorkshire Dales National Park Authority, Cragg Hill Road, Horton-in-Ribblesdale, Settle, North Yorkshire BD24 0HN, tel 01729 860481, @ £2.25 (+£2.00 p&p).

Maps: Ordnance Survey 1:50,000 Landranger series: 98, 99, 103, 104

Trains: Skipton, Settle & Dent are served by the famous scenic Leeds-Settle-Carlisle Railway.

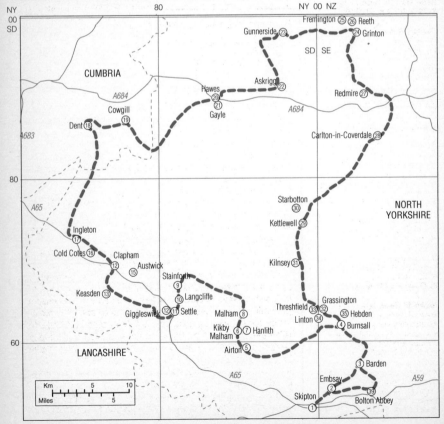

Skipton 1

National Grid Ref: SD9851

⚇ ⌾Craven Heifer, Sailor, Fleece, Elm Tree, Slaters' Arms, Wooley Sheep, Black Horse

Low Skibeden Farmhouse,
Skibeden Road, Skipton, N. Yorks,
BD23 6AB.
Actual grid ref: SE012524
C16th farmhouse with little
luxuries and fireside treats at no
extra charge.
Grades: ETC 3 Star,
AA 4 Diamond
Tel: 01756 793849 Mrs Simpson.
Fax no: 01756 793804
D: £20.00-£24.00 **S:** £25.00-£38.00.
Open: All Year
Beds: 3F 1D 1T **Baths:** 4 En 1 Sh
⌂ (12) 🅿 (5) ⅍⌷ 👱 ▥ Ⅴ ⬥ ⚵

Dalesgate Lodge, 69 Gargrave
Road, Skipton, N. Yorks, BD23 1QN.
Comfortable rooms, friendly
welcome. Special winter breaks
available.
Grades: ETC 4 Diamond
Tel: 01756 790672
Mr & Mrs Mason.
D: £17.50-£20.00 **S:** £20.00-£25.00.
Open: All Year
Beds: 2D/T 2S **Baths:** 4 En
⌂ 🅿 (2) ⅍⌷ 👱 ▥ Ⅴ ⚵

Bourne House, 22 Upper Sackville
Street, Skipton, N Yorks, BD23 2EB.
Edwardian townhouse, quiet loca-
tion, close to town centre, easy
parking.
Grades: ETC 3 Diamond
Tel: 01756 792633
Mr & Mrs Barton.
Fax no: 01756 701609
D: £16.00-£18.00 **S:** £17.00-£25.00.
Open: All Year (not Xmas/
New Year)
Beds: 1T 2D 1S
Baths: 1 En 2 Sh
⌂ (3) ⅍⌷ 👱 ▥ Ⅴ

Craven Heifer Inn, Grassington
Road, Skipton, BD23 3LA.
Country inn set at the gateway to
the Yorkshire Dales.
Grades: ETC 3 Diamond
Tel: 01756 792521 Smith.
Fax no: 01756 794442
D: £22.50 **S:** £44.95.
Open: All Year
Beds: 2F 13D 3T 1S
Baths: 16 En 3 Sh
⌂ 🅿 (99) ⅍⌷✗ 👱 ▥ & Ⅴ ⚵

Highfield Hotel, 58 Keighley
Road, Skipton, N. Yorks, BD23 2NB.
All ensuite homely rooms. 5 mins
town centre. Great dales location.
Grades: ETC 2 Star
Tel: 01756 793182 (also fax no)
Davis.
D: £18.50-£19.50 **S:** £25.00-£35.00.
Open: All Year (not Xmas)
Beds: 1T 7D 2S
Baths: 10 En
⌂ 🅿 ⌷✗ 👱 ▥ Ⅴ ⬥ ⚵

The Barn, Main Street, Skipton,
BD23 4ND.
Yorkshire Dales - Long Preston sit-
uated on the A65 Keighley to
Kendal road.
Tel: 01729 840426 Mrs Fleming.
D: £19.00-£21.50 **S:** £22.50-£25.00.
Open: All Year (not Xmas)
Beds: 1F 1D
Baths: 1 En 1 Sh
⌂ (2) 🅿 (5) ⅍⌷ ⼭ 👱 ▥ Ⅴ ⬥
⚵

Embsay 2

National Grid Ref: SE0053

⚇ ⌾Elmtree Inn, Mason Arms

Bondcroft Farm, Embsay, Skipton,
N Yorks, BD23 6SF.
Sheep and beef farm, well known
for trailing and breeding sheep
dogs.
Grades: ETC 4 Diamond
Tel: 01756 793371
Ms Clarkson.
D: £20.00-£22.50 .
Open: All Year
Beds: 1T 2D
Baths: 3 En
⌂ 🅿 (6) ⅍⌷ 👱 ▥ Ⅴ ⬥ ⚵

D = Price range per person
sharing in a double room

S = Price range for a single
person in a room

Barden (Skipton) 3

National Grid Ref: SE0557

Little Gate Farm, Drebley,
Barden, Skipton, N Yorks, BD23 6AU.
Tel: 01756 720200
D: £19.00-£19.00 **S:** £19.00-£19.00.
Open: Easter to Nov
Beds: 1F 1D 1T
Baths: 1 Pr 1 Sh
⌂ 🅿 ⅍⌷ 👱 ▥ Ⅴ ⬥ ⚵
Beautiful Grade I listed C15th
Dales farmhouse; all rooms look
down the valley to the River
Wharfe. We are a working
sheep-rearing farm, breeding our
own collies.

Howgill Lodge, Barden, Skipton,
N. Yorks, BD23 6DJ.
Actual grid ref: SE065593
Uninterrupted views over beautiful
Wharfedale. Once experienced,
you will return.
Tel: 01756 720655 Mrs Foster.
D: £27.00-£30.00 **S:** £32.00-£35.00.
Open: All Year (not Xmas)
Beds: 1F 2D 1T
Baths: 4 En
⌂ 🅿 (10) ⌷✗ 👱 ▥ Ⅴ ⬥ ⚵

Skipton to Ingleton

Skipton, one of the important market towns of the region, traces its roots to an ancient Anglo-Saxon settlement - its name means 'sheep farm'. Skipton Castle is one of the best-preserved medieval castles in Britain; at the centre stands a single yew tree planted in 1659. Also here are Holy Trinity Church, notable for the fifteenth-century bossed roof, and a museum of Craven, the North Yorkshire district in which the town lies. Out of Skipton the route heads northeast into **Wharfedale**. Here you will find the fifteenth-century Barden Tower, looking out across Barden Moor, before heading on to **Appletreewick** and the picturesque village of **Burnsall**. Then it's west through the beautiful limestone scenery of the Southern Dales into **Malhamdale**, where stand Malham Cove, a breathtaking 300-foot-high limestone natural amphitheatre, and the deep ravine of Gordale Scar. Close by you can find Janet's Foss, a waterfall with overhanging trees. The route passes to the south of **Malham Tarn**, an upland lake with a nature reserve protecting many species of waterfowl, and takes you west-wards around the imposing mass of **Fountains Fell** and into **Ribblesdale**. Here you cycle south alongside the famous Leeds-Settle-Carlisle Railway line, through the typically pretty Dales villages of Stainforth and Langcliffe into **Settle**. From here it's northwest to **Clapham**, continuing to Ingleton with **Ingleborough**, one of the so-called Three Peaks, on your right: remains of a Celtic settlement can be found at the gritstone summit by anyone wishing to take time out and make the climb.

Burnsall 4

National Grid Ref: SE0361

|○| ◁ Fountain

Burnsall Manor House Hotel,
Burnsall, Skipton, N. Yorks,
BD23 6BW.
Comfortable, friendly, relaxed.
Good food, ideal base for walking.
Tel: **01756 720231** (also fax no)
Mr Lodge.
D: £24.50-£28.50 **S:** £24.50-£28.50.
Open: All Year
Beds: 5D 3T
Baths: 5 En 1 Pr 2 Sh
⛺ 🅿 (9) ⠀⠀⠀⠀⠀⠀⠀⠀🖤

Holly Tree Farm, *Thorpe,*
Burnsall, Skipton, N. Yorks, BD23
6BJ.
Actual grid ref: SE014617
Quiet, homely Dales sheep farm.
Tel: **01756 720604** Mrs Hall.
D: £18.00-£20.00 **S:** £18.00-£20.00.
Open: All Year (not Xmas)
Beds: 1D 1S
Baths: 1 Sh
⛺ (5) 🅿 (2) ⠀⠀⠀⠀⠀⠀⠀⠀🚲

Airton 5

National Grid Ref: SD9059

🔺 **Airton Quaker Hostel,** *Airton,*
Skipton, North Yorkshire,
BD23 4AE.
Actual grid ref: SD904592
Tel: **01729 830263**
Under 18: £3.00 **Adults:** £5.00
Self-catering facilities, Showers,
Dining room, No smoking
Attached to C17th meeting house in
quiet Dales village close to
Pennine Way.

Kirkby Malham 6

National Grid Ref: SD8961

|○| ◁ Victoria

Yeoman's Barn, *Kirkby Malham,*
Skipton, North Yorks, BD23 4BL.
Tel: **01729 830639**
Mrs Turner.
D: £20.00-£25.00 **S:** £25.00-£25.00.
Open: All Year (not Xmas/New
Year)
Beds: 2D
Baths: 2 En
⛺ (5) ⠀⠀⠀⠀⠀⠀🖤
Converted C17th barn, large oak
beams, newly decorated bedrooms.
Warm welcome, tea tray on arrival,
open fire. Market towns of
Skipton, Settle and Hawes all near-
by. Malham Cove, Janets Foss and
Gordale Scar - all suitable for the
weekend walker.

D = Price range per person
sharing in a double room

Hanlith 7

National Grid Ref: SD9061

|○| ◁ Buck

Coachmans Cottage, *Hanlith,*
Malham, Skipton, N. Yorks,
BD23 4BP.
C17th cottage with beautiful view.
Every comfort.
Tel: **01729 830538** Mrs Jenkins.
D: £23.00-£23.00 .
Open: Easter to Dec
Beds: 2D **Baths:** 2 En
⛺ (10) 🅿 (3) ⠀⠀⠀⠀⠀⠀🖤

Malham 8

National Grid Ref: SD9062

|○| ◁ Listers, Buck Inn

🔺 **Malham Youth Hostel,** *John*
Dower Memorial Hostel, Malham,
Skipton, North Yorkshire, BD23 4DE.
Actual grid ref: SD901629
Tel: **01729 830321**
Under 18: £7.75 **Adults:** £11.00
Self-catering facilities, Television,
Showers, Shop, Laundry facilities,
Drying room, Security lockers,
Cycle store, Parking, Evening meal
at 7.00pm, WC, Kitchen facilities,
Breakfast available, Credit cards
accepted
Superbly located purpose-built
hostel close to centre of pic-
turesque Malham village, in the
middle of caving, walking and
cycling district.

Eastwood Guest House, *Malham,*
Skipton, North Yorkshire, BD23 4DA.
High quality bed and breakfast in
central village location.
Tel: **01729 830409** Mrs McIntyre.
D: £20.00-£25.00 **S:** £18.00-£30.00.
Open: All Year
Beds: 1F 1T 1D **Baths:** 3 En
⛺ ⠀⠀⠀⠀⠀⠀🖤

Stainforth 9

National Grid Ref: SD8267

🔺 **Stainforth Youth Hostel,**
Taitlands, Stainforth, Settle, North
Yorkshire, BD24 9PA.
Actual grid ref: SD821668
Tel: **01729 823577**
Under 18: £7.75 **Adults:** £11.00
Self-catering facilities, Showers,
Lounge, Dining room, Drying
room, Cycle store, Parking,
Evening meal at 7.00pm, Facilities
for disabled people, No smoking,
Kitchen facilities, Breakfast avail-
able, Credit cards accepted
Georgian listed building with fine
interior, set in extensive grounds
with grazing paddock, a short walk
from the village. Central for many
walks, including the Pennine and
Ribble Ways, and the Yorkshire
Dales Cycleway.

Langcliffe 10

National Grid Ref: SD8264

Bowerley Hotel & Conference
Centre, *Langcliffe, Settle, BD24 9LY.*
Country house hotel in 3 acres, bar,
restaurant, warm welcome.
Grades: ETC 2 Star
Tel: **01729 823811** Ralph.
Fax no: 01729 822317
D: £25.00-£29.00 **S:** £32.00-£39.00.
Open: All Year
Beds: 2F 8T 6D 2S
Baths: 18 En
⛺ 🅿 (50) ⠀⠀⠀⠀⠀⠀🖤
🚲

Settle 11

National Grid Ref: SD8163

|○| ◁ Golden Lion, Crown, Royal Oak

Liverpool House, *Chapel Square,*
Settle, N. Yorks, BD24 9HR.
Actual grid ref: SD822635
Situated in quiet area yet within 3
mins' walk town square.
Grades: AA 3 Diamond
Tel: **01729 822247**
Mr & Mrs Duerden.
D: £19.00-£23.00 **S:** £19.00-£20.00.
Open: All Year
Beds: 4D 1T 2S
Baths: 2 En 2 Sh
⛺ 🅿 (8) ⠀⠀⠀⠀⠀⠀🚲

The Yorkshire Rose Guest House,
Duke Street, Settle, North
Yorkshire, BD24 9AW.
Comfortable family run establish-
ment close to town centre/station.
Relax.
Grades: ETC 3 Diamond
AA 3 Diamond
Tel: **01729 822032**
D: £15.00-£23.50 **S:** £15.00-£23.50.
Open: All Year
Beds: 1F 1T 2D 1S **Baths:** 2 En 1 Sh
⛺ 🅿 (6) ⠀⠀⠀⠀⠀⠀🚲

The Oast Guest House,
5 Penyghent View, Church Street,
Settle, N. Yorks, BD24 9JJ.
High standards with a Yorkshire
welcome await you.
Tel: **01729 822989** (also fax no)
Mr & Mrs King.
D: £18.50-£23.00 **S:** £15.50-£17.50.
Open: All Year
Beds: 1F 2D 2T 1S **Baths:** 3 En 3 Sh
⛺ 🅿 (4) ⠀⠀⠀⠀⠀⠀🖤

Always telephone
to get directions to
the B&B - you will
save time!

Giggleswick 12

National Grid Ref: SD8164

⊮ ◖ Black Horse, Hart's Head

Yorkshire Dales Field Centre,
Holme Beck, Raines Road,
Giggleswick, Settle, N. Yorks,
BD24 0AQ.
Actual grid ref: SD813641
Excellent cooking - comfortable
well-appointed converted barn.
Tel: **01729 824180** (also fax no)
Mrs Barbour.
D: £10.50-£10.50 **S:** £10.50-£10.50.
Open: All Year
Beds: 6F 2S **Baths:** 5 Sh
⌕ ₱ (7) ⊬ ⌷ ⊁ ✕ ♨ ▥ Ⅴ ▮ ∦

Keasden 13

National Grid Ref: SD7266

Lythe Birks, Keasden, Lancaster,
LA2 8EZ.
Converted barn in its own grounds
overlooking Three Peaks.
Grades: ETC 3 Diamond
Tel: **015242 51688** Mrs Phinn.
D: £19.50-£19.50 **S:** £25.00-£25.00.
Open: All Year **Beds:** 2D 1T
⌕ ₱ ⊬ ⌷ ⊁ ✕ ♨ ▥ Ⅴ ▮ ∦ ⚲

Clapham 14

National Grid Ref: SD7469

◖ Goat Gap Inn

Arbutus Guest House, Riverside,
Clapham, Lancaster, LA2 8DS.
Situated in heart of village, over-
looking river. Excellent food and
parking.
Grades: ETC 4 Diamond,
AA 4 Diamond
Tel: **015242 51240** Mrs Cass.
Fax no: 015242 51197
D: £20.00-£26.00 **S:** £20.00-£36.00.
Open: All Year
Beds: 2F 1D 2T 1S
Baths: 5 En 1 Pr
⌕ ₱ (6) ⊬ ⌷ ⊁ ♨ ▥ Ⅴ ▮ ∦ ⚲

Goat Gap Inn, Newby, Clapham,
Lancaster, LA2 8JB.
300-year-old inn within sight of the
Three Peaks.
Tel: **015242 41230**
Mr & Mrs Robb-Cummings.
Fax no: 015242 41651
D: £24.00 **S:** £35.00.
Open: All Year
Beds: 1F 4D 1T **Baths:** 4 En 2 Sh
⌕ ₱ ⌷ ⊁ ✕ ♨ ▥ Ⅴ ▮ ∦ ⚲

Flying Horseshoe Hotel, Clapham,
Lancaster, LA2 8ES.
Actual grid ref: SD733678
Friendly and family run. Great food
and drink. Free fishing.
Grades: ETC 2 Star
Tel: **015242 51229** (also fax no)
Mr & Mrs Perrow.
D: £20.00-£25.00 **S:** £27.50-£32.50.
Open: All Year
Beds: 3F 3D 1T
⌕ ₱ (50) ⌷ ⊁ ✕ ♨ ▥ Ⅴ ▮

Austwick 15

National Grid Ref: SD7668

Christine Macdougall,
Dalesbridge, Austwick, Settle,
N Yorks, LA2 8AZ.
Friendly relaxing ensuite B&B.
Outstanding views and a great
atmosphere.
Grades: ETC 3 Diamond
Tel: **015242 51021** MacDougall.
D: £24.00-£24.00 **S:** £29.00-£29.00.
Open: All Year
Beds: 1F 3T 1D 1S
Baths: 4 En 1 Sh
⌕ ₱ (60) ⊬ ⌷ ⊁ ✕ ♨ ▥ Ⅴ ∦
⚲

Cold Cotes 16

National Grid Ref: SD7171

⊮ ◖ Goat Gap Inn

Moorview, Cold Cotes, Clapham,
Lancaster, LA2 8HS.
Beautiful detached house, peaceful,
comfortable, wonderful views and
great breakfast.
Tel: **015242 42085** Mrs Lupton.
D: £18.00-£20.00 **S:** £20.00-£24.00.
Open: All Year (not Xmas)
Beds: 2D 1T
Baths: 2 En 1 Sh
⌕ (1) ₱ (3) ⌷ ⊁ ♨ ▥ Ⅴ ▮ ∦ ⚲

Ingleton 17

National Grid Ref: SD6973

⊮ ◖ Bridge Hotel, Craven Heifer, Marton Arms,
Wheatsheaf

▲ *Ingleton Youth Hostel, Greta*
Tower, Sammy Lane, Ingleton,
Carnforth, LA6 3EG.
Actual grid ref: SD695733
Tel: **015242 41444**
Under 18: £7.75 **Adults:** £11.00
Self-catering facilities, Showers,
Lounge, Dining room, Drying
room, Cycle store, Parking,
Evening meal at 7.00pm, No smok-
ing, WC, Kitchen facilities,
Breakfast available, Credit cards
accepted
The hostel has been refurbished
recently, and is ideally placed for
family holidays, being on the edge
of the Yorkshire Dales National
Park. It is also a good base for
climbers, pot-holers and walkers of
all levels.

▲ *Barnstead Bunkhouse Barn,*
Stacksteads Farm, Ingleton,
Carnforth, Lancashire, LA6 3HS.
Actual grid ref: SD686724
Tel: **015242 41386** **Adults:** £8.00
Facilities for disabled people

Ingleton to Redmire

From Ingleton you head north through **Kingsdale**, and cross into Cumbria with **Whernside**, another of the Three Peaks, towering to your right and **Gragareth** to the left - you are now in **Deepdale**, one of the most scenic parts of the cycleway. Deepdale leads into **Dentdale**, which shelters the picturesque village of **Dent**, with its cobbled streets. From Dent it's east to **Cowgill** and then across the Leeds-Settle-Carlisle Railway line and back into North Yorkshire. Here you cycle northeast through **Widdale**, with Widdale Fell on the left, to **Hawes**, the main market town of **Wensleydale**, renowned for its eponymous cheese. Worth a visit here is the Dales Countryside Museum, tracing the history of many local industries. There is also a National Park Information Centre. A little to the north of the town is Hardaw Force, the highest above-ground single-drop waterfall in England, and further along the same detour you can find the Buttertubs, a striking group of natural wells. From Hawes you head east through Wensleydale along the banks of the River Ure to **Askrigg**, and then north, climbing steeply across the heather moorland of Askrigg Common, before descending into **Swaledale**, one of the most idyllically beautiful (famous for its distinctive breed of sheep). This rugged landscape, marked by the famous Dales dry stone walls, forms the backdrop for a string of pretty villages before you head south at **Grinton**, climbing over Grinton Moor and then descending back into Wensleydale at the village of **Redmire**. Close to here stands Bolton Castle, dating from 1379, where Mary, Queen of Scots was imprisoned in the late sixteenth century.

The Dales Guest House, Main Street, Ingleton, Carnforth, North Yorkshire, *LA6 3HH.*
Tel: **015242 41401** Weaire.
D: £19.00-£22.00 **S:** £19.00-£22.00.
Open: All Year
Beds: 1T 3D 1S **Baths:** 5 En
🛏 🖛 🗖 ⽊ ✗ 🕮 🛇 ♿ 🚲
A friendly welcome, cosy rooms with views and substantial home cooked meals await you, an ideal base for exploring the Dales, Forest of Bowland and Lakes. Special price breaks are available and various activities can be arranged for small groups.

Springfield Country House Hotel, Ingleton, Carnforth, Lancs, *LA6 3HJ.*
Grades: ETC 3 Diamond
RAC 3 Diamond
Tel: **015242 41280** (also fax no)
Mr Thornton.
D: £23.00-£25.00 **S:** £23.00-£25.00.
Open: All Year (not Xmas)
Beds: 1F 3D 1T
Baths: 5 En 1 Pr
🛏 🖤 (12) 🖛 🗖 ⽊ ✗ 🕮 🛇 ♿ 🚲
Detached Victorian villa; large garden at rear running down to River Greta. Patio, small pond & waterfall. Home grown vegetables in season. Front garden with patio and conservatory.

Bridge End Guest House, Mill Lane, Ingleton, Carnforth, Lancs, *LA6 3EP.*
Georgian Listed building, riverside location adjacent to Waterfalls Walk entrance.
Grades: ETC 3 Diamond
Tel: **015242 41413** Mrs Garner.
D: £19.00-£22.00 **S:** £25.00.
Open: All Year
Beds: 3D
Baths: 3 En
🛏 (8) 🖤 (8) 🗖 ✗ 🕮 🛇 🚲

Thorngarth House, Ingleton, Carnforth, North Yorkshire, *LA6 3HN.*
Country house surrounded by green fields. Wonderful food, open fires.
Tel: **015242 41295** (also fax no)
Mr Bradley.
D: £22.00-£35.00
S: £22.00-£35.00.
Open: All Year
Beds: 4D 1T
Baths: 4 En 1 Pr
🖤 (5) 🖛 🗖 ✗ 🕮 🛇 ♿ 🚲

Riverside Lodge, 24 Main Street, Ingleton, Carnforth, *LA6 3HJ.*
Splendid Victorian house, terraced gardens leading to river. Superb views.
Grades: ETC 3 Diamond, AA 3 Diamond
Tel: **015242 41359**
Mr & Mrs Foley.
D: £21.00-£24.00 **S:** £30.00-£30.00.
Open: All Year (not Xmas)
Beds: 7D 1T **Baths:** 8 En
🛏 🖤 (8) 🖛 🗖 ⽊ 🕮 🛇 ♿ 🚲

Ingleborough View Guest House, Main Street, Ingleton, Carnforth, Lancashire, *LA6 3HH.*
Lovely Victorian house with picturesque riverside location. excellent accommodation and food.
Tel: **015242 41523** Mrs Brown.
D: £19.00-£20.00 **S:** £25.00-£28.00.
Open: All Year (not Xmas)
Beds: 1F 2D 1T
Baths: 2 En 2 Pr
🛏 🖤 (6) 🗖 🖛 🕮 🛇 🚲

Dent   18

National Grid Ref: SD7086

▲ **Whernside Manor,** Dent, Sedbergh, Cumbria, *LA10 5RE.*
Actual grid ref: SD725858
Tel: **015396 25213**
Under 18: £5.00 **Adults:** £5.00
Self-catering facilities, Television, Showers, Grounds available for games, Drying room, Cycle store, Parking
Set in the grounds of a historic house - excellent situation.

Rash House, Dent Foot, Dent, Sedbergh, Cumbria, *LA10 5SU.*
Actual grid ref: SD6690
Charming C18th farmhouse situated in picturesque Dentdale.
Tel: **015396 20113** (also fax no)
Mrs Hunter.
D: £16.00-£18.00 **S:** £18.00-£20.00.
Open: All Year (not Xmas)
Beds: 1F 1D
Baths: 1 Sh
🛏 🖤 (2) 🗖 🖛 ✗ 🕮 🛇 ♿

Garda View Guest House, Dent, Sedbergh, Cumbria, *LA10 5QL.*
Village centre, friendly family house. Hearty breakfasts, walking information available.
Tel: **015396 25209** Mrs Smith.
D: £17.00-£17.00 **S:** £17.00-£17.00.
Open: All Year (not Xmas)
Beds: 2D 1T 1S
Baths: 1 Sh
🛏 🖤 (2) 🗖 🖛 🕮 🛇 ♿ 🚲

Stone Close Tea Shop, Main Street, Dent, Sedbergh, Cumbria, *LA10 5QL.*
Actual grid ref: SD705868
C17th oak beamed tea shop with log fires.
Tel: **015396 25231** Mr Rushton.
D: £17.00-£25.00 **S:** £19.50-£49.00.
Open: Feb to Dec
Beds: 1F 2D 1S
Baths: 1 En 1 Sh
🛏 🖤 (4) 🖤 🗖 🖛 ✗ 🕮 🛇 ♿ 🚲

Smithy Fold, Whernside Manor, Dent, Sedbergh, Cumbria, *LA10 5RE.*
Actual grid ref: SD725859
Small C18th country house.
Tel: **015396 25368** Mrs Cheetham.
D: £17.50-£17.50 **S:** £17.50-£17.50.
Open: All Year (not Xmas)
Beds: 1F 1D 1T
Baths: 1 Sh
🛏 (4) 🖤 (6) 🗖 🖛 ✗ 🕮 🛇 ♿ 🚲

Little Oak, Helmside View, Dent, Sedbergh, Cumbria, *LA10 5QY.*
Oak-beamed studio for two, warm welcome, pretty, unspoilt village.
Tel: **015396 25330**
Mr & Mrs Priestley.
D: £18.00-£18.00 **S:** £18.00.
Open: All Year (not Xmas)
Beds: 1D
🖛 🗖 🛇 🖤 🚲

Syke Fold, Dent, Sedbergh, Cumbria, *LA10 5RE.*
Actual grid ref: SD726859
Peaceful country hose with stunning views. Quiet location 1.5 miles east of cobbled Dent.
Tel: **015396 25486** Mrs Newsham.
D: £21.50-£23.00 **S:** £21.50-£23.00
Open: Feb to Nov
Beds: 1F 1D
Baths: 2 En
🛏 🖤 (2) 🖛 🗖 🖛 ✗ 🛇 🚲

The White House, Dent, Sedbergh, Cumbria, *LA10 5QR.*
House in picturesque Dales village. Quiet location, garden, superb walking.
Tel: **015396 25041** Mrs Allen.
D: £17.00-£18.00 **S:** £17.00-£18.00
Open: Easter to Oct
Beds: 1D 1T 1S
Baths: 2 Sh
🖤 (2) 🖛 🗖 🖛 🕮 🛇 ♿

Cowgill   19

National Grid Ref: SD7587

🍽 🍺 Sportsman Inn, George & Dragon

The Sportsman's Inn, Cowgill, Dent, Sedbergh, Cumbria, *LA10 5RG.*
Family owned freehouse 1670, scenic location, rooms overlooking River Dee.
Tel: **015396 25282**
Mr & Mrs Martin.
D: £17.50-£23.50 **S:** £17.50-£23.50
Open: All Year
Beds: 1F 2D 3T
Baths: 3 Sh
🛏 🖤 (10) 🖛 ✗ 🖛 🕮 🛇 ♿ 🚲

Scow Cottage, Cowgill, Dent, Sedbergh, Cumbria, *LA10 5RN.*
Actual grid ref: SD774853
Attractive and comfortable 250-year-old Dales farmhouse, set in beautiful countryside.
Tel: **015396 25445**
Mrs Ferguson.
D: £16.00-£17.00 **S:** £19.00-£25.00
Open: All Year
Beds: 1D 1T
Baths: 1 Sh
🛏 (12) 🖤 (4) 🖛 🖛 ✗ 🕮 🛇 ♿

Pay B&Bs by cash or cheque and be prepared to pay up front.

Hawes 20

National Grid Ref: SD8789

⚫ ◀ White Hart, Herriot's Hotel, Board Hotel, Fountain, Stone House, Wensleydale Pantry

▲ **Hawes Youth Hostel,**
Lancaster Terrace, Hawes,
N Yorks, DL8 3LQ.
Actual grid ref: SD867897
Tel: 01969 667368
Under 18: £6.90 **Adults:** £10.00
Self-catering facilities, Television,
Laundry facilities, Lounge, Games
room, Drying room, Cycle store,
Evening meal at 7.00pm, No smoking, Kitchen facilities, Breakfast
available, Credit cards accepted
Friendly and attractively refurbished purpose-built hostel overlooking Hawes and Wensleydale.

The Bungalow, *Springbank,*
Hawes, N. Yorks, DL8 3NW.
Large bungalow, excellent views,
quiet, off road parking.
Grades: ETC 2 Diamond
Tel: 01969 667209 Mrs Garnett.
D: £18.00-£20.00 .
Open: Easter to Oct
Beds: 2D 1T **Baths:** 2 En 1 Sh
🛏 (4) 🅿 ⛄ 🛏 ⚓ 🎢 📖 Ⅴ 🔌 ⟳

Ebor House, *Burtersett Road,*
Hawes, N. Yorks, DL8 3NT.
Actual grid ref: SD876897
Family-run friendly and central.
Off road parking and cycle store.
Grades: ETC 3 Diamond
Tel: 01969 667337 (also fax no)
Mrs Clark.
D: £17.00-£20.00 **S:** £19.00-£25.00.
Open: All Year (not Xmas)
Beds: 2D 1T 1S **Baths:** 2 En 1 Sh
🛏 (5) ⚡ ⛄ 🛏 ⚓ 🎢 📖 Ⅴ ⛄ 🔌 ⟳

The Green Dragon Inn, *Hardraw,*
Hawes, N. Yorks, DL8 3.
A 100ft waterfall in spectacular
back garden.
Tel: 01969 667392 Mr Stead.
D: £23.50-£27.50 **S:** £24.50-£28.50.
Open: All Year (not Xmas)
Beds: 2F 2T 4S **Baths:** 16 Pr
🛏 🅿 (30) ⛄ 🛏 ✗ ⚓ 📖 Ⅴ 🔌 ⟳

Overdales View, *Simonstone,*
Hawes, N Yorks, DL8 3LY.
Friendly welcome. Lovely views,
peaceful surroundings, comfortable
beds good food.
Tel: 01969 667186 Mrs Sunter.
D: £16.00-£18.00 **S:** £18.00-£20.00.
Open: Easter to Oct
Beds: 1F/T 1D 1S **Baths:** 1 Sh
🛏 🅿 (5) ⚡ ⛄ 🛏 📖 Ⅴ 🔌

Barney Fors, *Hawes, N. Yorks,*
DL8 3LS.
Grade II Listed ex-farmhouse, now
comfortable guest house, in beautiful setting.
Tel: 01969 667475 Mrs Harpley.
D: £25.00-£28.00 **S:** £40.00-£45.00.
Open: Easter to Nov
Beds: 3D **Baths:** 2 En 1 Pr
🛏 (7) 🅿 (8) ⚡ ⛄ 🛏 📖 Ⅴ 🔌 ⟳

Redmire to Skipton

From Redmire it's east to **Wensley**, which gave the Dale its
name, from where anyone interested can make a detour to see
the imposing ruins of Middleham Castle, dating from 1170, for a
short time the home of Richard III. At Wensley you cross the
Ure and begin the climb southwards through **Coverdale**, the
meadows at the bottom giving way to windswept fells. A steep
descent to the Park Gill Beck stream leads to the village of
Kettlewell. From here you cycle south through Upper
Wharfedale, below Kilnsey Crag, a great limestone overhang,
and through Grass Wood, a swathe of ancient woodland which
is now an important conservation area, to **Grassington**, a
village with a Georgian cobbled central square, on the site of a
seventh-century settlement. Here you will find the Upper
Wharfedale Museum. Now it's downdale back to Burnsall, and
retracing your tyre-tracks to Appletreewick and Barden Tower
you go on to **Bolton Abbey**. Here stand the ruins of Bolton
Priory, a twelfth-century Augustinian foundation which fell victim
to the Dissolution, one of the sites in the North of England
painted by Turner and hyperbolised by Ruskin. From here you
return to Skipton.

Steppe Haugh Guest House,
Townhead, Hawes, N. Yorks,
DL8 3RH.
Actual grid ref: SD869898
C17th house offering a wealth of
character and atmosphere.
Tel: 01969 667645
Mrs Grattan.
D: £18.00-£26.00 **S:** £20.00-£23.00.
Open: All Year (not Xmas)
Beds: 3D 1T 1S
Baths: 5 En
🛏 (7) 🅿 (6) ⚡ ⛄ 🛏 ⚓ 🎢 📖 Ⅴ 🔌 ⟳

Gayle 21

⚫ ◀ Board, Fountain, Crown, White Hart

Blackburn Farm/Trout Fishery,
Gayle, Hawes, N Yorks, DL8 3NX.
Idyllic location. Quiet, rural but
within walking distance of Hawes.
Grades: ETC 3 Diamond
Tel: 01969 667524 Ms Moore.
D: £17.00-£18.00 .
Open: Easter to Oct
Beds: 2D
Baths: 1 En 1 Pr
🅿 (4) ⚡ ⛄ 🛏 ⚓ 🎢 📖 Ⅴ 🔌 ⟳

East House, *Gayle, Hawes,*
N. Yorks, DL8 3RZ.
Actual grid ref: SD871892
Delightful house. Superb views,
ideal centre for touring the dales.
Grades: ETC 4 Diamond
Tel: 01969 667405
Mrs Ward.
D: £18.00-£21.00 **S:** £18.00-£18.00.
Open: Feb to Nov
Beds: 1T 1D 1S
Baths: 1 En 1 Sh
🛏 🅿 ⚡ ⛄ 🛏 📖 Ⅴ 🔌 ⟳

Gayle Laithe, *Gayle, Hawes,*
N. Yorks, DL8 3RR.
Modern, comfortable, converted
barn. Ideal for touring, cycling and
walking.
Tel: 01969 667397 Mrs McGregor.
D: £16.00-£17.00 **S:** £16.00-£17.00.
Open: Easter to Nov
Beds: 1D 1T 1S **Baths:** 1 Sh
🛏 🅿 (2) ⛄ 🛏 📖 Ⅴ 🔌 ⟳

Askrigg 22

National Grid Ref: SD9491

⚫ ◀ Kings Arms, Crown Inn, George & Dragon, Rose & Crown

Milton House, *Askrigg, Leyburn,*
N. Yorks, DL8 3HJ.
Lovely old dales family home situated in Askrigg village in beautiful
countryside.
Grades: ETC 3 Diamond
Tel: 01969 650217 Mrs Percival.
D: £19.00-£21.00 **S:** £25.00-£30.00.
Open: All Year (not Xmas)
Beds: 3D
Baths: 3 En
🛏 (10) 🅿 (3) ⚡ ⛄ 🛏 ⚓ 📖 Ⅴ 🔌 ⟳

Thornsgill House, *Moor Road,*
Askrigg, Leyburn, N. Yorks,
DL8 3HH.
Situated in quiet corner in Askrigg,
famous for 'All Creatures Great and
Small'.
Grades: ETC 4 Diamond
Tel: 01969 650617 Mrs Gilyeat.
D: £22.00-£22.00 .
Open: All Year
Beds: 1D 1T 1S **Baths:** 2 En 1 Pr
🛏 (10) 🅿 (3) ⚡ ⛄ 🛏 ✗ ⚓ 📖 Ⅴ 🔌 ⟳

Winville Hotel & Restaurant ,
Main Street, Askrigg, Leyburn, N Yorks, DL8 3HG.
C19th Georgian hotel in centre of Herriot village.
Tel: **01969 650515** Mr Buckle.
Fax no: 01969 650594
D: £24.00-£28.50 **S:** £24.00-£38.50.
Open: All Year
Beds: 4F 4D 2T
Baths: 10 En
🛏 🖪 (18) ⬜ ⛌ ✕ 🔥 ⅢⅢ Ⅴ ⓐ ⚡

Carr End House, *Countersett, Askrigg, Leyburn, North Yorkshire, DL8 3DE.*
Charming C17th country house. Idyllic situation, warm, comfortable. Excellent food.
Tel: **01969 650346** Mrs Belward.
D: £20.00-£22.00 **S:** £20.00-£22.00.
Open: All Year (not Xmas)
Beds: 1F 2D
Baths: 2 En 1 Pr
🛏 🖪 (7) ⛌ ⬜ 🔥 ⅢⅢ Ⅴ ⓐ ⚡ ⚲

Gunnerside   23

National Grid Ref: SD9598

🍴 🍺 Oxnop Hall

Oxnop Hall, *Low Oxnop, Gunnerside, Richmond, N. Yorks, DL11 6JJ.*
Oxnop Hall is in an environmentally sensitive area. Stone walls and barns.
Tel: **01748 886253** Mrs Porter.
D: £24.00-£31.00 **S:** £24.00-£34.00.
Open: All Year (not Xmas)
Beds: 1F 3D 1T 1S
Baths: 6 Pr
🛏 (7) 🖪 (6) ⛌ ⬜ ✕ 🔥 ⅢⅢ Ⅴ ⓐ ⚡

Grinton   24

National Grid Ref: SE0498

▲ **Grinton Lodge Youth Hostel,**
Grinton Lodge, Grinton, Richmond, N. Yorks, DL11 6HS.
Tel: **01748 884206**
Under 18: £6.90 **Adults:** £10.00
Self-catering facilities, Television, Showers, Laundry facilities, Lounge, Games room, Drying room, Cycle store, Evening meal at 7pm, WC, Breakfast available, Credit cards accepted
A useful stopover for the Coast to Coast path and the Yorkshire Dales Cycleway. Harkerside Moor has traditional drystone walling and field barns. The hostel itself was once a shooting lodge and retains its log fires among other original features.

S = Price range for a single

person in a room

Fremington   25

National Grid Ref: SE0499

🍴 🍺 Bridge Inn, Kings Arms

Broadlands, *Fremington, Richmond, DL11 6AW.*
Actual grid ref: SE046989
Peaceful village setting 5 mins from Reeth, spectacular views, comfortable accommodation.
Grades: ETC 1 Diamond
Tel: **01748 884297** (also fax no)
Mrs Rudez.
D: £19.00-£19.00 **S:** £27.00-£27.00.
Open: All Year
Beds: 1D 1T 1S **Baths:** 1 Sh
🛏 (12) 🖪 (4) ⛌ ⬜ 🔥 🔥 ⅢⅢ ⬇ Ⅴ ⓐ ⚡ ⚲

Reeth   26

National Grid Ref: SE0399

🍴 🍺 Kings Arms Hotel, Bridge Inn, Black Bull, Buck Hotel

Elder Peak, *Arkengarthdale Road, Reeth, Richmond, N Yorks, DL11 6QX.*
Actual grid ref: SE036999
Friendly welcome. Good food. Peaceful, beautiful views. Ideal walking, touring.
Grades: ETC 3 Diamond
Tel: **01748 884770** Mrs Peacock.
D: £17.00-£17.00 **S:** £17.00-£20.00.
Open: Easter to Oct
Beds: 1D 1T **Baths:** 1 Sh
🛏 (5) 🖪 (2) ⬜ 🔥 ⅢⅢ Ⅴ ⚡ ⚲

Arkle House, *Mill Lane, Reeth , Richmond, North Yorks, DL11 6SJ.*
Old Georgian house full of character located alongside Arkle Beck.
Grades: ETC 4 Diamond
Tel: **01748 884815**
D: £20.00-£25.00 **S:** £25.00-£27.50.
Open: All Year
Beds: 1F 1D **Baths:** 2 En
🛏 🖪 (2) ⛌ ⬜ 🔥 ⅢⅢ Ⅴ ⓐ

2 Bridge Terrace, *Reeth, Richmond, N. Yorks, DL11 6TP.*
Actual grid ref: SD041991
Dry-cured Gloucester old spot bacon, local bread, fresh fruit, yoghurt.
Grades: ETC 1 Diamond
Tel: **01748 884572** Mrs Davies.
D: £16.50-£17.50 **S:** £20.00-£22.00.
Open: Easter to Nov
Beds: 1D 1T **Baths:** 1 Sh
🛏 ⛌ ⅢⅢ ⓐ ⚡ ⚲

The Black Bull, *Reeth, Richmond, N. Yorks, DL11 6SZ.*
In Yorkshire Dales National Park. On Inn Way.
Grades: ETC 3 Diamond
Tel: **01748 884213** (also fax no)
Mrs Sykes.
D: £20.00-£25.00 **S:** £20.00-£37.50.
Open: All Year
Beds: 1F 1T 7D
Baths: 6 En 1 Pr 2 Sh
🛏 ⬜ 🔥 ✕ 🔥 ⅢⅢ Ⅴ ⓐ ⚡ ⚲

Redmire   27

National Grid Ref: SE0491

🍴 🍺 Bolton Arms

Briar House, *Redmire, Leyburn, North Yorkshire, DL8 4EH.*
Actual grid ref: SE046909
Comfortable C18th farmhouse, 'James Herriot' country. Good walking, cycling, touring.
Tel: **01969 622335**
Mr & Mrs Patterson.
D: £16.00-£18.00 **S:** £20.00-£22.00.
Open: All Year
Beds: 1F 1T 2D **Baths:** 3 Sh
🛏 🖪 (4) ⛌ ⬜ 🔥 ⅢⅢ Ⅴ ⚡

Carlton-in-Coverdale   28

National Grid Ref: SE0684

Abbots Thorn, *Carlton-in-Coverdale Leyburn, N. Yorks, DL8 4AY.*
Grades: ETC 4 Diamond
Tel: **01969 640620** Mrs Lashmar.
D: £18.00-£25.00 **S:** £28.00.
Open: Jan to Dec
Beds: 2D 1T **Baths:** 2 En 1 Pr
🛏 (12) ⛌ ⬜ 🔥 🔥 ⅢⅢ Ⅴ ⓐ ⚡ ⚲
Relax and unwind at our comfortable traditional Yorkshire Dales home. Oak-beamed guest lounge with open fire on those chilly evenings. Indulge yourself in our fabulous dinners. Superb scenery, terrific touring, wonderful walking. All bedrooms have beautiful views over glorious Coverdale.

Kettlewell   29

National Grid Ref: SD9772

🍴 🍺 Queen's Head, Race Horses, King's Head, Bluebell

▲ **Kettlewell Youth Hostel,**
Whernside House, Kettlewell, Skipton, North Yorkshire, BD23 5QU.
Actual grid ref: SD970724
Tel: **01756 760232**
Under 18: £6.90 **Adults:** £10.00
Self-catering facilities, Television, Showers, Lounge, Drying room, Cycle store, Parking Limited, Evening meal at 7.00pm, No smoking, Kitchen facilities, Breakfast available, Luggage store, Credit cards accepted
Large house right in the middle of pretty Wharfedale village of Kettlewell, ideal for families and small groups.

Lynburn, *Kettlewell, Skipton, N. Yorks, BD23 5RF.*
Well preserved property with well tended grounds. Peaceful surroundings.
Grades: ETC 3 Diamond
Tel: **01756 760803**
Mrs Thornborrow.
D: £19.00-£20.00 **S:** £25.00-£25.00
Open: Mar to Oct
Beds: 1D 1T **Baths:** 1 Sh
🛏 (12) 🖪 (2) ⬜ 🔥 ⅢⅢ Ⅴ ⓐ ⚡

All rooms full and nowhere else to stay? Ask the owner if there's anywhere nearby

---

Langcliffe Country House,
Kettlewell, Skipton, N. Yorks,
BD23 5RJ.
Grades: AA 4 Diamond,
RAC 4 Diamond
Tel: **01756 760243** Mr Elliott.
D: £45.00-£50.00
S: £65.00-£70.00.
Open: All Year (not Xmas)
Beds: 1F 2T 2D
Baths: 5 Pr 1 En
🛇 🄿 ⅊ 🗙 ⛁ 🏃 🗙 ⛫ 🃏 🔥 Ⅴ 🐾 ⚡
Kettlewell in Upper Wharfedale.
Traditional stone house with beautiful gardens. Ensuite bedrooms.
Elegant lounge with log fire.
Conservatory restaurant serving superb food in a panoramic setting.

Starbotton 30

National Grid Ref: SD9574

🄼 ⛊ Fox

Fox & Hounds Inn, Starbotton,
Skipton, N. Yorks, BD23 5HY.
Traditional cosy Dales inn.
Tel: **01756 760269**
Mr & Mrs McFadyen.
Fax no: 01756 760862
D: £27.50-£27.50
S: £35.00-£35.00.
Open: Mar to Dec
Beds: 1D 1T
🄿 (12) ⅊ 🗙 🦮 🗙 ⛫ 🃏 Ⅴ ⚡

Kilnsey 31

National Grid Ref: SD9767

🄼 ⛊ Tennant Arms

Skirfare Bridge Dales Barn,
Kilnsey, Skipton, N. Yorks,
BD23 5PT.
Actual grid ref: SD971689
Tel: **01756 752465** (also fax no)
Mrs Foster.
D: £8.00-£8.00
S: £8.00-£8.00.
Open: All Year
Beds: 5F 1T
Baths: 3 Sh
🛇 🄿 (8) 🗙 🃏 🐾 ⚡
Converted stone barn in beautiful limestone countryside of upper Wharfedale, ideally situated for outdoor activities. Centrally heated.
25 bunk beds, drying room, kitchen, common room, all inclusive. Catering by arrangement.
Individuals or school groups.
Off-road parking. No pets.

The Grid Reference beneath the location heading is for the village or town - *not* for individual houses, which are shown (where supplied) in each entry itself.

Grassington 32

National Grid Ref: SE0064

🄼 ⛊ Black Horse, Devonshire, Old Hall, Foresters' Arms

Mayfield Bed & Breakfast, Low
Mill Lane, Grassington, Skipton,
N. Yorks, BD23 5BX.
Actual grid ref: SE000635
Beautiful Dales longhouse. Guest rooms overlook fells and river.
Tel: **01756 753052**
Mr & Mrs Trewartha.
D: £22.00-£25.00 **S:** £25.00-£25.00.
Open: All Year
Beds: 1F 1D 1T
Baths: 1 En 1 Sh
🛇 🄿 (5) ⅊ 🦮 ⛫ 🃏 Ⅴ ⚡ 🐾

Town Head Guest House, 1 Low
Lane, Grassington, Skipton,
N. Yorks, BD23 5AU.
Actual grid ref: SE040799
Friendly guest house at the head of the village between cobbled streets and moors.
Tel: **01756 752811** Mrs Lister.
D: £25.00-£25.00 **S:** £30.00-£30.00.
Open: All Year (not Xmas)
Beds: 3D 1T
Baths: 4 En
🄿 (3) ⅊ 🃏 ⛫ 🃏 Ⅴ

Lythe End, Wood Lane,
Grassington, Skipton, N. Yorks,
BD23 5DF.
Actual grid ref: SE000647
Modern stone detached house, stunning views, quiet village location.
Tel: **01756 753196** Mrs Colley.
D: £22.00-£25.00 **S:** £30.00-£30.00.
Open: All Year (not Xmas)
Beds: 1F 1D **Baths:** 1 En 1 Pr
🛇 (12) 🄿 (2) ⅊ ⛫ 🃏 Ⅴ ⚡ 🐾

All rates are subject to alteration at the owners' discretion.

Craiglands, 1 Brooklyn,
Threshfield , Grassington, Skipton,
BD23 5ER.
Elegant Edwardian house offering quality accommodation and superb breakfasts.
Grades: ETC 4 Diamond
Tel: **01756 752093** Mrs Wallace.
D: £21.00-£26.00 **S:** £20.00-£28.00.
Open: All Year (not Xmas)
Beds: 2D 1T 1S
Baths: 3 En 1 Pr
🄿 (3) ⅊ 🃏 🏃 ⛫ 🃏 Ⅴ ⚡ 🐾

Kirkfield, Hebden Road,
Grassington, Skipton, N. Yorks,
BD23 5LJ.
Large house in own gardens.
Panoramic views of Wharfe Valley.
Tel: **01756 752385** Mr Lockyer.
D: £18.00-£25.00 **S:** £20.00-£20.00.
Open: All Year
Beds: 3F 1T 1S
Baths: 2 En 1 Pr 1 Sh
🛇 🄿 (8) ⅊ 🃏 🗙 🃏 ⚡ 🐾

Burtree Cottage, Hebden Road,
Grassington, Skipton, N. Yorks,
BD23 5LH.
Old cottage, comfortable rooms, lovely garden. Ideal walking/touring centre.
Tel: **01756 752442** Mrs Marsden.
D: £17.50-£17.50 .
Open: Mar to Oct
Beds: 1D 1T
Baths: 1 Sh
🛇 (10) 🄿 (2) ⅊ 🃏 ⚡ 🐾

Springroyd House, 8a Station
Road, Grassington, Skipton,
N. Yorks, BD23 5NQ.
Actual grid ref: SD980631
Conveniently situated, friendly family home.
Tel: **01756 752473**
Mrs Robertshaw.
D: £18.00-£20.00 **S:** £20.00-£22.00.
Open: All Year
Beds: 1D 2T
Baths: 1 En 2 Sh
🛇 🄿 (3) ⅊ 🃏 🦮 ⛫ 🃏 Ⅴ ⚡

New Laithe House, Wood Lane,
Grassington, Skipton, N. Yorks,
BD23 5LU.
A converted barn situated in the picturesque village of Grassington.
Tel: **01756 752764**
Mrs Chaney.
D: £21.00-£24.00 **S:** £25.00-£40.00.
Open: All year (not Xmas)
Beds: 1F 4D 2T
Baths: 4 En 1 Pr
🛇 🄿 (7) 🃏 ⛫ 🃏 ⅊ Ⅴ 🐾

Threshfield 33

National Grid Ref: SD9863

|o| ⌁ Old Hall, Foresters

Grisedale Farm, Threshfield, Skipton, N Yorks, BD23 5NT.
Friendly traditional Dales farmhouse near Grassington with beautiful rural location.
Tel: **01756 752516**
Mrs Kitching.
D: £15.00-£18.00 **S:** £20.00-£20.00.
Open: All Year (not Xmas/New Year)
Beds: 1T 1D
Baths: 1 Sh
ॐ �ₚ (2) ❑ ★ ♨ Ⅲ. Ⓥ ✦ ♻

Pay B&Bs by cash or
cheque and be prepared
to pay up front.

Bridge End Farm, Threshfield, Skipton, N Yorks, BD23 5NH.
Aga cooking, large garden, fishing, snooker and music rooms.
Tel: **01756 752463** Mrs Thompson.
D: £22.00-£26.00 **S:** £23.00-£27.00.
Open: All Year (not Xmas)
Beds: 1F 1D 1T 4S **Baths:** 6 En
ॐ �ₚ (8) ⌇ ❑ ✕ ♨ Ⅲ. Ⓥ ♠ ✦ ♻

Linton 34

National Grid Ref: SD9962

▲ *Linton Youth Hostel, The Old Rectory, Linton, Skipton, North Yorkshire, BD23 5HH.*
Actual grid ref: SD998627
Tel: **01756 752400**
Under 18: £6.90 **Adults:** £10.00
Self-catering facilities, Wet weather shelter, Dining room, Drying room, Cycle store, Parking, Evening meal at 7.00pm, No smoking, WC, Kitchen facilities
C17th former rectory in own grounds, across the stream from the village green, in one of Wharfedale's most picturesque and unspoilt villages.

Hebden 35

National Grid Ref: SE0263

|o| ⌁ Clarendon

Court Croft, Church Lane, Hebden, Skipton, BD23 5DX.
Grades: ETC 2 Diamond
Tel: **01756 753406** Mrs Kitching.
D: £17.50 **S:** £17.50-£20.00.
Open: All Year
Beds: 2T **Baths:** 1 Sh
ॐ �ₚ (4) ❑ ★ ♨ Ⅲ. Ⓥ ♠ ✦ ♻
Family farmhouse in quiet village close to the Dales Way.

All rooms full and
nowhere else to stay?
Ask the owner if
there's anywhere
nearby

Key to Entries

- ☜ Children welcome (from age shown in brackets, if specified)
- 🅿 Off-street car parking (number of places shown in brackets)
- ⌘ No smoking
- 📺 Television (either in every room or in a TV lounge)
- 🐾 Pets accepted (by prior arrangement)
- ✗ Evening meal available (by prior arrangement)
- �V Special diets catered for (by prior arrangement - please check with owner to see if your particular requirements are catered for)

- ▥ Central heating throughout
- ♿ Suitable for disabled people (please check with owner to see what level of disability is provided for)
- ❄ Christmas breaks a speciality
- ♨ Coffee/tea making facilities
- ▲ Youth Hostel
- ⌂ Camping Barn
- █ Packed lunches available
- ⁄⁄ Drying facilities for wet clothes and boots
- ⚲ Safe cycle storage

The location heading - every hamlet, village, town and city mentioned in this directory is represented on the path map within each section.

Use the National Grid reference with Ordnance Survey maps and atlases. The letter(s) refer to a 100 kilometre grid square. The first two numbers refer to a North/South grid line and the last two numbers refer to an East/West grid line. The grid reference indicates their intersection point.

● **Penny Hassett**   **12**

National Grid Ref: PH2096. ●

These are the names of nearby ── ● ¶◎ ♨ Cat & Fiddle, The Bull
pubs and restaurants that serve food in the evening, as suggested by local B&Bs.

The Old Rectory, Main Street, Penny Hassett, Borchester, Borsetshire, BC2 3QT.
C18th former rectory, lovely garden.
● **Grades:** ETC 3 Diamond
Tel: **01048 598464** Mrs Smythe.
D: £18.00-£22.00 **S:** £20.00-£27.50 ●
Open: All Year
Beds: 1F 1D 1T ●
Bathrooms ── ● **Baths:** 1 Pr 2 Sh
En = Ensuite   ☜(4) 🅿(2) ⌘ 📺 🐾 ✗ ▥ �V ♿ ❄ ♨ ⚲
Pr = Private
Sh = Shared

D = Price range per person sharing in double room
● **S** = Price range for a single person in a room
Bedrooms
F = Family
D = Double
T = Twin
S = Single

Grades - The English Tourism Council (**ETC**) grades B&Bs for quality in Diamonds (**1 Diamond** to **5 Diamond**, highest) and hotels in Stars (**1 Star** to **5 Star**). Bord Failte (**BF**, the Irish Tourist Board) grades guest houses in Stars (**1 Star** to **4 Star**); the Northern Ireland Tourist Board (**NITB**) rates them as **Grade A** (higher) or **B**. Both grade hotels in Stars (**1 Star** to **5 Star**). Both Tourist Boards for Ireland inspect B&B accommodation annually - such premises are entitled to show that they have been approved (**Approv**). Scottish and Welsh Tourist Board (**STB** and **WTB**) grades have two parts: the Star rating is for quality (**1 Star** to **5 Star**, highest), the other part designates the type of establishment, e.g. B&B, Guest House (**GH**), Country House (**CH**) etc. Ask at Tourist Information Centres for further information on these systems. The Automobile Association (**AA**) and Royal Automobile Club (**RAC**) both use, throughout the British-Irish Isles, the same system of Diamonds and Stars as the English Tourism Council.